The Anglican Parochial Clergy

A Celebration

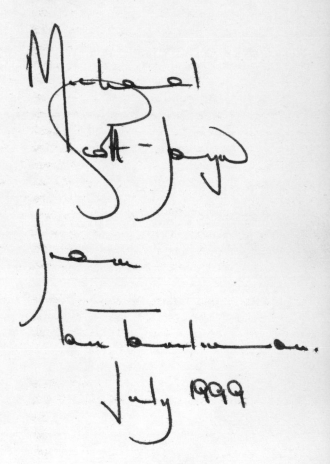

Michael
Scott-Joynt

from

Iain Tonbridge.

July 999

Michael Hinton

The Anglican Parochial Clergy

A Celebration

'But we have this treasure in earthen vessels, that the excellency of the power may be of God, and not of us.' (II Corinthians 4.7)

SCM PRESS LTD

0 334 02672 5

First published 1994
by SCM Press Ltd
9–17 St Albans Place,
London N1 0NX

Second impression 1996

Typeset by Regent Typesetting, London
and printed in Great Britain by
Mackays of Chatham, Kent

Dedicated to the people of
the parish of St Andrew, Shepherdswell, Kent

Contents

Acknowledgments

I am grateful to a number of publishers for permission to quote from copyright material: Darton, Longman and Todd for W.H. Vanstone's *Love's Endeavour, Love's Expense* (p. 115); John Murray (Publishers) Ltd for John Betjeman's 'Sunday Afternoon Service in St Enodoc Church Cornwall', *Collected Poems* and 'Blame the Vicar', *Church Poems* (p. 141 and 337); Macmillan for R.S. Thomas, 'Via Negative', *Later Poems* (p. 351). My thanks go also to Hodder and Stoughton for providing the photograph of David Watson.

Christopher Lewis, now Dean of St Albans, has given me invaluable encouragement and advice. I have relied heavily upon the facilities provided by Dr Williams's Library and St Deiniol's Library, and on their helpful staffs. Linda Foster of SCM Press has been a congenial editor. My greatest debt, however, is to my wife; and the fact that this is a common experience of authors will not prevent me from saying so.

Foreword

An empty book is like an Infant's Soul, in which
anything may be written ... I have a mind to fill
this with profitable wonders. (Traherne, 1.1)

The present decade has seen a turning-point in the history of the ministry of
the Church of England; the early years of the next century may see two others
of even greater significance. The priesting of women will certainly affect the
ministry's nature. At first women will be expected to fit into a tradition created
by men; in due course they will inevitably modify it. Looking further into the
future, the continuing numerical decline of the Church makes both disestablishment and the complete breakdown of the parochial system more likely.
By far the biggest issue facing the Church is whether these changes are to be
facilitated or resisted. The Church's response will in large measure be determined by the view she takes of the proper use of the clergy.

This is, therefore, an appropriate time to look back over four centuries of
parochial ministry. By doing so it may be possible to learn lessons for the future
– to distinguish the essential elements of the parish priest's role from the
fortuitous ones, to assess the parochial ministry's capacity for change, to make
judgments about the continuing value of the parochial system and of the
Establishment so far as it is related to that system.

But this book was occasioned less by concern for the future than by affection
for the past. It is, as its title indicates, a celebration; a celebration, at a time
when their future is in question, of a group of men who have had a greater
influence than any other on the quality and texture of English life. They are a
very mixed bag; that was to be expected. As Gibbon wrote: 'The theologian
may indulge the pleasing task of describing Religion as she descended from
Heaven, arrayed in her native purity. A more melancholy duty is imposed on
the historian. He must discover the inevitable mixture of error and corruption
which she contracted in a long residence upon earth among a weak and
degenerate race of beings.' Melancholy the task of surveying the parochial
clergy of the Church of England may in some respects be; but there is also
much to lift the heart. 'Celebration' *is* the right word.

Part One consists of two chapters. 'The Background' sketches the history of
the parochial ministry over the past four centuries, and places each of our
twenty-six principal characters (asterisked for convenience) in his context.
'A Portrait Gallery' supplies biographical material.

Part Two is the substance of the book. Any organization of inherently intractable material is bound to be contrived, but there is a rough logic in the arrangement of chapters. Dealt with first are those aspects of clerical life most likely to produce diversity; then those most likely to produce similarity; and finally those likely to penetrate the soul most deeply. An Afterword ventures some reflections about the future.

Well over four hundred clergy are mentioned, but only twenty-six play major parts and only a further sixty are referred to at any length. The central figures have been selected because they span the centuries; because they represent a great variety of character, qualities, backgrounds and churchmanship; because we know a good deal about them; and in order to supply the indispensable flavour of individual personality.

The word 'spirituality' is used frequently, but not in the ethereal sense sometimes attached to it. Here it means the effects of living in terms of an understanding of the nature and will of God. Spirituality in this sense is part and parcel of the trivial round, the common task. If we explore the whole of a parish priest's manner of life it should be possible to discover how far his Christian commitment coloured and controlled his thought and conduct; and on what belief structure that Christian commitment was founded. As befits a book about the professionally religious, that voyage of discovery is the central theme.

No apology is necessary for the use of novelists and poets. Some have been clergy themselves, others the children of clergy, others acute observers of the clerical scene. Their insights penetrate as deeply as those of historians and diarists. Occasionally too the writing of clergy who were not parish priests has been used, because it illuminates the attitudes which their parochial brethren have adopted or have been expected to adopt. There is, however, little about clergy who were only briefly or nominally parish priests. The concern is with men who were shaped, whether in life or literature, by years of concentrated parochial ministry. Many are not as well known as they deserve to be, not least because the material about them is in books long out of print. It is an act of piety as well as a pleasure to resurrect their memory.

Nor is any apology necessary for the extent to which I have used quotations. The clergy should be allowed to speak for themselves as much as possible. Their trade, after all, is words, and most of them have had plenty to say.

It may appear that the nineteenth century has been given more than its fair share of space. There are two reasons for the apparent imbalance. First, the century supplies vastly more material than any other. Secondly, the parochial ministry reached its zenith then; a book about the ministry must reflect the fact.

There is very little about women deacons. The problems here have been the short period of time since the first ordinations in 1987 and the lack of opportunity so far afforded women to make a characteristic contribution to ordained ministry. Since the ordained ministry of women began so recently it will not, I hope, be thought inappropriate that I habitually use masculine terms when writing of ministers in general.

I write as one who stands both outside and within the parochial clergy. I worked as a layman in schools for thirty-five years. Then I was ordained, and in 1985 came to live and work as a full-time non-stipendiary minister in the village of Shepherdswell in Kent, a parish within a larger benefice. The ensuing years have been for the most part intensely happy, and have left me with a deep sense of the value and rewards of parochial ministry; but I have remained an outsider in the sense that my position has been ambiguous. I have worked with the stipendiaries without being one of them: a status which has had its discomforts, but which has, in my view at least, helped me in writing this book.

My intention is, then, to observe parish priests engaged in ministry and life; to discover how they have interpreted their professional and personal responsibilities; and to assist the reader in forming judgments about the past and the future of parochial ministry. My own conclusions are for the most part positive. Echoing the quotation on the title page I would say that, though the men considered have been earthen vessels, the excellency of the power of God has none the less been manifested through them.

I have taken the opportunity afforded by this re-printing to rectify a number of mistakes and misprints in the hardback edition. I am grateful to reviewers and correspondents who have drawn my attention to some of them.

The text has not been revised to take account of recent events: notably the consequences of the priesting of women and the measures necessitated by the Church Commissioners' mismanagement of the church's resources. It does not appear to me, however, that the happenings of the past few years invalidate the arguments of my Afterword. Rather, they reinforce them.

M.G.H
July 1996

PART ONE

Setting the Scene

I

The Background

I will not by the noise of bloody wars and the
dethroning of kings advance you to glory; but by
the gentle ways of peace and love. (Traherne 1.4)

Since the Middle Ages the whole of England has been divided into parishes,
the smallest units of ecclesiastical administration. This book is about the clergy
who have cared for those parishes since the religious upheavals of the sixteenth
century established the Church of England as an autonomous communion.

The parochial clergy have been appointed by higher ecclesiastical authority,
by the Crown and other officers of government, by Oxford and Cambridge
colleges, by the affluent laity and by trusts. Until modern times the right to
presentation could be bought and sold like any other piece of property; and
throughout history the diocesan bishop has had only a limited influence on
appointments. This system has left room for a great variety of personnel and
practice, but has rarely allowed those most affected by an appointment – the
parishioners – much say.

The clergy serving the 9500 or so parishes of the 1560s were a motley crew.
Some had clung to their posts since the reign of Henry VIII. They had
accepted without overt protest Henry's breach with Rome, his dissolution of
the monasteries and his cautious reforms of liturgy and practice; then the
radical lurch towards Protestantism under Edward VI; then the return to Rome
under Mary; then the renewed breach under Elizabeth I. Some were ex-monks,
whose parishes were their pensions. Some were followers of Zwingli or Calvin
and longed to convert the whole Church to their way of thinking. Some were
still Roman Catholics at heart, and hankered after the pre-Reformation past.

At the time of Elizabeth's accession in 1558 there were not enough clergy to
go round. Mass ordinations rectified that problem but made another, of a
generally low calibre, worse. Many parish priests lacked education, or even the
elementary knowledge essential to their calling.

As the century wore on the situation improved. More graduates entered the
parochial ministry; more clergy (though by the 1580s still well under half) were
licensed to preach; parsons who clung to Roman Catholic practice were hauled
into line. A distinctive Anglican tradition began to appear, thanks in part to the
writing of John Jewel and Richard Hooker, in part to the regular use of the
Book of Common Prayer. Bernard Gilpin* provided a shining example of what a
parish priest could be under the new dispensation. Unlike him, however, most

parish priests were badly paid, partly because much of the Church's capital wealth had fallen into the hands of the laity, and partly because parochial income was plundered by lay rectors and higher ecclesiastical authority. Poverty encouraged pluralism (the holding of more than one living) and its corollary non-residence. Another difficulty was that some of the better-educated clergy were Puritans, at odds with much in Church life which reflected its Catholic traditions.

The accession of James I encouraged the Puritan clergy to state their case in the Millenary Petition of 1603. At the Hampton Court conference in 1604 the king decided against them. Bolstered by royal support, Arminian (High Church) ideas made headway, and the Church continued to develop a distinctive ethos: neither wholly Protestant nor wholly Catholic but borrowing freely from both traditions.

> But dearest Mother ...
> The mean thy praise and glorie is,
>   And long may be.

George Herbert*, who wrote those lines, (in 'The British Church') sketched an ideal for contemporary parochial ministry in his *A Priest to the Temple*. William Laud, Archbishop of Canterbury from 1633 to 1645, served the same cause in harsher fashion. He harried the Puritans, and infuriated many laity by his attempts to recover the Church's plundered revenues. Under his peremptory guidance the Church consolidated her position until the abrupt reversals brought about by the Civil Wars, the Commonwealth and the Protectorate.

Between 1642 and 1660 more of the clergy were persecuted and displaced than at any other time. By the best calculation, 2425 benefices were sequestered, and large numbers of unbeneficed clergy were also uprooted. The victims included some rascals; but for the most part the sufferers were ejected for loyalty to the Crown, to Laudian practice or to the Prayer Book.

At the Restoration hundreds of clergy sought their own again. For this reason, or because conscience bade them go after the 1662 Act of Uniformity, 1760 Puritans left their parishes and reinforced the ranks of nonconformity. They did not lack congregations, since Dissent was now tolerated, initially grudgingly but more generously as time went on. Other clergy of Puritan sympathies, such as Ralph Josselin*, retained their parishes and reluctantly conformed. The age produced in Thomas Traherne* a priest whose remarkable spirituality has been fully appreciated only in modern times.

The Church had returned in 1660 politically weakened, its fortunes more than ever tied to those of the Crown. This was the heyday of the doctrine of the Divine Right of Kings, a circumstance which made for embarrassment when King James II energetically advanced the cause of Roman Catholicism. The

Glorious Revolution of 1688 preserved the clergy from the Roman Catholic threat; but deprived the Church of the Nonjurors, who, having sworn allegiance to the Stuarts, were not prepared to break their oaths. They numbered only 400 or so, but included many men whom the Church was poorer for losing. Even the parochial clergy who remained in post were for the most part grudging supporters of the new dynasty; the eighteenth century was an age of Whig bishops and Tory incumbents.

With increasing agricultural prosperity, and thanks to the surrender to the Church by Queen Anne of taxes previously reserved for royal use, clerical incomes rose. The eighteenth-century clergy were better educated and from a higher class of society than their predecessors. It is significant that one in six of the parochial clergy at the end of the century had held a fellowship in an Oxford or Cambridge college; and that about a half of all graduates were ordained (Virgin, 133, 135). The ideal of 'a gentleman in every parish', personified in the genial figure of James Woodforde*, had found its time.

The eighteenth-century Church was not as moribund as is sometimes suggested. At the grass roots it was 'intimately involved in the life of the people, providing a great deal of their justice, acting the unenviable role of moral policeman, settling their disputes over legacies, protecting their rights, educating their children, and even pioneering much that has come to be known as social security' (Arthur Warne, *Church and Society in Eighteenth-Century Devon*, David & Charles 1969, 9). The two great religious movements of the century, Methodism and the Evangelical Revival, adorned by such men as William Grimshaw*, John Fletcher* and John Newton*, were nurtured in the bosom of the Church, even if she proved an unsympathetic mother. By the early nineteenth-century the number and quality of men coming forward for ordination were higher than ever before.

On the other hand the disparity of clerical incomes remained a problem, as did pluralism and non-residence. Some parishes were not served at all; others only by a starveling curate paid a pittance by an absentee incumbent. Nepotism abounded. Training for the ministry was almost non-existent. While few of the clergy were grossly immoral, many were uninspired and uninspiring, minor gentry in gown and bands. Boswell remarked approvingly of one such: 'his size and figure and countenance and manner were those of a hearty English squire, with the parson superimposed' (quoted Cragg, 128). Jane Austen's Edmund Bertram (in *Mansfield Park*) is no more than a purveyor of refinement to the upper classes and of kindness to the lower.

In the eighteenth and early nineteenth centuries the clergy had to contend with more public hostility than ever before or since. Thomas Secker (1693–1768), a future Archbishop of Canterbury, reflected: 'Christianity is now railed at and ridiculed with very little reserve, and its teachers without any at all. Against us our adversaries appear to have set themselves to be as bitter as they can, not only beyond all truth, but beyond all probability, exaggerating without mercy' (Cragg, 127). In the early nineteenth century two Radical publications – the *Episcopal Gazette* and the *Church Examiner* – were wholly devoted to anti-clerical propaganda. The bishop of Bristol's palace went up in flames during the riots at the time of the Great Reform Bill. It is against this background that we must see the tragic career of the upright but flawed John Skinner*.

Criticism and a renewed ardour within the Church herself had their due effect. Early nineteenth-century parish priests such as Sydney Smith* and Henry Fardell* took their duties more seriously than their predecessors had done, and structural change did away with some of the worst abuses. Parochial provision had become hopelessly out of conformity with the distribution of population, especially in the new industrial towns. After the Napoleonic Wars ended in 1815 a vast new church-building programme began, supported both by government and by private money. By 1857, 612 new churches had been opened. Parish priests of extraordinary quality, such as Arthur Stanton* and Robert Dolling*, gave their lives to service in the slums. A far larger proportion of the Church's resources was now devoted to urban areas; though even today two-thirds of the clergy serve one third of the population, and those looking for normative Anglicanism would be most likely to find it in villages and small towns.

The number of parishes doubled between 1850 and 1900. Legislation dealt effectively with a variety of longstanding abuses. Diocesan boundaries were changed and new dioceses created. A part of the incomes of bishops and of cathedrals was used to extend and strengthen the parochial system. Theological colleges to train ordinands were opened. Effective action was taken against non-residence and there was less pluralism than at any time before or since. Church schools were opened in thousands and almost everywhere the Church supplemented the harsh and scanty welfare provision afforded by the State.

Most important of all, the numbers and quality of the parochial clergy rose to unprecedented heights. There were 10,718 clergy in 1831, 17,621 in 1851, 24,232 in 1891; though it has to be added that this increase was not fully proportionate to the increase in population over the same period (Russell 83, 241–2). Walter Hook* set an example of brilliantly productive urban ministry; Charles Kingsley* of the parson as social thinker and writer; Robert Hawker* of creative eccentricity. At a less distinguished level there were thousands of humble and dedicated priests such as Francis Kilvert*. Significantly it was a Dissenter who remarked: 'We believe the Anglican clergy to be the most pernicious men of all within the compass of the church; but also the most sincere, the most learned, the most self-denying' (Chadwick, *VC* 1.230–1). The impetus for improvement came from an increased religious seriousness, which was itself both cause and effect of a greater seriousness within the nation as a whole. If one consequence was more religious controversy, about the relationship of the Church with the State and about the relations of Churchmen with each other, that was in itself a sign of life. Religious market forces were also at work, as church, chapel and the newly tolerated and resurgent Roman Catholic church vied for custom.

The Evangelicals were an increasingly potent force among the clergy, gifting the church with their patron saint in the person of Charles Simeon* and with such devoted if limited ministers as William Andrew*. As the nineteenth century wore on Anglicanism was enriched by the Tractarians and their successors the Anglo-Catholics – clergy who sought to revivify the Church by claiming her ancient heritage of doctrine and practice and by returning the eucharist to the central place in worship. John Keble* was to the Tractarians what Simeon was to the Evangelicals, William Bennett* a pattern of the Anglo-Catholic parish priest. Both Evangelicals and Anglo-Catholics were disturbed by the growth of biblical criticism and liberal theology, of which the brothers Augustus and Julius Hare* were early proponents and the great urban priest Samuel Barnett* a later one. Despite their disagreements, Evangelicals, Anglo-Catholics and Liberals all contributed to the vitality of the greatest age the Church of England has ever known.

But stormy waters lay ahead. The agricultural depression of the 1880s bore heavily on the clergy. Incomes, linked to tithes or to money which represented the commutation of tithes, had risen steadily from 1700 to about 1838; then they had levelled out; now they plummeted. Congregations, which had failed to keep up with the growth of population throughout most of the nineteenth century, began to decline in absolute terms towards the end of it. The Church had never really gained the working-class; now it began to lose the middle class. The clergy were as devoted as they had ever been; but the trend of the times was against them. The larger part which the State played in providing education and welfare was both an index of the Church's failure and a reinforcement of it. New ideas – Darwinism, Marxism, German biblical scholarship – eroded traditional belief, and two World Wars and economic change tore the old social fabric apart. Despite the heroic efforts of such priests as Dick Sheppard* in the earlier part of this century and David Watson* in the latter, the clergy have fought a losing battle ever since.

During the twentieth century the Church has purged herself of many of the abuses and weaknesses of the past. While remaining established she has become substantially self-governing. She is no longer the Tory party at prayer; though she is sometimes described as a church of readers of the *Daily Telegraph* led by readers of *The Guardian*. Lay participation and democratic procedures have been introduced at every level from the parochial upwards. Gross disparities in clerical income have been done away, and stipends are now almost uniform throughout the country. Though they are not generous, they offer security and are bolstered by the provision of a free house and of working expenses. A national system of clerical pensions has been introduced. It is harder than it used to be for an unworthy minister to cling to his post. The eucharist has become the central act of worship. A modern liturgy is available though not compulsory. Varieties of practice reflect churchmanship without arousing the strong feelings of previous generations. Women have been admitted to the diaconate, and will soon be admitted to the priesthood. Yet in a real sense all these reforms have been in vain.

The most important single characteristic of the Church of England in the twentieth century has been the catastrophic numerical decline in its active membership. In 1993, though about a quarter of all babies were still given Anglican baptism and the clergy still conducted a high proportion of marriages and most funerals, the Church could claim only 1.2 million regular worshippers, 2.3% of the population. Like other historic institutions she had been marginalized, and was no longer a pervasive influence on national life.

With the decline in the number of worshippers has come a decline in the number of clergy, in part because of lack of money to pay them, in part because of fewer vocations. This decline too, from 25,235 in 1901 to 12,905 in 1971, shows no sign of abating. It is anticipated that in the year 2000 the church will be 1000 short of the 10,000 men and women needed to maintain the existing parochial structure.

In 1991 England was divided into 13,099 parishes, but into only 8906 benefices – combinations of parishes. There were over 400 team ministries in which several clergy served a number of parishes collaboratively under the leadership of one of their number; and over 100 group ministries in which several incumbents or priests in charge worked together under a chairman. The work of the parochial clergy was supplemented by that of about 1700 priests in specialized or sector ministries, such as hospital and industrial chaplaincies. In addition the retired clergy, who outnumbered those in post, performed an indispensable supportive role.

Expedients adopted to recruit clergy and maintain the parochial system have included part-time ministerial training courses, the use of non-stipendiary ministers (unpaid clergy) who may or may not be full time, the use of local ministers raised up by their own parishes and confined to them, and a greater reliance on the ministry of the laity. It is a question for some, however, whether these devices will suffice to maintain the parochial system even in an attenuated form.

The clergy who serve parishes today are drawn from a greater variety of backgrounds than in the past, but recruits from the working-class are still rare. The average age is high. Less than half are graduates and most make no pretensions to scholarship. If they excel in anything, it is usually pastoral care. They are as conscientious and respectable as they have ever been. They tend to individualism, but less than formerly to eccentricity. By the public at large they are regarded with amused indifference, tinged in the case of people who have actually come across them with regard. Their congregations, though less deferential than in the past, are usually content to accept their leadership, to tolerate their inadequacies, and to treat them affectionately. They stand in need of such kindness, since they are confronted with a host of intractable problems: the relentless advance of secularism, the financial and administrative burdens connected with one or several parishes, the requirement to balance the needs of their congregations against those of the wider community, the inadequacy of resources, the lack of time. They are sustained chiefly by their spirituality, and in this respect, as in many others, join hands with the four centuries of their predecessors.

2

A Portrait Gallery

If he might have had but one request of God Almighty,
it should have been above all other, that he might be a
blessing to mankind. (Traherne, 4.32)

This portrait gallery serves two purposes. First, it contains introductory biographies of the 26 parish priests who feature most prominently later on. The content of each biography is determined by the nature of later references. Secondly, it contains basic information about the 60 other priests who are mentioned on several occasions. In Part Two the first appearance of a priest in either category in a chapter or section of a chapter is asterisked, with one or two asterisks respectively.

Henry Alford (1810–71): Vicar of Wymeswold, Leicestershire, from 1838 to 1853. Later served Quebec Chapel, Marylebone, and became Dean of Canterbury. A leading biblical scholar.

William Wayte Andrew
Born in 1805, Andrew had a chequered early life. His father went bankrupt when his son was sixteen, and Andrew was for a time apprenticed to a draper. But uncles left him property, and thereafter he had independent means. Despite a lack of academic qualifications he was admitted to St Mary Hall, Oxford. He underwent an evangelical conversion, and on graduating spent a year reading divinity. With some difficulty he persuaded bishop Bathurst of Norwich to ordain him, and served first as curate of Gimingham, Norfolk. In 1834 he married Ellen Wickes. Later the same year he took the curacy of Witchingham. In 1835, through the influence of his parents-in-law, he was presented to the tiny living of Ketteringham, Norfolk. He remained there until two years before his death in 1889.

Andrew was a zealot, certain of his own salvation and tireless in the offer of salvation to others. His blazing sincerity and whole-hearted dedication were not tempered by doubt or by respect for the views of other people. He was angular and lacked empathy. He was no intellectual. It was said with some justice that he appealed chiefly to women and to weak men. But he was a devoted pastor and a teacher who touched the hearts of many who at first resisted him. He was narrow, awkward and intransigent; but he had a touch of holiness as well.

J. C. Atkinson (c.1817–c.1900): Incumbent of Danby, Cumberland from 1847 until his death. As well as various learned works he wrote the delightful and atmospheric *Forty Years in a Moorland Parish*.

Sabine Baring-Gould (1834–1924): Influenced in his youth by Charles Lowder (qv), he taught in Woodard schools for a time and was ordained in 1864. In 1881 he took over the family living of Lew Trenchard, Devonshire, and was squire and parson there until his death. He was an immensely prolific popular author, and, of course, wrote *Onward, Christian Soldiers.*

Samuel Barnett

Samuel Augustus Barnett was born in 1844 in Bristol, where his father owned a foundry. In 1862 he entered Wadham College, Oxford, graduating in law and history in 1865. After a couple of years' teaching he paid a visit to the USA which, he said, 'knocked all the Toryism out of me'.

Barnett took orders in 1867, and served his title as curate of St Mary's, Bryanston Square, London. In 1870 he met Henrietta Rowland, a young woman from an affluent background who had become a parish visitor. After some hesitation she agreed to marry him. The young couple took over St Jude's, Whitechapel, which the Bishop of London described to them as 'the worst parish in my diocese, inhabited mainly by a criminal population' (Barnett, 1.68). They threw themselves into their ministry with exemplary vigour. In due course they moved on to a wider stage and became national figures in the field of social issues. Barnett was a prolific writer, and eventually an influential one. He had a genius for publicity, illustrated by the way he used the activities of Jack the Ripper to draw attention to conditions in Whitechapel.

The Barnetts spent their own money generously, and were able to attract large sums from affluent people living elsewhere. More important still, they persuaded men and women of the middle and upper classes to work in the parish, and to identify themselves with its needs. Out of this identification came in 1884 Toynbee Hall, the first urban settlement.

Exhausted, Barnett resigned his parish in 1894. He remained warden of Toynbee Hall and canon of Bristol Cathedral (a post to which he had been appointed in 1893) until 1906. In that year he became a canon of Westminster Abbey, continuing to support the causes to which he had given his life until his death in 1913. His widow survived him for thirteen years. She remained active in public life, eventually receiving the CBE.

In early life Barnett was not prepossessing. His appearance was uncouth, his manner diffident and uneasy. He was simultaneously shy and aggressive, and insensitive in personal relationships. These deficiencies were redeemed by what his wife thought his central characteristic, humility. She wrote of 'the meek acquiescence with which he bore every delinquency when it affected himself'. Humility did not, however, inhibit him from vigorous or even violent action; he broke a walking-stick over a boy who misbehaved on an organized holiday.

Barnett had other virtues. His extraordinary patience sustained him in failure and disappointment. He fearlessly challenged all those who damaged the quality of life of parishioners, whether individuals, companies or public authorities. As he grew older his nature was refined by marriage, experience and grace. He evoked virtue by assuming it. One Toynbee Hall resident asked another: 'Is Barnett sincere? he seems to flatter one.' 'If you think,' the reply came, 'you will see that his "flattery" consisted in expecting great things from you' (Barnett, 1.317).

In a sermon after Barnett's death, the Dean of Westminster said: 'Men spoke of Canon Barnett as a "Modernist", and if the slang term be applicable to one who laboured in the Church of Christ to put an end to the mediaeval tyranny of the Schoolmen over the intellect and reason of the Church, the mediaeval disregard of the working classes, the mediaeval contempt of laymen's representation on the councils of the Church, then he was a "Modernist" for whose work and example let us thank God' (Barnett, 2.369).

William Bennett

William Bennett was born in 1804, and educated at Westminster School and Christchurch, Oxford. He was ordained deacon in 1828 and priest in 1830. He married Mary Franklin in 1828. Of their three daughters, one died in infancy; their only son died at the age of 20.

After three London curacies and a spell as minister of Portman Chapel Bennett was appointed to the new church of St Paul's, Knightsbridge, consecrated in 1843. His parish of some 12,000 souls included some of the richest and some of the poorest streets in London. He proved himself a first-rate pastor and organizer, and used gifts from his affluent parishioners to build the church of St Barnabas, Pimlico, for his indigent ones. The church was consecrated in 1850, but almost immediately became a storm-centre because of Bennett's churchmanship. Brought up as a low churchman, he had been much influenced by the Oxford Movement, and was among the first of those who articulated its teaching by way of ornaments and ceremonial. His practices brought him into conflict with his bishop as well as with some of the public, and a few months after St Barnabas's consecration he was forced to resign. In 1852 he became, at the invitation of Lady Bath, vicar of Frome, Somerset. In this small town he resumed his Catholic practices, and, overcoming initial opposition, built up a hugely successful parish. He remained there until his death in 1886.

Bennett was energetic, courageous and pugnacious. His friends described his good looks, his charm and courtesy, his abstemiousness, and the lavish generosity with which he subsidized his projects from his own pocket. A meticulous organizer and a careful and thorough teacher, he combined strong and clear principles with personal kindliness and charity. It was typical of him that, when one of his curates at St Barnabas's converted to Rome, he labelled him as a schismatic and an apostate and publicly pronounced him excommunicate; typical too that when the priest returned to the Church of England Bennett gave him a curacy at Frome.

A prolific pamphleteer and an enthusiastic controversialist, Bennett survived unperturbed a prosecution brought because of his views on the Eucharist. He was one of the most attractive of the early Anglo-Catholics: of unimpeachable piety, a strong leader and a model parish priest.

Richard Benson (1824–1915): In 1850 appointed vicar of Cowley, near Oxford. He presided over the parish's expansion from a village to a suburb, and was the founder of the Society of St John the Evangelist, of which he was also the first superior. An austere Anglo-Catholic.

Edward Bickersteth (1786–1850): After service with the Church Missionary Society, he became in 1830 rector of Watton, Hertfordshire, where he conducted a model ministry until his death. The 'most colourful and godly of the evangelical clergy' (Chadwick, *VC* 1.441), a prolific author and hymnodist and a founding member of the Evangelical Alliance.

Patrick Bronte (1777–1861) Perpetual curate of Haworth, Yorkshire, from 1820 to his death. Father of the novelists.

George Bull (1799–1867): While curate of Byerley, near Bradford, from 1826 to 1840 he became a leading supporter of the Ten Hours movement, and was also active in other attempts to serve the interests of working-class people. He became an incumbent for the first time in 1840 and served in two working-class parishes in Birmingham and in one rural parish.

George Carey (1935–): From a working class background he obtained a first degree and a doctorate from London University. Vicar of St Nicholas, Durham, from 1975 to 1982. He then became in succession principal of a theological college, Bishop of Bath and Wells, and Archbishop of Canterbury.

Roy Catchpole (1946–); One of the few Anglican clergy who have graduated to ordination from prison. He has spent most of his ministry in parishes in Nottinghamshire.

Christopher Chavasse (1884–1962): After a curacy in St Helen's and war service, he became vicar of St George's, Barrow-in-Furness (1919–22) and rector of St Aldate's, Oxford (1922–8). Later Master of St Peter's Hall and Bishop of Rochester.

Francis Close (1797–1882): In 1824 he became curate and in 1826 incumbent of Holy Trinity, Cheltenham. Here he conducted a ministry so energetic and authoritarian that it has been said: 'No English city has come nearer Calvin's Geneva than Close's Cheltenham' (Hennell, 121). In 1856 he became Dean of Carlisle.

William Cole (1714–1782): A wealthy antiquary, ordained in 1745. He left a detailed diary of the years 1766 and 1767, during which he was incumbent of Bletchley and then of Waterbeach, Cambridgeshire.

L. John Collins (1905–82): A curate in Whitstable from 1928 to 1929. He spent the rest of his life in non-parochial posts, latterly as a canon of St Paul's. A founder of Christian Action and a leading member of the Campaign for Nuclear Disarmament.

John Conybeare (1843–1931): A member of a distinguished clerical family, he was incumbent of Barrington, Cambridgeshire, from 1871 to 1898.

George Crabbe (1754–1832): Initially an apothecary, he became curate of Aldeburgh, Suffolk, in 1782, and of Stathern, Leicestershire, 1785–9. He held the livings of Muston, Leicestershire, and of nearby West Allington, Lincoln-shire, 1789–1814. In the latter year he became rector of Trowbridge, Wiltshire, holding also Croxton, Leicestershire, until his death. An important poet.

Mandell Creighton (1843–1901): From 1875 to 1884 vicar of Embleton, Northumberland; thereafter professor of ecclesiastical history at Cambridge. Later bishop successively of Peterborough and of London.

George Denison (1805–96): Vicar of East Brent from 1845 until his death. From 1851 archdeacon of Taunton. A sturdy high churchman. He is thought to be the prototype of Trollope's archdeacon Grantley.

Robert Dolling

Robert William Radclyffe Dolling was born in 1851 in County Down. He attended Harrow and Trinity College, Cambridge, without distinction. In early manhood he fell under the influence of Arthur Stanton (qv), and began to demonstrate his extraordinary gift for befriending. Admitted to Salisbury Theological College in 1882, he was ordained deacon in the following year. Nominally licensed to a country curacy, he gave his time to a Mission in Stepney. After ordination to the priesthood in 1885 he took over the Winchester College Mission at St Agatha's, Landport, Portsmouth. He served there for ten colourful and productive years.

In 1895 Dolling fell out with Bishop Randall Davidson, and resigned. A period without a parish followed; he used part of it to write his book *Ten Years in a Portsmouth Slum*. In 1898 he became vicar of St Saviour's, Poplar. He was by now nationally famous and much in demand, but he found his own parish a hard nut to crack. His health failed and he died in 1902 at the early age of fifty-one.

Dolling's reluctance to read had stood in the way of conventional success at his theological college. That makes the more remarkable the principal's description of him: 'There was some singular – as it were mesmeric – force of pure humaneness, genuine sympathy, philanthropy, brotherliness, about him, amounting to a sort of genius ... [he had] a marvellous insight into character – a wonderful warmth and tenderness of love.' Dolling once said: 'The human are so ungodly and the godly are so inhuman; that is the difficulty.' A friend remarked that Dolling's greatest talent was the marvellous combination he evinced of the human and the godly within himself (Osborne, *Dolling* 41, 149).

Henry Fardell

Fardell was born in 1795. He married Eliza, a daughter of the bishop of Ely, Bowyer Sparke. They had four children. Already a Prebend of Ely Cathedral and incumbent of Waterbeach, Cambridgeshire, he became vicar of Wisbech in the same county in 1831. He retained all these offices until his death in 1854.

Conscious of his wealth and pluralism, Fardell embarked upon a diary 'to answer any questions that may be put relative to Parochial Residence, and to give an answer to such doubts as might otherwise arise relative to the discharge of Parochial duties' (Fardell, 1). The diary, which he kept from 1831 to 1853, lacks consistency and continuity but provides a vivid picture of conscientious pastoral ministry.

In his preface to his diary Fardell wrote: 'NB Censure not ... none know what the anxieties of a Parochial clergyman are, but a Parochial Minister' (Fardell, 1). Certainly he did not spare himself anxieties. Hard-working, devout, upright and systematic himself he was intolerant of the absence of those virtues in others. He was prepared to make a stand on principle even at the price of unpopularity. He was meticulous to a fault. His editor says, justly, that he evokes our affection and our respect, but that one would have hesitated to have become his curate (Fardell, 144).

John Fletcher

Jean Guillaume de la Flechere was born in Nyon in Switzerland in 1729. In 1749 he travelled to England to learn the language, and in 1752 he became tutor to the son of Thomas Hill, a Shropshire country gentleman, a post he held until 1759. During this period he englished his name. More importantly, he joined the Methodist movement, and, like John Wesley, experienced a deepening and widening of faith which transformed his life.

After some hesitation, Fletcher offered himself for the Anglican ministry, and was ordained deacon and priest in close succession in 1757. In 1760 he became vicar of Madeley in Shropshire, having refused another parish on the grounds that 'there is too much money and too little labour' (Macdonald, *Fletcher* 57).

Madeley was large and populous, inhabited chiefly by colliers and ironworkers. The town was, to quote one of Fletcher's biographers, 'remarkable for little else than the ignorance and profaneness of its inhabitants, among whom respect to man was as rarely to be observed, as piety towards God!' (Benson, *Fletcher* 51). Some responded with hostility to their vicar's attempts to evangelize them, but many were won over. Fletcher was soon preaching to vast congregations, and turning the parish into a model of pastoral and devotional life.

In the years which followed Fletcher combined his parochial ministry with the headship of Lady Huntingdon's seminary at Trevecca. When the controversy between the Calvinist and Arminian wings of Methodism compelled his retirement from that office, he took to his pen and proved to be a master of vigorous and charitable polemic. A long illness in 1776–7 drove him to Switzerland where he continued to preach and teach so far as the authorities would allow. His health partially restored, he returned to England in 1781; and shortly afterwards proposed to, and was accepted by, Mary Bosanquet. Fletcher died in 1785, but his wife continued his work in the parish throughout the thirty years of her widowhood.

Fletcher's chief claim to fame lay in his holiness. Melville Horne, one of the young people whom Fletcher loved to teach, and who later became his curate, wrote of him: 'I know not which most to venerate, his public or private character. Grave and dignified in his deportment and manners, he yet excelled in all the courtesies and attentions of the accomplished gentleman. In every company he appeared as the least, the last, and the servant of all. From head to foot he was clothed with humility; while the heavenly-mindedness of an angel shone from his countenance and sparkled in his eyes. His religion was without labour and without effort, for Christianity was, not only his great business, but his very element and nature. As a mortal man, he doubtless had his errors and failings; but what they were, they who knew him best would find it difficult to say, for he appeared as an instrument of heavenly minstrels, attuned to the Master's touch' (Macdonald, *Fletcher* 177–8).

Thomas Fuller (1608–61): Curate of St Benet's, Cambridge (1630–3), rector of Broadwindsor, Dorset (1634–42), curate of the Savoy Chapel (1642–3), curate of Waltham Abbey, Essex (1649–58) and rector of Cranford, Middlesex (1658–61). A prolific, witty and influential writer.

Cyril Garbett (1875–1955): Successively curate (1899–1909) and vicar (1909–1919) of Portsea, Hampshire. Later Bishop of Southwark and of Winchester, and Archbishop of York.

Samuel Garratt (1817–1906): He served curacies in Islington and Grappenhall, Cheshire, and was then incumbent successively of Holy Trinity, Waltham Cross (1845–50); Trinity Church in the parish of St Giles-in-the-Fields (1850–67); and St Margaret's, Ipswich (1867–1895). A leading Evangelical.

Bernard Gilpin

Born in 1517, Gilpin was a younger son of a Westmoreland country gentleman. He entered Queen's College, Oxford, in 1533, already intending to take orders. He was caught up in the intellectual ferment associated with the New Learning, and gradually moved from a reforming Catholic position to a Protestant one. In 1552 he accepted the parish of Norton, near Stockton, and, because it was a royal living, was commanded to preach before the court. His attack upon abuses in church and state did him good as well as harm in the reign of Edward VI, but his evolving theology placed him in jeopardy during the Marian persecution. He was protected by his friend bishop Tunstall of Durham, who in 1557 appointed him to the huge parish of Houghton in which two or three thousand people were scattered over fifty square miles. Summoned to London in 1558 to account for his opinions, he was saved from the stake by the death of Mary. He returned to Houghton, and refusing all offers of preferment stayed there until he died in 1584.

Gilpin was the founding father of Anglican parochial ministry, a paradigm of devoted and sacrificial endeavour. His success was due to his character. One of his biographers describes him: 'He had no servile appliances, he would have his means good as well as his ends. His behaviour was ever free from levity, obliging without meanness, insinuating without art; he condescended to the weak, bore with the passionate, complied with the scrupulous; in a truly apostolic manner he became all things to all men.' In addition, he was humble, tolerant over inessentials, and a good business man who used his income in the service of others. Naturally quick-tempered, he taught himself restraint; of serious disposition, he was a delightful companion. 'Cheerfulness was in his soul because it was in good health.'

He had friends among great men who admired his integrity. The same integrity also earned him powerful enemies; like many other saintly people he passed much of his life in conflict. Scrupulous almost to a fault, his conscience made decisions in matters of faith difficult for him. He was categorical about his central, Protestant, intention: 'My chiefest comfort and endeavour was to preach Christ, and salvation through Christ, plainly and sincerely, and to comfort myself in the most sweet promises of Holy Scripture, and in pouring out my prayers to God' (Collingwood, *Gilpin* 131, 284, 40).

William Grimshaw

Grimshaw was born of peasant stock in Brindle, Lancashire, in 1708. He attended Blackburn Grammar School and Heskin Free School. At Christ's College, Cambridge he lived the customary careless undergraduate life. He was ordained deacon in 1731 and after a short curacy at Littleborough in the parish of Rochdale, Lancashire, moved to Todmorden in the same parish. He was priested in 1732. In 1734 he experienced an awakening, which delivered him into a long spiritual struggle, but which eventually led him to a secure trust in the redeeming work of Christ.

Grimshaw was overwhelmed with grief at the death of his first wife in 1739 after only four years of marriage. He was scarcely more fortunate in his second marriage which lasted only from 1741 to 1746. But in 1743 he had moved to Haworth, nominally a daughter parish to Bradford. Haworth was a small, highly insanitary town of perhaps 2000 inhabitants, one of the most important centres of the worsted industry. Its inhabitants were stubborn, independent, inured to hardship, and capable of deep and lasting loyalty.

It did not take long for Grimshaw to make a favourable impression upon them. His plainness and bluntness; his capacity for hard work and the seriousness with which he took his responsibilities; his indifference to material things and the colourful quirks of his character; above all his blazing sincerity and the power and enthusiasm of his preaching: secured him a large congregation drawn both from the locality and from farther afield. He was not content, however, with the people who came to him. He spent a large part of his time on the move, preaching in homes or in the open, and more often than not outside his own parish. He was prepared to tramp miles to address a handful; but he frequently spoke to vast numbers. He was a Methodist in disposition and technique even before he met the Wesleys and became a leading member of the revival they led.

Grimshaw's robust health failed in the late 1750s and he died in 1763. Wesley did him no more than justice when he said: 'A few such as him would make a nation tremble. He carries fire wherever he goes!' (Baker, *Grimshaw* 264).

Thomas Hancock (1832–1903): F.D. Maurice persuaded him to seek ordination and he held four curacies between 1861 and 1875, offending congregations equally because of his socialism and because of his Anglo-Catholicism. In 1883 he found his niche in the lectureship attached to St Nicholas, Cole Abbey, London.

Augustus and Julius Hare

The brothers Hare were born in Italy, Augustus in 1792, Julius in 1795, but came to England when their father inherited the family estate at Hurstmonceaux in Sussex. Augustus went to Winchester, Julius to Charterhouse; Augustus to New College, Oxford, Julius to Trinity College, Cambridge. Both became dons; both were ordained; both were broad churchmen; they collaborated in writing a book *Guesses at Truth*.

In the late 1820s their paths diverged. Augustus fell in love with Maria Leycester, daughter of a parish priest, and married her in 1829. They went to the tiny parish of Alton-Barnes, Wiltshire, where they conducted a conscientious ministry until Augustus died in 1833. Julius remained a don until, somewhat reluctantly, he took over the family living of Hurstmonceaux in 1832. He remained there until his death in 1855, from 1840 holding also the post of archdeacon of Lewes. After Augustus's death, Maria Hare came to live in the parish. In 1844 her brother-in-law married her friend Esther Maurice, sister of F.D. Maurice.

Both Hares had brilliant minds. Augustus was lazy and light-hearted in early life, and a noted practical joker at university. Ordination and marriage steadied him, however, and he made great efforts to come to terms with the nature and needs of his rural parishioners.

Julius was the more open, pugnacious and demonstrative of the two; it was said of him that he was often loved, frequently detested, but never ignored. His lengthy visits to Germany acquainted him with the development of theological ideas and biblical criticism there, and he contributed to their introduction into this country. He was first and foremost a scholar. The parish took second place in his affections. He had no gifts of popularization as a preacher and was an ineffective pastor. He was aware of these deficiencies and they frequently depressed him; but, unlike his brother, he did not change.

Robert Hawker

Born in 1803, Hawker came of clerical stock. Largely self-educated, he obtained a place at Pembroke College, Oxford, in 1823. In the same year he married Charlotte I'ans, aged 41. She had means, but it was a love-match, and Hawker cared devotedly for his wife in her old age. She died in 1863 and in 1864 Hawker married Pauline Kuczynski, twenty years his junior, by whom he had three daughters. Again, the marriage was very happy.

Transferring to Magdalen Hall after his marriage, Hawker graduated in 1828. Made deacon in 1829 and ordained priest in 1831, he served a curacy at North Tamerton near his wife's house at Whitstone, Cornwall. He was then preferred to the remote, bleak and scattered parish of Morwenstow in the same county. His parishioners were mostly farmers, labourers and servants, many of them Methodists; there were no wealthy or powerful inhabitants to set an example of churchgoing or to enforce it. The local economy was declining, as was the population; in his later years Hawker was ministering to well under 1000 people. Wages were low and employment not plentiful; disease and extreme poverty were endemic.

Hawker strove mightily to serve his people. One of his flock said of him: 'Lovely gentleman he was ... say what you like he was a good man' (Brendon, *Hawker* 213). Unfairly however, his continuing fame rests more upon his complex character, his unusual opinions and his carefully cultivated idiosyncrasies than upon his work as a parish priest. A struggle raged within him 'between pride, vanity, dogmatism, irascibility, malice, superstition and courage, charitableness, humour, affection, humaneness, piety' (Brendon, *Hawker* 232). His wide reading and his delight in nature fed his capacity for intense intuitional experience and prompted his considerable output of poetry. He totally rejected the scientific materialism of his age, and had a vivid and literal belief in the supernatural. Adept at self-dramatization, he was consciously eccentric in dress and manner, an exhibitionist and an inveterate romancer.

Hawker was tortured by the hostility of local farmers, by the misery with which he was surrounded, and by the dreadful necessities associated with the regular shipwrecks on the nearby coast. He quarrelled with every member of his family except his wives, and with most of his friends. He was subject to depression and persecution mania. Attracted to the Roman Catholic church by its anti-scientific certainties, he was received into it a few hours before he died in 1875.

Stewart Headlam (1847–1924): The most outspoken, perceptive and clear-headed of the priestly Christian Socialists of the nineteenth century. He was from 1872 to 1873 curate at St John's, Drury Lane, and from then until 1878 curate at St Matthew's, Bethnal Green.

George Herbert

Herbert was born of mixed Anglo–Welsh stock in 1593. His father, Richard Herbert, an influential country gentleman of Montgomeryshire, died when he was three years old. George was cared for by his mother and, when she re-married, by his step-father Sir John Danvers. In 1601 the large, open-hearted and pious household moved to London. George attended Westminster School, where his enthusiasm for church music was fostered and where he came into frequent contact with the saintly Lancelot Andrewes, then dean of Westminster Abbey. He pursued his studies with distinction and in 1609 entered Trinity College, Cambridge, as a Westminster scholar.

Herbert obtained an excellent first degree, became a sublector and fellow of his college, and subsequently occupied other university posts including that of orator. He began to write the verse, unpublished in his life-time, on which his literary reputation depends. He was, however, handicapped by poor health, which became a continuing problem.

About the year 1617 Herbert began the study of divinity, and in his Latin verse acted as an apologist for the Church of England. A brief interlude as MP for the family borough of Montgomery decided him against the life of affairs. He was ordained deacon in late 1624. In 1626 he became a non-residentiary canon of Lincoln Cathedral, and prebendary without cure of souls of Leighton Ecclesia, Cambridgeshire.

In 1629 Herbert married Jane Danvers, cousin to his step-father, and in 1630 accepted the rectory of Fugglestone-with-Bemerton, near Salisbury. He was instituted in April and ordained priest the following September. He had two years of ministry before his health fell into a final decline. He died in March 1633. His elder brother wrote of him: 'His life was most holy and exemplary, in so much that about Salisbury where he lived beneficed for many years, he was little less than sainted: He was not exempt from passion and choler, being infirmities to which all our race is subject, but that excepted, without reproach in his actions' (Charles, *Herbert* 176).

There is little first-hand information about Herbert; Walton's famous *Life* is unreliable. But his poetry witnesses to his deep Christian devotion; and the picture of the devout priest in his posthumously published work *The Priest to the Temple, or, The Country Parson* may well (despite the charming disclaimer in the preface) have been a self-portrait. That is the assumption here.

Robert Herrick (1591–1674): Incumbent of Dean Prior, Devonshire, 1629–47 and 1662–1674. Author of poems both secular and sacred.

Walter Hook

Walter Farquhar Hook was born in 1798. He was unhappy at his schools, which included Winchester; solitary during his time at Christchurch, Oxford. In 1821 he was ordained deacon, in 1822 priest. He was curate to his father in the parish of Whippingham, Isle of Wight, until 1826 when he became perpetual curate of Moseley. In 1829 he took over the parish of Holy Trinity, Coventry, and in the same year married Anna Delicia Johnstone, who was a calming and restraining influence on him for the rest of her life (she died in 1871). In 1836 he began his notable incumbency at Leeds, setting a standard for the conduct of a large urban parish which has probably never been equalled and certainly never improved upon. Hook stood in the old tradition of high churchmanship, and spoke for it with as much vigour as others did for Tractarianism or Evangelicism. In youth a rigid Tory, his experience of the sufferings of the working-class made him their protagonist and trusted friend. He was impulsive, tactless and dictatorial; unashamed of the tears which he frequently shed; sometimes in the highest of spirits, sometimes dreadfully cast down. His biographer likens him to Samuel Johnson in his massive frame, 'in occasional twitchings and contortions of the face, fits of depression, a choleric temper, a constitutional dread of dying, and an antipathy to foreigners'. 'He was at once an active pastor, an eloquent preacher, a laborious student, a voluminous letter-writer, an able historian, a witty humorist, a wise practical moralist, and earnest Christian, an ardent patriot, and, every inch of him, a sturdy Englishman' (Stephens, *Hook*, 449, 570, 576).

Richard Hooker (*c*.1554–1600): The immensely learned apologist of the Elizabethan Settlement. Successively incumbent of Drayton Beauchamp, Buckinghamshire (1584), Boscombe, Wiltshire (1591), and Bishopsbourne, Kent (1595).

Arthur Hopkinson (*c*.1875–1960): Vicar of St Catherine's, Nottingham, 1904–9, and then rector of Winchfield until 1917, vicar of Banstead until 1929 and vicar of St Augustine's, Bournemouth until 1939.

Harold Hosking (1919–): He spent the whole of his ministry in Cornwall. His incumbencies included Penwerris (1953), St Mawgon-in-Pyder (1956), Newlyn (1961), Newquay (1969) and Redruth (1974–84).

Charles Jenkinson (1887–1949): The son of a dock labourer he became Conrad Noel's (qv) secretary and active in trade union affairs. After the First World War he read law at Fitzwilliam College, Cambridge, and trained for the ministry at Ripon Hall. In 1926 he became incumbent of St John and St Barnabas, Holbeck, Leeds. Elected to Leeds City council in 1930 he was from 1933 to 1936 an exceptionally effective chairman of the Housing Committee. He moved with his parishioners to the new housing estate at Belle Isle, resigning in 1947 when he became Leader of Leeds City Council.

William Jones (1754–1821): From 1780 to 1801 curate and from 1801 to 1812 vicar of Broxbourne, Hertfordshire. Clerical diarist.

W. Rowland Jones (*c*.1892–): After a Methodist upbringing he was ordained into the Church of England in 1920. He held a series of curacies, and was perpetual curate of St Hilda's, Audenshaw, from 1930 to 1952. After an unhappy continental chaplaincy and a further curacy he returned to Methodism.

Ralph Josselin

Josselin was born in 1617 at Roxwell in Hertfordshire. While he was still young, his father sold the family estate and moved to Bishop's Stortford. His mother died in 1624, but his father ensured that he had a good education at Bishop's Stortford school and at Jesus College, Cambridge. In 1636 his father, who had re-married, died leaving him only a small inheritance.

Josselin spent a couple of years teaching and then in 1639 became curate at Olney in Buckinghamshire. He was ordained deacon three months later, and priest (or, as he preferred to call it, minister) in February 1640. Later the same year the offer of a ministry at Cranham, Essex, enabled him to marry Jane Constable. After less than a year at Cranham, Josselin moved for health reasons to Earls Colne, Essex, a small town of some 1100 inhabitants. He stayed there until he died in 1683.

On 8 August 1644 Josselin wrote in his diary: 'Many things I have omitted that may be found in my notes, almanacks: etc. But now henceforwards I shall be more exact and particular' (Josselin, 15). In this way he marks a transition from condensed autobiography to entries never more than a few days apart. For nearly four decades thereafter he recorded his life in such detail that the published diary amounts to nearly 650 large pages.

Josselin's involvement in the main stream of history takes up only a small fraction of the diary. Most of it is devoted to the fabric of his daily existence. It tells of his devotion to, and of his suffering at the hands of, his wife; of the joys and tribulations which his children brought him; of his own and his family's health; of his finances; and of his life as a farmer and a clergyman.

Of particular importance is the fact that, in a manner almost unique among clerical diarists, Josselin recorded what were for him the spiritual implications of every aspect of his life. God spoke to him through everything, and he referred everything back to God. We do not have to guess at the spirituality to which he aspired; he lays it before us.

Josselin was upright, hard-working, thoughtful, self-critical, learned and serious-minded. He was a shrewd business man, who built up a solid estate through many vicissitudes. He loved his family, and meant well by them even when he did not handle his relationships with them successfully. He was humourless and unimaginative, and an inveterate worrier. He was almost pathetically grateful for the kindness of others, and felt coldness or slights acutely; wanting very much to be accepted, he often laid himself open to rejection. He displayed in abundance the strengths and the weaknesses of his Puritan creed. His editor remarks: 'He ... does not emerge as lovable, or even endearing – his conscientious and suffering figure simply stands before us, to wonder at, pity, and for all its frailty, respect' (Josselin, xxvi). I beg, at least in part, to disagree. Anyone who admits us to his essential humanity and to the crevices of his soul as fully as Josselin earns the love which is the appropriate response to vulnerability.

John Keble

Keble was born in the small town of Fairford, Gloucestershire, in 1792. He was educated at home, until in 1807 he obtained a scholarship to Corpus Christi College, Oxford. He obtained the rare distinction of a double first class honours degree, and in 1811 became a fellow of Oriel College. Ordained in 1815, he combined curacies and college posts until 1823, when he gave himself wholly over to parochial ministry. After two more short curacies he returned to Fairford to help his ageing father. In 1827 his book of poems *The Christian Year* was published, and proved phenomenally popular.

In 1831 Keble was elected Professor of Poetry at Oxford. In 1833, provoked by a bill proposing the suppression of ten Irish bishoprics, he preached the assize sermon on national apostasy which inaugurated the Oxford Movement. For the remainder of his life he was involved in the developments and controversies which ensued.

His personal circumstances changed when his father died in 1834, and when, in 1835, he married Charlotte Clarke. The marriage, though childless and darkened by illness, proved intensely happy. In 1836 he became vicar of Hursley in Hampshire, a scattered rural parish of some 1300 souls. Here he remained until his death in 1866. In addition to his local ministry he played a large part on a wider stage, through his writings, through his personal contacts with friends and sympathizers, and most of all because of his reputation for saintliness.

Francis Kilvert

Robert Francis Kilvert was born in 1840, one of the six children of Robert Kilvert, rector of Hardenhuish and later of Langley Burrell in Wiltshire. After a private education, he entered Wadham College, Oxford, reading history and jurisprudence, and leaving with a fourth class honours degree. He was ordained deacon in 1863 and priest in 1864. He served a curacy under his father, and then another from 1865 to 1872 under Richard Lister Venables, vicar of Clyro in Radnorshire. From 1872 to 1876 he returned to his father's parish, and then, after a brief spell as incumbent at St Harmon in Radnorshire, he was presented to Bredwardine, on the Wye in Herefordshire. In 1879 he married Elizabeth Anne Rowland, only to die a month later.

Kilvert kept an extensive diary, of which the greater part was destroyed after his death. There remained twenty-two notebooks, covering the years 1870–9, which were edited and published in part by William Plomer. Their quality has earned Kilvert a devoted following.

Kilvert had strong feelings and for most of the time no one in whom he could fully confide. Hence his diary became his confidant. He entrusted to it his profound love of nature and his susceptibility to feminine charm; his delight in his work and his sympathetic perception of suffering and poverty; his brilliant powers of observation and his fascination with the dramatic and unusual.

The diary reveals Kilvert as ingenuous and unworldly, hard-working and sociable, lively and humorous. An ex-parishioner wrote of him: 'All the people welcomed him to their homes for he always seemed to bring happiness with him.' The diary also indicates that he possessed darker strains of character which he controlled only with difficulty. He spoke of himself as an 'angel satyr' and an acquaintance said of him: 'Yes, he was a good man; if he had not been a good man he would have been a very dangerous man' (Grice, *Kilvert* 229, 218).

His religious faith was so much a part of him that he was the least pietistic of men. Neither learned nor theologically minded, he found God in the encounters of daily life and, especially, in nature. He entered with zest into the duties of a country clergyman, and performed them conscientiously and with unaffected kindliness. For the legion of his admirers, both his early death and the loss of the bulk of his diaries are major tragedies; but his short and largely undocumented life does not prevent him from being a figure both intriguing and immensely attractive.

Edward King (1829–1910): Curate for a short time at Wheatley, Oxfordshire in 1855. He then followed an academic career. As Principal of Cuddesden Theological College from 1863 to 1873 he was also incumbent of the parish. He became Bishop of Lincoln in 1885.

Charles Kingsley

Charles Kingsley was born in 1819. He was a delicate child, and did not enjoy his time at a preparatory school in Clifton. He was happier at Helston Grammar School, then known as 'the Eton of the West', and at King's College, London, where he went at the age of sixteen after his father had accepted the parish of St Luke's, Chelsea. In 1838 he entered Magdalene College, Cambridge.

By this time Kingsley had lost an earlier piety. He led a dissipated life at Cambridge until he met and fell in love with Fanny Grenfell. His conversion followed, and, having obtained a respectable degree, he was accepted for ordination by the Bishop of Winchester. He served a curacy at Eversley in Hampshire, a country parish consisting of some 750 souls. When his financial problems and the objections of Fanny's family had been overcome, he married her in 1844. Later the same year he became rector of Eversley.

Kingsley was a devoted and hard-working priest. He also campaigned vigorously on behalf of the poor. Although his 'socialism' was little more than a generous indignation on behalf of the oppressed, it was enough to earn him some notoriety and to stand in the way of his preferment. Things improved when his energetic patriotism at the time of the Crimean War and a run of popular novels earned him the favour of the royal family. He combined with his parish the posts of chaplain in ordinary to the Queen and professor of modern history at Cambridge. In the latter capacity he tutored the future king Edward VII.

In 1862 he published the book by which he is best remembered, *The Water Babies*. In 1864 his criticisms of J.H.Newman (qv) provoked the latter to write a crushing rejoinder, his *Apologia pro Vita Sua*. In 1869, after many disappointments over preferment, he was given a canonry at Chester, where he was an enormously popular preacher. In 1873 Gladstone offered him a stall at Westminster, a post which he held until his death in 1875.

Kingsley was a man of astonishing energy with a vast number of interests. However, he was plagued with ill health and subject to periods of acute depression and collapse. His passionate nature and his ready sympathies ensured that he passed much of his life amidst controversy, and he suffered accordingly. His life was never easy or settled, and it is doubtful whether he ever found spiritual peace; but few parochial clergy have been so well known in their life-time, or so effective in stirring the consciences of their countrymen. As for his spiritual capacity, a contemporary said of him: 'He was man of prayer and piety, filled with a personal, even passionate, love for Christ, whom he realized as His Friend and Brother in a fashion almost peculiar to the saints' (Osborne, *Dolling* 34).

Cosmo Lang (1864–1945): Curate at Leeds Parish Church (1890–3), and vicar of Portsea, Hampshire (1896–1901). Later Bishop of Stepney and Archbishop both of York and of Canterbury.

Charles Lowder (1820–80): Curate at St Barnabas, Pimlico (1851–6). For the rest of his life he conducted mission work within the parish of St George's in the East, building the Church of St Peter's, London Docks. One of the greatest of the Anglo-Catholic slum priests.

Alexander Mackonochie (1825–87): A leading Anglo-Catholic. After two curacies he was in 1862 put in charge of the newly built church of St Alban's, Holborn. He was singled out for persecution by the Church Association, and eventually resigned his incumbency in 1882. After a brief interlude in another parish he continued to work unofficially in St Albans parish until his death.

Charles Marson (1859–1914): He served for two years under Samuel Barnett (qv) at St Jude's, Whitechapel, then ran through three further curacies in a single year because of the scandal given by his social radicalism. Two brief incumbencies followed; he gave further offence by becoming an ardent Anglo-Catholic. In 1894, Lord Roseberry offered him Hambridge in Somerset. Here he conducted a combative ministry until his early death.

John Mitford (1781–1859): Incumbent of three Suffolk livings, Benhall, from 1810, Weston St Peter's from 1815, and Stratford St Andrew from 1817 until his death. A literary scholar; widely suspected of unbelief and sexual malpractice.

John Henry Newman (1801–90): Vicar of St Mary's, Oxford 1828–43. A leader of the Oxford Movement. He became a Roman Catholic and eventually a Cardinal.

James Newton (1714–86): Rector of Nuneham Courtenay, Oxfordshire, from 1736 until his death. His diaries for the years 1759–60 and 1761–62 have survived.

John Newton

Newton was born in 1725. His father was a sea captain, who treated him with considerable severity. His mother was a devout dissenter who laid the foundations of his religious life but who died when John was only six.

Newton went to sea with his father in 1736. Thereafter, for many years, his habits of life fluctuated between the fragmentary piety instilled by his mother and the reaction against it occasioned by his nautical experience. He served in both the Royal and the Merchant Navy, latterly on slave ships. The hardships and dangers of the life pointed him to conversion, as did his marriage in 1750 to Mary Catlett ('Polly'). He felt no moral objection, however, to further voyages as captain of a slaver.

In 1754 ill health compelled Newton to resign his command, and in the following year he became a tide surveyor at Liverpool. By now he was leading a deeply committed Christian life. However, he was twice refused ordination into the established Church, and only his wife's opposition prevented him from starting his own dissenting congregation in Liverpool.

In 1764 Lord Dartmouth's interest secured him Anglican ordination and the curacy of Olney, Buckinghamshire, a small market town where the principal industry was lace-making. His devoted ministry soon filled his church, and his influence was extended by his publications. The wealthy evangelical merchant John Thornton became his friend and supporter, and the poet William Cowper moved to Olney to be near him.

In 1780 Thornton presented Newton to St Mary Woolnoth, an important City of London parish. He used his position in the capital to good effect. He was prominent in the campaign against the slave trade, his earlier experiences enabling him to supply the factual detail which the reformers needed. He was a director of the Sierra Leone Company which settled freed slaves. He was on the committee of the Church Missionary Society, and helped found the London Missionary Society and the British and Foreign Bible Society.

In 1790 Newton lost his dearly-loved wife, and later had to endure the prolonged mental illness of his niece Betsy whom he and Polly had adopted and brought up. He continued preaching until a few months before his death in 1807. Even when a shadow of his former self he was treated with a reverence which he richly deserved.

Newton is one of the most attractive of Anglican parish priests. Self-taught, both academically and in the school of harsh experience, he sat lightly to party lines. He retained close links with the Methodists and with the dissenting churches throughout his life. He described himself as a Calvinist, but hated theological rancour. He lacked both a systematic theology and an ordered mind; but his sermons and writings were full of shrewd observation and practical wisdom. His vivid recollection of the sinfulness from which he had been rescued made him compassionate almost to a fault in his dealings with others. He refused to surrender to orthodoxy when it told against his deep sense of the love of God. His capacity for love embraced his wife, his adopted daughter, his servants, his parishioners, and the vast numbers of other men and women who turned to him for guidance, and who found in him a tenderness rooted in a deep humility.

Conrad Noel (1869–1942): Strongly socialist and strongly Anglo-Catholic, and not a man to compromise, Noel found bishops unwilling either to ordain him or to retain his services after ordination. In 1910, however, Lady Warwick offered him the parish of Thaxted, Essex, where he remained, a controversial and charismatic figure, for the remainder of his life.

William Paley (1743–1805): He demonstrated early in life the outstanding academic gifts which made him the foremost expositor and apologist of the century. He held a large number of livings, chiefly in the Carlisle area, and was for a time archdeacon and chancellor of the Carlisle diocese. Later in life he became subdean of Lincoln cathedral.

Octavius Pickard-Cambridge (1828–1917): He spent most of his adult life as curate, then rector, of the family living of Bloxworth, Dorset. An eminent naturalist.

Joseph Price (*c*.1736–1807): Originally a dissenting minister, he held livings in Norfolk, retaining them when he moved to Kent in 1767 as vicar of Brabourne. In 1786 he became vicar of Herne, remaining there until his death. One volume of his diary, covering the years 1769 to 1773, has survived.

Jack Putterill (1892–*c*.1979): Early in life he fell under the influence of Conrad Noel (qv) whose daughter he married. After various curacies he returned to Thaxted in 1925 to help Noel. In 1937 he became incumbent of St Andrew's, Plaistow. When Noel died in 1942 he succeeded him at Thaxted and remained there until his retirement in 1971. An active Socialist and deeply interested in the arts.

Richard Randall (1824–1906): He was his father's curate at Binfield, Berkshire, 1847–51, and then became Henry Manning's successor at Graffham-cum-Lavington, Sussex, when Manning seceded to Rome. He was vicar of All Saints, Clifton, 1868–92, and then became Dean of Chichester. A leading Anglo-Catholic.

Nicholas Rivett-Carnac (1927–): His father, from whom he inherited a baronetcy, was an admiral. After holding a commission in the army, and working in the City, he was converted and called to minister to the urban poor. From 1972 to 1989 he was in charge of St Mark's, Kennington.

John Robinson (1919–83): He served a curacy at St Matthew, Moorfields, Bristol, under Mervyn Stockwood (qv). Thereafter his career was academic save for the years 1959–69 when he was Bishop of Woolwich. The author of *Honest to God*.

John Rous (1584–1644): A clerical diarist whose record covers the years 1625–43. From 1623 until his death he was incumbent of the tiny parish of Santon Downham, Suffolk.

Dick Sheppard

Hugh Richard Lawrie Sheppard was born in 1880, the son of a minor canon of Windsor. He was educated at Marlborough College, which he hated, and at Trinity Hall, Cambridge. There he did very little work, but led an active social life and took an interest in Oxford House, Bethnal Green, a university mission. Spells as manager of a boys' club and as bishop Lang of Stepney's secretary convinced him that his gifts lay with people, and he offered himself for the priesthood. He was trained at Cuddesdon, and after ordination in 1907 returned to Oxford House as chaplain and, later, head. He wore himself out, and resigned in 1911. After two curacies in Mayfair and a brief spell as an army chaplain he was from 1914 to 1926 the phenomenally successful vicar of St Martin's-in-the-Fields in Trafalgar Square. Later in life he was successively dean of Canterbury and a canon of St Paul's; he was a leading figure in the pacifist movement of the inter-war period. When he died in 1937, 100,000 people filed past his coffin.

Sheppard was the most widely influential parish priest the Church of England has ever known. He combined practical creativity of the highest order with exceptional business capacity and a passionate pastoral sense which enabled him to make close relationships with vast numbers of other people. He was a populist of the first order who was never afraid to espouse controversial causes. His deep personal devotion and his irresistible charm retained him a host of friends among those most likely to be shocked by his impatience with organized religion, while his radicalism won him unlikely allies. The King and Queen worshipped at St Martin's; George Lansbury and Bernard Shaw spoke there. He was the establishment's darling as well as the establishment's gad-fly.

All this was costly. Throughout his life he was plagued with illness, in part psychosomatic. He was beset with depression and self-doubt, and his high ambitions subjected him to frequent disappointment.

Sheppard's sufferings were the price he paid for his personality and achievements. The effect he had on his contemporaries is summed up in two remarks. A friend said of him: 'The love Dick so lavishly bestowed on us, and in bestowing called forth, was the nearest approximation to the love of Christ that any of us are likely to see this side of the grave.' Rose Macaulay wrote: 'When Dick Sheppard died, the world's temperature seemed to drop' (Scott, *Sheppard* 50, 227).

Charles Simeon

This most famous of Evangelicals was the son of a wealthy Reading attorney. He was born in 1759, and at the age of seven went to Eton. In 1779 he went on to King's College, Cambridge, where, in his first term, he was converted. In 1782 he became a fellow of his college and was ordained deacon. After he had cared for St Edward's, Cambridge, for a few months in the absence of the incumbent, the Bishop of Ely nominated him to the parish of Holy Trinity, Cambridge. The appointment was unpopular with his parishioners and for several years they harrassed him severely. They were not being merely vindictive; Simeon had still much to learn and much in himself to change.

He was ordained priest in 1783. By this time he was attracting bigger congregations, including many people from outside the parish; though it was a long time before the church was full. When it became so, his hearers were in large part undergraduates, to whom, and in particular to ordinands, Simeon devoted the bulk of his time. The outcome was that a stream of enthusiastic young Evangelicals issued from Cambridge. At first they had to be content with obscure parishes, but in due course Simeon's purchase of advowsons opened wider opportunities to them.

Simeon became, after much trial and error, a great preacher. He was not a scholar, but he was a clear thinker and possessed deep spiritual insight. He was also vastly industrious. He took his teaching from the Bible, and to all intents and purposes from the Bible only; and in this respect too was deeply influential. He was one of the most active early members of the British and Foreign Bible Society, of the Church Missionary Society, and of the London Society for Promoting Christianity among the Jews. Unlike other Evangelicals, however, he did not espouse the cause of the abolition of the slave trade; nor indeed that of any other social reform.

Simeon remained an outsider for much of his life. For reasons both creditable and discreditable, he was an easy man to dislike. In the early years of his ministry he was ostracized by respectable townspeople, and he was detested by many dons. He deliberately shunned society. His readiness to co-operate with Dissenters made him an object of suspicion. He was exposed to the obloquy which anyone who takes the Christian faith seriously attracts from those whose commitment is demonstrated by comparison to be shallow.

In due course, however, his achievements and his virtues won him the recognition so long denied him. When he died in 1836 the town closed its shops and the university suspended its lectures; his funeral was the most impressive in the history of Cambridge. This was proof enough of a remark made a couple of years before his death, that 'so great a change has taken place in men's hearts that at this moment there is not a more popular man in the whole university than the venerable minister of Holy Trinity Church' (Hopkins, *Simeon* 213).

John Skinner

John Skinner was born in 1772, the son of a Hampshire gentleman. He was educated at Cheam School, Trinity College, Cambridge, and Greys Inn. He was ordained deacon in 1797 and priest in 1799. After a couple of west country curacies, he became rector of Camerton, Somerset in 1800, remaining there for the rest of his life. In 1805 he married Anna Holmes, by whom he had five children. He committed suicide in 1839.

Camerton was a mining village seven miles from Bath. In 1811 there were 151 houses in the parish, and a population of 786. Skinner took his duties seriously and found his flock a constant strain. His difficulties in dealing with them were accentuated by a background of domestic unhappiness. A Tory by temperament and conviction, he viewed with alarm and despondency the political and religious tendencies of his day. For over thirty years Skinner kept a journal, in which he described with dogged and painful honesty the uneven tenor of his daily life. From his writing a detailed picture of his character emerges.

Skinner was able, scholarly, courageous and devout; a high churchman of the traditional kind, with a clear and coherent view of what should constitute Anglican faith and practice. He served his flock conscientiously, caring for their physical as well as their spiritual needs. But he was cursed with a temperament which constantly worked against his very genuine good intentions. He was hot-tempered, peremptory and inflexible; over-zealous in pursuit of evil-doing, over-sensitive to the hostility of those he offended. He was quick to perceive real or imagined injuries, constantly able to find fresh evidence to justify his deep pessimism. He was a depressive who gradually succumbed to paranoia. He is a fascinating example of a high-minded and well-meaning clergyman whose work was hamstrung by unfortunate traits of character which he was incapable of subduing or controlling.

Sydney Smith

Smith was born in 1771, the son of a business man who did not treat him well. He went to school at Winchester, which he hated, and in 1789 to New College, Oxford. He was ordained deacon in 1794 and priest in 1796. A dispiriting curacy at Netheravon in Wiltshire was succeeded by a tutorship which took him to Edinburgh, where he was one of the founders of the influential periodical *The Edinburgh Review*.

In 1800 he married Catherine Pybus. The family moved to London, where Smith led an active social and literary life among Whig families. In 1806 his political friends secured him the Chancery living of Foston-le-Clay, Yorkshire. In the years that followed, a prebendal stall at Bristol and a living held in plurality, helped him financially as he brought up his four surviving children, and in 1828 he was able to exchange to the more convenient Chancery living at Combe Florey in Somerset. When the Whigs came in in 1832 he secured, in addition, a canonry at St Paul's.

In an age when most clergy were as a matter of course Tory, Smith was unusual in being a Whig. He was unique as a clerical humorist. Charles Greville wrote of him: 'It is almost impossible to overrate his wit, humour, and drollery, or their effect in society ... If there was a fault in it, it was that it was too amusing' (Bell, *Smith* 196–7). Many thought him too light-hearted for a clergyman. He was indeed worldly, but he did not betray his profession when he was practising it.

Smith summed himself up in a letter written about a year before his death in 1845: 'I am living among the best society in the metropolis, and at ease in my circumstances; in tolerable health, a mild Whig, a tolerating Churchman, and much given to talking, laughing and noise. I dine with the rich in London, and physic the poor in the country, passing from the sauces of Dives to the sores of Lazarus. I am, upon the whole, a happy man, have found the world an entertaining world, and am thankful to Providence for the part allotted to me in it' (Bell, *Smith* 217).

Nicolas Stacey (1927–): Rector of Woolwich from 1959 to 1968. After his resignation he worked mostly outside church structures.

Arthur Stanton

Born in 1839, Arthur Henry Stanton was one of the twelve children of a wealthy cloth merchant of Stroud, Gloucestershire. After an undistinguished academic career at Rugby and Trinity College, Oxford, he prepared for the ministry at Cuddesdon theological college. He was ordained deacon in 1862 and priest in 1864.

Oxford confirmed Stanton in the Catholic leanings he had possessed since boyhood. He became curate to A.H. Mackonochie (qv) in the parish of St Alban the Martyr, Holborn, and stayed there for the rest of his life. His attachment to St Alban's, which was at the centre of the ritualistic troubles of the century, his stubborn independence and his outspoken support for Anglo-Catholicism and socialism made him a marked man.

Stanton was mercurial, courageous and combative. His verbal violence, which did him much harm and which he moderated as he grew older, was in itself deplorable, but stemmed at least in part from his disregard for personal consequences. Often exposed to criticism and injustice, he did not find it easy to accept either. He was over-sensitive and prone to resentment, an indisciplined subordinate and not always an easy colleague. His spirits were often buoyantly high, but when frustrations multiplied he could descend into unrelieved gloom.

Stanton also possessed almost irresistible charm and humour, boyish warmth and simplicity, and a genius for sympathy. His qualities were illuminated by his holiness. He was a wealthy man but he spent almost nothing on personal possessions, and lived the plain life of the clergy house. He was a superb preacher, with a message equally evangelical and eirenic. He was infinitely accessible. Vast numbers came to see him, men more than women, the poor more than the well-to-do, the young more than the old. He was confessor to many of the clergy, and conducted a huge pastoral ministry by correspondence. He had a particular affinity for the wretched and the degraded. He was as gentle in dealing with individuals as he was stringent in condemning sin in the abstract. Many were kept from crime because 'Dad would take it so to heart' (Russell, *Stanton* 196). It was said of him, as of St Francis de Sales, that if you wished to secure his friendship you had only to do him an injury. One urchin, to whom he had refused a shilling, pleaded 'It was I, Dad, who sneaked your watch'. Stanton regarded him silently for a minute, and then handed over the money, saying 'Well, I think that does deserve a bob' (Russell, *Stanton* 198).

Stanton never married, and the whole of his great capacity for love was poured out on the ne'er-do-wells of Holborn. He loved indiscriminately, and was in return loved as few priests have been. He was the most influential curate in the history of the church of England.

Laurence Sterne (1713–68): Vicar of Sutton-on-the-Forest, Yorkshire, 1738–59. Perpetual curate of Coxwold, Yorkshire, 1760–8. Author, most notably of *Tristram Shandy*.

Mervyn Stockwood (1913–): Curate and vicar of St Matthew Moorfields, Bristol, 1936–55, and vicar of Great St Mary's, Cambridge, 1955–60; then Bishop of Southwark. One of the more colourful of twentieth-century churchmen.

Thomas Traherne
He was born, son of a shoemaker, in Hereford about 1636. In 1652 he entered Brasenose College, Oxford, receiving his MA in 1661. By this time he had in 1657 become rector of Credenhill, Herefordshire. In 1667 he became in addition private chaplain to Sir Orlando Bridgman and minister in the parish church of Teddington. He received a BD in 1669, and died in 1674.

During Traherne's lifetime only one work of his – a polemic – was published; a book on Christian ethics came out soon after his death. His fame rests upon poetry and prose which remained in manuscript until our own century. He was one of the great metaphysical poets; he wrote the work now called his *Centuries* as instruction for a pious lady.

Centuries consists in part of Traherne's spiritual autobiography, in part of spiritual instruction. It is remarkable because of the stress he lays on the desirability and possibility of happiness, and because of his insistence that God is revealed through the contemplation of his creation. He has been accused, perhaps not unjustly, of unorthodoxy and even of pantheism; but his thought provides a welcome counterbalance to the preoccupation with sin and moral conflict characteristic of most of his contemporaries.

William Vanstone (1923–): Service in two parishes in Manchester in the 1950s and 60s was distilled into theological reflection in the widely influential *Love's Endeavour, Love's Expense*. Later a canon of Chester.

Arthur Wagner (1824–1902): Perpetual curate and later vicar of St Paul's, West Street, Brighton, from 1850 to his death. A leading Anglo-Catholic, and a benefactor of staggering generosity.

Henry Wagner (1792–1870): Father of the above. Vicar of Brighton from 1824 until his death. He was strong-minded and generous. Both qualities contributed to an extensive development of church life in Brighton during his incumbency, the first to frequent contention with Dissenters and Radicals.

Tom Walker (1933–): From 1970 to 1991 he was vicar of Harborne Heath, Birmingham. In 1991 he became archdeacon of Nottingham.

David Watson
David Christopher Knight Watson was born in 1933. He attended Bedford Preparatory School and Wellington College, and did his national service as an officer in the Royal Artillery. In 1954 he went up to St John's College, Cambridge, to read Moral Sciences. During his first year there he was converted and became an enthusiastic Evangelical and member of the Cambridge Inter-Collegiate Christian Union. In 1955 he decided to offer himself for ministry and from 1957 spent two not altogether happy years at Ridley Hall, Cambridge, asserting his 'simple gospel' against biblical criticism and liberal theology.

Watson served his first curacy under the priest who had converted him, John Collins, at St Mark's, Gillingham, a tough working-class parish. A second curacy at the Round Church, Cambridge, was for various reasons less happy, and led him to seek a deeper quality of Christian life. He found it in the charismatic experiences which were to be of immense significance to him but which made him a suspect figure in Evangelical circles. At this time he began to suffer acutely from the asthma which was to plague him for the rest of his life. In 1964 he embarked upon a marriage with Anne MacEwan Smith which was to exact a high price from both of them but also to prove deeply rewarding.

In 1964 Watson accepted a curacy within the parish of Holy Trinity, Heworth, with responsibility for St Cuthbert's, a church with few parishioners but well situated for a ministry to students at the new university of York. He and Anne developed a strategy based on extensive prayer, careful teaching, family worship and enormous stress on relationships. Growth began and accelerated. In 1973 numbers necessitated, and the diocesan authorities facilitated, a move to St Michael-le-Belfrey, close to York Cathedral. Watson became vicar, an appointment which confirmed him in a previously wavering allegiance to the Church of England.

Watson built up a pattern of worship, combining teaching, music, dance and drama, which many found deeply fulfilling. He secured a sense of fellowship and participation in prayer enriched by charismatic experience. A report on his work testified: 'What comes across is the sheer weight of testimony upholding the word preached by the word received, believed in and being lived by so many happy but ordinary people who are part of proclaiming in themselves' (quoted Saunders, *Watson* 241).

Watson had an extensive ministry outside his parish. He became the most effective evangelist the English churches possessed and also produced a steady stream of books. In 1982 he decided to devote himself entirely to evangelism. He and his family left York for London where he planned to work under the auspices of the specially created Belfrey Trust. Shortly after the move however, he was diagnosed as having cancer. He died in 1984.

Samuel Wesley (1662–1735): Rector of Epworth, Lincolnshire 1695–1735. Father of John and Charles Wesley, and husband to the formidable Susannah.

Gilbert White (1720–93): He spent a great part of his life living in Selborne, Hampshire, and was four times, for a total of fifteen years, curate in charge there. Famous for *The Natural History of Selborne*.

Harry Williams (1919–): A curate in two London parishes 1943–8. After an academic career in Cambridge he became a monk of the Community of the Resurrection in 1970. A major spiritual writer.

Joseph Williamson (1895–1988): After a working-class upbringing, he was ordained in 1920. A variety of posts at home and overseas followed. He was vicar of St Paul's, Dock Street, London from 1952 to 1962.

Francis Witts (1783–1854): Rector of Upper Slaughter, Gloucestershire, from 1808 until 1854, and vicar of Stanway, in the same county, from 1814 to 1854. Extracts from his diary, covering the period 1820 to 1852, have been published. He was a conscientious central churchman, an active magistrate and local administrator, and a convinced Conservative.

Nathaniel Woodard (1811–91): Curate of New Shoreham, Sussex from 1847, and from 1870 canon of Manchester and rector of St Philip's, Salford. A leading Anglo-Catholic and founder of the Woodard schools.

James Woodforde

Woodforde was born in 1740. His father was rector of Ansford and vicar of Castle Cary, in the county of Somerset. After his education at Winchester and New College, Oxford, he was for a short time a fellow of the college. In 1763 he was ordained deacon and in 1764 priest. He served as a curate in Somerset for several years, mostly in his father's parishes. From 1773 to 1776 he was back at New College, but in the latter year he moved to the parish of Weston Longueville, Norfolk, a village of some 360 souls, where he served as rector until his death in 1803.

We know a great deal about Woodforde because of the diary he kept from 1758 to 1802. It is a daily record of extraordinary minuteness, from which emerges a vivid picture of country life in the eighteenth century and a fascinating portrait of Woodforde himself. He gives first place to the company he kept, to the doings of his family, and to the often gargantuan meals he ate. But he also tells us how the rest of his time and money were spent; about the state of his health; about the weather; and from time to time about public affairs. About his opinions and feelings there is relatively little, but enough to enable him to step off his pages and into the affections of his readers.

We learn from Woodforde's diary how little an eighteenth-century parish priest could do without losing his own self-respect or forfeiting that of his parishioners. For the most part he pursued the occupations of a country gentleman with a secure income and a small, manageable estate, serenely unconscious that his interpretation of his responsibilities might be open to question.

It is only fair to add that Woodforde's cure was very small, and that, being comfortable himself, he seems to have made those around him comfortable too. Occasionally he fell out with individuals; especially as he grew older he was prone to fits of bad temper and despondency; but in general he was open, uncomplicated and kindly. He shared the interests and presuppositions of his parishioners as fully as the customs and rhythms of their lives.

Woodforde is a paradigm of one sort of Anglican parish priest. He was too well integrated into his local community to offer any kind of challenge to it. There was little in his own life to call others to a serious examination of theirs. But such influence as he had was stabilizing and softening; likely to make his parishioners more contented with their lot, and a little more conscious of the divine dimension in their lives.

George Woodward (1708–90): Rector of East Hendred, Berkshire, from 1744 to his death. Letters which he wrote to his uncle between 1753 and 1761 have been published. They reveal him as conscientious within strict limits, as active in his pursuit of the main chance, as a loving husband and father, and as a convivial and unintellectual man.

PART TWO

A Celebration of the Clergy

3

Domestic Life

As pictures are made curious by lights and shades,
which without shades could not be so: so is felicity
composed of wants and supplies; without which
mixture there could be no felicity. (Traherne, 1.41)

Marriage

It has never been universally believed that Church of England clergy should marry. Queen Elizabeth I hankered after a celibate ministry, and the Injunctions of 1559 laid it down that no clergyman should marry unless his bride had proved acceptable to the bishop and to two justices of the peace. It was not until 1604 that a wife's position was firmly established in law; and well into the seventeenth century George Herbert* (himself a married man) wrote: 'The country parson, considering that virginity is a higher state than matrimony, and that the ministry requires the best and highest things, is rather unmarried than married' (Herbert, 200).

This view appeared again in the nineteenth century. One of the early Tractarians, Frederick Faber, wrote while he was still an Anglican: 'I honour the celibate so highly, and regard it so eminently the fittest life for a priest, that ... I should prefer ... to live a virgin life, and to die a virgin' (Faber, 43). In 1855 Charles Lowder** founded the Society of the Holy Cross, which offered among its three rules one for celibates. The practice of celibacy eventually became so normative in leading Anglo-Catholic parishes that when H.C. Firth of St Alban's, Holborn, decided upon marriage he resigned his incumbency. It was said of a certain Father Bristowe of Bagborough that he used to try and persuade clergy wives to leave their husbands, and boasted of the separations he had caused (Pickering, 187, 186).

Celibacy, however, has rarely been chosen on the grounds of its intrinsic superiority. Charles Simeon* remained unmarried partly because he would otherwise have lost his Cambridge fellowship, partly because he thought his income insufficient for the married state, partly because observation convinced him that marriage and a family were as likely to bring unhappiness as happiness, and partly because celibacy left him free for the work to which God had called him (Hopkins, *Simeon* 68–9). The young Walter Hook* declared that he would never marry because he would want his wife to conform to George Herbert's model of a woman who would dress sores and wounds with her own hands. 'Now I could never bear to have those dressed with my wife's hands; therefore I must remain a bachelor' (Stephens, *Hook* 83). In due course he saw things differently.

Very naturally, mere inclination has played a part. One is never sure how far to believe Robert Herrick**, but he spoke for others if not for himself when he wrote:

> Suspicion, Discontent and Strife,
> Come in for Dowrie with a Wife. (Herrick, 13)

Some have chosen celibacy; others have had it thrust upon them. Cyril Garbett**, seems to have had his hand refused while he was Vicar of Portsea, Hampshire. His biographer comments that this was perhaps just as well, 'because he would have found it extremely difficult to fit a wife into his time-table' (Smyth, *Garbett* 453). Francis Kilvert* remained unmarried for far longer than he would have wished, less because of young ladies' reluctance than because of their fathers' objections.

The mutual society, help and comfort which the *Book of Common Prayer* gives as the third of God's purposes in ordaining matrimony have been supplied in ways other than through marriage. Robert Herrick declared:

> A Sister (in the stead
> Of Wife) about I'le lead;
> Which I will keep embrac'd
> And kisse, but yet be chaste. (Herrick, 13)

James Woodforde* was looked after by his niece Nancy and by female friends and servants. Not only did they see to his creature comforts but they ministered to emotional needs as well. He much enjoyed their teasing, even when it included almost tearing his wig to pieces and making him an apple pie bed (Woodforde, 1.299, 302). Robert Dolling* was accompanied through-out his ministry by two or three of his five sisters, and for most of it by a devoted housekeeper (Osborne, *Dolling* 49). Less conventionally, Joseph Price** of Brabourne, considered taking one Polly Weatherley as a 'companion'. That her duties would not have been confined to housekeeping is suggested by the fact that he felt he would have to 'make provision' for her (Price, 20).

Arthur Stanton* was supported by the life of St Alban's clergy house, which he shared with the incumbent and with his fellow-curates. A book remains to be written about the importance of these communities in the history of the Church of England. At Portsea around 1900 Cosmo Lang** had up to sixteen curates, some living in the vicarage, some in houses nearby. They were bound to him and to each other by a common vocation, a common life, a common background (public school, university, and ministerial training at either Cuddesdon or Wells), and by the discipline which the vicar exercised. They developed a formidable team spirit; literally, in the sense that they turned out a cricket XI capable of beating strong sides from the Armed Services. Lang said that he forbade his curates to marry, and that if one did so he would get rid of him. What he demanded of others he imposed on himself. Queen Victoria once asked him why he did not marry. His first reply was that he could not afford it; his curates cost too much. Pressed, on the grounds that a wife would be worth more than one or two curates, his rejoinder was 'No doubt, ma'am, but there is this difference: if a curate proves to be unsatisfactory I can get rid of him. A wife is a fixture' (Lockhart, *Lang* 117–19, 166, 131).

But we have been looking at exceptions. Most parochial clergy have married. Their motives have varied from the purely pragmatic to the deeply spiritual. The great Elizabethan scholar and parish priest Richard Hooker** wrote: 'Experience hath found it safer that the clergy should bear the cares of honest marriage than be subject to the inconveniences which single life imposed on them would draw after it' (quoted in More, 667). If George Herbert's country priest decided on marriage 'his choice of his wife was made rather by his ear, than by his eye; his judgment, not his affection found out a fit wife for him, whose humble and liberal disposition he preferred before beauty, riches, or honour ... His wife is either religious, or night and day he is winning her to it' (Herbert, X). The saintly Edward King**, single himself because he 'never felt called to anything else' advised a priest that he was quite free to marry – if he thought a wife would be helpful to his ministry (King, *Letters* 109).

Different criteria influenced Sydney Smith*. 'As for the lady,' he wrote to a friend, 'she is three years younger than me, a very old friend of mine – a good figure and *to me* an interesting countenance, of excellent disposition, extremely good sense, very fond of music, and me – a wise, amiable woman such as without imposing, specious qualities will quietly for years and years make the happiness of her husband's life' (Bell, *Smith* 24). Smith did not consider the question of religion at all, or perhaps took it for granted. By contrast William Jones**, of Broxbourne, was desperately torn when he met an elderly spinster of fortune who despised religion. On the one hand he was attracted both by her looks and by her fourteen thousand pounds. On the other: 'How ... can I have a thought of her? Better perhaps for me to marry a decent woman, who fears God, with a small fortune or without any' (Addison, 81–2). In the event the lady married someone else.

Joseph Price was actively considering marriage during the period for which his diary survives. He was most drawn to Mrs Mary Lane, a distant relation and a wealthy widow twelve years his senior. He considered several other ladies, however, setting the money they would bring him against the possibility of losing Mary Lane's favour and the inevitable disqualification from a fellowship at his college, Peterhouse. It was a disadvantage that two of the ladies he had in his sights were nonconformists, though for religious reasons only in a restricted sense: 'I would rather live with a papist than with a Methodist or strict, free thinking, dissenter.' He was also conscious of the constraints of marriage, noting in a table containing the pros and cons of one lady: 'Taedium vitae will increase in this situation'. Eventually he proposed to Mary Lane, who refused him but retained him as her heir; perhaps the best of all outcomes from his point of view (Ditchfield, *Price* 19, 18, ch.2).

John Fletcher's* marriage was one both of love and of Christian compatibility. In 1781 he proposed to Mary Bosanquet, a lady ten years his junior, whom he had known and admired over a long period but whom he had not seen for fifteen years. His bride to be had been converted to Methodism early in life. Estranged in consequence from her family, she had created Christian communities at Leytonstone near London and at Gildersome near Leeds. Over the years her fortune, which had been the chief obstacle in Fletcher's mind to a proposal, melted away. They were married at the end of 1781, and settled at Madeley in 1782.

William Wayte Andrew* decided to marry because his vicar would not allow him to minister to young women and this was a serious constraint on his work. So for some weeks he made the choice of a wife the centre of his prayers. One day the name of a young woman with whom he was barely acquainted – Ellen Wickes – came into his mind, and thoughts of her grew on him. He made enquiries, continued to pray, and eventually approached Ellen's parents. They referred him to Ellen herself. 'She trembled and began to weep; and then begged a short time for prayer. The next morning they read together a chapter of St John's Epistle [sic]; and a few days after ... he received the letter of assent. He believed that he had been led to her almost by inspiration' (Chadwick, *Andrew* 27). The marriage was a happy one.

Another clerical marriage was of the stuff of which romantic novels are made. While a curate at Horbury in Yorkshire Sabine Baring-Gould** came across a sixteen-year-old mill girl, Grace Taylor. She was a totally unsuitable match but Baring-Gould fell deeply in love with her. He sent her to York to learn the customs and speech appropriate to a new life, and in 1868 they were married. They had fifteen children and lived happily together until Grace died forty-seven years later (Purcell, *Baring-Gould* 80–7).

Once undertaken, clerical marriages have been influenced both by the fact that they are between Christians, and by the fact that the husband is a priest. The ideal has been complementarity and close union, together with dedication to a common task. John Keble's* wife Charlotte possessed 'just sufficient poise and knowledge of the world to fill up what was lacking in her husband'. Her accomplishments and her outgoing nature enriched the Keble home, and gave it a quality of joyous love which enchanted guests, especially young ones (Battiscombe, *Keble* 165). John Newton* wrote in 1774: 'Since the Lord gave me the desire of my heart in my dearest Mary, the rest of the sex are no more to me than the tulips in the garden ... I ... am as prone to change as a weathercock. But, with respect to you, he [God] has been pleased to keep me fixed as the north-pole, without one minute's variation for twenty-four years, three months, and one day' (Martin, *Newton* 241).

The traditional Christian view has been that the God-given duty of a husband is to cherish, and of a wife to obey. As the Homily on the state of matrimony puts it: 'The husband ... ought to be the leader and author in love ... For the woman is a weak creature, not endued with like strength and constancy of mind.' For George Herbert, the husband was 'the good instrument of God to bring [his wife] to heaven' (Herbert, IX). Samuel Wesley**, of Epworth, wrote of his wife Susannah:

> She graced my humble roof, and blest my life,
> Blest me by a far greater name than wife;
> Yet still I bore an undisputed sway,
> Nor was't her task, but pleasure, to obey;

and of himself:

> Nor did I for her care ungrateful prove,
> But only used my power to show my love. (Addison, 107)

This was an inaccurate description of the Wesley marriage, but it stated a widely accepted ideal. Maria Bronte wrote to her husband, the formidable Patrick**, 'Nor do I fear to trust myself under your protection or shrink from your control. It is pleasant to be subject to those we love especially when they never exert their authority but for the good of the subject' (Colloms, 85). In *The Way of All Flesh* Samuel Butler described Mrs Pontifex's relations with her husband: 'her absolute submission, the perfect coincidence of her opinion with his own upon every subject and her constant assurances to him that he was right in everything which he took it into his head to say or do' (Butler, 99–100). In a more creative fictional relationship, Trollope's Mrs Crawley, stronger and wiser than her husband, exercised her influence in the background and unhesitatingly gave him public primacy (Trollope, *BT* passim). In the 1960s Anne Smith married David Watson* believing that a wife should submit to her husband (Brown, 82).

John Fletcher illuminated the true nature of traditional Christian wifely obedience on his wedding day. He had quoted scripture: 'Wives, submit yourselves to your own husbands.' Mrs Fletcher added: 'As unto the Lord'; to which Fletcher replied: 'Well, my dear, only in the Lord. And if ever I wish you to do anything otherwise, resist me with all your might' (Benson, *Fletcher* 279).

Spiritual considerations apart, there have been wives who would privately at least have agreed with Fielding's Mrs Adams. When Parson Adams quoted the Bible to secure her obedience, she replied that: 'it was blasphemy to talk scripture out of church; that such things were very proper to be said in the pulpit, but that it was profane to talk them in common discourse' (Fielding, 348). Mrs Adams spoke for others in the respect that in most clerical marriages personalities rather than principles have determined the relationship. William Oughtred, rector of Albury, Surrey, in the seventeenth century and a famous mathematician, was, according to Aubrey, forbidden by his penurious wife to burn a candle after supper, 'by which meanes many a good notion is lost, and many a probleme unsolved' (Aubrey, 2.110). In a happier seventeenth-century instance, Walton wrote of George Herbert and his wife Jane, whom he had married after three days' acquaintance: 'There was never any opposition betwixt them, unless it were a contest which should most incline to a compliance with the other's desires' (Walton, 199). While Susannah Wesley was usually prepared to obey a direct order from her husband, she was far more practical than Samuel and at least equally strong-willed. Their most famous son was conceived only because Samuel came to terms with his wife's Jacobite sympathies, and rescinded a vow not to share her bed until she renounced them.

Affection has made compliance easy; John Newton ended a letter to his Polly 'I am, My dearest, Your most affectionate and obedient – I meant obliged – husband, but I shall not scratch the word out.' But affection has also caused spiritual problems. Polly wrote: 'I worship My Golden Image ... what cause I have to fear that the Lord will punish me for My Idolatry.' Newton too feared that their married love might be idolatrous because so intense; but that did not prevent him from beginning what was probably his last letter to Polly: 'My dear, sweet precious beautiful own dearest Dear.' One doubts if God objected (Martin, *Newton* 255, 256, 326).

The spiritual hallmark of clerical marriages down the centuries has been the identification of the wife with her husband's ministry. Walton describes George Herbert writing to his wife after his institution to Bemerton: 'You are now a minister's wife, and must now so far forget your father's house, as not to claim a precedence of any of your parishioners; for you are to know that a priest's wife can challenge no precedence or place but that which she purchases by her obliging humility' (Walton, 203).

'Obliging humility' has often been the best description of the wife's role. William Cole** of Bletchley (a bachelor) wrote in 1766 of 'a proper Parson's Wife, visiting no where & taking Care of her Family Concerns' (Cole, 43–4). John Newton, lamenting the necessity of seeing to domestic business after Polly's death, told a colleague that for forty years he had not so much as bought a pair of stockings (Martin, *Newton* 346). Robert Hawker's* first wife Charlotte was described as admirable – 'busy, sympathetic, generous to others, yet "abstinence itself" where her own needs were concerned' (Brendon, *Hawker* 48). Walter Hook's wife Delicia compensated for his lack of tact and his incompetence in money matters. As well as bringing up five children and engaging in good works she wrote numerous devotional books, which she published under her husband's name (Stranks, *Hook* 32). In our own century Arthur Hopkinson** thought that his wife's chief contribution to his ministry was that she ran their home well (Hopkinson, 95). George Bernard Shaw's Candida spoke for many wives in real life when she said: 'I build a castle of comfort and indulgence and love for him (her clergyman husband), and stand sentinel always to keep little vulgar cares out' (quoted Christmas, 248).

The diary entry made by Francis Witts**, of Upper Slaughter, on the day of his wife Margaret's death in 1850 sums up what most parochial clergy have looked for in their wives: 'A virtuous loving wife, tender mother, good daughter, kind mistress, friendly neighbour, unaffectedly pious, patient and charitable, excellent in the management of her family, attentive to poor neighbours, prudent, amiable and sensible' (Witts, 174).

While the wife's first duty has been to her husband and family, it has also been assumed, and increasingly as the centuries have gone by, that she should play a part in parish life. The wife of George Herbert's country priest confined herself to the medical attentions which so disgusted Walter Hook. A century later wives visited more widely; Mary Fletcher accompanied her husband as he contended with the rough colliers and bargemen of his parish (Macdonald, *Fletcher* 174). A century later still wives were central figures in the life of the parish. The new combination of roles was described in dramatic terms by Charles Marson**, who wrote to his Chloe a month before their wedding in 1890: 'You are being dedicated to God anew and to the cooperation with and the strengthening of one of his faltering priests. For you this step is one of pain and anxiety and difficulty – a hard mission, an ascetic life … and at the end of the day perhaps only tired limbs and tears' (Reckitt, 106).

By the time Christopher Chavasse** was rector of St Aldate's, Oxford, in the 1920s, there was nothing odd about the fact that his wife Beatrice was pastor and confidante to the women of the parish. Meal-times were staff meetings (Gummer, *Chavasse* 90). A priest of our own day, W.H. Vanstone**, recalls that both his father and his mother 'were deeply absorbed in the life and work of the Church, and … allowed themselves … no other interest or pursuit except only the care and well-being of their children' (Vanstone, 3). David Watson's wife Anne became the prophetic and visionary member of the partnership; until precluded from ministry she played a leading role in a multitude of parish activities. She later became a parish elder (Watson, *YAMG*, chs 15 and 16). In one extreme case the wife effectively took over the parish. Mary Fletcher outlived her husband by thirty years. She stayed in the vicarage, chose the curate, spoke frequently in rooms and chapels though not in church, and led meetings (Macdonald, *Fletcher* 170).

In every respect save that there were no children the marriage of Augustus Hare* to Maria Leycester corresponded to the traditional Christian ideal. Maria's ambition was to be worthy both of Augustus and of God, without letting the lesser obligation stand in the way of the greater. She wrote in her journal after their engagement: 'His standard is that of Christian feeling and action, and to come up to it in every daily occurrence of life, will require that watchfulness must not slumber ... Oh, may I be enabled to fulfil this new post of life in such a manner as may become a real follower of Christ ... endeavouring as much as possible to put away self from every consideration, labouring for the good of others, submitting without a murmur to their will, and seeking so to temper the strongest feelings of my nature, that they may never draw me too much from higher thoughts, making me love the *creature* more than the *Creator*.' To her future husband she wrote: 'The highest gratification I can feel is when I have done anything to oblige or please Augustus, and the most painful sensation I can experience is having done anything he disapproves. Ought I not much more to feel this with my Saviour and my God?' (Hare, 1.239, 244).

Maria was a mature woman of thirty, and the high ideals of the engagement persisted into the marriage. In her correspondence she called her husband 'the Master' without apparent irony. She wrote rapturously to friends of his tenderness and consideration. In her journal, musings on her happiness were interspersed with penitential reflections. She played the piano and sang to him; in the mornings he taught her the Greek Testament, and in the evenings they read Cicero, Landor and Coleridge together. He introduced her to the higher criticism; she wrote a sermon which he preached.

They ministered together to the people of their parish, Maria as wholeheartedly as Augustus. He taught the men, she started a mothers' meeting; he started an evening school for boys, she a Sunday School for girls. He did most of the visiting, but she knew everything that was going on, and actively supported him. They celebrated a wedding anniversary by holding a children's dinner of bacon and potatoes followed by gooseberry pie. Like James Woodforde a few decades previously they had old men to dinner on feast days. Maria was not exaggerating unduly when she wrote 'we live as one family with our people' (Hare, 1.428).

The marriage did not have to stand the test of time. They married in June 1829, and Augustus died in February 1833. Maria wrote: 'That we have had five years [sic; perhaps she included their engagement] of love so perfect, and union so entire, is a blessing vouchsafed to so few; I would bless and praise God for having *lent* it to me so long' (Hare, 2.24).

The ideal of the dedicated clergy wife is not dead. In 1993 my wife Jean, still keeping at the age of sixty-four a motherly eye on five adult children and a grandmotherly eye on four infants, was caring single-handed for a five-bedroomed vicarage which contained a parish room and in which every church activity except worship took place; on Sundays six rooms were in use. She did the lion's share of the work in a large garden freely used by the parish, ran the Junior Church and a ladies' working party, helped with the two youth clubs and was on all the church care rotas. Ministerial confidences apart, she knew as much about the parishioners as I did, and, as in the Chavasse home, every meal was a staff meeting. My wife, however, represented an ideal which was no longer normative.

When Nicolas Stacey** went to Woolwich in 1959 a tearful deputation of ladies from the congregation called to resign their church offices so that his wife could take them over. Stacey refused their offer, and, taking a view which has become increasingly widespread, resolved that no clergy wife should run anything in the parish (Stacey, 124–5). In that instance the wives still played 'menial' (Stacey's word) roles in parochial life; but in recent times the idea of shared ministry has been giving way to that of the wife with a full-time job outside the Church, and a life of her own to live, or, occasionally, to those of the wife being an ordained colleague of her husband or the ordained member of the partnership. The implications of these new situations, so far as they bear on the nature of clerical marriage and on the nature of married ministry, are considerable. In Joanna Trollope's novel *The Rector's Wife* (Bloomsbury Publishing 1991) Anna, the wife of the title, seeks to reassert her stifled individuality. A sympathetic priest diagnoses her dilemma: 'The problem lies with the wives who discover, quite legitimately, that although bowing to the will of God of your own free will is one thing, bowing to it as translated to you by your husband, who has somehow assumed a monopoly on the first place with God, is quite another'. Anna herself raises the same issue in another form when she says to a friend 'being married to a priest … is rather like having a crucial relationship with someone who is always half turned away from you.' (pp. 140, 131). No longer is the life of the spouse necessarily subsumed in that of the minister; but no longer either is there always a sense of a common enterprise to which both partners are wholly dedicated. The new situation may make even more demanding a relationship already sufficiently so.

For clerical marriages are as subject to strain as any other, and in some ways more than most. The wives in Shelagh Brown's *Married to the Church* write of financial stringency, of the pressures created, especially for the children, by the public nature of a vicarage, of a never-ending shortage of time, of a competition for attention between parish and family, of expectations which could only be met by pretending to be someone other than oneself. The strain has become even more acute when the wife has paid employment but still tries to play a full part in the life of the parish, as several of the wives in Brown's book did. Analogous situations must surely occur when the wife is ordained and the husband not. Christian faith is no panacea for these problems, and it is significant that the rate of breakdown in contemporary clerical marriages is about the same as in the population as a whole.

David Watson writes movingly (in *You are My God*, passim) of the difficulties which he and his wife Anne experienced. In the early days of their marriage he expected a degree of support from her which she was not able to give. When they moved to St Cuthbert's, York, in 1965, the priority which Watson gave to parochial work and to his frequent outside engagements over the claims of his wife and children strained their relationship and drove Anne into a depression. The stresses of an experiment in an extended household brought the marriage to the brink of dissolution. (In a case known to the author a similar experiment was partly responsible for a divorce.)

The success of a clerical marriage is not guaranteed by the spiritual quality of the partners. Gilbert Shaw (1886–1967) was an outstanding if controversial spiritual writer and director, who ended his life as Warden of the Sisters of the Love of God. He married a deeply Christian woman by whom he had three children, but in 1924, a year before his ordination, decided to live as a celibate. Thereafter he nearly always lived away from home, and the times he spent with his family were full of strain. The marriage endured, but it cannot be said to have offered either party fulfilment (Hacking, *Shaw* passim).

Dick Sheppard* was deeply loving and profoundly lovable; but his marriage failed. In 1915 he married Alison Carver, who was twelve years his junior. She came from a wealthy family; she was beautiful, childlike, direct, imaginative and spoiled. At first the marriage went well. She enjoyed making a home for him and taking him out of himself; for his part he shielded her from anything tedious or tough. They had two daughters, but neglected them. Sheppard overworked, and Alison, faced with increasing responsibilities, cultivated helplessness as a survival technique. As Sheppard's health deteriorated they began to sleep apart and their sex life died away. Alison hated Sheppard's illnesses, played no part in his ministry, and led an empty and expensive social life. She rarely attended church and was attracted to spiritualism. Increasingly they went their own ways, never quarrelling but never coming to terms. Alison's behaviour provoked scandal and strained other people's marriages, and in 1937 she left her husband for the comic writer Archie Macdonell. Sheppard, who had always thought of her as a lost child who would eventually come home to security, blamed himself: 'How can I go and preach from the pulpit when I know that it must be because of me that she's left?' 'How can I ever preach love again?' Later he wrote: 'I think I can truly say that all that is in my heart now, over and above a great dull ache, is an infinite tenderness towards her, and an infinite sorrow that I failed her' (Scott, *Sheppard* 232, 233). When Macdonnell left Alison and she sought a reconciliation, he did not refuse; but he died before her return could be negotiated. The Dean of St Paul's did not allow Alison to attend the funeral (Roberts, *Sheppard*, and Scott, *Sheppard* passim).

The marriage of Samuel and Henrietta Barnett* stood on the border between traditional attitudes and modern ones. Without obviously defying convention, it was in fact an equal partnership. Husband and wife shared a philosophy and a ministry, each supporting the other and each undertaking specific responsibilities in the fields to which each was best suited.

Barnett married Henrietta Rowland in 1873. Yetta (as Barnett called her) was as determined and energetic as her husband; but, until he mellowed with age and learned the lessons she had to teach him, she was his superior in human relations. She had the self-confidence which social position, intelligence and affluence confer, and a delightful gaiety and sense of humour which took Barnett out of himself as he relaxed in her company. A friend spoke of her as a 'bright, piquante, fascinating personality'. On the debit side, she was plagued with ill health, with which it took time for Barnett to come to terms. She also said of herself: 'I am one of those women who are not fit for public work, and dislike and distrust all forms of conflict' (Barnett, 1.120; 2.294). She did herself less than justice, but her achievements would have been impossible without the encouragement of her husband; as his without hers.

The marriage was founded securely upon a shared faith. Each of them found God in the other. Before they were married Barnett wrote to Henrietta 'It is strange, that sense of God between us. I feel you with me as I feel Him. I draw near to you as I draw near to Him' (Barnett, 1.46). As they found God in marriage, so they found him in life. Both of them felt that they were not 'religious', and in one sense they were right. They found their true vocation in serving the Christ in other people, and especially in the poor.

They shared a passion for self-improvement. They spent their honeymoon visiting cathedrals; on cold days Barnett read to his wife from Maurice's lectures on the Epistles, Lecky's *History of Rationalism*, and treatises on political economy. On a convalescent holiday years later they read Jowett's *Plato* together. Henrietta was discovered by a friend reading her way through Aristotle.

From the beginning they worked as a team. In the early years at St Jude's Barnett would decide on his sermon subject on Mondays, and develop his theme throughout the week, with Henrietta listening and criticizing at every stage. She was no tame panegyrist. ' "On Mondays", I used to say, "it is simple, fit for a coster; on Saturdays only a philosopher could understand it" ' (Barnett, 1.79). In his awe-inspiring humility Barnett was quite prepared to consign his week's work to the flames at her behest.

Their profound intimacy is illustrated by the respect with which Barnett regarded his wife's psychic powers. She told with pride the story of how he once got up at 5.30 a.m. on a bleak morning to convey to a doctor her intuition of the correct diagnosis in the case of a sick friend. 'I never heard of any other man who would get up and go out at that hour in that weather because his wife had an idea' (Barnett, 2.223).

In important aspects of their work Henrietta complemented her husband. He was the rigorous theoretician and sometimes ruthless fighter; she the softening influence constantly drawing his attention to human factors. He found it hard to tackle sexual issues; she became a regular visitor to Lock wards, and conducted a vigorous ministry among prostitutes and unmarried mothers. More generally, Barnett suggested the ends and she provided the means. The widowed Henrietta recalled a day spent on the river at Oxford: 'the Canon sitting in the bow and I steering; a parable perhaps, for in our common work he saw and pointed out where to go, and I knew how to get there' (Barnett, 2.18).

It infuriated Barnett when his wife was regarded as a mere domestic manager; she for her part was perfectly ready to play conventional feminine roles when it served their joint purposes. At Toynbee Hall she was the only woman among a large number of men. On several occasions the democratically elected governing committee resolved to take the housekeeping away from her; each time, to her amusement, they besought her to take it over again. She had a genius for hospitality, mingling rich and poor at her table, and consciously setting out to secure the support of the affluent and influential. She wrote: 'with the motherliness of a young wife I decided that it would be good for him to have his ambition fired ... with a desire for the power which, following recognition, would give further opportunities of service and influence. With this end in view, I fearlessly invited to our tiny Whitechapel vicarage all the most intellectual people we met, who, when they had cleared away his hedges of mannerisms, recognized, revered and followed the real man' (Barnett, 1.145).

Henrietta had her burdens to bear. In the first years of their relationship Barnett's driving energy and dedication made him thoughtless and insensitive. His wife never forgot how, soon after she met him, he expected her to make an extended journey in a horse van with a drunkard at her feet. On holiday, he exhausted her by walking too fast and too far. Impatient with ill health in others, he could be 'comically fussy' about his own. There were arguments about his propensity for overwork. Henrietta had to reassure Barnett in his recurring self-distrust, and ensure that other people did not undervalue him to the extent that he undervalued himself.

On the other hand Barnett understood that they must keep time for each other. They took Fridays as a day off, to be spent in each other's company. They had no hesitation in absenting themselves from work for long periods. Barnett supported his wife heart and soul in her separate enterprises and sustained her sometimes flagging self-confidence. The result was that in the last years of her married life and in her widowhood Henrietta threw herself into two major causes. She was the moving force behind the establishment of Hampstead Garden Suburb, and she was so influential in reforming the way in which children in state institutions were treated that Mr Asquith called her 'the non-official custodian of the children of the State'.

They had no children of their own. In 1891 they adopted a seven year old girl whose parents had died. She was a great joy to them for ten years, but then she died. Henrietta wrote: 'from that date we understood children better, and the desolate pain of sorrowing parents has been ours' (Barnett, 2.145). Their loss was society's gain; had family life made a greater claim upon their energies they would not have been able to contribute as much as they did to the family life of others.

A resident of Toynbee Hall wrote: 'Mrs Barnett did more than refine male roughness, she gave Residents a new ideal of married life, that of the wife as an equal partner with her husband in work and thought' (Barnett, 2.43). Barnett, who believed that women should be on an equal legal footing with men, practised that principle in his married life. But the most remarkable thing about this marriage was that equal partnership went with a total identity of faith and philosophy, and with a profound mutual emotional support; so that Henrietta could say 'We ... were individual but interdependent' (Barnett, 1.348). In many respects the marriage provides a model for our own day and for the future.

Children and Family Life

Thomas Fuller**, wrote in his *Worthies of England*: 'There goeth a common report, no less uncharitable than untrue, yet meeting with many believers thereto, as if clergymen's sons were generally signally unfortunate, like the sons of Eli, Hophni and Phinehas, dissolute in their lives, and doleful in their deaths' (Fuller, *WE* 1.78). The Eclectic, the clerical society John Newton* founded at St Mary Woolnoth, took as a topic for discussion 'Why do ministers' children so often prove to be bad?' (Martin, *Newton* 323). Newton's great contemporary William Grimshaw* had a son John who resisted attempts to apprentice him to a trade, who accepted neither discipline nor the necessity of hard work, and who shortened his life by drunkenness and debauchery. Patrick Bronte's** son Branwell, devastated by a fatal love affair, took to drink and to opium, and contracted debts which dogged the family until he died at thirty-one (Colloms, 90–91).

Plenty of clergy have been tried hard by their families. Some have failed them. John Skinner*, left to bring up his three children after their mother's early death, was driven to despair by his sons, who had inherited his cross-grained temperament but not his sense of duty. His real and active concern for them was vitiated by the clumsiness with which he treated them, and, although relationships never broke down entirely, there were times when it was impossible for them all to live together in the same house. Joseph had a disastrous career at Sandhurst, Owen a temper which matched his father's. Both young men used religion as a weapon in their domestic battles. Skinner noted that Owen had said that he (John Skinner) 'was a Deist or a Socinian if I was anything'; and that Joseph, at that time very ill, had declared that: 'He did not like my doctrines ... since they were not the doctrines of the Church ... he expected to be saved by grace' (Skinner, 461, 462). They could have found no better way of wounding their father than by beating him over the head with the doctrines of the Methodists whom he spent so much time contradicting; so it is pleasant to record that Skinner was reconciled to Joseph, and ministered to him in the weeks before his death.

Skinner was a caring parent. Not all clerical fathers have been so. A famous story about Sabine Baring-Gould** alleges that he asked one of his fourteen children who her father was (Purcell, *Baring-Gould* 2). Dick Sheppard* never considered altering his life-style in order to accommodate his children; their tragedy was compounded because their mother behaved like their father. Patrick Bronte neglected his children before and after the early death of his wife, both because of his solitary character and because of his devotion to ministry. The girls were brought up simply and hardily at their father's command; but his authority was a remote one, and they hardly ever saw him (Gaskell, *Bronte* 38). Charles Kingsley* went into his clerical father's study only to recite his lessons. The corporal punishment used on him probably contributed to his lifelong stutter, and decided him never to beat his own children (Chitty, *Kingsley* 28). Kingsley's father was of course not unusual in his methods. Mrs Lynn Linton, a popular Victorian novelist, recorded her treatment at the hands of her bad-tempered father, parson Lynn of Crosthwaite: 'I do not suppose a week passed without one of these memorable outbreaks, with the rod and the dark closet under the stairs to follow' (Addison, 165). Samuel Butler, whose hated clerical father used to beat him too, made a shrewd psychological point when he suggested that the high standards demanded of a clergyman in public exact a price from his family. 'The clergyman is expected to be a kind of human Sunday ... the person whose vicarious goodness is to stand for that of others entrusted to his charge. But his home is his castle as much as that of any other Englishman, and with him ... unnatural tension in public is followed by exhaustion when tension is no longer necessary. His children are the most defenceless things he can reach, and it is on them in nine cases out of ten that he will relieve his mind' (Butler, 136).

Butler also thought that the fact that the clergyman is much at home places a special burden on his family (Butler, 130). Be that as it may, there is no doubt that the necessity of setting a good example has both been regarded as essential and has made for difficulties. George Herbert* insisted: 'The parson is very exact in the governing of his house, making it a copy and a model for his parish' (Herbert, X). Two of the charges brought against Robert Bayley, vicar of Oadby, Leicestershire, when he was being investigated after the first Civil War, were that he let his children play on Sunday, and that his wife was infrequently in church (Matthews, *Walker* 231). James Woodforde* was caused pain and embarrassment by his niece and housekeeper Nancy, who attended church only irregularly, sometimes not even at Easter (Woodforde, 2.240 and passim). R.W. Evans, vicar of Heversham, Westmoreland, and author of a mid-nineteenth-century clerical handbook, wrote: 'It is not enough ... that the clergyman must be personally holy and diligent; the family must also be holy and regular; if not it is a continual contradiction to his power of government, and encourages rebellion against him' (Evans, 205–6). David Watson* decided that the witness he was trying to give in York required that he remove his children from fee-paying schools and send them to local authority ones; a decision which bore heavily upon him and them, and which he later reversed (Saunders, *Watson* 153, 224).

The task of setting an example is not made easier by the fact that the family live their life in the public view. Evans again: 'While others may have secrets, his [household] can have none. You must submit to having your hours of rising and retiring known; the hours and qualities of your meals known; yea, and the nature of your studies known; the conversation at your table to be known, your guests to be known, everything to be known' (Evans, 200–201).

The openness to observation of the clerical home has been increased by the obligation of hospitality. While at Olney, John Newton* once wrote in his diary for May 'free from company for the first time since 20 January'. He issued an open invitation to dinner to any of his congregation who had walked six miles or more to church. Parishioners could stay to tea after evensong, and remain for a house meeting which could number up to seventy (Martin, *Newton* 218). Robert Walker, curate of Seathwaite, Cumberland, for sixty-six years in the eighteenth century, and bringing up a large family on a pittance, offered a meal every Sunday to those of his congregation who had come a distance (Addison, 126).

A proper balance between generosity and frugality has been expected. Herbert counselled against the 'very visible' sin of luxury (Herbert, III), and Skinner commented tartly after dinner at a colleague's home: 'French dishes and French wine in profusion. I hope such feasts will not be repeated often, or I am sure I shall not be one of the guests' (Skinner 252).

Despite the difficulties, many clergy and their wives have set a good example of Christian family life. One of the charming aspects of the Kilvert* diaries is the picture they paint of the affectionate household at Langley Burrell, with its daily prayers, family croquet, Francis showering 'sweet kisses' on his sister, and Francis's father reading aloud 'that wild and powerful book *Lorna Doone*' in the evenings (Kilvert, 2.269, 317, 283). W.H. Vanstone** remembers that: 'it was the evident belief of my parents that the good care of their children was among their most important duties as members and leaders of the Church; and, on the other hand, that the proper care of children included their training and involvement in the life of the Church' (Vanstone, 3). The effect in that case was to encourage the son to follow in his father's vocation and to become, in due course, one of the most distinguished spiritual writers of our day. John and Charlotte Keble*, childless themselves, delighted to welcome children into their home, to the extent that when Keble took nephew Tom for tuition fun predominated over work. Keble used to write standing at the mantelpiece of his sitting-room, surrounded by the comings and goings of a busy household, and ready to break off at any moment to see to the needs of a parishioner or to join in family games (Battiscombe, *Keble* 192–3, 318). There are countless similar examples of happy and devoted clerical homes, where love was infectious and where the children grew up to walk as their parents did. Woodforde's father, grandfather and great-grandfather were all clergymen. Thomas Phelps (1814–1903), rector of Ridley, Kent, could claim a grandfather, father, uncle, brother, son and grandson of the cloth (Loo, *Phelps* 23).

As he waited for the stake, the Marian martyr Rowland Taylor wrote to his son in terms which would be conventional were it not for the circumstances: 'See that thou fear God always. Flee from all sin and wicked living, be virtuous, serve God with daily prayer, and apply thy book ... see that thou be obedient to thy mother, love her and serve her; be ruled by her now in thy youth, and follow her good counsel in all things. Beware of lewd company, of young men that fear not God but follow their lewd lusts and vain appetites. Fly from whoredom, and hate all filthy living, remembering that I thy father do die in the defence of holy marriage ... when God shall bless thee, love and cherish the poor people, and count that thy chief riches is, to be rich in alms; and when thy mother is waxed old, forsake her not, but provide for her to thy power ... for so will God bless thee, and give thee long life upon earth, and prosperity' (Foxe, 6.692).

Taylor's Protestant devotion cost his son a father. In less dramatic ways the religious commitment of clerical parents has often born hard upon children. Leigh Richmond, the evangelical rector of Turvey in Bedfordshire at the beginning of the nineteenth century, forbade his family all games of chance, fishing, field-sports, dancing, theatre-going, novels, oratorios and intimacy with servants or other unsuitable persons. The children rose very early and from 6.00 a.m. read and prayed with their father. He conducted what he called his Home Mission: a correspondence with his children which continued whether he himself was at home or not. In a typical letter he reminded a child of his brother's recent death, and of his dying words; and asked: 'Has the affecting thought "I must live forever in heaven or hell" suitably impressed your mind? ... You are a sinner, and without a gracious Saviour, you must perish' (Hart *ECCP* 65–6).

The way Samuel and Susannah Wesley** brought up their children has attracted unfavourable comment, largely because of Susannah's remark that she had taught her children to 'cry softly' when they were beaten. Under closer scrutiny the life of the Wesley home yields much that is admirable, even if out of harmony with the attitudes of a more permissive and hedonistic age.

Susannah was a deeply devout woman, who since the age of twenty had kept a vow to spend two hours a day in prayer and meditation. She bore nineteen children, of whom ten reached adulthood. Despite spending much of her married life pregnant or nursing, she exercised a close personal supervision over her family. According to her own account (admittedly given in old age, when memory may have confused the actual with the ideal) six hours a day were spent in domestic school. The children learned the ancient languages from their father, but otherwise were educated by their mother. Living a disciplined devotional life herself, she expected the same of them. As soon as they could speak they learned the Lord's Prayer which they said morning and evening. As time went on they learned a prayer for their parents, collects, a short catechism and portions of scripture. Before they got their breakfast they had read or heard the psalms and Old Testament reading for the day, and said their private prayers; in the evening the process was repeated with the reading from the New Testament. In addition Susannah gave each child personal religious instruction.

The children were governed by a code of table manners which sounds draconian but which, as in the case of the requirement that they should whisper if they wanted anything, numbers no doubt necessitated. 'They were so constantly used to eat and drink what was given them,' Susannah recalled, 'that when any of them was ill, there was no difficulty in making them take the most unpleasant medicine, for they durst not refuse it, though some of them would presently throw it up' (Ayling, *Wesley* 23). Of a piece with table discipline were 'by-laws' such as that no sin should pass unpunished and that personal property should be rigorously respected.

But it was also a by-law that owning up to an offence exempted the offender from a beating. Those beatings for which the children were taught to cry softly began very early in life 'by which means they escaped abundance of correction which they might otherwise have had' (Ayling, *Wesley* 22). Acts of exceptional obedience were commended and rewarded. In some respects the Wesley parents were enlightened and even genial. The girls were given the same education as the boys. Unusually for the age, the children ate with their parents. The regime allowed for cards, dances and visits to local fairs. It is significant of the relationships established that Wesley used to regard his mother as his spiritual mentor even while he was at University; and that in later years Susannah reproached herself for having loved John too much.

Like wives, children have been expected to share the father's ministry. Unmarried daughters in particular have given themselves over to good works. When the Evangelical Edward Bickersteth** became rector of Watton, Hertfordshire, in 1830, he deputed his unmarried daughters to establish a working school for young women and adult evening schools for young men (Hennell, 36). William Barnes (1801–86), the Dorset scholar, poet and parson, divided his parish into four; he visited two areas each week and expected his two daughters living at home to visit the other two (Colloms, 142). Miss Ellison, in Flora Thompson's Lark Rise, visited more often than her father, lavishing an unappreciated care and kindness on the villagers (Thompson, 221–2).

The opportunity for daughters to lead lives of their own has often been severely limited by presumptions of Christian propriety which fathers took for granted and which the daughters themselves often freely accepted. Margaret Oliphant's Hester Maydew 'lived contentedly in the old rotten tumbledown vicarage, doing the same thing every day at the same hour year after year, serving her father and the parish, attending all the church services, visiting the schools and the sick people.' Mrs Oliphant commented: 'I hope good women who live in this dutiful routine get to like it, and find a happiness in the thought of so much humble handmaiden's work performed so steadily; but to the profane and the busy it seems hard thus to wear away a life' (Oliphant, *CC* 8). Nor has it been easy to leave home. Samuel Wesley constantly frustrated his daughters' attempts to marry, with unhappy results. Charlotte Bronte was forced to defer her marriage because of her father's opposition; he depended on her as his only surviving child, and although she eventually prevailed on him to agree to the match it was on the understanding that her husband would be curate at Howarth until Patrick died (Colloms, 93–4).

Only in modern times has the typical clerical household consisted of a nuclear family. In the past the membership frequently included other relatives and almost always servants. When Herbert and his wife moved into Bemerton Rectory three orphaned nieces joined them; there were also four maid-servants and two man-servants (Charles, *Herbert* 154–5). The Rectory was enlarged in the later nineteenth century to hold a family of six, and ten indoor and four outdoor servants (Hammond, 48). James Woodforde had Nancy, and five living-in servants. Keble's sister Elizabeth lived with him during the last part of her life; he referred to her and Charlotte Keble as 'his two wives'. George Sumner, the later Archbishop, employed seventeen servants when he became rector of Old Alresford in 1851. His wife Mary, founder of the Mothers Union, was said never in her life to have put on her own stockings (Hammond, 61). Kilvert kept four or five servants during his bachelor days at Bredwardine (Grice, *Kilvert* 125–6). The far from affluent Charles Garbett, vicar of Tongham, Surrey, from 1869 to 1895, employed seven (Smyth, *Garbett* 31).

The distinction between relations and servants has sometimes been blurred. Herbert said of the country parson: 'To his children he shows more love than terror, to his servants more terror than love; but an old good servant boards a child' (Herbert, X). Ralph Josselin* employed his sister Mary as a servant before finding her a similar post with his patron. John Newton retained in his service three elderly servants who spent much of their time looking after each other in their illnesses; Newton remarked: 'I shall always think myself more obliged to them than they can be to me, and I hope nothing but death shall part us' (Martin, *Newton* 337).

Terror has had its place too. Woodforde dismissed a servant after nine years' service 'which ... is much too long for any Norfolk Servant for they will then get pert, saucy and do as they please' (Woodforde, 4.124). George Woodward** dismissed an 'active, diligent and neat' maid as soon as her pregnancy was discovered; he retained two other servants who wished to marry only on the understanding that should the birth of children cause inconvenience the couple would leave his service (Woodward, 82, 128). James Newton** beat one servant 'for not keeping the Cows', and 'Horse whipt' another for reasons he did not record (James Newton, 151, 72). William Cole**, who was kindly enough to invite an ex-servant to dine with him, also cudgelled young Jem Wood for taking too long over an errand. Dr Pettingal (1708–81), rector of Stoke-Hammond, Buckinghamshire, neglectful of advice given in the *Homilies* which he no doubt regularly read to his congregation, beat a maid severely enough for her to seek legal redress; a fellow-clergyman excused him 'for kicking his Maid, because she was a very bad one' (Cole, 24, 95, 115, 118, 154, 253, 256).

Contiguity could lead to other excesses. Cole recorded that his neighbour and frequent dining companion Thomas Goodwin, rector of Loughton, was guilty of indecent advances to his maids, while Goodwin's much younger wife was thought to be overly fond of her menservants (Cole, 9, 270–9).

In well-regulated clerical households the servants have been included in the spiritual arangements, and have attended family prayers. John Skinner decided in 1824 that he should hold morning as well as evening prayers for them; he sometimes read them a sermon. He insisted that they should attend church, a regulation which once cost him a cook (Skinner, 353). Josselin blessed servants on their arrival. Oliver Rouse, rector of Tetcott, Devonshire, in the early nineteenth century, dismissed a man-servant because he refused to learn the collect for the day (Brendon, *Hawker* 164).

A conscientious parson felt himself responsible for his servants' morals; in particular for preserving the maids' virginity. James Woodforde parted with his Sukey after she conceived, but in typically kind-hearted fashion gave her a present on top of her wages. More personally embarrassing was the conduct of his nephew Bill Hammerton, who had a liaison with another of his maids. 'I told Bill ... that I should have nothing more to do with him ... He was very low ... and cried much' (Woodforde, 1.232, 237, 238). William Kingsley, parson of South Kilvington, near Thirsk, in the mid-nineteenth century, deterred the local lads by a notice 'Man-traps are set at night in these grounds'; he explained to his friends that the man-traps were his maids (Colloms, 229). Robert Hawker* vetted his maids' followers and dismissed his farm manager for seducing the maids of his neighbours; another Cornish parson of the period was murdered by a parishioner whom he had forbidden to come courting (Brendon,

Hawker 165–7). Francis Kilvert's vicar at Clyro, Mr Venables, was deeply upset when his married coachman proved responsible for the pregnancy of a kitchen-maid (Kilvert, 1.144, 1.154).

Robert Dolling* interpreted his domestic responsibilities in his own distinctive fashion. He shared his home in Portsmouth with a shifting population of lodgers, numbering between fourteen and thirty. Some were men discovering whether they had a vocation to work in the slums; most were sick in body, mind or soul. Only Dolling knew the full circumstances of each lodger; most were referred to solely by a nickname. The rules of the house were: be punctual for meals; do not annoy each other except with Dolling's permission; be in by 10.15 p.m. Lodgers could leave when they wished, and steal if they could find anything worth stealing (Dolling, *TY* 75).

There have been modern equivalents to the extended households of the past. While they were in York David and Anne Watson had two children to care for; at Anne's suggestion, they also took in up to eight other people many of them afflicted with serious personal problems. There was a common purse and minimal provision for personal spending; as a result a number of people were able to give themselves to ministry without undue concern about money. Although Watson and his wife regardèd themselves as joint house-parents they also tried to disperse authority by encouraging every member of the community to speak the truth in love. The pressure these arrangements created was intense. Watson himself suffered from the lack of privacy, from a lack of control over his personal belongings, from personality clashes with other residents and from resentment from members of his congregation at what they saw as a privileged relationship. He found it necessary to erect a partition in the rectory hall, separating his study and office from the rest of the house, and living much of his life in isolation from the rest of the community (Saunders, *Watson* 154). None the less, the community survived for eight years, held together by daily prayers, by regular household meetings, by Anne's enthusiasm and by huge self-sacrifice. Watson's judgment on the experience was that, through its pain and brokenness, through the vulnerability of the members of the household to each other, the grace of God was clearly seen, and capacity for ministry enhanced (Watson, *YAMG*, ch. 12). Nicholas Rivett-Carnac** undertook a similar experiment when he became priest in charge of St Mark's Kennington in 1972. He was a bachelor at the time, and relied upon a group of Christian friends to support him in providing a home for a changing population of the unstable. Incomes were pooled and possessions held in common. The scheme broke down after eighteen months, but inspired a number of more cautious enterprises within the parish (Cooke, chs 9 and 13).

We turn to Ralph Josselin for a detailed picture of relationships between father and children in a clerical home.

He rejoiced in the birth of his children, valuing them 'above gold and jewells'; but they also tried him sorely. His wife had ten live births. Two sons died in infancy, a daughter at eight, a daughter at nineteen, and a son at twenty-nine. The other five children outlived him. When baby Ralph died at ten days old in 1648, Josselin was able to thank God because the outcome had been expected; because the death was easy; because he and his wife had not yet learned to love Ralph deeply; and because the baby was destined for 'the land of rest, where there is no sickness nor childhood but all perfection'. Soon afterwards he was writing that their mourning was over. In 1650, however, he and his wife lost another baby, and eight-year-old Mary. He wrote 'many times I find the memory of my deare babes bitter as death, and no rest till my meditacions rest on god, who is my present peace, oh how happy are they, that have a god in their difficulties to goe unto, I will rejoyce under the shaddowe of thy wings.' When the nineteen-year-old Ann died in 1673 he wrote: 'god hath taken 5 of 10. lord lett it be enough ... bee reconciled in the blood of thy son my saviour and make all mine thine' (Josselin, 203, 113–14, 119, 210, 568).

The living caused him even more tribulation than the dead. Especially when the children were young, it was unusual for them all to be well. Often the angel of death hovered close by; Josselin recorded with dread the incidence of small-pox and the plague in the neighbourhood, and his expectations that certain illnesses might prove fatal. Four of his children did contract smallpox; fortunately they all recovered. He took childish naughtiness very seriously – 'the follies of my young children awakened mee to see the sad effects of our fall in Adam, how operative corruption is tainting of us.' He was put to heavy expense when he apprenticed his sons in London, and to much distress when they were unhappy, eventually returning home. Tom settled down and opened a shop, but died young. John, 'whose behaviour suggests a violent attempt to attract to himself the love and concern that were likely to have been centred on his ailing elder brother' (Macfarlane, *Josselin* 118), was a serious and continuing problem. He refused to settle to anything; was given to swearing, drink and bad company; repeatedly ran away, on one occasion stealing money from his mother and sister; and made promises of amendment only to break them. His father tried threats and promises with an equal lack of success, recording with hope occasional periods of quiescence, and with despair the relapses which invariably followed. Towards the end of his life Josselin learned a kind of resignation, and recorded that John had married without his parents' knowledge with only eight words of comment: 'god pardon his errors, pray god blesse him' (Josselin, 402, 618, 631, 634).

The daughters who survived childhood gave him other but lesser worries. They too put him to considerable expense, since he sent them away to school, and provided for them both before and at their weddings. Jane, the eldest, and Elizabeth and Rebecca, the youngest, made good marriages, and gave him little to complain of. Anne was sickly throughout her life; sent to London to go into service she quarrelled with her mistress, and eventually returned home to die at the age of nineteen. Mary proved hard to marry off. She caused her father great concern by refusing four swains, but accepted a fifth before he died.

Josselin experienced the pressures which beset all devout and busy fathers. He reproached himself for deadness in family prayer and for failing to give the children sufficient religious instruction; and also for letting family affairs come between him and God (Josselin, 410, 307). Later on, as the children went their own way, he had another common parental experience, that of finding his advice unwelcome and unregarded.

There was a positive side to parenthood. Josselin occasionally referred to times of health and happiness – 'god hath given me much confort in my wife and children ... which hath made my bed a rest and a refreshing comfort unto mee.' He rejoiced in the 'towardlynes' of his children to learn, and in the providences of God which saved them from harm in accidents. 'god good in preserving An in a milke bowle, and Jane from swouning who let her fall in ... god gives his angels charge over us.' He was especially fond of his daughter Elizabeth, recording after she had visited him with her son: 'shee was with mee with sweetnes and content, that made her company pleasant to mee, I parted with her in all love. gods blessings with her.' Later in life he was able to take pleasure in grandchildren, and in the rare occasions when the whole family was together: 'I saw my six children togither on earth, blessed bee god, and lett us all bee togither in heaven.' In all, however, Josselin's quiverful constituted a cross, and he constantly turned to God for strength to bear it (Josselin, 93, 330, 639, 481).

Sexuality

The novels of Trollope follow the clergy into their bedrooms only to eavesdrop on conversation. Those of Susan Howatch, written in our own day, observe no such discretion; they insist, rightly, that the clergy like other men have to come to terms with their sexuality. As with other men too sexuality has driven them to extremes. In 1779 James Hackman, vicar of Wiveton in Norfolk, 'victim of insane love', shot and killed the mistress of the Earl of Sandwich, and was hanged for it (Barrow, 113).

Sexuality bulks large in clerical life partly because of the need to control it. Priests are expected to abide strictly by Christian sexual teaching, and are likely to have strong guilt feelings if they fall short. At the same time the clergy have more private access to women than the members of any but the medical profession, and in less clinical conditions than they; sexual misbehaviour is a betrayal of trust which must be expected to attract severe sanctions. All this makes for difficulties. As a sermon preached at an Archdeacon's visitation in 1787 put it: 'When a clergyman falls into the Arts of Seduction, and becomes Libertine by Profession ... he must be considered as no better than Satan in

Disguise' (Hart, *ECCP* 119). Joseph Price** was sorely harassed by a woman whom he called 'Jezebel' or 'la diablesse', with whom he had had a liaison, and who tried to blackmail him (Price, 15–16). Mrs Oliphant took it for granted in *The Perpetual Curate* that her hero Frank Wentworth could be ruined by an innocent but indiscreet association with the parish clerk's daughter. In real life John Robinson, curate in charge of Downe, Kent, in 1868 lost his reputation when he was alleged to have walked out with one local girl, and to entered the house of another 'supposed to have a bad character' (Desmond and Moore, 563–4). Roy Catchpole**, has given a vivid account of the agonies inflicted upon his family and himself by a false accusation that he had made a young parishioner pregnant (Catchpole, *GMDC* 104–43).

After the episode with his Jezebel, Joseph Price made other sexual arrangements. Looking back on the year 1771 he noted: 'My inclinations for marriage do not increase. I have as much c–nt [sic] as I want' (Price, 169). He was not untypical. Many clergy denied the satisfactions of marriage, or finding them insufficient, have sought relief elsewhere. In 1625 Joan Coxe of Benson, Oxfordshire, admitted that she had had a child by the curate John Shurlock. 'Mr Shurlock before and after the childe was begotten promised to marry her but he durst not do it until his father was dead' (Hart, *TCL* 73). The charges brought against Royalist clergy during the period 1642–60 frequently included sexual ones. Peter Allen, vicar of Tollesbury, Essex, was accused of 'living incontinently a long time with severall women', by one of whom he had a child. Timothy Clay, rector of Wickham St Paul, Essex, and another parson 'kept a noted whore with them … the most part of 2 daies and 2 nights, to the expense of above £5'. Robert Bankes, vicar of Rolvenden, Kent, was sequestered because he was 'very vitious in his conversation and hath laine hold of severall maides whom he hath found alone using very wanton and lascivious Dalliance with them, yea sometimes on the Lordes day' (Matthews, *Walker* 144, 148, 210).

In the next century James Newton** remained a bachelor rather against his will. Coy references in his diary imply that he took advantage of his frequent trips to London to visit prostitutes; it was a convenience that the ladies frequented places of public worship, and that he could follow them home therefrom (James Newton, 21, 73, 82, 113). In 1829 Edward Drax Free, rector of Sutton, Lincolnshire, was deprived on charges which included having 'illicit connections' with a string of maid-servants (Barrow, 137). The sexual athleticism of Harold Davidson, the rector of Stiffkey, Norfolk, earned him national notoriety in the 1930s. In a less dramatic case, the young Arthur Hopkinson** discovered, on taking up his first incumbency, that his parishioners included the mistress and children of a local colleague (Hopkinson, 144).

Howatch quotes Bishop Hensley Henson: 'The sexual appetite (which is the most insistent and the most important of our bodily desires) presses for satisfaction ... So we start with the certainty that sexual indulgence will be popular and that Christianity will be most difficult precisely at that point' (Howatch, *GI* 105). Most especially difficult because until recently two injunctions, additional to the fundamental ones of abstinence outside marriage and faithfulness within it, have formed part of Anglican teaching about sexual intercourse.

The first injunction has been against enthusiasm for the act of intercourse itself. Fielding's Parson Adams warned Joseph Andrews not to marry in order to indulge his carnal appetites. 'All such brutal lusts and affections are to be greatly subdued, if not totally eradicated, before the vessel can be said to be consecrated to honour. To marry with a view of gratifying those inclinations is a prostitution of that holy ceremony' (Fielding, 333). Adams was echoing the teaching of the foremost ethical primer of the age *The Whole Duty of Man*. Since marriage is 'aiming only at the subduing of lust ... it is very contrary to that end to make marriage an occasion of heightening and enflaming it' (*WDM*, 140). This attitude endured. In John Henry Newman's** novel *Loss and Gain*, written in 1847, Charles Reding, who speaks for Newman himself, favours celibacy over marriage because in marriage there is a greater danger of the sin of copulation for its own sake (Faber, 221–2).

Secondly, the Anglican Church, in common with most others, has until modern times opposed any kind of birth control save abstinence. *The Whole Duty of Man* teaches that the sole aim of sexual intercourse is to beget children, and that nothing may be done to avoid that outcome (*WDM*, 140). The size of clerical families has indicated that what the clergy have enjoined on others they have practised themselves. The liberal Samuel Barnett* held all contraceptive methods wrong save self-control (Barnett, 1.195). As late as 1920 the Lambeth Conference issued a strong warning against artificial contraception. Though the 1930 Conference sanctioned it in limited circumstances, Mervyn Stockwood** was a pioneer when, as vicar in the 1940s of the impoverished parish of St Matthew's Moorfields, Bristol, he pressed for contraception on the rates (Stockwood, 27). Later in the same decade, Harry Williams** at All Saints, Margaret Street, seeking advice for use in the confessional from leading Anglo-Catholics, was told that all artificial contraception was wrong (Williams, 126). He soon decided to take a more liberal personal view, but it was not until the Lambeth Conference of 1958 that the Anglican communion as a whole can be said to have pronounced contraception morally acceptable. By the 1960s Nicolas Stacey** was able to pioneer a family planning clinic in a hostel for the homeless to general approval. He wrote: 'If there is any connection between increasing human happiness and building the Kingdom of God, the work of God was being done in that clinic' (Stacey, 268–9).

In his *Speculum Sacerdotum*, a book of guidance for the clergy published in 1893, W.C.E. Newbolt writes: 'What is to give us ... spirituality? Is it not purity?' (Newbolt, 70). He goes on to argue that purity is the opposite of sensuality, which is not confined to inordinate sexuality but which includes it. His general point underlines the spiritual weight traditionally placed on sexual morality; the vagueness with which he writes illustrates the frequently held view that talk about sexuality is in itself somehow unclean. The eighteenth-century parish priest and novelist Laurence Sterne** attracted odium because of the sexual explicitness of his masterpiece *Tristram Shandy*. Samuel Barnett's wife attributed to teen-age experiences 'his shrinking from any talk, however pure and necessary, on sex questions' (Barnett, 1.8).

This reluctance to talk about sex has sometimes translated itself into a denial of sexuality itself. Shelley, writing of the economist Malthus, described him as 'a priest and therefore a eunuch'; and if Shelley be thought a tainted source, we need look no further than George Crabbe**. In 'The Borough' he writes of a vicar whose feeble advances impelled the girl he loved to turn to someone more vigorous:

> Yet our good priest to Joseph's praise aspired,
> As once rejecting what his heart desired.

Sydney Smith* made the same point in even fewer words when he remarked that there were three sexes – men, women and clergymen.

But it is not easy to deny the sexual urge, and long years of attempted continence could be full of strain. Samuel Butler's Ernest Pontifex was shocked to find 'that certain thoughts which he warred against as fatal to his soul, and which he had imagined he should lose once for all on ordination, were still as troublesome to him as they had been'. His over-vigorous approach to a girl he took to be a prostitute earned him a spell in jail (Butler, 256, 289–97). John Newton* took full advantage of the sexual opportunities provided by a slave ship until his conversion. Thereafter, admonished by religion and his love for Polly, he took precautions. 'Knowing the danger of my situation I resolved upon sighting a certain point of land to abstain from flesh in my food, and to drink nothing stronger than water, during the voyage; that by abstemiousness, I might subdue every improper emotion' (quoted Martin, *Newton* 111).

Newton met his sexual problems head on; Francis Kilvert* dealt with his obliquely. He underwent two common nineteenth-century experiences: he was introduced to sexuality in its nastier forms at his school, and he endured a long period of celibacy. Denied the realities of marriage, he retained in his view of the other sex an adolescent idealism which inhibited explicit sexual imagery. References to sexual temptation in the surviving parts of his diary are few and obscure. Instead, his sexual feelings found expression in three disparate respects.

First, he was a sentimental romantic, whose affections were easily aroused and sometimes enveloped in a cloud of religious feeling. An Irish girl hawker encountered on a train journey overwhelmed him with her beauty, and inspired a wild impulse to follow her. A pretty girl at a Church Congress aroused 'an evil thought' which was expelled only when she bowed at the name of Jesus. He conducted two love affairs before the one which led to his marriage, and when one of them came to an end preached a sermon of the deepest indiscretion on the text 'It is expedient for you that I go away' (Kilvert, 2.210–11; 2.383; 3.298–9).

Secondly he was fascinated by nakedness. He was excited by art gallery nudes and by bathing naked while ladies looked on (Kilvert, 3.109, 37–8).

Thirdly, his genuine and heart-warming affection for little girls was darkened by a preoccupation with flagellation. A small girl's bottom, exposed as she was put on a swing, attracted the comment that it was 'plump and in excellent whipping condition'. He records with ill-disguised relish the chastise-ment of young female parishioners, and once offered to whip an already much whipped little girl (Kilvert, 3.218; 3.60).

The psychological mechanism seems clear. Kilvert's conscious mind rejected explicit sexual temptation on religious grounds; his desires found their way to the surface by devious routes.

Clerical marriage has not necessarily opened the way to an unfettered expression of sexual feeling. Ralph Josselin*, who bemoaned the 'strange, prodigious uncleane lusts' of childhood, and a couple of episodes of what would nowadays be called heavy petting in his 'teens, went to his marriage a virgin. He and his wife Jane do not appear to have habitually slept together; Josselin twice records with gratitude that his wife joined him in bed. Their frequent illnesses and the processes of pregnancy and childbirth must have limited their sexual activity (in addition to giving birth to ten living children, Jane suffered at least five miscarriages). Josselin's generalized denunciations of himself include one or two specific references to lust, but there is no direct evidence to suggest either that his marriage was strengthened by a good sex life or that he regretted its absence. One entry reads indeed as if he blamed himself for making sexual demands (Josselin, 4, 118, 620, 357). He would have echoed the words of Oliver Heywood, a contemporary very like him in all respects save that he refused to conform at the Restoration: 'I am often jeolous lest my conjugal loue should degenerate into or be mixed too much with carnal and sensual delight, and beg often it may be spiritualized' (Heywood, 1.147).

Laurence Sterne, a debauchee before marriage, compensated for his wife's mental instability by joining the Demoniacs of Skelton Castle, whose ritual was 'blasphemous and priapic' and whose conversation consisted of 'bawdy and bravado'. In addition he conducted a series of affairs which may not have gone as far as intercourse but which considerably exceeded the bounds of discretion (Peter Quennell, *Four Portraits*, Hutchinson 1985, 132–86).

Charles Kingsley*, whose Fanny was more passionate than most, had to learn marital restraint: 'I long to be back in your arms, while all you long for, you cruel, cold, darling beauty is, I find, to sleep by my side!' (Chitty, *Kingsley*

137). Worse still was the experience of sexual loss when a wife died. At the age of twenty-seven, William Grimshaw* married a young widow, who died only four years later in 1739. Grimshaw plunged into a period of depression and imaginative torment, of which one element was lurid sexual temptations. 'He lusted after every woman he saw, and most extravagantly of all after the Virgin Mary' (quoted in Baker, *Grimshaw* 41). Desires he resisted staunchly in his waking hours returned to plague him in his sleep; very naturally, he had erotic dreams about his dead wife. It took him time to distinguish between what was within his control and what was not, and his sexual difficulties contributed to the spiritual turmoil which preceded his conviction that he had been justified by faith.

In 1741 Grimshaw married again, but his second wife died in 1746, exposing him afresh to sexual temptation: 'The smouldering fires of passion were liable to be fanned into flame by the touch of a feminine hand, or even by a visit to a bedfast woman parishioner.' He was, however, now better equipped to deal with his difficulties. He did so in part by asceticism, in part by incessant activity, but chiefly by way of his regular written covenants with God. He considered marrying again, but was content to abide by the toss of a coin: 'Heads I marry, tails I don't'. The coin came up tails (Baker, *Grimshaw* 85, 86).

In view of his struggles with his sexuality, it is not surprising that Grimshaw concluded that all forms of physical pleasure were at worst immoral and at best worthless, and retained in his parish disciplines which were dying out elsewhere. He rebuked adulterers in public, and employed the disciplinary powers of ecclesiastical law to punish fornication. Offenders came into church barefooted, wearing a white sheet and carrying a white wand; after the Gospel had been read, the fornicator stood on a seat and repeated a set form of repentance after the minister. Grimshaw did not confine his strictures to sexual malpractice; but it is reasonable to surmise that his harrying of sexual miscreants drew part of its urgency from his own experiences.

Grimshaw won his battles with his sexuality; so, if his own testimony is to be believed, did Robert Herrick**. During the 1620s, probably both before and after his ordination, Herrick wrote a large number of richly erotic poems in which he celebrated his mistresses. Opportunities for self-indulgence were not lacking, for he did not move to his Devonshire parish till 1629. But when his book *Hesperides* was published in 1648 the final couplet read:

> To his Book's end this last line he'd have plac't,
> Jocond his Muse was, but his Life was chast.

Herrick was suspected at one point of having fathered a child; but no disciplinary action was ever taken against him. Other clergy, then and since, have not been so lucky. For reasons both good and bad, sexual misconduct has attracted greater obloquy and more severe consequences than any other offence. John Mitford**, whose wife left him as soon as his child was born and who had a mysterious relationship with a twelve year-old village girl, once wrote: 'Will the God who made us what we are: who cursed us with evil instincts and strong passions, punish us because we are unable to resist their promptings?' (Colloms, 101). The answer church and society have returned to that question has been in the affirmative; and human as well as divine sanctions have been applied. Charles Kingsley's predecessor at Eversley had neglected his parish with impunity; but an indiscretion with a female parishioner forced him to flee the country. Harold Davidson, mentioned above, was formally un-frocked and ended his days as an entertainer in amusement parks. While this book was being written a vicar was deprived for adultery with his curate's wife.

On the other hand, the church authorities have sometimes dealt with sexual misconduct gently and sensitively, taking the view that a ministry is no more invalidated by this sin than by others; always assuming that it has not given public offence. Bishop Edward King** supported a young priest compelled to leave his curacy after 'visiting a bad woman' and 'getting into serious moral difficulties'. He sent him money, and wrote to him regularly and at length in his new curacy (Russell, *King* 235). Tolerance has sometimes been extended even to practising homosexuals. Charles Vaughan (1816–97) became head-master of Harrow and was offered a bishopric. He had, however, had a homosexual affair with a pupil, and was compelled by a parent who had discovered the offence to resign his headship and to refuse the diocese. Instead he became vicar of Doncaster and later dean of Llandaff. The circumstances were known to successive Archbishops; they did not prevent Vaughan from being regarded as a valuable adviser.

In general, however, the lot of the homosexual priest has been unenviable. Christian tradition, social attitudes and, until recently, the law have militated against sexual self-expression, and the choice has been between an often reluctant celibacy or sexual activity fraught with danger. Edward King warned his clergy: 'Love we must but so as to be in heaven together ... The greatest bar to friendship is any kind of sinful love' (Elton, *King* 55). A married woman deacon who parted from her husband after discovering her lesbian orientation kept the circumstances secret for fear of losing her job (Treasure, 51–2).

Some homosexual priests have found their way to celibacy as a vocation. One told his story in the *Church Times* (2 November 1990). Perceiving his orienta-tion, he took it for granted he would remain celibate, till at thirty-five he fell in love. He was rejected and spent ten years in 'a hell of longing, loneliness, self-pity and sexual frustration'. Then at a Church Congress he had an experience of the unconditional love of God which dispelled most of his suffering. Later still, after having rejected another man's advances, he experienced Christ in the eucharist as his constant and ever-loving spouse. He had been surprised by joy.

Numbers of parochial clergy have taken a more permissive view. Their position is summed up in the statement of conviction of the Gay Christian

Movement (now the Lesbian and Gay Christian Movement (LGCM)) set up in 1976. 'Human sexuality in all its richness is a gift of God gladly to be accepted, enjoyed and honoured as a way of both expressing and growing in love, in accordance with the life and teaching of Jesus Christ; ... it is entirely compatible with the Christian faith not only to love another person of the same sex but also to express that love fully in a personal sexual relationship.'

It is frequently said that a high proportion of the clergy are homosexuals. Malcolm Johnson, Rector of St Botolph's, Aldgate, from 1974 to 1992 started a support group for gay clergy in 1975 which attracted between 70 and 100 to its meetings (*Church Times*, 12 February 1993). The LGCM's first president was a parish priest, Peter Elers, incumbent from 1973 to 1984 of Thaxted, Essex, married with four adopted children, but a declared homosexual whose bishop supported him against objectors. The Movement's formation had been made possible by changes in the law respecting homosexuality, changes concerning which the influence of the Church of England had been for the most part on the liberal side. But it is one thing to argue that homosexual activity by consenting adults in private should not be a legal offence; another to suggest that it should no longer be regarded as a sin; and yet another to say that the clergy should be free to conduct such relationships in public. Most of the clergy are still uneasy with arguments which give homosexual relationships the same spiritual status as marriage. When Peter Elers conducted a service of blessing for two lesbian couples he was required to give a solemn undertaking not to repeat the ceremony. In 1988 the church authorities compelled the LGCM to vacate an office in the tower of St Botolph's, Aldgate, on the grounds that the use of church property gave its aims credence. A bishop, reported in *The Guardian* of 10 April 1991, was explicit about the compromises into which current attitudes force him. If he were wise, he said, he would employ no gay clergy, but in fact he has a number in his diocese, some notably devout and sensitive. They could be tolerated and discreetly supported unless their orientation became a matter of public scandal. Then it was no longer possible to defend them.

That bishop's problems were not eased by the pronouncement later the same year of the House of Bishops that 'in our considered judgement the clergy cannot claim the liberty to enter into sexually active homophile relationships' (*Issues in Human Sexuality*, Church House Publishing 1991, 45). As the protests which followed made clear, the pronouncement laid a heavy spiritual burden on some gay clergy; however, had the bishops come to the other conclusion they would have created spiritual difficulties for the Church as a whole.

In one case it is possible to study in detail the interweaving of sexuality and spirituality, and their effect upon each other (for what follows see Chitty, *Kingsley*, passim).

In 1839 Charles Kingsley met Fanny Grenfell, one of four orphaned sisters, and was deeply attracted by her plump and youthful prettiness. However, social convention and the sisters' intention of joining a religious community founded by the Tractarian Pusey stood in the way of a close relationship.

Kingsley was wrestling with his own sexuality. It seems possible that he had homosexual proclivities which he suppressed by laying enormous stress on 'manliness'. He led a wild life during his second year at Cambridge, and on one occasion sought the services of a prostitute. This lapse filled him with shame and self-disgust, and contributed to a spiritual crisis in 1840 where he sought Christ but could not feel that he had regained his faith. He was intent on an absolute commitment and was repelled by what he saw as the tepid religion of his family. He flirted with the idea of becoming a monk, but decided that he had no vocation to celibacy. He was by now writing regularly to Fanny. In one letter he stressed his unworthiness but added: 'You are to me a middle point between earthly and ethereal morality. I begin to love good for your sake. At length I will be able to love it for God's sake' (Chitty, *Kingsley* 58). In January 1841 he kissed Fanny for the first time; soon afterwards she confessed her love for him, and three days later he announced his conversion in these terms: 'I feel, Fanny, that I am under a heavy debt to God and how can I pay this better than by devoting myself to the religion I have scorned, making of the debauchee a preacher of purity and holiness' (Chitty, *Kingsley* 60).

Soon after his conversion, Kingsley decided to seek ordination. He was equally critical of his father's low churchmanship and of the Tractarianism to which the Grenfell sisters adhered. He inveighed against Fanny's 'Manicheanism', by which he meant any suspicion of the pleasures of the flesh which her Puseyite associations might have given her. He need not have worried; her passion matched his own.

The path of love did not run smoothly, since Kingsley had no income and Fanny's sisters were strongly opposed to the match. The lovers were separated, and for a period agreed not even to correspond with each other. Denied ordinary expression, their sexual feelings found a variety of outlets, all with religious associations.

As a curate at Eversley, Kingsley threw himself into his work, but despite fasting, sleeping on the floor, and rising in the middle of the night to pray, he was unable and perhaps unwilling to exorcize fantasies about Fanny's body. He started a biography of St Elizabeth of Hungary, intended as a wedding present; it was the vehicle for sketches of a naked woman with Fanny's body under torture. He sent to Fanny other sketches in which they were shown embracing naked. He and Fanny joined in weekly festivals and fasts. On Thursdays they lay in imagination in each other's arms, on Fridays Kingsley stripped and scourged himself. Fanny did not go so far, but Kingsley wrote to her enthusiastically about the fasting and the hair shirts they would share in marriage. He envisaged himself praying outside her door while she whipped herself or was whipped by her maid. He would hear her confession: 'You shall come to me some morning when we can ensure solitude and secrecy, come as a penitent barefoot, with dishevelled hair, wearing one coarse garment only and then I will, in God's name, solemnly absolve you. Afterwards I will bathe you from head to foot in kisses and fold you in my arms' (Chitty, *Kingsley* 80). After their engagement they shared mortifications such as wearing chains in their beds; and confessed to each other that they felt closer to God when naked.

Kingsley was intent on sanctifying his sexual feelings. 'Matter is holy, awful glorious matter. Let us never use the three words *animal and brutal* in a degrading sense. Our animal enjoyments must be religious ceremonies' (Chitty, *Kingsley* 80). He had confessed the episode with the prostitute to Fanny, and had offered her an unconsummated marriage if that were her wish. Convinced that it was not, he suggested that for the first month of their marriage they should abstain from full sexual intercourse in order to purify their bliss and prepare the way for its prolongation in heaven.

They were married in 1844. They abided by the resolution to postpone intercourse, but there is no evidence that other austerities were continued or initiated. The realities of human intimacy replaced them.

Kingsley tackled the problems created by his sexual feelings in three ways. He tried to exorcize them by self-discipline; he tried to sanctify them by theological argument and by associating them with religious practice; and he gave vent to them as fully as his conscience would allow. Even had the conventions of the age not rendered it difficult, he would not have engaged in intercourse before marriage, but he admitted no other restraints. He recorded contentedly: 'We did all we could before we were one!' (Chitty, *Kingsley* 82).

Eroticism distorted the spiritual dimension of the relationship, but behind the extravagances of overheated sexual feeling lay something truer and deeper. It is easy to dismiss Kingsley's thought and practice during the period before marriage as nothing more than an attempt by a highly-sexed man to come to terms with frustration by dreaming up and acting out fantasies with a religious colouring; but that would do him less than justice. His love for Fanny helped him make his peace with God; and the profound sexual attraction he felt for her was an essential element in a lifelong affection which survived great vicissitudes, and which was the basis for a deeply Christian marriage. They often caused each other distress; they often wore each other out; but they meant everything to each other. The twin pillars on which their union rested were their compatibility as lovers and their shared religious commitment.

Health

Until very recent times, most people have been unwell for much of their lives. An account of Charles Kingsley's* health serves to illustrate the point. He was a delicate child and a stammerer, an affliction which dogged him all his days. He was withdrawn from school at the age of sixteen with mild cholera which permanently affected his liver. Soon afterwards, living in London, he acquired a congested left lung which gave him constant trouble and which was further damaged when he became an addictive smoker at Cambridge. After his final exams in 1841 he had the first of a series of breakdowns. Others occurred in 1848, 1849, 1851, 1852, 1853, 1855, 1856, 1859 and 1864; each put him out of action for weeks or months. His general health began to decline from 1863; he was a martyr to toothache, and his 1864 collapse was associated with an ulcerated intestine. He was very ill on an American lecture tour in 1874, and pneumonia carried him off in 1875 at the age of fifty-five.

Two centuries before Kingsley, Ralph Josselin* recorded his medical history in clinical detail and with morbid enthusiasm. His proclivity to colds and allied chest complaints does not earn him much sympathy from an age which still has to endure them; but he suffered from other ailments which modern medicine would have disposed of in short order. From October 1648 to May 1652 he was afflicted with a suppurating navel and from 1673 to his death in 1683 with an infected leg. Toothache and 'ague' were frequent companions; so were problems with his bowels and his urine. None the less he lived to sixty-seven, which suggests that for his era he was a basically healthy man.

Josselin accommodated his state of health within his spiritual scheme with as much facility as he did every other aspect of his life. He thought sickness a deserved chastisement, and was therefore able to give thanks when, as with a cold, the chastisement was gentle. A sore tongue reminded him that God could rob him of any member at His pleasure, and that he was called to use this one to God's praise. His suppurating navel evoked reflections about patience and submission, and he saw occasional improvements as an answer to prayer. When the navel healed up for a time he was concerned lest he should relapse into vanities and 'contemplative lusts'. When soreness recurred he saw it as a justified punishment. Hearing of some one else who had died of this ailment, he expressed his confidence in God's intention of curing him. He went on: 'I shall praise him, and being thus fixed in heart upon him I enjoy sweet peace.' Perhaps he did; it seems more likely that he felt he ought to (Josselin, 77, 144, 157, 159–60).

With ill health in such generous natural supply, it is surely unnecessary to invite it. John Fletcher* probably damaged his constitution by his austerities, but the Anglican tradition has not favoured harmful asceticism. George Herbert*, while enjoining fasting, insisted on exceptions: 'For it is as unnatural to do anything that leads me to a sickness ... as not to get out of that sickness, when I am in it' (Herbert, X). The common sense of this view is underlined by the havoc which ill health can wreak on ministry. John Skinner's* irascibility, which did great harm both to family and to parish life, was in part the effect, as also an occasion, of the insomnia which plagued him. As James Woodforde* grew older, his physical and emotional ailments, which included 'blind' and bleeding piles and 'oppressed spirits', kept him almost permanently at home.

To some extent Woodforde had himself to blame for his incapacity. His eating and drinking were excessive. He wrote rather shamefacedly: 'I am afraid I eat too much, my Appetite being perhaps too great for health.' In a similar vein he recorded that a daily pint of port had done him great harm; he was sleeping much better after only two or three glasses of wine (Woodforde, 3.205). He was not the only parson to have succumbed to the temptations of the table. John Newton* struggled without much success against gluttony and corpulence; so did Charles Simeon*. Sydney Smith* grew enormously fat; dieting in old age, he remarked that he looked as if a curate had been taken out of him (Bell, *Smith* 217).

In 1801 Woodforde attributed an improvement in his health to the fact that he had given up smoking (Woodforde, 5.344). With the same end in view, John Skinner gave up wine (Skinner, 383). Not every parson has been so wise. Many have compensated for difficulties elsewhere in their lives by smoking and drinking to excess. Dick Sheppard*, though plagued by asthma, smoked fifty or sixty cigarettes a day. Geoffrey Beaumont, a much loved priest of our own day, was always a heavy smoker and became an alcoholic in reaction to the difficulties he experienced in his Camberwell parish. He dealt with his problems by becoming a monk (Williams, 261–2).

The temple of the Holy Spirit has been damaged not only by self-indulgence but also, more pardonably, by medication. George Crabbe** became addicted to medically prescribed opium. John Skinner is said to have used it 'in the pangs of neuralgia' (Skinner, 505). So did Charles Tennyson Turner (1808–79) (brother of the poet Tennyson) who suffered badly from depression and neuralgia. He broke himself of the habit before he took over the family livings of Caister and Grasby and married, but the strains of parish and domestic life caused a relapse. His wife left him until he again overcame the addiction. Thereafter they served their parishes admirably (Colloms, 154–65).

If Robert Hawker* originally took opium for medical reasons he probably prescribed it himself. Like many other people of his time he used it to deal with conditions to which medical knowledge offered no other remedy; in his case neuralgia and insomnia. He was probably not aware of opium's addictive nature, and valued the sense of well-being as well as the freedom from pain which the drug gave. He must have realized, however, how destructive its long-term effects were, since he tried at great physical cost to break the addiction in the months before his second marriage. How far the paranoia and melancholia which afflicted him were the causes and how far the effects of the drug it is impossible to tell; but, at the very least, his life and ministry were adversely affected.

A priest's health is often at risk because of his ministry. William Grimshaw* died of typhus contracted while sick visiting. Cyril Garbett** remembered his father and mother visiting during a diphtheria epidemic in their parish of

Tongham, and being forbidden to go near them on their return; his father later died of an infection picked up visiting (Smyth, *Garbett* 26, 41). The great Anglo-Catholic Charles Lowder**, working in Wapping, was frequently ill, partly because of constant strain and partly because of the foul atmosphere and dreadful food (Ellsworth, *Lowder* 70). A multitude of clergy have succumbed to illness caused by overwork. Even though he was still only in his early thirties, Walter Hook* had a breakdown which incapacitated him for months while he was at Holy Trinity, Coventry. Samuel Barnett* paid for his efforts in White-chapel and for the criticism which his methods attracted with frequent spells of illness and depression.

Because God's ways are not man's, bad health is not invariably destructive. W.C.E. Newbolt in his handbook for ministry *Speculum Sacerdotum* taught that sickness could be God's way of preventing the priest from becoming too identified with his work. Or, if the ailing priest continued his ministry, 'It may be ... God's will for us, that the shadow of the Cross should be shed abroad from our lives by the fierce glow of sorrow within; that the pain which burns there, consuming our strength, should throw into strong relief the message of the sombre Cross, and the message should be the message of our lives rather than the message of our lips' (Newbolt, 277).

Newbolt's first point was exemplified in the experience of David Watson* when he was at St Cuthbert's, York. He was a martyr to asthma, and in 1966 the combined effects of his work as parish priest and missioner completely disabled him. Much against his will he had to take three months rest. Deeply depressed at the outset, he concluded: 'My natural strength had failed, and I had to release to the Lord all that had become very dear to my heart. It may be that I had come to love the Lord's work more than the Lord himself ... I had to hand back everything ... to the Lord, and humbly, with empty hands, ask for his mercy, healing and grace.' His insight was justified by the remark which greeted him on his return: 'Your absence has been such a blessing to us!' (Watson, *YAMG* 87–8).

In illustration of Newbolt's second point, it was said of Patrick Bronte** that his sermons were never so effective as when he preached during blindness caused by a cataract (Gaskell, *Bronte* 278). Bronte, however, was not in pain; Nicholas Byfield, incumbent of Isleworth, Middlesex, in the early seventeenth century, was. He preached twice each Sunday and catechized twice a week for many years and until five weeks before his death, though suffering agonies from a stone which proved at his post-mortem to weigh thirty-three ounces (Hart, *CC* 144). George Eliot's hard-working Mr Tryon, a consumptive, declared: 'I think I should not be a long lived man in any case; and if I were to take care of myself under the pretext of doing more good, I should very likely die and leave nothing done after all' (Eliot, *SCL* 326). The agnostic Eliot understood as well as any believer the redemptive effects of suffering volun-tarily accepted.

More generally, ill health can increase spiritual effectiveness and depth. A parish priest who died in 1991, Gonville ffrench-Beytagh, rector of St Vedast's in the city of London, suffered from severe depression. The condition contributed to the deep perceptiveness which made him a masterly spiritual director and writer (*Guardian* obituary 14 May 1991). Dick Sheppard's friend and biographer R. Ellis Roberts wrote of him: 'In many ways ... Sheppard showed the marks of sanctity: surely in this struggle, so bitter, so dark and solitary, against cruel and disabling illness, there was most conspicuously that heroic and supernatural virtue which it is the strange privilege of the saints to exhibit under the tormenting discipline of agony' (Roberts, *Sheppard* 181).

Sickness in the parson's family can be as incapacitating or as instructive as sickness in the parson himself. John Keble* was surrounded by people who needed nursing – his mother, his father, his sisters, his wife. Almost all the women of the Keble family led what the novelist Charlotte Yonge called 'a sofa life'. There were long periods when Keble could not leave home because of sickness, and long periods when he accompanied his wife in search of a better climate than that of his parish. His alleged indolence must be seen in the light of these responsibilities. Patrick Bronte and his children began their lives at Haworth under the shadow of the cancer which carried off his wife Maria, and which set the tone for the sombre years which followed. George Crabbe wrote in 'The Borough' of a curate with nine children condemned to penury in a seaside parish because of his wife's ill health:

> A wife grown feeble, mourning, pining, vex'd,
> With wants and woes – by daily cares perplexed;
> No more a help, a smiling, soothing aid,
> But boding, drooping, sickly and afraid.

A priest of our own time, Tom Walker**, practises the healing ministry within an evangelical and charismatic tradition which expects great things from petitionary prayer. The illness of Rachel his teen-age daughter, characterized by wasting away and sleeplessness, proved testing because prolonged. 'It was so much easier to be the minister of healing to others than it was to be the "wounded healer" experiencing months of seemingly unanswered prayer' (Walker, 99). Rachel herself was put under pressure by friends who appeared to imply that her condition was perpetuated by her own lack of faith. Finally, when the family were near breaking-point, Walker and Rachel experienced the authority and the peace of God in prayer in a profound way, and the condition disappeared. Walker concluded that it was necessary for the situation to seem hopeless humanly speaking for the glory to be given to God.

Ministry and spirituality are shaped by illness; still more by bereavement. The tragic and destructive elements in the character of John Skinner were aggravated by the death of his wife Anna in 1812 after only seven years of marriage. He wrote of her death-bed: 'All her thoughts, which have anything to do with this world, are now directed to me; she declares that the only wish she has to live longer is that she may continue to console me, and when she thinks how desolate I shall be, if left alone among the ill-disposed people of Camerton, without any friends to whom I may confide my cares, or who may soothe my mind when too much irritated by their misconduct, she feels indeed most wretched, and hopes and begs she may be spared.' She was not spared; Skinner wrote poignantly: 'I was quite alone; but still the Comforter was with me' (Skinner, 72, 73).

Although the greatest, the loss of his wife was far from being the only bereavement Skinner had to suffer. He wrote in 1813 when he was forty-one: 'The mortality in my family has been great indeed, as I have lost my wife and child, two sisters and a brother, two great-uncles and my father-in-law.' Nor was that all. Of the four children surviving when he wrote, two were to predecease him. The death of his favourite child Laura in 1820, at the age of fourteen, was particularly hard to bear. Her anguished father wrote: 'I know not how I shall support this last blow. I have borne up against the malice and injustice of mankind with fortitude, but on this point I am most vulnerable and weak. Yet the loss alone is mine. The dear angel will be removed from a bad and troublesome world before she has smarted from its baseness and ingratitude' (Skinner, 3–4, 134).

In her well-known essay on Skinner, Virgina Woolf writes: 'These losses, though they served nominally to make him love God the better, in practice led him to hate men more' (Skinner, 5), a harsh but just judgment. A negative reaction to bereavement is an example of the double-edged nature of suffering, which sometimes stifles Christian virtues and sometimes nurtures them. Even the saintly Keble lost much of his innocence and gaiety when his sister Mary-Anne died; thereafter the depression inherent in his character rose more frequently to the surface.

There are examples of the opposite process too. Josselin, contemplating a family bereavement, wrote to a friend: 'I have thoughts of my sweetest Daughter now with comfort, who have had thoughts of her like the bitterness of death' (Macfarlane, *Josselin* 221). Henry Alford** wrote to a friend after the death of a son: 'I find myself the greatest comfort in reflecting that my dear boy has attained by a shorter and more merciful way the perfection after which we amidst many errors and sorrows are still striving ... I have found too that the fact of our dear children having wrestled with and overcome death seems more than ever to remove all terror from the prospect of our own struggle with him' (Alford, 191–2). Charles Lowder was changed by the death of his mother. Previously he had been bleak, reserved and sparing of praise; now he became gentler, more genial and more affectionate (Ellsworth, *Lowder* 126).

A sense of shared faith lightens the burden of bereavement. When William Grimshaw's daughter Jane died at school at Kingswood at the age of thirteen, her father was reconciled to his loss by assurances that she died in a state of grace. Skinner's grief at Laura's death was tempered by the manner of her dying. She daily read the appointed psalms and lessons, and retained 'the natural benevolence of her disposition'. Her father wrote: 'I cannot look upon her but with a degree of veneration' (Skinner, 134).

Josselin denied himself any sense of communion with the dead; that, he thought, must await the general resurrection (Josselin, 114). Others have sought such a communion in varying ways. John Newton felt seven years after his wife's death that 'the Lord has healed the wound He made', but she was still almost continually present to his waking thoughts (Martin, *Newton* 329). John Fletcher's widow wrote a year after his death: 'What part of our union can heaven dissolve? ... Clear as light it appeared before me, that heaven could not dissolve anything which agreed with its own nature' (Addison, 111). She was not the only Evangelical with a powerful belief in the communion of saints. The great Evangelical parish priest, Henry Venn (1796–1873), later secretary of the Church Missionary Society, denied that his union with his wife had been broken by death; during dull committee meetings he used to hold 'sweet converse' with her (Hennell, 73). In another tradition, John Keble remained convinced after his sister Sarah's death that she continued to love him and interest herself in his welfare (Battiscombe, *Keble* 38). Both sentiment and experience stood in the way of accepting the Protestant doctrine of the unreachability of the dead.

Finance

When James Newton** discovered in January 1760 that he had won nothing with the thirteen tickets he had purchased in the National Lottery, he was provoked to a typical piece of moralizing: 'Had a great Prise fallen to my Lott, its possible I might have missappl'd it ... if so its better for me to be without it & I am content & I dont set my Heart upon Riches, but on the Service of God and may I ever continue so to Do. A great Fortune wont make a Man Happy ... Let us suit our Minds to our Fortunes & moderate our Desires & then both Rich and Poor may do tollerably Well' (James Newton, 81–2).

In this manner he subdued his chagrin. He was touching on a tender topic. As an index of spirituality, a man's use of his purse ranks second only to his use of time. The enormous variations in the incomes of the parochial clergy have illustrated the temptations and opportunities associated with every level of wealth and poverty.

Trollope paints a vivid picture of contrasting clerical circumstances in the persons of Archdeacon Grantley, snugly ensconced at Plumstead Episcopi, and of Mr Crawley, perpetual curate of Hogglestock, trying vainly to support his wife and family on £130 a year. He did not exaggerate the differences to be found in reality. At one extreme of clerical income, the parish of Doddington,

Cambridgeshire, was worth £7300 by the early nineteenth century, more than most bishoprics (Virgin, 47). At the other extreme, parson Mathson of Patterdale in the Lake District served his parish for sixty years at the turn of the eighteenth and nineteenth centuries on a stipend initially of twelve and later of eighteen pounds a year (Addison, 129).

In the past disparities in clerical incomes were not thought inappropriate. Thomas Fuller** believed 'maintenance of ministers ought to be plentiful, certain, and in some sort proportional to their deserts' and that 'it is unequal that there should be an equality betwixt all ministers' maintenance' (Fuller, *HS* 218, 219). Sydney Smith* wrote a pamphlet late in life, when he himself had secured a comfortable income, arguing that an equal distribution of resources, which would have given every clergyman a stipend of about £250 a year, would fail to attract able men tempted into ministry by the thought of the prizes to be won (Bell, *Smith* 178–9). Egalitarian twentieth-century spirituality has rejected these arguments. Pay scales are now uniform, and differentials narrow.

Plenty of clergy have sought financial advantage without a pang, either as a good in itself or as an element in a wider good. Sydney Smith chose his wife because she united 'fortune, understanding and good disposition in a degree that makes an alliance desirable' (Bell, *Smith* 22). The eighteenth-century rector George Woodward** wrote with respectful wonder about Bernard Gilpin's* refusal to become a pluralist, and commented: 'He seems to have been a very good man, but of a more squeamish conscience than the clergy appear to be nowadays' (Woodward, 59).

Until modern times a substantial proportion of clerical income came from tithes. Their assessment was complex and their weight sometimes heavy, facing the incumbent with the choice of insisting on his dues at a cost to his relationships with his parishioners, or of forgoing them at a cost to his pocket. The sixteenth-century priests who claimed tithes on fallen apples and wild cherries were unlikely to have enhanced their spiritual reputations (Hart, *CC* 66). John Earle's Grave Divine behaved differently: 'He is not base Grater of his Tythes, and will not wrangle for the odd Egge' (Earle, 24). William Grimshaw* was of the same mind, saying to his parishioners: 'I want nothing more than your souls for God, and a bare maintenance for myself' (Baker, *Grimshaw* 13). John Fletcher* excused Quakers their tithes. He 'did not choose to take from them by force, what they did not think it lawful to give him' (Benson, *Fletcher* 332). George Crabbe** used to say of poor defaulters: 'Let it be – they cannot afford to pay so well as I can to want [be without] it – let it be' (Crabbe, 1.200).

James Woodforde* had very little difficulty in getting his tithes, partly because he held an annual Tithe Frolic – a dinner and entertainment at which the tithes were paid – and partly because his demands were modest. His successor doubled them (Woodforde, 5.413n). Nearly a century later Francis Kilvert* used Woodforde's methods with equal success; possibly because, as he dryly commented, some small-holders ate the value of their tithe in bread and cheese (Kilvert, 3.366–7). Faced with more intractable parishioners and displaying his genius for confrontation, John Skinner* ceased for a time to hold a tithe dinner, 'for I never could with comfort set down with people to eat with them who I knew would pervert every word that I said and do me every injury in their power behind my back' (Skinner, 62). Skinner was for ever engaged in battles over tithe, souring his relationships with landowners and tenants from the lady of the manor downwards. (Skinner, 272–5, 282–3). Worse still was the experience of Fairfax Francklin, rector of Attleborough, Norfolk. During the agricultural unrest at the end of 1830 he was intimidated at a vestry meeting by a mob of labourers who demanded a 50% reduction in tithes. Francklin refused, and had, after four hours, to be rescued by friends. Similar incidents were frequent at the time, and created antagonisms which made normal ministry impossible (Virgin, 11). As late as 1935 there was a demonstration against tithes in Kent, with a deputation to a local rector and the burning in effigy of the Archbishop of Canterbury (Barrow, 199).

Until modern times parish priests retained the fees paid them for the occasional offices – the so-called surplice fees. The sums paid varied with the wealth of the parishioners concerned. Ralph Josselin* received £2 from the two fathers for conducting a wedding – 'god in mercy requite their love and bounty' (Josselin, 413). Woodforde, paid two guineas for a funeral, thought it 'very handsome' (Woodforde, 3.15). He often returned the fees paid by poor people, sometimes with an additional gratuity. Clergy in populous parishes could earn vast sums from fees. In 1838 the vicar of St Giles-in-the-Fields earned £764 16s 6d from funerals, the rector of St George's, Hanover Square, £597 17s (Chadwick, *VC* 1.327).

The search for income has taken forms which have eroded the time and energy available for ministry. Many clergy have farmed their glebe. Henry Fielding's Parson Trulliber 'was a parson on Sundays, but all the other six might more properly be called a farmer' (Fielding, 194). Robert Hawker* created a prosperous farm out of his seventy-two-acre glebe and the additional fields he rented; he needed the income because he was notably improvident in other respects (Brendon, *Hawker* 162–4). Very many parochial clergy have taken pupils or run a school in the vicarage, as did William Jones** of Broxbourne; many, such as Sabine Baring-Gould**, have supplemented their stipends with their pens; some have practised as physicians; in Elizabethan times it was not uncommon to use the parsonage as an ale-house. His parishioners complained in 1646 of Peter Waterman, rector of Wootton Rivers, Wiltshire, that he 'doth suffer his wife to sell matheglin [mead] in his house' (Matthews, *Walker* 381). In 1824 Bishop Blomfield of Chester discovered a parish priest who was postmaster in a large town (Clark, 51). It took an Act of Parliament in 1817 to curb the worst abuses.

The most notorious method of increasing clerical income has been by way of pluralism – holding more than one living. Sometimes this has been a device to secure affluence, as in the case of Benjamin Barker who acquired the advowsons for Shipdam and All Saints, Rockland, in Norfolk and presented himself to both livings. In the 1830s his income was £2307 a year (Virgin, 185). Sometimes it has been necessary for survival, as in the case of Robert Hanson, vicar of Rasen Drax in the Lincoln diocese in Elizabethan times, whose living was worth only £8 per annum and who obtained a neighbouring living of the same value (Hart, *CC* 46). In this case, as in many others, it was possible for one man to serve both livings. Where it was not, the incumbent was expected to provide a curate at his own expense, or to pay the incumbent of a nearby parish to do duty. Henry Fardell*, who possessed a prebendal stall at Ely Cathedral and a living at Waterbeach as well as Wisbech St Mary, maintained a curate at Waterbeach (Nicholas, *Fardell* 1).

Although pluralism has been regarded as a scandal, it has sometimes been a commonsense response to a lack of means. Attempts to abolish it during the Commonwealth and Protectorate foundered because the income of single parishes would not support the incumbent. Where the populations involved are small, it is hard to make a case against it. The modern Church of England has re-introduced it on a large scale, in part because of lack of clergy, in part because of an inability to pay them.

It is easy to look askance at the mercenary considerations which have bulked large for many clergy, but we need to remember their necessary outgoings. There have been taxes specifically directed at their order; in the sixteenth century they were still liable to first fruits and tenths, and payments during visitations from authority. They paid a higher rate of subsidy than the laity and a charge for armour and munitions (Hart, *CC* 48).

As members of the professional class the clergy have been held, at least in the eighteenth and nineteenth centuries, in the iron grip of social expectations. The problem has never been better summarized than by George Eliot: 'Given a man with a wife and six children: let him be obliged always to exhibit himself when outside his own door in a suit of black broadcloth, such as will not undermine the foundations of the Establishment by a paltry plebeian glossiness or an unseemly whiteness at the edges; in a snowy cravat, which is a serious investment of labour in the hemming, starching and ironing departments; and in a hat which shows no symptoms of taking to the hideous doctrine of expediency, and shaping itself according to circumstances; let him have a parish large enough to create an external necessity for abundant shoe-leather, and an internal necessity for abundant beef and mutton, as well as poor enough to require frequent priestly consolation in the shape of shillings and sixpences; and, lastly, let him be compelled by his own pride and other people's, to dress his wife and children with gentility from bonnet-strings to shoe-strings. By what process of division can the sum of eighty pounds per annum be made to yield a quotient which will cover that man's weekly expenses?' (Eliot, *SCL* 44).

The cost of bringing up children to be gentlemen or ladies has been very considerable. John Skinner calculated that the annual expense of educating his three children when they were in their teens was about £400; later, when they were young adults, it amounted to £500 (Skinner, 235, 293).

The clergy have to provide for their old age, and for the needs of their wives and infant children should they pre-decease them. Robert Grimshaw's* generosity with his money was made easier by the fact that his children had substantial inheritances settled upon them. Centrally funded clerical pensions are a twentieth-century invention. In the past, most priests died in office, or, if they retired, came to an agreement with their successor by which they received a proportion (usually a third) of benefice income until death. An alternative was to accept an undemanding country living. George Bull** retired from an inner city Birmingham parish to Almeley in Herefordshire for the last year of his life.

Clergy in the past had to find expenses which nowadays are met from other sources. A curate's stipend came from the pocket of the incumbent; so did the upkeep of the chancel; so did the cost of maintaining and improving, and sometimes of purchasing, the parsonage; so did many of the charges which nowadays would fall on the Parochial Church Council, the diocese or the Church Commissioners.

Personal almsgiving and hospitality have always been expected of the clergyman; in the past, not only as a personal Christian duty but as a proper redistribution of the income which his parishioners afforded him. It was a regulation in the sixteenth century that a clergyman should give to poor relief one-fortieth of the income of any parish in which he was not resident (Hart, *CC* 48). George Herbert* tithed his tithe to provide money which his wife gave to the poor (Walton, 216). About a tenth of Ralph Josselin's* expenditure was on charity, hospitality and books (Macfarlane, *Josselin* 4.1). Dryden's Good Parson was

> ... contented to be poor.
> Yet of his little he had some to spare,
> To feed the famished, and to clothe the bare
>   (Dryden, quoted Christmas 51).

John Fletcher gave away the whole of the £100 a year he received from a private property in Switzerland. Offered his expenses on a visit to Dublin, he distributed them among the poor. 'The profusion of his charity ... is scarcely credible: it constantly exhausted his purse; it frequently unfurnished his house, and it sometimes left him destitute of the most common necessities' (Benson, *Fletcher* 84). Robert Hawker* gave doles on both a regular and an indiscriminate basis. He did not exclude Dissenters, remarking: 'I like to give them a little comfort in this world, for I know what discomfort awaits them in the next' (Brendon, *Hawker* 116). When Alexander Mackonochie** was driven from St

Alban's, Holborn, in 1882 his congregation's parting gift of £1800 was invested in an annuity for fear that otherwise he would give it away (Towle, *Mackonochie* 265). A priest of our own century, Charles Jenkinson** of Leeds, though a married man, kept only so much of his stipend as sufficed for a frugal existence. He refused fees for the occasional services, and spent most of the £1500 a year he earned as chairman of the Stevenage Development Corporation on his church of St Silas, Hunslet (Hammerton, *Jenkinson* 181).

However, lavish giving has been less common than a more cautious approach. James Woodforde had an income of rather over £400 a year. He had five servants and three horses, kept open house for his social equals, and was liberal with his niece and nephews. He had his charitable routines. On St Thomas's day each year he gave the poor people of the parish (40–50 in number) 6d each; on Christmas Day he had a group of poor old men to dinner, and gave each a shilling to take home to their wives; on St Valentine's Day all the local children received a penny. As we have seen, he did not bear heavily upon his parishioners for their dues; nor was he a severe landlord to his Somerset tenants (Woodforde, 3.135). He records numerous acts of personal charity. The total impression left by the diary is of unassuming kind-heartedness. None the less, it cannot be said that Woodforde was a generous giver. In a typical year, 1791, he gave away a total of £3 14s 4d, together with some remission of fees, some gifts in kind, and a few monetary gifts of an unspecified size – perhaps between 1% and 2% of his income.

In a more general sense the parson's income was until this century regarded (though only occasionally used) as an opportunity for serving his parish rather than as the means of supporting himself and his family. The response of some clergy to this situation has been generous to a degree. Bernard Gilpin spent almost all his annual income of £400 on his parishioners. Walter Hook, while perpetual curate of Moseley, practised personal frugality so as to be able to spend liberally on his parish from his stipend of £150. He drank raspberry vinegar instead of wine, and ate pork instead of beef or mutton (Stephens, *Hook* 83). William Bennett* spent so freely on his parish of Frome that in the last year of his life he was unable to afford a summer holiday (Bennett, 237). Robert Landor, brother of Walter Savage Landor and vicar of Birlingham, Worcestershire, from 1829 to his death in 1869, lived on his small private income, and devoted his stipend to charities and to the maintenance of his church (Colloms, 47). Cosmo Lang** at Portsea used the whole of his stipend to pay his tribe of curates; he lived on the tiny profits from running the clergy house, and on the fifty pounds a year he received as a fellow of All Souls. He used to say that the real value of the parish was minus nine hundred pounds a year (Lockhart, *Lang* 114, 118–19).

Arthur Wagner** lived a life of personal austerity and gave away the greater part of his considerable wealth. He spent between £60,000 and £70,000 on building churches, and a further vast sum on their staffng and maintenance.

He maintained St Mary's Home, a local charity staffed by the nuns of the Order he had created, and including in its activities a home for repentant prostitutes, a dispensary, a home for the aged, an orphanage, a day-school and a visiting association providing relief for the poor. He spent £40,000 on building homes for the poor, and dispensed charity to individuals on the grand scale. He was still worth £50,000 when he died, but his giving had for some years been constricted by poor health, and the obituary which suggested that without that constraint he would have beggared himself was probably correct (Wagner, 130–7).

Priests with private means have sometimes used them not to augment their stipends but to replace them. Arthur Stanton* worked unpaid, supporting himself from his private income, very little of which he spent upon himself. Some of Lang's curates at Portsea took no more than their keep (Lockhart, *Lang* 118). Dick Sheppard* took only half his stipend at St Martin's in the Fields, thus emulating the church's eponymous saint, who gave half his cloak to a beggar (Scott, *Sheppard* 67). Nicolas Stacey**, Rector of Woolwich in the 1960s, paid for his staff and expenses out of his stipend, and pledged the whole of his capital in order to launch a re-building scheme (Stacey, 112–13).

Other priests with private means have used them to raise their own standard of living, sometimes to unwarrantable levels. Benjamin Newton, rector of Wath, Yorkshire, from 1814 to 1830, kept his own pack of greyhounds, dined on venison, turtle and champagne, and bought his port by the £100 pipe (Virgin, 81–2).

In modern times the equivalent of a private income is often a wife in paid employment. In her contribution to *Married to the Church* Jeanette Kitteringham speaks for many when she writes that her income has meant family holidays, extras for the children and a heated vicarage (Brown, 65). The church also relies increasingly upon non-stipendiary ministers, who give their time for love, and who derive their income from a non-ecclesiastical source. Richard Rogers, a pensioner ordained in his late 60s, served the village of Coldred in Kent in the 1990s as an unpaid assistant priest, and from 140 inhabitants secured a regular congregation of 30.

The Christian tradition has always and rightly included a suspicion of clerical affluence; nor have the laity been slow to advocate a simplicity of life for their pastors which they have not necessarily thought appropriate for themselves. The clerical response has been various. George Herbert admonished the country parson to 'slight and disesteem' wealth and to avoid luxury (Herbert, III). John Skinner wrote himself a memorandum to show that his income in 1832 of £478 was not over-great, despite an outcry suggesting that clerical incomes should not exceed £200. His argument was purely financial – that the capital which had purchased him the living and which he had since sunk in it would have purchased an annuity bringing much the same return (Skinner, 448–9). Trollope's Mary Thorne says dryly: 'I tell you that as the clergyman tells you to hate riches. But though the clergyman tells you so, he is not the less anxious to get rich himself' (Trollope, *DT* 78).

'I've no face to go and preach resignation to those poor things in their smoky air and comfortless homes, when [meaning "should"] I come straight from every luxury myself. There are many things quite lawful for other men, which a clergyman must forego if he would do any good in a manufacturing population like this.' So George Eliot's Mr Tryon, justifying his decision to live in poverty among his flock (Eliot, *SCL* 306). He put his finger on a sore point. Clergy who have not been well off by middle class standards have often been better off than their own parishioners; and the difference has given offence. Robert Hawker had what he regarded as a grossly insufficient stipend of £365 a year, an income about twenty times as great as that of a Cornish labourer. When he built himself a house he had this verse inscribed over the front door:

A House, a Glebe, a Pound a Day,
A Pleasant Place to Watch and Pray.
Be true to Church – Be kind to poor,
O Minister, for ever more.

He laid himself open to an anonymous riposte:

How different now the times we see
Since Jesus dwelt in Galilee,
And did poor fishermen prepare
His Holy Gospel to declare.
No scrip or purse were they to take
But suffer for the Master's sake,
And not a single word did say
Of House or glebe, or pound a day.
    (Brendon, *Hawker* 87–8)

It is only fair to point out that, had Hawker had to exist on the eight shillings a week which was the agricultural wage in Morwenstow during his time there, he would have had no opportunity or energy for anything save the necessities of survival.

A lack of means can have unpleasant consequences. John Earle's raw young preacher, 'whose friends and much painfulness may prefer him to thirty pounds a year' would have had to content himself with a chambermaid for a wife (Earle, 23). Samuel Wesley** spent time in prison for debt. One nineteenth-century parish priest, the perpetual curate of Forest Hill, Oxfordshire, spent eight months in a debtors' prison for owing less than £10;

unable to get out of debt, he was later deprived and died in prison (Hammond, 49–50). The saintly Edward King**, while admitting a priest who had been jailed for debt to Holy Communion as a penitent, refused to allow him to celebrate (King, *Letters* 101). The burden thrown on wives has sometimes been extreme. George Eliot's Milly Barton was not alone in putting patches on patches and re-darning darns (Eliot, *SCL* 99). Fanny Kingsley* wrote to her husband: 'I chafe you ... you chafe me ... When we are out of debt, poetry will return!' (Chitty, *Kingsley* 125).

Most of the parochial clergy have been poor rather than rich by the standards of the educated and professional classes of their day; not least of course because of the wholesale way in which the laity have from time to time plundered the church. The Elizabethan country priest lived no better than the majority of his flock. In the following century the clerical diarist John Rous** transcribed a set of verses entitled *The Scholler's Complaint* (Rous, 115–17) which lamented the poverty of a learned clerk. This unfortunate failed to obtain a fellowship or to secure the good offices of the great; so:

Into some country village
Nowe I must goe,
Where neither tithe nor tillage
The greedy patron
And coached matron
Sweare to the Church they owe;
But if I preach and pray too on the suddaine,
And confute the Pope too, extempore without studying,
I've tenne poundes a yeere, besides my Sunday pudding.

The only escape lay out of the parochial ministry and into school-teaching.

Rous's clerk was out of the ordinary only in that he was more learned than most. At the beginning of the seventeenth century 40% of parishes were impropriated – that is, the tithes were paid to laymen who made over what was often a derisory proportion to the parish priest (Hill, 86). At the beginning of the eighteenth century half the parishes in England were worth less than fifty pounds a year, and twelve hundred worth less than twenty (Cragg, 126). Oliver Goldsmith's village priest was 'passing rich with forty pounds a year'.

The circumstances of the clergy improved after the creation of Queen Anne's Bounty in 1704, and on the back of the advance of agriculture from the eighteenth to the later nineteenth century, but thereafter the situation again changed for the worse. With the agricultural slump at the end of the century the value of tithes plummeted. Edward Bligh, rector of Rotherfield, Sussex, was getting an income of £500 from tithes in the 1860s, of a third less in the 1880s (Colloms, 30). By the first years of the twentieth century almost one parish in two was supplementing the parson's other income with a voluntary

Easter offering (Russell, 48). In 1918 the Bishop of London issued a public appeal on behalf of the poor clergy of his diocese, many of whom were said to be facing bankruptcy and starvation because of the rising cost of living (Barrow, 190). Cyril Garbett**, taking over Southwark in the following year, found clergy in the diocese who were paid less than road-sweepers, and made it his first financial objective to ensure a minimum stipend of £400 (Smyth, *Garbett* 152). Yet, as late as 1939, 5000 parochial clergy were still being paid less than that sum (Hastings, 70). In the 1980s Roy Catchpole** was not alone in claiming Social Security in order to bring his family up to the poverty-line (Catchpole, *GMDC* 123).

If the plight of incumbents has sometimes been sad, that of curates has often been harsh beyond tears. Elizabethan curates were usually paid less than £10 per annum (Hart, *TCL* 55). John Garbrore, curate of Stane, Lincolnshire, was excused visitation fees in 1604 'in meare pitty' because his stipend was only twenty shillings a year (Hart, *CC* 82). Thomas Fuller pointed out in the seventeenth century that the 'miserable and scandalous stipends' afforded curates by their fellow-clergy explained the niggardliness with which the laity treated incumbents in unendowed parishes, 'seeing such who knew most what belonged to the work allowed the least wages to the ministry' (Fuller, *CH* 3.480). He was thinking of such sufferers as John Streating, curate of Ivychurch, Kent, whose parishioners complained that, after twenty-six years of service, he was receiving only £30 of the £200 which accrued to the absentee incumbent (Hart, *TCL* 94).

Most curates, of course, did the work of absentee clergy, often pluralists. There were recurring attempts to end or minimize this abuse; Rous's learned clerk noted in 1641:

> Bigamy of steeples is hanging matter,
> Each must have one, and curates will grow fatter.
>   (Rous, 116)

Until the nineteenth century, however, pluralism persisted on a large scale. William Law's Cognatus, 'a sober, regular clergyman of good repute ... cannot serve both his livings himself, so he makes it matter of conscience to keep a sober curate upon one of them, whom he hires ... at as cheap a rate as a sober man can be procured' (Law, 129). That rate was no more than twenty or thirty pounds a year. When John Newton* went to Olney, he had to pay part of benefice income to the absentee vicar, and was left with about £38 a year, a quarter of what he had earned as a tide surveyor. The situation has been little better in the case of curates whose incumbents have not been absentees. When Cyril Garbett went to Portsea in 1899 to serve under Cosmo Lang he was paid £110 a year, of which £80 was deducted for board and lodging (Smyth, *Garbett* 111).

Nothing, however, is more impressive, and more characteristically Christian, than the witness of a minister living contentedly with restricted means. The income of the sixteenth-century Puritan John Carter, Rector of Belstead, Suffolk, rarely rose above £20 per annum, despite the best efforts of his parishioners, but his comment was that 'he sought not *theirs* but *them* and so was content' (Hart, *CC* 143). In the same century Simon Lynch was given a small living at North Weale near Epping, worth £40 a year; offered Brent Wood Weale, with three times the income, he replied 'he preferred the weal of his parishioners' souls before any other Weale whatsoever', and stayed where he was for sixty-four years (Fuller, *Worthies* 1.523). The eighteenth-century evangelical Thomas Jones was driven from parish to parish because of his opinions until, in 1785, Charles Simeon* settled him in the hamlet of Creaton, Northants, with a stipend of £25 a year. He served forty-six homes for nearly fifty years, lodging in the inn because he could not afford to live elsewhere. When his books earned him a little money, he built six almshouses. He also founded the Society for Poor Pious Clergymen which assisted married curates (Jones himself was a single man) and which distributed £35,000 in eighteen years (Balleine, 83).

But the effects of poverty are not necessarily spiritually advantageous, as Trollope demonstrates unforgettably in the character of Mr Crawley. George Crabbe describes (in 'The Borough') an elderly and impoverished curate with nine children in terms which make one wonder if Trollope had read him:

A man so learn'd you shall but seldom see,
Nor one so honour'd, so aggrieved as he;
Not grieved by years alone; though his appear
Dark and more dark; severer on severe:
Not in his need – and yet we all must grant
How painful 'tis for feeling age to want:
Nor in his body's sufferings; yet we know
Where time has plough'd, there misery loves to sow;
But in the wearied mind, that all in vain
Wars with distress, and struggles with its pain.

In real life, Robert Hawker was, to say the least, not improved by lack of means. It is unclear how badly off he actually was – he was both reckless and generous in using the money he had – but he harped endlessly on his poverty and engaged in shameless mendicancy to alleviate it. In his defence it must be said that he spent considerable sums, including his first wife's inheritance, on social amenities in his parish and on charity; but it must also be said that he was unscrupulous if not dishonest over financial matters. Perhaps he was impelled by his paranoia rather than by real want; but in any event it is in money matters that he appears in the least attractive light. His case demonstrates that there is a considerable difference between the lack of means accepted as part of a vocation and lack of means experienced as threatening or crippling.

Modern stipendiaries are exempt from most of the personal financial problems which beset their predecessors. They do not own their homes, but nor do they pay for their upkeep. They are neither indecently affluent nor excruciatingly poor. Their income, although in increasing part derived from their congregations, is sanitized as it flows through the channels of the quota and the diocesan board of finance. They are not expected to subsidize the work of their parishes; indeed, considerable pressure is exercised on their behalf to ensure that their expenses are paid. Their charitable giving is a matter of personal conscience, and state provision meets, at least in part, the needs of their indigent parishioners. They are usually and necessarily inveterate fund-raisers, but not in any obvious way on their own behalf. By historic standards they are fortunate.

Recreation and Attitude to Nature

A priest's recreation can be seen as a concession to human weakness – a means of recovery from and preparation for the sterner business of life; or as an opportunity for the minister to meet his people in relaxed circumstances as he shares their leisure; or as a necessary part of what it is to be human, a participation in the sweetness of life which ensures a proper perspective on the rest of it.

George Herbert* held the first view with a tincture of the second. The parson, though generally sad because he knows nothing but the cross of Christ 'sometimes refresheth himself, as knowing that nature will not bear everlasting droopings, and that pleasantness of disposition is a great key to do good ... Wherefore he condescends to human frailties both in himself and others: and intermingles some mirth in his discourses occasionally, according to the pulse of his hearer' (Herbert, XXVII).

Condescending to frailty has been thought particularly acceptable when coupled with the need to preserve health. The Victorian Henry Liddon allowed the parish priest two hours daily as 'an amply sufficient allowance of time for a walk or recreation'; though he added severely 'if indeed his parish does not give him sufficient exercise' (Liddon, 42). Charles Simeon* compensated for his addiction to the pleasures of the table by his passion for riding. Simeon also swam, as did Francis Kilvert* whenever he had the opportunity. The tradition of clerical enthusiasm for this form of exercise was still alive in Oxford when I was up in the late 1940s; a section of the Cherwell, reserved for male nude bathing, was known as Parsons' Pleasure.

There have been health reasons for holidays too. Dick Sheppard* followed a recurring cycle of frenzied over-commitment leading to collapse and a compulsory holiday imposed by sickness and the need for convalescence. Samuel Barnett* took his wife on a trip round the world after she had had pneumonia (Barnett, 2.130). Augustus Hare* was in search of better health in Italy when he died there. It is astonishing how many Victorian clergy sought to restore their constitutions by exposing themselves to the discomforts of extended overseas travel.

The idea that a parish priest should take a week-day off arrived on the scene only in modern times. In the past, the clergy, like the laity, took Sunday as their day of rest, if indeed they took one at all. R.W. Evans, himself a country parish priest, wrote in *The Bishopric of Souls*, published in the mid-nineteenth century, 'The Lord's day ... is his [the clergyman's] holiday ... not only his mind has repose, but his body also enjoys rest from the weariness of long walks, and from going from house to house' (Evans, 99). Some clergy have denied themselves even that latter respite. Herbert's country parson used Sunday afternoons to reconcile neighbours at variance, to visit the sick, and to exhort backsliders (Herbert, VIII). Robert Dolling* claimed that he had not had a day off for four years before the opening of his new church at Landport (Dolling, *TY* 165).

Taking holidays has not been universal practice. Ralph Josselin* occasionally visited relations, but never went on holiday in the modern sense. William Jones** noted in 1799 that in nineteen years of 'servitude' he had been absent from his parish for no more than two or three Sundays (Hart, *ECCP* 57). A century later, Bartholomew Edwards, rector of Ashill, Norfolk, was absent from his church on only three Sundays in thirty years, before he died in 1889 in his hundredth year (Hammond, 68). The record of J. Edmond Long, rector of White Roothing, Essex, from 1893 to 1925, was even more extraordinary. He was never out of his parish on a Sunday, and missed taking services through illness only once or twice (Addison, 220).

From the eighteenth century onwards, however, the tendency has been for every parson who could afford it to leave his parish for extended periods. Every three years or so Woodforde returned to his native Somerset for several months, taking advantage of the entertainment London had to offer on the way. While in the West Country he performed occasional duties and saw to family business, but on the whole lived an even easier life than he did in his parish. John Skinner* took holidays, spending five weeks on the Isle of Wight in 1818 and the inside of a fortnight at Weston-super-Mare in 1832 (Skinner, 114, 441). John Keble* went away with his family for several weeks each summer; so did Henry Fardell* with his. Kilvert did likewise; he belonged to the generation which was beginning to make extensive use of the railways. Arthur Stanton* took regular continental holidays, and on one occasion visited America.

Short excursions have been even more common. Woodforde used to combine pleasure with business on his trips to Norwich, on one occasion making the journey in order to see an execution. Skinner appears in his most agreeable light taking young people to see the Cheddar Gorge and Wells Cathedral. Kilvert's life was studded with social outings such as picnics. John Conybeare**, incumbent of Barrington, Cambridgeshire, in the latter part of the nineteenth century was a pioneer cyclist who used to ride around with his wife perched on a seat in front of him (Colloms, 255).

Some kinds of recreation have been thought to be professionally hazardous. R.W. Evans wrote in *The Bishopric of Souls*: 'Amusement ... means a change of occupation, which, while it relieves the mind of its burden, does neither derange its spiritual frame, nor give any colour of reasonable offence to other minds.' The clergyman should, he thought, eschew any recreation, even fishing, at which serious minded parishioners looked askance. 'What right minded man,' he asked, 'can but be offended at the sight of a clergyman at a race, at a theatre, at a ball, at a hunting party, at a shooting-party, at a public festival, at any meeting of the world in its professedly worldly character?' (Evans, 222, 221).

Individuals made their own adjustment to these stringent views. William Andrew* believed that dining out was an unwarrantable intrusion upon parish duties; but his opinion was a minority one. One of the pleasures Josselin allowed himself was a convivial evening with friends. Woodforde's life revolved round visits to and from, and dinners with, his local acquaintance. Indeed, his social life was so full that at one point he, the most sociable of men, professed himself 'heartily weary' of it (Woodforde, 1.83). Jane Austen took it for granted that the clergy in her novels would participate fully in polite society.

Attitudes to other domestic and personal pleasures have varied widely, Numbers of the clergy have availed themselves of the pleasures of the table. Robert Hawker* was unusual in eating relatively little and drinking neither wine nor spirits. Two of his near neighbours, John Davis of Kilkhampton and Oliver Rouse of Tetcott filled their diaries with enthusiastic comments about food and drink; as, of course, did Woodforde. It was said in the nineteenth century that the difference between a low and a high church clerical household was that in the former the food was good, in the latter the wine.

Alcohol has presented special problems, partly because of its social function. As a young parson in Oxfordshire, John Pierce, who in 1594 became Archbishop of York, 'drowned his good parts in drunkenness, conversing with his country parishioners'. Given advice, he reformed (Fuller, *CH* 3.152). Herbert taught that a parson should avoid all forms of 'luxury ... a very visible sin' but especially the most popular vice of drinking, 'into which if he comes he prostitutes himself both to shame and sin' (Herbert, III). Drunkenness was the moral charge most frequently brought against the clergy evicted between 1642 and 1660 (Matthews, *Walker* passim). John Hurt, vicar of Horndon on the Hill, Essex, was said in 1643 to have persuaded parishioners to drink with him after Sunday afternoon service and to have been 'lately unable to take service on Sunday his face being so battered and beaten after a drinking bout' (Matthews,

Walker 155). Kilvert attributed his frequent bad headaches to over-indulgence in wine (Kilvert, 1.38). It was not, however, until 1892 that the Clergy Discipline Act made it possible to deprive an incumbent for drunkenness. Alfred Harris, vicar of Stoke near Rochester, was one of the first to suffer under this regulation (Barrow, 172–3). The temperance movement of the nineteenth century commanded considerable clerical support; it was hard to minister to the Band of Hope if one did not subscribe to their principles.

Public houses presented other and related difficulties. The Injunctions of 1559 bade priests avoid alehouses, cards and dice. Not only was this regulation widely ignored but some priests kept ale-houses themselves. In the following century, Herbert reinforced the prohibition: 'Neither is it for the servant of Christ to haunt inns, or taverns, or ale-houses, to the dishonour of his person and office' (Herbert, III). When J.C. Atkinson** was secretary of the agricultural show he had to go to meetings in public houses. To show respect for his presence the farmers would not drink, and laid aside their pipes, until business was concluded (Atkinson, 28). By contrast, Hugh Mansfield Williams, parish priest at Shepherdswell in Kent from 1974 to 1985, was a daily visitor at the public house which adjoined the Vicarage, and was so loved there that a memorial seat was installed after his death. The issue here, as so often in parish life, has been between a witness against social evil and identification with the common life of the locality. When William Proctor, rector of Stradishall, Suffolk, was charged in 1644 with tippling, he gave the reasonable reply that 'In giving men drink he became all things to all that he might win some' (Matthews, *Walker* 341).

Ambivalence over the propriety of alcohol has been echoed in the case of smoking. It has always been suspected of being unhealthy, and frequently condemned as being improper. King James I's views on the subject are well known. The seventeenth century author John Aubrey commented: 'Within these thirty-five years 'twas scandalous for a divine to take tobacco' (Aubrey, 2.181); which suggests that the practice was becoming increasingly common when he wrote. A century later Woodforde smoked a pipe and John Newton* was a heavy smoker. Dr Samuel Parr, the learned perpetual curate of Hatton, Warwickshire, in the eighteenth century, would light up his pipe in the vestry during breaks in the service (Barrow, 117). A book of etiquette laid it down in 1855 that: 'One must never smoke, without consent, in the presence of a clergyman, and one must never offer a cigar to any ecclesiastic over the rank of curate' (Hammond, 203). By contrast, much of Robert Dolling's* pastoral work was conducted among the clouds of tobacco smoke always to be found in gatherings of nineteenth-century working-class men, and to which he made his own generous contribution. In this, as in much else, the middle class has been more censorious. Frank Fenwick, the eponymous cleric in Trollope's *The Vicar of Bullhampton* ventures to light a cigar in London only because 'Everybody is out of town' (Trollope, *VB* 479). Susan Howatch's Charles Ashworth voices views prevalent in low church circles in the 1930s when he says: 'I think clergymen ... should always avoid smoking when they're wearing their clerical collar. Such habits project the wrong image on the ecclesiastical screen' (Howatch, *GI* 145).

Domestic amusements have fallen under the ban in only the smallest number of cases. Ralph Josselin frequently played chess with his friends (Josselin, 114). William Paley** was an enthusiastic whist player (*DNB*). Woodforde was happy to play cards for money, to lay wagers with his friends and family, to participate in the State lottery, to attend balls and to dance at them. He noted, however, that his father refused to play cards in Passion Week, 'which [abstention] I think is not amiss' (Woodforde, 1.73). Skinner too was prepared to play cards for money, and frequently did; though, typically, he wrote after a successful evening at the table: 'I hate card playing most decidedly; it is a great loss of time, not to say worse of it.' He hated balls even more, though he attended them without dancing and ensured that his children were given dancing lessons. He played Christmas games with the young people of his and other families, and was sorry he had not learned to play chess when young. He helped his son build a boat, and remarked, possibly with intent, after an evening of music 'the young people seemed much to enjoy themselves' (Skinner, 300, 180–1, 179, 122, 302, 307).

For some clergy, dancing has been an integral part of hospitality. George Eliot's Mr Osgood was no 'pale-faced memento of solemnities', but an exemplar in the dance as in all social duties (Eliot, *SM* 158). Jack Russell (1795–1883), perpetual curate of Swymbridge, Devon, from 1832 to 1880 and a famous hunting, boxing and wrestling parson, once led the Princess of Wales out to dance at Sandringham (Barrow, 163). Conrad Noel** organized dancing on the Vicarage lawn on Sundays (Reckitt, 150).

In contrast, William Andrew was typical of Evangelicals in abhorring dancing (and also cards). Christopher Chavasse**, a leading Evangelical of our own century, told a conference that he had never been taught to dance. He represented a strong strain in Evangelical thinking, which banned dancing altogether; or, at most, allowed quadrilles, the lancers and Sir Roger de Coverley on the grounds that they were games not dances (Addison, 134). David Watson* clashed with the residue of this tradition when he tried to make use of liturgical dance.

Chavasse also said at the same conference that he had never been to a theatre in his life (Gummer, *Chavasse* 129). Here he was on common ground with many of his colleagues. In the late 1840s the Evangelical Samuel Garratt** refused the offer of a music-hall for services at a time when his church at Waltham Cross was being repaired because: 'I could not do it without seeming ... to acquiesce tacitly in the usual employment of the room' (Garratt, 50). The immediate cause of the radical Stewart Headlam's** dismissal from his curacy in 1878 was a lecture in which he called theatrical entertainment 'pure and beautiful', and encouraged the young to attend music-halls (Norman, 99, 109). In contrast, Woodforde, Skinner and Kilvert were all theatre-goers. Dolling said: 'Not that I have one word to say against theatres. "Thank God", I suppose most of us can say, "for lessons we learnt in them which we would never have learnt in church"' (Osborne, *Dolling* 37). Dick Sheppard arranged special services for actors and actresses and played a leading role in the productions of the St Martin's Players (Roberts, *Sheppard* 101–2). By the 1950s John Hester, rector of Soho, was ministering to performers not only in conventional theatres but also in strip clubs (Hester, ch. 3).

Twentieth-century controversies about the propriety of using Bible stories for entertainment were foreshadowed by John Newton's disapproval of 'The Messiah' which was performed as part of a Handel Commemoration at Westminster Abbey in the 1780s. Newton was provoked into preaching a series of fifty sermons based on the oratorio's libretto. The poet Cowper put the point of objection more succinctly:

Man praises man. Desert in arts or arms
Wins public honour; and ten thousand sit
Patiently present at a sacred song,
Commemoration-mad; content to hear
(O wonderful effect of music's power!)
Messiah's eulogy for Handel's sake. (Macdonald, *Fletcher* 299)

The advent of the novel set another snare for clerical consciences, contributing to the wider problem of what it was proper for a clergyman to read. One of the first great English novelists, Laurence Sterne**, was himself a parish priest, but his masterpiece *Tristram Shandy* was denounced by contemporaries on moral grounds. James Woodforde read Smollett's racy *Roderick Random* without being moved to protest (Woodforde, 2.175), but George Eliot's Rev. Archibald Duke thought the immense sales of *Pickwick Papers* 'one of the strongest proofs of original sin' (Eliot, *SCL* 92). Francis Kilvert, on the other hand, was an enthusiastic reader of novels, as of literature generally; his reading included the work of another clerical novelist, Charles Kingsley*.

Opinion has been less divided about the propriety of scholarly pursuits as a form of recreation. The library has been as often a refuge as an armoury. Skinner was an enthusiastic classicist and antiquarian, who believed that his parish of Camerton stood on the site of Camulodunum, home of the father of King Caractacus. He spent a rainy morning reading Caesar's Commentaries and Horace's Epistles; he frequently conducted digs despite the obstructiveness of uncomprehending landlords; and he pursued his obsession with etymology in the face of teasing from his colleagues and a lack of enthusiasm on the part of publishers. He confided to his journal: 'To me indeed study has been a shield and a safeguard against the evils of life, for when I find myself ruffled either by the knavery or the ingratitude of my fellow creatures I retire to my books and to my private meditations, as a hermit would do to his cell' (Skinner, 169, 271–2).

Outdoor games have been seen as innocent amusements, as a way of using up energies which might otherwise find less reputable expression, and as a means of identification with parishioners. They have also been viewed less favourably. The nineteenth-century *Clergyman's Instructor* quoted with approval remarks made by Bishop Edmund Gibson in 1724: 'The laws of the church in all ages have restrained clergymen from many freedoms and diversions, which in others are accounted allowable and innocent: being either such exercises as are too eager and violent and therefore unagreeable to that sedateness and gravity, which become our function: or such games or sports which frequently provoke to oaths and curses, which we can neither decently hear, nor, at that time, seasonably reprove; or such concourses and meetings as are usually accompanied with jollity and intemperance, with folly and levity and a boundless liberty of discourse ... among which temptations it is by no means proper to trust so nice and tender a thing as the reputation of a clergyman' (*CI*, 304).

These contrasting views have been held in the case of the most English of games, cricket. When Henry Venn became a priest in 1749 he gave up the game, saying 'I will never have it said of me "Well struck, parson"' (Barrow, 99). John Mitford** on the other hand regarded cricket 'with the vision of an artist and the reverence of a disciple', which was more than could be said of his attitude to Christianity. Octavius Pickard-Cambridge** taught his sons to be competent cricketers and, as time went on, the whole village of Bloxworth was drawn into the game. The local team shone in competition, and the rector forged a bond of unity with his people (Colloms, 105, 71). While his health permitted, Dick Sheppard was an enthusiastic cricketer, who played for the I Zingari club. In 1939 Frank Gillingham, a parish priest who had played for Essex for twenty-five years, was appointed a chaplain to the King (Barrow, 202).

As these examples show, the ideal which prevailed was that of the sporting parson whose spiritual standing was enhanced by his prowess with bat, ball or oar. The first Oxford Boat Race crew consisted exclusively of ordinands. Christopher Chavasse's vast popularity as a curate in St Helens in the years before the First World War arose in large part from the fact that he played rugby league for the town's team, the 'Saints' (Gummer, 43).

Gentler sports have almost always been found acceptable. Skinner took his sons skating, and played bowls (Skinner, 229, 238). Kilvert engaged in croquet and archery, both sports he could share with ladies. J. Edmund Long, mentioned above, wrote detective novels; many clergy have been avid readers of the genre. The clergy have also been noted for their enthusiasm for railways, whether in the direct sense immortalized in the film *The Titfield Thunderbolt* or indirectly in their mastery of Bradshaw. Model railway layouts have been found sufficiently frequently in the lofts of parsonage houses for the Canterbury diocesan surveyor in the 1980s to warn clergy against overloading joists. Probably the most widely known parish priest of recent times has been Wilbert Vere Awdry, vicar of Ementh, Norfolk, from 1953 to 1965, author of the much-loved children's books *The Railway Series*.

Gardening has always been regarded as the most amiable and inoffensive of clerical recreations. *The Clergyman's Instructor* quoted Burnet, the seventeenth-century bishop as saying 'his friends and his garden ought to be his chief diversions, as his study and his parish ought to be his chief employments' (*CI* 166). Burnet's contemporary, Robert Herrick**, loved flowers, visualizing violets springing from the memorial urn of his maid Prudence Baldwin. (He was using poetic licence; Pru outlived him.) John Keble was an enthusiastic gardener. George Denison** began his day in his garden and greenhouse before church at 8.00 a.m. Even William Andrew allowed himself time to garden, though, typically, he had twinges of conscience about it.

A love of gardening is one facet of a love of nature; neither has been universal. Like most farmers Josselin did not garden. He recorded the weather in strictly utilitarian terms, with an occasional account of a phenomenon and an occasional pious reflection, and wrote nothing about landscapes; his concern was his crops. At the other extreme was his contemporary Thomas Traherne*, for whom the proprietary enjoyment of the created world was the key to a right sense of values. 'The Sun serves us as much as is possible, and more than we could imagine. The Clouds and Stars minister unto us, the World surrounds us with beauty, the Air refresheth us, the Sea revives the earth and us. The Earth itself is better than gold because it produceth fruits and flowers. And therefore in the beginning, was it made manifest to be mine, because Adam alone was made to enjoy it' (Traherne, 1.14).

Traherne sees man's understanding of and delight in nature as his contribution to a 'circulation' by which God's gift is re-created and returned to Him; in his poem 'Providence' George Herbert sees man as nature's intercessor:

Man is the world's high Priest: he doth present
The sacrifice for all; while they below
Unto the service mutter an assent,
Such as springs use that fall, and windes that blow.

He goes on to describe and extol the interdependence of things both animate and inanimate, and to conclude that the very nature of nature constitutes a hymn of adoration:

All things that are, though they have sev'rall wayes,
Yet in their being joyn with one advise
to honour thee.

Kilvert's diary is read largely for its loving and delicate descriptions of the natural world. He wrote of Easter Eve 1870: 'I awoke at 4.30 and there was a glorious sight in the sky, one of the grand spectacles of the Universe. There was not a cloud in the deep wonderful blue of the heavens. Along the Eastern horizon there was a clear deep intense glow neither scarlet nor crimson but a mixture of both. This red glow was very narrow, almost like a riband and it suddenly shaded off into the deep blue. Opposite in the west the full moon shining in all its brilliance was setting upon the hill beyond the church steeple. Thus the glow in the east bathed the church in a warm rich tinted light, while the moon from the west was casting strong shadows. The moon dropped quickly down behind the hill bright to the last, till only her rim could be seen sparkling among the tops of the orchards on the hill. The sun rose quickly and his rays struck red upon the white walls of Penllan, but not so brilliantly as in the winter sunrisings' (Kilvert, 1.89).

That morning Kilvert rose at 5.00 a.m. and worked on his Easter sermon. He spent the rest of the day on pastoral duties, and on admiring the efforts of the local people as they adorned church and graveyard with flowers. As he walked home after choir practice he noticed that 'the decked graves had a strange effect in the moonlight and looked as if the people had laid down to sleep for the night out of doors, ready dressed to rise early on Easter morning'. The next day was 'the happiest, brightest, most beautiful Easter I have ever spent', with the weather, the large congregation at morning service, and the local customs of decking the churchyard and wearing something new for the day all contributing to Kilvert's joy (Kilvert, 1.95).

Unlike Traherne, Kilvert was not capable of analysing his reactions to nature, and formulating a consequential system of thought; but innumerable passages in the diary show that in the undifferentiated whole of his experience his awareness of nature and his awareness of God infused and illuminated each other, and found a common expression in the life and practice of the rural church. 'How many of us hear the wheat at night praising God, or in the droning of bees hear the music of angels over a repentant sinner? Few suspect that the cooing dove is "making intercessions for us with groans that cannot be uttered".' The diary identifies the natural world with the nature of man. Kilvert saw near Clyro a blackbird dead in a gin fixed to a post, and thought it part of the creation which, according to Paul in Romans 8, 'groaneth and travaileth in pain'. 'Somehow the suffering creature reminded me of the Saviour upon the Cross. I felt as if some sin of mine had brought him there' (Grice, *Kilvert* 232).

Others besides Kilvert have identified with the animal kingdom. Augustus Toplady, an eighteenth-century parson best known for composing 'Rock of Ages', thought all animals would go to heaven, and was upset when John Newton enquired whether fleas were included (Pollock, *AG* 162). Kingsley and Hawker agreed with Toplady.

Country priests have had, of course, to come to terms with the unsentimental realism with which their people have regarded their flocks and herds; have indeed often shared it. Kilvert was disgusted to find the daughters of the vicar of Newchurch assisting in the castration of lambs, 'but I made allowance for them and considered in how rough a way the poor children have been brought up, so that they thought no harm of it, and I forgave them' (Kilvert, 1.127). Other priests have found the animal kingdom puzzling rather than inspiring. John Henry Newman** used to speak of it as a 'disturbing mystery' (Faber, 43). He would have sympathized with Bishop Gore who, on meeting William Temple taking a party of children to the Zoo, exclaimed 'I hate the Zoo; it turns me into an atheist in twenty minutes'.

We sometimes look in vain for any sense of the sacredness of the animal creation. Flora Thompson remembered how Rector Ellison visiting Lark Rise would admire collections of birds' eggs, and even condescend to accept a rare specimen. He would have echoed the local saying 'Where there's no sense there's no feeling' (Thompson, 152). Sometimes insensitivity has been in the cause of science. Stephen Hales, perpetual curate of Teddington, Gloucestershire, in the eighteenth century for more than fifty years, mangled conscious animals in order to investigate blood pressure (Addison, 83–4). Gilbert White** was quite happy to kill animals and birds in pursuit of his researches, and mostly describes them in severely objective terms; only very occasionally does a theological reflection creep in. He writes of the tortoise: 'It is a matter of wonder to find that Providence should bestow such profusion of days, such a seeming waste of longevity, on a reptile that appears to relish it so little as to squander more than two-thirds of its existence in a joyless stupor.' He was prepared to concede, however, when his small niece insisted that the 'pleasing murmur' of far off rooks at eventide was the sound of their prayers, that she spoke 'in the true spirit of physico-theology' (White, 213, 227–8).

Lack of compassion for animals opened the way to a tolerance of, or enthusiastic participation in, field sports. George Crabbe** writes in 'The Village' of a dying man in a poor-house who seeks spiritual consolation. Unfortunately his parish priest is:

> A jovial youth, who thinks his Sunday's task
> As much as God or man can fairly ask;
> The rest he gives to loves and labours light,
> To fields the morning, and to feasts the night;
> None better skilled the noisy pack to guide,
> To urge their chase, to cheer them or to chide

Crabbe was painting from life. Woodforde refused to leave his dinner to bury an infant who had been brought to the church gate without his knowledge; but left it when he had an opportunity to course a hare. He loved fishing, and made pastoral use of a good day out by giving the bulk of his catch to the poor of the parish (Woodforde, 2.285, 301; 1.310). Skinner taught his sons to fish and shoot, and engaged in both sports himself. Edward King**, advised a young clergyman to go on a shooting holiday: 'I am not saying this out of false kindness ... but because I do value so highly a natural growth in holiness ... and I dread the unnatural, forced, cramped, ecclesiastical holiness, which is so much more quickly produced.' He did, however, anticipate that his friend would outgrow his desire for the sport (Addison, 190). In 1980 BBC television showed a programme about Peter Fluck, incumbent to a group of Lincolnshire parishes, who was a keen shot and on good terms with the local hunt.

There has indeed been a strong tradition of clerical huntsmen, described by disapproving Evangelicals as 'mighty Nimrods of the cloth' (Virgin, 110). It was recorded of Thomas Bird, vicar of Somerby, Leicestershire, during the Commonwealth, that 'he did ride on huntinge in his perambulation after a hare, in his surplice, and leapt over a gate and so teare his surplice, that the parish was inforced to provide a new surplice for him to read prayers in, and to keepe the old one for him to hunt in' (Matthews, *Walker* 232. It is only fair to note that Bird denied the allegation.). That incumbent was hunted in his turn by a committee investigating scandalous ministers, but other clergy have followed the sport scatheless. The sporting parson Jack Russell rejected his Bishop's request that he should give up his hounds, but suffered no penalty (Colloms, 39). Kingsley, enthusing about 'manliness', discovered it in participation in blood sports, which, he declared, had 'unutterable and almost spiritual charm' (Norman, 37). An elderly incumbent Charles Slingsby, was in 1912 killed by a fall from his horse while hunting. When a memorial window to him was unveiled at Moor Moncton church, Yorkshire, Cosmo Lang**, by then Archbishop of York, said during his address 'Hunting is a sport which develops some of the finest qualities of human courage and endurance' (Barrow, 182). In 1979 the Hunt Saboteurs Association disrupted a service at Preston, Lancashire, on the grounds that the Rector, Roland Meredith, was a follower of the Bleasdale hounds (Barrow, 232).

Other clergy, such as Bartholomew Edwards mentioned earlier in this section, have renounced hunting. Young William Hornby, one of the succession of squarsons who served St Michaels-on-Wyre, Lancashire, from 1789 to 1919 obeyed his bishop's instructions and gave up hunting after his ordination (Colloms, 14–15, 36). Robert Hawker did not hunt and gave up shooting early in his ministry. He deplored the fact that colleagues did not follow suit (Brendon, *Hawker* 159). Kilvert was disgusted by rook-shooting, and noted: "'What a fine day it is. Let us go out and kill something. The old reproach against the English. The Squire has just gone by with a shooting party"' (Kilvert, 2.86). However, what he confided to his diary he did not say in public. Very few rural priests, even if they have renounced field sports for themselves, have condemned them in their parishioners.

Even those clergy who in other circumstances have killed animals for fun, have relished God's creation in their intimacy with and love of their pets. Woodforde operated upon a cat with a broken rib: 'It grieved me much to see the poor creature in such pain. ... and therefore made me undertake the above, which I hope will preserve the life of the poor creature' (Woodforde 1.81. On the other hand, he hanged a greyhound when it ran away with a neighbour's meat – 4.103). One of the most attractive passages in Skinner's diary reads: 'After dinner this evening there were lying on the floor before the fire my three dogs and a pet lamb of my daughter's, also a large cat, and at the window presented itself a tame jackdaw; all these different creatures were perfectly quiet, and to all appearances good friends.' He wrote Latin inscriptions for the tomb-stones of his children's pet pigeon and dog (Skinner, 429, 268). Cosmo Lang, when he was vicar of Portsea, took his dog with him when he gave sick communions (Lockhart, *Lang* 119–20). In 1959 Mervyn Bazell, rector of Chedzoy, Somerset, got into trouble with his parishioners for bringing his terrier into church. He declared: 'I regard all animals as God's creatures and I would never turn any animal out of a church.' His bishop declined to proceed against him (Barrow, 217–18, *Crockford's Clerical Directory*).

Robert Hawker taught that 'a fondness for [the] society of animals and pleasure in watching their familiar affections is a native and natural impulse with good and kind and holy men'. He kept up to nine cats, several dogs, and two deer named Robin Hood and Maid Marion. The dogs and cats followed him into church, and he objected neither to their presence nor to that of animals belonging to his parishioners. He once called out when a retriever was about to be removed: 'Let him be ... there were dogs in the ark'. One of his cats went on walks with him, and he had a singular capacity for attracting wild birds and controlling horses. He is said to have excommunicated a cat for catching a mouse on a Sunday, but that seems out of character (Brendon, *Hawker* 142–4).

No doubt Hawker, like many other people, compensated for failures and difficulties in human relations by forming close ties with animals. But his affinity with the wider creation represents a truer spirituality than that of the clergy who have regarded nature and the animal kingdom as fit for nothing but exploitation. In the conflict of thought and attitude between clergy who have simply used nature and those who have reverenced it, contemporary sympathies are with the latter group; and, even after allowing for the fact that most clergy have been country people and most modern moralists urban, this is a welcome instance of our own age proving spiritually perceptive.

4

Scholarship, Doctrine and World View

> A Divine includes a Philosopher and a Christian;
> a Christian includes a Divine and a Philosopher; a
> Philosopher includes a Christian and a Divine. Since
> no man therefore can be ... a perfect Christian unless
> he be a Divine, every man ought to spend his time in
> studying diligently Divine Philosophy. (Traherne, 4.3)

Scholarship

Ralph Josselin* was clear that scholarship was an essential part of his spiritual equipment. He was shocked when he heard a separatist preaching against learning. He regarded the purchase of books as a moral duty, on a par with giving to the poor. He read many Protestant divines and at least one Catholic, often in Latin. He read Josephus. In 1644 he resolved to practice Hebrew and Greek daily; as with so many of his resolutions, this one lapsed and in the case of Hebrew had to be renewed more than once (Josselin, 34, 276, 143, 25, 54, 77, 140).

He was, of course, saturated in the Bible. Direct quotations occur only occasionally in the diary, but almost every entry gives the sense of a mind tuned to the scriptures. He wanted to produce a work of biblical scholarship, and in 1649 he embarked upon a reconciler, an attempt to bring into accord those passages in scripture which appear contradictory. The project lasted for only a few months; references to it in the diary cease while he was still embroiled with the Pentateuch.

For several years in the 1650s, and to some extent thereafter, he engaged in millenarian speculation. He read widely, and played with the numbers in Revelation, Daniel and Ezekiel; proving to his own satisfaction that the Second Coming was not far off. Such ideas were in the air at the time, and they do not seem to have deflected his life from its ordinary course.

In the field of learning as in many others he found cause to reproach himself – with the waste of time which could have been devoted to study, with allowing disinclination for study to prevail over his better instincts, with allowing study to be crowded out by his other obligations. None the less as he grew older he appears to have read less; a not uncommon phenomenon among the clergy.

When he was being true to his intentions, Josselin stood in a great tradition. While few clergy have agreed with William Jones** that a parson's first duty is to his books and that his needy parishioners should have only so much time as he can spare from them (Hart, *ECCP* 57), the ideal of the learned parson, bringing spirituality to his scholarship and scholarship to his spirituality, runs like a golden thread through Anglican history. Bernard Gilpin* was guided by exact scholarship to the pattern of thought which sustained his teaching and pastoring. Thomas Brightman, rector of Hawnes, Bedfordshire, in the reign of James I, always carried a Greek Testament, every fortnight reading the whole of it (Aubrey, 3.260). Bryan Walton, rector of St Martin Orgar and of Sandon, Essex, although sequestered during the Civil War period, produced in 1657 a six volume Polyglot Bible, containing the text in Hebrew, Greek, Latin, Syriac, Ethiopic, Arabic, and Persian, together with a wealth of supportive material (Matthews, *Walker* 61; *ODCC*). Thomas Clarke, rector from 1766 to 1793 of Chesham Bois, a Buckinghamshire village with only twenty-four houses, was called 'a walking Synopsis' by a fellow Evangelical – 'he gives you the opinion of every commentator, and then gives his own, which is worth all the rest put together'; he trained a multitude of young men for Orders (Balleine, 82). Julius Hare* boasted a library of 14,000 volumes in his home at Herstmonceaux.

Even secular scholarship has been thought to fit the clergy better for their work. Fielding's Parson Adams proved himself a cleric to a doubting host by bombarding him with reflections on Homer to the extent that 'the gentleman, … so far from entertaining any further suspicion … now doubted whether he had not a bishop in his house' (Fielding, 225–8). William Stubbs (1825–1901), who laid the foundation of his immense historical learning while he was rector of Navestock, Essex, from 1850 to 1866, was a popular parish priest, but was offered preferment and eventually a mitre because of his scholarly rather than his ministerial gifts. The same was true of another great historian, Mandell Creighton**.

Given the intellectually restricted circumstances in which priests have often pursued their ministries, scholarship has been a necessary enlargement of their lives, keeping them in touch not only with the wider aspects of their own faith but also with the community of the well-educated and cultured. Thomas Taylor Lewis (1801–58), a conscientious minister to the village of Aymestry in Herefordshire, was also a considerable and widely respected geologist and antiquarian. Richard Watson Dixon (1833–1900), incumbent successively of two northern villages, was a well-known historian and poet, and a friend of Gerard Manley Hopkins, Robert Bridges and Dante Gabriel Rossetti (Colloms, 112–23, 210–23).

As we have already seen, it has been quite possible to combine scholarship with conscientious ministry. John Stevens Henslow, rector of Hitcham, Suffolk, in the early nineteenth century, was also professor of botany at Cambridge. He resided in his parish in order to serve it properly, returning to Cambridge only to lecture. Charles Darwin, his greatest pupil, admired him for his learning, his moral example and his benevolence to his parishioners

(Chadwick, *VC* 2.16–17). William Barnes (1801–86), a largely self-taught poet, antiquarian and philologist who knew sixty languages, was the much-loved rector of Carne, Dorset, for twenty-four years. A village woman told his daughter: 'There, miss, we do all o' us love the parson ... he be so *plain*. Why, bless you, I don't no more mind telling o' 'un all my little pains and troubles than if he was my grandmother' (Colloms, 143). Octavius Pickard-Cambridge**, who was known as 'the Father of British Spiders' because of his work as a naturalist, presided over the family living with assiduous authority (Colloms, 56).

But scholarship has its dangers, most obviously that of distracting the priest from his parochial duties. Thomas Fuller** confessed that he found so much delight in the writing of history that he was afraid he had neglected pastoral work in consequence (Addison, *WDF* 206). William Oughtred (1574–1660), rectory of Albury, Suffolk, for fifty years, was famous as a mathematician, astrologer and alchemist; but, Aubrey reported, 'I have heard his neighbour ministers say that he was a pittiful preacher; the reason was because he never studied it, but bent all his thoughts on mathematiques' (Aubrey, 2.105). Threatened with sequestration as a royalist Oughtred reformed; there was no like constraint on George Crabbe's** Author-Rector:

> ... his delight
> Was all in books; to read them, or to write;
> Women and men he strove alike to shun,
> And hurried homeward when his tasks were done.

John Mitford** was a literary scholar, who retained his parishes chiefly because he needed their income (Colloms, 104). Perhaps more forgivably, Henry Alford**, one of the fathers of the Revised Version, turned his parish over to a curate in order to secure seven hours a day for his biblical work (Alford, 195).

Crabbe's Author-Rector fell into another trap of scholarship – a pre-occupation with the recondite and unhelpful:

> Of questions much he wrote, profound and dark,
> How spake the serpent, and where stopped the ark;
> From what far land the Queen of Sheba came;
> Who Salem's priest, and what his father's name.
>   ('The Parish Register')

Ralph Josselin was only one of many clergy who have sunk into the bog of millenarian speculation. Thomas Brightman, mentioned above, discovered personal references to Thomas Cromwell, Archbishop Cranmer and Lord Burleigh in the book of Revelation (Aubrey, 3.260). Over three hundred years later Samuel Garratt** was informing correspondents that texts in the prophets, gospels and epistles indicated that the end of the current dispensation was near, and identifying the Russian Empire of his day with the Third Woe in Revelation XI (Garratt, 136, 157).

Scholarship can be corrosive of faith, as the questioning mind usurps the primacy of the trusting heart. John Earle, later to be a bishop, wrote that the sceptic in religion 'finds doubts and scruples better than resolves them, and is always too hard for himself. His learning is too much for his brain; and his judgment too little for his learning, and his over-opinion of both spoils all. Pity it was his mischance of being a scholar; for it does only distract and irregulate him and the world by him ... His whole life is a question, and his salvation a greater, which death only concludes, and then he is resolved' (Earle 67–8).

Worst of all, scholarship has served as the handmaid of odium theologicum. When learning has come in at the door charity has often flown out of the window. John Walker (1674–1747), rector of two Exeter parishes for most of his life, laboured monumentally to produce his *Sufferings of the Clergy during the Grand Rebellion 1642–60*; but he was not content to allow his facts to speak for themselves. 'His prejudices were violent, and so also was the language he used to express them' (Matthews, *Walker* xi). He would have been advised to follow the view of Walter Hook*: 'Bishop Jebb, my Gamaliel, used to tell me not directly to oppose error, but to exhibit the beauty of the opposite virtue; not e.g. to preach against infidelity, but to bring prominently forward the love of the Gospel' (Stephens, *Hook* 433).

But if scholarship has its dangers, so does the lack of it. A proportion of the clergy have been disabled for their work by a lack of basic intellectual skills. In Tudor and Stuart times many were drawn from the labouring trades, and received no instruction in their responsibilities. Bishop Hooper of Gloucester discovered in 1550 that 186 of the 300 clergy in his diocese could not recite the Ten Commandments and that 34 could not name the author of the Lord's Prayer (Melinsky, 97). A visitation of three Archdeaconries in the diocese of Lincoln in 1576 found 374 clergy who were sufficiently qualified in sacred learning and 432 who were not. It was thought to demonstrate an improvement in intellectual quality when Archbishop Whitgift discovered in the first years of the next century that over half his men were now licensed to preach (Hart, *CC* 25, 60). Aubrey describes Thomas Hobbes, father of the great political scientist, and vicar of Westport, Wiltshire, as an ignorant 'Sir John' who 'could only read the prayers of the church and the homilies; and disesteemed learning ... as not knowing the sweetness of it' (Aubrey, 1.323).

In the eighteenth and nineteenth centuries, when nearly all clergy were graduates, attempts to assess their academic qualifications were frequently perfunctory. James Woodforde* was recommended for ordination after half an hour's questioning. None the less he thought himself hard done by. The questions were 'hard and deep ... I had not one question that Yes or No would answer' (Woodforde, 1.25). Walter Hook recalled that the whole of his examination in Divinity at Oxford in 1821 consisted of proving 'the errors of the Roman Catholics in worshipping relics and the folly of the Jews in wearing phylacteries ... together with something about the doctrine of the Trinity' (Stephens, *Hook* 28). The following year the Hon. George Spencer, son of an earl, was told by the fawning clerical examiner for the diocese of Peterborough that it was impossible 'that I could ever entertain any idea of subjecting a gentleman with whose talents and good qualities I am so well acquainted as I am with yours, to any examination except one as a matter of form' (Virgin, 138). When Christopher Chavasse** was ordained deacon in 1910 he had not read a single serious theological work (Gummer, *Chavasse* 41). It is against this background that we must understand the stress laid on formal education and proper testing in more recent times; against it too that we must judge the force of the frequent modern assertion that clerical training should be predominantly practical and pastoral.

It has been said that a good scholar must practise almost as incessantly as a good violinist. Whether that is true or not, it is certain that many clergy have failed themselves and their congregations by setting their books aside once their ministry began. Frequently, disinclination for study has gone with a more general indolence. It is characteristic of James Woodforde's attitude towards his duties that he only very occasionally bought or read a book, and that when he did it was often a novel. While Robert Hawker* spent all his spare time mulling over theological and antiquarian works, his clerical neighbours engaged in no intellectual activity more strenuous than that of reading newspapers and periodicals, and playing cards with the ladies (Brendon, *Hawker* 158).

There have been great souls in the tradition of the Curé d'Ars who have managed very well without even a tincture of scholarship. Robert Dolling* never read books because he reckoned that he had better things to do with his time. But Dolling possessed superb gifts which compensated for a lack of learning; and even he had to ask his scholarly curate and later biographer, C.E.Osborne, to talk theology with him for an hour a day and to prepare many of his sermons (Dolling *TY* 234). How much he was helped is another matter. Archbishop Lang** remembered him visiting St Mary's, Oxford, with a carefully prepared manuscript. Part way through it, he confessed that it had been written for him by a friend better able to speak to University men; he then threw it aside and 'poured forth an impassioned plea for brotherliness towards the poor and outcast, and closed with a long, fervent, and very moving extempore prayer'. That, Lang remarked, was Dolling all over (Lockhart, *Lang* 110–11.).

Scholarship, then, is a double-edged weapon. Those who wield it can wound themselves and others; but those who do not possess it are often at a disadvantage. It has been a constant struggle to prevent the writing of this book from distracting me from parochial duties; on the other hand, the work has enriched my thought and refreshed my mind. I like to think that, on balance, my parishioners have gained.

Doctrine and World View

We turn to the effect of changes in the intellectual climate upon clerical spirituality, and consider three areas of thought. They are closely related, but can be distinguished as the growth of the critical attitude to the Bible, developments in the scientific world view, and changing attitudes to dogma.

The great Anglican teachers have always insisted that the Bible must be understood in the light of learning and reason. There has rarely been a disposition to handle it totally uncritically. Charles Simeon* took his religion from the Bible, and, so far as he could contrive, from the Bible alone. 'I love the simplicity of the scriptures,' he said; 'I wish to receive and inculcate every truth precisely in the way and to the extent that it is set forth in the inspired Volume.' But even Simeon was ready to point out passages which could not possibly be taken literally, and admitted that while 'no error in doctrine or other important matter is allowed; yet there are inexactnesses in reference to philosophic and scientific matters because of its popular style.' He thought the book of Job a poem which was in part allegorical rather than literal (Hopkins, *Simeon* 175, 177, 121).

Simeon was not untypical in the flexibility which he brought to exegesis. The seventeenth-century Royalist Robert Levet, vicar of Wood Ditton, Cambridgeshire, defended total submission to royal authority by assuring a parishioner that the story of Shadrach, Meshach and Abednego 'was but a fable' (Matthews, *Walker* 83). Thomas Traherne* wrote of Genesis that it is not 'to be believed, that God filled all the world with creatures before he thought of man; but by that little fable he teaches us the excellence of man' (Stranks, 118).

Simeon's was, however, the last generation in which it was still the general practice to treat the text of the Bible with undifferentiated respect. For him and for his predecessors the Bible was 'penned by one and the self-same Spirit' (Herbert, IV). There was no question of impugning the text; the scholarly task was to draw out its Christian significance. But then came the critical revolution of the nineteenth century. It was to inspire contrasting reactions.

There were those who welcomed it. Henry Alford**, whose Greek Testament, begun when he was vicar of Wymeswold, was his great scholarly achievement, spoke warmly of German scholars and added: 'I have been painfully struck as I have advanced in my work with the dishonesty of our English commentators in concealing difficulties, or solving them in a manner which must be even to themselves unsatisfactory' (Alford, 174–5). Maria, wife of the liberal Augustus Hare*, summarized his views on historicity: 'In everything that was of the slightest importance to the conveying the knowledge of God ... there the Spirit dictated ... but the mere historical detail cannot with all its variations and inconsistencies be dwelt on as every *word* inspired by God.' Her husband reflected on the similarities between discrepancies in the accounts of the death of the statesman Huskisson in a railway accident and in those of events in the gospels, and wrote to a clerical friend afflicted with doubt: 'I am disposed to say to any Christian who vexes himself about such questions as that of Jonah and his fish, for instance, "What matter whether the story be literal or allegorical, so long as we believe in Jesus and his tomb, and know that He rose from it triumphantly?"' (Hare, 1.328, 339–40).

For a long time, however, the majority view was the other way. John Keble's* opinion was that men who had difficulties over scriptural inspiration were too wicked to be reasoned with (Battiscombe, *Keble* 62–3). The mildly liberal *Essays and Reviews*, published in 1860, provoked the unsuccessful prosecution of two of its authors, H.B. Wilson, rector of Great Staughton, Huntingdonshire, and Rowland Williams, a university teacher who was also beneficed in the Salisbury diocese (Chadwick, *VC* 2.75–83). Robert Hawker complained that the book would 'foam infidelity over the land' (Brendon, *Hawker* 225). He spoke for his brethren, 11,000 of whom signed a declaration maintaining 'without reserve or qualification the inspiration and Divine authority of the whole canonical scriptures, as not only containing, but being, the Word of God' (Flindall, 179). Sabine Baring-Gould's** book *The Origin and Development of Religious Belief*, published in 1869–70, which argued that, since it was no longer possible to believe either in an infallible Bible or in an infallible Church, Christianity must be proved true by the way in which it catered for human needs, was condemned by all sections of the religious press (Purcell, *Baring-Gould* 92). Later in the century George Denison** thundered against the mildly liberal publication *Lux Mundi*: 'I tremble for the coming Century, building up itself on the indifference and infidelity of this Century, and comforting itself upon false grounds.' For Denison '"Real faith" enables a man to take up the Bible ... as a book wholly different from any other book, and to say "Here is my *law*"' (Denison, 339, 81).

Another brake upon clerical acceptance of biblical scholarship was a pastoral one – a fear of scandalizing the laity. John Skinner* horrified a Methodist, ministering with him at a sick-bed, by assuring him that the English Bible contained mistakes of translation (Skinner, 79). By the middle of the nineteenth century the clergy were being reminded that they did not use the same scriptures as the parishioners they were visiting: 'You use the scriptures in the sense in which they were understood by the persons to whom they were written ... they use them in the sense which suits the prevailing mind of our own times ... to understand the scripture yourself, and to exhibit in plain language and in a clear light to grosser intellects, are two very different accomplishments' (Evans 58–9, 151). Things became even more difficult as the corrosive effects of the new learning began to be felt. It was natural that men who had themselves found it hard to come to terms with it should think twice before exposing their parishioners to its influence. This attitude stood in the way of accepting new translations as well as new interpretations. R.W. Evans advised: 'If you come across a Bible passage which the Authorized Version translates inaccurately it is far from prudent to state that there is any difference; choose another passage instead' (151). Henry Alford, one of the begetters of the Revised Version, insisted that they must 'let the venerable aspect of antiquity, even with its rust and unseemliness, continue to hang about the thing of all others which most we honour'; but, bolder than some others, he went on: 'Let all absolute misapprehensions and blunders of translation be corrected fearlessly at once' (Alford, 121). He was more radical than many other clergy. The Revised Version was not authorized for use in churches until 1899, fourteen years after its publication.

For those who strove to be both good pastors and intellectually honest, the spiritual conflict engendered by biblical scholarship could be a bitter one. In his book of guidance for clergy *Speculum Sacerdotum*, published in 1894, W.C.E. Newbolt agonized over the problems created by textual criticism and over the fact that it was no longer possible to say that certain stories were 'true'. He pictured the parish priest despondently reading the latest biblical review 'telling us that Holy Scripture is no doubt inspired, only that the sparks of Divinity must be caught as best they may from the friction of diverse aims and contending parties which contributed to its composition, and bidding us, when we have separated the several constituent threads which make up the narrative, gauged the direction of the prophetic mind, allowed due weight to the love of the supernatural, and the exaggeration of affection, to enjoy whatever remains as a precipitate of inspiration'. All this is pastorally destructive. 'Men look for truth ... not probability, in those who professionally study a revelation from another world' (Newbolt, *SS* 104–5, 153–4).

Gradually a more critical attitude to scripture became the norm. Even Robert Hawker admitted that the Bible contained errors of translation, though he denied that they impaired it as a 'code of salvation' (Brendon, *Hawker* 226). Stewart Headlam**, radical in this as in all else, denied verbal inspiration (Norman, 103). By the later nineteenth century Bishop William Stubbs, in most respects an undeviating conservative, was telling ordination candidates that they need not believe that the sun stood still over Gibeon and that a good deal of the Bible could only in very indirect ways be regarded as integral to God's revelation (Hammond, 112). A century later still I conducted a weekly Bible study group for parishioners, at which the critical approach to the Bible was explained and commended. A few of the group felt threatened from time to time; for most the discussions were a liberation.

The critical approach to scripture came more naturally to those who had come to terms with the scientific and philosophical changes of their day. Here too the parochial clergy were confronted with challenges which were both personal and pastoral.

For James Woodforde* – and in this he was typical of his time – Nature spoke of God, both in the sense that the contemplation of creation filled men with awe, and in the sense that science had shown that matter was subordinate to Mind (N. Sykes in *Theology*, vol. 38, 104–5). For Woodforde's contemporary Gilbert White** too there was no problem. He followed the teaching of John Ray and William Derham, who were the principal progenitors of physico-theology. This was a Christian approach to science which saw the observation and analysis of nature as ways of demonstrating God's beneficence (White, 40n). White was freed to write with the utmost objectivity because of his underlying assumption that he was demonstrating the workings of the divine design.

In the following century, however, the men of science were often – though by no means always – to be found among the critics of Christian belief. Charles Darwin was slow to publish his views on evolution and natural selection, partly because of the hurt he knew they would give to his many clerical friends. He was right to be cautious. His *Origin of Species* weakened or destroyed the faith of many Christians. A clergyman named Brownjohn resigned his parish because he thought his belief in evolution incompatible with his office; he later made a public protest against Frederick Temple's confirmation as Archbishop of Canterbury because of the latter's acceptance of evolution (Chadwick, *VC* 2.23). George Sketchley Ffinden, rector of Darwin's own parish of Downe, Kent, wrote that he 'had been long aware of the harmful tendencies to the cause of revealed religion of Mr Darwin's views' and that he trusted 'that God's Grace might in time bring one so highly gifted intellectually and morally to a better mind.' Even Darwin's friend and teacher J.S. Henslow, rector of Hitcham and professor of botany at Cambridge, while admiring much that the book contained, thought that it pushed hypothesis too far. He concluded: 'Darwin attempts more than is granted to Man, just as people used to account for the origin of Evil – a question past our finding out' (Desmond and Moore, 614, 487–8).

By contrast, Octavius Pickard-Cambridge**, who corresponded with Darwin over the sexual habits of spiders, remained untroubled by his great contemporary's theories (Colloms, 73). Richard Church, incumbent of Whatley, Somerset, and later a distinguished Dean of St Paul's, hailed Darwin's work (Addison, 191). Charles Kingsley*, who thought 'this progress of society in the present day is really of God', also believed that 'it is the scientific go-aheadism of the day which must save us' (Norman, 38). He wrote enthusiastically to Charles Darwin that he was awed by *The Origin of Species*. It was 'just as noble a conception of Deity, to believe that He created primal forms capable of self-development ... as to believe that He required a fresh act of intervention to supply the lacunas which He Himself had made' (Desmond and Moore, 477). Stewart Headlam took the same line; evolution was 'creation, by means of gradual, orderly development' (Norman, 103).

Thoroughgoing supernaturalism in the face of changing scientific and philosophic thought remained – and remains – an option. It was possible to ignore intellectual change altogether, a course adopted by some Evangelicals; Thomas Arnold described a typical Evangelical as 'a good Christian with a low understanding, a bad education and ignorance of the world' (Chadwick, *VC* 1.451). Thomas Hardy's Mr Clare, 'an Evangelical of the Evangelicals ... had in his raw youth made up his mind once for all on the deeper questions of existence, and admitted no further reasoning on them thenceforward' (Hardy, 217). It was always possible to refer everything back to first causes. A leading Evangelical preacher, Henry Melvill, at the time incumbent of the Camden chapel, Camberwell, wrote in 1838: 'I do not believe it the result of properties which, once imparted, operate of themselves, that vegetation goes forward and verdure mantles the earth: I rather believe that Deity is busy with every seed that is cast into the ground, and that it is through his immediate agency that every leaf opens, and every flower blooms' (Whale, 112).

Robert Hawker saw scientific explanation as accounting only superficially for natural phenomena. It was 'young men in white garments ... the Battalions of the Lord of Hosts ... [who] each with delegated office fulfil what their "King Invisible" decrees; not with the dull, inert mechanism of fixed and Natural Law, but with the unslumbering energy and the rational obedience of Spiritual Life' (Brendon, *Hawker* 226). Hawker's most recent biographer describes him as an anachronism from the Middle Ages; but he did no more than echo in vivid terms the conviction of many clergy, then and since, that the laws of nature describe without explaining. John Polkinghorne, briefly parish priest of Blean, Kent, during a career of great scientific distinction, argued in 1986 that theology explains the source of the rational order and structure which science assumes and confirms (John Polkinghorne, *One World*, SPCK 1986, 97).

It is one thing, however, to see God behind nature, another to believe Him active within it. George Herbert's* country parson reminded his flock that just as God ordered the sun to stand still and fire not to burn in biblical times, so he was capable of destroying the harvest of a farmer who failed to acknowledge his dependence upon the divine assistance (Herbert, XXX). Ralph Josselin* too saw God's direct intervention everywhere, and this view persisted. A friend wrote of Robert Hawker: 'He believed that God was continually present with his people and that his Presence was revealed in ordinary events of human life ... unlike most of us, Hawker was not ashamed openly and continually to ... say of anything that happened unexpectedly or opportunately or strangely, that it was God's doing' (Brendon, *Hawker* 152–3). At the end of the nineteenth century Henry Liddon was telling his fellow clergy: 'Miracle simply asserts

God's right to act with unfettered freedom in the world which He has made' (Liddon, 184).

On the other hand, as early as 1680 George Hickes (1642–1715), vicar of All Hallows, Barking, was arguing that miracles were confined to biblical times. Their purpose had been to establish divine truth, and now they were no longer necessary (More, 68–9). Some eighteenth-and nineteenth-century clergy concluded that the accumulating certainties of science told against the likelihood of miracles. Miracles had indeed occurred in biblical times, but were not necessary now. Concerned about the charismatic movement led by Edward Irving, Charles Simeon declared 'are we all to possess the power of "working miracles, and speaking divers kinds of tongues"? No; the time for such things is long since passed ... no such power exists at this day' (Hopkins, *Simeon* 185). John Skinner was moved by a visit to a Ranters' camp meeting in 1828 to preach a sermon in which he too asserted that the age of miracles was over (Skinner, 336). It remained a question for the clergy just quoted in what terms they were to explain God's workings in the world, for example in answers to prayer and in the personal guidance of individuals, if direct supernatural intervention were to be ruled out.

Another problem created by the inexorable advance of scientific knowledge was the doubts it threw upon scripture. In 1838 the dilemma was well expressed by Henry Melvill, mentioned above. 'There has been much anxiety felt in modern times by the supporters of revelation, on account of alleged discoveries in science, which apparently contradict the Mosaic record of the creation. We had been accustomed to conclude with the Bible for our guide, that this globe was not quite six thousand years old; that, six thousand years ago, the matter of which it was composed was not in existence, much less was it the home of animal or vegetable life. We had been accustomed to think that, unless man had fallen, there would have been no decay and no death in this creation, so that every beast of the field would have walked in immortal strength, and every tree of the forest waved in immortal verdure. But modern science is quite counter to these our suppositions and conclusions: for the researches of the geologist oblige us to assign millions, rather than thousands, of years as the age of this globe, and to allow it to have been tenanted by successive tribes of living things long before the time when man was summoned into being.' Melvill's view was that the findings of science were conclusive and that previous interpretations of scripture might need modification. He asserted, however, that 'Science may scale new heights, and explore new depths; but she shall bring back nothing from her ... excursions which will not, when rightly understood, yield a fresh tribute of testimony to the Bible' (Whale, 111). His words were of course no more than an assertion.

Not all clergy were so eirenic. At the Church Congress of 1867, Archdeacon Denison denounced the claim of science to equal the Bible as a road to truth, and declared 'Those who accept the Bible do not investigate truth, they receive it'. The remark was greeted both with cheers and with cries of 'no! no!' (Chadwick, *VC* 2.25). Great quantities of clerical time and trouble went on attempts to reconcile scientific knowledge with the biblical text. John Keble, arguing with the geologist Buckland over the tendency of his subject to cast doubt on Archbishop Ussher's dating of the Creation in 4004 BC claimed, in a manner reminiscent of the elder Goss, that it was conceivable and indeed certain that God had made the fossils during the six days recounted in Genesis 1 (Brendon, *Hawker* 52). Samuel Butler's Theobald Pontifex was in the same tradition when he composed a sermon showing that 'so far as geology was worth anything at all – and he was too liberal entirely to pooh-pooh it – it confirmed the absolutely historical character of the Mosaic account of the Creation as given in Genesis' (Butler, 71). Today, of course, it is a bold, not to say a foolhardy, biblical scholar who either champions the sacred text against the received opinions of scientists or strives to reconcile it with them.

Changes in philosophy, like those in scientific thought to which they are often closely linked, can be seen as threatening to Christianity. Aubrey reported of Edward Davenant (d. *c.*1679), vicar of Gillingham, Dorset, and a great mathematician, that he could not endure to hear of Cartesian philosophy: '"for", sayd he, "if a new philosophy is brought in, a new divinity will shortly follow"'; 'and', reflected Aubrey, 'he was right' (Aubrey, 1.201). Such apprehensions had substance when the new philosophy was a liberal one. The Whig Latitudinarian clergy were of this tendency and attracted a scathing attack from Henry Sacheverell in his pamphlet *Character of a Low Churchman* (1701): 'He believes very little or no Revelation, and had rather lay his faith upon the substantial Evidence of his own Reason than the precarious Authority of Divine Testimony ... He thinks the Articles of the Church too Stiff, Formal and Straitlaced a Rule to confine his Faith in. He looks on the censuring of False Doctrine as a dogmatic Usurpation, an Intrusion upon that Human Liberty which he sets up as the Measure and Extent of his Belief' (Balleine, 138n).

Liberalism, however, survived Sacheverell. William Paley** taught that, since the Thirty-Nine Articles contained 'about 240 distinct propositions, many of them inconsistent with each other', they should be regarded merely as 'articles of peace' (*DNB*). In 1772 and 1774 a group of Anglican clergymen known as the Feathers Tavern Association, and including in their number John Conant, incumbent of two Kentish parishes, petitioned the House of Commons against compulsory subscription to the Thirty-Nine Articles (Price, 119–20). The petitions failed but the views which they represented were reinforced in the nineteenth century by the new critical scholarship. The brothers Hare significantly entitled a joint publication *Guesses at Truth*, and some of the clergy began to see inherent virtues in uncertainty and disagreement. In her novel *The Perpetual Curate*, Mrs Oliphant describes a conversation between two clerical brothers, Gerald and Frank Wentworth. Gerald, who is on the point of entering the church of Rome, complains that 'in England it seems to be the rule of faith that every man may believe as he pleases'; to which Frank replies by defending 'a Church happily so far imperfect, that a man can put his life to best account in it, without absolutely delivering his intellect up to a set of doctrines' (434–5). Stewart Headlam thought that religious doubts were 'probably of divine inspiration', and that the real spiritual danger lay in submission to authority (Norman, 103). It is significant of a changed atmosphere that the Clerical Subscription Act of 1865, which required only a general assent to the Thirty-Nine Articles, passed almost without opposition.

At times, however, conservatives rallied to the defence of ancient values. In 1852 George Denison wrote to another clergyman: 'When I spoke of "objective truth", what I meant by it … is, the body of truth delivered to us by the Creeds, with the interpretation affixed of the essential meaning of each Article by Catholic tradition … That a branch of the Catholic Church should admit … the very slightest departure from … such interpretation … would amount … to a forfeiture of its Catholic character.' Ten years later he poured scorn on the notion that the educated and the uneducated might have differing notions of what constituted truth: 'The use and application of intellect, and the culture of it in those to whom it has been given … is simply that of confirming themselves and others in the implicit acceptance of what has been revealed.' In 1872 he strongly opposed Archbishop's Tait's proposal that the use of the Athanasian Creed be made voluntary, and in 1891 was writing to his wife: 'We are clearly come to a time in which Objective Truth is set aside to make room for subjective Truth, that is … the truth of God and simplicity of Faith is set aside for every man's "View" of what is meant by "Faith". It is the last step in the road to General Disbelief … it hides itself in the plausibility and sentimentality of the time' (Denison, 13, 80, 124–5, 351).

This view of doctrine became harder to hold as time went by. More and more clergy came to the view of Samuel Butler's Ernest Pontifex 'that it matters little what profession … a man may make, provided only he follows it out with charitable inconsistency' (Butler, 322); or shared the secret thoughts of Ernest Raymond's Canon Humbert Welcome who, as he stood before his confirmation classes, 'was troubled now and then at having to teach them much which he could no longer believe, but happy to be teaching these dear young things to be good' (Raymond, 175). At the time when Raymond wrote his novel, soon after the Second World War, relativism was becoming respectable. Mervyn Stockwood** quoted words of A.J. Balfour to summarize his own theological position:

> Our highest truths are but half-truths,
> Think not to settle down for ever in any truth.
> Make use of it as a tent in which to pass a summer's night,
> But build no house in it, or it will be your tomb. (Stockwood, 91)

Contemporaries, living in an age when the scientific world view and intellectual liberalism have become orthodoxy, may be tempted to suppose that those who resisted their influence on religious thought were reactionary. It is important to point out, therefore, that when, under the pressure of scepticism and rationalism, a sense of the numinous is lost, the spiritual baby has been thrown out with the intellectual bath water. The problem remains as it was described by Bishop Tait at the height of the controversy about *Essays and Reviews*: 'the great evil is that the liberals are deficient in religion and the religious are deficient in liberality' (Battiscombe, *Keble* 330). The modern mind, like the mind of any past age, is culture-conditioned, with its own deficiencies and blind spots; and the spiritually minded are called to what P.L. Berger, in *A Rumour of Angels*, calls 'cognitive deviance' – a refusal to see the world in precisely the same terms as does the prevailing habit of mind. I myself, finding cognitive deviance both difficult and indispensable, constantly remind myself of Dean Inge's remark that he who marries the spirit of the age soon finds himself a widower.

We turn to changing clerical attitudes to dogma, taking as our example the relative emphasis laid upon the severity and upon the love of God.

A phenomenally successful devotional work entitled *The Practice of Piety*, published anonymously in the early seventeenth century, was probably written by Lewis Bayly (d.1631), then Bishop of Bangor, and based upon sermons delivered when he was incumbent of All Saints, Evesham. References to the love of God in this book are few; the emphasis is upon the outraged and inflexible divine judge. Christ is seen, not as the self-revelation of the Father, but as the one upon whom is visited the punishment which the sinner most justly deserves. 'The wicked transgresseth and the just is punished; the guilty is let escape, and the innocent is arraigned; the malefactor is acquitted and the harmless condemned; what the evil man deserveth, the good man suffereth ... Man sinneth and God dieth' (Bayly, 698).

By contrast, one of the most widely admired devotional books of recent years, W.H. Vanstone's** *Love's Endeavour, Love's Expense*, perceives God as most perfectly made known in the love of the suffering Christ:

Drained is love in making full;
Bound in setting others free;
Poor in making many rich;
Weak in giving power to be.

Therefore He Who Thee reveals
Hangs, O Father, on that Tree
Helpless; and the nails and thorns
Tell of what Thy love must be.

Both Bayly and Vanstone are typical of their time; the tendency over the centuries has been away from an emphasis on judgment and towards an emphasis on love. But in every age too there have been those who have withstood the tendencies of their time as well as those who have reinforced them.

It has been widely believed by the clergy – as indeed the Athanasian Creed, which according to the *Book of Common Prayer* should be recited annually at thirteen major festivals, commands them to believe – that a great part of the human race are destined – or even predestined – to damnation of the sort zestfully described in *The Practice of Piety*. 'To the damned nothing remaines but hellish torments, which knows neither ease of pain, nor end of time. From the Judgment Seat thou must be thrust by Angels ... into the bottomless Lake of utter darkness, that perpetually burns with fire and brimstone. Whereunto ... there shall be such weeping, woes and wailing that ... it shall seem unto thee a Hel [sic], before thou goest into Hel, but to hear it' (Bayly, 84–5). John White, Rector of Barsham in Suffolk during the reign of James I, declared: 'we certainly knowe by the scriptures and without controversie believe, no small part of mankind, in God's decree and eternal purpose, to stand reprobate and rejected from salvation ... from all eternitie prepared ... to destruction' (Hart, *CC* 73–4). Even the sunny pages of Traherne's *Centuries* are shadowed by the occasional reference to hell; though, typically, his hell is psychological rather than physical (1.48).

There views persisted. William Paley was forbidden by the head of his Cambridge College to defend the thesis 'Eternal punishment contradicts the attributes of divinity' at his degree viva voce, and was required to take the opposite position (*DNB*). The Evangelical Samuel Walker of Truro urged his hearers in 1755 'to think of the body dwelling in flames! ... And this is but the half, perhaps the lesser half of man's eternal misery' (Hart, *ECCP* 43). William Grimshaw* taught, with some of the ancient Fathers, that a part of the happiness of the redeemed would consist in contemplating the misery of the damned. James Woodforde 'lent Dr Clarke a pamphlet called a sure Guide to Hell ... and a very good moral book it is, taken properly' (Woodforde, 1.33). John Skinner attempted to reform a drunken thief and deter a would-be suicide by warning them of the torments to which they might be exposed in another world. He told a parishioner who claimed not to believe in hell that 'there was an end to all reformation if he had brought his mind to this belief' (Skinner, 64–5, 75, 44).

John Henry Newman's** Anglican sermons, phenomenal in their influence, were founded on a deep sense of the vileness of sin and of its appalling consequences in the next world; hence on an appeal to fear. A hearer wrote: 'Under God's grace, I will raise my superstructure of love upon a solid groundwork of holy *fear* – the *beginning* of wisdom, the persuader of men' (Faber, 183n). Similarly, John Keble insisted on the doctrine of eternal punishment largely because he thought that the ordinary man was kept from sin not by love of God but by fear of hell. 'There is never a boy or girl going up and down the street but can catch in a moment the idea of there being no Hell and apply it when tempted to deadly sin' (Battiscombe, *Keble* 326). William Andrew* fell out with one of his congregation at Witchingham because he taught that men were born in sin and deserved eternal wrath from the moment they were born (Chadwick, *Andrew* 31).

In the traditional view, God's punishments bulked large in this world as well as in the next. In one of his regenerate moods Robert Herrick** wrote:

Make, make me Thine, my gracious God,
Or with thy staffe, or with thy rod;
And be the blow too what it will,
Lord, I will kisse it, though it kill:
Beat me, bruise me, rack me rend me,
Yet, in torments, I'le commend Thee. (Herrick, 343)

On the gentler side we find George Herbert adjuring God:

Throw away Thy rod,
Throw away Thy wrath;
O my God,
Take the gentle path.
Then let wrath remove,
Love will do the deed;
For with love
Stony hearts will bleed. (from 'Discipline')

A little later we find William Dunkin, vicar of St Laurence, Ramsgate, Kent, teaching (and getting into trouble for it) that those preaching too much about judgment should have their tongues clipped, for God was a God of mercy (Matthews, *Walker* 215). We find Thomas Traherne writing: 'By Love alone is God enjoyed, by Love alone delighted in, by Love alone approached or admired. His nature requires Love, thy nature requires Love. The law of Nature commands thee to Love Him: the Law of His Nature, and the Law of thine' (Traherne, 1.71).

John Dryden, in his 'The Character of a Good Parson', described his subject in this way:

He preached the joys of heaven, and pains of hell;
And warned the sinner with becoming zeal;
But on eternal mercy loved to dwell.
He taught the gospel rather than the law;
And forced himself to drive; but loved to draw. (Christmas, 50)

John Fletcher*, deflected from being a minister early in life because he felt unable to accept predestination, wrote that the truth on which he fed was that God is love; 'and love in us, being His image, is the sum and substance of all moral and spiritual excellence' (Macdonald, *Fletcher* 15, 143). He gave up his superintendance of Lady Huntingdon's seminary at Trevecca because he insisted against her on 'the possibility of salvation for all men' (Benson, *Fletcher* 140). Patrick Bronte**, preaching at the funeral of his curate Willy Weightman, said approvingly: 'He thought it better and more scriptural, to make the love of God rather than the fear of hell, the ruling motive for obedience' (Colloms, 89). Francis Kilvert* 'abhorred' the Athanasian Creed, presumably because of its stress on damnation (Kilvert, 3.27). Stewart Head-lam, who had had to leave his first curacy because he had spoken of the possibility of pardon in a future state (Reckitt, 62), told the East London Secular Society in 1876 that eternal punishment was 'a horrid doctrine'; on another occasion he called it 'a monstrous libel upon God' (Norman, 102). By the early twentieth century, W.B. Hankey, of St Mary's, Graham Street, a strict Anglo-Catholic, was teaching that God will find a place in his kingdom for non-Christians who have had no opportunity to be anything else (M.K.C. Strong (ed.), *The Church of the Saints*, 1907, 25). Conrad Noel** was a universalist; he used to say of Roman Catholics that they believed not in All Souls Day but in *some* Souls Day (Reckitt, 163).

Sometimes the maturing of personal spirituality has led to a lighter emphasis on judgment and a heavier on love. Thomas Fuller wrote of William Perkins, preacher in St Andrew's parish, Cambridge in the sixteenth century: 'He would pronounce the word "damn" with such an emphasis as left a doleful echo in his auditors' ears a good while after ... [but] ... in his older age he ... remitted much of his former rigidness; often professing that to preach mercy was the proper office of the minister of the gospel' (Fuller, *HS* 80). John Newton, who would in early life have accepted the view that 'a God all mercy is a God unjust', concluded as he grew more compassionate that God must be at least as compassionate as he was (Martin, *Newton* 364).

In the early years of his ministry, Charles Simeon was a judgmental preacher. As love assumed a central position in his life, this characteristic disappeared. He said 'Love should be the spring of all actions and especially of a minister's.' He was appalled by the censoriousness he found among Christians and wrote: 'I regard love as wealth; and as I would resist a man who should come to rob my house, so would I a man who would weaken my regard for any human being' (Hopkins, *Simeon* 65, 171, 134).

John Henry Newman once wrote: 'What counts with each of us is not the beliefs to which we give notional but those to which we give real assent.' Clergy loyal, as clergy are expected to be, to the traditional teaching of the church, have always had to balance ideas of judgment against those of mercy, ideas of retribution against those of reconciliation. Temperament, theology and the spirit of the age have all played a part in shaping the emphases of individuals; but at the deepest level it has been personal spirituality which has been the determining factor.

5

Running a Parish

You are God's joy for willing what He willeth.
(Traherne, 1.53)

A contemporary said of the notorious John Mitford**: 'He is no more fit to be a parson than I am to be the Angel Gabriel'; a modern author that: 'His lack of religious conviction in no way interfered with the overall supervision of his parish responsibilities' (Colloms, 102, 107). Those comments throw into sharp relief the distinction between the spiritual and the institutional functions of the parish priest.

What should be the relation between them? The theologian Jürgen Moltmann urged the clergy of the diocese of Canterbury at their 1989 conference to 'forget about the Church and think about the Kingdom'. He was advising them to give second place to the machinery which they service, and first place to the objectives which the machinery exists to serve. The ideal is unexceptionable and liberating, but it has never been easy for the parochial clergy to live up to it. On the other hand, it may be that running a parish can be an exercise in creative spirituality; that serving the Church and seeking the Kingdom can be made to coincide. This chapter explores these issues.

One scans Ralph Josselin's* diary in vain for any indication that his parish involved him in financial or administrative affairs. But even for his time he was an exception. There are two chapters in George Herbert's* *A Priest to the Temple* concerning these matters – 'The Parson's Church' and 'The Parson with his Churchwardens'. With regard to the church, Herbert taught, it is the priest's duty to see to its state of repair, its cleanliness, its state of decoration and its furnishings. This was not an onerous task for Herbert himself, since he was a wealthy man; but for large numbers of his predecessors and successors it has been a burden, sapping them of energy and diverting them from the care of souls. Until modern times the upkeep of the chancel was the responsibility of the incumbent, of the nave that of his parishioners; the need for resources for the former and the lack of authority to ensure the latter pressed heavily on many clergy. Few were as fortunate as James Woodforde*, whose Oxford college (patron of his living) paid for chancel repairs after a storm (Woodforde, 1.242, 248, 252, 269). Unhappy in a different way were the clergy serving churches in the hands of neglectful lay impropriators; they had no means at all of ensuring the good order of the building which was the centre of their worshipping life.

An ill-maintained or ill-ordered church has usually meant a neglectful or defeated priest. In one of his rare ecclesiastical references Gilbert White** of Selborne wrote regretfully 'we have many livings of two or three hundred pounds a year, whose houses of worship make little better appearance than dove-cotes' (White, 64). Francis Kilvert* recorded his first experience of St Harmon's: 'My heart sank ... like a stone as I entered the door. A bare cold squalid interior and high ugly boxes for seats, a three-decker pulpit and desk, no stove, a flimsy altar rail, a ragged faded altar cloth, a singing gallery with a broken organ, a dark little box for a vestry and a roof in bad repair, admitting the rain' (Kilvert, 3.289).

More positively, the restoring or building of churches has been a statement of spiritual commitment. George Herbert planned and contributed to the restoration of three churches – Leighton Bromswold, Fugglestone and Bemerton. Walton reports him as saying of his decision at Leighton Bromswold to place the reading desk and the pulpit at equal heights that 'they should neither have a precedency ... but that prayer and preaching, being equally useful, might ... [have] ... an equal honour and estimation' (Walton, 193). John Keble* rebuilt Hursley, designing the pews so that it was almost impossible not to kneel when praying (Battiscombe, *Keble* 286). Robert Hawker* re-built Morwenstow; typically, he deliberately used both good and bad materials to symbolize Catholic inclusiveness (Brendon, *Hawker* 95). William Bennett* built St Barnabas, Pimlico from the subscriptions of the rich in order to serve the urban poor. At Leeds Walter Hook* demolished the parish church and built a new one. He not only provided more accommodation but secured that a substantial proportion of it was free. The church was designed for congregational participation, and beautified on the principle that 'a handsome church ... [is] ... a kind of standing sermon' (Stephens, *Hook* 229). In modern times George Carey**, later to become Archbishop of Canterbury, undertook a massive and costly reconstruction of his church of St Nicholas, Durham, as an essential element in the introduction of a new style of ministry and worship. Not everyone was pleased with the result, but a visitor said to Carey: 'As I wandered round your warm, brightly lit ... building it seems to say, "you are loved and accepted, a member of God's family; he is your heavenly Father and wants you to enter into fellowship with him", and I leave encouraged knowing that he cares for me' (Carey, 145–6).

Over the centuries the demands on the minister as a general fund-raiser have expanded and then contracted. They expanded as the church assumed greater responsibilities for education and welfare within the parish and for missionary work outside it; and contracted as the secular community took over many of the church's responsibilities. The heaviest obligations were undertaken by the great Victorian parish priests. Charles Lowder** built two churches, opened several schools, social agencies and a Working Men's Institute, and had to find most of the money for his Mission himself. His personal preference was for working with individuals, and the constant need to raise money sat heavily on him. One of his colleagues recalled: 'It was a small matter that sometimes he could not pay the curates, but it became a very painful difficulty that he often was not able to pay even the school teachers.' He became so disheartened that at one point it took the joint efforts of his (clearly dedicated) curates to prevent him from resigning (Ellsworth, *Lowder* 123). No wonder W.C.E. Newbolt writes: 'Many a priest who could have faced cheerfully the ordinary routine of the parish, has found himself quite broken down by the annual burden of a sum of money which must be raised to finance the current schemes of his parochial administration' (Newbolt, 42).

Until 1868 it was in principle possible for a parish to raise money for ecclesiastical purposes by levying a compulsory church rate authorized by a vestry meeting which all local residents were entitled to attend. These meetings were often lively affairs. They gave local Dissenters and dissident Anglicans a golden opportunity to state their grievances. Wise clergy, especially in the towns, were slow either to ask for a rate or to enforce it rigorously once granted. Henry Fardell* described the situation in Wisbech in 1841: 'The following have declared they will not contribute to a rate: All the Dissenters ... and a great number whose names I am unable to recollect. Another party object to a voluntary contribution, & another say they will only give provided there is a rate, which is as much to say they will only give what the law compels them to give – and another party seem unwilling to give at all.' Fardell incurred much odium that year by refusing to attend a vestry meeting. In 1845 he presided at a meeting which granted a rate by a substantial majority, and was disgusted when the local justices refused to proceed against Dissenters who refused to pay (Fardell, 114–15).

Fardell's troubles were minor compared with those of Henry Michell Wagner** at Brighton. There, between 1835 and 1852, vestry meetings gave Dissenters and Radicals the opportunity to express their opposition to the principle of a compulsory rate, to keep it at a level well below what was necessary, and, on several occasions, to prevent it being levied at all. Eventually the vicar, who had insisted on the compulsory rate because it was the law of the land, put expediency before principle and headed a voluntary subscription to pay for major repairs to his church of St Nicholas, which was falling into serious disrepair (Wagner, 61–74). The pastoral harm the church rate inflicted was one of the reasons for its abolition.

Direct giving for parochial purposes through a Sunday offertory is a relatively modern practice. For most of our period offertories were for charity. An attempt in East London in the 1840s to raise money to run newly built churches by weekly collections was thought to be popish and was abandoned when it proved unsuccessful (Chadwick, *VC* 1.329). Attitudes changed later on, and direct giving has become the most favoured method of fund-raising, for both practical and theological reasons. David Watson* revolutionized the finances of St Cuthbert's, York, by insisting on the principles that it was positively immoral to go to unbelievers for money and incumbent on believers to give generously in return for the salvation freely given them (Saunders, *Watson* 106–7). Nicholas Rivett-Carnac**, serving an inner city London church, presided over an increase of giving from £2000 in 1972 to £150,000 in 1988. Just as the congregation were expected to tithe their personal income, so the parish gave away well over a tenth of what it received (Cooke, *Rivett-Carnac* 200).

Other methods of money-raising have involved moral questions; chiefly whether gambling and entertainment are permissible. Astonishingly, William Grimshaw* invested in the state lottery; he won, and the proceeds went towards building a Methodist chapel (Baker, *Grimshaw* 222). William Bennett made no use of pew rents or the parish rate at St Barnabas, Pimlico, and abolished church rates in Frome. He refused to raise money by way of entertainments. Instead he asked for it to be given and got it, no doubt in part because he was a lavish giver himself. The Evangelical Samuel Garratt** wrote in 1902 that he believed at aiming at spiritual ends by spiritual means, and deprecated 'amusement, the fancy fair, the bazaar, the carnival, the theatrical entertainment, farces and all kinds of frivolities, by means of which people who ... do not care enough for what concerns God's work to give without a quid pro quo, may be led to open their purses' (Garrett, 119). Cuthred Compton, vicar of Shepherdswell, Kent, in the 1920s, supported a fete to raise funds for church heating, but resisted the request for an annual event on the grounds that it was spiritually necessary to rely for the most part on 'real giving' (*SPM* Sept. 1922). In the 1930s Archbishop William Temple appealed to his clergy to have no raffles or lotteries at their bazaars (F.A. Iremonger, *William Temple*, 1948, 445). By contrast, at Woolwich in the 1960s Nicolas Stacey** started bingo, and felt it was one of the few occasions on which he met his parishioners' needs as well as his own (Stacey, 156–8). In the same period Christian Stewardship campaigns were often based on the principle of relying solely on direct giving; most stewardship parishes eventually succumbed again if not to the financial then to the social attractions of fetes and bazaars. By the 1990s my own parish of Shepherdswell was following almost universal practice by relying chiefly on direct giving but also by having fund-raising events for church and charity at which small-scale gambling was permitted.

Like getting, spending has a moral dimension. Clergy have usually thought it a part of their responsibility to encourage their congregations to give to causes outside their own neighbourhood. Kilvert recorded a well attended Church Missionary Society meeting at Langley Burrell, and noted that the parish had raised £18 1s od for the Society that year (1874). 'We hope some year to raise it to £20' (Kilvert, 3.99–100). It was part of the tradition of the impoverished parish of Portsea under its great reforming vicars to give generously to foreign missions. At St Cuthbert's, York, in David Watson's time, an annual gift day raised enough money to support a missionary in Taiwan (Saunders, *Watson* 115). However, some parish priests have had to contend with what might be called the Jellyby syndrome: R.W. Evans commented in the mid-nineteenth century that the laity were more likely to support overseas missions than the local school (Evans, 175–6).

We turn to administration, and first to relations with parochial officialdom. George Herbert adjured the country parson to impress upon his church-wardens the dignity and the responsibility of their office, 'it being the greatest honour of this world, to do God and His chosen service' (Herbert, XXIX). The wardens' duties were and are onerous. In the past they had civil as well as ecclesiastical duties and they have been expected to keep a watchful eye on the incumbent himself. As well as enquiring into every aspect of the minister's discharge of his professional duties, Archbishop William Laud's Visitation Articles of 1635 enquired whether he was incontinent, a drunkard, a gambler, a swearer, unscholarly, kept bad company 'or is otherwise offensive or scandalous'. When wardens were given such ample opportunity to inform on their minister, his effectiveness and peace of mind would largely depend upon his relations with them.

Relations can be uneasy. William Jones** of Broxbourne clashed with a churchwarden named Rogers, who did his best to prevent him from being promoted from curate to vicar, and who cut the church bell-ropes while a peal was being rung in honour of Jones's institution (Hart, *ECCP* 57–8). When Charles Simeon* was appointed to Holy Trinity church, Cambridge, the wardens arranged for locks on the proprietary pews, so that when the normal occupants stayed away no one else could occupy their seats. The congregation was confined to the aisles and the edges of the church. For several years the wardens also prevented Simeon from holding an evening service (Hopkins, *Simeon* 38, 43).

John Skinner* had trouble with his wardens, as with almost everyone else. He was exasperated by their ignorance and incompetence, and above all by their failure to attend church; in their absence there was misbehaviour which he would have relied on them to correct. But a parish priest has not had to be cantankerous to have trouble. When Walter Hook went to Leeds the wardens, anxious to keep the church rate as low as possible, refused expenditure on tattered surplices and dog-eared service hooks, and grumbled about the increased sums spent on sacramental wine as the congregation grew larger (Stephens, *Hook* 224). Dick Sheppard* parted company acrimoniously with a churchwarden whose custom it was to enter St Martin's just before the communion and to leave immediately afterwards (Scott, *Sheppard* 74).

Until modern times it was not a requirement that wardens should be Anglicans. Nicholas Blundell, a Lancashire country gentleman and a Roman Catholic, was elected churchwarden at Sefton in 1714. He worked hard at his duties, possibly hoping that the church would be restored to Roman Catholic worship should the Stuart line be restored (Blundell, 125). Robert Hawker had a Dissenter as a warden. In Leeds, in 1842 and 1843, the local Chartists thought it worth their while to control the election of wardens. Walter Hook handled the situation with his usual dexterity, declaring to a meeting in 1843 'that he had never had such honourable, straightforward and gentlemanly church-wardens, and that he could not wish for better unless they were to give him members of the Church of England' (Chadwick, *VC* 1.336).

The other key official used to be the parish clerk. He had to be able to read, write and sing; he made the practical arrangements for worship; he wore a surplice and led the congregation in the responses and the psalms. James Woodforde treated well the three clerks who served him during his time at Weston Longueville, and had few complaints to make of them. They did odd jobs for him, frequently dined in his kitchen and received gifts from him. When 'poor old James Smith' was dying, Woodforde supported him with money and an occasional visit. William Cole** had a clerk who was 'a quiet good-tempered man', and whom he treated very kindly; but unfortunately he was a hopeless drunkard for whom a deputy had constantly to be found (Cole, 30). Skinner found it impossible to get a clerk to his liking. One, James Widcombe, embezzled money and was committed to prison. Skinner lamented, in terms which parish priests down the centuries have echoed, 'I am like the captain of a king's ship sent to sea with a bad crew, and no officer I can rely on' (Skinner, 383–4).

The vestry elected both civil and ecclesiastical officers. James Widcombe, as well as being clerk, was the elected overseer of the poor, and was able therefore to rob both priest and parish.

In more recent times the link between the civil and the ecclesiastical parish has been broken. In the countryside, parish councils replaced vestries for civil purposes in 1894. Parochial church councils, at first optional bodies instituted by progressive incumbents such as W.A. Fremantle of St Mary's, Bryanston Square, under whom Samuel Barnett* served his curacy, became statutory everywhere after the First World War. Nowadays, while in law the wardens are elected by parishioners as a whole, in fact they are chosen by and from the faithful, as are the other church officers. This does not mean however that the parish priest is spared the problems of his predecessors. Infuriated by one of his parochial church council at Portsea, Cyril Garbett** sent for him and began their conversation by declaring: 'What is the matter with you, Mr –, is that you're a humbug'. Mr – transferred his allegiance to another parish (Smyth, *Garbett* 104). Arthur Hopkinson**, Vicar of Banstead, Surrey, in the years after the First World War, dreaded PCC meetings, and spent wakeful nights before them (Hopkinson, 91). Roy Catchpole** has described the organizational havoc and emotional trauma created by church officers using resignation as a personal weapon (Catchpole, *GMDC* 43).

In the whole of his five volume diary James Woodforde makes only two references to general parochial administration. In his book of guidance to the clergy, *The Bishopric of Souls*, published in 1856, R.W. Evans mentions it once, disparagingly. But even before Evans wrote his book, parishes were developing systems of organization, education and welfare which demanded considerable administrative skills and which took priests away from the functions for which they had been ordained, sometimes with their actice connivance, sometimes to their regret. In time, as the state took over initiatives which the church had pioneered, some demands lessened, but others took their place. In the twentieth century, and increasingly as the century has gone on, the parish priest has needed the skills related to the steady growth of participatory democracy and the accompanying stress upon consultation and meetings; to the growing bureaucratization and regulation of life; and to the need to work with and through secular institutions, especially in the field of social service. The parish priest who retains his chairmanship of a local church school's board of governors is caught up in a network of time-consuming obligations which are acceptable only if he manages to hold the end steadily in view despite the increasing complexity of the means. Nor does the Church herself set a good example. Many clergy must feel inclined to echo the words of Thomas Hancock**: 'the saddest characteristic of the Church in our age is an utterly preposterous faith in mere organization' (Reckitt, 20). Since this defect is one to which women are less prone than men, it may be the Church will suffer less from it in the twenty-first century.

Traditionally the parish priest has led his people from the front. When the young Christopher Chavasse** went to Barrow in 1919, he began by telling his parishioners to expect no immediate changes; and then within months turned the whole parish upsidedown. He justified his alterations by claiming that they had been imposed upon him by enthusiastic parishioners. Some resentment was aroused among those who were conscious of the true state of affairs, but since so many of the changes were obviously for the better the bulk of his people supported him. His biographer comments dryly: 'If the art of leadership is to make others believe that what you want is what they have suggested, Christopher Chavasse was a great leader' (Gummer, *Chavasse* 74).

The laity have indeed often preferred strong leadership. When the idealistic Edward Miller tried to set up a Church Council in his remote Warwickshire parish of Butler's Marston where he served from 1868 to 1879, he was told that everyone would prefer to leave decisions to him. A missions committee lasted a few years and then fell apart amid a welter of jealousies, leaving the parson to take over. An attempt to establish a reading room committee in his next parish of Bucknell, Oxfordshire, failed in the same way (Colloms, 53).

Some clergy have led through persuasion, others through personality. By his own account, Walter Hook would never press change upon his people, but would teach them until they said to him 'How inconsistent you are! Why do you not do as you tell us you ought to do?;' to which his reply was 'Oh very well; if you wish it I will do so and so' (Stephens, *Hook* 357). His biographer writes of Dick Sheppard: 'Besieged by doubts about almost everything he did, a basic, overriding certainty carried his PCC staunchly with him; sometimes they even had ideas of their own' (Scott, *Sheppard* 107).

Two great Evangelicals involved their people in leadership, and suffered for it. Charles Simeon organized a team of twelve lay 'stewards', who managed the church finances and led six 'societies' which met for Bible study and fellowship. At first he was always present at meetings, but in time the pressure of other responsibilities and of bad health led to long absences. Left to itself, the system threw up a number of lay people who, without Simeon's knowledge or permission, became itinerant preachers. Simeon's attempt to restrain them led to a long and debilitating row (Hopkins, *Simeon* 47–9).

At St Michael's, York, in the 1970s David Watson and his congregation commissioned a group of male elders to share pastoral responsibility; later the parish was divided into areas, with area groups meeting for prayer, study and mutual support. The pastoral life of the parish could not have been sustained without delegation, and there were great spiritual gains. It is likely, however, that the dissensions and the schism which followed, although similar to many which occur in large evangelical and charismatic congregations, were facilitated by Watson's desire to share his authority (Watson, *YAMG* chs 15 and 16).

One whole dimension of administration is determined by the numbers to be ministered to. In the past, parishes varied vastly in size; in the mid-nineteenth century the parish of Leeds boasted a population of 150,000, that of Childerley, Cambridgeshire, of 54. Nowadays numbers vary less, but whereas the average parish of the past contained a few hundred souls, a priest nowadays is responsible for a population of thousands. Dr Johnson's remark, that a London parish was a very comfortless thing, for the clergyman seldom knew the face of one in ten of his parishioners (quoted Martin, *Newton* 275), is now of wider application. A priest is able to perform his duties only because the great majority of his people make no call upon his services – but that in itself is a perpetual challenge. He can seek consolation in words of Walter Hook: 'The cure of 20,000 souls would not be to me more arduous than of 9,000; for why? in either case it is impossible to attend to them all, and God does not require impossibilities at our hands' (Stephens, *Hook* 178).

Large teams serving large parishes have not been uncommon. Robert Bickersteth, who became Rector of St-Giles-in-the-Fields, London, in 1850, had a team of seven curates, five readers from the Church Pastoral Aid Society and seven London City missionaries (Hennell, 60). In 1864 Henry Michell Wagner, vicar of Brighton, presided over nineteen churches, nine of which had been built by himself and his family; a contemporary referred to his kingdom as 'a bishopric within a bishopric' (Wagner, 59). When Christopher Chavasse went to St Helens in 1910, a population of 23,000 was served by a parish church, four mission churches, five or six clergy, and sufficient Church Army captains and lady workers to make an almost daily check upon parishioners (Gummer, *Chavasse* 40). By contrast, Walter Hook met the needs of his 150,000 parishioners by creating by Act of Parliament seventeen other parishes in the city of Leeds, to all of which he as Vicar of Leeds was patron.

On a more modest scale, many Victorian parish priests dealt with the influx of a working-class population by erecting one or more mission churches within the parish, and employing curates to care for them. This was the course adopted by the liberal John Ellerton, incumbent of Barnes, Middlesex from 1876 to 1884. To serve the poor district of Westfields within his parish, he purchased for £80 an iron church holding two hundred people and no longer required in inner London, and transported it to its new home (Whale, 141–3).

The ministry of clergy in large parishes unblessed with sufficient assistance can be distorted by the weight of their duties. Before Hook went to Leeds, most of the occasional offices for the whole town were conducted at the parish church. His predecessor, together with his curate, spent three and a half hours every day taking marriages; baptized and churched in bulk twice a day; and conducted burials two or three times a day (Stephens, *Hook* 222). Even today, when clerical services are less in demand, funerals can absorb an unconscionable proportion of a town priest's time.

The problem of numbers has a second aspect – that of the proportion of parishioners who take part in church life. In the early part of our period this was not, in one sense, a difficulty, since church attendance was legally enforceable. Josselin, noting in 1663 'divers of the ruder sort of people hearing', commented 'the statute of paying 1s when absent from divine service is more than the feare of gods command' (Josselin, 500). But, from the end of the seventeenth century, the voluntary principle was slowly established, first in fact and then in law, and the clergy had to rely more and more on their own efforts if they were to have full churches.

To measure results in terms of numbers is in principle quite wrong. J.B. Lightfoot, Bishop of Durham from 1879 to 1889, forbade his clergy to count heads lest they should be unduly elated or depressed (Melinsky, 162). Few clergy, however, have been holy enough to follow his advice. Some have had the stimulus of 'success'. The Evangelical Edmund Knox, incumbent of Kibworth Beauchamp, Leicestershire, in the 1880s, filled the 550 seats in his church on Sunday evenings from a population of 1500. The small town also supported three other places of worship (Chadwick, *VC* 2.161). People queued for hours to get into St Martin's in the Fields when Dick Sheppard was vicar (Roberts, *Sheppard* 100–1). When Mervyn Stockwood** took over at St Matthew's Moorfields in 1941 his first Sunday evening People's Service attracted some thirty people. Six months later the numbers had doubled and then doubled again; soon the church was full to overflowing (Stockwood, 43).

The 'success' of some has made the 'failure' of others harder to bear. Clergy have always been anxious about the size of their congregations. Josselin lamented in 1647 'congregacion growes very thinne, oh lord doe not give my flocke over to loosenes and error' (Josselin, 93). Skinner was upset when attendances at Camerton, with its population of 800, sometimes dropped below 100. Robert Dolling* was oppressed, when he moved to Poplar in 1898, by his failure to persuade his new parishioners to worship in the numbers he was accustomed to at Landport or when he preached elsewhere. He reported sadly that on a Sunday evening he might expect no more than 200 out of a population of 10,000; 'the religious instinct is not there' (Osborne, *Dolling* 311, 313).

The modern priest is confronted with the perpetual challenge of the contrast between his actual and his potential congregation. At Shepherdswell in 1993, when the population was 1800, total Sunday attendances at two services could be as few as 60 and rarely exceeded 100. Although numbers were larger for great festivals, it was because more of the regular congregation made an effort to attend.

The most soul-destroying circumstance for a parish priest is that of a perpetually declining or obstinately minimal congregation. 'My congregation', said a late nineteenth-century vicar sadly, 'is waiting for me in the churchyard' (Chadwick, *VC* 2.160–1). The Kentish rural incumbent of the 1960s whose congregation was invariably in single figures and who took to drink was not untypical either in his experience or in its outcome.

The decline of congregations in modern times was not initially due to a lack of either quantity or quality in the clergy. The decline in fact began when both were improving. C.F.G. Masterman said at the end of the nineteenth century: 'If the works done in South London today ... had been done in Sodom and Gomorrah, they would have repented in dust and ashes' (Chadwick, *VC* 2.238). But, far from repenting, Londoners stayed away in droves, and in greater numbers as time went on. Eventually the situation provoked the sort of reaction described in the 1960s by Hunter Davies. A London curate, in a parish with a staff of six, reported that sixty years before his church had congregations of 550 in the evening and 400 in the morning. Now the numbers were 150 and 180, and it took the whole efforts of the staff to prevent them from getting smaller. The curate himself was going to become a full-time teacher in a comprehensive school, and work as a priest in the remainder of his time. In that way, he felt, he would be more Christianly useful (Hunter Davies, *The Other Half*, Panther Books 1968, 155–6; internal evidence suggests that the curate was Jeremy Hurst, who served with Nicolas Stacey at Woolwich).

Behind all these difficulties lies one huge sociological factor, which can be summed up in two aphorisms. Mervyn Stockwood observed that it would take a saint to empty a church in Surrey; while it has been famously remarked that the Church of England never lost the industrial working class, because it never gained them. As Horace Mann wrote in his census of religious worship in 1851 (which estimated that about half the population was not in church on any single Sunday): 'More especially in cities and large towns it is observable how absolutely insignificant a portion of the congregation is composed of artisans' (Flindall, 133). The clergy in urban working-class parishes have had to come to terms with that fact. They have not shirked the challenge; but it would be too much to say that they have met it. Even the most successful of the nineteenth-century slum priests brought no more than a fraction of their people into church. Chadwick tells the story of the urban clergyman who provided work for his unemployed parishioners. To show their gratitude, they attended church as a body – once (Chadwick, *VC* 2.262). At the beginning of this century 34.5% of the population of South Kensington worshipped regularly in an Anglican church; the percentage in Somers Town was 1.6 (Hastings, 66).

In the countryside too, the tendency has been for labourers to stay away from church, except when drawn in by a priest of exceptional powers or driven in by social pressures. Walton's charming picture of ploughmen resting at their work to join in prayer when the Bemerton church bell tolled, if true, describes an untypical situation (Walton, 213). Clergy responding to a bishop's Visitation in 1738 reported habitual non-attendance among 'the lowest ranks' (Russell, 30). Mandell Creighton** said that the difference between a Russian and an English peasant was that the one swears and gets drunk and goes to church, while the other swears and gets drunk and does not go to church. At Lark Rise, Oxfordshire, at the end of the nineteenth century, while nine out of ten of the villagers received the rites of passage at the parish church, only the children and a dozen of their elders attended regularly. 'The rest stayed at home, the women cooking and nursing, and the men, after an elaborate Sunday toilet ... eating, sleeping, reading the newspaper, and strolling round to see how their neighbours' pigs and gardens were looking' (Thompson, 209). It is only fair to report by way of contrast that Cyril Garbett remembered most of the popula- tion of Tongham coming to his father's church at least once a Sunday without any obvious coercion (Smyth, *Garbett* 31); and that the country clergyman R.W. Randall**, said in old age that he had seen no saintliness of life that exceeded the deep religion of the English peasant, and that sometimes when he was giving them communion he wanted to kneel down and kiss their horny hands (Chadwick, *VC* 2.167).

A priest saved work by the small size of his immediate flock is likely to have a conscience about the rest of his parishioners. They remain his responsibility and a charge upon his time and efforts. He may be as ineffective as Mr Ellison of Lark Rise whose response to the failure of his people to come to church was to berate those who actually attended (Thompson, 211). He may make huge and often unavailing efforts to increase numbers. He may engage in social service; a more altruistic course in the twentieth than in the nineteenth century, because the likelihood of those served becoming involved in church life is less.

In some circumstances a traditional ministry is still possible. Serving only

1800 people, I have been able to minister to the community at large: by general visiting, by visiting everyone at turning-points in life, and by being active in village secular life. I have been in a distinguished but fading tradition.

The problems of running a parish are hugely increased when a priest is responsible for more than one of them. Throughout Anglican history, this situation has obtained as often as not. Pluralism can lay such financial and administrative burdens on a priest that his whole ministry is warped. In the past a pluralist could always find curates to share his work with him. But in modern times that is not so. A single priest may have to care for as many as six or seven parishes; the care of as many buildings and Parochial Church Councils can leave him unable to minister in a personal way even to the relatively small numbers of churchgoers characteristic of the situation. I said to a Somerset priest responsible for five parishes 'I suppose your biggest problem is visiting'. 'No', was the reply; 'I don't do any; my biggest problem is administration.'

Despite the foregoing it could be argued that there is no necessary conflict between the spiritual and the institutional functions of the parish priest. Bernard Wilson, vicar of Portsea from 1901 to 1909, was both a devoted and highly successful pastor and an enthusiastic man of business. Not resting content with subsidizing the parish from his own considerable private means, he laboured to put its finances on a sound footing. After a long day in his parish he looked forward to spending the hours around midnight on the church accounts. He is alleged to have said: 'Let the laity by all means look after the doctrine, if only they will leave the finance to the clergy.' He was a phenomenon; but he died, worn out, at fifty-two (Smyth, *Garbett* 77).

Wilson has not been the only priest to find positive stimulus in the administrative aspect of his work. Samuel Barnett opposed the breaking up of large parishes, because he thought that they gave men with organizing powers their opportunity. Otherwise 'the best men ... become Bishops, and then they are apt to be strangled by their own gaiters' (Barnett, 1.194). William Bennett at Frome was an excellent teacher and pastor; but at the same time he zestfully controlled three curates, twelve district visitors, several schools and a vast number of welfare and devotional organizations. A curate wrote: 'Mr Bennett's love of order and method was very remarkable, and showed itself in every detail. Schools, classes, dispensary, provident clubs, soup kitchen, blanket and other charities were all in perfect working order, and his authority was felt in all the details of their management' (Bennett, 206).

In general the most effective parish priests have been those who have have not shirked the administrative and financial requirements of their office, but have subsumed the institutional within the spiritual, procedures within relationships. Mrs Barnett ascribed the lack of friction at St Jude's to the number of social occasions which oiled the wheels of parochial organization (Barnett, 1.16). Mervyn Stockwood laid the foundation for his extensive achievements at St Matthew Moorfields, Bristol, by assiduous visiting and socializing (Stockwood, 41). A friend pointed to one of the reasons for Dick Sheppard's achievements when he remarked that, in spite of his genius for organization, he had a deep distrust of all institutions (Roberts, *Sheppard* 120).

An account of the work of three parish priests illustrates how organizational gifts can serve spiritual ends in the differing circumstances presented by the passage of the centuries.

Bernard Gilpin's* parish of Houghton covered some fifty square miles. It contained between two and three thousand people distributed among at least sixteen villages and many isolated homes. Taking account of the parish's scattered nature, he held open house on Sundays throughout the winter, setting up tables for gentry, for farmers and for labourers. His living was worth £400 a year – a vast sum for the time – and he vigorously asserted his financial rights against those who sought to infringe them. He lived frugally himself, and used his income for the benefit of his people. He repaired and extended his rectory, and lodged there a score of the boys attending the Grammar School he had founded. He supported several students at university. He provided pensions for twenty-four of his poorest parishioners, and on Thursdays invited the poor to eat at his house. He distributed charity wherever he went, being best pleased when it was an incentive to industry, as when he gave his horse to a peasant who had lost one of his team and could not afford to buy another. He adjudicated among his flock to prevent them going to law.

For the most part Gilpin was a pastor and teacher; he spent much of his time on preaching tours in other, neglected, northern parishes. His management of his parish consisted in using his income to set up a miniature welfare state. Nothing else was called for or conceivable in the circumstances of the time (Collingwood, *Gilpin* passim).

Robert Dolling took over the Winchester College Mission of St Agatha's, Landport, in 1885. He served an impoverished population of 5000 people. There were fifty-one public houses and at least fifty brothels in the district.

In 1891 Dolling reported: 'We have put into the army 39 young men, into the navy 57 young men. We have emigrated to Australia, America and elsewhere 63. We have started in life over 100 young men who lived with us. We have reformed 25 thieves just out of gaol. We have sent to service and into shops about 100 girls. 25 girls have passed through our training home for from two to five years; there are 19 in it now. We have turned many drunkards into self-respecting, church-going people. We have rescued 144 fallen women, and got them into Homes. We have maintained, and are maintaining, in preventive Homes 124 children, snatched from the brink of ruin. We have shut up in the district over 50 brothels and have changed the whole aspect of the place. We house 6 old couples free of rent. We feed for a halfpenny a meal 180 children and 25 old people free twice a week during the winter. We teach over 500 children in our Sunday-schools, and 600 in our Day-schools. We have a large gymnasium, clubs for "rough lads" and "smooth lads", for intellectual young men and for card-playing old men. We have "socials" for our factory girls, mothers' meetings for our older women. We have a nigger troupe, an acrobatic troupe, dancing-class, and glee club; a sewing-class; a large temperance society and Band of Hope; a lending library, and three penny savings banks' (Osborne, *Dolling* 163–4).

It was typical of Dolling that he described his achievement in terms of people. In his ten years he provided the organizations and the buildings, including a new church, which made the achievement possible; but he would never have thought of assessing his work in those terms.

His theology, which was practical rather than theoretical, was incarnational. 'The secular and spiritual elements should interpenetrate in one religious unity of social life.' Although he came to disbelieve in 'salvation by clubs' and to put his principal effort into building up family life, he provided a plethora of social and recreational activities. He horrified some of his fellow-clergy by using dancing as a way of bringing young people together in controlled circumstances and by setting up a 'Communicants' Dancing Guild' (Osborne, *Dolling* 48, 99).

His conception of his wider responsibilities to his people brought Dolling into the public arena. He joined with a group of other clergy to set up a Vigilance Committee which lobbied the Town Council to secure a closer supervision of public houses. He was a crusader against sexual immorality, getting many brothels closed by making representations to landlords. He brought pressure to bear on the authorities through facts and figures collected by the Portsmouth Social Purity Organization. He was a member of the local School Board and of the Board of Guardians, but disliked workhouses, as he did 'all herding and cataloguing of human beings' (Osborne, *Dolling* 165). He never hesitated to express his views on political issues. He opposed Alfred Harmsworth, the gruesome newspaper magnate, when he stood for parliament at Portsmouth in the Conservative interest; though it was typical of him that he later became Harmsworth's close friend, and prevailed on him to pay for the boys' camps he organized at Broadstairs.

It was impossible to accuse Dolling of neglecting the spiritual well-being of his people in his passion for their social welfare. That worship should speak to them was his chief concern. Earlier in life he used to remark that Rome had retained the grandeur of worship and Dissent the simplicity; but that the Church of England had lost both. At St Agatha's his ritualism exceeded the bounds of legality; but so in a different direction did the informal Mission services which he held weekly after Evensong. Dolling taught that 'ceremonial ... could be safely employed with fitting dignity when it was felt to be not the swathings of a dead Christ, but the robe of a living one' (Osborne, *Dolling* 50, 116).

Dolling's work depended upon financial support from outside the parish. First and foremost he turned to Winchester College, but not to the College alone; he reckoned that he spent a day a week 'begging'. In his ten years at Landport he raised £50,000 from sources inside and outside the parish. When he was short of money he would call his people to a day of prayer from 5.30 a.m. to 10.00 p.m. Unlike other great Victorian priests he did not have substantial private means; he wrote that he went to St Agatha's poor and came away poorer still, because he had had to sell his library (Dolling, *TY* 52–3, 182).

He gave very little time to administration. His normal daily routine was to rise at 5.30 a.m. to call those of his household who had to get off to work. He went back to bed to read or write till 6.00 a.m., and spent the next hour in private conversation with other members of the motley crew who gathered round him in the parsonage. Between 7.00 a.m. and 8.30 a.m. he celebrated twice and read morning prayer. A clerk would take down correspondence as he ate breakfast, and he spent the whole morning seeing individuals. The afternoon and early evening were used flexibly, and after a church service of some kind at 7.30 p.m. he visited parish clubs until bed-time (Dolling, *TY* 95–6).

Dolling did not shirk office work but he hated it. As his prose style indicates, he did not possess a facile pen, and the days when he wrote his reports to subscribers were gloomy ones when everyone kept out of his way. His secretary had the task of correcting his spelling. He deployed a large staff in the district, but gave them the sort of free hand he demanded for himself. He quoted with approval a priest who had said to him: 'Don't make plans for your parish, let your parish make plans for itself' (Dolling, *TY* 234, 17). However, he did have a genius for conceiving large-scale ideas for the welfare of his people, and for enthusing others to assist him in implementing them.

It was in human and in spiritual qualities that Dolling excelled. An old Wykehamist said: 'Dolling did not *teach*, so much as *exist*. One found oneself glad to be with him, and realized that one was glad because he was good' (Osborne, *Dolling* 280). His goodness was robust. He was a man's man, with no time for pietism or religious frippery. He was quick-tempered and not averse to using his fists if the situation called for it. He did not hesitate to break regulations if they prevented him from serving God or man. Like his mentor Arthur Stanton* he was an unrepentant individualist; like Stanton he never considered converting to Rome because he would have been incapable of the necessary obedience.

Dolling was full of warmth and humour, addressing his congregation at St Agatha's as 'my dears', and enjoying nothing better than rowdy social evenings with the soldiers, sailors and working men who flocked to him. He had a gift for bringing the classes together, and was equally at home with the rough diamonds of Landport and the polished young men of Winchester College. He had a Christlike tenderness for the fallen and disadvantaged. He offered sanctuary to those most pathetic of men, the inebriate clergy; and had a special place in his heart and home for those such as the blind mental defective who learned comic songs so as to make a contribution to communal life. He lived as he taught: 'to believe that some one loves me is akin to believing God loves me'. At the same time he was a realist, writing that 'all boys from fourteen to sixteen are cruel and disagreeable', and that 'the real difficulty of work like this is that it makes tremendous demands on one's own personality, and that the larger part of the expenditure is in vain' (Dolling, *TY* 81, 34, 33).

Dolling had a special devotion, less common in his day than in our own, to the human Christ, the workman of Nazareth. This devotion was both a reflection of and an inspiration for his love of individuals for themselves. People felt that he cared for *them* rather than seeing them as fodder for salvation. He never proselytized; instead he provided religious opportunities. Since he was not committed to success, he remained detached from consequences. His enforced resignation from St Agatha's was a shattering personal blow, but he exercised his extraordinary influence over his people to the last, and in a remarkable way. 'No single one said "Because Mr Dolling has left, I leave". They knew their duty was to Christ and his Church not to me' (Dolling, *TY* 223).

If Dolling's ministry at Landport is an example of the institutional being subsumed within the spiritual, that of Nicolas Stacey at Woolwich is an example of spirituality finding new methods of expression in a changing world (see Stacey passim for what follows).

Stacey spent much of his time at Oxford University competing in athletics at the highest level, and sharpening the qualities of aggression, determination and single-mindedness which he was later to bring to ministry. After Cuddesdon he served a fruitful curacy at St Mark's, Portsea; 'I am glad to have been trained in the norm from which I now deviate' (Stacey, 49). In his next post as domestic chaplain to the Bishop of Birmingham he developed a flair for journalism and an impatience with the structures of the church which he took with him to his first incumbency as Rector of Woolwich, where he served from 1959 to 1968. When he took the parish over, it was at a low ebb; when he left it it was much changed, but far from what Stacey had originally planned.

He deployed considerable resources. He attracted a team of outstandingly able curates and lay workers, with whom he shared his authority in a way almost unheard of then or since. They worked under a demanding spiritual discipline, and enormously hard.

Finance was a constant problem, not least because Stacey hated committee work, and got on badly with the diocesan bodies which controlled resources. He obtained money from private donations and from a charitable trust, but relied largely upon freelance journalism to pay the salaries of his team. At one point he pledged the whole of his personal capital in order to expedite his building plans. These involved closing one of the parish's three churches and turning the mother church of St Mary into a multi-purpose building, including offices, a coffee house and a lounge. It immediately became a centre of an intense social and pastoral life.

Stacey accepted that secular provision for education and welfare was now such that the Church had only a marginal role to play. Instead he and his team concentrated upon the spiritual and the pastoral. An intensive programme of house to house visiting was greeted first with incomprehension, then with warmth, but almost never with a readiness to come to church. As the clergy acquired personal case-loads of families who needed frequent support, general visiting tailed away.

The parish maintained the usual organizations, and pioneered others, such as a branch of the Samaritans. It undertook charitable fund-raising, using methods which demonstrated Stacey's skill in attracting publicity. This skill was deployed in a variety of ways; Stacey had his own column in the local paper, and the parish was constantly in the news. Stacey was instrumental in founding the Woolwich Council of Churches. He not only preached ecumenism and the rationalization of resources, but took Methodist and Baptist ministers, and, less formally, a Roman Catholic priest on to his team. Overcoming enormous legal difficulties he was able to arrange for St Mary's to be shared by the local Presbyterian congregation.

Stacey believed that his position as Rector of Woolwich obliged him to play his part in the wider life of the borough. He worked closely with the local MP and with the leaders and officers of the Borough Council; his team kept in touch with industry and with local services; they all worked as chaplains in the hospital.

The congregation Stacey had inherited was a small one, three-quarters of them elderly and female, and half living outside the parish. Less than half of one per cent of parishioners worshipped at an Anglican church, and those who did were not socially representative. To change this situation the ministry team embarked on a series of initiatives, including the work already mentioned, the reform of worship, the creation of house groups, educational and social programmes, and a Christian Stewardship campaign concerned with the use of time, talents and money. Enormous care was take with the rites of passage. The total effect was to double Sunday congregations from 50 to 100, but of the extra 50 most were lapsed church people who lived outside the parish. Nor was the team able to resist the decline occurring everywhere, but especially in London, in the numbers of children attending Sunday School or being confirmed. Stacey often felt like a general without an army.

The conclusion which Stacey drew from his first four years was that the Church in its then form was irrelevant, at least in Woolwich and places like it. If he and his team had failed, having been given resources of which other parishes could only dream, what hope was there for less favoured clergy? When he published his thinking in a newspaper article he aroused a storm of protest from fellow-churchmen, and was confirmed in his view that the vision which might match the resources of the Church to the task which now presented itself was almost entirely lacking. He tried therefore to implement on a small scale the policy he was recommending for urban churches everywhere. St Mary's would continue on its ecumenical, multi-purpose way; but most of the team would take secular employment, and work within the Church structure for only a part of their time. The laity would be trained to take over much of the work previously done by the clergy. His PCC agreed, and the experiment was tried. The congregation did not diminish, but the wider pastoral work of the previous years was abandoned.

Stacey was no longer responsible for the life of the worshipping congregation, but he continued as chairman of the team, which grew to twelve because of the eagerness of others to join it. He oversaw a further development of St Mary's building. A Youth Centre and a licensed bar were provided in the crypt, offices for the Council of Social Service in the side aisles, and a re-furbished worship area in the nave. With the help of a group of City professionals he developed a Housing Association which pioneered the building of low-rent flats with money largely provided by the Greater London Council. He arranged for a family planning clinic to be set up in the local hostel for the homeless.

After seven years at Woolwich and at the age of forty, Stacey wanted a fresh challenge. He was offered no other employment within the Church, and so was compelled, not altogether reluctantly, to look outside it. For the remainder of a distinguished career, while remaining a priest, he held secular posts.

Stacey's character was very different from that of most twentieth-century Anglican parish priests, though not dissimilar from that of some of the great Victorians. By his own account he was impetuous, outspoken, mercurial, easily bored and easily irritated; it was easy to accuse him of arrogance and showmanship. He was also courageous, dynamic, hard-working, a brilliant organizer and publicist, and a creative thinker of the first order. His personal religious commitment remained unwavering; his doubts were about Church structures not about God's self-revelation in Christ. No doubt his personal defects contributed to his failures, but there is no reason to believe that they were its chief cause.

In his first years at Woolwich Stacey seemed to prove that the traditional resistance of the English urban working class to Anglicanism had become insurmountable. What had worked after a fashion a century or half a century before worked no longer. So far as the spiritual aspirations of his parishioners were concerned, he and his team had shown, to use the words of one of them, that the church was needed but not wanted. So, in his later years he pioneered a response to that situation, demonstrating how much could be accomplished by a group of devoted Christians supporting each other through the community of faith, and working with and through secular organizations.

The great Victorian Henry Liddon wrote: 'The conversion, the building up of souls, one by one; this is our real business' (Liddon, 216). Judged by that criterion, and other traditional ones, Stacey lacked priestly spirituality.

Although he did not shirk the fundamental duties of the parish priest's vocation he was not satisfied by them. He expected measurable achievement and was incapable of remaining detached from consequences. But, judged by the standard set by Moltmann and quoted at the beginning of this chapter, he evinced a spirituality appropriate to his circumstances. He could not serve God and his fellows to the extent he wished within the traditional confines of parochial life; so he and his parish broke new ground. They forgot about the institutional Church, and thought about the Kingdom.

6

Place

As there is a time, so there is a place for all things.
Everything in its place is admirable, deep and glorious;
out of its place like a wandering bird, is desolate and
good for nothing. (Traherne, 2.55)

The Parish

'A melting Sermon being preached in a Country church, all fell a weeping,
except a Country man, who being ask'd why he did not weep with the rest?
"Because" (says he) "I am not of this Parish"' (*Delights and Pastimes*, 1697,
quoted in the *Oxford Book of Humorous Prose*).

The Church of England has always been territorial; not simply in the sense
that the boundaries of the denomination originally coincided with those of a
nation state, but also in the sense that the parochial system has been, in the
words of Archbishop Runcie, 'a statement about God's concern for nation as
well as church, communities as well as congregations, daily life as well as
worship' (*Church Times*, 3 February 1989). Originally the whole local population were expected to look to the parish priest as their spiritual leader; when
this situation no longer obtained, the parish priest came to regard himself as the
whole local population's servant.

The territorial principle has other implications. Parishes have always
differed, and the most strenuous attempts to produce uniformity have never
ironed those differences out. The priest has stamped his individuality upon the
community, and the community has retained its individuality with or without
the approval of the priest. The wise priest has learned from his people, as they
from him, and both have been changed in the process.

Territorial spirituality has manifested itself in a thousand ways. For
example, James Woodforde's* diary contains a spirited account of beating the
bounds at Weston Longueville, a procedure which included the renewal of
boundary markers and the distribution of drink and tips from parson and
squire to all who joined their progress (Woodforde, 1.280 1). James Hervey,
incumbent of Weston Favell, Northamptonshire, from 1752 to 1758, who had
been one of the first Oxford Methodists, flatly refused on principle to work
outside his parish (Balleine, 67). In *The Natural History of Selborne* Gilbert
White** preserves for ever the local environment in which he lived and
worshipped. In *Forty Years in a Moorland Parish*, J.C. Atkinson** describes
with a love born of countless hours spent and miles traversed among his people

a way of life based on myth, legend and superstition to which he accommodated himself as sensitively as any missionary on foreign shores. One family, the Hills, provided rectors for Buxhall, Suffolk, in an unbroken line for four hundred years (Barrow, 212).

It is hard to appreciate the isolation and idiosyncrasy of many rural parishes in the past. The people of Robert Hawker's* Morwenstow were without commerce, culture or communications. He said of them: 'A visit to a distant market-town is an achievement to render a man an authority or an oracle among his brethren.' More tellingly still he wrote to a friend: 'Did you ever hear that for every 100 miles you live from London, you must reckon yourself a century back from your own date? We, therefore, who are 250 miles off, are now in the year 1610 in all that relates to agriculture and civilization' (Brendon, *Hawker* 65, 29–30).

Like people, like priest. Hawker's rich crop of eccentricities flourished because the remoteness of his parish left him free to cultivate them. More generally, isolation has often been a condition of ministry. That fact, combined with the sense that parochial affairs are small beer, has constituted a disincentive to a conscientious performance of duty. It took an act of parliament to persuade Sydney Smith* to take up residence at Foston-le-Clay.

On the other hand, the patient acceptance of the routine of parish life has been a powerful school of souls. 'Here is the imprisonment to work, which makes a man cheerfully recognize that his own parish is his first work, and not the excitement of itinerant preaching, or spasmodic or sporadic work in other fields of labour' (Newbolt, 25). So W.C.E. Newbolt; and in a chapter in *Speculum Sacerdotum* significantly entitled 'Obscurity' he writes: 'Do not let us seek the empty glory of fame ... Let us seek the real comfort and happiness of being known to a few' (248). This was the path chosen by Arthur Stanton* when, after a string of episcopal censures, he concluded: 'I never could think again that I should consider myself a prophet in the Anglican Israel. I felt I must keep as quiet as I could, and do all that I could for St Alban's, Holborn, and that was to be my ministry' (Osborne, *Stanton* 169). In fact the path he chose was not the one he followed; he wielded more influence from his parish than most bishops from their palaces.

But plenty of parish priests have remained truly obscure; as St Paul might have said of them, they have been 'unknown yet well known' (II Cor.6.9). As I look at the list of parish priests preserved in Shepherdswell church I reflect that not one of them has created even the faintest stir in the wider world; but that every one of them in his day has been the most familiar figure in the village. Leslie Paul puts into the mouths of parishioners the words: 'We are glad he is there, so long as he does not bother us too much ... It means that ... the joyous and tragic ultimates, birth and death, growth and decay, happiness and disaster, the depth experiences ... are *some one's* care. The line to God is open.'

Paul goes on: 'The spire points the way. When my church, All Saints in

Battersea, burnt down, the people from the back streets thronged round shouting "our church is burning!" *Our* church? They never attended. But it was still *our* church' (Paul, 95). As befits a territorial faith, Anglican spirituality is inextricably bound up with local buildings. Clergy who regret their role as custodians of ancient churches are out of tune with a spirituality of place which has a deep sense of both time and eternity. Sabine Baring-Gould** treasured the tiny church at Lew Trenchard so much that he chose as his funerary inscription 'Paravi lucernam Christo meo' – 'I have prepared a lantern for my Christ' (Purcell, *Baring-Gould* 5). John Betjeman writes of St Enedoc, Cornwall:

> So soaked in worship you are loved too well
> For that dispassionate and critic stare
> That I would use beyond the parish bounds.

There is a second building in most parishes which breathes the spirituality of place. It is the parsonage. In one of the most delightful of his poems Robert Herrick** describes his home, including the lines:

> Low is my porch, as is my Fate,
> Both void of state;
> And yet the threshold of my doore
> Is worn by th'poore,
> Who thither come, and freely get
> Good words, or meat. ('A Thanksgiving to God for His House')

The beggar at the door is only one example, and not the most important, of the significance of a priest living among his people. The tradition that the parsonage stands for hospitality and availability has been a hallmark of Anglicanism.

Like other virtues, this one can be costly. Roy Catchpole** writes of a parishioner: 'Mrs Macaulay called at the vicarage on average twenty-three times a day over a period of eighteen months. Every time the door-bell went it was either Grandma or one of the tiny minions she sent on errands. I was a bank, a confessor, a doctor's surgery, a post office, a counselling centre, a councillor, welfare rights advisor …, a teacher, guide, priest (sometimes), comforter, grocer, lawyer, junk shop, clothier, restaurant, first aid post and a hundred other things' (Catchpole, *GMDC* 6).

Samuel and Henrietta Barnett* set out to make their home accessible to their parishioners. Mrs Barnett adapted the vicarage so that the poor could enter her luxuriously furnished drawing-room without having to negotiate their way past a servant at the front door. She furnished the drawing-room itself so that the dirt and infestations brought in from the streets could easily be dealt with. The vicarage was available not only for the Communicants' Society but also for frequent parties where rich and poor mingled freely. A parishioner wrote: 'I wonder if Mrs Barnett has ever quite realized how much propaganda work was done for *education* by sharing her beautiful things with us' (Barnett, 1.152). She did realize; behind the warm hospitality lay a pastoral policy.

But church and parsonage are emptied of meaning if no priest inhabits them. Non-residence has been a recurring and disgraceful phenomenon in Anglican history. Over and over again clergy have either left their parishes without a minister of any kind or have put in a curate to do all the work for a fraction of the emoluments. Richard Greenham, incumbent of Dry-Drayton, Cambridgeshire, in the later sixteenth century summarized the case against the non-residents when he wondered how they could take any comfort in their wealth: 'For, methinks,' saith he, 'they should see written on everything which they have, Pretium sanguinis, the price of blood' (Fuller, *CH* 3.147). Jane Austen's Sir Thomas Bertram made the same point when he said of his clerical son Edmund: 'He knows that human nature needs more lessons than a weekly sermon can convey, and that if he does not live among his parishioners and prove himself by constant attention their well-wisher and friend he does very little either for their good or his own' (Austen, *MP* 188).

In the eighteenth century less than half of the parishes of England had a resident incumbent. Sometimes the cause was a dilapidated parsonage, sometimes the absence of one; when an official survey was made in 1835, 1728 parsonages were said to be unfit to live in, and 2878 parishes had none. Even so conscientious a parson as William Andrew* could find no place to reside within his parish boundaries. Octavius Pickard-Cambridge** was unable to reside in his parish during his curacy in Scarisbrick, Lancashire, because the chief landowner was a Roman Catholic who refused to allow an Anglican lodging on his estate (Colloms, 56). In the 1850s the conscientious and zealous Mr Colbourne of St Matthias's, Bethnal Green, would not reside because he would not 'subject his children to the trial of growing up in a sewerless, fever-ridden alley amid a gin-drinking, fornicating rabble' (Chadwick, *VC* 1.331).

Most frequently the reason for absenteeism has been pluralism, which as we have already seen has been a recurring feature of the Anglican scene, and which ceased to be a significant one only for a brief period in the latter part of the nineteenth century and the earlier part of the twentieth. Sometimes a resident curate did the pluralist's work, but often the parish remained unserved except in the most residual sense. In the early nineteenth century Hannah More reported from Somerset that in her own parish no clergyman had resided for forty years, and that in the neighbourhood there were thirteen adjoining parishes without so much as a resident curate between them (Purcell, *Baring-Gould* 39). At that time Lewes in Sussex was called the Rookery, because of the number of black-coated clergy who rode thence on a Sunday to do duty in the surrounding villages (Hammond, 45). When Augustus Hare* arrived at Alton-Barnes he found that the nearby church of Alton-Priors had a service only once every three weeks and that no other notice was taken of the parishioners. He therefore did Sunday duty alternately morning and evening in the two churches with a congregation drawn from both parishes (Hare, 1.296–7). Robert Hawker was the first resident incumbent at Morwenstow for a century.

In recent times absenteeism has again become a feature of church life, as priests have been required to look after several parishes, of which they can reside in only one. The sense of identification with the local community has been attenuated, and attempts to persuade disparate communities that having a priest in common has in some way united them have been only modestly successful.

Even a resident parson can show little sense of place. Both clergy and people have often failed to honour their local heritage. When the young J.C. Atkinson was taken by his predecessor into Danby church, Yorkshire, he found the altar rickety and worm-eaten, and covered with rags which had once been green baize and with crumbs from the Sunday School teachers' meals; nor did the minister remove his hat (Atkinson, 44–5). Descriptions of dilapidated and uncared for churches pepper the records of visitations; the parson himself was not necessarily to blame. A parson is, however, responsible for his own behaviour in church; and Trollope was repeating a common observation when he commented that 'of all persons clergymen are the most irreverent in the handling of things supposed to be sacred ... When a parson takes lay friends over his church on a week day, how much less of the spirit of genuflexion and head-uncovering the clergyman will display than the layman!' (Trollope, *LC* 167).

The practice of locking churches, common in past centuries as in our own, has been a further example of a defective spirituality of place. John Skinner* locked his church, and used his control of the key as a weapon in his constant battles with his bell-ringers (Skinner, 208). By contrast, W.H. Hudson, used to having to borrow church keys, found that the vicar of Coombe, Devonshire, left his church open day and night, not least so that tramps could use it as a refuge (quoted Christmas, 249). George Carey** in our own time opened the city centre church of St Nicholas, Durham, and left it unmanned. There was occasional theft and damage, but harder to bear was the necessity of cleaning up rubbish and excrement. Carey consoled himself with the reflections that service entails risk, and that cleansing the sacred place was a way of showing love for the incarnate Christ (Carey, 19). Nicholas Rivett-Carnac** experimented with leaving his church of St Mark, Kennington, open day and night, with single members of his congregation on duty there, as a witness to the parish's commitment to deprived and homeless. Eventually he decided that the dangers were too great and the demands on the cleaners unacceptable (Cooke, 81–2, 104). The country church of Shepherdswell has been left open since 1991, with a daily trickle of local people and visitors using it for devotion and refreshment and with only one instance of minor damage.

The parochial principle has encouraged certain less desirable clerical characteristics. One of the main themes of Mrs Oliphant's nineteenth-century novel *The Perpetual Curate* is the friction created by the fact that the Curate, Frank Wentworth, works in the parish of Carlingford without the incumbent's consent. But when Wentworth takes over the parish: 'He was now in his own domains, an independent monarch, as little inclined to divide his power as any autocrat ... secure that no parson nor priest should tithe or toll in his dominions, and a great deal more sure ... that henceforth no unauthorized evangelization should take place in any portion of his territory' (Oliphant, *PC* 540). The author of a handbook for the clergy wrote: 'the diligent country parson walks or drives about his parish, not without a decided feeling of authority and ownership' (quoted Russell, 129). A.G. Edouart, the vicar of St Michael's, Burleigh Street, London, put an end for a time to the hugely successful evangelical Exeter Hall services held in his parish, despite the fact that his own bishop approved of them (Balleine, 162–3; Russell, 94–5).

Some priests have been faced with an opportunity which was also a temptation. They have been the squarson, the principal landowner as well as the incumbent. Members of the Hornby family served the little parish of St Michaels-on-Wyre, Lancashire, from 1789 to 1919 as 'paternalistic vicars and humane landlords' (Colloms, 14–15). Edward Winnington-Ingram, father of the later Bishop of London, was rector and squire of Stanford, Worcestershire, for forty-six years (S.C. Carpenter, *Winnington-Ingram* 8). Charles Tennyson Turner, brother of the poet Tennyson, succeeded an uncle as parson and squire of Caister and Grasby, Lincolnshire. He and his wife had no children, and adopted the parish as their family. They rebuilt the church and built a vicarage, which was open to all at festivals. He visited assiduously during a smallpox epidemic and was unsparing in his charity to the needy. To counter drunkenness he purchased the village inn, and put in a reliable landlord. In an area where witchcraft was still common, loyalty to religious practice, so far as it existed, was a personal tribute to the Rector (Colloms, 155–9).

So far we have seen examples of squarsonic power being used benevolently. But the other possibility also existed. Octavius Pickard-Cambridge reigned unchallenged at Bloxworth, since although he was not technically the squire the village belonged to his family. On the whole he was benevolent, but a labourer who missed church would find the rector at his door, impatient of excuses and threatening him with the loss of his cottage (Colloms, 68).

Jeremy Taylor wrote: 'Entertain no persons into your assemblies from other parishes ... lest the labour of thy brother be discouraged and thou thyself be thought to preach Christ out of envy, and not of good will' (*CI*, 73). Despite Taylor's admonition, it has proved hard to confine evangelical and pastoral zeal within the boundaries of a single parish, especially in the face of neglect and lassitude elsewhere. Bernard Gilpin* itinerated far and wide; so did Robert Grimshaw*. John Berridge (1716–93), incumbent of Everton, Bedfordshire, from 1755 until his death, was itinerant to such an extent that his bishop threatened to imprison him. William Andrew dispensed charity and pastoral care in neighbouring parishes, and drew his flock from a vastly wider area than his own.

Andrew wrote of himself: 'I have ever been rather a congregational than a parochial minister' (Chadwick, *Andrew* 49). The congregational principle has always been hard to resist in towns, and has been encouraged by the growth of 'party' churches. Only eight of David Watson's* huge membership at St Michael-le-Belfry came from his parish; in order to cater for his people he set up Area Groups which met in other parishes all over York (Saunders, *Watson* 137). The congregations of All Saints, Margaret Street, and All Souls, Langham Place, are eclectic; the churches serve worshippers with liturgical and doctrinal preferences rather than parishioners with a local loyalty. In the countryside, however, where the choice has usually been between attending the local church or staying away altogether, wise priests have been slow to suggest divisive innovations.

At the end of the twentieth century the parochial system still exists, though in an attenuated and often ineffective way. Its retention grows increasingly problematic; but its value, and hence the spiritual function of the clergy who serve it, has been given classic expression by Archbishop Runcie in the speech already quoted: 'If the parochial system is at root not a statement about boundaries and residential areas and neighbourhoods but instead about God's reign over the whole of society, we ought not to let it go merely because it is facing challenges from the way in which society is developing' (*Church Times*, 3 February 1989).

Social Position and Relationships

Introduction

Flora Thompson describes the seating in Lark Rise church in the 1880s: 'The Squire's and clergyman's families had pews in the chancel, with backs to the wall on either side, and between them stood two long benches for the school-children, well under the eyes of authority. Below the steps down into the nave stood the harmonium ... and round it was ranged the choir ... Then came the rank and file of the congregation, nicely graded, with the farmer's family in the front row, the Squire's gardener and coachman, the school mistress, the maidservants, and the cottagers, with the Parish Clerk at the back to keep order' (Thompson, 210).

Traditionally the seating arrangements in parish churches have reflected the social relationships of the congregation. Most of what seating there was in the sixteenth and seventeenth centuries was reserved for the affluent, though there might be benches against the wall for the weak. As pews became more common so did the custom of individuals of higher station constructing their own, sometimes enclosed within high walls and with arrangements for heating and refreshment. It was alleged in 1842 that the squire at Tong church 'has built a pew in the Chancel; when the Ten Commandments are begun, a servant regularly enters at the chancel door with a luncheon tray' (Hammond, 80–1). Henry Alford** described the pews at Wymeswold in the 1840s: 'Facing all ways, and enclosed in boxes of all heights, the congregation were placed in every position of advantage for observing the dress or habits of their neighbours, and of disadvantage for concentrating their attention upon any one subject or employment' (Alford, 140). In the 1850s pewholders at Islington parish church refused to open their doors to let operatives sit by them (Hennell, 66). It was thought to be one of William Bennett's* great triumphs that he was able to get rid of the pews at Frome without serious resistance (Bennett, 183).

Pew rents provided income for parishes, and although nineteenth-century reformers such as Walter Hook* set an example by getting rid of them they persisted until well into the twentieth century. There was stubborn resistance to their abolition. John Sharp, Sabine Baring-Gould's** vicar during his first curacy at Horbury, Yorkshire, spent a fortune on law cases occasioned by his determination to eliminate the private pews, resembling an array of horseboxes, which filled his church (Purcell, *Baring-Gould* 59–60, 86). The toughest battle Dick Sheppard* had to fight with his congregation at St Martin's was over the abolition of reserved pews (Roberts, *Sheppard* 99). Christopher Chavasse** thought it a great triumph when all the seats at St Aldate's, Oxford, became free in 1923 (Gummer, *Chavasse* 88).

Seating presented problems of precedence and protocol. James Woodforde* was embarrassed when the squire's brother's mistress took his seat in the chancel without asking permission (Woodforde, 1.285). Some nineteenth-century churchwardens found allocation, their responsibility, so unpleasant a task that they asked a clergyman from a parish nearby to undertake it (Hammond, 82). Henry Fardell's* wardens had to assert their independence against a gentleman who claimed a pew in right of the purchase of a house (Fardell, 128). An observer commented with astonishment that when William Bennett opened St Barnabas church the rich actually sat side by side with the poor (Bennett, 62).

Arrangements for church seating illustrate the sense of hierarchy and social subordination which the Church of England has perpetuated and which the clergy have for the most part sought to instil. The intention has been served in a variety of ways. Generations of ordinary people have sat in church surrounded by memorials to their betters, often buried within the sacred walls.

Generations of children have learned, in the words of the catechism, 'To honour and obey the King, and all that are put in authority under him: To submit myself to all my governors, teachers, spiritual pastors and masters: To order myself lowly and reverently to all my betters.' As recently as 1991 a parish priest in rural Warwickshire, seeking to make changes, was told by his people that he must obtain the approval of the local gentry, even though none of them was a churchgoer (personal information).

Mr Ellison of Lark Rise might have been behind the times, as Flora Thompson thought, when he preached in the 1880s that 'God, in His infinite wisdom, had appointed a place for every man, woman, and child on this earth and it was their bounden duty to remain contentedly in their niches' (212); but similar sentiments have issued from a thousand pulpits for the great part of Anglican history, and have died away recently only because society has changed, and the church with it. It is hard to dissent from a remark by the nineteenth-century Socialist priest Llewelyn Davies: 'Few will doubt that the Church of England greatly needs the help of divine grace to preserve it from an undue reverence for station and property' (Chadwick, *VC* 2.156).

The ordering of church life has reinforced and sanctified social gradations; and the resources of the Church of England have been deployed disproportionately in favour of the privileged. Even today, the Church bears marks of its past; whether it be in the formal styles applied to the clergy, in the lavish provision of chaplains for Oxford and Cambridge colleges, or in the assiduous if frequently unavailing attention paid to the spiritual needs of the royal family.

Spirituality has wrestled with social distinction, but has not overcome it. George Herbert* wrote:

A peasant may believe as much
As a great clerk and reach the highest stature;
Thus doth Thou make proud nature bend and crouch
While grace fills up uneven nature.

None the less his country parson does some of his duties with gritted teeth. 'Neither disdaineth he to enter into the poorest cottage, though he even creep into it, and though it smell never so loathsomely. For both God is there also, and those for whom God died: and so much the rather doth he so, as his access to the poor is more comfortable [the word means "comforting"], than to the rich; and in regard of himself, it is more humiliation' (Herbert, XIV). Behind the impeccable sentiments lurks the same sense of class as appeared overtly in the requirement by the bishop of Norwich in his 1639 synod that communicants should form into ranks in order of precedence with the 'best of the parish' kneeling at the altar rails (Hart, *CC* 99).

The sense of class has manifested itself in the spiritually disabling attitudes of snobbery and prejudice. Joseph Price** of Brabourne did not speak for himself alone when he wrote: 'A kind reception from a good family makes me well pleased with myself and raises my spirits;' but not every clergyman would have added as he did: 'what weakness!' (Price, 11). The gentle Francis Kilvert* showed uncharacteristic malevolence in his comments on the miners' strike of 1873. He wrote of 'the baneful tyrannical influence of that cursed Union' and referred with approval to a proposal to import Chinese coolies to work the British mines (Kilvert, 2.316; Grice, *Kilvert* 248). Nor has snobbery been confined to the clergy's view of the laity. John Collins** remembered from his time at Westcott House in the 1920s that the Principal would read the list of new entrants: 'A.B., Eton and King's College; C.D., Winchester and New College; E.F., Marlborough and Corpus Christi, Cambridge ...' Then there would be a pause, and he would continue: 'X.Y.,' followed by a clearing of the throat – 'Bradford Grammar School and Keble: be kind to him, boys' (Collins, 45).

But the clergy have not been totally unaffected by the spiritual egalitarianism which co-exists with reverence for social gradation in the pages of the New Testament; by Paul's words that in Christ 'there is neither Jew nor Greek, there is neither slave nor free, there is neither male nor female; for you are all one in Christ Jesus' (Gal. 3.28). There has been a tension between a respect for persons in the sense in which the phrase is used in the Authorized Version, and a belief in the ultimate value of each individual; a tension which has been partially resolved in principle only in modern times, to the extent that the ideology of democracy resonates with the idea of equality before God.

When it has existed, the clergy's sense of people's equality before God has evinced itself in three ways. The first has been to claim that, in matters pertaining to their vocation, ministers stand in equal judgment over everyone. Fielding's Parson Adams, 'though he paid all submission and deference to his superiors in other matters, where the least spice of religion intervened ... immediately lost all respect of persons. It was his maxim, that he was a servant of the Highest, and could not, without departing from his duty, give up the least particle of His honour and His cause to the greatest earthly potentate' (Fielding, *JA* 368). As a curate, William Bennett preached graphically on the way in which the affluent, attending church, left their servants outside waiting for them (Bennett, 24).

Secondly, many priests have believed that, if the poor are to know their place, the place of the clergy is to be often with them. On the eve of a prison visit another saintly fool of literature, Goldsmith's Vicar of Wakefield, says: 'If these wretches ... were princes, there would be thousands ready to offer their ministry; but in my opinion, the heart that is buried in a dungeon is as precious as that seated on a throne' (Goldsmith, 251). Sabine Baring-Gould tells the story of an old parson discovered in the servants' hall by the squire's lady two days after he had ended a visit upstairs: 'Like Persephone, madam,' he declared, 'half my time above, half in the nether world' (quoted Christmas, 220–1).

Thirdly, a priest thinking it impossible or undesirable to challenge the social order may also think it his duty to stand clear of it. The principle is that of that most rigidly hierarchical of organizations the Royal Navy, where a chaplain has no rank; or, it might equally be said, every rank. He shares the rank of the person to whom he is ministering. This is the spirit lying behind Liddon's remark that: 'It is fatal for an ordained man to hold the faith of Our Lord Jesus Christ with respect of places or respect of persons' (Liddon, 108).

. But even a priest trying to stand clear of the social order is still firmly embedded in the church's own hierarchy and power structure. Until modern times church order and the social order overlapped and deeply influenced each other; even today a connection remains. A parish priest's place in the scheme of things can be defined by ecclesiastical as well as by secular relationships. So in order to investigate in more detail the entanglement of the parochial clergy with the social structure, and the spirituality of their responses to that entanglement, we shall in this section look at relationships with bishops and with colleagues as well as with patrons and parishioners; then, in two other sections, at appointments and at Establishment.

Patron

'There is still a greater man belonging to the church, than either the parson or the clerk himself. The person I mean is the Squire; who, like the King, may be styled Head of the Church in his own parish.' Thus the poet William Cowper in the eighteenth century (quoted Hart, *ECCP* 86). He was describing a situation which has obtained in many rural parishes until modern times. If the parson has had freehold he has been afforded some personal protection; but his effectiveness has been largely determined by his relationship with his patron.

There have been parish priests who have conducted their ministry under terms of humiliating servitude. William Harrison, who died in 1593, complained about financial exactions 'in Essex, where a minister taking a benefice (of less than twentie pounds in the Queenes Bookes) was forced to pay to his patronne twentie quarters of otes, ten quarters of wheat, and sixteene yeerlie of barlie' (Goodenough, 42). Addison's famous essay (*The Spectator*, no. 112) makes it clear that Sir Roger de Coverley ruled the roost in 'his' church as everywhere else on his estate. In the letter quoted at the beginning of this sub-section, Cowper wrote of churches where the congregation might be kept waiting an hour after the proper time for the squire to arrive, and where the sermon was timed to last as long as the squire's nap (Hart, *ECCP* 86). Until 1898 a parish priest might be installed under the terms of a bond of resignation, which committed him to resign after a fixed term. Robert Browne was appointed to Lullingstone, Kent, in 1864 on the understanding that he would resign at a month's notice if either of the patron's two sons should be ordained. Fortunately for him, neither was (Loo, *Phelps* 131). The insecurity which these arrangement implied has been resurrected in the later twentieth century, when more and more priests hold parochial positions for a period limited by contract.

In such circumstances a parish priest has been well advized to deal discreetly with a patron's shortcomings and to respect his prejudices. George Crabbe** in his poem 'The Squire and the Priest' tells the story of a dissolute squire who seeks the compliance of the nephew he has placed in the local living. He advises the young man:

> Shun all resemblance to that forward race
> Who preach of sins before a sinner's face ...
> Yet there are sinners of a class so low,
> That you with safety may the lash bestow;
> Poachers and drunkards, idle rogues, who feed
> At others' cost, a mark'd correction need;
> And all the better sort, who see your zeal,
> Will love and reverence for their pastor feel;
> Reverence for one who can inflict the smart,
> And love, because he deals not them a part.

The nephew, who has fallen under evangelical influence, ignores this advice and 'announces the power of grace', infuriating the squire and dividing his congregation. The poem ends with the parish in disarray. Similarly Addison graphically spells out the sort of consequences which squire and parson at loggerheads might produce. 'The parson is always at the squire, and the squire, to be revenged on the parson, never comes to church. The squire has made all his tenants atheists and tithe-stealers; while the parson instructs them every Sunday in the dignity of his order, and insinuates to them, almost in every sermon, that he is a better man than his patron' (*The Spectator*, no. 112).

In a real life instance James Newton** of Nuneham Courtenay remained quiescent when his patron, Lord Harcourt, moved village and rectory a mile and a half away from the church, and rebuilt the latter so that it ornamented in a way acceptable to eighteenth-century taste the landscape visible from his new country seat. The outcome was a building designed to be looked at rather than used. Congregations fell away and catechizing ceased. The spiritual well-being of the parish had been sacrificed to the whim of a rich man (James Newton, xvii-xix).

Some clergy have hugged their chains. Jane Austen's egregious Mr Collins toadied to Lady Catherine de Bourgh. 'The rector of a parish has much to do ... he must make such an agreement for tythes as may be beneficial to himself and not offensive to his patron ... he should have attentive and conciliatory manners towards everybody, especially towards those to whom he owes his preferment' (Austen, *PP* 121). Daughter and sister of clergymen, the clear-eyed Jane had every opportunity to draw from life. The clergy were as apt to grovel to their betters as was anyone else in need of patronage; and as likely to suffer from failing to do so. Thomas Fuller** was glad to leave Waltham Abbey after a witticism about the wife of his patron the Earl of Carlisle had been taken amiss; he was able to move to Cranford because of the protection of Lord Berkeley, whom he referred to a his Maecenas (Addison, *WDF* 247). Many parish priests were in effect chaplains to great men; sometimes formally, as in the case of Thomas Traherne* who left the care of his living of Credenhill in order to be chaplain to Sir Orlando Bridgeman, Lord Keeper of the Great Seal, sometimes informally, as in the case of Henry Michell Wagner**, whose duties as vicar of Brighton took second place to those of being tutor to the Duke of Wellington's sons for so long as the latter responsibility lasted (Wagner, 39).

Often patron and parson have worked closely together. Sir William Heathcote at Hursley, John Keble's* parish, refused to let to non-churchmen and appears to have made attendance at church a condition of tenancy (Battiscombe, *Keble* 173–4). Lord Lyttleton presented his younger brother William to Hagley, Worcestershire, in 1847; he remained there until his death in 1884, working in harmony with the rest of the family, and following the policy of declared conservatism and inconspicuous change which works best in most rural parishes (Chadwick, *VC* 2.153–4). Only one situation could be more harmonious – when, as was the case with the Hastings family at Martley, Worcestershire, for well over a century, the patron presented himself (Hastings, 69–70).

We can study in instructive detail the relations between William Andrew* and his patron Sir John Boileau (for what follows, see Chadwick, *Andrew* passim).

Andrew became incumbent of Ketteringham in 1835. The parish was tiny. In 1831 there had been only 28 inhabited homes, and a population of 215. The church stood close to Ketteringham Hall, the owner of which was the local landlord and patron of the living. In 1835, the Hall's owner was living abroad in poverty and the Hall itself was occupied by a tenant. Andrew had the opportunity to establish himself without opposition.

In 1838 the Hall's new owner, Sir John Boileau, took up residence. Sir John was wealthy, learned, liberal and civilized; active in public affairs and in good works. He was an excellent landlord, though also a strict disciplinarian. He was deeply devout. He led daily prayers in his home; read his family sermons in the liberal tradition on Sunday evenings; prepared his footmen for confirmation; and visited, relieved and prayed with the poor and sick. Not without justice he called himself father of the parish. But he was determined to be master on his own estates. It was not long before he clashed with the equally strong-willed Andrew. The vicar rebuked the patron for Sabbath-breaking and permitting dancing in his home. The patron, more by accident than design, occasioned the eviction of the vicar from his rented house.

Sir John then went abroad until 1841. When he returned, he embarked upon a series of alterations and improvements to the church; he took it for granted that he had the right to do this without consultation. He built a school-room and paid for a schoolmistress. He then denied Andrew the use of this building, save on the condition that people from outside the parish were excluded. He felt strongly that people should attend their own parish church, as he did; Andrew felt that he should feed hungry sheep whatever their fold. The parson thought the squire should not engage in and encourage worldly vanities; the squire thought the parson should not preach at such length and in so personal a fashion. Eventually there was an enormous row, when Andrew refused as a godparent a lady to whom he had denied the sacrament. Sir John involved the bishop; the latter treated Andrew with the greatest delicacy, but none the less requested him to back down. Other concessions followed. To all intents and purposes Sir John now controlled the parish, referring to Andrew on one occasion as 'my clergyman'.

Then Sir John overstepped himself. In order to prepare the chancel vault for his wife, who was very ill, he removed the coffins from it and buried them in the graveyard. A relative of one of the dead objected; and after months of humiliating publicity the coffins were returned. Sir John felt Andrew could have prevented him making a fool of himself; Andrew felt that Sir John's overbearing attitude had left him no choice but to accept the plan. Matters were made worse by Mrs Andrew's overt hostility to the squire.

The effect of the episode was to encourage Andrew to show more independence. Sir John had also to contend with divided allegiances within his own family. His daughter Caroline, always active in good works within the parish, found herself drawn towards Andrew's spirituality, and began to meet him secretly for prayer. When her father discovered what was going on, by way of her disinclination to attend the servants' ball, he forbade her to speak to Andrew. Caroline, then in her twenties, obeyed him implicitly until the order was in due course rescinded.

One remarkable aspect of this stormy relationship is the fact that personal communication between squire and parson never broke down completely. Not only did they meet and co-operate on public occasions, but Andrew visited Sir John when he was ill, and ministered to the family when a younger son was killed in the Crimean War. After Sir John's wife died in 1862 Andrew was a frequent visitor, though his efforts to help Sir John were only partially effective; the squire found his ministrations clumsy and unsympathetic. But his two other unmarried daughters also fell under Andrew's spell, and as he grew older and more dependent upon them, he accepted their Sabbatarianism. He placed himself under Andrew's spiritual direction and abandoned liberal authors for evangelical ones. He still disliked much about the vicar's sermons and opinions, but: 'He had succumbed, in some part, to the courage, the integrity, and the perseverance of the vicar ... but still more to the insistent cry of the human soul, in the end, for the consolation of the spirit' (Chadwick, *Andrew* 177–8).

The conflict between these two deeply religious men took place on three battlefields. There was a power struggle, with the patron claiming, in effect, to control everything in the parish save the conduct of worship. There were disagreements over principle: Andrew was an ardent Sabbatarian and condemned as unchristian worldliness what Boileau saw as innocent amusement; Boileau thought the parish church was for parishioners, Andrew that it was for all who wished to attend it. There was a clash of personalities, which could have been most destructive of all, save that on both sides there was a firm intention to live as a Christian should. It is easy to imagine how in other circumstances conflict could have culminated in alienation, and dislike have developed into hatred. That the outcome was different is a tribute to the spirituality of the protagonists.

Parishioners

When I came to the Kentish village of Shepherdswell in 1985 I was intrigued to discover that there were parishioners, usually male and invariably elderly, who called me 'sir'. These parishioners were not churchgoers; they represented a tradition of social subordination which was almost dead within the Church herself, but which had deep roots in the English past.

The parochial clergy of the sixteenth century were often of the same class as the bulk of their parishioners. Over the next three centuries the intention, frequently achieved, was that the parish priest should be in the social sense a gentleman. As late as 1950 a novelist could depict clergy as horrified that a new colleague had been the manager of a boot shop and did not possess a degree (Raymond, 24). Since then, however, the clergy have slipped back in the social stakes; while still predominantly drawn from the middle class, they serve a more middle class society. They have been increasingly ill advised to expect deference.

In the unquestioningly hierarchical society of the past, the effectiveness of the clergy depended in large part on the position they occupied on the social ladder. The day labourers, serving men, ostlers, glovers, drapers, tallow-chandlers, shoemakers, soldiers and fishermen who filled the ranks of the clergy in Elizabethan times lacked the resources or social confidence to stand up to the nobility and gentry; the same must be said, despite a notable precedent, of carpenters (Hart, *CC* 24). The wife of John Conybeare** was once talking to a lady about Holman Hunt's *The Shadow of Death*, which showed Christ in the workshop at Nazareth. 'I do not like having forced on me,' the lady remarked, 'that Our Lord was a working man and his Mother a peasant woman' (Colloms, 257–8).

The better education and relative prosperity of the clergy from the seventeenth century onward brought a higher standing and with it solid advantages. 'Sordid circumstances and economic anxieties do not always confirm religious faith, social equality and neighbourly propinquity do not always create love, and a slight elevation above the traditional habits of the countryside might elevate a parson a little above some very ugly things – above much grossness of life, above the enjoyment of such pleasures as bull baiting, badger drawing and cock fighting, above barbarisms and superstitions, such as the lingering belief in witchcraft' (Clark, 33). An analogous point was made by Cecil St John, the old curate in charge in Margaret Oliphant's novel of that name. Trying to overcome the diffidence of the rector who is to replace him he says: 'Which is best for them [the parishioners] to have, a man who is well off, whom the farmers and masters will stand in awe of, and who will be able to help them in trouble – or a poor man who has to struggle for himself, who has nothing to spare, and no great influence with any one?' (Oliphant, *CC* 118). Frank Fenwick in Trollope's *Vicar of Bullhampton* was a case in point. Socially and intellectually able to match the local landlord, the Marquis of Trowbridge, he was equally prepared to quarrel with him in a good cause and to make friends with him again in the interests of the people whom he served and who were the Marquis's tenants.

On the other hand, social superiority could militate against sensitive ministry. Fielding's Parson Adams met a gentleman who told him that: 'The parson of our parish, instead of esteeming his poor parishioners as part of his family, seems rather to consider them as not of the same species as himself. He seldom speaks to any, unless some few of the richest of us; nay, indeed, he will not move his hat to the others. I often laugh when I behold him on Sundays strutting along the churchyard like a turkey-cock through the rows of his parishioners, who bow to him, with as much submission, and are as unregarded, as are a set of servile courtiers by the proudest prince in Christendom' (Fielding, 203–4). John Skinner* voiced a common view when he wrote after visiting a bereaved labouring family: 'Happy it is that people in the lower ranks of life are not possessed of the same sensibility as their superiors' (Skinner, 248). The reaction of a servant girl visited by the nineteenth century parson Legh Richmond was: 'Sir, I take it very kind that you have condescended to leave the company of the rich and converse with the poor' (Chadwick, *VC* 1.514).

Parson Adams claimed that 'he looked on all those whom God had entrusted to his care to stand to him in that relation [as children]' (Fielding, 203). Such an attitude transmuted social distinction into a spiritual relationship; but the transmutation has rarely been complete, or even attempted. George Woodward** of East Hendred wrote of his farmers' tithe feast: 'I am always heartily glad when it is over; for it's very disagreeable sitting for half a day among such sort of folks' (Woodward, 114). After a ride with a friend's gardener the young John Henry Newman** commented: 'Pony went well, and so did Meacher's tongue. Shoot them both. They will never be better than they are now' (Faber, 243). After the agricultural riots of 1830, John Keble* reproached himself and his fellow clergy for their failure to act as mediators between the farmers and their men, declaring that parsons should 'shrink less from intercourse with tradesmen and farmers' (Battiscombe, *Keble* 133); a remark which throws a flood of light upon his own attitudes. Robert Dolling* described a typical public school and university parson in a sermon: 'Five percent of his parishioners, his equals, he does understand; fifteen per cent, those hungering after gentility, he may guess at; the eighty per cent he is practically hopeless with' (Osborn, *Dolling* 212).

Plenty of clergy have seen it as their duty to reinforce social distinction. Charles Kingsley* loved to talk with 'inferiors' but preserved his dignity as their superior. He wrote smugly to Fanny: 'The lower orders worship me and *never* take liberties' (Chitty, *Kingsley* 95). Mr Ellison at Lark Rise 'would preach eternal punishment for sin, and touch, more lightly, upon the bliss reserved for those who worked hard, were contented with their lot and showed proper respect to their superiors' (Thompson, 212).

While hierarchy endured, there were ways of robbing it of its sting. Walton noted of Richard Hooker** that he 'was of so mild and humble a nature, that his poor parish clerk and he did never talk but with both their hats on, or both off, at the same time' (Walton, 153). Walter Hook* relied on simple friendliness. Trying to wean a labourer from drink he promised that if the other would refrain from alcohol for a year, so would he. 'How,' said the man, 'shall I know that you are keeping your word?' 'Nothing easier,' replied Hook, 'You ask my missus and I'll ask yours' (Stranks, *Hook* 90–1).

Graduated hospitality had its part to play. William Cole** of Bletchley moved naturally among the gentry; but on Sundays he had farmers to dine with him, and members of the lower orders frequently ate in his kitchen (see, for example, Cole, 82). But graduated hospitality could be used against the parson as well as by him; Joseph Price** of Brabourne noted that a fellow-clergyman had said that the gentry were 'not fond of seeing the clergy when they had their best and genteelest company' (Price, 154).

With all his defects, James Woodforde* managed his relations with his parishioners well. He unquestioningly accepted the social hierarchy, and was clear about his own place within it. His normal intercourse was with the gentry, including his fellow clergy. With them he socialized endlessly, and the only personal presences and absences at church he noted, apart from those of his own family, were of the Custances, the Micklethwaites and, occasionally, the wealthier farmers. On the other hand, the fact that the lower orders also took hierarchy for granted enabled Woodforde to be on friendly terms with them without worrying about his dignity.

Some clergy have been actually more at home with the poor. Francis Kilvert wrote one Palm Sunday: 'In the afternoon I had the happiness to have all the poor people to myself. None of the grand people were at church because of the snow. So of course I could speak much better and more freely' (Kilvert, 2.157).

Kilvert may have felt intimidated by his social superiors, but Samuel Barnett*, who was intimidated by no one, also preferred the poor. He wrote to his future wife that he was wearied by the affectation and unreality of the rich, and sometimes felt that nothing but 'hard words and cruel cuttings' could help them. He added with his usual profound self-knowledge: 'I am too fond of giving hard words to trust myself to teach them in this way' (Barnett, 1.52).

As modern times approached, servile manners began to die away, and the clergy no longer expected them. Kilvert noted with amusement that a mother rebuked her daughter for not curtseying as she handed him his hat, and that 'old fashioned' folks still called him 'your honour' and 'your reverence'. 'Old Sarah Williams and a few more of the old people still salute one with, "Your servant, sir", ... after a few more years this will never be heard' (Kilvert, 2.98, 79). Twentieth-century social egalitarianism has completed the process he anticipated.

When neither party has threatened the other, Christian affection has spanned social differences. On 20 December 1810 John Skinner buried James Britten, aged 70. Britten had worked as a day-labourer for the whole of his life, bringing up a family on a wage of seven shillings a week, which he never asked to have increased. Latterly he had been plagued by rheumatism, and had with great reluctance accepted 1s 6d a week from the parish, supplementing it with his own labour. A few months before his death he had dug up a potato field for Skinner, always remembering, when making his claim for wages, to deduct for time lost because of rain or disability. Over the years Skinner 'was so much pleased with his industry, contented disposition and constant attendance to his religious duties, I occasionally had opportunities of rendering him some little assistance ... Every Sunday he dined at the Parsonage for upwards of two years ... always grateful, modest, unassuming, it was with difficulty one could get him to make any little want known, so fearful was he of giving trouble.'

Britten had often said to Skinner that 'most happy should he be if the Almighty would please to take him before he got too infirm for work, as he knew not what he should do without some employment, and he could not bear to think of being a burden to others'. He had his wish, dying after only a few days' illness. He had been a pattern parishioner, devout, unquestioning and uncomplaining; validating by his virtues the system under which he lived, and arousing in his parish priest the generous and protective feelings which he was rarely able to exercise. Small wonder that Skinner determined to pay for a gravestone reading:

Here lieth James Britten
who was what every true Briton should be,
An honest, Good Man,
...

Reader
May thou both live and die as he did. (Skinner, 58–9)

Bishop

It would be pleasant to record that the relationship between parish priests and their fathers in God has invariably been marked by intimacy and mutual trust, by wise guidance on one hand and by a growth in grace and spiritual effectiveness on the other. George Herbert* expressed this ideal when he wrote that the country parson should honour his diocesan both in word and behaviour, and resort to him in any difficulty, whether in his studies or in his parish (Herbert, XIX). Unfortunately the reality has often been otherwise, partly and inevitably because of the personalities involved and partly and less excusably because of the institutional nature of the Church of England.

From the point of view of the parochial clergy, the most prominent characteristic of the episcopate has been remoteness. Dioceses have been large, suffragans appointed in numbers only over the past century, and the time of bishops given to politics, administration and scholarship – to anything other than pastoral care. The situation was at its worst in the eighteenth century, when an elderly episcopate spent the parliamentary season in London and for the most part preferred the comfort of their studies to the rigours of travel round their sees. Even in the reforming nineteenth century, Cyril Garbett's** father, vicar of a parish within four miles of Farnham Castle, received only two visits from the Bishop of Winchester in the twenty-six years of his incumbency.

Remoteness has not been simply a matter of geography. It has also been a consequence of the exercise of authority. The Church of England has inherited from the mediaeval church a tradition of prelacy which has tolerated large dioceses and which has placed greater weight on the exercise of power than on that of love. Many great bishops such as Whitgift and Laud have been more notable for their political and administrative than for their spiritual capacities; those like Edward King have been rare. Consequently, a characteristic emotion of the clergy in the presence of their bishop has been unease. Even the cheerful and secure James Woodforde*, who passed several pleasant social occasions with his Bishop, wrote after one of them: 'Upon the whole we spent an agreeable Day, but must confess that being with our equals is much more agreeable' (Woodforde, 2.104). George Woodward** commented with refreshing honesty on the failure of his Bishop to call on him: 'I can't say, that a visitant of this rank would have given me a very extraordinary pleasure, any otherwise than that I should have been in hopes, that sometime or other he might have taken into his head, to have paid for the trouble he had given me' (Woodward 45).

The clergy's reservations about their diocesans have not been merely perverse. Cyril Garbett**, when Archbishop of York, was attentive to his parish priests but also intimidated them. They felt that his visits were of inspection rather than encouragement; the way in which he rationed his time often meant that, just as a priest was preparing to open his heart, the Archbishop would get up to go. His peremptory manner inhibited communication and led to serious misjudgments on his part which sometimes sent a clergyman away from an interview broken-hearted. At an earlier stage in his career, as Bishop of Southwark, he had been more intimidating still, terrifying even senior clergy to the extent that one confessed he could hardly pluck up the courage to ring the bell of Bishop's House.

On the other hand when, as with Garbett, severity and strong leadership were combined with deep devotion and the will to love, remoteness did not entirely inhibit pastoral care. At Southwark, after compelling an incumbent to resign because of drunkenness, he took every step necessary for his treatment and rehabilitation. At York, he listened patiently to the bitter and silly accusations of a priest in serious personal trouble, and wrote 'I must try to help him'. Arriving at a parish with a deed of resignation for a vicar who had been reported by two archdeacons for writing cheques which could not be met, he found a young couple hopelessly ignorant of finance and in the hands of a money-lender, and resolved to clear their debts. A priest harassed for four years by a religious maniac was eventually provoked into ringing the Archbishop direct; the matter was sorted out within twenty-four hours with the aid of the local Chief Constable, and the priest mildly rebuked for not invoking the Archbishop at an earlier stage. The clergy concerned in these cases would not have held Garbett's Arctic disposition against him (Smyth, *Garbett* ch.VI and ch.XIV).

Sometimes relationships have been built on stronger foundations than the social kindness which delighted Skinner and Woodforde or the practical helpfulness which mitigated Garbett's severity. Edward King moved from his country palace into Lincoln in part because, as he remarked, it was not every poor parson who could afford half a crown for a cab fare. He invited his clergy to an annual retreat in the Cathedral, and corresponded endlessly with those in difficulty or doubt. His accessibility was legendary, his philosophy summed up in one of his letters: 'It is my great wish ... to help on clergy of the diocese into peaceful communion with God, that they may then be enabled to do the same for their people' (King, *Letters* 122). Emanating love himself, he made it easy for his clergy to love him in turn. When he was brought before the Archbishop of Canterbury for alleged ritualism, one of his clergy wrote supportively: 'As one of the Evangelical clergy of the Diocese, and one who has received innumerable kindnesses at the hands of your Lordship, I wish ... to assure you of my unfeigned love to your person and sincere regard to your office' (Russell, *King* 158).

When Samuel Garratt** was working among the large Irish community in the London parish of St-Giles-in-the-Fields in the 1850s he wished to conduct parts of his services in Irish. He approached bishop Blomfield, for his permission, only to be told that the law forbade it. 'Then the Bishop looked up with a kindly smile and said, "I will tell you what I would do if I were you. I should have the service all the same. Only you must not say that the Bishop of London gave you leave."' Garratt wrote: 'The kindly and sensible advice gave me a lesson for life' (Garratt, 231–2). The lesson was, of course, that the clergy should be prepared to experiment without embarrassing their bishop by asking for his formal approval. In so far as the Church of England has adapted itself to the needs of the centuries, it has done so largely because of the readiness of bishops to trust their clergy to discern the spiritual needs of their parishes and to respond appropriately to them. Despite William Grimshaw's* extra-legal activities and the attempts of other clergy to delate him, he was protected by successive archbishops. Archbishop Gilbert asked Grimshaw to preach before him and said: 'I would to God all the clergy in my diocese were like this good man!' (Baker, *Grimshaw* 132).

A century later, Bishop Jackson of London, though totally averse to ritualism, also knew a good priest when he saw one, and dealt tactfully and patiently with Charles Lowder**. He went to great lengths to accommodate him and to avoid driving him into a corner. He twice ensured that attempts to proceed against him by law came to nothing, and though the relationship was an edgy one Lowder was preserved from the kind of harrassment to which Alexander Mackonochie** had been exposed under Bishop Tait. A later Bishop of London, Walsham How, consulted by Samuel Barnett* about his proposal for informal worship hours, replied: 'On the whole, Barnett, I think the best thing I can do is to wink' (Barnett, 1.275).

The clergy have frequently needed episcopal protection from their parishioners. A rich and influential landowner wrote to Bishop Talbot of Winchester to complain of Arthur Hopkinson**, Vicar of Banstead, Surrey, in the 1920s. The bishop's charming reply concluded: 'I hope you will not find it necessary to alienate yourself from your vicar, your church, and (may I say?) from myself' (Hopkinson, 93).

The young Mervyn Stockwood** was fortunate in his diocesan, Bishop Woodward of Bristol. He supported Stockwood in the considerable difficulties of his curacy (including the threat of arrest after a political sermon), and offered him a lift to one of the outdoor political meetings on behalf of the Christian Socialists at which Stockwood regularly spoke and which earned him the soubriquet of the 'Red traitor' from a senior local clergyman. When he offered Stockwood Moorfields, Bishop Woodward accepted his illegal condition that he should have a free hand to run the parish on an ecumenical basis. He winked at Stockwood's cavalier attitude to faculties, remarking on one visit to St Matthew's: 'I always have to play Nelson here as I never know what illegalities you and your curates have been up to!' His gentle handling preserved for the Church a talented priest whose career he could quite easily have shattered either by direct action or by standing aloof (Stockwood, 30, 35, 36, 39, 117).

When he became a Bishop, Stockwood supported Nicolas Stacey**, almost as stormy a petrel as he had been, when Stacey had problems with one of his staff (Stacey, 68).

The two men's relationship was not, however, always easy, partly because they were so alike, partly because Stockwood, in assuming a bishop's responsibilities, felt bound to accept constraints which as a parish priest he was able cheerfully to ignore. Stacey thought that Stockwood promised more than he could deliver, thus pointing up the problem that a bishop's power is in many respects severely limited. Even Garbett could not override the parson's freehold. When an elderly and incompetent incumbent resisted a suggestion that he should resign by replying: 'Your Grace, you are an old man and so am I, and if you will give the lead by retiring, I will follow your example,' Garbett could do no more than leave in silence (Smyth, *Garbett* 385). It is little wonder that a modern author has written: 'The bishop is called to martyrdom ... [for example to] ... rejection, misunderstanding and deferential defiance, particularly by disgruntled clergy ... "His authority is swathed in impressive impotence"' (Melinsky, 157).

Just as there have been priests who have been encouraged to reach their full spiritual stature by their bishops, so there have been those who have been constrained and diminished by them. Robert Dolling* had both experiences, and it is worth recounting them at some length.

In *Ten Years in a Portsmouth Slum* Dolling wrote of time spent at university 'that it is a time of acquiring character for the priesthood, hardness, endurance, mental struggle, intellectual activity, no one but a Bishop can imagine.' His general point apart, he had reason to sound sour about bishops. He had felt compelled by episcopal pressure to resign his phenomenally successful ministry at St Agatha's, Landport. He still owed £3000 personally for parish enterprises, and: 'I am paying for the church in which I shall never minister again, for an increased playground for the school in which I shall never teach again, for the bad house [a brothel he had bought] next the parsonage, so that it may be enlarged, though I may never live there again, for an organ for the new church' (Dolling, *TY* 86, 182).

It would be easy to tell Dolling's story so as to paint the conduct of bishops in the darkest colours. While he was still a deacon he built up in his own inimitable fashion St Martin's Mission in the parish of Holy Trinity, Stepney. Ordained priest in 1885, he sought to have the mission district turned into a parish. Bishop Temple of London, the future archbishop, insisted, however, on licensing him as a curate of Holy Trinity. He was within his rights; but he was in effect saying that Dolling deserved no greater freedom of action than any other young clergyman. Dolling resigned, and soon afterwards went to Landport. His biographer comments: 'It was on the altar of red-tape that his work [in London] ... was sacrificed' (Osborne, *Dolling* 58).

Ten years later Randall Davidson, another future Archbishop, had just taken over the diocese of Winchester when the question of licensing the new St Agatha's church, Landport, was referred to him. A tangled dispute ensued over a third altar within the church intended specifically for the celebration of masses for the dead. Eventually Davidson ruled that Dolling must discontinue the practice of masses for the dead, and must observe the *Book of Common Prayer* rubric requiring three communicants other than the priest. Dolling resigned; the bishops closed ranks against him. It was not until 1898 that he was offered another living.

Dolling presented the bishops responsible for him with a considerable dilemma. On the one hand, his work among the poor was beyond praise; indeed, almost beyond emulation because it depended so much on his personal character. But on the other hand that very character made him a turbulent subordinate and an inveterate rule-breaker. His biographer writes, rather disingenuously, that he did not 'at any time actually defy the bishops, as he was always ready to resign should episcopal remonstrances with which he disagreed become episcopal commands which he could not conscientiously obey' (Osborn, *Dolling* 172). Another way of putting it might be to say that he dared his bishops to take him on.

The craggy Temple can perhaps be pardoned for failing to perceive in the young Dolling a quality which entitled him to special treatment; his first two bishops in the diocese of Winchester treated him with extreme sensitivity. Both Bishop Browne and Bishop Thorold were Evangelicals, who abhorred many of Dolling's practices; both had their brushes with him; but both accepted a great deal of which they disapproved because they admired Dolling's work. Looking back on his time at St Agatha's after his resignation (and no doubt making implicit comparisons) Dolling regretted any harsh things he had said about Bishop Thorold. 'A passion for the poor consumed his [the bishop's] heart' (Dolling, *TY* 164).

Even Davidson was not as heavy-handed as the narrative above suggests. He was new to the diocese; he relied on advice given by the rural dean, who was hostile to Dolling; in an interview Dolling betrayed his lack of theology by saying things which confirmed Davidson's worst fears about his attitude to prayers for the dead; Dolling was in fact thinking of resigning in any event, in order to take a much-needed rest. Not unnaturally he resented the way Davidson treated him; but the responsibility for his departure did not lie entirely upon one side. Dolling's sympathetic biographer summarized the problem when he wrote 'Dolling could be no doubt on occasion very difficult, but this was only because of his own indomitable zeal' (Osborne, *Dolling* 58). His troubles were tragic in the true sense, in that they arose for the most part from conflicts between good men.

Colleagues

George Herbert* thought that the country parson should keep 'good correspondence with all the neighbouring pastors round about him, performing for them any ministerial office which is not to the prejudice of his own parish. Likewise he welcomes to his house any minister, how poor or mean soever, with as joyful a countenance, as if he were to entertain some great lord' (Herbert, XIX).

Good correspondence has often prevailed, the common vocation serving as a bond of union. At a purely social level the clergy have looked to each other for congenial company, especially since, in rural areas, the choice of dinner companions has been very limited. Ralph Josselin*, William Cole**, James Woodforde*, John Skinner* and Francis Kilvert* constantly visited, or were visited by, other parish priests. However, propinquity has also had negative effects. Robert Grimshaw's* own vicar, Benjamin Kennet, tried unavailingly to get him suspended for his extra-parochial activities (Baker, *Grimshaw* 131), and a young clergyman living locally affixed a paper to the door of John Fletcher's* parish church charging him with 'rebellion, schism, and being a disturber of the peace' for preaching outside his own parish and in dissenting meeting houses (Benson, *Fletcher* 66. The first charge was true, the second false.).

Local clerical meetings for prayer, Bible study and discussion have a long history. Josselin records many in the period before the Restoration, ranging from consideration of 'divers particulars in reference to church government, but came to no conclusion' to 'baptizing of persons that are not in church state'. On the latter discussion Josselin commented: 'My brethren and I are none of the nimblest disputants, but exercise will quicken us I hope.' After 1660 things were less happy. What had been 'freindly and comfortable and profitable' in 1647 was marred by 'janglings' in 1678 (Josselin, 95, 105, 107, 92, 615). In 1817 Skinner recorded that one of the regular meetings of local clergy was largely given over to conversation lamenting the prevalence of Dissent. He went on: 'I only wish our Meeting were better attended and more systematic. If a paper were to be written against each meeting ... it might be better than delivering our crude opinions ... without sufficient consideration' (Skinner, 111). Kilvert, attending a ruridecanal conference in 1874 on the topic 'How to work a parish', noted that several clergy described enterprises in their own parishes in glowing terms. In addition one priest spoke 'strongly' in favour of the clergy confining themselves to their own parishes, another 'in bad taste' against dissenters and a third 'unwisely' on the Contagious Diseases Act (Kilvert, 2.435–6). All of this suggests that over the centuries local clerical meetings have been what they remain, occasions which conscience suggests should be used for considered discussion but which have in fact been devoted to informal mutual support and to letting off steam.

The members of the hierarchy who have given rank and file clergy the most support have been rural deans. Parish priests themselves, with little or no coercive powers and with a limited period in office, they have rarely had administrative or political axes to grind. Robert Hawker*, when he was a rural dean, initiated the practice of holding ruridecanal synods and persuaded his bishop to hold diocesan ones (Brendon, *Hawker* 157). Nicolas Stacey** urgently represented the plight of his overstretched colleagues to his bishop (Stacey, 254).

The clergy have also supported each other through organizations based on principles other than contiguity. In 1855, Charles Lowder** founded the Society of the Holy Cross whose objects were to promote a stricter rule of life among the clergy, to establish home missions to preach the gospel to the poor, and to defend and extend Catholic faith and practice. The SHC encouraged clergy to go into retreat, and supported them in ritualistic practices; its members incurred much episcopal obloquy (Ellsworth, *Lowder* passim). Those in the Catholic tradition in our own day have sometimes become Franciscan tertiaries or, if single, members of the Oratory of the Good Shepherd.

The Evangelicals were earlier in the field. John Fletcher founded the Society of Ministers of the Gospel, an association to promote spiritual life and ministerial efficiency. Its members met for two days twice a year (Macdonald, *Fletcher* 88). The London Evangelical clergy used to meet at the Eclectic Society, founded in 1783, for discussion (Balleine, 46). Charles Simeon* arranged summer house-parties for like-minded clergy and their wives; they were marked, he felt, with 'solemnity, tenderness, spirituality and love' (Hopkins, *Simeon* 119–20).

Herbert's second requirement, that the clergy should support one another in their daily work, has been general practice. All our clerical diarists did duty for colleagues and found colleagues ready to do duty for them. Sometimes there was a kind of shunting effect, caused by difficulties of travel; a parson would do duty for his neighbour so that he in turn could do duty for some one else (see, for example, Woodforde, 1.275). This mutual support was, and still often is, given out of good will; there have also been paid substitutions, and clergy who have eked out a meagre living or supplemented a pension by undertaking them.

When Herbert required that his parson should greet all other ministers as 'great lords' he assumed a fraternity of order which would ignore differences of wealth and standing. Such a sense of fraternity has in fact not always been apparent. In particular there has often been a gulf fixed between incumbents with the freehold and their less fortunate colleagues; and between incumbents generally and their curates.

It has frequently been the case that a large parish or group of parishes has been served by a team of clergy under the leadership of one of them. In the early nineteenth century the parish of Bradford was served by a parish church and thirteen others, each cared for by a curate. Leadership was not always sensitive. George Bull** resigned his care of his newly-built church of St James because the vicar of Bradford refused him both independence and the fees for occasional services (Gill, *Bull* 128–131). Walter Hook* took the unusual step of dividing Leeds into independent parishes, retaining only the patronage. He sacrificed a large part of his income from fees and also much of his power over his colleagues, a step which caused him considerable grief in the case of the rebellious Anglo-Catholic parish of St Saviour's (Stranks, *Hook* 65, 97–100). The policy of Edward Jacob, vicar of Portsea at the end of the nineteenth century, was more typical; he re-built the mother church, built four daughter churches, and had a staff of ten curates (Lockhard, *Lang*, 116–17).

In modern times the shortage of clergy and the alleged loneliness of single-handed incumbents have led to the growth of group and team ministries. The successful operation of such schemes has depended upon the personalities and the wisdom of those concerned; since clergy have tended to be individualists and parishes individualistic, the happiest arrangements have been those with a maximum of devolved responsibility.

I had a friend from teaching days, an exceptionally sane and well-balanced person, who entered the ministry in his thirties and who was driven into a nervous breakdown by his incumbent during his first curacy. I was also personally involved as a layman when a curate was forced into resignation by his vicar and abandoned by his bishop. Fortunately, the bishop's successor took a different line, and the clergyman in question was salvaged.

Such examples, which could be multiplied indefinitely, illustrate the degree of dependence of curates upon incumbents, and the consequences of the relationship being a poor one. In the past, of course, a curate was not as a rule the assistant of a resident incumbent, but his substitute. Often his disregarded substitute; asked by the Bishop of Norwich what was the name of his curate for the two parishes he held in the diocese, Joseph Price** was unable to remember (Price, 3).

A curacy has been fraught with hazards. It was common practice in the eighteenth century for incumbents to fail to license their curates; in this way they could avoid the Act of 1713 which set a minimum stipend and could dismiss the curate at a moment's notice (Hart, *TCL* 112). E.B. Ellman was ordained in 1838, and accepted the curacy at Berwick in Sussex. The rector, Harry West, allowed him to live in the rectory and paid him £40 a year; on that income he had to buy pigs instead of books and send the vegetables from his garden to market. West lived in Lewes, eight miles away. In the six years of Ellman's curacy he never visited him. Instead he harassed him: on the large scale by trying to make him pay the rates, which he had originally promised to pay himself; on the small scale by removing a clock from the rectory on the grounds that it was not usual to provide one (Virgin, 216).

There have been, of course, more productive relationships. Charles Simeon's attitude to his curate Henry Martyn, later a famous missionary, might be characterized in modern terms as tough love. The older man told the younger that he knew as much about the trials and temptations of the Christian life as of the distances of the planets; that his views on sacred subjects were 'wrong'; that he should read public worship with more solemnity and devotion. Later Simeon dissuaded Martyn from pressing his suit on Lydia Grenfell, whom Martyn dearly loved and whom he wished to accompany him to India. None the less, Martyn was devoted to Simeon and found a growing happiness in working with him (Hopkins, *Simeon* 146–8).

The curates of Cosmo Lang** at Portsea 'respected him a lot and feared him a little'. They called him 'Sir', and when they wished to see him about anything, made formal appointments (Lockhart, *Lang* 119). Cyril Garbett** was subjected to this regime for two years. He then served for eight under Bernard Wilson, who adopted a very different policy. His curates, a diverse bunch, were thrown back on their own resources and expected to use their own initiative. Garbett said of him: 'His clergy felt that he trusted them completely, that he looked on them as comrades in the work ... He had a remarkable power of gaining the affection of his men. In almost every one of his curates there was some quality which attracted him, and which he drew out, so that all felt bound to him by some common interest or sympathy' (Smyth, *Garbett* 78).

Garbett learned a great deal from Wilson, but when he succeeded him his fear of being regarded with insufficient respect by his erstwhile fellow-curates and the natural austerity of his temperament made him a remote and severe taskmaster. Tales abound of his obsessive insistence on punctuality and of the tongue-lashings which he administered. He insisted that his curates spend their mornings in study, their afternoons (after an hour of recreation) in visiting, and their evenings either in attending clubs or in more visiting. Sermons were carefully scrutinized in advance, and junior curates had to present to the vicar a weekly 'Washing List', which accounted for every hour in the preceding week. On the other hand, Garbett insisted each man took a full day a week off, behaved with kindness and sympathy when a curate was ill, and apologized on the rare occasions when he convinced himself that he had been in the wrong. His curates were not fond of him, but they deeply respected him and looked back on their time at Portsea as a superb training (Smyth, *Garbett* 107–26).

Faults have not always been exclusively on the incumbent's side. James Woodforde was plagued by the behaviour of Mr Cotman, a curate he appointed to do duty for him in his latter years. Cotman failed to turn up on several occasions; was once too late for the service to take place and once began it so early that only a few people were there; and once turned up without a sermon. Woodforde was very relieved when he gave notice (Woodforde, vol. 5 passim).

More galling still were the experiences of John Hepworth, who became vicar of Harewood, Yorkshire, in 1699. He found a curate, William Cheldrey, already securely in place, and had neither the means to remove nor the strength to subdue him. Cheldrey secured the affections of Hepworth's widowed daughter, and took full advantage of the ill health which prevented Hepworth from doing regular duty and which gave his curate the leading role in the conduct of the parish's affairs. The patron, John Boulter, heartily disliked Cheldrey but was not prepared to cast him adrift. In the event the cuckoo took over the nest. The right of presentation reverted to the Archbishop of York, and, when Hepworth vacated the living in 1704, Cheldrey was given his place (Hart, *ECCP* 139–144).

Henry Fardell* both sinned against his curates and was sinned against by them. During his twenty-two years at Wisbech he had no less than ten, and approved of only one. His high sense of duty and his pernickety nature made him a difficult man to work for, and if he spoke to his curates in the same terms as he wrote about them relations must have been perpetually strained. He constantly complained to his diary about the neglect of duty of the two who served him longest, Messrs King and Jackson, chronicling unwarranted absences and failures to visit, to complete returns and to keep in touch with him. These offences, however, paled into insignificance beside those of Mr Montion who tried to 'raise a party in the Parish'; of Mr Calder, who 'formed an improper acquaintance' with the local drinking set; of Mr Copeman whom he thought idle and factious and whom he had to keep under 'great restraint'; and, above all, of Mr Fowell who managed to create a breach between his rector and the Bishop (Fardell 130–35).

Looking back at the end of his ministry Arthur Hopkinson** wrote: 'From the curate's side I knew the comradely vicar, the inspiring vicar, the aloof but trusting vicar. From the vicar's side, I knew the incompetent but lovable curate, the self-centred and partially efficient curate, and the brotherly-disciple curate.' He concluded that the first essentials for a happy relationship were that the vicar should trust the curate and give him responsibility and a free hand; and that he should consult him daily and about everything. The model, he thought, was supplied by Paul's letters to Timothy; though for completeness it would also be necessary to have Timothy's letters to Paul (Hopkinson, 155–7).

Appointments

A familiar joke concerns the priest offered promotion who buries himself in an agony of prayerful consideration while his wife gets on with the packing. Neither the clergy nor their wives have been guided exclusively by the main chance over questions of preferment; but spirituality has always had to contend with worldliness.

Few have been as high-minded as M.H. Close who resigned Shangton, Leicestershire, in 1857 because of 'scruples as to the propriety of holding a benefice under lay patronage' (Chadwick, *VC* 2.207); or as Thomas Hancock** who in 1872 refused the offer of a parish from Lord Halifax on principle: 'You are the Lord and Patron ... let the people elect me' (Reckitt, 7). Sydney Smith* was being realistic rather than cynical when he wrote: 'A clergyman always attends first to those who have any preferment to give away, and though I am so full of preferment that I can hold no more, the old habit prevails' (Bell, *Smith* 166). Throughout Anglican history clerical appointments have been made on a highly personal basis. Even today the bureaucratic methods of appointment and promotion usual in other large organizations take second place to acquaintance and the predilections of individuals.

Patronage has often been a prerequisite of orders. Bishops have been reluctant to ordain men without evidence that a post awaited them; and they have refused to ordain men they have found personally unacceptable. On the whole, however, first curacies have not been too hard to come by, though easier for some than others. Walter Hook* and Francis Kilvert* served with their fathers, while Charles Kingsley* was indebted to his father for his first post at Eversley. James Woodforde* was offered his curacy at Thurloxton by a university acquaintance; after only a few months he too moved to his father's parish. By contrast, John Newton* was twice refused ordination, partly because of his informal education and partly because of his Methodist connections. It was only when he came to the notice of Lord Dartmouth, that he was enabled to go to Olney. George Crabbe** was ordained, after an irregular education, only because of the patronage of Edmund Burke (Crabbe, 1.98). William Andrew* was rebuffed by a prospective vicar for being too evangelical, and displeased Bishop Bathurst of Norwich at interview. His chance came when his Evangelical connections secured him the offer of the curacy of Gimingham; though he might still have been refused ordination had not a friend introduced him to the bishop's chaplain who was to examine him (Chadwick, *Andrew* 19–21). Offered a title, Conrad Noel** was refused ordination by bishop Ryle of Exeter because of his alleged pantheism. When, during his first curacy, he delivered a series of lectures on Catholic Socialism, his bishop refused to ordain him priest and dismissed him from his post (Dark, *Noel* 45).

Charles Simeon* despaired of finding a suitable first curacy, and thought of putting out an advertisement, to read: 'A young clergyman, who felt himself an undone sinner, and looked to the Lord Jesus Christ alone for salvation, and desired to live only to make that Saviour known unto others, was persuaded that there must be some persons in the world whose views and feelings on this subject accorded with his own, though he had now lived three years without finding so much as one; and if there were any minister of that description he would gladly become his curate and serve him gratis' (Hopkins, *Simeon* 33). He was not driven to that extreme; indeed, unless a short period standing in for an incumbent may be so described, he served no curacy at all. His father secured him the incumbency of Holy Trinity, Cambridge, through his friendship with the bishop of Ely, despite the facts that he was still a deacon, had not yet taken his degree and had only the most minimal experience.

As this example illustrates, incumbency, like curacy, has depended upon connections. A fellowship at an Oxford or Cambridge college used to provide a golden but not a certain opportunity. James Woodforde was presented to Weston Longueville by his colleagues at New College, Oxford, after a contested election which he won by 21 votes to 15 (Woodforde, 1.143). John Skinner's* uncle purchased the living of Camerton for him. Henry Fardell* was appointed to Wisbech by his father-in-law, Bowyer Sparke, the bishop of Ely. So many of this prelate's relations held ecclesiastical office in his diocese that it was said that a man would find his way through the Fens by the light of the Sparkes in the stubble (Fardell, 136). John Mitford** held three Crown livings simultaneously because of the efforts of his distant relative Lord Redesdale, Lord Chancellor of Ireland (Colloms, 99). George Denison** was given East Brent by his brother, the Bishop of Salisbury, who happened at the time of the vacancy to be administering the diocese of Bath and Wells (G.A. Denison, *Notes of My Life*, 1878, 93). Sydney Smith was offered the Chancery living at Foston in 1806 because during a brief Whig administration his friend Lady Holland approached the Lord Chancellor over the dinner table (Bell, *Smith* 72–3). A priest of our own century, W. Rowland Jones**, who was a strong supporter of the Labour party, was offered only curacies for the first ten years of his ministry; when a Labour government came in he was offered livings by both the Prime Minister and the Lord Chancellor (Jones, 122–3).

The road to incumbency has often been stony, and a high proportion of the clergy have fallen by the wayside. In the early nineteenth century, about 20% of the clergy remained curates for the whole of their lives and a further 25% left parochial work (Virgin, 140). Lack of influence could be fatal. Fielding's Parson Adams, promised a living by a patron whom he had supported politically, lost his chance when the relation on whom he had relied for influence died (Fielding, 167). Adams did eventually receive an incumbency, but Margaret Oliphant's Cecil St John was less fortunate. Curate in charge in one parish for twenty years, he was thrust out at the age of sixty-five by the death of the incumbent, and only his death preserved him from yet another curacy. His fatal defect had been passivity. The lack of drive which did not hinder his pastoral ministry made him reluctant to engage in the badgering necessary for preferment (Oliphant, *CC* passim). Tragic outcomes have not been unknown. In 1902 the elderly F.J. Bleasby entered Tiverton workhouse after having made 470 unsuccessful applications for a curacy (Barrow, 176).

Few clergy have been content with their first incumbency; many have been prepared to do whatever was necessary to secure advancement. In the early eighteenth-century so many clergy obtained Kentish parishes through marrying the female members of the family of Archbishop William Wake that it used to be said that 'a parson must be asleep who doesn't marry a Wake' (Price, 83–4). John Flowerdew Colls, rector of Laindon, Essex, from 1853 paid several thousand pounds into his bishop's private account to secure a move to Kent. The bishop died before a move could be arranged, and Colls lost his money (Loo, *Phelps* 124–9). James Layton was the curate and only priest in three Norfolk parishes from 1802 to 1830. In 1830 he put his name forward for the rectory of St Peter's, Sandwich. This presentation was by popular election, and Layton had to face a contest. He disliked the idea: 'I hate a contest for shopkeepers favor – I hate a struggle as it were upon the very steps of a Pulpit – & most of all to be beaten in the struggle and kick'd down.' However, he swallowed his pride: 'I have applied for votes in Hospitals, Almshouses, Workhouses and Alehouses – in Tanyards & in Coalships; have stayed the labourer with his barrow or mortar hod – have discussed points of Creed with an Unitarian Brewer's servant ... & a Methodist barber.' His efforts and his local connections prevailed, and he was elected (Virgin, 246).

Numbers of clergy have been involved in the embarrassments of public canvassing. The valuable living of Painswick in Gloucestershire was, in the early nineteenth century, in the hands of the local householders. The incumbent was appointed by election, with the unedifying result that vacancies reproduced the worst features of contemporary parliamentary elections. Francis Witts** reported that: 'On a recent occasion the place presented all the intrigue, bustle and chicanery of a contested borough; legal assessors, counsel, and attorneys, bribery, bold swearing, clamour and warm excitement ... disorder, drunkenness and all the concommitments [sic] of a contested election, with great expense in agency, treating and the like, has hitherto been the rule of the place' (Witts, 145–50).

However, open endeavour has been less common than more discreet though not necessarily less humiliating methods. George Woodward** of East Hendred maintained his acquaintance with his relation the duke of Grafton and his professional superior the bishop of Salisbury with a self-interest equally undisguised and unrewarded (Woodward, passim). Joseph Price**, whose search for preferment was almost obsessional, endeavoured to ingratiate himself with the Yorke family by writing a funeral oration on the death of Lord Hardwicke in 1764 which was as sycophantic as it was empty. He persevered in commending himself to the family and it was a blow when Charles Yorke, Lord Hardwicke's son, died only three days after accepting the appointment, rich in ecclesiastical patronage, of Lord Chancellor. 'The breaking of a blood vessel discomforts all my glittering hopes, and tells me I must die Vicar of Brabourne' (Price, 35, and see ch. 3, passim).

Clergy have found various ways of commending themselves to those with patronage to offer. Joseph Price alleged that William Langhorne (1721–72), perpetual curate of Folkestone from 1753, was given the post by Archbishop Herring because he had, while in Yorkshire, preached against the Jacobite rebellion of 1745; and that John Gostling was given Milton, near Canterbury, because his father had showed the patron, a martyr to gout, how to put his leg on a chair without causing himself pain (Price, 137, 131). W.R. Hay, responsible with another clerical magistrate for loosing the yeomanry at the Peterloo massacre of 1819, was given the plum benefice of Rochdale by a grateful government (Virgin, 120). More scandalous still were the means by which Edmund Keene obtained Stanhope, Durham, in 1740. He had promised to marry the patron's illegitimate daughter in return for his appointment; but once installed he jilted her, and paid her £600 instead (Barrow, 97).

Since so much has depended upon good will, it has been a bold or foolhardy clergyman who has given the establishment offence. William Paley** was never offered high office, despite his outstanding intellectual qualifications, because of his latitudinarianism (*ODCC*). Sydney Smith's support of Catholic Emancipation closed the doors of preferment to him except when a Whig government was in power. He recorded a conversation in which 'a poor clergyman whispered to me that he was quite of my way of thinking, but had nine children. I begged he would remain a Protestant' (Bell, *Smith* 123). Arthur Stanton was told by the Bishop of London that if he joined Alexander Mackonochie** at St Alban's, Holborn, he need never expect preferment. The bishop was right. In the whole of his ministry Stanton was offered only one living – in Chicago (Russell, *Stanton* 34, 264. Stanton, however, was offered the post of prebendary at St Paul's Cathedral just before he died. He refused it). Nicolas Stacey** attracted sufficient odium at Woolwich in the 1960s for his bishop to predict accurately that he would not be offered another post in the Church of England (Stacey, 218, 283).

Precluded from advancement by prejudice against them, the holders of unpopular views have sometimes been salvaged by eccentric patrons, by party organizations or by the sheer force of their learning and sanctity. William Bennett*, forced out of St Barnabas, Pimlico because of his ritualism, was given sanctuary at Frome by Lady Bath. Lord Rosebery offered the socialist and Anglo-Catholic Charles Marson** another Somerset parish, Hambridge. Similarly, Conrad Noel, who had spent many years either as a curate or without a post because of his socialist views, was appointed to Thaxted by Lady Warwick, who was almost unique among the aristocracy in sharing his opinions. In the early nineteenth century Evangelicals were usually condemned either to curacies or to tiny parishes. William Romaine, the great Evangelical preacher and scholar, was not offered an incumbency in his chosen city of London until the age of 52; then, in 1764, the parishioners of St-Andrew-by-the-Wardrobe with St Anne, Blackfriars, elected him their rector despite his refusal to canvass. It was to help those who thought as he did that Charles Simeon set up the trust to buy presentations which bears his name.

Preferment may also be precluded by factors the minister concerned can do nothing about. It is said that the entry 'W.I.' on a diocesan file is fatal; the letters stand for 'Wife Impossible'. (I must confess that my only authority for this story is Howatch, *SR* 29.) It is certain that large numbers of posts are and will for the indefinite future be closed to women clergy because of their sex.

In modern times, and in profound contrast to the more distant past, canvassing for a move has been thought to be unspiritual. A priest, convention requires, should wait to be asked. Samuel Garratt** wrote: 'I was willing to serve Him anywhere, but I must be sent by Him.' This principle took him from a parish where his wife's health was endangered into a period of enforced idleness while he waited to see if anyone would offer him employment.

Eventually the possibility of a curacy arose. He would have disliked the post but would have accepted it had not he been offered at the same time exactly what he wanted, in the shape of a large slum parish (Garratt, 37).

However, the system of waiting to be approached has not obviated the importance of contacts and of influence; has perhaps even increased the element of the lottery. Nicolas Stacey claims to have secured a number of jobs for clergy simply because of chance meetings with bishops in process of filling vacancies (Stacey, 283).

Especially in modern times some vacancies have been advertised. I was told in the 1950s that no clergyman with any sense of self-respect would answer an advertisement; but since then attitudes have changed. At a Dover deanery chapter meeting in the early 1990s every stipendiary priest present took up an offer of a regular mailing of the Appointments Adviser's list of vacancies.

It would of course be ridiculous to suggest that merit has played no part in preferment. Conscientious bishops and patrons have at least applied the negative test, of not offering posts to their connections if they thought them undeserving. Thomas Fuller** wrote of his Good Patron: 'If he can by the same deed provide for God's house and his own family, he counts it lawful; but on no terms will prefer his dearest and nearest son or kinsman, if unworthy' (Fuller, *HS* 87). The system has served many devoted and excellent men; Bernard Gilpin* went to Houghton because of his friendship with Bishop Tunstall, but Tunstall could hardly have done better. None the less the presumption for the greater part of Anglican history has been that those with influence have first claim on vacancies, and that merit of itself is insufficient. After Sydney Smith had accepted Foston the Lord Chancellor wrote to him: 'I should be ... taking a merit ... which I have no claim to, if I were not to say that I should have given the living to the nominee of Lord and Lady Holland without any personal consideration; at the same time I can add very truly that I thought myself most fortunate indeed that the friend they selected was so deserving' (Bell, *Smith* 73). That put the situation in a nutshell. Influence was what mattered; being deserving was an agreeable extra.

The right to appoint – the advowson – was, until this century, a saleable commodity, and since it guaranteed an income for life it was usually bought or sold according to market rules. Jane Austen's hero, young Edmund Bertram, was deprived of the prospect of a family living because the presentation had to be sold to cover his elder brother's debts. Fortunately a second family living was held for him by a clergyman who resigned as soon as Edmund was old enough to take it over (Austen, *MP* 16–7).

This market system was subject to market sharp practice. A nineteenth-century clergyman bought the advowson to a parish where a vacancy was soon to occur. He presented himself, and then discovered that the glebe land was full of brick earth. This he sold. He then sold the advowson, and sought to resign the parish. His bishop, who discovered what had been going on, refused to accept his resignation; whereupon the clergyman bought another advowson, presented himself to the parish, and thus vacated his previous parish automatically (Chadwick, *VC* 2.211).

Sometimes we can observe in some detail the thought processes of clergy offered or considering other posts. The prospect of moving from Earl's Colne to nearby Hinningham threw Ralph Josselin* into an agony of mixed motives and tortured syntax. When the possibility arose in 1659 he noted 'lord I am thine to dispose of as thou pleasest, yett if it please thee make my lot comfortable at Colne, yett not my will but thy will be done.' He meant that his preference was to stay in his present post, if the financial problems which dogged him there could be resolved. A few days later he wrote: 'I earnestly sought god to direct mee in my going or staying at Colne, things seeme to worke out my remove, and my heart is much loosned from the place lord if soules require me here, and thy glory lie most in it, lett me not goe but lette mee not bee barren or unfruitfull in thy worke.' To paraphrase, he felt that circumstances were now pointing him to a move to which he was less disinclined than in the past; but his preference was still to stay if he could be useful. The issue disappeared from his diary when, after a positive offer from Hinningham, his patron at Earl's Colne, Mr Harlakenden, offered him an extra £20 a year to stay, 'an act of love', Josselin joyfully recorded, 'not easily matcht evidencing his zeale to god and love to my ministry' (Josselin, 438–9).

Cyril Garbett** went through torture when the time came for him to move on from his first curacy at Portsea. The possibility of a country parish where he would have plenty of time for study and writing provoked from a colleague whom he consulted a robust defence of the possibility of combining parochial and intellectual work in all circumstances. It included sentences which it is almost impossible to imagine anyone directing to the austere Garbett, even in his youth: 'I should always be ready to hand to check any propensity to over-parochialism. I should run down and pinch your bottom (mind you don't cease to have one when you become a vicar) and tell you to become intellectual again' (Smyth, *Garbett* 84).

In 1908 Archbishop Lang, who had been Garbett's vicar, offered him Goole. Garbett accepted, only to be offered the parish of Portsea in which he was serving as a curate a few weeks later. He had been initially convinced that God was calling him to Goole; but now he was cast into an agony of indecision, seeing powerful arguments both for and against accepting this new offer. Money does not seem to have been a factor; had it been so he would certainly have refused Portsea, where the whole of the vicar's stipend and a considerable sum besides were devoted to parochial uses. He consulted both Archbishops and his fellow-curates; but eventually told his Bishop, Ryle of Winchester, that he would stay at Portsea only if ordered to do so. The order was given; Garbett ran the parish with an iron hand and with considerable success until his elevation to the episcopate (Smyth, *Garbett* 85–97).

There is an inevitable collision between human nature and institutional characteristics on the one hand, and Christian ideals of service and abnegation on the other. It is easy for clergy who have been well served by the appointments system to retain a spiritual integrity which has not been put to the test. It is correspondingly hard for those ill-treated to avoid bitterness and disillusion. For the most part it has been the former group who have emerged into the view of history; but there is also plenty of evidence to show that the Anglican system of appointments has left a trail of blighted lives and twisted souls. The only thing to be said in its defence is that every possible alternative has almost as many disadvantages.

Establishment

In 1913 the Church Council of the parish of Shepherdswell, Kent, decided to build a hall. The parish magazine explained that it would be 'available to all who care to hire it, irrespective of their religious or political views, provided that nothing be said or done contrary to the principles of the Church of England or subversive of the authority of the King' (*SPM*, April 1913). The conditions illustrate both the commanding social influence which the Church of England claimed until weakness made the claim a mockery, and the close link with civil government natural to an established Church.

Until well into the nineteenth century the identification of Church and State was almost universally taken for granted. William Warburton, incumbent of Brent Broughton, near Newark, and also Frisby, Lincolnshire, wrote in his book *The Alliance of Church and State* (1736) that society would fall apart without the cement of religion. The state made an alliance with the majority church, and, in recompense for favours accorded her, the church upheld the civil power (Virgin, 143). What was true on the grand scale was true also on the small. The clergy serving the country's ten thousand parishes influenced daily life at least as much as the secular authorities, and worked hand in hand with them to serve a common cause.

The Church's liturgy has always evinced the intimacy between Church and State. Up to 1858 the *Book of Common Prayer* contained services to commemorate the day of Charles I's execution and (as a pair) the defeat of the Gunpowder Plot and the Glorious Revolution of 1688. To this day it contains a service to celebrate the day of the monarch's accession, and a plenitude of prayers for the royal family. On 5 November 1768 James Woodforde* 'read Prayers ... being ... the day on which the Papists had contrived a hellish plot in the reign of King James the first, but by the Divine hand of Providence were fortunately discovered'; on 30 January 1785 he 'read the Service for King Charles's Martyrdom'; on 29 May 1769 he 'read prayers this morning at Castle Cary ... the Restoration of Charles II from Popish tyranny' (Woodforde, 1.81; 2.173; 1.86).

In 1842 Henry Fardell* overbore the objection of his curate that 'the service was not often read', and adapted the normal Sunday worship to incorporate the Martyrdom. A few months later he did the same to commemorate the Restoration (Fardell, 118–19). The tradition continues. *The Alternative Service Book* of 1980 includes among its lesser commemorations that of King Charles the Martyr.

Loyalty to the monarch has been a natural product of the establishment. In the seventeenth century torrents of clerical ink and floods of clerical eloquence were devoted to the defence of the Divine Right of Kings. Personal devotion persisted even when the Stuarts had been banished and royal authority was ebbing away. Woodforde's diary is for the most part a laconic document; it took the royal family to evoke prolixity and the lyric mode. In March 1789: 'I read Prayers and Preached this Afternoon at Weston Church – Also read with the greatest Pleasure a Prayer composed on the Occasion of the restoration of His Majesty's Health, which I received this Morning. I return also to thee O Lord my private but most unfeigned Prayer of thanksgiving for the same. And may so good a King long live to reign over us – and pray God that his amiable and beloved Queen Charlotte may now enjoy again every happiness this World can afford, with so good a Man, and may it long, very long continue with them both here and eternal happiness hereafter. This is the ardent and most fervent Prayer of one of their most sincere subjects for the best of Kings and Queens.' Seeing the royal family on a visit to Sherborne provoked a long and ecstatic description of a 'Dies Memorabilis'. Substituting actions for words, he celebrated Queen Charlotte's birthday in 1780 by firing a triple-charged blunderbuss and by giving three cheers (Woodforde, 3.89, 126–9; 1.272).

Henry Fardell read prayers celebrating the birth of royal princes and princesses, and on 5 June 1842 'preached a sermon on the occasion of the late wicked attempt to shoot our beloved Sovereign' (Fardell, 5). Francis Kilvert* anxiously charted the news about the illness in 1871 of the not notably pious Prince of Wales. When recovery came he quoted (or composed) this remarkable piece of verse:

> Men met each other with erected look,
> The steps were higher that they took,
> Each to congratulate his friend made haste
> And long inveterate foes saluted as they passed. (Kilvert 2.95–9)

Woodforde, Fardell and Kilvert were conservatives. But even the sturdy social reformers George Bull** and Robert Dolling* did not lag behind them in monarchist zeal. Bull 'defended the throne and the aristocracy because he never faltered in his belief that nothing in the constitution stood in the way of changes necessary to secure social justice'. When the Prince of Wales married in 1863 Bull organized a breakfast for 1700 children and provisions for the bed-ridden

(Gill, *Bull* 115, 147). Dolling was as loyal to the monarchy as he was enthusiastic for the Empire (Osborne, *Dolling* 314–15).

In their allegiance to the monarchy the clergy have of course reflected public sentiment as well as helped to create it. The same might be said of their patriotism. George Woodward** celebrated the victory of Louisburg in 1758 by providing a bucket of ale for the bell-ringers (Woodward, 111). John Skinner offered to take up arms during the invasion scare of 1803, but after advice from his bishop withdrew to the more mundane task of recruiting, 'nevertheless resolving privately to learn the Broad Sword exercise, to be prepared in case of emergency' (Skinner, 10–11). Charles Kingsley* celebrated the Crimean War with a tract which assured the troops in action that the British army was God's army; he manifested the enthusiasm for bloodshed common among those who have had no experience of it (Chitty, *Kingsley* 169–70). When the First World War broke out archbishop Randall Davidson had to work hard to dissuade clergy from enlisting as fighting men (Hastings, 46).

Few clergy have taken the pacifist line of Arthur Stanton*, who spoke out against the Russo-Turkish war of 1878; or would have written with him: 'I hate war on principle … I would stand on the same platform with the Devil, if the Devil would advocate peace' (Russell, *Stanton* 184). One who did was Samuel Barnett* who at the height of anti-Russian sentiment in 1876 organized a public meeting to protest against jingoism. During the Boer War of 1899–1902 Toynbee Hall was divided against itself, with Barnett and his wife both firmly on the side of the Boers (Barnett, 2.39).

With patriotism have come xenophobia and racism. Charles Kingsley managed a disgraceful double when he observed of the Irish peasantry: 'To see white chimpanzees is dreadful; if they were black, one would not feel it so much' (Chitty, *Kingsley* 209).

A priest of the established Church has had only a restricted choice between overt identification with the machinery of civil government and a position of relative independence. He has had certain statutory civil responsibilities. In the seventeenth century he was required by law to be present when a rogue was whipped, could license sick people to eat flesh on fish days, could prosecute recusants if his wardens failed to do so, and had to certify that a dead person had been buried in a shroud made of sheep's wool. James Woodforde, in common with other parish priests, was in effect employed as a tax collector between 1783 and 1794, when a stamp duty was imposed on baptisms, marriages and burials (Russell, 142; Woodforde, 2.96–7). To this day the clergy have been extensively used as witnesses to identity and to character.

Anglican clergy have also been the agents of government, and until modern times the only agents (with the exception of a brief period after an Act passed by the Barebones Parliament in 1653) in solemnizing and recording marriages. The task has not been without its embarrassments. In the eighteenth century the

Bastardy Act imposed penalties upon the putative father unless he chose to marry the woman who had named him. The priest who performed the ceremony was part of a machinery designed to save the community welfare payments. Some resented their role. Even the complacent Woodforde noted after tying the knot for a reluctant swain: 'It is a cruel thing that any Person should be compelled by Law to marry ... It is very disagreeable to me to marry such Persons' (Woodforde, 2.197). John Skinner had a similar experience. The girl was near her time, but the father wanted a payment of two guineas for going through the ceremony, and was only with great difficulty persuaded to accept his fate free of charge (Skinner, 63–4).

For many clergy it has been a natural thing to assume the responsibility of civil magistracy. Archbishop William Laud encouraged parish priests to become magistrates in order to raise their social standing (Roger Lockyer, *Tudor and Stuart Britain* Longmans 1964, 253). In Georgian England one in four magistrates was a clergyman and one in six clergymen a magistrate (Virgin, 94). William Paley** spared time from his studies and the care of his parishes to serve as an irascible JP (*DNB*). The standard nineteenth-century book on the office of a JP was written by Richard Burn, vicar of Orton, Westmoreland (Clark, 35). Sydney Smith* and Henry Fardell were vigorous magistrates.

The occupation was not without hazard. In 1816 John Vachell, vicar of Littleport, Cambridgeshire, an unpopular magistrate, saw his vicarage wrecked before his eyes (Virgin, 8). In 1873 two clerical magistrates, Thomas Harris and W.D. Carter, incurred national obloquy when, after considerable hesitation, they sent 16 women to prison for trying to intimidate blacklegs brought in during a strike (Clark, 249–50).

The anomalies involved in this combination of roles did not pass unobserved. Charles Simeon* thought pastoral ministry must suffer. In addition clerical magistrates 'are likely to be snared into secular habits by their brother justices, or else to be hated and doubly opposed by them' (Virgin, 125). 'The offices are so far distinct,' declared W.L. Bowles, vicar of Bremhill, Wiltshire, from 1804 to 1850, 'that, except in cases of necessity, and for the good of the community, I would not wish to see a Minister preaching on Sunday, and sending a poacher to prison, or taking the examination of a frail parish damsel, on Monday.' Yet he was a magistrate himself (Virgin, 115).

R.W. Evans taught in *The Bishopric of Souls* that a clergyman should not be a magistrate. It was, however, right for him to use information obtained from visiting to help the civil authorities, and he should use his spiritual authority for such secular purposes as preventing riots. He advised his readers: 'Accustom yourself ... not to draw the line between the law of the kingdom of heaven, and the law of the kingdom of this world; for the latter flows, however defiled be the stream, from the pure fountain of the former' (Evans, 26, 229, 236, 247). As time went on, the clergy withdrew from the magistracy. In 1873 there were still 1043 clerical magistrates, in 1906 less than 40.

Parochial clergy have held civil offices other than that of magistrate. Woodforde was a commissioner of the Land Tax. After the 1834 Poor Law Amendment Act, many parish priests became active members of the local Boards of Guardians. Henry Fardell was chairman of the Wisbech Board (Fardell, 2). C. Dodson, chairman of the Andover Board, enforced the Act so harshly that he was the subject of a Parliamentary enquiry. By contrast Brooke Lambert, curate and later incumbent of St Jude's, Whitechapel, used his membership of a Board to mitigate the Act's evil effects (Clark, 159–60); as did Samuel Barnett, and in the following century Jack Putterell** at Thaxted (Putterell, 49).

Parish priests have served the establishment in a further and most important way. As this book abundantly illustrates, they were for centuries the main national repository of education and culture; adding substance to the claim that the Church represented the moral and spiritual aspect of society as a whole. State and Church, it was often argued, were interdependent. The civil authorities were restrained and guided by the teachings of the Christian faith; the Church sustained and sanctified the secular order. George Herbert's* country parson counted among his responsibilities the inculcation in every social class of virtues which would support and enrich the commonwealth (Herbert, XXIII). Two and a half centuries later the radical Stewart Headlam** believed so deeply in the identification of Church and nation that he hated Dissenters as schismatics (Reckitt, 74).

This ideal was not an ignoble one when compared with modern attempts to maintain the social order through bureaucratic regulation, penal sanctions and the use of force. There has been a tradition stretching back to the New Testament by which Christians have been expected to be good citizens; a more questionable but defensible tradition stretching back to Constantine by which the Church has lent aid and comfort to the State. In practice, however, the relationship between the State and the Church of England has been one-sided. The State has dominated the Church, and used her as its instrument. James I's remark 'no Bishop, no king' is well known; he made it for entirely secular reasons. Equally significant was his remark at the Hampton Court Conference of 1604: 'I [sic] will have one doctrine, one discipline, one religion, in substance and in ceremony' (Fuller, *CH* 3.206). Because religious practice was the cement which held society together and which subjected the people to their rulers, it was to be determined by the Crown. The clergy must be content to be subordinate in ecclesiastical as in civil matters. Thomas Fuller** wrote in his *Church History*: 'Every Convocation in itself is born deaf and dumb; so that it can neither hear complaints in religion, nor speak in the redress thereof, till first Ephphatha, "Be thou opened", be pronounced unto it by commission from royal authority' (Fuller, *CH* 2.400).

The powers over the Church which the Crown exercised passed to Parliament, which has not hesitated to use them. Ralph Josselin* commented disapprovingly on a sermon extolling the work of the parliamentary commissioners of 1656: 'I saw no beauty in the day, neither doe I joy to see ministers put under the lay power, and thus on their own head [viz. with their approval] ... lord remember us for we are become a reproach' (Josselin, 363). Even in quieter times than the seventeenth century Parliament has wielded a heavy hand. For example, in 1850 an attempt to place decisions about Anglican doctrine in the hands of the bishops was voted down in the House of Lords. In 1874 the Public Worship Regulation Act sought to curb the alleged excesses of ritualists. Even clergy who disapproved of ritual extremism writhed under this evidence of the raw power of state over church. George Denison** of East Brent thought the cure worse than the disease, because of its Erastian nature. But the problem did not go away. Dick Sheppard* was a leading light of the Life and Liberty Movement which sought greater autonomy for the Church. He was deeply disappointed by its anaemic outcome, the Church Assembly (Roberts, *Sheppard* 118–20). As late as 1927 the House of Commons rejected the Revised Prayer Book, leaving the clergy with the choice of staying with a *Book of Common Prayer* which many of them believed did not meet the needs of their time, or of ignoring the law in the interests (as they saw them) of their parishioners. The limited delegation of powers to General Synod in recent times has come only when the Church has ceased to be a powerful (though remaining a significant) force in national affairs.

For the most part, however, if the Church has not hugged her chains, she has worn them without complaint. The clergy have practised, and the laity have been taught, submission and quiescence. *The Homilies appointed to be read in Churches*, published in 1562 and providing a source for addresses for centuries thereafter, include a sermon in six parts against disobedience and wilful rebellion, and teach that subjects ought to be 'obedient, not only to their good and courteous, but also to their sharp and rigorous, Princes'. Robert Harris, vicar of Hanwell, Oxfordshire, declared in a London sermon in 1622: 'Happy that state wherein the cobbler meddles with his last, the tradesman with his shop, the student with his books, the counsellor with state, the Prince with the sceptre and each creature lives in his own element' (Barrow, 39–40). A thousand sermons have underlined the teaching of *The Whole Duty of Man* that rulers were entitled to active obedience; and, until the Church found herself imperilled by the policies of James II, a thousand sermons underlined the book's further teaching, that if the state enjoined anything contrary to God's commands subjects might refuse obedience but must not rebel (*WDM*, 232–3). In 1820, Charles Simeon, preaching on the accession of George IV, proclaimed that 'religion and loyalty are inseparable ... to inquire whether any or what circumstances would justify a departure from this rule (that the powers that be are ordained of God and are to be obeyed) ... is ground which a minister of the Prince of peace is not called to occupy' (Hopkins, *Simeon* 194).

Establishment has not only made the Church of England a junior partner of the

State; it has associated her with a continuing characteristic of the social order which Thomas More observed in the sixteenth century. 'When I consider and weigh in my mind all these commonwealths, which nowadays anywhere do flourish ... I can perceive nothing but a certain conspiracy of rich men procuring their own commodities under the name and title of the common-wealth. They invent and devise all means and crafts, first how to keep safely without fear of losing, that they have unjustly gathered together, and next how to hire and abuse the labour of the poor for as little money as may be.'

By identifying themselves with the State the clergy have identified them-selves with the rich and powerful. At best, they have been the instrument by which the few have sought to placate the many; at worst, one by which they have sought to subjugate them. Even reformist clergy have set strict limits to their zeal. For all his polemics on the condition of the poor, Charles Kingsley remained a social conservative. The poor must be relieved; but it was the function of the upper classes to make the necessary arrangements. Gibbon remarked with his usual delicate irony: 'So intimate is the connection of the throne and the altar that the banner of the church has very seldom been seen on the side of the people.' In a more local context many a landowner would have echoed the words of the Squire in Margaret Oliphant's *The Perpetual Curate*: 'The eldest [son] the squire, the second the rector. That's my idea ... of Church and State' (Oliphant, *PC* 444). A nineteenth-century intellectual described the village clergy as 'black dragoons' (Colloms, 23).

The use of religion as an instrument of social control has often been quite overt. The Duke of Wellington attended church once every Sunday except when in London: 'I consider that the attendance at divine service in publick is a duty upon every individual in high station, who has a large house and many servants, and whose example might influence the conduct of others' (quoted Chadwick, *VC* 1.515). Putting the same point the other way round John Skinner, commenting on misbehaviour in and absences from church, noted: 'Things are come to a sad state, and it proceeds from the total unconcern of the superior orders to religion; but this cement, once taken away from the building of the Constitution, it will soon sink under its own weight' (Skinner, 404–5). In 1828 a devout lady complained of a sermon of which she otherwise approved that it 'was rather calculated to raise the discontent of the poor, than to exercise the charity of the opulent' (Wagner, 23). Later in the nineteenth century the trade unionist Joseph Arch was convinced, with much evidence to support him, that the distribution of charity by squire and parson was a means of exerting political pressure (Colloms, 28).

In 1848, in one of his more prophetic moments, Charles Kingsley claimed that the Bible was being reduced to a 'mere special constable's hand-book, an opium dose for keeping beasts of burden patient while they were being overloaded' (quoted Clark, 29). His was a minority view. John Masefield describes the drunken Saul Kane railing at the local parson:

'You teach the ground-down starving man
That Squire's greed Jehovah's plan ...
(Better a brutal starving nation
Than men with thoughts above their station).'

Masefield puts this reply into the parson's mouth:

'You think the Squire and I are kings
Who made the existing state of things,
And made it ill. I answer No,
States are not made, nor patched; they grow,
Grow slow through centuries of pain
And grow correctly in the main ...
You think the Church an outworn fetter;
Kane, keep it, till you've built a better.' ('The Everlasting
   Mercy', quoted Christmas, 272–3)

Masefield's parson rather than Charles Kingsley spoke for the clergy as a whole. As the well-educated spokesmen of the possessing classes they have been cast in the role described in Niebuhr's *Moral Man and Immoral Society*: 'Since inequalities of privilege are greater than could possibly be defended rationally, the intelligence of privileged groups is usually applied to the task of inventing specious proofs for the theory that universal values spring from, and that general interests are served by, the special privileges which they hold.' Charles Simeon was representative of the general complacency when he declared of the British constitution of his time: 'Under the whole heaven there never was a country where the laws were more equitably, more impartially dispensed ... the peace and security which we of this happy land enjoy, under the domination of the laws, are not exceeded by any people under heaven, and are equalled by very few' (Hopkins, *Simeon* 198). Edward Bickersteth**, in a sermon delivered in 1844, suggested that the pouring out of the sixth of the bowls described in the book of Revelation could be seen in 'the spread of lawlessness, infidelity and superstition, in *Chartism, Socialism*, [author's italics] and open or half-disguised popery' (Hennell, 46).

For every Anglican clergyman who has seen the social order as unjust and sought to change it there have been a hundred who have seen it as God-given and who have sought to uphold it. The methods used or approved by the majority have ranged from a robust use of force to sensitive acts of charity which have justified the system at the same time as they have relieved the individual. Instances of the latter approach occur throughout this book; here are some of the former. In 1766 Mr Risley, rector of Tingewicke, Buckinghamshire, shot a highwayman dead; he was tried but acquitted (Cole, 60). James Woodforde 'heartily concurred' in vigorous measures taken against public disturbances, though he refused to take an active part because he 'did not think it consistent with the Character of a Clergyman'; he was relieved when in a time of hardship the poor remained 'very patient and submissive' (Woodforde, 4.313–14: 5.290). During the agricultural riots of 1830 Robert Wright, rector of Itchen Abbots, Hampshire, raised a small army to defend the local threshing machines. In a battle with rioters 40 or 50 were taken prisoner, and the rest put to flight (Virgin, 9).

To take a more extended example: Augustus Hare's* wife wrote that 'his respect for "the powers that be" ... prevented his sanctioning for a moment any insubordination of feeling or undue exaltation of the lower above the higher class'. This attitude was put to the test during the agricultural riots of 1830, when a group of labourers from elsewhere came to Alton-Barnes. Maria Hare gave them money to prevent damage to their home, while Augustus followed them to the nearby home of farmer Pile, and tried to reason with them. The rioters, however, started breaking up Pile's threshing machine; and when the farmer, arriving home, tried to prevent them, they dragged him off his horse, beat him, and smashed his furniture. Hare retreated, and an attempt to summon local assistance by ringing the church bell evoked no response. The rioters went off of their own accord, to be pursued and captured by the Yeomanry. 'And so ended our siege,' Maria wrote, 'which it must be owned was as little resisted as ever enemy was' (Hare, 1.290, 353).

Hare played his part in identifying the ring-leaders, who were severely punished. His wife was convinced that the rioters were wastrels who spent their money in beer-shops. She was glad that no one from Alton-Barnes took part, but claimed 'they all rejoice secretly at what is to bring them greater wages' (Hare, 1.354). Not unnaturally, one would have thought; the Hares' devoted ministry had shown them how poor their parishioners were and how harshly they were oppressed. But she had been badly frightened; and there was no room in her mind, or in that of her husband, for the idea that the rioters might have had a case. The rich, the Hares thought, had a moral duty to care for the poor; but the poor had no right to make demands upon the rich. When Augustus Hare's brother Julius* visited the parish soon afterwards, he preached strongly against the sin of civil unrest.

Establishment has had a further implication. Until very recently the Church of England has been partisan in a clear and distinctive sense. While governments of every party have been able to make clerical appointments from the ranks of their own supporters, the clergy as a whole have remained overwhelmingly of the right. Like Charles Simeon they have 'read the Bible ... through blue-tinted glasses' (Hopkins, *Simeon* 52). The influential Evangelical Francis Close** of Cheltenham said: 'The Bible is conservative, the Prayer Book conservative, the Liturgy conservative, the Church conservative, and it is impossible for a minister to open his mouth without being conservative' (Hennell, 107).

It could be taken almost for granted in the eighteenth century that a clergyman would be a Tory (not, of course, at that time an absolute synonym for being a conservative). In rural parts the belief persisted; in 1858 the parishioners of Huntspill in Somerset were shocked to discover that their new incumbent was of another persuasion (Chadwick, *VC* 1.515). James Woodforde was thankful that an arrangement by which 'young Baker of Cawston' was to become his curate fell through, because he had discovered that 'the whole Family are very violent Democrats indeed' (Woodforde, 5.195). Writing about the Chippenham election of 1874 Francis Kilvert made his sympathies plain: 'The Radicals have had a fair field and have been beaten' (Kilvert, 2.408–10). Octavius Pickard-Cambridge** worked hard for the Tory cause in Dorset, and was an active member of the Primrose League (Colloms, 71). Flora Thompson remembered Mr Ellison of Lark Rise denouncing 'a mild and orthodox Liberalism ... as "a bloody cause"' (Thompson, 212). It was not the least of Robert Dolling's eccentricities that he supported Radical election candidates on the grounds that the Bible demanded concern for the weak and helpless (Osborne, *Dolling* 131); not the least of Samuel Barnett's that he became president of his local Liberal Association.

The clergy have been supporters of Toryism; the Tory party has been the natural champion of the Church. The clergy felt a profound sense of betrayal when a Tory government espoused the cause of Catholic Emancipation in 1829. Churchmen believed, correctly, that the status of the Church of England as the spiritual aspect of the state was being eroded; and believing that, they were blind to the injustices, above all in Ireland, which that status had created. John Skinner wrote in apocalyptic strain after the great fire in York Cathedral in February 1829: 'If the visible signs and prefigurations of the Almighty obtained now, as they did in the time of the Jews, I should denominate the burning of York Cathedral a token and omen of the destruction of a great part of the Protestant Church – the purest and most enlightened ... establishment of any in Christendom' (Skinner, 379–80).

The lot of the priest not of the right has often been hard. Part at least of the misfortunes of W. Rowland Jones**, a self-styled 'misfit priest' of our own century, can be ascribed to his socialism. Support of a Labour candidate during one of his many curacies led to parishioners complaining to the bishop. Preaching socialism from the pulpit contributed to the short duration of another curacy; throwing his church open to a workers' meeting during the General Strike to that of a third. After he had given offence by 'preaching politics' in his next parish, his bishop was glad to see him shunted sideways into an unlicensed ministry. When he was offered a living by Ramsay Macdonald in 1930 he was received grudgingly by his bishop and treated with formal remoteness thereafter (Jones, passim).

By his own account Jones was an awkward customer; and by his own account too there were those within the Church who did their best for him. But a priest equally outspoken in the opposite direction, as plenty have been, would not have had so uncomfortable a time. Mervyn Stockwood**, whose support of the Labour party during his ministry in Bristol hindered though it did not prevent his preferment, put the matter in a nutshell when he wrote: 'The trouble is, if a priest of the Church of England supports Conservative causes he is not accused of partisanship; it is another matter when his sympathies lie on the other side' (Stockwood, 34–5).

There have been times when the fact that the clergy were ranked with a particular party has evoked a hostility which has hampered their ministry or exposed them to danger. Samuel Wesley** of Epworth was consigned to Lincoln gaol for a debt of £30 at the instance of a friend of a Whig candidate in the general election of 1705 (Ayling, *Wesley* 19). Henry Michell Wagner**, vicar of Brighton from 1824 to 1870, spent much of his ministry at odds with many of his parishioners partly because Brighton was a Whig and Radical stronghold. At a time before the introduction of the secret ballot, he was always the first to vote at elections, passing through noisy and hostile crowds in order to do so (Wagner, 87). At the time of the Reform Act of 1832 clergy were subject to abuse and the threat of assault. Near Bristol a curate had to run the gauntlet of a hostile crowd in order to baptize a dying baby (Chadwick, *VC* 1.26). An election mob jeered at John Skinner, who reacted characteristically: 'I stopped my horse and demanded by what authority they insulted me ... I declared that if they continued their insults whatever it might cost me I would shew at Court there was one true Englishman remaining, for I would horse-whip the first person I could lay hold of, whatever the remainder of the mongrels might do to me afterwards. I laid my hand on my whip and not a voice was heard.' Another gentleman intervened and Skinner returned home unscathed (Skinner, 479).

Because the natural tendency of Anglican liturgy and teaching has been to maintain the status quo, it has been a common cry from the right that the clergy should 'keep out of politics'; that is, refrain from anything which might weaken the effects of a generally conservative posture. On the whole the clergy have obliged, with an effect noted by Robert Dolling: 'The subservience of the Church of England ... to the interests of political Conservatism, and her timid hesitancy ... or total apathy where social wrongs ought to have been rebuked, have largely forfeited for her the confidence of those who are in any sense leaders of their fellows in intelligence among the working classes of this country' (Osborne, *Dolling* 123).

Conscious of the harm which identification with Toryism has done, some clergy have seen it as their duty to stand aside from party politics, though not necessarily to refrain from comment upon political issues. John Newton* thought politics 'a pit that will swallow up the life and spirit, if not the form of religion ... If I was to add another article to our Litany it might run "From poison and politics, good Lord, deliver me"' (Martin, *Newton* 345). Charles Simeon told a questioner 'I do not think clergymen have much to do with politics'; and on another occasion said: 'Politics in general have very little to do with religion, because politics are seldom founded upon truth.' None the less, he had to take some interest in the subject, because his opinion was often asked for; and as we have already seen his general posture was unbendingly conservative (Hopkins, *Simeon* 195).

Later in the same century, R.W. Evans wrote: 'To say ... with the vulgar cry, that he [the parish priest] has nothing to do with politics, is either the absurdity that such cries generally are, or is one of those propositions, which is true in one sense, and false in another.' The clergyman, he thought, should take a 'clear and decided, holy and disinterested' view of political issues, looking at measures rather than supporting a party. He should be slow to denounce public measures concerning the Church herself from the pulpit; he was too obviously an interested party (Evans, 241, 247–8, 252). In another book of advice for the clergy W.C.E. Newbolt wrote: 'It surely must be the part of the minister of God to show where religion comes in ... in questions of the day' (Newbolt, 214). They were signalling a change of view which reached its apogee in the life and teaching of the great William Temple.

In modern times many parish priests have felt that they served all their people best by being unpartisan. It has been hard, however, to retain a reputation for objectivity while also commenting upon public affairs. I wrote an article for my parish magazine at the time of the 1987 general election. After pointing out that there were Christians who felt able in conscience to support each of the main parties, I suggested that Christians should take three factors into account when voting: parties' and candidates' concern about the arms race and the danger of nuclear war; the debt burden of the Third World; and the state of the deprived in our own society. I was dubbed a socialist by one parishioner, a communist by another. It is fair to add that neither was a churchgoer.

There is another implication of the establishment which is not unique to it, but which its special character exacerbates. The Church is an institution – a structured organization sustained in part by the use of coercion. Every denomination has institutional characteristics, but, because of the establishment, the Church of England more than most. Robert Dolling, the most uninstitutional of men, saw this clearly. He thought the Church of England a class-ridden Church, a complacent Church, an unenthusiastic Church, a hidebound Church (see, for example, Osborne, *Dolling* 305–8). He was not far wrong. While Christianity can be lived only in community, its spirit is relational not institutional. It follows that the clergy servicing the institutional machinery are likely to be corrupted by the task. Trollope's Archdeacon Grantley, rector of Plumstead Episcopi, is a paradigm of the clergyman governed by considerations appropriate to the protection of an institution, and only occasionally given pause for thought by the intrusion of Christian conscience.

The drawbacks of the establishment have led some clergy to conclude that it should be dispensed with. One who viewed it without enthusiasm was John Keble*. At first sight, his attitude seems at odds with his general conservatism, but it arose from a high view of the Church which saw her as representing in England the Catholic Church as a whole, and which denied the State any regulatory authority over her. For Keble, Church and State were independent and separable. Because of her Catholic heritage, the Church did not need the additional standing which came from a formal connection with the State. As early as 1827 Keble contended: 'Establishment is not on the whole as great a benefit to men's spiritual interest as one has been led to think.' Because he was able to contemplate disestablishment, he viewed with equanimity both the issue of Catholic Emancipation and the Gorham judgment (Battiscombe, *Keble* 126, 154–6, 302. For a discussion of the judgment see p.253.).

Other high churchmen followed where Keble led. They objected to the State services described earlier in this section partly because of the sentiments they contained and partly because they did not believe them to have ecclesiastical authority. 'How is this, Mr Wingfield', asked Bishop Blomfield of a London curate, 'that you would not read the 5 November service?' 'My Lord,' came the reply, 'it is not a church service but a state service, and I could not conscientiously read it' (Chadwick, *VC* 1.491). William Bennett* was highly critical of the royal supremacy, which he saw as no more than a cloak for the supremacy of the House of Commons. 'The government of the Church ... comes simply to this – that she is governed by her enemies' (Bennett, 248).

The long drawn out prosecution of the ritualist Alexander Mackonochie**, culminating in a hearing before the Judicial Committee of the Privy Council, led both him and his fiery disciple Arthur Stanton to conclude that disestablishment was a prerequisite of church freedom. Mackonochie wrote: 'Let the State send forth the Church roofless and penniless, but free, and I will say "Thank you".' Stanton was a founder member of the Church League for promoting the separation of Church and State, a pressure group prepared to contemplate disendowment as well as disestablishment (Russell, *Stanton* 107, 178). Robert Dolling likewise detested Erastianism: 'He regarded it as the death of true Christianity, as fettering the Church, regarded as a part of the great Catholic Society, and also tending to numb and check the efforts of personal and enthusiastic religion.' His biographer felt he could have taken words of John Wesley as his own: 'Let the Establishment stand or fall as God wills, but let us build the city of God.' When he realized, however, the danger that a disestablished Church might fall into the hands of her wealthy laity, his enthusiasm for it cooled (Osborne, *Dolling* 209, 299).

The majority of the clergy have believed, however, that the balance of advantage lies with establishment. Walter Hook*, who had originally favoured disestablishment had convinced himself by the early 1830s that: 'My error consisted in thinking only of the purity of the Church. I would far sooner myself live in a Church unshackled by the State; but then we must look to the indirect good; to the forming a religious atmosphere. It is something to provide a religion for quiet, unreflective classes of society, who, but for an Establishment, would be respectable Nothingarians' (Stephens, *Hook* 110).

In a related form, Hook's argument continues to have force. By the end of the twentieth century the establishment has become so attenuated that its survival depends more upon political inertia than upon principle. But parish priests continue to accept responsibility for the well-being of all their parishioners, Anglican or not, Christian or not. As one of them wrote: 'The Church ... is not to be seen as a community of the saved but as a saving community for the building of the Kingdom of Heaven ... I was not instituted as a chaplain to a congregation but as incumbent to a parish' (George Burgon, in *The Guardian*, 15 September 1992). This remains the special witness of the Anglican parish priest; a ministry to the nation, costly because on the whole unrequited, which moulds the spiritual character of those who undertake it. It has been said that Roman Catholic priests do not need to smile because they know what their job is, while Anglican clergy are always smiling to conceal the fact that they do not. The observation is wide of the mark. If Anglican clergy are enthusiastic smilers (as observation suggests) it is not because of insecurity but because they minister to people who for the most part need every encouragement to make use of them.

After my first few years of parochial ministry, I needed a theology which would validate the use of that large part of my time which was spent with and for people unlikely to be drawn to Christian faith in its fullness. I was not content to regard that time as wasted, or as useful at an exclusively secular level, or as an investment producing dividends only in the case of the tiny minority who were drawn into active membership of my congregation. I concluded that this part of my ministry was a contribution to the priestly task of the Church in sweetening and sanctifying the whole world, in diffusing grace throughout society; not as a preliminary to a Christian takeover, but so that God could work in hearts which did not fully accept him.

7

Prophecy

Souls are God's jewels, every one of which is worth
many worlds. (Traherne, 1.15)

Introduction

In his book *The Service of a Parson*, published in 1965, Edward Carpenter writes: 'By and large the priest in the parish must be more patient, more tolerant, more understanding than the prophet or rebel is inclined to be' (p. 20). His point was echoed by Archbishop Runcie in an article written for the clergy: 'You might be a prophet sometimes but, I think, rarely are prophets found within institutional ministries' (Canterbury School of Ministry, occasional paper 10, autumn 1990). It seems that both pastoral considerations and the necessities of serving an institution militate against prophecy.

Some parochial clergy have in fact prophesied in the traditional sense, and have suffered for it. But, in another sense of 'prophecy', the rest have been prophets too. Henry Liddon, in a sermon delivered in 1868, argued that: 'the prophetical office ... lives on, although its message is stereotyped for all time since the appearance of the Redeemer ... The heavenly origin of the message and the disinterested philanthropy of its promulgation mark off the prophetic office of the Church from all human teacherships' (Liddon, 49). In other words, the patient proclamation to each generation of the Christian verities is a prophetic activity. It is with prophecy in this wider sense that this chapter is chiefly concerned.

Preaching

Until quite recent times sermons were the chief source of information and instruction for simple people, and one of their few opportunities for entertainment. They have bulked large in the culture of the educated too. Dr Johnson thought no library complete without its stock of them. Pepys and Gladstone were inveterate sermon-tasters. The sales of popular sermons were phenomenal. Walter Hook's* 'Hear the Church', preached before Queen Victoria, went into 28 editions and 100,000 copies were sold (Stephens, *Hook* 251).

The very significance of preaching has sometimes limited the clergy's freedom to engage in it. As wise Thomas Fuller** remarked: 'Those who hold the helm of the pulpit always steer people hearts as they please.' A proclamation of 1548 forbade preaching altogether, except by licence from the Lord Protector or the Archbishop of Canterbury (Fuller, *CH* 3.112; 2.357). It was enforced only for a few weeks but throughout the sixteenth century preachers needed a special licence, which in the 1580s less than half of them possessed (Hart, *CC* 29; H.W. Davies, *The Early Stuarts*, Oxford 1959, 69). In 1623 King James I issued regulations setting clear limits to preachers' choice of topics and to their manner of dealing with them: for example, forbidding preaching 'in any popular auditory deep points of Predestination, Election, Reprobation, or of the Universality, Efficacy, Resistibility or Irresistibility of God's Grace', and preachers 'to fall into bitter invectives and undecent railing speeches' (Fuller, *CH* 3.357). Bishops are entitled to debar clergy from preaching, and have often done so. To mention three examples: the teaching of the admirable Puritan Hugh Clark, vicar of Wolston, Warwickshire, at the turn of the seventeenth century, led his listening bishop so to writhe in his wrath as to prompt a churchwarden to offer him cushions. The bishop departed declaring to the congregation: 'This is indeed a hot fellow, but I will cool him.' Thereafter he forbade Clark to preach or to expound the scriptures. It is pleasant to record, however, that the two men later became good friends (Hart, *CC* 144). In 1868 the Bishop of Chichester inhibited the Evangelical J. Knapp of St John's church, Portsea, from preaching in his diocese because he had preached in a Baptist chapel (Wagner, 79). At the other ecclesiastical extreme Alexander Mackonochie,** embroiled in prosecutions for ritualism, was inhibited in 1869 by the Bishop of Ripon (Towle, *Mackonochie* 203).

The contents of sermons have often been dictated by government. In 1620 James I ordered the Bishop of London to tell his clergy to preach against 'the insolency of our women and their wearing of broad-brimmed hats, pointed doublets, their hair cut short or shorn'. Under Charles I in 1626 the instruction was to preach that refusal of financial support to the Crown was sinful (Hill, 76).

It used to be an acceptable and was often a recommended alternative to preaching that the parish priest should read from the *Books of Homilies* issued in 1547 and 1571, or from the popular devotional work *The Whole Duty of Man* (see, for example, *CI* 276). The *Books of Homilies* were normative; the King's Directions of 1623 laid it down that preachers should be guided by them and by the Thirty-Nine Articles (Fuller, *CH* 3.356). When John Fletcher* went to Madeley in 1760 he allayed local suspicion by reading a homily among his early addresses. 'By this means I stopped the mouths of many adversaries' (Benson, *Fletcher* 60).

Fletcher also stopped mouths by reading some of the sermons of Archbishop Ussher. He was following common practice. In the eighteenth century it was thought 'enthusiastic' (a term of severe condemnation) always to write one's own sermons. It was more fitting to buy and read those of others (Virgin, 144). William Paley** advised his pupils, if they had to preach every Sunday, 'to make one sermon and steal five' (*DNB*). As a curate, Walter Hook followed the common practice and read the sermons of others (Stephens, *Hook* 48). Often the sermons were those of great men such as Archbishop Tillotson. James Woodforde* used Tillotson but condensed him for his rural congregation (N. Sykes in *Theology*, vol. 38,100). Some parish priests were suppliers. Arthur Roberts, the Evangelical rector of Woodrising, Norfolk, from 1831 to 1886, published seventeen volumes of village sermons which were widely used; on holiday, he heard his address on an eclipse of the sun preached twice in separate churches (Chadwick, *VC* 2.176–7).

Preaching other men's sermons can be evidence of laziness rather than humility. John Earle's young raw preacher has 'the notes of Sermons, which taken up at St Mary's [the university church at Oxford] he utters in the country ... His writing is more than his reading; for he reads only what he gets without book' (Earle, 22). Francis Witts** commented: 'the composition of original sermons is far too much neglected; disuse begets distrust of one's own powers, and a disinclination to the labour' (Witts, 87). John Trusler, a former curate of St Clement Danes in the Strand, made a comfortable fortune in the 1770s out of printing 150 sermons in imitation handwriting and selling them at a shilling each (Barrow, 108). In the same century a worldly-wise man, who proposed to set his son up for life by settling him in a parish, said to him: 'All that will be expected of you is to read prayers and preach a sermon, which will cost you threepence once a week, or by a visit to the metropolis you can lay in a stock of manuscript sermons which will last you for the whole of your life' (Martin, *Newton* 208). Thackeray's parson Crawley in *Vanity Fair* adopted the even cheaper expedient of having his sermons written by his wife.

For good reasons or bad then addresses in church have often consisted of other men's flowers, and have often been stamped with the prescriptive authority of the church rather than with the personal spirituality of the speaker. John Keble* was in the tradition when he advised a friend: 'Don't be original' (Battiscombe, *Keble* 175). None the less, most conscientious clergy have, if only from time to time, heeded the advice given by Bishop Sprat in 1695: 'Every person who undertakes this great employment, should make it a matter of religion and conscience to preach nothing but what is the product of his own study and of his own composing' (*CI*, 224).

For some clergy, particularly Evangelicals, preaching has been the heart of their ministry. William Grimshaw* never preached less than twenty times a week, and once thirty-one times (Baker, *Grimshaw* 107). Charles Simeon* produced *Horae Homilectae*, a publication in twenty-one volumes containing 2536 sermon outlines covering the whole Bible (Hopkins, *Simeon* 60). Alexander Baring-Gould, uncle of Sabine** and a vicar in Wolverhampton, tolerated morning and evening prayer only because they 'prepared the soul for the sermon' (Purcell, *Baring-Gould* 50). However, the Evangelicals had rivals. Alexander Mackonochie once preached twenty-three sermons in a week, and would sustain up to six sermon courses simultaneously (Towle, *Mackonochie* 219).

The care and labour devoted to sermons has varied but has often been immense. The proverb in Thomas Fuller's time was 'Saturday the working day, and Monday the holiday of preachers'. Fuller himself praised Andrew Marvail, a minister in Hull, 'a most excellent preacher, who ... never broached what he had new brewed, but preached what he had pre-studied some competent time before' (Fuller, *Worthies* 240). 'I got up this morning at two o'clock,' wrote James Woodforde in 1764, 'to get or make a sermon for Farmer Bertelet's funeral this afternoon, and by twelve o'clock I had finished almost all of it.' He did not appreciate effort on this scale, and avoided preaching when he could. On a visit to Somerset he refused an invitation because he had brought no sermons with him (Woodforde, 1.36–7; 2.37). Charles Simeon prefaced each sermon with not less than twelve hours study (Hopkins, *Simeon* 67). Walter Hook usually wrote his sermons out in full, and also advocated learning them almost by heart (Stephens, *Hook* 578). Nicolas Stacey** at Woolwich laid it down that each member of staff should go over his sermon with a colleague before it was delivered. A second incentive to careful preparation was the requirement that the preacher should expose himself to questioning at coffee after the service (Stacey, 129–30).

If sermons are to be personally and carefully composed, and the writing fitted into a busy ministry, it may be desirable to repeat them. Bishop Sprat recommended the creation of a yearly or two yearly cycle of sermons, revised and polished on each occasion they were repeated (CI, 232–3). George Crabbe** read his stock of sermons on a rotation, each sermon coming up triennially (Mills, *Crabbe* xxi–xxii). James Woodforde repeated his sermons after two or three years (N. Sykes in *Theology*, vol. 38, 101, 105, 343). George Eliot's Mr Gilfil 'had a large heap of short sermons, rather yellow and worn at the edges, from which he took two each Sunday, securing perfect impartiality in selection by taking them as they came, without reference to topics.' Nor did his parishioners object. '"We've had a very good sermon this morning," was the frequent remark, after hearing one of the old yellow series ... for to minds on the Shepperton level it is repetition, not novelty, that produces the strongest effect' (Eliot, *SCL* 121, 125). I myself was intrigued to discover that sermons preached a first time without visible effect were sometimes deeply appreciated by the same auditors on (did they but realize it) a second hearing. I came to the obvious conclusion that what speaks to a person's condition on one occasion may be quite valueless on another.

Preparation need not stand in the way of inspiration. When Henry Alford** was at Wymeswold he preached three times each Sunday. He might write up to six pages of notes beforehand, but went into the pulpit with nothing but a Bible (Alford, 107). Early in his ministry Arthur Stanton* wrote his sermons out; later on he wrote them in outline; but he preached without a manuscript of any kind. Charles Simeon found that if he repeated his Cambridge sermons from memory in the villages which he visited he could achieve greater 'familiarity and homeliness of style' (Hopkins, *Simeon* 50).

The Holy Spirit might seem to have the clearest field in the case of a preacher who speaks extempore, relying on a well-stocked mind and a prayerful life. Josselin, who aimed 'to digest my sermons into my head,' often recorded that 'god was mercifull to mee in giving mee strength and freedome for his Sabbath'. After the victory at Naseby in 1645 'the lord was pleased in some measure to raise up my heart in the worke, and helpe mee with many expressions and unstudied meditations, for which his name be praised' (Josselin, 410, 166, 42). Even the more pedestrian John Skinner* found that while preaching he 'could with great ease to myself make allusion to passages connected with the subject of which I treated in the Lessons of the day. I feel convinced that with a little practice, I could express myself without any kind of hesitation; not that,' he hastily added, 'I ever mean to adopt extemporaneous preaching' (Skinner, 267–8). His disclaimer was of his age; anything other than a script rigidly adhered to savoured of Methodism. One of the causes of offence given by George Eliot's saintly Evangelical Mr Tryon was his habit of preaching extempore (Eliot, *SCL* 263).

The practice does have dangers; witness the criticism levelled at another of George Eliot's clergymen, Amos Barton: 'When he tries to preach wi'out book, he rambles about, and doesn't stick to his text; and every now and then he flounders about like a sheep as has cast itself, and can't get on its legs again' (Eliot, *SCL* 48). Francis Kilvert* sometimes preached extempore to his own satisfaction, sometimes emphatically not. He noted that sermons of this nature rarely lasted less than half an hour. His comment, 'Half an hour seems like five minutes when you are talking or preaching', (Kilvert, 2.48) explains the occasional reserve with which congregations regard the free flow of the Spirit. A friend once reminded William Andrew* of the riddle: 'Why is an extempore sermon like a ring? because it is endless' (Chadwick, *Andrew* 91).

Expounding chapters of scripture, Ralph Josselin 'did not write them downe being so much overlayd with businesse' (Josselin, 185). Extempore preaching can, as in this instance, be forced upon the preacher; it can also be the product of indolence and contempt for the congregation. A parishioner explained why he sat only once under John Ellerton, rector for thirty-two years round the turn of this century of White Roothing, Essex: 'He got up into that old pulpit, stared at us all ... and said "Well now, what am I going to talk to you about this morning?" It wasn't for me to tell him, so I didn't go again' (Addison, 220).

Prepared or unprepared, written or extempore, a sermon stands or falls as much on delivery and personality as on the thinking behind it. Thomas Fuller said of Richard Hooker** 'such was the depth of his learning, that his pen was a better bucket than his tongue to draw it out.' Hooker spoke quietly and gestured not at all; 'the doctrine he delivered had nothing but itself to garnish it'. Since he also spoke in long sentences 'driving on a whole flock of several clauses', he frequently bored and bewildered the less intelligent of his auditors (Fuller, *CH* 3.138, 141). George Herbert's* country parson 'procures attention by all possible art, both by earnestness of speech ... and by a diligent and busy cast of his eye on his auditors, with letting them know that he observes who marks, and who not' (Herbert, VII). John Fletcher 'spake as in the presence of God, and taught as one having divine authority. There was an energy in his preaching which was irresistible. His subjects, his language, his gestures, the tone of his voice, and the turn of his countenance, all conspired to fix the attention, and afflict the heart' (Benson, *Fletcher* 70). William Bennett* wrote his sermons on large sheets of paper with very few lines on each page, and with a notation by each word to show how it was to be pronounced. He appeared never to look at his manuscript, and preached gravely and seriously, with frequent pregnant pauses (Bennett, 265–80).

John Henry Newman's** sermons were delivered in what Kilvert's father called 'the sweetest voice I ever heard' (Kilvert, 3.244), compared by another auditor to 'a fine strain of unearthly music'. He uttered a sentence or two rapidly and clearly and then paused. Those pauses gave rise to electric effects; as when, after picturing the incidents of Christ's passion, Newman broke the ensuing silence with the words: 'Now I bid you to recollect that He to Whom these things were done was Almighty God' (Faber, 187–8). Richard Benson** preached at great length and made no intellectual concessions to his hearers, but a poor, uneducated woman came to hear him again and again. Asked why she replied: 'That gentleman just opens heaven to me and I can look right in' (Woodgate, *Benson* 54). At a more mundane level Walter Hook advised: 'If your sermon is not in your opinion a good one, deliver it as if you *thought* it was a good one' (Stephens, *Hook* 578).

R.W.Evans deplored 'what is called a rant ... Should you ever be transported into such fits depend upon it that you have either indulged an evangelical impetuosity of mind, or you are methodical [viz like a Methodist] amid your madness.' He went on to advise against gestures (Evans, 109–10). He spoke from the long tradition of restraint which has made much Anglican preaching inoffensive at the price of making it ineffective. Oliver Goldsmith remarked: 'Men of real sense and understanding prefer a prudent mediocrity to a precarious popularity; and fearing to outdo their duty, leave it half done. Their discourses ... are ... dry, methodical, and unaffecting: delivered with the most insipid calmness; insomuch that should the peaceful preacher lift his head over the cushion, which alone he seems to address, he might discover his audience, instead of being awakened to remorse, actually sleeping over this methodical and laboured composition' (*Essays*, quoted Christmas, 83). But restraint has also been a method of giving due weight to content. The speech of Earle's Grave Divine 'is not help't with enforce'd action, but the matter acts it selfe. Hee ... beats upon his Text, not the Cushion making his hearers not the Pulpit groane' (Earle, 24. One is reminded that an eighteenth century nickname for a clergyman was 'a cushion thumper').

Old Hannah Whitney told Kilvert that Parson Williams of Llanbedr, though a brawler and a drunkard, was 'a capital preacher … He used to say … in his sermons, "My brethren … don't you do as I do, but you do as I say"' (Kilvert, 2.134). On the whole, however, technique stands or falls by the person behind it. George Herbert put the point at its strongest when he wrote: 'The character of his [the parson's] sermon is holiness; he is not witty, or learned, or eloquent, but holy' (Herbert, VII). John Keble had deficiencies as a preacher, but they mattered little because, as an inhabitant of Hursley observed, he 'was outside the church what he professed to be within it' (Battiscombe, *Keble* 43).

John Newton* is an example of a preacher whose effect depended upon what he was rather than upon what he said or how he said it. In his early days as a clergyman he was ineffective both when speaking impromptu and when reading a text. The best his friend William Cowper could find to say of his later preaching was that it was 'plain and neat'. Another admirer said: 'He appeared to least advantage in the pulpit … He did not generally aim at accuracy in the composition of his sermons, nor at any address in the delivery … his utterance was far from clear and his attitudes ungraceful.' Yet even in extreme old age, when he would ramble for fifty minutes, he attracted devoted hearers who found his sanctity infectious (Martin, *Newton* 209–10, 232: Pollock, *Newton* 181).

Newton was conspicuous for his humility; so was William Grimshaw, who summarized his preaching intentions as 'debasing man and exalting my dear Lord'. He had no patience with those who 'to gain the vain admiration of the ignorant and the praise of men, affect in their preaching high-flying words, pompous language, rhetorical strains and philosophical terms'. He sought instead to be 'a soul searching, a soul winning, and a soul enriching minister, one who maketh the hard things easy, and dark things plain'. Confessing himself a sinner, he made it easy for others to acknowledge their own sin (Baker, *Grimshaw* 119). Keble evinced humility in a different way; discovering on one occasion that he had created a great impression, he deliberately preached badly on the next, 'lest,' Newman recorded, 'in his former sermon he had so handled a sacred subject as to lead his audience to think rather of him than of it' (Battiscombe, *Keble* 175). Keble would have approved of Sterne's Parson Yorick who observed: 'To preach, to show the extent of our reading, or the subtleties of our wit – to parade in the eyes of the vulgar with the beggarly accounts of a little learning, tinseled over with a few words which glitter, but convey little light and less warmth – is a dishonest use of the poor single half hour in the week which is put into our hands –' Tis not preaching the gospel – but ourselves' (Sterne, 314).

The great exceptions apart, delivery and integrity need the support of substance. A preacher should have something to say, both in general and in particular. In general, he is proclaiming Christian truth; in particular, he should make it accessible to his hearers by embodying the abstract in the concrete. The cerebral Julius Hare* 'generally preached for an hour to a nodding audience' (Kilvert, 2.376n). By contrast Herbert's country parson 'tells ... stories and sayings of others, according as his text invites him; for them also men heed and remember better than exhortations' (Herbert, VII).

William Grimshaw's rough speech and homely illustrations spoke to his North Country listeners. He used 'market language', rendering Psalm 48.14 'they who have this God for theirs shall never want a pound of butter for eightpence, or three pints of blue milk for a halfpenny, as long as they live.' He was capable of genuine eloquence and humour: 'Does the flesh tempt you? Flee and pray. Does the world tempt you? Watch and pray. Does the Devil tempt you? Resist and pray.' 'Think not to dance with the devil all day, and sup with Christ at night: or to go from Delilah's lap to Abraham's Bosom' (Baker, *Grimshaw* 119, 120, 121).

The preacher should be master of his material and also the servant of it. It was said of Francis Close** that: 'His mode of giving out ... his text says "Look at that – not at me; that is the important thing: come and let us see what it meaneth"' (Hennell, 109). Close was at the opposite pole from those stigmatized by Bishop Hart of Tuam in 1742: 'It has given me disgust to observe in some preachers a certain affectation of choosing such texts as appear remote and foreign to their subject, that by this means they may have opportunity of showing their wit and ingenuity in fetching that out of a text which nobody imagined could be in it' (*CI* 336). Simeon taught that the text was to be given 'its just meaning, its natural bearing and its legitimate use'. The point of a passage should come out naturally, 'like the kernel of a hazel-nut; and not piecemeal, and after much trouble to your hearers, like the kernel of a walnut'. 'My endeavour,' he declared, 'is to bring out of scripture what is there, and not to thrust in what I think might be there. I never wish to find any particular truth in any particular passage. I am willing that every part of God's blessed Word should speak exactly what it was intended to speak' (Hopkins, *Simeon* 57).

Simeon asked of each sermon: 'Does it uniformly tend

TO HUMBLE THE SINNER
TO EXALT THE SAVIOUR
TO PROMOTE HOLINESS?' (Hopkins, *Simeon* 62)

The Evangelical tradition, however, has sometimes tended to concentrate on the first and second of those objectives. One of Grimshaw's hearers described him in verse:

See, there he stands! the pious crowds among,
Celestial eloquence flows from his tongue:
Lo! on his reverend brow the frowns arise,
And from his tongue the awful threat'ning flies.
He tells the sinner what must be his doom;
He thunders out the awful wrath to come ...
But now his face a milder aspect wears,
And conscious pleasure in his eye appears;
He points the sinner to the Lamb of God,
And tells the virtue of atoning blood. (Baker, *Grimshaw* 127–8)

For such as Grimshaw the central function of preaching has been to convict the auditor of his sinfulness and then to offer him the redemption wrought by the cross. The evangelist John Berridge of Everton, Bedfordshire, advised Charles Simeon in 1794: 'When you open your commission, begin with ripping up the audience ... Lay open the universal sinfulness of nature, the darkness of the mind, the forwardness of the tempters, the earthliness and sensuality of the affections ... When your Hearers have been well harrowed ... then bring out your CHRIST.' Such a message was sometimes delivered with more force than sensitivity. Simeon's vehemence in the early days of his ministry prompted some of his parishioners to complain to the bishop; but later he learned better, and warned ordinands against 'preachers who act like butchers; they cut at sin as if they did not feel any mercy for sinners'. By then, like John Newton, he had no time for 'angry and scolding preaching', and taught an attitude 'which expresses kindness and love, and not that which indicates an unfeeling harshness ... Let your preaching come from the heart. Love should be the spring of all actions and especially of a minister's. If a man's heart is full of love he will rarely offend. He may have severe things to say but he will say them in love' (Hopkins, *Simeon* 63–5). A century earlier, in yet more outspoken days, Ralph Josselin had noted that when he preached on not delaying repentance, 'as it was with affection on my part, so was with affection heard' (Josselin, 426). While the gentle John Fletcher 'was faithful in proclaiming the day of vengeance to the disobedient, he neglected not to proclaim liberty to the captives, performing both ... parts of his duty with fidelity but the latter only with alacrity and cheerfulness' (Benson, *Fletcher* 56–7). Walter Hook was within the same kindly tradition when he declared: 'I hate your preachers who are always dealing in hell and damnation; I am sure they can never have experienced the difficulties with which most people have had to contend' (Stephens, *Hook* 165).

In other respects wise preachers have avoided a negative emphasis. Both Jeremy Taylor and a later seventeenth-century bishop, Sprat, advised against 'controversial divinity'; though Sprat thought it in order to attack Roman Catholicism and to speak against those who denied the fundamental Christian verities (*CI*, 226–7). In the mid-nineteenth century R.W. Evans took the same line: 'The conflicting opinions of men ... should come as little as possible under your notice; and in refuting them, your most prudent plan will be ... not to state it [the error] and refute it in direct terms, but earnestly to press the opposite truth ... to meet it' (Evans, 142).

Kierkegaard wrote: 'A sermon is not a play written by God, acted by the preacher and observed by the congregation. It is much more that the preacher is the playwright, the congregation is the company of actors and God is the audience.' Certainly, the congregation is an active constituent in the process of preaching. The preacher learns what he has conveyed from the reaction he evokes; the Spirit passes back to him in the response of the congregation. Harry Williams** describes his hearers at St Barnabas, Pimlico, his first parish: 'I ... felt I had a good deal to teach these dear simple people. With the greatest possible kindness they made me realize that it was I who was the dear simple person. They listened ... with true Christian indulgence, paragons of patience who knew it would be wrong to discourage a young deacon. By their forbearance, by the very affability of their faces while I spoke, they brought me as painlessly as possible to the recognition that, compared with them, I knew next to nothing of life' (Williams, 107). While a curate at St Matthew's, Moorfields, John Robinson** spoke in a sermon of 'the eschaton entering history'. During the following week a rough and ready member of the congregation, Charlie Hodder, asked Mervyn Stockwood** 'What was Dr Robinson on about last Sunday – eskimos and history?' Thereafter, when vetting Robinson's sermons, Stockwood's query by any obscurity read 'What *will* this mean to Charlie Hodder?' (James, *Robinson* 34).

Nothing lends wings to a minister's preaching more than the sense that he is effective. Attendance can be the index. While Thomas Fuller was incumbent of Broadwindsor in Dorset his summertime congregations could not be contained within the church; they stood outside while their minister preached from the church steps (Hart, *CC* 161). More often, however, the telling thing is the reaction of individuals or of the whole congregation. Ralph Josselin was delighted when he had 'a very cheerfull audience', and when a sermon on steadfastness wrought with such effect on a woman inclined to defect to the Quakers that 'shee resolved never to heare them more' (Josselin, 531, 373). Francis Kilvert recorded that a well-used harvest sermon so touched a congregation that the collection constituted a record. 'Vaughan said I had drawn water out of stony rocks and had hit the Newchurch farmers as hard as Moses hit the rock' (Kilvert, 2.53). More spectacularly, John Berridge who in his own phrase 'prattled of Jesus', turned sections of his congregations into howling maniacs. Berridge, properly cautious, could not decide whether these effects came from God or the devil; in due course they ceased to appear (Balleine, 69).

The supportive listener reassures the preacher that his weaknesses do not destroy his value as a mouthpiece for the Word. Fuller wrote that the good parishioner 'sets himself to hear God in the minister' (Fuller, *HS* 85), and Keble echoed the thought when he said: 'All sermons are good' (Stranks, 262). He

meant of course that no sermon is so bad that a devout hearer cannot obtain
benefit from it. As George Herbert put it:

> Judge not the preacher; for he is thy judge:
> If thou mislike him, thou conceiv'st him not.
> God calleth preaching folly. Do not grudge
> To pick out treasures from an earthen pot. ('The Church Porch')

Other factors have favoured a spiritual symbiosis between speaker and hearers.
For example, it used to be possible to assume continuity of attendance. The
clergy could preach series of sermons in the confidence that their auditors would
hear most of them. John Skinner preached his way through series on the
Evidences of Christianity, the Lord's Prayer and the Creed. At Portsea Cosmo
Lang** held vast congregations spellbound with courses on the gospels, the
epistles, the prophets, the creeds, the sacraments, the beatitudes, and the
doctrine and history of the Church. A course on Isaiah lasted nearly eighteen
months (Lockhart, *Lang* 121, 124). One is lost in equal admiration for the
stamina of the preacher and for that of the congregation.

Stamina has been equally evinced in tolerance of length. Michael Ignatieff has
asserted (in a series of television programmes entitled 'The Three Minute
Culture') that the attention span of people nowadays, conditioned by constant
exposure to vivid brevities, is three minutes. Congregations of the past gave their
clergy the opportunity to be more expansive. Ralph Josselin never preached for
less than one hour, and sometimes for four or five. Puritan sermons were of
course noted for their length; but most clergy in the past were given to substantial
addresses. It was one of the articles of accusation against Edward Salter, rector of
St John, Stamford, Lincolnshire, when he was ejected from his living in 1644
that he preached for only half an hour (Matthews, *Walker* 256). Henry Fardell*
thought the congregation slighted when a curate preached for only a quarter of an
hour (Fardell, 121). Confronted with a congregation largely of Chartists at St
James, Bradford, George Bull** preached for nearly two hours on the equal
iniquities of rich and poor, and held his hearers throughout (Chadwick, *VC*
1.335).

That was, however, a special occasion, warranting an otherwise intolerable
length. The demands the clergy have made on their hearers have sometimes
stood in judgment upon them. William Andrew resolved in 1842: 'I determine by
God's help I will digest my sermons better.' His aim was to keep them to thirty
minutes, but a prepared sermon might last sixty-five minutes and an extempore
one as much as an hour and a quarter (Chadwick, *Andrew* 56, 91). Invited by
William Bennett to preach for twenty minutes, George Denison** read for two
hours from a pamphlet on the Public Worship Regulation Act of 1874, desisting
only at 11 p.m. when a lady in the congregation fainted (Bennett, 262).

The advantages of brevity have not been overlooked, though ideas of what constitutes it have varied from century to century. Herbert wrote: 'The parson exceeds not an hour in preaching, because all ages have thought that a competency, and he that profits not in that time, will less afterwards' (Herbert, VII). Nicholas Andrews, seventeenth-century incumbent of St Nicholas, Guildford, and of Godalming, Surrey, preached against long sermons, saying: 'Peters sword cut off but one eare, but long Sermons like long swords, cut off both at once' (Matthews, *Walker* 348). John Newton advised against preaching more than an hour. 'Perhaps it is better to feed our people like chickens a little and often, than to cram them like turkeys till they cannot hold one gobbet more. Besides, over-long sermons break in upon family concerns, and often call off the thoughts ... to the pudding at home, which is in danger of being over-boiled' (Martin, *Newton* 210). By the later nineteenth century twenty minutes was thought to be a desirable minimum. Anything less was short-changing the congregation, more than forty minutes a cause for bitter complaint (see Trollope, *LC* 166, 757). A century later still those figures had been more than halved.

The minister is sometimes torn between what he thinks it his duty to teach and what he knows will be acceptable. Skinner, mourning a congregation of less than a hundred, wrote: 'If I were to commence a new system as an evangelical teacher, the Methodists would attend; but I cannot prevail upon myself to do evil to work no good, unless it be good to gratify one's vanity by procuring full benches at the expense of one's principles' (Skinner, 442). By contrast, local dissenters would come to hear Keble preach, declaring that this indeed was the gospel (Battiscombe, *Keble* 43).

The issue of appropriate content arose in an acute form when the nineteenth-century Chartists sought to exhibit their strength and to influence public opinion by appearing in large numbers at church services. At Manchester 150 of them listened quietly to a sermon on obedience to the constituted authorities. At St Stephen's, Norwich, however, when the clergyman preached to a huge crowd on contentment with the state of life in which we find ourselves, sticks were waved and there were cries of: 'You get £200 a year, come and weave bombazine' (Chadwick, *VC* 1.335).

It has been said that a preacher's job, like that of a journalist, is to comfort the afflicted and to afflict the comfortable. Some have been happier with one task, and some with the other. Brave or foolhardy souls have not hesitated to risk hostility and even violence in proclaiming the truth as they saw it. The sixteenth-century Puritan Hugh Clark, vicar of Oundle, Northants, reproved his people severely for their profanation of the Sabbath; to the extent that 'a lusty young man' visited him one morning intent on murdering him. Fortunately conversation won him round (Hart, *CC* 144). In the following century John Vicars, vicar of Stamford, suffered severe ecclesiastical sanctions for saying that it was a 'greate sinne' not to hear two Sunday sermons if two were available, and that the minister who failed to preach twice would be 'fryed in hell' (Hart, *CC* 103). At the height of the riots at St Barnabas, Pimlico, in 1850 William Bennett preached extempore on death and judgment to such effect that he not only subdued his hearers but turned the tide of protest (Bennett, 114–21). It was said of Thomas Hancock**: 'When preaching to the respectable middle class of St Stephen's, Lewisham, he would examine and dissect "the sacred rights of property"; when preaching to the socialist members and supporters of the Guild of St Matthew he would uncover the evil of man-made schemes for the salvation of society.' He said in 1870 that it was the task of the Church 'to take the scorned and hated side in those conflicts of our time in which we are obliged to share'. Hancock was one of those clerics who, occupying no pigeon-hole themselves, succeed in annoying almost everyone. During his curacies his preaching caused some of his congregation to leave because they thought he was no Protestant, and others because they thought he was no Catholic (Reckitt, 2–3, 8).

There is a tension between prophecy and pastoring which can bear hard on the parish priest. Bishop John Robinson retreated to Arncliffe in the Dales during university vacations when he was chaplain of Trinity College, Cambridge, and fulfilled the functions of parish priest there. He visited assiduously, and tried (somewhat clumsily) to come to terms with local people. When, however, at Christmas 1982, during the Falklands War, he preached about commitment to peace, he gave such offence that his ministry was damaged (James, *Robinson* 273–4). At least his motives were of the best. It is not possible to be equally sure about Robert Shepard, rector of Hepworth, Suffolk, who was charged in 1643 with stigmatizing his parishioners in catechizing and preaching as 'Black-mouthed hell-hounds, Limnes of the Devill, Fire-brands of Hell, Plow joggers, Bawling doggs, Weaverly Jacks, and Church-Robbers, affirming that if he could terme them worse he would' (Mattews, *Walker* 344).

On the other hand, a truly Christian congregation has been able to sustain and profit from frank speaking on the part of its minister. One of my own people called a sermon 'squirm-making', and meant it as a compliment.

Special questions arise when the pulpit is used to belabour individuals. Francis Abbot, vicar of Poslingford, Suffolk, in the 1630s pointed at the wife of a substantial parishioner and shouted: 'When your husbands are gone abroad you send for your comrades, and then you play the wantons … and you are not ashamed to come into the house of God with your whorish face' (Hart, *CC* 106). Abbot was a Puritan, and it was chiefly of Puritans that the Bishop of London was thinking when at the Hampton Court Conference of 1604 he complained about sermons being 'pasquils [lampoons], wherein every discontented fellow may traduce his superiors'. James I agreed that 'the pulpit is no place for personal reproof' (Fuller, *CH* 3.205); a principle set in a wider context by Jeremy Taylor writing later in the century: 'Every minister … ought to concern himself in the faults of them that are present, but not of the absent … In the reproof of sins be as particular as you please … but meddle with no man's person … so doing he shall exasperate the man but never amend the sinner' (*CI* 74–5). Practical good sense here went hand in hand with Christian love. Neither was exhibited by Parson Williams of Llanbedr, who is said to have preached at the funeral of a farmer with whom he had quarrelled on Isaiah 14.9: 'Hell from beneath is moved for thee to meet thee at thy coming' (Kilvert, 2.135). That story smells of the lamp; but there is no doubt that one of Sir John Boileau's servants said to William Andrew: 'O sir, how hard you do strike Sir John in your sermons! I really do not know scarcely how to sit sometimes in my seat' (Chadwick, *Andrew* 91).

John Newton remarked: 'Dr Pulpit is my best physician'; never averse to preaching, he did so even on the day of his dearly loved wife's death. But others have found that preaching exacts a price. 'Sermon preaching makes me feel lonely,' wrote Samuel Barnett*; 'there is always reaction, a sense of failure. It is a grand position to be able to talk to people on their highest interests, but all kinds of doubts and hopes haunt one to make one depressed' (Barnett, 2.331).

Perhaps the greatest trial the preacher can undergo is one which Barnett often endured, congregational imperviousness. The blame may of course be his own. 'Sleep at my bidding crept from pew to pew,' observed Charles Churchill, curate at Rainham, Essex, in the middle of the eighteenth century (Addison, 62). But the most devoted of preachers can be confronted with apathy. 'No great incouragment in the audience,' lamented Josselin in 1655; 'oh how deadly and drowsily men heare the word' (Josselin, 346). John Skinner, after having preached to an overflowing congregation on the sudden death of a parishioner, was cut to the quick when the ringers immediately adjourned to the belfry for a 'merry peal' (Skinner, 167). Robert Hawker* used to tell the story of how he had once burned a large number of sermons and used them, to no avail, to fertilize turnips. 'Barren, all barren, like most modern discourses; not even posthumous energy' (Brendon, *Hawker* 96). 'People are never better for sermons, at least not often', wrote Arthur Stanton to his sister (Russell, *Stanton* 103).

Hawker had better reason for pessimism in his circumstances than Stanton in his; but a certain caution about the value of sermons is in the Anglican tradition. George Herbert wrote in 'The Church Porch':

Resort to sermons, but to prayers most;
Praying's the end of preaching.

A century later George Woodward** wrote: ''Tis a difficult matter to convince country people, or indeed others of a better education, that their main business at Church is to attend to the prayers rather than the sermon, which is the lowest part of the service' (Woodward, 82). A century later again Walter Hook said about an alteration to his church 'by the proposed plan we shall get 1200 more kneelings. I use the word in preference to the term sittings, that persons may be reminded that they come to church not to sit and hear a sermon, but to kneel before their God in prayer' (Stephens, *Hook* 229). Robert Hawker, who believed in the Real Presence of Christ in the Eucharist, would not preach 'in my Master's presence' (Brendon, *Hawker* 97). For these priests, and those who thought like them, church attendance was primarily an opportunity to worship God, and only secondarily an opportunity to be instructed.

Nor has the Church of England thought of sermons as the only component of prophecy. Jeremy Taylor wrote in his episcopal charge of 1661 'by preaching, and catechizing, and private intercourse, all the needs of the soul can best be served; but by preaching alone they cannot' (Thornton, 237). 'Though sermons give most sail to men's souls,' wrote Fuller, 'catechizing layeth the best ballast in them, keeping them steady from being "carried away with every wind of doctrine" ' (Fuller, *WE* 1.134). We turn therefore to other elements of the teaching ministry.

Teaching

Catechizing has now been consigned to history, but for centuries it was the accepted way of inculcating Christian teaching, chiefly but not exclusively into the young. The *Book of Common Prayer* requires that catechizing should take place after the second lesson at evening prayer on Sundays and Holy Days; canon law, before the modern revision, in the half-hour before evening prayer. Sometimes catechizing replaced the sermon, sometimes supplemented it. Walton describes George Herbert* as catechizing according to the requirements of the Prayer Book (Walton, 207). Herbert himself devoted a chapter of *A Priest to the Temple* to the subject. He expected 'all the doctrine of the catechism; of the younger sort, the very words; of the elder, the substance.' The young were to be catechized in public, with their elders present: 'that parents and masters ... may when they come home, either commend or reprove, either reward or punish'. In a wholly modern way he condemned rote learning and commended the use of questions and answers, by which the catechizer 'once he get the skill of it, will draw out of even ignorant and silly souls the dark and deep points of Religion'. He was also realistically aware 'that at sermons and prayers, men may sleep or wander; but when one is asked a question, he must discover [viz. reveal] what he is'. Catechizing benefits the minister too. Unlike sermons, it cannot 'inflame or ravish'; but: 'Whereas in sermons there is a kind of state, in catechizing there is a humbleness very suitable to Christian regeneration, which exceedingly delights him ... for the advancing of his own mortification' (Herbert, XXI).

Ralph Josselin* catechized the youth of his parish from time to time, in he 1640s using the catechism provided by the Westminster Assembly, and in the 1660s that in the *Book of Common Prayer* (Josselin, 282, 517). With eighteenth-century moderation William Cole** of Bletchley and Lawrence Sterne** catechized the local children during Lent (Russell, 132). John Keble* had no sermon at Sunday Evensong, but catechized the boys and girls on alternate Sundays, summing up their answers for the benefit of the listening adults

(Battiscombe, *Keble* 176). Walter Hook* catechized a thousand Leeds children every Sunday afternoon (Stephens, *Hook* 349), Cosmo Lang** fifteen hundred on his first Sunday in Portsea (Lockhart, *Lang* 120).

The fame of William Bennett* as a catechizer was such that the Prince Consort came twice to hear him. A pupil wrote: 'Mr Bennett, after the second lesson, stood on the lectern steps and explained the meaning of each sentence. We had to take notes and write out the texts, which had to be learned by heart for the following Sunday, when each in turn was questioned. Sometimes we had as many as a dozen texts to learn, besides the divisions of the subjects, of which we had to make notes.' When he moved to Frome, Bennett's Sunday School teachers were given copies of a manuscript book containing his teaching; they had to see their classes during the week to prepare them for the forthcoming Sunday. The course, which lasted two years, was a compulsory requirement for confirmation (Bennett, 268ff.).

Other clergy have tackled confirmation preparation in other ways. Notified of a confirmation, James Woodforde* preached about it, examined those who came forward, and then gave them their tickets of permission. John Skinner's* approach was similar. He relied on the religious education given in his Sunday School, and was disgusted when two of his ex-pupils proved to have completely forgotten their catechism, and not to know the Lord's Prayer (Skinner, 284). Henry Venn, the Evangelical vicar of Drypool, Hull, from 1827 to 1834, gave three lectures a week in church for a month beforehand to the 160 candidates who came forward for the first confirmation after his arrival. During the week before the confirmation itself he spent six hours a day in church so that he could speak to the candidates individually (Hennell, 71). Francis Close** of Cheltenham gave seven Friday lectures (Hennell, 111). Robert Hawker* gave instruction every evening for four weeks (Brendon, *Hawker* 99). Charles Kingsley's* confirmation classes at Eversley were so popular that the hunt servants offered to repeat them (Chitty, *Kingsley* 95). The admirable Bernard Wilson at Portsea organized post-confirmation classes with a registered attendance, and personally visited absentees (Smyth, *Garbett* 76).

In common with numbers of his contemporaries, Walter Hook conducted district classes for adults which gave a general religious education. A visitor described one: 'Through narrow, crooked, crowded streets we reached a shabby old building, and went up by a rickety staircase to a dirty, half-lighted schoolroom. Some 50 or 60 poor men and women were assembled there. There was a small organ, and part of the Liturgy was sung. Then the vicar read a chapter from St John's Gospel, and made a plain and familiar exposition of it. After this he entered into friendly and familiar conversation with the people ... Then he called their names, and they came one by one and laid a penny or twopence on the table by him as their weekly contribution to the District Library of Religious Knowledge. Lastly he asked me to dismiss them with the blessing' (Stephens, *Hook* 349).

The teaching ministry has been confined neither to spiritual matters nor to children. In the nineteenth century it was customary for the clergy to assume a responsibility for the general education of adults. In fiction, George Eliot's Mr Cleves got together the working men of his parish once a week to give them 'a sort of conversational lecture on useful practical matters, telling them stories, or reading some select passages from an agreeable book'; and her Mr Tryon opened a religious lending library in his parish (Eliot, *SCL* 94, 263). In real life, Charles Kingsley, who discovered when he arrived at Eversley that not a single local labourer could read, held evening classes at the rectory three times a week, and cottage lectures for the elderly and infirm twice (Chitty, *Kingsley* 95). While he was at Coventry Walter Hook began a Religious and Useful Know-ledge Society, which combined a library with lectures and other cultural activities. Its non-political nature commended it to the support of affluent citizens alarmed by the more partisan atmosphere of Mechanics' Institutes (Stranks, *Hook* 36–7).

Francis Kilvert* edified and entertained his parishioners at Clyro with lectures and penny readings. He records one successful evening when 'I spoke about Noah's vineyard and drunkenness, the Tower of Babel, Babylon and the confusion of tongues, the Tongue Tower, the death of the Emperor Napoleon III and the Great Coram Street Murder'; he does not mention the common theme uniting these disparate topics. He insisted on a high moral tone, refusing permission for a 'low and coarse' song to be sung, and invoking the local policeman to evict the disgruntled artiste (Kilvert, 2.335–6, 309).

Unfortunately, not all clergy were as positive in their approach as those just mentioned. George Sketchley Ffinden, rector of Downe, Kent, when Charles Darwin was living there, tried but failed to prevent the naturalist and his wife from opening a reading room for the villagers (Desmond and Moore, 625). No doubt Ffinden was concerned about Darwin's likely choice of books. Standards were stringent – John Keble was compelled to withdraw Scott's *Old Mortality* from the reading-room he opened in Hursley (Battiscombe, *Keble* 180).

The general education of young people has been as important as that of adults and has lasted longer as an element of Church life. At Olney, John Newton* eventually attracted two hundred children to his meetings for them; at an earlier stage he wrote: 'I have twenty lambs, every one of which is worth more than all the cattle that will be in Smithfield these seven years' (Martin, *Newton* 217–8). Sabine Baring-Gould** left a vivid account of the life of the mission which he opened in Horbury Brig in 1864. Activities included Night School four times a week, twice for young men and twice for young women. The instruction consisted of the three Rs. A further evening was devoted to credal instruction (Purcell, *Baring-Gould* 68). At Portsea in the first years of this century Bible classes for men, boys and girls were associated with clubs; for the youngsters attendance at the club was conditional upon attendance at the Bible class, for the men not. The boys' clubs, usually led by athletic curates, specialized in team games. They enlivened the lives of many working-class people, though the links between the Christianity of the Clubs and that of the parish church were sometimes flimsy (Smyth, *Garbett* 105–6).

Arthur Stanton* did not aspire to that kind of organized club life. He met with his boys on a Sunday evening. 'We don't play any games,' he said; 'the only game they know is to spit into a fire: we just sit around the fireplace.' He told with relish the stories of how he tempted them into a Good Friday service with the promise of hot cross buns; and how his Vicar's sister had come to see his lads, and how they had inspired her to continue her thirty years' work with boys in Suffolk. 'I'd decided,' she said, 'that it was quite hopeless and that I'd give it up. But when I'd seen your boys, all I can say is that mine are like angels by the side of them, so I'm going on.'

At the age of seventy, Stanton was still having forty rough lads to tea each Sunday, big ones one week and small ones the next, and complaining that the police 'harass us . . . not that we ever do anything wrong according to our own ideas, which unfortunately don't square with theirs'. The quality of relationship he created is exemplified by a story he told of visiting a lad dying of pneumonia. 'I said, "Jim, dear boy, you've had a rough time of it; you've never had a home; you've never learnt a trade ... you've been in and out of prison; and now I want to tell you that the good God is going to take you home to be with Him." And he looked up into my face and said, "Well, that's all right, ain't it Farver?" And I said, "Well, dear boy, if you think it's all right, then it will be all right." And then ... he put his arms up round my neck ... and kissed me. And after that I couldn't say any more. And next time I went he was gone' (Russell, *Stanton* 254–5, 279, 257–8).

In more recent times many clergy have thought it their duty to run open youth clubs, with little or no worship or overt religious teaching. In the 1970s John Ruffle, vicar of Emmanuel parish, Weston-super-Mare, was running 'a club for the unclubbable' in the centre of the town. He was content if an evening passed off without violence and if a youngster or two chatted with him about religious or moral matters. Harold Hosking**, vicar of Newlyn, Cornwall, from 1961 to 1971 ran a similar club, finding it a hard and thankless task. He tells the story, however, of a well-dressed man getting out of his car many years later and bringing two teenagers across the road. He did not speak to Hosking directly, but said to his children: 'This is the man I often spoken to you about, who used to open up his church hall for us ... I don't know how he put up with us lot ... but he did more good than he'll ever know' (Hosking, 61). At about the same period David Watson*, curate at St Mark's, Gillingham, used to pray before Youth Club night in the words of Jeremiah 1.8: 'Be not afraid of their faces, for I am with you to deliver you, says the Lord' (Watson, *YAMG* 44).

A compromise between the formal and the informal teaching of youth has been the work of the uniformed youth organizations, such as the Church Lads

Brigade and the Scout and Guide movements. Many a curate has found himself serving the kingdom by way of drill and camping, first aid and firelighting. Harry Williams** was given premature experience of purgatory by his scout troop; providentially his worst boy jumped through a plate glass window, with permanently sobering effects on the rest (Williams, 112). An even more unlikely scoutmaster was John Robinson**. While he was a curate his enthusiasm for pot-holing once left him stuck below ground while a friend was stuck with erecting camp above it (James, *Robinson* 29).

In *The Parson's Handbook*, a widely read handbook first published in 1899, Percy Dearmer wrote: 'The Prayer Book knows nothing of Sunday schools, which became a necessity owing to the want of diligence on the part of the clergy' (p. 449). He did not hold this rather grudging attitude alone. George Denison** of East Brent saw no place for them 'except as a means of gathering together those children for Church whose parents do not take them' (Denison, 259). Dissenting Sunday Schools have tended to be bigger and more effective than Anglican ones.

But Dearmer did less than justice to those clergy who used the Sunday School as a preparation for catechizing. Bennett's practice has been described above; Keble followed a similar policy. Skinner set up a Sunday School in his parish, in part to teach reading, but chiefly to instruct children in the catechism on which they were examined after Sunday morning service (Skinner, 36).

Sunday Schools were also founded for more general purposes. John Fletcher* set up schools with paid teachers to teach reading, writing and the principles of religion. He supplemented their work by meeting two or three hundred children one week-day evening in order to give them further instruction himself (Macdonald, *Fletcher* 175–6). He was a pioneer in an activity which Evangelicals took especially seriously. Their Sunday Schools usually opened from 10.00 a.m. to 5.30 p.m., with teachers who were paid a shilling a week. They were widely suspected of teaching sedition and atheism (Balleine, 94–6), and objection was taken even to their professed objectives. 'Give me a servant as can nayther read nor write ... and doesn't know the year o' the Lord as she was born in,' declared George Eliot's Mr Tomlinson; better by far, he thought, the days when children used their Sundays to go birds-nesting (Eliot, *SCL* 247–8).

The Evangelicals were not deterred, and in time won many imitators. During the nineteenth century they instituted special Children's Services and the Children's Scripture Union was founded in 1879 (Balleine, 164). Kilvert taught a class in the family dining-room before morning church (1.29). Similarly the Anglo-Catholic clergy held children's masses, as George Dolling* did at Landport (Dolling, *TY* 51).

The numbers attending Sunday Schools in their heyday were phenomenal, both absolutely and proportionately. At their strongest, in the 1880s, about seventy-five per cent of children were attenders (Chadwick, *VC* 2.257). In 1878

St Paul's parish, Manchester, had 1865 children on the books (Chadwick, *VC* 2.260). Because he insisted on high standards of behaviour, Dolling had 'only' five or six hundred in his School at Landport (Dolling, *TY* 51). In his first curacy in Nottingham, Arthur Hopkinson** found 1400 children in the Sunday School; his own class numbered 100 (Hopkinson, 137). The tiny Kentish village of Shepherdswell could boast an Anglican Sunday School of sixty in 1912; with a Methodist chapel and its attendant Sunday School in the village too, it is fair to surmise that every child in the village attended one or the other (*SPM*). The actual teaching was overwhelmingly in the hands of the laity, to the extent that the clergy sometimes felt excluded; many Sunday Schools were inefficient and some were bear-gardens; but, as prime movers of the life of their parishes, the Victorian clergy could claim to have made a huge contribution to literacy, to religious knowledge, and, though less certainly, to religious commitment.

There have been Sunday Schools for adults as for children. In 1841 Henry Fardell* set one up 'to induce persons to attend the afternoon Service'. Instruction and a lending library were provided, and the elderly encouraged to attend to listen to others reading. The School attracted respectable numbers – forty-five soon after its opening – and continued for a number of years (Fardell, 124). As a curate in Leeds in the 1890s Cosmo Lang had charge of the 'A division' – eighty to a hundred young men in their twenties and thirties who met each Sunday afternoon. At Portsea he ran a Men's Conference, attended by many men who had only the flimsiest church connection, on Sunday afternoons, and a Bible class for women, with a membership of some two or three hundred, on a week-day (Lockhart, *Lang* 98, 124).

These tremendous achievements are now history. Sunday Schools have been overtaken by modern education and vitiated by modern hedonism; the very name has fallen into disrepute, and children still in touch with the faith are as likely as not to attend Junior Church or a family service. In Shepherdswell the Sunday School of sixty has given place in a village three times as large to a Junior Church of twenty. But the work the clergy and their helpers have wrought then and now on their charges is touchingly illuminated in a letter written to Samuel Garratt** when he left Holy Trinity parish, Waltham Cross, in 1867: 'You have been our friend and helper in every sorrow and need, and always watching so tenderly over us. Above all, our hearts are full that you have taught so many of us to know Jesus ... O God bless you dear Sir ... for all the happiness and joy in Christ through your teaching and preaching, for our happy Christian fellowship with one another, and how you have taught us by word and example to love those who do us wrong. We would like to ask your forgiveness for the trial we must have caused you many times, but we *know* you forgive us all' (Garratt, 74).

The connection between ministry and school-teaching has always been a close one; to the extent that many parochial clergy have engaged in both. Some have been deeply seized of the work's importance: Fielding's Parson Adams 'thought a schoolmaster the greatest character in the world' (Fielding, 258). Others have adopted the profession from earthier motives. Ralph Josselin was schoolmaster at Earls Colne from 1650 to 1658; not an unduly onerous task if the numbers were habitually close to the 8 he recorded in 1650, and if he was constantly able to use school hours as he did at the outset, as times of personal study. He undertook the work largely in order to provide an education for his eldest son Thomas; but the diary makes it clear that his chief interest in it thereafter lay in the income it afforded him. With his usual painful self-criticism he noted on relinquishing the school: 'I begge pardon from god that I attended no better to it while I had it' (Josselin, 206, 208, 421).

By contrast, Robert Walker, who served as curate of his native village of Seathwaite, Cumberland, for sixty-six years until he died in 1802 at the age of 93, was in church for eight hours a day five days a week offering teaching to the local children. He used the communion table as his desk and filled the moments he could spare from his charges with spinning (Addison, 127). William Grimshaw* took over the teaching in the local school when necessary, and constantly supervised its work (Baker, *Grimshaw* 78). John Keble invariably spent two hours a day teaching in Hursley school (Battiscombe, *Keble* 178). R.W. Evans wanted the school to be the 'vestibule of the church', and delivered himself of the striking remark that the parson was likely to find it a peaceful haven compared with the homes of adult parishioners (Evans, 178–9). Charles Kingsley arranged for an intelligent young man to be sent off to Winchester Training College; whence he returned to spend the rest of his life running the village school (Chitty, *Kingsley* 95). Francis Kilvert taught in Clyro school, going in three times a day before the visit of a Government inspector, and helping to secure a record grant of £36 10s od (Kilvert, 1.371, 386).

Henry Fardell threw himself with his usual energy into supporting the schools of Wisbech. He was chiefly concerned with the two National Schools (that is with the boys' and girls' schools founded under the auspices of the Anglican National Society). Sunday attendance, with its concomitant church-going and catechizing, was a condition of admission. Fardell taught regularly in the boys' school, on one occasion lecturing for an hour and twenty minutes on the liturgy of the Church. He was deeply involved in managing both schools and in examining the children; he arranged for them to be fed in bad times, provided an annual treat, and was the instigator of a plan to open an infants' school. Occasionally he joyfully recorded evidence of progress among the children; more often he lamented low standards of discipline, attendance and achievement, and the poor quality of the teaching. He was very evidently the moving force in the education of the local poor, determined to ensure the pervasive influence of Christian teaching and practice, and taking it for granted that the teaching staff should dance to his tune.

Working in less favourable circumstances than Fardell, Robert Hawker could claim a similar achievement. He provided both the inspiration and the finance for St Mark's school, Morwenstow. When the school was deprived of its government grant under the system of payment by results, he raised or supplied the whole of the income required for its continuance. He cajoled and bullied parents into sending their children, and taught regularly in the school himself. Like Fardell, he saw education as a civilizing and restraining force, a way of inculcating true religion and of strengthening the social fabric. He was not concerned to produce intellectual liberation. He said 'Happy they who only know enough to believe'; and thought schooling 'should be dogmatic. Tell a child it is so, never why'. Judging by the level of literacy it produced, his school was a good one; but the aim was to replace the chains of ignorance with the silken fetters of predigested learning (Brendon, *Hawker* 88–92).

There has been a long tradition of clergy housing pupils in their own homes. Francis Kilvert's father ran a school at Hardenhuish which was attended by Augustus Hare, the biographer of his namesake (Grice, *Kilvert* 12–3). Gladstone and Macaulay received a part of their education in the homes of clerical tutors. Of another an ex-pupil wrote: 'Mr Abbott was in some respects a marvellous man. He managed the entire school himself, without the aid of a single usher. He duly flogged us; played cricket with us; punctually reported us to our parents, and in addition to these unassisted labours, he was actually sole curate of the large parish of St Lawrence, the mother church of Ramsgate' (Russell, 185–6, 190–1).

Francis Close is an example of the clergyman as a founder of schools. He replaced dames' schools with larger and properly organized infant schools; he enlarged the local National School; he founded a commercial school, Cheltenham College (the boys' public school), and a Training College. He believed that education was a good in itself, but he also had other axes to grind. First, he was anxious to create Evangelical institutions which would serve as a counterpoise to Tractarian ones. When Cheltenham College was opened he promised: 'We would never have any master at the school but such as embraced the religion of the Liturgy, the religion of the Homilies, the creed of the Martyred Reformers in the true and literal sense.' Secondly, he wanted to keep education in the hands of the Church: 'The great barrier against the progress of revolutionary principles among the working classes is the salutary influence of the clergy, greatly exercised through the medium of the children' (Hennell, 112–17).

One parish priest left an astonishing educational memorial. Nathaniel Woodard** became curate at New Shoreham, Sussex, in 1847. In the years which followed he created a succession of schools, eventually eleven including one girls' school, which were carefully graded to cater for every level of income among the middle classes. His motives were explicitly religious; the schools were to be Christian brotherhoods, with non-teaching chaplains whose function was to direct each pupil's spiritual life. With considerable practical wisdom

Woodard remarked that 'a greater degree of confidence will be inspired by a clergyman who has nothing to do with *teaching* and *punishing*'. More controversially, it was one of the chaplain's principal functions to prevent masturbation and homosexuality: 'Most of our youth,' thought Woodard, 'grow into life familiarized and reconciled to living in the most deadly sin' (Heeney, 63). Since the Woodard schools were for the most part for boarders, he was probably right about his own charges.

James Fraser, the second Bishop of Manchester wrote in the 1860s: 'But for the zeal and activity of the clergy and their large sacrifices, not only of money, but of labour and time, in three fourths of the rural parishes of England there would be either no school at all, or at best only the semblance of a school' (Clark, 125). What the clergy achieved was astonishing, but it was not enough. If all children were to receive some kind of education the state must play a larger part; and if the Church no longer provided the means for schooling she could no longer dictate the terms on which it was given.

Some clergy believed passionately that religion was so important that education without it would spell an end to 'patriotism, honour and morality' (Newbolt, 250); others believed equally passionately that education was so important that, if the church could not provide it, it was sssential that the state should. William Bennett built or restored a number of schools at Frome, but eventually handed them over to the local School Board. 'If the State will civilize them,' he said, 'we may be able to make Christians of them' (Bennett, 255–6). The other point of view was represented by George Denison of East Brent who would never allow a government inspector into the local school, and who wrote that 'a school board is the most powerful engine of future indifference, latitudinarianism and infidelity'. He emphatically denied that it was possible to divide educational content into the religious and the non-religious; and dealt with the problem of Dissenters desiring schooling for their children by insisting that every child admitted at East Brent should be baptized and received into the Church of England (Denison, 31, 36, 117–18, ch. xi).

The generally positive impression the preceding pages have given of the clergy's attitude to education is not the whole picture. It is well known that progress towards universal primary education was slowed by controversy between Churchmen and Dissenters and between Christians and secularists. Thomas Bere, the curate of Blagdon, Somerset, forced Hannah More to close her local Sunday School on the grounds that the schoolmaster taught Calvinist doctrines and employed Methodist practices; when he had succeeded he illuminated the rectory, rang the church bells and remarked jubilantly 'The Church has carried it' (Hart, *ECCP* 84; J. and M. Collingwood, *Hannah More*, Lion 1990, 96–8). Plenty of parish priests have shown as little regard for the educational as for the economic well-being of their people. Even when the regard has been there, respect for the lay teaching staff has sometimes not. The early battles of the National Union of Teachers were usually with overbearing parish priests. A Victorian inspector of schools ruminated that he recalled some instances of a schoolmistress being received at a clergyman's table, but almost none of a clergyman shaking hands with or talking familiarly with a parochial schoolmaster (Hammond, 158).

To conclude this and the preceding section, we consider three teaching ministries, of which two were exceptional and one typical.

Even before his appointment to Houghton, the parish which made him famous, Bernard Gilpin* had shown his mettle. In a sermon before the court he had fired a broadside against the abuses of the age. He denounced the mis-appropriation of benefices (the way in which lay patrons of livings took most or all of the income for themselves); bad appointments made by reason of nepotism or favouritism; non-residence and pluralism; the decay of learning; and the unchecked avarice of the rich. 'When Christ suffered His passion, there was one Barabbas, St Matthew calls him a notable thief, a gentleman thief, such as rob nowadays in velvet coats; the other two were obscure thieves, and nothing famous. The rustical thieves were hanged, and Barabbas was delivered. Even so now-a-days the little thieves are hanged that steal of necessity, but the great Barabbases have free liberty to rob and spoil without all measure' (Collingwood, *Gilpin* 48–9).

Gilpin's words were lent wings by his deeds. Going abroad soon afterwards, he handed over the whole income of his parish, which for a legal reason he could not resign, to his replacement. Later, because he was uncertain about the propriety of holding the posts of incumbent of Easington and Archdeacon of Durham together, he resigned both. When he was appointed to Houghton he refused to take a canonry as well.

Despite the scattered nature of his parish, Gilpin was soon getting large congregations. But it was not his parishioners alone who benefited from his preaching. Annually he set off on tours through neglected parishes, including those in the wildest border country. He preached in churches when they were available, in barns when churches were not. Despite his outspoken comments on local morals he passed safely everywhere; once, when his horses were stolen, the thief returned them as soon as he learned who the owner was.

As Gilpin travelled, he recruited for the Grammar School he had founded and endowed. A score of the pupils boarded at his rectory, mostly free of charge. He supported several students at university. In this, as in so much else, he blazed a trail for others to follow.

The teaching ministry of Augustus Hare* provides a model on the smallest scale. His parish of Alton-Barnes in Wiltshire consisted of about a hundred souls, though he also ministered to the people of the adjacent parish of Alton-Priors, which had no resident priest. The parishioners were either labourers or small farmers; there were no other gentry, no shops, not even a public house. Most of the labourers were very poor, and the circumscribed nature of life in this isolated hamlet can be easily imagined. When Hare arrived there, no one in Alton-Barnes could read. 'The poverty of their minds, their inability to follow a train of reasoning, their prejudices and superstition, were quite unknown to him.' At first he did not connect with them save through his earnestness: 'Mr Hare does *long* to save our souls'. Then he learned how to simplify and to rely on the Bible: 'how our minister does *grow*' (Hare, 1.287, 293).

Hare took his Sunday sermons seriously. He did not start writing them until Saturday because he feared that otherwise they would dominate his week. He adopted the dominical style, using short words and Saxon English and peppering his argument with rural illustrations. The contrast with his brother Julius Hare* was marked. After Julius had preached, his sister-in-law commented that he was too much the scholar: 'I long for him to be thrown more into the world, that, by mixing with different classes of society, his theories may become less visionary' (Hare, 1.349).

Augustus Hare never hesitated to improve the occasion. When there was no sermon on a Sunday morning, he would expound the Old Testament lesson. At the funeral of a young girl he asked: 'Which ... hours ... did she now look back on with most pleasure and delight – those spent in idleness and wasted in folly, or those devoted to her God?' In similar vein he would ask parents during baptismal instruction 'Do you wish your child to be an angel in heaven, or a *devil in hell*?' (Hare, 1.427; 1.307).

The rectory was too small for meetings, so Hare conducted a Bible studies class, mostly attended by old men, in a barn. The barn was peppered with holes covered with sackcloth; teacher and taught attended wrapped up against the cold. In due course the barn was warmed with a laundry stove and served also as the schoolroom, replacing the school in a private house which the Hares had founded. Husband and wife also ran Sunday and evening schools for young people. Pretty well the whole child population must have attended the Sunday School – on New Year's day 1833 fifty-six children received prizes in return for their attendance tickets.

The Hares encountered one perennial problem. 'How hard it is,' Maria lamented, 'to give them the least notion of religion, except as one of forms and outward acts.' Teaching on its own would not answer, but character and charity might. So: 'Any surly or ungracious behaviour towards himself was ... a stimulus to show a more than usual degree of loving-kindness' (Hare, 1.334, 295).

Samuel Barnett* was no preacher. His sermons were academic and impersonal, their content determined by his own preoccupations at the time he delivered them, and not by the needs of his hearers (Barnett, 1.25). Yet, and it was a fact recognized by those who dissented from many of his ideas, he was one of the few truly prophetic figures which the Church of England has produced.

A year after the Barnetts had started work in the parish of St Jude, Whitechapel, in 1873 they could point to these achievements: 142 children in schools; 50 students in adult classes learning such subjects as French and Latin; a girl's night school; and a lending library. This was the beginning of a remarkable educational ministry, directed towards both the young and adults.

Barnett opened church schools and personally taught religion in them on four mornings a week, instructing the teachers as well as the pupils. Mondays in term-time began with prayers at the vicarage for clergy and teachers. Fees were what parents could pay, and parents were fully involved in school life and activities. In many ways Barnett was in advance of his time. He objected to cramming – his aim was to engage interest. Volunteer teachers enlarged the curriculum and handicrafts were introduced. (This illegal activity cost his schools their government grant.) There were play classes from 5.00–7.00 p.m. and continuation classes for school leavers. He even tried unsuccessfully to introduce co-education, to ensure that girls were treated on an even footing and to improve male behaviour towards them.

Henrietta Barnett's night schools for girls were more successful in creating relationships than in providing formal education. 'I recall one evening when the gas was suddenly turned off, the heads of teachers wrapped in table-cloths, and the whole class, with wild whoops, tore down the stairs into the street. Fights between the girls were frequent, and enjoyed by both combatants and onlookers. The language they used is best forgotten; their unconquerable and communicable dirt led to the Verminous Persons Bill; ... their deficiency in self-control made teaching almost hopeless; but their hearts were good, full of tenderness, quick to respond to what was kind, and they were ready – until they forgot – to be responsible for any and every thing they were trusted with. What friendships grew out of that rough stony soil, and how we laughed at and with them!' (Barnett, 1.102–3).

True to their principle of supporting secular attempts to enrich life, both Barnetts were School Board managers. In 1884 Barnett set up the Education Reform League 'to infuse more life into the dry bones of state-aided Elementary Education'. He argued for a school leaving age of 15 or 16 and for universal free education. Mrs Barnett was an active manager of District Schools, the vast institutions into which uncared for children were decanted. Her experiences convinced her that 'no one can love six hundred children', and she became secretary of the State Children's Association, founded 'to obtain individual treatment for children under the Guardianship of the State'.

From 1875 Barnett began using his connections with Oxford, and especially with Balliol College under Jowett, to interest university men in the condition of the poor. The outcome was Toynbee Hall, set up in 1884 to provide a lodging for men ready to work with the poor and a place for such work to be done. Barnett was its first Warden. The Memorandum of Association defined its aims, in part, as: 'to provide education and the means of recreation and enjoyment for the people of the poorer districts of London and other great cities; to inquire into the condition of the poor and to consider and advance plans calculated to promote their welfare' (Barnett, 1.309).

From Toynbee Hall sprang a vast enterprise in adult education, staffed by the residents and by others of the educated and socially conscious class. Barnett's aims in this enterprise were social and moral. 'The object is that there may not be so many wretched, homeless people on Commercial Street doorsteps, so many unemployed half-fed in their single-roomed homes, so many neighbours full of envy, hatred and uncharitableness; that work may not be so destructive of mind, and that the problems of capital and labour may not be settled by bullets. The memory of this object will make the students feel in honour bound to become servants' (Barnett, 1.341). It would be hard to imagine a more Christian approach.

Evangelism

An essential component of prophetic ministry is evangelism; partly conceived of in terms of converting those afar off but rooted in the desire to convert those who are nigh. The need has always seemed great. Clerical gloom about the spiritual state of one's contemporaries has been perennial. In 1657 Ralph Josselin* wrote: 'the heart of the nacon never lesse regardful of god, they mind themselves, their lusts, their opinions their own designes no time nor heart to mind or regard the things of christ.' A like pessimism has been a constant feature down the centuries, and many a parish priest has prayed to be blessed as Josselin was: 'god was good to mee this day in holding out the mercy of god through christ to sensible sinners' (Josselin, 400).

The most cautious form of evangelism has been the holding of services in unconsecrated buildings. Since the practice had been pioneered by Methodists and was illegal, the nineteenth-century clergy who adopted it had to proceed with caution. Schoolroom services for the poor were originally entitled 'lectures', and services in houses were often an extension of the visitation of the sick. Walter Hook* used a sail loft at Whippingham for services for fishermen, sailors and others (Stephens, *Hook* 45). R.W. Evans advocated calling the neighbouring poor into the home of a sick person for a short service (Evans, 144). George Bull** of Byerley lectured at a variety of places on Sunday evenings, and held a regular Monday lecture at the home of a widow (Gill, *Bull* 55).

For most of our period, open air evangelism was the prerogative of Dissenters and Methodists. The practice is said to have been revived among Anglicans by John Cale Miller, the Evangelical rector of Birmingham 1846–66 (Balleine, 159). In the 1850s A.C. Tait, then Bishop of London, founded a diocesan home mission, through which the clergy were encouraged to preach in the open or in unconsecrated rooms. In the 1880s some parish priests took advantage of the bands of the newly created Salvation Army, and marched through the streets with them as they made their way to church (Chadwick, *VC* 2.286, 294). At St Helen's during Christopher's Chavasse's** time there, he attracted congregations by inducing one of his fellow-curates to pursue him through the streets shouting 'Stop thief!' The fleet-footed Chavasse outpaced the crowd which joined in the chase until he brought them into a square where a band and Church Army evangelists would be waiting for them (Gummer, *Chavasse* 42).

Where Evangelicals led Anglo-Catholics were not slow to follow. Until inhibited, Arthur Stanton* was among the most effective missioners in the country. His work was generally conducted within the walls of the local church, but he had a gift for enticing what one observer called those 'of the very poorest and reprobate description' to hear him there. On occasion he would stand in the street throwing his surplice in the air to attract attention; when a crowd had gathered he would preach to them on the spot, afterwards leading them into church. Mission services were often eucharistic, often highly informal. In 1869 at St Columba's, Kingsland Road, London, 'a procession wound out into the lighted nave, those who formed it singing at the top of their voices a most enthusiastic mission hymn to a very catching tune. First came Father Stanton in cassock, surplice, and tippet, singing lustily, and behind him followed a crowd, and oh! *such* a crowd of working men. Shoe-makers in leathern aprons, as if they had just left their benches; one man, a carpenter or joiner, with his linen apron tucked round his waist, and a basket full of tools on his shoulder; then a lame man hopping along on crutches; then costers out of Hoxton, roughs out of the Kingsland Road; a sprinkling of respectables, and sundry women of every description' (Russell, *Stanton* 93, 112, 110).

Cyril Garbett** threw the whole of his vast energy into the Portsea Parochial Mission of 1913. It might have been thought that a campaign which attracted over a thousand communicants to a final week-day Eucharist at 5.00 a.m. on a cold December morning and which was at least partly responsible for the 360 candidates for the next Confirmation could be counted a success; but Garbett, a supreme realist, recognized that the Mission's true success had been among those already in touch with the church. He concluded that the systematic pastoral work which constituted the daily life of his parish precluded the possibility of remarkable success at the time of a Mission. What he proved on a large scale at the beginning of the century, I confirmed in a small way at the end of it. A mission to Shepherdswell preceded by two years of preparation galvanized the existing congregation; but it would be hard to show that it added a single soul to its number.

The most well-known English evangelist of modern times was also, though increasingly only in name, a parish priest. David Watson* proved at York that he had remarkable powers of attracting a large congregation and of welding them into a spiritual community. It has to be said that he drew a large proportion of his hearers from other churches and from visitors, and that he failed, as have nearly all parish priests, to appeal to the bulk of working-class people; but those reservations set his achievement in perspective rather than derogate from it. It is not surprising that he was asked, and increasingly as time went on, to head evangelistic efforts elsewhere; to such as extent that he decided in due course to hand over the day to day responsibility for his parish to others, and later to leave it.

Watson's success derived from a spirituality rooted in a powerful devotional life, including a readiness to receive and use charismatic gifts. In addition he spent countless hours in study, and, without being highly intellectual, equipped himself formidably for his work. His addresses were the fruit of intensive labour, and he gave close attention to the technicalities of public speaking. Believing profoundly in the good news he was proclaiming he felt no need to argue or manipulate. He taught that evangelism was fundamentally a matter for the individual Christian and the local congregation, as he had himself shown in York. He realized the advantages of using drama and dance, and built up a team who accompanied and supported him. He learned to transcend the narrowly Evangelical attitudes which marked the first years of his ministry, and became widely acceptable to Christians from traditions other than his own. He was totally unmercenary, and the asthma which gravely hindered his ministry also tinged it with heroism (Saunders, *Watson* ch. 18).

The Church will always need charismatic figures such as Watson, who act as a focus for missionary endeavour and who are beacons of hope for other Christians struggling in apparently unfruitful fields. Recent research has shown, however, that it is the long slow process of Christian education which is the real seed-bed of commitment. Infinitely more has been done for evangelism by clergy patiently slogging away in their parishes than by glittering figures speaking to vast crowds; indeed, whatever fruit the latter have gathered they usually owe to the former. I recall a dozen young people going forward at a Billy Graham crusade. They were all baptized, all churchgoers, all members of Sunday School or the Church youth club; they were using the occasion to declare a commitment for which a lifetime had prepared them.

A new instrument of evangelism appeared in the mid-nineteenth century and was almost universally employed by the 1880s. It was the parish magazine, supplemented as time went on by local or national inserts. Many magazines have been shrines to the trivial and the fatuous, but far larger numbers of people have exposed themselves to their parish priest's influence by reading him than by listening to him. Sheppard's own magazine, *The St Martin's Review* covered national and world as well as parochial affairs, received contributions from many of the most distinguished figures of the day, was read by an average of 50,000 people, and was an opinion former of major importance (Roberts, *Sheppard* 107–11).

Nicolas Stacey found in the 1960s that an assiduous wooing of the press, combined with writing a column for a local paper, benefited his parish at the price of earning him unpopularity with his fellow-clergy, who resented his high profile. He also had a couple of bruising experiences of the capacity of television to distort and trivialize, and of the massive reaction which a few minutes on the screen can evoke. There is an inevitable tension between the advantages which publicity confers and the spiritual dangers which seeking publicity involves; Stacey secured the one but did not entirely avoid the other (Stacey, 174–8, 216–22).

With one major exception, parish priests have played little part in the representation of the Christian faith in the national media. The exception was Dick Sheppard. The first service to be broadcast from a place of worship came from St Martin's on the feast of the Epiphany 1924, and was the precursor both of monthly services from St Martin's itself and of all the broadcast services which have taken place since. In addition Sheppard was a prolific journalist, writing for a variety of dailies and periodicals, and for several years having a column in the *Sunday Express* (Roberts, *Sheppard* 11–3, 227–8).

We turn to overseas endeavour. A fascinating sequence of entries in Josselin's diary refers to missionary work among Red Indians undertaken from the late 1640s by the Society for the Propagation of the Gospel in New England. His enthusiasm for the work was fanned by the contemporary theory that the lost ten tribes of Israel might be found among them, and hence that their conversion was a necessary preliminary to the Second Coming. Josselin resolved in 1651 that if he received some arrears due to him he would 'make the lord a sharer with it for his worke in new England to the summ of £5'. When he appealed to his parish for the same cause in 1653 both rich and poor responded and he eventually raised the very considerable sum of £54 (Josselin, 119n., 238, 238n., 263, 290, 291, 292, 299).

During succeeding centuries overseas missions were regarded with suspicion. John Skinner* was of his age when he wrote in 1830: 'Methinks they had better strive to mend matters at home, instead of going abroad to unsettle the minds of their fellows' (Skinner, 441–2). A like caution informed the mind of George Eliot's lawyer Dempster who, in the course of a tirade against the pernicious practice of Sunday lectures, declared: 'We are not to be poisoned with doctrines which ... pick a poor man's pocket of the sixpence with which he might buy himself a cheerful glass after a hard day's work, under pretence of paying for bibles to send to the Chicktaws!' (Eliot, *SCL* 282).

Mr Tryon, who had aroused Dempster's ire, was an Evangelical; and it was they who were first prominent in the cause of overseas missions. Charles Simeon* was, more than any other individual, the founder of 'The Society for Missions to Africa and the East', later known as the Church Missionary Society. He was also its foremost recruiting officer, a substantial fund-raiser and the teacher, friend and adviser of Henry Venn, a notable secretary of the Society (Hopkins, *Simeon* 151–2).

In addition, Simeon was an enthusiastic advocate of the conversion of the Jews. This enterprise had deep roots. In 1655 Josselin had been glad to hear rumours that the Jews were to be re-admitted to England (as in fact they were). He noted: 'The lord hasten their conversion, and keep us from turning aside from Christ to Moses of which I am very heartily afraid' (Josselin, 358). Simeon did not share that fear, but he was a strong supporter of the London Society for Promoting Christianity among the Jews. He found the money for a chapel in Amsterdam to facilitate work among the city's 30,000 Jews, and worked hard to save converts from the evil consequences of being cut adrift from their community. Friends thought his preoccupation with this work almost obsessional; Simeon would no doubt have replied that he was doing no more than continuing the work of his beloved St Paul (Hopkins, *Simeon* 187–9).

Evangelism, whether at home or overseas, takes its toll of the evangelist. Thomas Fuller** wrote: 'The preaching of the word in some places is like the planting of woods, where, though no profit is received for twenty years together, it comes afterwards' (Fuller, *HS* 78). At least he anticipated results. My own experience of ministry has convinced me of the truth of Bernard Shaw's remark in the preface to *Androcles and the Lion*, that it is a great mistake to think that the bulk of people are potentially devout; it is only a small percentage who are really interested either in their own souls or in those of other people. I have constructed a personal theology which concedes Shaw's point; countless other clergy have been heavily burdened because they have proceeded on other assumptions.

Social Teaching

The dominant tradition of social teaching in the Church of England has consisted of general admonitions to the poor to respect the existing social order and to the rich to soften its ill effects. A preacher in 1602 put the matter in a nutshell. 'God made some rich and some poor that two excellent virtues might flourish in the world: charity in the rich and patience in the poor' (Barrow, 32). Predominantly 'A Christian's duty to his neighbour was seen as duty to specific persons, to particular individuals who were in need' (Stranks, 286). The need for a social gospel has been further obscured by a stress on the primacy of personal salvation. Robert Hawker* declared of slavery: 'So that you save the whole man, never heed his fettered limb' (Brendon, *Hawker* 33).

In this section, then, we deal with a minority of exceptional figures, prophetic in the true sense of the word, and hence out of step with their contemporaries. None is to be found before the nineteenth century.

One way to secure alterations in social conditions is to describe them. This was the path chosen by Sydney Godolphin Osborne, rector of Durweston, Dorset, from 1841 to 1875. A stream of letters to *The Times* and other published work laid bare the condition of the agricultural poor, to the horror of many of his readers, and to the fury of landowners and the local MP. He taught that the Church should 'preach the plain truth boldly, that God will not have the poor oppressed in body or in soul' (Colloms, 201).

Osborne's reputation was enhanced when he went out to serve as a chaplain during the Crimean War. His habit of signing his writings by his initials SGO earned him the soubriquet of 'Sincere, Good and Outspoken' from his admirers. His critics dubbed him 'a popularity hunting parson' and complained about him to his bishop and the patron of the living; but he was protected by his aristocratic connections and his freehold. Behind those impregnable defences he continued to support social reform, and to deal with a postbag of personal problems so heavy that it nearly crushed him. He was, however, no revolutionary; at the time of the Chartist agitation he wrote: 'Let us have power to earn fair wages wherever we can get work; let us have decent dwellings wherever we are forced to live; give us power to worship our God on the day He appoints; let us have a chance of rearing our young ones in their duty to Him in Heaven and to the rulers on earth; and no Chartists will ever drive us to disturb the country by asking for changes which would pull the rich down and make the poor still poorer.' He is an admirable example of the compassionate conservative who thinks a due care for the poor both a Christian duty and the best way of preserving the existing social order (Colloms, 204, 186–208).

Osborne was brother-in-law to another and better-known reformer, Charles Kingsley*. Like Osborne, he had seen in what manner many of his parishioners were forced to live, and had found their circumstances intolerable. Observing agricultural misery at first hand, he acquainted himself with its urban counterpart largely by reading; and campaigned vigorously to ameliorate both. He was a popular and widely read novelist, who sugared the bitter pill of fact with a thick coating of fiction, and who contributed to the changes in public attitudes which made social reform possible. He gave qualified support to the Chartists.

Again like Osborne, Kingsley was ultimately a conservative. He was a social paternalist who did not believe in democracy and who romanticized the Crown and the landed classes. He disliked the Manchester Radicals, whose emphasis on social and economic competition he saw as socially destructive. Factory life was essentially inhuman, in that men were treated like machines. Men should be freed to be their true selves; they should not be humiliated by alms, fettered by ignorance and abject poverty, or enslaved by their employers. When he called himself a 'Christian Socialist' he meant that he believed in 'co-operative associations, education, sanitary reform, recreation and religion' (Norman, 45).

Kingsley underwent the common metamorphosis of becoming less radical as he grew older and more successful. Stewart Headlam**, a truly prophetic figure, barely falls within the ambit of this book, because his Socialist and Anglo-Catholic views, together with the provocative way in which he expressed them, contributed to his extrusion from parochial ministry after only six years, and to his failure to secure any parochial post thereafter. Edward Norman writes of 'his sense of the damage done to the interior lives of men by their wrong social priorities, their inability or unwillingness to elevate collective needs above individual, and their blinkered cultural perspectives, which made men mistake the transient for the permanent in human orders of society'

(Norman, 99). He also taught that all work for humanity was 'of Christ'. Jesus 'revealed himself not as the teacher of religion but as the Servant of Humanity' (Reckitt, 64). Headlam was regarded as so dangerous a character that Robert Dolling* nearly lost his post at Landport simply because he invited him to speak there (Osborne, *Dolling* 125–6).

By the end of the nineteenth century a considerable minority of clergy had become deeply interested in social issues and were prepared to consider radical methods of tackling them. For example, in 1878 William Lewery Blackley, who, after serving in Southwark, had for health reasons moved to a country parish, wrote an article in *The Nineteenth Century* proposing a system of National Insurance (November issue). In the previous year Headlam had founded the Guild of St Matthew which became a national propagandist Socialist organization, founded on 'the belief that mere commercialist Individualism is inadequate and morally unsatisfactory as a solution of the problems presented by the vast inequalities in the distribution of wealth, and of the opportunities for legitimate human development' (Osborne, *Dolling* 123). A more broadly based group was the Christian Social Union, founded in 1889, with a bishop as its president; it was a sign of changed times that when Cyril Garbett** (who had been much influenced by seeing Dolling at work in Landport) proposed to resign from the Union on ordination, his bishop, Randall Davidson, dissuaded him (Smyth, *Garbett* 43, 465). In the 1890s the Christian Socialist H.C. Shuttleworth and his assistant Thomas Hancock** preached a social gospel in the London parish of St Nicholas, Cole Abbey, and filled a previously empty church (Chadwick, *VC* 2.281). After four curacies, Hancock was out of work from 1875 to 1883 and was never an incumbent. Some words of his perhaps explain why: 'The preacher of the Gospel may go a great way in attacking the prejudices of his hearers, and be patiently tolerated, but let him even seem to lay a hand upon their most sacred idol, and he will find that the fanatical intolerance he has aroused is fundamentally a religious intolerance ... what the sepulchre of Jesus Christ was to our fathers in the Middle Ages, property is to us in this age' (Reckitt, 8).

The greatest Anglican social teacher of the twentieth century, William Temple, was only briefly and incidentally a parish priest. The most important Anglican social documents, *Faith in the City* and *Faith in the Countryside* were fathered by another Archbishop, Robert Runcie. But these great men evinced as well as contributed to a changed atmosphere in which a social (though not necessarily a Socialist) gospel was increasingly seen as part of the whole teaching of the Church. Gilbert Shaw, working in Poplar in the 1930s and more radical than most, concluded that 'the foundations of our society are at fault, for they are of gold not God' . . . The dying world needs one thing – a revolution to put God in the Centre of its social life, to proclaim again the living Gospel as good news for the poor and as having a living contact with every part of life' (Hacking, *Shaw* 54). Mervyn Stockwood** was overtly a

Socialist in his days as a parish priest, though he remained sceptical of the ultimate transforming power of secular arrangements, and defined politics as 'the science of deferred repentance' (Stockwood, 77). Stockwood's socialism was both a response to and a reason for ministry in a working-class parish, and for the most part the proponents of a social gospel have found themselves most at home in such surroundings, and most likely to be appointed to them. The most notable exception was Conrad Noel**, who preached full-blooded Socialism from his base in the tiny town of Thaxted, Essex, between 1910 and 1942. Both what he stood for and the forces arrayed against him were symbolized by the riots provoked in 1921 and 1922 by his insistence on hanging the Red Flag and the flag of Sinn Fein in his church (Conrad, *Noel* 110–20). The ideals which Noel stood for were continued in differing circumstances by priests such as Alan Ecclestone (1904–92), who served the industrial parish of Darnall, Sheffield, from 1942 to 1969. Ecclestone was a member of the Communist party from 1948 to 1988. Seeking 'to understand the Church as the seedbed of a new human society', he used a weekly parish meeting, open to everyone, as a forum for the discussion of public affairs, the arts and philosophy (*Guardian*, 16 December 1992).

The socialist priest Charles Marson (1859–1914) wrote: 'The clergy and the clergy alone can, if they have the grace of the Holy Ghost, not only hear the cry of the poorer nation, but can reach the ears of the [upper] classes and carry the truth to them' (Reckitt, 121). It has been one of the stranger changes in the spiritual vocation of the Anglican clergy that, from being a class of men identified with the preservation of the existing social order, they have sometimes become among its more articulate critics.

In his social teaching one clergyman was by any standards a prophet, and was recognized as such in his life-time. Samuel Barnett* worked out and implemented a developed social policy based on a liberal theology. In his own time he was widely criticized, but the ideas he pioneered were to become a new orthodoxy.

Barnett's starting point was that everyone is 'a human being in whom is Christ', and that everyone must be treated accordingly. Each human being is uniquely valuable and each should be brought to the full flower of his or her potentiality. Each also retains a personal responsibility for his or own life and must not be assisted in evading that responsibility.

The great obstacle in the way of personal growth is not suffering but sin; so 'anything which mars the grandeur of human life must be brought under a converting influence'. The aim is not to fit people for the life to come but to enrich life now. 'Christ gives joy not by promising a future good, but by making us able to enjoy the present' (Barnett, 1.76, 40). The kingdom of God on earth is to be found in fellowship and social action.

Long before David Sheppard used the phrase, Barnett exhibited a 'bias to the poor'. He was in constant touch with the wealthy, the powerful and the influential, but solely so that he could enlist them in his battle against spiritual and physical deprivation. He and his wife declared that living among the rich made them more indignant for the poor. They could not bear the condescension with which the gospel was sometimes taken to the lower classes by the higher ones, especially when the implication was that favours depended upon a co-operative response.

Barnett spoke of the 'sin of patronage', and based both evangelism and social work on personal relations. One of the large number of affluent women whom he enlisted to help him wrote: 'Mr Barnett does not want us to be district visitors or preach to them [the poor] or anything like that, but be really a friend to them, and so perhaps lead them to God without their knowing' (Barnett, 1.105).

Barnett was concerned not so much to alleviate need as to foster self-respect and independence; and to this end he followed a policy over charitable assistance which required ruthlessness and courage as well as dedication and perseverance. 'A man's soul was more important than a man's suffering ... it was spiritual murder so to act as to nullify for him the results of his own actions' (Barnett, 2.230).

Barnett appreciated the importance of accurate information if social evils were to be tackled effectively. He inspired Charles Booth to write his monumental and influential book *The Life and Labour of the People*, and he set up the Inquirers' Club which sought out the facts about the condition of the poor.

In 1906 Barnett wrote to a friend: 'Does not the rising sun of Labour dispel all wintry thoughts and make you feel young?' His engagement with politics and his contacts with the Labour movement modified Barnett's thought. In later life he called himself a socialist. He began to appreciate that 'what was wanted was not palliatives for individuals' suffering, but remedies for society's disease'. He viewed with contempt the attempts of the affluent to purchase public peace by lavish donations to charity at times of social unrest. He engaged in public criticism of the luxury which existed alongside poverty and which was condemned by it. He approved of the introduction of state old age pensions and of unemployment relief because the benefits were universal and did not carry the old implications of begging and degradation. He supported the universal provision of the essentials of civilized life. He supported 'free breakfasts to all children in elementary schools, free medical relief, national registry offices free alike to employers and employed, free picture galleries, libraries and swimming-baths, free fresh air, free water, cheap if not free transit, and universal pensions' (Barnett, 2.195, 233, 281).

The fact that Barnett became a widely respected national figure did not exempt him from attacks from his fellow-clergy. They girded at him for his 'socialism', his defence of trades-union action, his frequent approval of strikes, his claims for equality for women (Barnett, 2.346). Above all, they accused him of abandoning religion for politics.

But that reproach was entirely misplaced. Amidst all their large scale activity Barnett and his wife never lost sight of spiritual fundamentals. Many of their contemporaries misunderstood them because, as Henrietta once said, they aimed at permeation rather than conversion. Their pastoral work, although immensely elaborate, was based on personal relationships. Henrietta said of Toynbee Hall that its methods were spiritual rather than material, and that its trust was in friends linked to friends rather than in organization. Although a brilliant organizer, Barnett was never seduced by organization. At a late stage in their ministry at St Jude's he and his wife went to the Bishop of London and offered to abandon all that they had achieved there, including Toynbee Hall, and to begin again in another East End district, building a church and conducting a ministry at their own expense. Their intention was to escape the large-scale organizations they had created and to return to the simplicities of personal ministry. Unaccountably, Bishop Temple, having promised to give his decision in writing, never did so.

Barnett wrote: '"One by one" is the phrase which best expresses our method, and "the raising of buried life" is that which best expresses our end' (Barnett, 1.320). In his creative energy, his respect for individual souls, his social and moral far-sightedness and his rich view of what constitutes a fulfilled Christian life he was among the very greatest of urban parish priests.

8

Priesthood

Are not praises the very end for which the world
was created? (Traherne, 3.82)

Corporate Worship

Whatever else a parson does or refrains from doing, it is unthinkable that he
should not lead public worship. It is his most characteristic activity.

A priest represents his people to God and God to his people. He prays for
them in private and public, he guides and teaches them individually and
collectively. But his representative function is most apparent as he leads
corporate worship; and all the more so if he transcends the attitude, held
unthinkingly by the bulk of the laity, that the value of worship consists in its
effect on the worshippers.

'I had discovered – or, rather, I had been shown – that the importance of the
Church lies in something other than its service to, or satisfaction of, the needs
of man.' W.H. Vanstone's** experience on a housing estate in the 1950s led
him to believe that 'the Church is what man is and does when he recognizes
what is happening in the being of the universe' (Vanstone, 16, 99). The Church
exists to respond to the love of God by offering back love on behalf of mankind.
Worship is a summation and expression of that responsibility. As John Keble*
also taught, church-going is a service due to God rather than a means of
edifying men (Battiscombe, *Keble* 175).

The consequences of believing otherwise can be dire. In 1827 poor John
Skinner* confided to his journal: 'I am free to confess that Sunday, which used
to be the most interesting day of the week, is now become the most irksome. I
feel perfectly assured I am not of the least service to the people among whom I
am placed' (Skinner, 304). God had been worshipped; but, because his people
had apparently not benefited, Skinner perceived no value in what he had done.

On the whole, however, the clergy have had no doubt of the intrinsic
significance of worship, and have clung jealously to their right to lead it.
Though in Elizabethan and Jacobean times the clerk was allowed to read the
first lesson or the epistle, he could get into trouble if he presumed further
(Hart, *CC* 75). On a Sunday in 1863, on the sudden illness of an officiating
curate, a congregation adjourned to the schoolroom and a layman took the
service, reading a printed sermon. The reaction was extreme. The layman's
vicar called the occasion 'an illegal parody', and the archdeacon reminded him
of the fate of the Israelite who sacrilegiously touched the ark. Such attitudes

have been modified only slowly. In the 1870s it was still uncommon for the laity to be entrusted with reading the lessons, and it was only in the 1880s that licensed Readers became common. In 1884 Wilson Carlile, founder of the Church Army, was almost howled off the platform of a Church Congress because he urged that laymen should be allowed to lead prayers in church (Chadwick, *VC* 2.164, 298).

Objection to lay participation has arisen in part from sacerdotalism, in part from fears about lack of expertise. Yet there has always been a built-in safeguard against abuse. The dominant characteristic of Anglican worship has been the use of set forms, whether those of the *Book of Common Prayer* or those of the *Alternative Service Book*. The traditional spirituality of the clergy has been indelibly affected by the cadences of the *Book of Common Prayer*. Robert Sanderson (1587–1663), rector of Boothby Pagnell, Lincolnshire, for forty years, told Izaak Walton that 'the collects were the most passionate, proper and most elegant expressions that any language ever afforded, and so interwoven with instructions, that they taught us to know the power, the wisdom, the majesty, and mercy of God, and much of our duty both to him and our neighbour'; and that the psalms were 'the treasury of Christian comfort, fitted for all persons and necessities' (Walton, 271). His enthusiasm had been forged in the flames of harsh experience; he had been forcibly prevented from using the Book during the time of the Commonwealth and Protectorate (Hart, *CC* 118).

Sanderson spoke for most Anglicans save the Puritans, of whatever party. Although the Evangelical John Newton* was prepared to make alterations to the set order if he thought circumstances justified it, he defended the Prayer Book against the criticisms of Dissent by pointing out that the Dissenters themselves sang hymns over and over again:

> Crito freely will rehearse
> Forms of pray'r and praise in verse:
> Why should Crito then suppose
> Forms are sinful when in prose? (Martin, *Newton* 212)

Charles Simeon* too was devoted to the Book, saying 'no other human work is so free from faults'. He 'felt the prayers of our church as marrow to my soul.' He took enormous trouble with reading the service; a listener noted how he 'prayed the prayers'. He said 'all the preaching in the universe will be of no use without prayer ... A congregation uniting fervently in the prayers of our Liturgy would afford as complete a picture of heaven as ever yet was beheld on earth.' (Hopkins, *Simeon* 213, 42).

Devotion to the Prayer Book has sometimes led to an under-valuing of other forms of worship, or to a lack of capacity for them. Robert Sanderson told Izaak Walton that the 'putting up to God [of] these joint and known desires [in the collects] ... could not but be more pleasing to God, than those raw, unpremeditated expressions to which many of the hearers could not say Amen' (Walton, 271). Likewise Charles Simeon declared: 'If all men could pray at all times as some men can sometimes, then indeed we might prefer extempore to precomposed prayers' (Hopkins, *Simeon* 213). James Woodforde* was never easy if he departed from set forms. 'I prayed for poor James Burge this morning, out of my own head, hearing he was just gone off almost in a consumption. It occasioned a great tremulation in my voice at the time' (Woodforde, 1. 63–4).

Enthusiasm for the Prayer Book has become less marked in modern times, especially among clergy reaching out to the unchurched. Henrietta Barnett* described herself as 'one of those unfortunate people who, while passionately spiritually hungry, cannot find food in the old forms and time-hallowed words, which have to me lost their significance by a reiteration which pays no regard to changing conditions.' She was the moving force behind the non-liturgical Worship Hours held from 8.30 to 9.30 p.m. on Sunday evenings at St Jude's (Barnett, 1.273). At St Martin's in the Fields Dick Sheppard* sometimes omitted the creed, drastically cut the psalms, and introduced silence and extempore prayer (Scott, *Sheppard* 110). At St Matthew's, Moorfields, in the 1940s Mervyn Stockwood** introduced a Sunday evening People's Service, held after Evensong was over, and consisting of four hymns, a Bible reading, prayers and an address (Stockwood, 43). In the 1960s David Watson* introduced a Family Service, based on a Church Pastoral Society form, at St Cuthbert's, York (Saunders, *Watson* 105). In the 1970s George Carey** introduced informal worship with extensive lay participation, together with modern hymns, music groups, dance, and eventually a totally redesigned church building at St Nicholas, Durham. He did so at cost both to himself and to others. He was subjected to a torrent of criticism, and a proportion of his congregation departed. Only the conviction that he and those who supported him were under the guidance of the Spirit sustained him; the outcome was a larger and more vital church community (Carey, passim).

On the whole, however, the clergy have remained loyal to liturgical worship, if not to the *Book of Common Prayer*. Convocation authorized the use of the *Revised Prayer Book* of 1928, despite its rejection by Parliament, and it was widely employed until the experimental orders of Series 1, 2 and 3 and their outcome the *Alternative Service Book* of 1980 replaced it in clerical favour. The new book supplied a liturgical framework which the vast majority of the clergy were prepared to use as they grappled with the needs of modern congregations. Watson used it as the basis for worship at St Michael-le-Belfrey (Saunders, *Watson* 134). I found a positive preference among my congregation at Shepherdswell in 1985 for its introduction for the principal Sunday service.

A devotion to liturgical worship need not necessarily imply loyalty to the formularies of the Church of England. For more than a century there have been parishes where the order followed has been that of Rome. An example is that of

St Saviour's, Hoxton, which was so Romanized by E.E. Kilburn, its incumbent from 1907 to 1923, that it became indistinguishable from a Roman Catholic church. The clergy at St Saviour's rejected any kind of State control and regarded the *Book of Common Prayer* as an alien form of worship imposed by Parliament. They also resisted the authority of their bishop, and, since he was the gentle Arthur Winnington-Ingram, they got away with it (Carpenter, *Winnington-Ingram* 170–5). They were representative of that form of Anglo-Catholicism which W.S. Pickering has called Anglo-Papalism; a form of spirituality which, as history has progressed, has stranded a now dwindling number of clergy in the no man's land between the Council of Trent and the Second Vatican Council.

The use of a liturgy has conferred a certain objectivity upon Anglican worship. Frank Wentworth, Mrs Oliphant's perpetual curate, did not 'carry his personal feelings ... into the pulpit with him, much less into the reading-desk, where he was interpreter, not of his own sentiments and emotions, but of common prayer and universal worship' (Oliphant, *PC* 533). How far this objectivity has been a cause and how far a consequence of the English clerical character is a matter for speculation. According to his biographer, John Keble regarded emotion as the Jews regarded Jehovah, as a God not to be mentioned. In his case reserve was elevated to the level of a virtue, and sobriety was of the essence of the via media:

> Thus souls by nature pitched too high,
> By suffering brought too low,
> Meet in the Church's middle sky,
> Halfway twixt joy and woe. (Battiscombe, *Keble* 143, 112)

The sheer extent of public worship has been an indication of the primacy given to it. William Bennett* wrote about a typical Sunday at St Paul's, Knightsbridge, in 1846: 'We have an average of 120 communicants; we commence the service at eleven and seldom conclude before half-past two. At half-past two the congregation come in for evening service at 3, women for churching, children for baptism; so that we are occupied with very little intermission, from 11 to 5 ... in the presence of a congregation of seldom less than 1700 persons in the morning and 1200 in the evening; and withal the second Evening Service following closely after at half-past six. Very frequently the clergy have not time to take off their robes between the Communion Service and the Evening Service.' This demanding sequence was preceded by an early celebration and by sung Matins (Bennett, 41). In 1881 George Denison**, in the Somersetshire village of East Brent, was conducting 25 services a week (Denison, 250). In the village of Shepherdswell, near Dover, in 1912, with a single-handed incumbent and a population of about 500, there was on Sundays Matins and Evensong, Holy Communion once, twice or thrice, depending on the Sunday of the month, a children's service in the afternoon, and an afternoon men's service in a private house. The Sunday School met twice. On Saints' days there was Holy Communion and Evensong, and morning prayer was read publicly on every week day. As late as the 1960s, the vicar of the same village took Sunday services at 8.00 a.m., 9.30 a.m., 11.00 a.m. and 6.30 p.m. and, once a month, at 11.30 a.m. as well. He read the office daily at 7.30 a.m. and 6.30 p.m. and on Holy Days there was communion at 7.00 a.m. and 10.00 a.m. (*SPM*).

The clergy have exerted themselves at length as well as frequently. Ralph Josselin* noted that on a day when God was good to him he was four hours in church, and that on a public fast he was there for six (Josselin, 321, 331). The principal Sunday service for the greater part of our period was morning prayer, followed by the litany, the ante-communion (that is, the first part of the communion service) a sermon or homily, and occasionally by the remainder of the communion service; a marathon not to be speedily completed. Francis Witts**, attending a service conducted by Francis Close** which included a communion, noted that it lasted for three and three-quarter hours; the fact did not prevent him from going on almost immediately to an act of worship in another Cheltenham church (Witts, 15). The Act of Uniformity Amendment Act of 1872, which reflected as well as permitted a change in practice, allowed for the separation of the service into its constituent parts (Russell, 60).

Enthusiasm for frequent or extended services, or the ability to provide them, has not been universal. Sunday evening services became unusual during the eighteenth century; their re-appearance was a consequence of the Evangelical revival (Chadwick, *VC* 1.407). There have been many parishes at many times where there has been only one act of worship a week or less; many served by priests also responsible for other churches, or with a low view of what was required of them. Woodforde offered his people a single Sunday service, and although he was not prepared to go on holiday unless he could find a *locum tenens*, he frequently cancelled worship for other reasons. Services were abandoned in cold weather, when repair work was going on, and when the parson was indisposed. Woodforde's curates, taken on when he thought himself too old and ill to lead worship in person, also sometimes missed church without providing substitutes.

Woodforde and his curates are not isolated examples, nor the worst ones. W. Finch, fellow of Trinity College, Cambridge, held nearby Barrington from 1770 to 1835, together with two other parishes. There was an afternoon service scheduled at Barrington once every three weeks, but only if adults appeared in addition to the clerk; if there were only children there, Finch would give them sweets and send them home. The Eucharist was not celebrated for a period of twenty-five years (Colloms, 253). George Bayldon, vicar of Cowling, Yorkshire, from 1850 to 1894, would go to the vestry on Sundays, and if anyone appeared in church, and only then, would conduct a brief service (Chadwick, *VC* 2. 178). Even these derelictions pale, however, beside those of the Cornish vicar of the 1870s who rejected his bishop's request that he should take the services held in his own church, on the grounds that a neighbouring incumbent was always ready to stand in for him. His personal contribution to worship was to stand at his garden gate and chat with his parishioners as they filed out of church (Goodenough, 113).

In modern times even conscientious clergy have thought it inappropriate or found it impossible to make the lavish provision of the past. In Shepherdswell in the 1990s, working under the constraints of a team ministry, I offered my parishioners no more than two services on a Sunday and one on week-days; a remarkable contrast even to the 1960s. For the most part, however, the smaller number of services has been due to lack of enthusiasm on the part of the laity rather than on that of the clergy. Quantity is less important than quality; and quality depends in large measure upon the response of the congregation. George Herbert's* country parson used all means to create a sense of reverence. He insisted on 'a straight and steady posture' in his people and that the responses were to be given 'not in a huddling or slubbering fashion, gaping, or scratching the head, or spitting even in the midst of the answer, but gently and pausably [that is, dwelling on the words], thinking what they say'. Nor would the parson tolerate the habit among the gentry and nobility of arriving late for service; if admonition would not reform them, they were to be brought before a church court just like anyone else (Herbert, VI).

Congregational behaviour has sometimes offended, sometimes reflected, the clergy's view of propriety. Ralph Josselin was distressed when his people kept their hats on during the singing of psalms (Josselin, 152). Charles Simeon was saddened by the reluctance of the people at Holy Trinity to sing (Hopkins, *Simeon* 41). By contrast, an observer at the opening of William Bennett's church of St Barnabas commented on the segregation of the sexes 'strictly according to the early Christian use ... so that no thoughts of earthly custom should intrude, but each [sex] in its peculiar sanctity should worship ... looking upward to the choir of angels' (Bennett, 62).

It has not always been easy to maintain the dignity of worship in the face of the behaviour of individuals. In 1647 Josselin 'tooke notice of the rudenes of divers of the congregacion, reproved them and incouraged the officers to punish them' (Josselin, 94). William Grimshaw* chided anyone in his congregation who fell asleep during worship, and personally chased out stray dogs (Baker, *Grimshaw* 213). Woodforde was confronted at Castle Cary by one Thomas Speed who 'came into the Church quite drunk and crazy and made a noise ... called the Singers a Pack of Whoresbirds and gave me a nod or two in the pulpit'; Speed was taken into custody and haled before a magistrate (Woodforde, 1.101). Skinner once threatened to stop a service he was taking for a colleague when the people in the gallery 'made ... a constant hawking, in the manner an audience at a theatre expresses disapproval of an actor'. There were those in his own congregation who fell asleep with their legs up on the pew, or who refused to stand when others did (Skinner, 42, 55–6). When William Bennett first went to Frome, he had to contend with a galleryful of boys who ate, fought and gossipped; to the noise they made was added that of their master's cane, as he vainly endeavoured to restore order (Bennett, 199).

Pre-eminently, however, it is the minister's own example which sets the tone for worship. That example has sometimes been lacking. It is difficult for the clergy, constantly engaged in public worship, to remain recollected. Josselin was as conscientious as a minister could be; but he confessed to his diary that he had stopped dead in the middle of the blessing, thinking he was giving it for the second time, 'so weake and fraile is my memory from my heedlesnes' (429).

Most churchgoers have their stories of priestly eccentricities which have obtruded to the detriment of public worship. Robert Hawker* was partially hidden from his people by the rood screen, and perhaps it was just as well. He would range round the chancel, reading the service now in English, now in Latin, and occasionally prostrating himself before the altar. At one time he was liable to fainting fits which interrupted the service and frightened his congregation. Later he suffered from 'neuralgic diorrhea', which impelled him to precipitate if temporary departures (Brendon, *Hawker* 96, 174).

There have of course been positive examples too. According to Walton, George Herbert explained the nature and structure of the service to his people, and the significance of standing or kneeling. He paused after each collect to give time for reflection (Walton, 207, 210, 212). William Bennett insisted on a constant atmosphere of reverence; at Frome conversation in the vestry before a service was banned (Bennett, 203).

The adjuncts of worship give it much of its aura, and not a little of its significance. The minister's garb has always had implications beyond the sartorial. The standard dress for most of our period was, for the service, the surplice worn with an academic hood and bands, and for the sermon the academic gown. The records of Elizabethan visitations abound, however, with references to clergy evading the wearing of the surplice. Early in the following century it was alleged of Thomas Wooll, Vicar of Boston, Lincolnshire, 'that the surplis hath been tendred to him and he in scorn maketh it his cushion to sit on' (Hart, *CC* 37–8, 61). For Puritans, of course, a surplice was a rag of popery, and symbolic of everything in the Church of England with which they were at odds. However, they observed other conventions. Josselin, who never wore a surplice if he could avoid it, once noted: 'I preacht without a cap, god preserve mee.' Left to himself, he wore a gown and cassock (one of which lasted thirty-five years), and once dreamt that he had been humiliated by appearing without his bands (Josselin, 639, 576–7, 364).

The function of a surplice as a badge of party endured. In the nineteenth century High Churchmen wore it in the pulpit while Evangelicals maintained the tradition of wearing a gown. The Evangelical Samuel Garratt** justified

the gown because a preacher was 'addressing the congregation as an ambas-
sador for Christ, not the servant of the congregation speaking in their name,
but the servant of God speaking in His name'; and thought the Tractarians
wanted the surplice worn 'in order to diminish the importance of preaching by
making it a mere adjunct of the service' (Garratt, 243). Mr Courtenay of the
parish of St Sidwell's, Exeter, was harrassed by huge mobs on two successive
Sundays in 1845 because he wore a surplice in the pulpit (Chadwick, *VC*
1.219–20). As the century went on, however, attitudes mellowed. Even Samuel
Butler's cautious Theobald Pontifex set aside his bands and master's gown and
wore the surplice in the pulpit (Butler, 402).

Originally the surplice was usually worn over everyday dress (Josselin was
an exception), and it took time for the cassock to be accepted when it was re-
introduced in the nineteenth century. Francis Kilvert* poked fun at a colleague
who wore it as a daily garb (Kilvert, 3.197). Cosmo Lang**, who often crossed
from Vicarage to Church at Portsea in his cassock, was accused of practising
'celibacy openly in the street' (Lockhart, *Lang* 126).

The most contentious issue of the nineteenth century was the wearing of
Eucharistic vestments; not unreasonably, because they clearly had doctrinal
implications. Hawker, who was perhaps the first Anglican in modern times to
wear vestments, did so as part of a policy which included frequent communion
services and teaching the doctrine of the Real Presence (Brendon, *Hawker* 96–
7). As Catholic practice spread so did the wearing of vestments; to this day they
carry doctrinal overtones.

Like dress, ceremony has been taken very seriously. John Rous** heard a
Mr Gane of Becham, Norfolk, preach in 1632: 'Among those he made liable to
God's fearfull judgment ... he named adulterers, oppressors, atheists, those
that bowed not at the name of Jesus, and (I thinke also) those that were covered
at divine service' (Green, *Rous* 69). Gane was of course attacking Puritans, who,
in addition to the offences remarked upon, refused to stand at the Creed, or to
use the sign of the cross at baptism or wedding rings.

Ceremony can be seen, as William Bennett saw it, as an expression of the
sacramental nature of the Christian faith and as a means of teaching doctrine:
'God in his mercy has ever made religion sacramental, in order that it might
accord with the nature of man's life ... Thus, then, I contend for externals ...
for the things of God in his worship ... they cannot be too great, too glorious,
too magnificent ... In bowing to the altar ... what is the doctrine conveyed?
The presence of God, and at the altar His presence in a most special manner'
(Bennett, 188, 189).

But ceremony can also be seen as, or become, an obsession with frippery.
Kilvert was disgusted by an Ascension Day service he observed at St Barnabas,
Oxford, at which processions, vestments, banners, and incense were freely
employed (Kilvert, 3.319–20). When in our own century Fr Algy Robertson,
newly vicar of St Ives, Huntingdonshire, abandoned the Asperges, his

predecessor accused him of 'jeopardizing the Catholic religion' (Pickering, 143).

Ceremony should be seen in context. The heartily realistic Robert Dolling considered that 'the ceremonial at the Sung Mass ... could be safely employed ... when it was felt to be not the swathings of a dead Christ, but the robe of a living one.' Dolling also wrote, with a typical disregard of syntax: 'I believe you want two kinds of worship – one very dignified and ornate, which enables them to realize that they are making an offering to the Lord of Heaven and Earth, the other very simple and familiar, that they are talking to a loving Father who knows all their needs and wants to help them' (Dolling, *TY* 207). He was himself no slave to detail, and boxed the ears of a ritualistic youth who objected to the way he held his hands at the altar (Osborn, *Dolling* 109, 116).

Much of nineteenth-century ritualism was developed because it was said to be popular, especially among the urban poor. Certainly men such as Bennett, Charles Lowder** and Dolling attracted large and loyal congregations; but it is uncertain whether they did so because of the ritual they employed or because of their personal spiritual qualities. Ritual has been by no means a panacea. When in late Victorian times the vicar of Northmoor Green, Somerset, a village with a population of 800, started wearing vestments, his congregation sank to three (Chadwick, *VC* 2.322). As the nineteenth century wore on, it was the educated middle class who provided the bulk of the congregations of ritualistic churches.

Over ceremonies, as over much else, the wings of the church have borrowed from each other. We have frequently observed Anglo-Catholics conducting services of Evangelical simplicity. Reciprocally, nineteenth-century Evangelicals introduced surpliced choirs, and twentieth-century Evangelicals have outdone most ritualists by introducing dance. Following the example of Watson at York, George Carey did so at St Nicholas, Durham in the 1970s. Carey saw dance as a way of involving the body in spirituality, and of assisting spontaneity in worship (Carey, 40–43).

Many clergy have thought it less important to secure the ceremonial which they personally favoured than to consider the susceptibilities of their congregations. These susceptibilities have sometimes been acute. At Margaret Chapel (later All Saints, Margaret Street) the introduction of alms bags in 1839 was thought 'a perilous novelty' (Bennett, 191). Low Church people objected to Sabine Baring-Gould's** hymn 'Onward Christian Soldiers' because of the lines:

With the Cross of Jesus
Going on before. (Purcell, *Baring-Gould* 71)

Cosmo Lang disarmed suspicious parishioners at Portsea by respecting their insistence that the altar candles should never be lit (Lockhart, *Lang* 121). W.C.E. Newbolt spoke for many clergy when he wrote: 'it will require very earnest thought, and very fervent prayer, before any question of mere ritual ... can be put in the same scale of importance as the church-going of a pious man' (Newbolt, 220).

Describing his time in the rural parish of Winchfield (1909–17), Arthur Hopkinson** put another view. He decided to start as he intended to go on, and wore vestments on his first Sunday. He argued that country people will 'never, never' be ready for change; but they may perhaps get used to it (Hopkinson, 113–14). The argument is questionable. Nicolas Stacey** tells the story of a new vicar, who on his first Sunday replaced the traditional altar with a table in the nave; the resulting shock-waves damaged his ministry for two years (Stacey, 128).

Second only to liturgy and more important than ceremony in glorifying God and uplifting the congregation has been music. The best has sometimes been available. In Elizabethan times Richard Mulcaster, incumbent of Stanford Rivers, Essex, introduced his congregation to the music of William Byrd, who lived nearby (Addison, 32). Conrad Noel** persuaded Gustav Holst to help with his choir at Thaxted. At All Saints, Margaret Street, in the 1940s Cyril Tomkinson presided over masses by Mozart, Schubert, Saint-Saens, Gounod, Palestrina and Viadana; the superb choir sang evensong daily to plainsong (Williams, 117–18).

Usually, however, the music has been of a more modest character. Until the nineteenth century the psalms were sometimes said, sometimes sung in a metrical version, such as those of Sternhold and Hopkins or Tate and Brady. Thomas Fuller** wrote of these versifiers that their 'piety was better than their poetry; ... they had drunk more of Jordan than of Helicon' (Fuller, *CH* 3. 380). The early custom was for the congregation to repeat the psalms, a line at a time, after the clerk (Goodenough, 108). At Lark Rise in the 1880s it was still the practice for the rector and the congregation, led by the clerk, to read the psalms verse and verse about (Thompson, 210). The Anglican chant came in, amidst controversy, in the 1850s and 1860s. Sung services were sometimes thought Papistical. The Bishop of London tried to do away with them at St Paul's, Knightsbridge, after Bennett's resignation, but was frustrated by the congregation's insistence on continuing (Bennett, 141–2).

Before singing hymns became general practice, additional psalms were often sung between the sections of the service. The Wesleys produced the first hymn books in the modern sense. Later in the century Augustus Toplady (1740–78) vicar of Broad Hembury, Devonshire, and author of 'Rock of Ages', published *Psalms and Hymns for Public and Private Worship*; and with the help of the poet Cowper, John Newton wrote a hymnbook for his congregation at Olney. On the whole, however, hymns were for long frowned upon. In the eighteenth century they were thought to be Methodistical; as late as 1820 the Bishop of Peterborough forbade them throughout his diocese (Balleine, 182). Later still, as the

Evangelical Samuel Garratt noted, the clergy of his party largely abandoned them, on the grounds that the Prayer Book did not provide for them and in order to retain the legal advantage in their struggles with the Anglo-Catholics (Garratt, 251).

But the trend was the other way. Tractarians discovered the virtues of traditional hymnody in translation, and clergy of all parties used hymns in mission. Of those we have already encountered, Henry Alford** wrote several hymns including 'Come ye thankful people come'; Percy Dearmer wrote 'Jesu, good above all other'. Other parish priests wrote hymns which remain immensely popular: Henry Francis Lyte (1793–1847), perpetual curate of Lower Brixham, Devon, 'Abide with Me' and 'Praise, my soul, the King of Heaven'; Henry Hart Milman (1791–1868), vicar of St Mary's, Reading, 'Ride on, ride on, in majesty'; William Walsham How (1823–97), rector of Whittington, Shropshire, 'For all thy saints'; John Earnest Bode (1816–74), incumbent of Castle Camps, Cambridgeshire, 'O Jesus, I have promised' (see *The Penguin Book of Hymns*, ed. Ian Bradley, 1989, passim). Another prolific author was John Ellerton (1826–93), a leading liberal churchman who spent most of his life as a parish priest. He wrote some eighty hymns, including 'The day thou gavest, Lord is ended' (Whale, 132–7).

The new hymns had to be made generally available. The decisive step was the publication of *Hymns Ancient and Modern* in 1861. The editor was a High Church parish priest, Sir Henry Baker (1821–77), of Monkland, Herefordshire, and author, among other hymns, of 'Lord, thy word abideth' and 'The King of love my shepherd is'. In the twentieth century the controversy has been between those who cling to hymns now made familiar by decades of use, and those, such as David Watson and George Carey, who seek to supplement or replace them with words and music said to be more appropriate to our age.

Incumbents have always had considerable influence on what is sung and on the manner of singing it. In 1801 the Rev. J.G. Sherer of Blandford Forum issued a long printed address to his parishioners deprecating the singing of 'God save the King': 'Where is that congregation of Christian people who would not turn with trembling and abhorrence from peals of rude and bacchanalian sound bursting upon their senses in their devotional exercises?' (B.G. Cox, *The Parish Church of SS Peter and Paul Blandford Forum*). The fact that John Keble was totally unmusical meant that nothing was done about the notoriously bad Hursley choir (Battiscombe, *Keble* 318). In Francis Close's Cheltenham psalms, canticles and responses were all sung from 1844, but Close stigmatized intoning as 'a fad ... absurd, unEnglish, unProtestant and undevotional' (Hennell, 111). Richard Randall** alienated his congregation at Lavington by insisting on the use of plainsong and intoning (Briscoe, *Randall* 95).

In past centuries the music was often in the hands of the parish clerk. When, as frequently happened, the congregation were reluctant to participate, the singing consisted of a duet between parson and clerk. Poor old Js Smith, Woodforde's clerk, 'made a shocking hand of it ... much laughed at' (Woodforde, 3.292).

Substitutes for the clerk have presented problems too. 'Difficult, disappointing, distracting folk are choirs ... [to be in charge of them requires] a great deal of prayer, watchfulness and inflexible severity' (Hammond, 85). Thus W.C.E. Newbolt, whom we have met frequently in these pages as a dispenser of counsel to the clergy. Certainly a love of music does not necessarily go hand in hand with a desire for harmony. Woodforde had trouble both with the singers at Castle Cary, who sang psalms chosen with malevolent intent, and with those at Weston, who threatened resignation even though he had given them a guinea to buy books (Woodforde, 4.22). Skinner constantly quarrelled with the Camerton singers, as of course with everyone else. The singers gave him cause. They interrupted catechizing, and turned up for service drunk; when reprimanded they left in a body, threatening to decamp to the Meeting House. On the other hand, when they had returned they attracted a larger congregation (Skinner, 36, 200, 203, 233, 398). Even in the little Eden of Alton-Barnes, quarrels with the singers occasionally deprived Augustus Hare* of a sung service. Robert Dolling lost his choir at Landport when he exchanged Matins for Mass, and had to recruit another (Dolling, *TY* 211).

The singers usually operated from the gallery; so did the early choirs. George Denison's choir at East Brent, which included women and girls, sat in the organ loft (Denison, xi–xii). One of Walter Hook's* innovations was to put his choir into the chancel. Thomas Phelps, rector of Ridley, Kent, from 1840 to 1893, enlarged the chancel of his church in the 1850s so that it could hold a choir (Loo, *Phelps* 118).

Placing the choir in the chancel encouraged the practice of robing them, as Phelps did. People came from far and wide to see the surpliced choir created by John Sharp, Sabine Baring-Gould's incumbent at Horbury. In 1887 a surpliced choir of women at Skelton-in-Cleveland was denounced by Henry Liddon as grotesque (Chadwick, *VC* 2.178, 216), but less sexist views gradually gained ground. Mervyn Stockwood's choir girls at St Matthew's Moorfields wore French-lavender purple and were known as 'Stockwood follies' (Stockwood, 45).

The use of the choir as a way of attaching young people to church life is a practice of long standing. Sabine Baring-Gould, trying to civilize his slum district at Horbury, would ambush the boys who pelted his Mission and conscript them; his difficulty in persuading them not to eat oranges or toffees has been a recurring one (Purcell, *Baring-Gould* 68).

For most of our period voices were supported, if at all, by a gallimaufry of instruments. Sometimes the clerk would be the accompanist, playing a pitch-pipe or a barrel organ (Goodenough, 108). Presumably it was a barrel-organ which Anthony Hoggett, the Puritan incumbent of Northill, Bedfordshire, in

Elizabethan times sold for forty shillings (Barrow, 29). William Cole**
imported a bassoonist for special occasions (Cole, 119, 261). When Samuel
Butler's Theobald Pontifex took over his parish, the music was provided by a
cello, a clarinet and a trombone (Butler, 93). At George Eliot's Shepperton,
when the choir sang an anthem 'the key-bugles always ran away at a great pace,
while the bassoon every now and them boomed a flying shot after them'
(Eliot, *SCL* 43). The general nineteenth-century tendency was for organs or
harmoniums to replace the orchestras of the past. Simeon, who had had a hymn
book privately printed for his congregation, installed a barrel-organ in 1794,
later replacing it with an ineffective pipe organ (Hopkins, *Simeon*, 40–1). The
energetic William Charlton Frampton, rector of Moreton, Dorset, from 1840 to
1898, found the music at the beginning of his incumbency provided by a mixed
adult choir and by a bass viol, a bassoon, two or three clarinets, and others 'of
a like harsh character which ... well accorded with the rough and inharmonious
voices which they accompanied'. He purged both the orchestra and the choir,
and was able after five years to introduce a harmonium and after eight an organ.
A surpliced choir and choral services followed; but in 1858 the Rector's elder
brother, who had succeeded his father as patron of the living, assumed the
leadership of a group who objected to choral services, and secured their
abolition. Eventually they were reintroduced, but not until after the organ had
been disposed of. Thereafter the choir were accompanied by another
harmonium (*Short History of St Nicholas, Moreton* 1984, 9–10).

The conservatism which resisted the introduction of pipe organs has in
our own century resisted their replacement. George Carey had the utmost
difficulty in getting permission for an electronic organ, installed to save money
for the major re-ordering of the church building at St Nicholas, Durham, in the
1970s. He was, however, fortunate in a congregation which, unlike others of
our time, responded positively to the use of instruments to supplement the
organ (Carey, 96–9, 37–8).

At the end of the day it is the *spirit* of worship which the priest hopes to
summon up, for his own benefit and for the benefit of those whom he serves;
and the Spirit blows as it wills. Harold Hosking, looking back upon informal
services in the Fishermen's Mission in Newlyn, Cornwall, in the 1950s,
reflected: 'Of one thing I feel sure, the act of worship in some great cathedral
where a choir was singing something by Bach, Byrd, Tallis or Handel could not
have been heard more readily before the Throne of Grace than members of the
Fishermen's Rest singing "Will your anchor hold?" while Willie Mallon
struggled with his arthritis at the American organ' (Hosking, 39–40).

The Eucharist

The Church of England's search for the via media has never been more clearly
illustrated than in the history of attitudes to the Eucharist. In Elizabethan times

the emphasis was upon the destruction of Popish superstition; the parochial clergy were admonished, for example, to put the communion wafer into the hand rather than the mouth, and not to lift up the elements to be adored (Hart, *CC* 37). On the other hand, Richard Hooker** took a high view of the Eucharistic Presence: 'This hallowed food, through concurrence of divine power, is in verity and truth unto faithful receivers instrumentally a cause of that mystical participation, whereby, as I make Myself wholly theirs, so I give them in hand an actual possession of all such saving grace as My sacrificed Body can yield and as their souls do presently need, this is to them and in them My body' (Hooker, *Laws of Ecclesiastical Polity*, quoted in More, 463).

By the reign of James I communions were becoming more infrequent, though they were still well attended. Puritan influence was growing, and was exemplified by Jeremy Dyke, parson at Epping, Essex, who taught: 'The less glory in the altar the more glory to God, who perfects His power in weakness, His glory in outward meanness'. When Archbishop Laud ordered the holy table to be placed at the east end of the chancel and railed off, Dyke provided railings, but left the table in the middle of the chancel lest it be thought to be an altar. Yet he took a high view of the significance of the Eucharist. 'Sacraments have the promise of Christ's presence, and His blessing, and are the excellent and powerful instruments of the Holy Ghost, to do more than all the golden, glittering, glorious, and specious inventions, and pompous services of man are able to do' (Addison, 45–8).

Puritans were challenged by Arminians, the High Churchmen of the early seventeenth century. Under Arminian influence old practices, such as bowing to the altar, turning east for the Creed and mingling water with the sacramental wine, returned. So did the custom of kneeling to receive the sacrament, though not without opposition; the incumbent of Sudbury, Suffolk, had to present several parishioners before the Star Chamber for disturbances engendered by his refusal to allow them to communicate sitting (Hart, *CC* 75, 102). One of the standard accusations brought against the clergy investigated during the period 1642–60 was that they had insisted on their parishioners kneeling at the altar rail, thereby driving many of them away (see, for example, Matthews, *Walker* 209–10).

George Herbert's* country priest celebrated the Eucharist five or six times a year: at great festivals, before and after harvest, and at the beginning of Lent. The sacrament, open to all old enough to distinguish sacramental from common bread, was preceded by careful instruction, and conducted with a proper reverence. The elements were 'of the best, not cheap or coarse, much less ill-tasted [ill-tasting] or unwholesome.' Those receiving might be either seated or kneeling: 'The feast ... requires sitting, because it is a feast, but man's unpreparedness asks kneeling' (Herbert, XXII). As to the nature of the sacrament itself, Herbert expressed a reverent agnosticism in his poem 'Holy Communion':

O gracious Lord, how shall I know
Whether in these gifts thou be so
As thou art ev'rywhere;
Or rather so, as thou alone
Tak'st all the lodging, leaving none
For thy poor creature there?

First I am sure, whether bread stay
Or whether bread do fly away
Concerneth bread, not me.
But that both thou and all thy train
Be there, to thy truth and my gain,
Concerneth me and Thee.

Later in the century Ralph Josselin* introduced the sacrament to the inner circle of his people in 1650 only after careful preparation. His account of the occasion is one of the most eloquent passages in his diary: 'Wee all sat round and neare the table, the bread was broken not cutt in blessing it, the lord poured out a spirit of mourning over Christ crucified on me and most of the company, and my soule eyed him more than ever, and god was sweete to me in the worke, no vain thoughts but wholly intent on the worke, no difficulty among ourselves, a savour on my spirit, but not that healing to my soule at present I desired, but I will waite on god in the way of his ordinances and bless his name and leave his manfestacions to his owne time, praising him that it was not empty to me' (Josselin, 236). Similar celebrations occurred regularly in ensuing years; after the Restoration, however, Josselin celebrated only at Easter, in a more perfunctory fashion, and with few communicants. He was not atypical; the Eucharist was about to enter a long period of eclipse.

In the eighteenth and early nineteenth centuries it was customary to celebrate the sacrament three or four times a year in the countryside, and rather more frequently in towns. However, plenty of parish priests fell short even of this modest standard. As late as the early 1830s a devout layman, going to church twice every Sunday, received the communion only twice in five years (Chadwick, *VC* 1.514). In the middle of the nineteenth century a high proportion of parishes still had a communion only four times a year. In 1874 Francis Kilvert* recounted a story of an archdiaconal visitation during which a parish clerk replied to an enquiry about the frequency of Holy Communion by blurting: 'Aw, we do never have he. We've got no tackling.' From direct observation he recorded with horror in 1875 that the sacrament had been administered in Foxham parish only five times in two years (Kilvert, 2.423–4; 3.197).

The infrequent communions of the period did not usually attract large attendances when they took place, partly because of a belief that they were intended for 'the quality' (Russell, 102). William Cole** of Bletchley had forty communicants at Easter 1766, but the usual figure during the period of his diary was under twenty (Cole, 29, 50, 132). James Woodforde* was pleased to get thirty communicants on Easter day 1786; two years later he attracted only twenty-three (Woodforde, 2.240; 3.13). John Skinner* recorded gloomily that at Easter 1829 there were only twelve communicants at Camerton, ten of them women; numbers were not much better in other years. Skinner tackled his clerk White after he had three times failed to remain for communion, to be told that he felt unworthy because of his feelings against those who had turned him out of the position of bailiff. Skinner's characteristic reply was to argue that if he himself could forgive the far worse injuries done him, White could surely do the same; especially since his salvation depended upon it (Skinner, 384, 306 – see also 325, 428).

We do not know whether White experienced a change of heart. If he did, he became part of a tiny minority. It was calculated that in 1832 no more than two and a half per cent of the population of the diocese of Lichfield ever communicated (Chadwick, *VC* 1.333). Kilvert reported the vicar of Fordington as saying that when he came to his parish in the 1820s no man had ever been known to receive the sacrament, with the exception of the parson, the clerk and the sexton. There were sixteen women communicants, but most of those ceased to attend when the parson refused to pay them for coming (Kilvert, 2.442). Kilvert himself was ecstatic when there were forty-one communicants at Langley in 1876, 'the largest number that I or anyone else had ever seen in Langley Church at once'. He was pleased when he got twenty communicants at Bredwardine on Easter Day 1878. Charmingly, he called them 'guests' (Kilvert, 3.258, 388).

Though clergy deplored small numbers of communicants, they had to take the chief responsibility for them. A long period of sacramental neglect had born bitter fruit. However, a devoted minister could reverse the trend. Twelve communicated at William Grimshaw's first communion at Haworth; numbers rose to five hundred in the winter and twelve hundred in the summer. Before the end of the eighteenth century the Evangelical curate of Creaton, Northamptonshire, Thomas Jones, had attracted the whole adult population of the village to his monthly celebration (Balleine, 83). John Keble* introduced a weekly Eucharist at Hursley after the consecration of the new church in 1848 (Battiscombe, *Keble* 295). James Skinner went to the tiny parish of Newland near Malvern, with only thirty-six resident families, in 1861. That year the sacrament was celebrated seven times. By 1867 it was being celebrated daily, always with communicants (Chadwick, *VC* 2.179). George Denison** instituted daily Eucharists at East Brent in 1874, and they became a common practice as time went on. Joe Williamson** at Stepney in the 1950s was typical of many other priests; his day began with Matins followed by a Eucharist and a time for private prayer and meditation (Williamson, 134).

As some of the examples just given illustrate, improvements in the nineteenth century were not solely the work of Tractarians. Charles Simeon* had been converted by an experience of the Holy Communion, and for the rest of his life he retained a deep reverence for what he always called the Lord's Supper. In his teaching he frequently referred the sacrament back its roots in the Passover and the Old Testament sacrificial system. Other Evangelicals of his time used language which would later have been seen as giving hostages to high churchmen. Edward Bickersteth** wrote *On the Lord's Supper* to encourage more frequent communion. He called the sacrament 'a solemn ordinance, designed for a perpetual exhibition ... of the atoning sacrifice of the death of Christ', and quoted with approval the words of another author claiming that we plead the merits 'of the same sacrifice here, that our great High Priest is continually urging for us in heaven' (Hennell, 41).

Mainstream clergy too rediscovered the Eucharist. Walter Hook* thought it the greatest of consolations to receive frequently; weekly if possible (Stephens, *Hook* 370). He celebrated from time to time in the afternoon or the evening to make the sacrament more accessible to the poor (Balleine, 161–2). Dick Sheppard* introduced a regular 10.15 a.m. Choral Communion at St Martin's in the Fields during the First World War, and drew personal strength from a daily Eucharist (Scott, *Sheppard* 74, 110). Thanks largely to the efforts of the Parish and People movement the Parish Communion became the most popular main Sunday service in the years after the Second World War, and its position was consolidated by the publication and widespread use of the *Alternative Service Book* of 1980. In one representative village parish, Shepherdswell in Kent, a monthly family communion was introduced in 1954, a weekly parish communion in 1963, and the *ASB* Rite A in 1986 (*SPM*, March 1954; September 1963).

The popularity of the Eucharist was enhanced by the discovery that it was an effective instrument of evangelism. Robert Dolling* argued that simply to confront people with the character of Jesus was to drive them to despair; far better 'to enable them, by the means which He Himself has ordained, to he partakers of His very nature ... some make the Blessed Sacrament the crown of their religion. I desired to make it the foundation as well' (Dolling, *TY* 119–120). George Carey** at Durham in the 1970s, discovered that, conducted in the fashion he favoured, it was the most popular of services; so he rejected the argument that it was an obstacle to outsiders, and made it a weekly main service, alternately in the morning and the evening (Carey, 39).

In the nineteenth century the wish to make the Eucharist the main Sunday service conflicted with the growing emphasis on fasting communion. At Frome William Bennett* moved the service back to the early morning for this reason; working-men who attended a 5.15 a.m. Communion were given coffee at the Vicarage before they went off to work (Bennett, 200). For some Anglo-Catholics fasting before communion became a burden or a fetish. Richard

Benson** would take his Sunday breakfast at 2.00 p.m. after two Eucharists and Matins. In the 1920s Arthur Hopkinson** presided over Matins and three Eucharists before eating breakfast at 12.15 p.m. (Hopkinson, 104). In the same decade the young Mervyn Stockwood** was told he would be refused absolution if he did not fast before communion (Stockwood, 15). At Cuddesden Theological College in the early 1940s there were ordinands who would not clean their teeth before the service, for fear of swallowing a drop of water (Williams, 94). Like other Anglo-Catholic practices, this one was dealt a body blow by alterations to the practice of the Church of Rome.

The insistence on fasting was one factor encouraging those Anglo-Catholics who took their cue from Tridentine Rome to adopt the practice of the non-communicating High Mass; even the relatively moderate Dolling recommended it to his people, partly to ensure that when they communicated they did so with adequate preparation. When Hugh Worlledge, incumbent of St Barnabas, Pimlico, in the 1940s, replaced High Mass with a Parish Communion, he was accused of selling the pass (Williams, 105). Some Anglo-Catholics adopted other Roman customs too, such as that of saying the canon of the Mass inaudibly. Some went the whole hog and adopted the Roman Missal. In the 1950s the Anglo-Papalist Hugh Ross Williamson was refused when he asked if he might celebrate at All Saints, Margaret Street; 'Because, my dear,' the vicar explained, 'you'll use that horrid Roman book and the rule here is music by Mozart, choreography by Fortescue [a Roman liturgiologist], decor by Comper, but libretto by Cranmer' (Pickering, 38).

One consequence of the new stress on the Eucharist has been an increase in the number of communicants. Total numbers have never been very high: in 1882, at the height of the Victorian religious effort, only eight percent of the population over the age of 15 were Easter communicants in the Church of England (Chadwick, *VC* 1.333). But where the Church has been strong the change has been dramatic. By the middle of the nineteenth century the practice of issuing tickets, still surviving in the countryside, had broken down in the towns. Bennett at Frome had at least twenty communicants every day (Chadwick, *VC* 2.314). In Shepherdswell, with a population of 500, there were 171 Easter communicants in 1921 (*SPM*, May 1922).

The significance of the Eucharist for the clergy has been apparent in the intimate circumstances of home communions. One of the most touching passages in James Woodforde's diary recounts how he gave communion to Billy Gunton, a servant accompanied by his mistress, in his parlour because the church was out of use at the time. 'It gave me great pleasure ... as it will ever give me pleasure to do anything in my power, that may give any satisfaction or ease to any person whatever, especially the distressed' (Woodforde, 4.275–6). Francis Witts** took the sacrament to 'an estimable old parishioner, now become very feeble', and was pleased that a lady of rank took the trouble to join them (Witts, 145). Kilvert, taking communion to Thomas Watkins, a Clyro parishioner, recorded the sick man's reflection: 'Last night I was thanking God that the Blessed Sacrament has come down to us through all the broils for 1800 years.' On the same errand to John Morgan, an old soldier, he found the veteran 'very quiet earnest and thankful' (Kilvert, 2.132; 1.87–8). I never feel more priestly than when taking communion to the sick and housebound; though this feeling contends with a sense of the extreme difficulty of concentrating when home communions follow each other in quick succession. The duty has its less attractive side. Both my predecessor and I have had to consume consecrated wafers spat out by senile worshippers.

The very significance of the Eucharist has made it a focus for disagreement. The name of the service was disputed in the nineteenth century, with Protestants violently objecting to the appellation of the Mass. Dolling defended its use on the grounds that it comprehended the whole of which all other names were but partial descriptions; but he was disingenuous in ignoring the overtones which the word had for most Englishmen (Osborn, *Dolling* 110).

Over a more substantial issue John Keble gave offence to his friends by a stanza in his poem 'An Address to Converts from Popery':

O come to our Communion Feast!
There, present in the heart,
Not in the hands, the eternal Priest
Will his true self impart.

It was not until he was dying that he authorized the replacement of 'Not' by 'As' (Faber, 99).

The doctrine of the sacrament has created notable controversy. George Denison joyfully provoked a prosecution in the 1850s by insisting that the wicked as well as the faithful received the inward reality of the sacrament (Chadwick, *VC* 1.492). Stewart Headlam's** offences included a socialist approach to the Eucharist as 'the Feast of National Emancipation ... the service which tells of brotherhood, solidarity, co-operation'. He also preached a provocative doctrine of representation: 'The Sacrifice which we offer is of Redemption for *all* mankind, not only of the pious few who may come to take their part in it' (Reckitt, 71). The general tendency in modern times, however, has been for a higher view of the sacrament to be taken. Hook summed up the position of many central churchmen then and later when he wrote to a friend about the doctrine of the Real Presence: 'Roman Catholics would call a paper £5 note real gold; Zwinglians would say it is only a bit of paper; Anglicans would say it is really and truly worth £5 for that is the sovereign's will' (Stephens, *Hook* 365).

But doctrine has attracted less controversy than practice. There was much ground to make up at the beginning of the nineteenth century if the sacrament was to be given due respect. It was common at the time to leave the disposal of the consecrated elements to the discretion of the clerk (Bennett, 20–21). Hook's churchwardens complained on the grounds of expense when he poured away the consecrated wine remaining after the service. Often the elements were taken to the congregation in their pews (Stephens, *Hook* 275). It is not surprising that nineteenth-century Anglo-Catholics, wishing to do the sacrament due honour, surrounded it with ceremonies unused for centuries. William Bennett provoked the 'surplice riots' of 1850 by such Romish practices as having two lighted altar candles, using the eastward position for celebrating, and using the sign of the cross; he was forced by bishop Blomfield to resign. John Purchas, who bought and ministered in the proprietary chapel of St James, James Street, Brighton, was condemned by the Judicial Committee of the Privy Council in 1871 for using Eucharistic vestments, incense, wafer-bread, a mixed chalice, altar lights and the eastward position. He defied the authorities and was protected from sanctions only by his sudden death in 1872 (Wagner, 77–81, 120–1).

The tide, however, was flowing in the ritualist direction. All over the country in the mid-nineteenth century parish priests were cautiously restoring and enlarging chancels, putting a cross behind the altar and candlesticks and flowers upon it (in one case with the proviso that the flowers must *not* be of the colour of the season) and occasionally wearing vestments. Bennett introduced incense and vestments at Frome in the 1860s in response to requests from his congregation (Bennett, 190, 200–1). It took time, however, for anything like a common mind to be reached over what was appropriate and what not. The enthusiastic Anglo-Catholic Nathaniel Woodard** refused to communicate at All Saints, Margaret Street, in 1865, because he disapproved of unleavened bread on the grounds that it lacked the accidents (in the Aristotlean sense) of ordinary bread. George Denison disliked the censing of individuals and always refused to wear a cope (Denison, 86, 291).

That the celebrant should stand to the north of the holy table, as the *Book of Common Prayer* enjoined, had been all but universal practice until well into the nineteenth century; John Henry Newman** and Richard Pusey followed the practice, and until recent times it was the position favoured by low churchmen. When George Illingworth, vicar of Shepherdswell, Kent, abandoned it in 1931 he called it a 'meaningless ceremony' (*SPM*, September 1931); but its significance for those who clung to it was that it minimized the sacrificial nature of the sacrament. Equally, the eastward position was a statement about the representative nature of the priest. In the years after the Second World War all parties tended to move their altars forward from the east wall, and to celebrate facing the congregation; a position with a different significance again.

Much of the nineteenth-century opposition to changes in Eucharistic doctrine and practice arose from a fear of sacerdotalism. For well over a century the clergyman had been seen, and had seen himself, as part and parcel of the professional and gentlemanly class. He had claimed no mystique, and had not separated himself from the life of polite society. Now things were changing. Both the greater seriousness of the clergy in general and the special emphases of Anglo-Catholics tended to set the clergyman apart. That in itself was no bad thing – perhaps it is no bad thing when it happens nowadays. But a stress on the dignity of orders can alienate people. Robert Dolling put the matter in perspective when he wrote: 'The ministry of the priesthood is in no danger of disproportionate exaggeration whenever it is exercised side by side with the prophet's insight and courage and the evangelist's zeal and love' (Osborn, *Dolling* 117).

The Office

When with the Virgin morning thou do'st rise
Crossing thy selfe; come thus to sacrifice:
First wash thy heart in innocence, then bring
Pure hands, pure habits, pure every thing.
Next to the Altar humbly kneele, and thence,
Give up thy soule in clouds of frankinsence.

Thus Robert Herrick** in his 'Mattens' (Herrick, 127). The clergy of the Church of England have always been expected to say morning and evening prayer, matins and vespers, daily, preferably in church. There have been those who have said the office and those who have not; those who have said it privately and those who have said it in public; and those who have and those who have not laid stress upon the importance of a congregation. We deal with each contrast in turn.

Some of the clergy who figure largely in this book used and valued the office. Dick Sheppard* thought it 'the best way he knew to be alert and responsive to the leadings of the Spirit' (Scott, *Sheppard* 110). Others may have used it, but, perhaps because they took it for granted, made no reference to it. James Woodforde* and John Skinner* are of this number. Others again, such as Ralph Josselin* and William Grimshaw* preferred altogether freer methods of personal worship.

Saying the office privately can mean saying it at home or in church without publicity; saying it alone or with one's family. Henry Liddon criticized those clergy who used only a truncated office as a basis for family prayers (Liddon, 8). Negative evidence places most clergy, if indeed they said the office at all, in the private category. A survey in 1743 found that of 836 churches in the province of York only 24 had daily services, and only 253 any kind of week-day service at all (Hart, *ECCP* 39). When the Tractarian F.M.R. Barker instituted a daily public service (presumably the office) at Bledington, Gloucestershire, in 1842, the Bishop asked other local clergy to remonstrate with him (Witts, 13). A survey in the diocese of London in 1906 found that in 232 churches out of 622 there was no daily service (Carpenter, *Winnington-Ingram* 194n).

By contrast, George Herbert* and his family read the office publicly in church on week-days at 7.30 a.m. and 6.30 p.m. They were joined by neighbours; and in Walton's famous words 'some of the meaner sort of his parish did so love and reverence Mr Herbert, that they would let their plough rest when Mr Herbert's saint's-bell rang to prayers, that they might also offer their devotions to God with him; and would then return back to their plough' (Walton, 212–13). Six o'clock Matins in church was not uncommon both in town and country in the eighteenth century; the clergy could expect a congregation (Addison, 121). Fielding's Parson Adams read the offices daily in church, though only his wife and the parish clerk joined him. John Sanford, incumbent of Dunchurch, Warwickshire, in the mid-nineteenth century, said morning prayer daily assisted by a congregation the average size of which was forty (Russell, 66). Walter Hook* introduced daily choral offices at Leeds. Richard Randall** secured a respectable attendance at a daily Matins at 6.00 a.m. in rural Graffham-cum-Lavington. In this parish both offices were sung daily with a surpliced choir (Briscoe, *Randall* 75, 128). In the 1980s a group of laity at Shepherdswell took turns in supporting me in saying public morning prayer.

How important is the presence of a congregation? Henry Alford** at Wymeswold introduced the daily offices as an experiment, but discontinued them because of lack of support (Alford, 146). Trollope poked gentle fun at the Tractarian Caleb Oriel who 'delighted ... in services at dark hours of winter mornings when no one would attend' (Trollope, *DT* 373). There is, however, a long tradition of saying the office as a representative act. The Caroline divines stressed its vicarious function (Thornton, 267). Robert Hawker*, who usually had no company or only that of his wife, prayed 'for the people, not with them even if they came, but as the Prayer Book means, for those whose labours and duties suffer them not to join, that the voice of the Minister may plead twice every day for the absent and occupied sheep'. For him the office was 'vicarious, intercessory and sacerdotal' (Brendon, *Hawker* 101–2). In our own century Arthur Hopkinson** used to say the offices in church daily in his country parish of Winchfield. Sometimes others joined him but in any event 'I knew ... that the men in the fields and the women in their homes liked to hear the bell, and to know that someone was praying for them' (Hopkinson, 114).

In his discussion of the value of the office Henry Liddon quotes from Bishop Cosin: 'We who are priests are called "Angeli Domini"; and it is the Angel's office, not only to descend to the people and teach them God's Will, but to ascend to the presence of God to make intercession for the people, and to carry up the daily prayers of the Church on their behalf' (Liddon, 15). That has been the chief public significance of the office; its personal significance has never been better expressed than by Martin Thornton: 'The Office is the supreme remedy for aridity and periodic spiritual sluggishness ... the Office, objectively said, recited even with boredom, constitutes necessary obedience: a satisfying discipline on which the weary soul may rest. All thoughts, affections, and devotion may be thrust upon the church itself; the arid soul has praised God, it is truly knit with Christ, lack of fervour notwithstanding. The Office is our daily gift to God through Christ, and the value of the gift lies in its acceptability to the recipient not its effect on the donor' (Thornton, 277).

There is an additional sense in which the office has bulked large in the spirituality of the laity; except when superceded by the Eucharist or by informal worship it has been the basis of Sunday public worship. Matins followed by the litany, ante-communion and sermon was the usual morning service until the nineteenth century; then, for the most part, Matins with hymns, intercessions and a sermon took its place. Evening prayer with catechizing and/or a sermon developed into Evensong, for long the best attended of all services though now in catastrophic decline. Whether the office, designed for other purposes, has proved satisfactory as a main Sunday service is a question which our own age appears to answer in the negative; but in its time it was the heart and centre of public worship, and as such has a permanent place in Anglican affections.

The Church Year

William Kethe, minister of Blandford Forum, Dorset, in Elizabethan times, saw the Church seasons as no more than a mixture of junketing and hypocrisy. In a sermon preached in 1570 he claimed that the candles of Candlemas were inducements to God to overlook the excesses of Christmas. Shrove Tuesday was marked with surfeit, for which Ash Wednesday was used to make recompense. Eggs were offered on Good Friday to gain Christ's Easter favour, and the sins of the following weeks were thought to be discharged by Rogation processions (Addison, 30).

Kethe spoke for other Puritans. Ralph Josselin* had a minimal sense of the Church year. At Christmas 1647, in the heyday of Puritan restriction, he wrote: 'People hanker after the sports and pastimes that they were wonted to enjoy, but they are in many families weaned from them.' After the Restoration of 1660, however, he records Christmas as a day when he preached and feasted his tenants. Before the Restoration he mentions Easter only once, in passing; thereafter it figures regularly, mainly because he was obliged by law to celebrate Holy Communion. No other season nor any saint's day appears in the diary (Josselin, 108, 539, 581, 588, 396).

In this respect the Puritans were out of step with normal Anglican practice. They were, however, in the mainstream over the observance of Sunday, which, interpreted in varying ways, has been a universal hallmark of serious churchmanship throughout our period. For a long time the law called for Friday observance too, since it imposed abstinence from meat-eating. This was, however, more for the benefit of fishermen than for the salvation of souls, and, despite the adjurations of the *Book of Common Prayer* and The *Alternative Service Book*, only a minority of clergy have taken Fridays seriously. Richard Hooker**, who often used to say that 'the life of a pious clergyman was visible rhetoric', locked himself in church to fast on Fridays, as also in Ember weeks (Walton, 155). Walter Hook* used to argue that if people kept Sunday as a feast they should keep Friday as a fast (Hook, 367–8). Hooker and Hook were exceptions.

Puritans apart, the clergy have, after their own fashion, invariably observed the seasons of the church year. James Newton** gladdened his parishioners' hearts by distributing 'among the poor of the parish a whole Sheep within a Triffle' on Christmas Eve (James, *Newton* 154). John Skinner* prepared himself devotionally for Christmas by meditating on Christ's sufferings, and by resolving: 'I can forgive, as I hope to be forgiven.' With his temperamental distaste for noisy pleasure, he deplored his bell-ringers' enthusiasm for celebrating the season: 'They had better retire within themselves, and commune with their hearts, and be still.' He was surprised when he got a good congregation on Christmas Day (Skinner, 305–6). Augustus Hare* attracted only two communicants other than his family on a snowy Christmas Day in 1829 (Hare, 1.329).

Robert Hawker* greatly enlivened Christmas at Morwenstow. When he arrived there carols had fallen almost out of use. Hawker wrote some new ones, and the church choir walked from house to house singing through the night of Christmas eve. The church was decked with holly and ivy provided by Church (as opposed to chapel) farmers; and the bells were rung (Brendon, *Hawker* 77). Francis Kilvert* described how at Langley Burrell in 1874 a Christmas text was made out of straw letters, and how ivy was used to decorate the church, with the blossom whitened with flour (Kilvert, 3.123–4). Washington Irving's book-worm parson allowed greenery, but insisted that his sexton remove mistletoe from the church because of its pagan associations (quoted Christmas, 135).

Candlemas Day marks the end of the Christmas celebrations. Robert Herrick** lovingly charted how the change of season was marked by changing decorations:

> Down with the Rosemary and Bayes,
> Down with the Misleto;
> In stead of Holly, now upraise
> The greener Box (for show). ('Ceremonies for Candlemass Eve')

Clergy faithful to the *Book of Common Prayer* have engaged in 'the cussing of a Ash Wednesday', as a character in George Eliot's *Silas Marner* calls the denunciations of the commination service (p. 131). Kilvert did so at Clyro in 1870, though he noted that the congregation was very small (Kilvert, 1.46). James Woodforde* kept Ash Wednesday 1799 by having salt fish and egg sauce for dinner (Woodforde, 5.167).

nes Woodforde

William Andrew

lney Smith

William Bennett

Arthur Stanton

Robert Hawker

rancis Kilvert

John Keble

Robert Dolling

Samuel Barnett

Henrietta Barnett

Lent, like Fridays, used to be by law a time of abstention from meat; Josselin noted in 1662 that corn was so short that flesh-eating was to be specially permitted (Josselin, 486). Wise Robert Herrick saw behind the regulation to the principle. The season inspired one of the most effective of his poems, which reads in part:

Is this a fast, to keep
The larder lean?
And clean
From fat of veal and sheep? ...

No: 'tis a fast to dole
Thy sheaf of wheat
And meat
Unto the hungry soul.

It is to fast from strife,
From old debate,
And hate;
To circumcize thy life.

To shew a heart grief-rent;
To starve thy sin,
Not bin;
And that's to keep thy Lent.

The observance of Lent slackened in the eighteenth century, but improved in the nineteenth, not least because of the efforts of the Tractarians. They were not, however, allowed to claim the whole credit for themselves. The ferociously Evangelical Francis Close** deprecated flattery of the 'Oxford novelists [innovators]', asserting 'There is no neglect of fast and feast in this town ... The bells of the Parish Church have always been muffled during Passion Week in accordance with my feelings and those of my predecessors' (Hennell, 111). Close would have rebuked John Keble's* deplorable slackness, deprecated by his own curate, in allowing penny readings to continue throughout the solemn season (Battiscombe, *Keble* 180).

The penitential seasons have been used to deepen devotion through additional observance. Arthur Stanton* presided over late night Monday evening services in Advent and Lent. They were of the plainest character, but the church was filled to its capacity by those eager to hear him preach (Russell, *Stanton* 231–3). Augustus Hare held dinner hour services on Wednesdays and Fridays in Lent, and on saints' days. At Clyro in Kilvert's time there was a Wednesday morning service during Lent; at Bredwardine he held well-attended Friday evening services in Advent. The need for systematic teaching and devotion was illustrated by a girl who told him that on Palm Sunday: 'Jesus Christ went up to heaven on an ass' (Kilvert, 2.146–7).

In the eighteenth century it was not uncommon to celebrate Holy Communion on Good Friday, an arrangement also envisaged in modern liturgical publications. Woodforde celebrated when he was a curate at Babcary in 1764. At Weston Longueville thirteen years later he was shocked to find no service on the day. He instituted one and attracted a 'tolerable good congregation'. To keep the fast he did not dine till 5.00 p.m. 'and then only eat a few apple fritters and some bread and cheese' (Woodforde, 1.36; 1.200–1). Kilvert gives a touching account of how on Good Friday 1877 he visited a young woman kept at home by her child, to take her a cross bun and to explain the meaning of the day (Kilvert, 2.163–5). Alexander Mackonochie** introduced the three hours devotion to London in 1865 (Towle, *Mackonochie* 102).

At Clyro, the folk decked the graves with flowers on Easter Eve (Kilvert, 2.166). The link between the life of the Church and the life of the earth has also found expression in the ceremonies of Rogation-tide. Richard Hooker is said never to have been happier than when, during Rogation processions, he exhorted his people to thank God for the blessings of the earth and to live in peace with each other (Addison, 36). George Herbert's* country parson 'is a lover of old customs, if they be good and harmless; and the rather, because country people are much addicted to them, so that to favour them therein is to win their hearts, and to oppose them therein is to deject them ... He loves [the Rogation] Procession and maintains it, because there are contained therein four manifest advantages. First, a blessing of God for the fruits of the field; secondly, justice in the preservation of bounds; thirdly, charity in loving walking and neighbourly accompanying one another, with reconciling of differences at that time, if there be any; fourthly, mercy in relieving the poor by a liberal distribution and largesse.' Indeed, the country parson insists that his parishioners should join him, and presents them at the church court if they fail to take heed (Herbert, XXXV).

The practice of marking great feast days by secular as well as religious activities has been employed at Ascension-tide. John Conybeare** describes how the day was kept at Barrington in 1872: 'Great day. All school to church, and treat in afternoon. Tea on lawn, and games. Sack racing and swing boat hired from village ... Band marched us back to church in grand style. Congregations 140 + 155 + 235 = 500, much largest yet.' The festival became the highlight of the village's spring. 'For weeks beforehand all the cottages were newly papered, painted and whitewashed outside. Daughters returned from their places as servants in the big houses, merry-go-rounds and booths for sweets and coconuts were erected on the green' (Colloms, 258). Richard Randall** persuaded the farmers of Graffham-cum-Lavington to give their men a holiday on this day; and, more unusually, on Ash Wednesday too (Briscoe, *Randall* 74).

Kilvert's reflections on Ascension Day were spiritual: 'To me afresh each Ascension Day there comes again a sense of loss, and it seems as if one had left the world and left it for the present comfortless.' Not surprisingly, he calls the Sunday after Ascension Day 'Expectation Sunday'. He also comments on the tendency of bees to congregate about the church windows on Ascension Day, and reports his father as saying that the bees were showing the people the way to church (Kilvert, 2.351; 3.20; 1.142–3).

Woodforde marked Whitsunday 1781 by celebrating the Eucharist, and persuaded his niece and housekeeper Nancy, whose religious enthusiasm left a good deal to be desired, to attend and to receive for the first time (Woodforde, 1.313). Kilvert describes customs connected with Whitsun: 'The hallowing of Churches on the stroke of twelve, mysterious visits to the graves of friends, scattering on the graves the last blooms of May, the letting loose of a white pigeon in honour of the Holy Dove, and maidens dressed in white waiting in silence in Church chancels as if in expectation of a celestial descent' (Kilvert, 1.352).

Brenda Colloms tells the story of a young High Churchman who headed a letter to his bishop 'The Rectory, St Timothy's day'; to receive in reply a letter headed 'The Palace, Wash day' (Colloms, 23). Trollope's Mrs Proudie regarded services on saints' days as 'rank papacy' (Trollope, *LC* 178). Defying the lady's shade, conscientious clergy of varied churchmanship have kept saints' days. William Cole**, a traditional High Churchman, said Matins on all the holy days given eucharistic readings in the *Book of Common Prayer*, and on some minor festivals such as St Valentine's day. Sometimes he lacked a congregation because the clerk forgot to ring the church bell. Woodforde was conscience-stricken when he forgot St Luke's day in 1766; 'As it was not done wilfully, I hope God will forgive it' (Woodforde, 1.61). Henry Fardell* was indignant when he discovered that it was not the custom at St Peter's, Wisbech, to observe St Thomas's day (then 21 December). He put matters right (Fardell, 116). One of the innovations of Daniel Wilson, an Evangelical who became vicar of Islington in 1824, was to mark every saint's day with a service (Balleine, 131).

Rogation-tide apart, Anglican practice long failed to echo the Jewish precedent of associating the ecclesiastical with the agricultural year. The deficiency was put right by the institution of harvest festival. In 1663 Ralph Josselin 'preacht two harvest sermons' (Josselin, 500); but Robert Hawker is often given the credit for the introduction of the harvest festival service. He began it at Morwenstow in 1843 in the hope of sanctifying the 'beer and tumult' of the past. He consciously harked back to the Old Testament model, hanging a sheaf of corn over his dining-table, and explaining to guests that it was the 'harvest wave-offering, presented at the altar and waved before the Lord at the Harvest Festival'. As his biographer remarks, 'he and his flock were thanking their Maker for freedom from famine for another year, for life itself' (Brendon, *Hawker* 77, 148–9).

Harvest festival services spread like wildfire. Kilvert lovingly describes the preparation of Clyro church in 1870 and 1871, an activity which involved all ages and both sexes. 'We had ten sheaves of wheat, barley and oats at the school and the children were busy between lessons teasing out the corn tiny and regular in little sheaves ready for me to make my crossed sheaves on the Church walls ... The Cabalva ladies ... came and put up their magnificent pulpit and desk hangings, violent flannel covered with beautifully worked designs in corn, a sickle and sheaf, IHS, Faith, Hope and Charity, represented by an anchor, a cross and a heart respectively. Bunches of purple grapes were mixed with the corn. A deep fringe of oats, flax and rye was looped up with bright red apples' (Kilvert, 1.227–9; 2.44–6). George Denison** reported on the 1883 Harvest Home at East Brent with pardonable pride and somewhat after the style of Mr Jingle: 'The people, indefatigable as soon as huge tents had been got up in rain, set to work, Vicarage and village to decorate; great work of high art; ... took £45 at the gate; subscriptions £68 ... will pay all expenses and leave some balance. Wonderful Punch, steam Merry-go-round, fortune-telling, various other amusements; teetotal drinks only – football etc.; ... two grand Balls ... had food over on Tuesday enough for poor parishioners' second meal Wednesday; ... dressing in best taste, manners and general demeanour perfect; no doubt an admirable institution; should be witnessed to be comprehended' (Denison, 278).

The intertwining of the secular and the sacred, however deplored by the rigorous, has been the natural outcome of a life where both were part of the natural order of things. The farmers of Goldsmith's Vicar of Wakefield's village retreat 'wrought with cheerfulness on days of labour, but observed festivals as intervals of idleness and pleasure. They kept up the Christmas carol, sent true love-knots on Valentine morning, ate pancakes at Shrovetide, showed their wit on the first of April, and religiously cracked nuts on Michaelmas eve' (Goldsmith, 39). Kilvert rejoiced in Mothering Sunday. 'All the country in an upturn going out visiting. Girls and boys going home to see their mothers and taking them cakes, brothers and sisters of middle age going to see each other. It is a grand visiting day' (Kilvert, 1.313).

Just as sacred days have been used for secular pleasures, so secular occasions have been given religious overtones. Woodforde read prayers on New Year's day (Woodforde, 1.61). There are frequent references in Josselin's diary during the pre-Restoration period to public days of humiliation (that is, of fasting and prayer); during the first Civil War such fasts occurred monthly (Josselin, 33). The proclamation of public fasts continued after the Restoration, and lasted into the nineteenth century. Woodforde read prayers on such days, and ate only salt fish and fritters (see, for example, Woodforde, 1.221; 5.244). When workmen in his parish of St Barnabas were prevented from earning on a national fast day in 1847 William Bennett* arranged for them to be paid from parish funds

(Bennett, 238). In due course fasts were replaced by less demanding national days of prayer. Josselin also mentions days of thanksgiving following military victories; it was to this secular drumbeat rather than to the church year that his ministry marched. Nowadays Remembrance Sunday, with its countless parades at war memorials and in churches, presents clergy with the challenge of finding something to say which will both do justice to the deep feelings of many of those involved and also set them in a Christian perspective. Nicolas Stacey** found himself in hot water when he suggested to a congregation of Old Contemptibles and members of the British Legion that the day was losing its appeal, and that it might well be replaced by a Peace Sunday (Stacey, 168).

Dedication day in many parishes was no more than an excuse for a revel. Hawker civilized it at Morwenstow writing in 1864: 'It used to be a time of drunkenness and riot, but it is very far from that now' (Brendon, *Hawker* 77). It was, however, an achievement on his part to keep the day's church connection. In Flora Thompson's childhood, the dedication feast had been entirely detached from its origins, and was celebrated at the inn in Lark Rise rather than at the church in Fordlow (Thompson, 230–1). All the more credit then to William Cole in the previous century. He succeeded in retaining Feast Sunday (a village festival originally on the feast-day of the church's patron saint but later fixed arbitrarily) for religious uses. He read Matins and Vespers, and preached twice, the only occasion during the year when he did so (Cole, 119).

The defeat of the sacred by the secular, now almost taken for granted, was in smaller measure a feature of the past too. Josselin remarked of the Christmas of 1675: 'All shops open, trade goeth, religion sad' (Josselin, 588). Kilvert lamented: 'Good Friday has now become a holiday and mere day of pleasure' (Kilvert, 1.89). John Skinner noted that the colliers and farmers worked as usual on Good Friday, and was scandalized to discover that a brother clergyman had employed workmen on his house during the day (Skinner, 325). Stanton, who had no objection to the theatre as such, was offended when theatres were opened during Holy Week (Russell, *Stanton* 24).

Over the centuries the Anglican clergy have sought, some in one way some in another, to couple the march of time with an awareness of the Christian story; to sanctify festivity and to bring worldly affairs under the discipline of spiritual routine. It has not been the least of their services to national spirituality that they have often been successful.

Rites of Passage

Baptism and Churching

George Herbert's* country priest believed baptism 'a blessing that the world hath not the like'. He baptized only in the presence of the whole congregation and constantly reminded them of the vocation to which baptism had called them. He permitted 'no vain or idle names, but such as are usual and accustomed', and (a second dig at his Puritan contemporaries) 'willingly and cheerfully' made the sign of the cross on the child, believing the ceremony 'not only innocent but reverend' (Herbert, XXII).

Ralph Josselin* practised infant baptism both before and after the re-introduction of the *Book of Common Prayer*, agreeing with colleagues that faith on the part of the parents was not a requirement in an established Church. He baptized both in public and in private; it appears that in his day privacy was a perquisite of the higher classes. He only once mentions an adult baptism, which suggests that most of his flock were brought to the font in infancy. He called the godparents of his own elder children 'witnesses'; there is no evidence that they played any significant part in the children's lives (Josselin, passim, especially 101, 271, 355, 397).

In the eighteenth and early nineteenth centuries private baptism was frequent. Jane Austen's clerical father George Austen, rector of Steventon, Hampshire, was following common practice when he baptized his daughter at home the day after her birth, and publicly received her into the Church a few months later (Park Honan, *Jane Austen*, Ballantine 1989, 22). When so many children died in infancy, and when Christian burial was refused to the unbaptized, there was much to be said for this procedure. James Woodforde baptized both at home (his or the parents') and at church. Domestic baptisms occurred the more frequently, and only occasionally because the child was in obvious danger of death. In keeping with his generally tender-hearted approach to his duties, he never refused to baptize 'spurious' [illegitimate] children (see Woodforde, 1.33; 1.74; 1.212; 1.248–9; 1.272; 1.320; 2.96; 2.153; 3.6; 3.60 and passim).

Relaxed and sometimes scandalous attitudes persisted. Sabine Baring-Gould** describes a cottage christening, with the parents, the god-parents and the parson sitting round a table on which had been set a bottle of rum, a pack of cards, a lemon and a basin of water. The basin was needed for the decently conducted religious rite, the rest for the conviviality which followed (Addison, 140). Francis Kilvert* was told that in the parish of Fordington, Dorset, in the 1820s the clerk responded to a request for water for a baptism by exclaiming: 'The last parson never used no water. He spit into his hand' (Kilvert, 2.442). John Skinner* referred with disgust to the practice of some of his colleagues of turning out their fonts and using them for garden decorations, substituting a 'foolish carved toy of wood'. He also objected to their practice of baptizing on week days, despite the preference of the rubric for Sundays and Holy Days (Skinner, 491, 293). A further abuse was the demand for a fee. Henry Fardell* was horrified to find that one of his curates had demanded 6d when poor women had requested the ceremony (Fardell, 121). Perhaps more pardonably, James Woodforde received five guineas for baptizing the child of Mr Custance, the local squire (Woodforde, 2.94).

Nineteenth-century seriousness and the influence of the Oxford Movement ensured that the significance of the sacrament was reinstated. Augustus Hare* made it a rule that parents should go to him before baptism for advice and instruction (Hare, 1.306). Henry Fardell refused private baptism except when the child was in danger of death; but considered a baptism public if the 'sponsors' (that is, the god-parents) were present (Fardell, 118–19). At Frome William Bennett* baptized only at Evensong, surrounding the rite with additional ceremonies designed to emphasize its significance (Bennett, 201–2). Robert Hawker*, in characteristic fashion, opened a usually closed church door 'for the escape of the fiend', and if the infant cried at the appropriate moment declared that the fiend had indeed departed (Brendon, *Hawker* 98).

Both doctrine and temperament impelled John Keble* to make the most of the occasion. Witnesses describe 'his loving care and intense seriousness', the kiss of peace which he gave the infant, and his apparent reluctance to part with him or her. He said to a friend: 'Those who christen little children have a right to love them'; and his attitudes so influenced his parishioners that he easily attracted two hundred signatures for a petition against the Gorham judgment (Battiscombe, *Keble* 292–3).

George Gorham was an Evangelical presented in 1846 to the parish of St Just with Penwith, Cornwall. Here his views and activities irritated Bishop Phillpotts of Exeter. When Gorham sought to transfer to the parish of Brampford Speke, Devon, Phillpotts refused to institute him until he had examined him on doctrine. The two men spent a total of fifty-two hours discussing baptismal regeneration. The outcome was that Phillpotts refused to institute Gorham. Gorham appealed to the courts, and after a long legal battle the judicial committee of the privy council decided that Gorham's views were not contrary to the formularies of the Church of England.

Phillpotts had insisted that infant baptism conferred regeneration unconditionally, Gorham had denied it. The legal decision had a double implication: first, that Anglicans were not bound to hold Phillpotts' doctrine; secondly, that a secular court had the right to define the doctrine of the Church of England. The first decision preserved the Church of England as a broad church; both presented High Churchmen with problems. The outcome was that a number of Anglicans, including some clergy, seceded to Rome (Chadwick, *VC* 1.250–71).

Protestant emphasis on the individual's assent to the work of grace within the soul has made infant baptism contentious for some Anglicans. The sixteenth-century Puritan parish priest and controversialist Thomas Becon argued that the child of a believer receives the Holy Spirit in the womb, and that water baptism does no more than testify to the congregation a process of regeneration which has already taken place (Bailey, *Becon* 107). In the early nineteenth century prayers implying the doctrine of regeneration were often omitted (Bennett, 21). Charles Simeon* included them but taught that regeneration was only 'the beginning of that process by which we are changed'. Edward Bickersteth** made a distinction between regeneration 'the seed of life implanted' and conversion 'the extension of life existing, by the turning of the soul to the only true Author and Giver of life' (Hennell, 42). Modern individualism has followed where Protestant feeling led. The London parish priest who chose in 1991 to have his baby dedicated rather than baptized preserved his child's future freedom of choice at the price of denying him full membership of the church. He had of course the justification that Anglican practice over confirmation makes the question about what constitutes full membership a difficult one to answer.

A second subject of controversy has been the availability of the sacrament. William Andrew* refused a baptism because a godmother was not a communicant (Chadwick, *Andrew* 97). Stewart Headlam** believed in baptism upon demand because it was 'the sacrament of equality' (Reckitt, 72). Some parish priests, especially Evangelicals, have thought it a mockery to baptize children whose parents and godparents have had little or no church connection; others, with a more organic view of Christian life, have baptized on request, and used the opportunity afforded for a (usually unsuccessful) attempt to associate the family more closely with the church community. Interestingly, Simeon was of the latter party, arguing that, like the Jewish rite of circumcision, baptism is a sign of membership of God's own community and not lightly to be denied (Hopkins, *Simeon* 181–2). A modern Evangelical, George Carey**, takes the view that baptism, even when the parents understand its meaning very imperfectly, anticipates the arrival of personal response. Even when faced with the rivalry of the house church movement which was drawing away many charismatics from the established church, he refused to rebaptize. He was prepared, however, to conduct a baptism by total immersion in the River Wear (Carey, 120–3).

The folk religion aspect of baptism has always bulked large. In the eighteenth and early nineteenth centuries it was seen by many laity and not a few clergy as a naming ceremony. The controversy in Sterne's novel about Tristram Shandy's name depends upon that assumption (Sterne, 323 and passim). It was common for the parson to attend at the home for naming soon after the birth, and for the family to come to church later (see, for example, Atkinson, 45n). William Cole** noted that he had baptized a little boy 'or rather received him into the congregation' after a previous private baptism; his phrasing suggests that he had to remind himself not to fall into the common confusion (Cole, 240). John Skinner noted in 1828: 'The people are now getting into the way of getting their children named ... in order to avoid bringing godfathers and godmothers to Church;' he also noted sourly that they would find excuses in order to get the parson to visit them, instead of coming to the parsonage for the naming (Skinner, 311, 312). When a new Vicar asked the people of Fordington, Dorset, why they brought their children to be baptized, he was told that a child dying without a name would 'flit about in the woods and waste places and could get no rest' (Kilvert, 2.442–3).

The 1836 Act introducing the civil registration of births created fresh confusion. Henry Fardell thought it necessary to preach a sermon on 'the impropriety of considering the registering of a child's name by the civil registrar as intended to supercede baptism' (Fardell, 120). Well into the nineteenth century Walter Hook* was writing: 'Nobody here [in Leeds] seems to have a notion that baptism is anything more than a form of registration. I think it my duty therefore to have it always administered with peculiar solemnity' (Stranks, *Hook* 62).

The folk religion aspect of baptism has created problems for clergy anxious to see the dignity of the rite respected. John Skinner had trouble with one godmother who disturbed the service with 'grunts and groans' and with another who was unable to make the responses and who admitted that she never came to church. He was so upset by the misbehaviour of a baptismal party and their failure to give the responses that he nearly abandoned the ceremony (Skinner, 376, 303, 309–10). I have encountered open irreverence in some baptismal parties, and witnessed a baptism from which the baby's mother stayed away in order to prepare the tea.

Twentieth-century parish priests have made huge efforts to give baptism its true significance. Nicolas Stacey** preceded a baptism with two visits from one of the parish priests and a mass rehearsal which included refreshments, a film strip, and a singing of the hymns to be used on the day. The baptism itself was a spectacular affair, using a specially written order of service and including a procession of mothers and babies, and other devices later included in *The Alternative Service Book*. The procedure concluded with a follow-up visit from a clergyman and annual visits for seven years from members of the congregation. The total effect from the hundreds of baptisms carried out in this way was that one family joined the regular congregation (Stacey, 146–9).

Modern methods of preparation for baptism would not have withstood for long the pressure of numbers characteristic of the past. Joshua Brooks, appointed chaplain of the Collegiate church in Manchester in 1790, was said to perform a hundred baptisms a day, and in addition twenty weddings (Barrow, 119). The three clergy at Leeds parish church before Hook's arrival conducted about 2000 baptisms a year. In 1902 the Anglican clergy were still baptizing two-thirds of all babies (the proportion in the 1990s was about a quarter). In the early 1940s there was a Bristol parson who baptized on demand for the price of a sixpenny registration card, and who had a notice outside his church reading: 'The church with a thousand baptisms a year' (Stockwood, 47).

The churching of women after childbirth has never been universal; Josselin, in common with other Puritans, appears never to have performed it, and other clerical diarists mention it only rarely. But when it occurred it carried overtones beyond those suggested by the Prayer Book title 'The Thanksgiving of Women after Childbirth'; overtones which reached back to the rite's origin in Jewish purification practice. The woman was expected to bring an offering, and, before the 1662 *Book of Common Prayer* substituted the requirement of decent apparel, to appear veiled. Robert Herrick** entitled his poem on the subject 'Julia's Churching, or Purification', and suggested that the purpose of the ceremony was to restore the woman's maiden purity.

Woodforde churched regularly, often returning the 6d fee in the case of poor women. Joseph Price** recorded that a colleague was considering refusing to church any woman who gave birth six months after marriage, unless the offending female did penance (Price, 41). In the early nineteenth century the ceremony did not necessarily take place in the church. Sometimes it was undertaken by the vestry fire, sometimes in the lady's bedroom. High church-men saw these practices, which breached the rubric, as abuses; it is equally possible to regard them as a commonsense accommodation to the lady's condition. Nineteenth-century rigorists refused to church the mothers of illegitimate children, and one clergyman claimed to have reduced the local illegitimacy rate by adopting this stance (Russell, 81–2).

Folk attitudes endured. A young mother asked Francis Kilvert if it would be in order for her to go to her father's funeral without first being churched (Kilvert, 3.220). When I was teaching in Lancaster in the 1950s it was still within living memory that a woman who had given birth was expected to make churching her first appointment on leaving her home; if other errands preceded that one, she covered her head with a tile. In Chorley, Lancashire, in the early 1960s a woman came home after giving birth without first being churched; her mother insisted that the chair she used on her return should be burnt (personal information). With the erosion of superstition has come the almost total disappearance of the traditional rite. In eight years in a Kentish village I have been asked to perform it only once: for a non-churchgoing mother at the prompting of the grandmother. Sadly, however, it has proved difficult to persuade even church-going mothers to use the thanksgiving service provided in the *Alternative Service Book*.

Confirmation

Confirmation has been the responsibility of the parochial clergy only to the extent that it has been their duty to prepare their people for it. They cannot be held responsible for its rarity in the past, and only indirectly for the length, confusion and irreverence which disfigured confirmations until well into the nineteenth century. William Cole** remarked: 'It is done in such a Hurry, with such Noise and Confusion, as to seem more like a Bear Baiting, than any Religious Institution' (Cole, 22). In 1794 James Woodforde* took seventeen candidates to a confirmation at which two hundred people were presented, and which lasted three and a quarter hours (Woodforde, 4.140). In 1830 a confirmation party travelling to Cambridge set out at 8.00 a.m. and got to church at 10.30. There they found themselves among a vast and ill-behaved crowd. The service began at 11.15, but the members of their group were not confirmed until 3.00 p.m., and they did not get away until 4.00 (Hammond, 170).

When a confirmation was in prospect it was urgently necessary to take advantage of the fact. William Cole was indignant because he was given only three weeks' notice; but he could not afford to let the opportunity slip (Cole, 22). During Augustus Hare's* brief stay at Woodhay an opportunity occurred, and no less than twenty-seven of the seventy inhabitants were presented (Hare, 1.272).

The clergy themselves have not always taken confirmation with the necessary seriousness. Richard Baxter, the seventeenth-century Puritan divine, was 'bishooped' with no examination and little ceremony (More, 449–50). A Fenland vicar of recent times is said to have presented his housekeeper annually (Williams, 83).

When the clergy have been willing and able, preparation has been meticulous and disorder minimized. John Keble gave weekly instruction for six months before the event; if a candidate was not well enough to come to him, he went to the candidate (Battiscombe, *Keble* 177). Henry Fardell* made detailed arrangements for confirmations at Wisbech, and in 1841 managed to secure the confirmation of 370 candidates at a service lasting less than two hours (Fardell, 121–3). Things improved still further as the nineteenth century went on, as travel became easier, and as bishops made a practice of visiting individual parishes. The Bishop visited Langley Burrell in 1873 to confirm twenty of the Kilverts' flock and some others, and Francis Kilvert* counted the day 'one of the happiest in my life . . . nice and quiet, no hurry, confusion or excitement and the behaviour of the young pupils was quiet and reverent in the extreme … The girls looked like twenty-one sisters, dressed chiefly in white' (Kilvert, 2.361–2).

Conscientious clergy have presented candidates with discrimination. In 1823 John Skinner* refused tickets to fourteen 'ignorant and ill-behaved' collier boys, but gave them to the schoolmaster's son and eighteen girls, though in one case only when she promised to amend recent improper behaviour (Skinner, 241). In 1841 William Andrew* approved only four of those presenting themselves; of the other eight he was prepared only to say that they were not immoral. To his sorrow all were confirmed. He took it hard when the Bishop declared that if any of the candidates were not under 'religious impression' the fault was not theirs but their pastors' (Chadwick, *Andrew* 55). The Bishop's judgment condemns most clergy then and since. It is notorious, and a source of lasting sadness, that the majority of the confirmed – or at least of the young confirmed – lapse.

Marriage

Anglican marriage discipline has been among the strictest in Christendom. The Canons of 1604 laid it down that a divorced couple should give a bond against re-marrying, and it was a subject for debate as the century went on whether a man who had put his wife away for adultery was entitled to re-marry (the question did not arise in the case of an injured woman, since she was not permitted to divorce her husband). It has been customary to refuse the sacraments to couples living together outside marriage – the saintly Bishop King** thought this essential (King, *Letters* 100); customary too to refuse the sacraments to the divorced and re-married. In the 1950s Mervyn Stockwood** persuaded Bishop Cockin of Bristol to lift such a ban on Sir Walter Monckton, a Cabinet minister; he also privately blessed Monckton's second marriage (Stockwood, 75). At about the same time, however, a parish priest who had conducted a service of blessing over divorcees was severely rebuked by Archbishop Garbett**. The full extent of Garbett's liberalism was to permit the 'innocent', and sometimes, after careful investigation, the 'guilty', party in a divorce to communicate (Smyth, *Garbett* 391–3).

Since the nineteenth century there has been a divergence between the marriage disciplines of State and Church, with consequent anomalies and problems. An Act of 1836 allowed marriages in a registry office or a dissenting place of worship in the presence of the registrar. The 1857 Divorce Act provided that a clergyman might refuse to marry the guilty party in a divorce, but must surrender his church if the couple could find a clergyman in the same diocese who would celebrate the wedding (Chadwick, *VC* 1.483). William Bennett* was always prepared to marry in church people already married in registry offices, but in no circumstances would he marry divorced persons (Bennett, 257–8).

Mervyn Stockwood was ready so to do (Stockwood, 32), setting an example which has been widely followed in recent decades. The sweeping changes in sexual behaviour in the later twentieth century have created difficulties for parochial clergy who wish both to be loyal to traditional Christian values and to behave sensitively and compassionately in individual cases.

John Skinner* gave advice to a young couple detained in church after their marriage by a shower of rain. He recommended them to find a home of their own as soon as they could, and to come to church (Skinner, 403). It has been only in modern times that more formal marriage preparation has become the custom. Nicolas Stacey** eschewed the current practice of preparing several couples together, an arrangement he thought more suitable in middle-class areas, and spent three sessions with each couple on their own. He succeeded, if in nothing else, in persuading grooms to hold their stag nights earlier than the night before the wedding; perhaps because he told couples that he would not conduct the service if he thought the man drunk (Stacey, 150–1).

Very often in the past, marriage preparation in the weeks before the wedding would in one major respect have come too late. 'A village wedding,' wrote John Keble*, 'is in general the most melancholy of all ceremonies to me' (Battiscombe, *Keble* 162). His sadness arose from the fact that the bride was usually in an advanced state of pregnancy. The situation might be worse still. William Cole** penned a graphic account of how he married a couple under protest because of the short notice they gave him, and then baptized their child and churched the mother immediately afterwards. He lamented: 'As the Discipline of our Church, through the practices of the Dissenters, is now so relaxed as to come to nothing, there is no Parleying with your Parishioners on any point of Doctrine or Discipline; for if you are rigid, they will either abstain from all Ordinances, or go over to the Dissenters' (Cole, 8–9). Skinner wrote mordantly: 'I had to marry a couple ... the bride was as round as a barrel and according to custom I suppose there will be a christening in the course of the honeymoon.' He was so delighted on another occasion to find everything 'comme il faut' that he returned the wedding fees to the bride so that she could buy some tea-things (Skinner, 409, 416). The twentieth-century clergy who lament the fact that many of the couples who approach them are already co-habiting are echoing the complaints of their ancestors. My own experience of being approached by the parents after a baptism with a request to arrange their marriage has not been very far from William Cole's.

Anticipation of nuptial delights has not been the only source of regret to parochial clergy called upon to conduct marriages. Skinner nearly stopped a wedding because the bride 'behaved so bad by laughing and other misconduct ... and the man who gave her away put on his hat in the midst of the church' (Skinner, 296). Arthur Hopkinson**, whose ministry spanned the first forty years of this century, was convinced that more than half of the weddings he conducted should not have celebrated in church, because of the carelessness with which the vows were regarded. Hopkinson also had to encounter the bitter resentment of those to whom he had refused a church wedding because they were unbaptized (Hopkinson, 150–51). He was doing no more than exercise the discipline of the Church as it then stood. It has been a relief to clergy of our own day that the Church's position has now been modified.

One modern clergyman had a distinctive method of marking out the marriages of committed Christians from those of others. At Belle Isle, Leeds, Charles Jenkinson** refused the use of the organ to any save communicant members of his parish's Free Will Offering Fund. He declared: 'We have organs and choirs in our churches not for our gratification ... but for the ... glorification of God in the Church's common worship. That worship is main-tained week by week and is open to all. To provide the adjuncts of such worship ... for the personal gratification or social glorification of people who persistently ignore it ... is ... to prostitute it. We shall not do it' (Hammerton, *Jenkinson* 148–9). It is a striking point of view.

Funerals

The spiritual opportunities presented by a death have sometimes been taken, sometimes not. James Woodforde* read prayers with and gave the sacrament to a lady before she died, but this was an exception rather than the rule with him (Woodforde, 4.206). In 1747 George White, curate of Colne and Marsden, Wiltshire, read the rite twenty times in one night over the graves of those who had been buried during his absence (Addison, *ECCP* 119n). It was quite customary at the turn of the eighteenth and nineteenth centuries for the first part of the burial service, which took place in church, to be omitted when a fee was not forthcoming, and for the body simply to be taken to the grave for committal (Bennett, 21–2, Stephens, *Hook* 87).

Not necessarily through their own fault the clergy have been associated with funerals far below any reasonable standard of reverence and decency. John Skinner* was so upset by the behaviour of some boys at funerals that he asked his clerk to beat them (Skinner, 329). In the early nineteenth century London graveyards were hideously overcrowded. Space for coffins was hard to find, and at times of epidemics the scenes at funerals were indescribable (Chadwick, *VC* 1.327). George Bull** attacked the custom of 'arvils' – drinking bouts which disfigured the occasion (Gill, *Bull* 111). Francis Kilvert* recorded how a funeral was hampered by a flood of water from a neighbouring grave and the sides of the grave falling in; 'moreover there was a deadly stench, enough to breed typhus fever ... we are terribly cramped for burying room now' (Kilvert, 3.151).

Conducting funerals has involved both physical and psychological dangers. William Cole** recorded how he had buried a man from another parish, who had died of smallpox: 'As even those [clergy] who had had it themselves, were afraid of carrying the infection to their Wives and Children.' Prudently, he insisted that the grave be half filled up before he read the service (Cole, 27). Robert Hawker* had the ghastly duty of burying the remains of those drowned in the shipwrecks which constantly occurred off the Cornish coast. Bodies were washed up in every stage of incompleteness and decay, and Hawker was strained to the limit by the conscientious care of them which he displayed. 'The constant threat of wrecks, and their occasional advent, meant that Hawker's life was spent in long periods of gnawing worry which culminated in moments of excruciating crisis.' He came to believe himself haunted by the spirits of the unburied dead. His sole consolation, expressed in a letter, was that: 'It always moves me to soothing thoughts, that no sooner is the bruised and broken and nameless stranger cast up by the sea than the Church greets him as a son and proclaims his right to inherit a glorified body and a life everlasting' (Brendon, *Hawker* 135, 131, 129).

With a firmness which was no less saddening for being logical, the clergy were in the past forbidden to use the burial service for the unbaptized. (Woodforde, 3.6). George Gorham, vicar of Walkeringham, Nottinghamshire, and son of the Gorham of Judgment fame, refused to bury anyone who had received a Methodist baptism (Russell, 80). One of the most heartbreaking passages in Hardy's *Tess of the D'Urbervilles* describes how a vicar, refused admission to the house to baptize Tess's baby, declined to give the child Christian burial even though Tess had baptized him herself. His humanity wrestled with his sense of order: 'He said "It will be just the same". How the Vicar reconciled the answer with the strict notions he supposed himself to hold on these subjects it is beyond a layman's power to tell, though not to excuse ... So the baby was carried in a small deal box ... to the churchyard that night, and buried ... at the cost of a shilling and a pint of beer to the sexton, in that shabby corner of God's allotment where He lets the nettles grow, and where ... the conjecturally damned are laid' (Hardy, 148). In due course Convocation ruled that prayers and scripture readings could be sustituted for the forbidden service; some clergy simply refrained from asking whether the dead person had been baptized (Hammond, 131). More recently still practice has been still further relaxed for pastoral reasons. When a five-year-old parishioner of my own died suddenly and tragically, it was some consolation to his distraught mother to learn that the fact he had not been baptized would not preclude Christian burial.

Suicide too has stood in the way of Christian burial. Francis Kilvert, recording the sad story of one Mary Meredith, who drowned herself, noted that it was expected that she would be buried without a service on 'the backside of the Church'. In fact Kilvert's kindly vicar, Mr Venables, buried her 'with the usual ceremony' (Kilvert, 2.48).

The burial of Dissenters raised other problems. Where the only burial ground was the churchyard, they should in law have been buried with the Anglican service, conducted by the parish priest. This arrangement was acceptable to some Dissenters, but by no means to all. Wise clergy were prepared to allow a silent interment; but almost unanimously the clergy resisted the proposal that dissenting ministers should be allowed to conduct the graveside service. None the less an Act to this effect was passed in 1880, with no more atrocious consequences than the resignation of one incumbent, and a declaration by George Denison** that he would not register non-Anglican burials (Chadwick, *VC* 2.202–7).

While doctrine and discipline stood in the way of human sympathy, that same sympathy sometimes persuaded the clergy to accept the customs of folk religion. J.C. Atkinson** told the tale of an old man who was buried with 'a candle, a penny and a bottle of port; the candle to light the road to Jerusalem, the penny to pay the ferry, and the port to sustain him on his journey' (Atkinson, 215).

It is sometimes said that death is the great leveller; Anglican funeral practice suggests the contrary. In 1657 Josselin conducted the funeral of a lady of quality. She was buried in the chancel with some ceremony, the sermon continuing till sundown despite (or perhaps because of) fears of infection from the corpse. On another occasion Josselin was upset when one of the Harlakenden family, 'noted for religion', was buried without a sermon (Josselin, 395–6, 455). In 1753 George Woodward** thought it his duty to make himself available for the burial of a lady from an affluent family, even though they were Roman Catholics (Woodward, 48–50). The contrast with the perfunctory ceremonies which have usually marked the passing of the poor is marked.

Until an act of the nineteenth century forbade the practice, intra-mural burial was a privilege of the superior classes. John Lewis, parson of Bagendon, Gloucestershire, from 1800 to 1845 ordered his curate to dig about in the chancel until he found a place in which the rector's brother might be buried. Reporting that the ground was already full of departed rectors the curate was instructed: 'Scrabble them all on one side; and while you're doing it, make room for me too' (Addison, 175).

Modern funerals are conducted with outward decency, but are sometimes robbed of significance by the religious ignorance or indifference of the mourners. Better a ceremony adapted to the true facts of the case. I was asked to preside over the funeral of a lady whom I had visited regularly but who was an avowed agnostic. I was encouraged by the family to share my own perception of the event; but for the most part the ceremony was avowedly secular, and, it appeared to me, spiritually more appropriate for being so.

Direction and Reconciliation

Thomas Fuller** wrote of Richard Greenham, parish priest of Dry-Drayton, Cambridgeshire, in the later sixteenth century: 'His master piece was in comforting wounded consciences. For, although Heaven's hand can only set a broken heart, yet God used him herein as an instrument of good to many, who came to him with weeping eyes, and went from him with cheerful souls. The breath of his gracious counsel blew up much smoking flax into a blazing flame' (Fuller, *CH* 3.147).

The priest's private spiritual ministry to individuals rivals in importance his role in public worship. 'The heavy stress Anglicanism lays on personal conscience and individual responsibility, far from minimizing the need for personal guidance, greatly increases it' (Thornton, 240). Direction is hidden from public view; yet it is immensely time-consuming, and might be termed the iceberg element in the clergyman's life. Cosmo Lang** at Portsea once had thirty-five private interviews of twenty minutes each on a single day (Lockhart, *Lang* 122). Despite working among a largely self-sufficient middle-class population, I have often found a single parishioner absorbing uncountable hours.

Much of Ralph Josselin's* ministry was to individuals. He had the common ministerial experience of being lifted up by evidence of having been helpful: 'Spoke with 2 in troubles of mind, whereof one professes much good gotten by my ministry, oh my god, it is a pretious comfort to heare of any workings upon the spirits, of any in these backe sliding days.' He wrote in sterner terms too: 'One with mee in trouble of minde, lord thou art acquainted with her estate, make her to see her vilnes to loathe her selfe, and to see thee her alone salvation' (Josselin, 59, 261).

In later life, when he had put behind him the didacticism of his early ministry and had achieved spiritual maturity, John Newton* was much in demand as a counsellor. He has been called the St Francis de Sales of the Evangelical movement (Balleine, 73). He had a huge circle of correspondents to whom he wrote quarterly, and gave his time generously to individuals in conversation. He seasoned his advice with common sense and humour. He told the unduly introspective to take holidays and to refresh themselves with sea bathing and country air. Asked if he supported a plan for a prayer circle on Sunday evenings he replied, 'Yes, but not too literally, when I have been preaching and nine p.m. comes round I find myself more disposed for supper and bed than prayer.' He told a woman rejoicing that she had won a lottery: 'Madam, as for a friend under temptation I will pray for you.' The young William Wilberforce visited him in search of spiritual comfort, and wrote afterwards: 'Was much affected in conversing with him – something very pleasing and unaffected in him … he encouraged me – though got nothing new from him … except a good hint, that he never found it answer to dispute' (Martin, *Newton* 302, 306).

Charles Simeon* was in the same tradition of sensitive guidance. He disliked, though he did not eschew, guidance by correspondence: 'If I *speak* with a man, I can stop when I see it is doing harm; I can soften the truth so as not to fly in the face of his cherished views … Written words convey ideas … but they cannot convey exact feelings … You cannot *hesitate* upon paper; you cannot *weep* upon paper; you cannot *look* kindness upon paper.' He was much involved in the spiritual turmoils of undergraduates; contending, for example, with the profound feelings of guilt and depression which his own religious tradition did much to instil. He said: 'When people come to me in deep distress of mind, my first inquiry is as to the state of their bodily health … My next … is whether some social or domestic trial be not preying on their spirits … these two inquiries dispose of nine-tenths of such applications. Not above a tenth of those who attribute their depression to religious causes are really under conviction of sin.' In words which see him join hands with modern counselling practice he wrote: 'Be not hasty to offer advice to those who are bowed down with a weight of trouble. There is a sacredness in grief which demands our reverence; and the very habitation of a mourner must be approached with awe' (Hopkins, *Simeon* 124–9).

For all his drive and vigour, Walter Hook* was a sensitive counsellor, wary of classifying people as saints or sinners. 'I know that my own growth in grace has been very slow and gradual; and therefore I am desirous of encouraging others, who … are still going on … Encourage, excite, animate such persons; don't say say to them "You must be damned because you are not better than you are"; but say "I am glad to see that God is merciful to you: now try if you cannot make a little further spring in the straight and narrow path"' (Stephens, *Hook* 165). Robert Dolling* too was a great counsellor. He employed both sacramental and non-sacramental methods to help those who came to him.

They included failed priests who were restored by his tenderness and benevolence (Osborn, *Dolling* passim).

Dick Sheppard* was a supreme exponent of this role. It is ironic that the wife who eventually deserted him supplied a tender description of his gift: 'He knew almost at once when he saw a person, whether they had a burden on their heart, and he couldn't rest until he had taken their burden on himself. He couldn't just be sympathetic like an ordinary friend. He had to actually bear the burden and be hurt by its weight.' Sheppard had a lifetime habit of writing at night to those whom he had seen during the day; sometimes as many as a hundred letters and notes at a time (Scott, *Sheppard* 118).

Written direction has played a large part in many clergy's lives. Walter Hook found time to correspond with his 'spiritual children', writing between ten and thirty letters a day (Stephens, *Hook* 413). Charles Kingsley* wrote huge numbers of long and thoughtful letters to those afflicted by doubt or seduced by the attractions of Rome (Chitty, *Kingsley* 115–16). Some idea of the labour involved, and of the style sometimes adopted, can be gathered from a letter which Henry Alford** wrote to a girl who had attended the parish school at Wymeswold and who was now in domestic service: 'I have received two letters from you, and have been much pleased with them. I am sorry to hear you are not so well again. I was afraid that you would not be able to undertake a place so soon after your illness; you have been wonderfully raised up as it is, and you should be very thankful to your gracious Father and God who has brought you out of the jaws of death almost to health and strength again. You must never forget that you are the Lord's child and bought with Christ's most precious blood; be sure to endeavour to adorn the doctrine of God your Saviour in all things, by meekness and patience, by faith and hope, by prayer and praise, by humility and holiness. Think on yourself as one for whom Christ has died, how precious must such a one be to Him, and how earnestly should you strive to keep that robe of His spotless righteousness with which His grace has clothed you. I am writing this to you as being a child of God which I hope and trust you are, and will continue; if you fall away to this wretched world, God's promises and His inheritance will cease to be yours, and what a thing that would be. I shall never cease praying for you, that you may endure unto the end, and be found among the elect of the Lord, at His glorious coming to take His kingdom. God bless you, and give you a large measure of His Holy Spirit. I am your affectionate Minister, and brother in the Lord' (Alford, 169–70). Austere comfort; but a generous gift of time to one small parishioner.

The practice of sacramental confession survived the Reformation. Izaak Walton thought that Richard Hooker** and one Dr Saravis were confessors to each other. Saravis heard Hooker's confession and gave him communion before his death (Walton, 160). In 1622 Francis White (*c.*1564–1638), rector of St Peter's, Cornhill, taught, in controversy with a Roman Catholic, that private confession, though not necessary for the remission of sins, was 'a godly discipline, consonant to Holy Scripture and anciently practised by the Primitive church' (More, 515). In the middle of the century Dr Vane of Crayford, near London, was accused of preaching 'that is was necessary for every man to confesse his sinnes to the Priest' (Hart, *CC* 120). The enormously popular devotional treatise *The Whole Duty of Man*, published in 1658, instructed its readers, as did the *Book of Common Prayer*, that if they found themselves unable to make their peace with God on their own they should consult a minister. Indeed, 'we are generally so apt to favour ourselves, that it might be very useful for most, especially the more ignorant sort, sometimes to advise with a spiritual guide' (*WDM* 70–2).

The issue of sacramental confession became a hotly contested one in the nineteenth century when Anglo-Catholics first re-introduced the practice and later insisted on it. The Tractarians employed the practice sparingly. John Keble* advocated it within his parish, not so much because it benefited the penitent, as because it gave the priest an insight into the spiritual needs and problems of his people. When Charlotte Keble was thought to be dying she communicated but there was no suggestion that she should make her confession (Battiscombe, *Keble* 179, 258). Arthur Stanton* was one of the greatest confessors of his time, but he offered the sacrament rather than required it. Nathaniel Woodard** provided it at his schools, but as a voluntary discipline, undertaken with the permission of parents (Heeney, 64).

In the nineteenth century the clergy who offered the confessional could expect to be traduced and harrassed. Nathaniel Woodard lost his first charge, St Bartholomew's, Bethnal Green, in 1843 because of a sermon advocating the practice (Heeney, 55). Another notable case was that of Arthur Wagner** who heard in 1865 the confession of a young woman named Constance Kent to the murder of her step-brother five years earlier. The murder had created great interest, and when Constance's public confession revealed that she had confessed privately a Protestant storm broke. It is hard to see why, since it had been Wagner's religious influence which impelled the girl to disclosure; but the issue quickly became whether Wagner could be compelled to reveal what Constance had said to him in the confessional. Legal opinions varied; Wagner himself was determined to remain silent; but the question was never resolved because Constance pleaded guilty at her trial. The affair focussed Protestant objections to the sacrament. The matter was raised in Parliament; a public meeting in Brighton resolved among other things that sacramental confession was 'contrary to the spirit of the Church of England, a violation of privacy and the sanctity of domestic life, an infringement of personal liberty, a fruitful source of immorality ... grossly corrupting those who make it and extremely pernicious to those who receive it'; and Wagner was attacked by ruffians in the street (Wagner, 105–18).

As time went on, sacramental confession became more widely acceptable, and some Anglo-Catholic clergy began to insist on it. The parish magazine of a village in the Lichfield diocese around 1900 contained the instruction: 'You will come to the church sometime before Easter and make your confession in the hearing of God's priest' (Pickering, 79). Harry Williams** describes how, at Cuddesdon theological college in the 1920s, the readiness to make one's confession was equated with total self-dedication to God (Williams, 94). I remember from my youth how, just as Evangelicals urged the absolute necessity of instantaneous and declared conversion, so Anglo-Catholics insisted on that of confession; in both cases the pressure applied was intense.

The practice of hearing confessions has not been confined to Anglo-Catholics. Nathaniel Woodard recalled that 'in 1827 when I was preparing for my first Communion I went and told my sins which pressed upon my conscience to a very Low Church clergyman in London, who urged me to do so, and who had hundreds of others applying to him' (Heeney, 53). Walter Hook took a typically robust attitude to confession: 'The Church of Rome makes it the rule – we the exception. The Church of Rome commands it; the Church of England permits it … The great aim of the priest who hears confessions should be to enable the person to do without his confession, as the aim of a doctor should be to enable his patient to do without a doctor' (Stephens, *Hook* 411, 579). W.C.E. Newbolt took it for granted in a book of advice to the clergy, *Speculum Sacerdotum*, published in 1894, that sacramental confession would be offered and practised, and wrote warmly and positively about it. Dick Sheppard habitually heard confessions (Scott, *Sheppard* 109).

Direction, formal or informal, is an essential element in Christian life; the clergy, who provide it for others, are well advised to secure it for themselves. The necessity of making a sacramental confession is best expressed in the familiar formula: all may, some should, none must.

9

Pastoring

He conceived it his duty and much delighted in the
obligation, that he was to treat every man in the whole
world as the representative of mankind, and that he
was to meet in him, and to pay unto him all the love
of God, Angels and Men. (Traherne, 4.27)

The Care of the Laity

As the very word 'pastoral' suggests, the pastoral ideal has usually been a
paternalistic one. Paternalism has considerable virtues; when the parish priest
is superior in background, education and income to the majority of his people it
is difficult and perhaps wrong to eschew it. George Herbert's* country priest
was 'a father to his flock ... as fully as if he had begot his whole parish'
(Herbert, XVI). 'Surely,' wrote Bishop Blomfield of London in 1834, 'it is not
possible to estimate at too high a rate the moral influence which is exerted by a
well educated and pious man stationed in the midst of a poor, unenlightened
population, labouring solely for their good ... inquiring with tenderness and
delicacy into their wants and woes, and devising methods for their relief;
assisting, superintending, perhaps conducting, the education of their children;
contriving and facilitating methods of economy and humble independence'
(Clark, 143). Though I work in a different age and in differing circumstances, I
think the local convention by which I am called Father Michael not inappropriate (I must confess, however, that I foresee a problem when my woman
deacon colleague is priested).

Paternalism gives standing. The priest has often been the natural mediator in
disputes among his parishioners. George Herbert's country parson 'endures
not that any of his flock should go to law; but in any controversy, that they
should resort to him as their judge'. He spends part of every Sunday 'reconciling neighbours that are at variance' (Herbert, VIII, XXIII). In 1770 James
Woodforde* called together the warring families in Castle Cary and persuaded
them to end the law suits going on between them (Woodforde, 1.98).

Ralph Josselin* records well over a score of instances of mediation. He dealt
with disputes between landlords and tenants, between creditors and debtors,
between father and son, between a working man and a soldier who had
wounded him. He was prepared to use his own money to speed the process of
reconciliation, and intervened to bring law suits to an end. He writes of one
quarrel: 'An arbitration between sisters was submitted to mee, the lord in
mercy helpe mee to walke in wisedome uprightly. I desire to deliver a poor
shiftles one from the hand of another that would oppresse, and yet [sic] to

releive the oppressed'; of another: 'Made an end of all difference ... oh how I rejoyce to doe good to a person that gives mee no respect, lord for thy sake, I shall deny my selfe through grace.' His work as a mediator was one of the most productive parts of his ministry. The spirit in which he undertook it is summed up in his reflection when he had made up 'divers quarrels': 'Lord ... blesse mee who desire peace with thee, and love it, and for thy sake with all others, remember the peacemakers for the sake of the prince of peace' (Josselin, 356, 382, 457; see also passim, and especially 104, 107, 278, 288, 361, 409, 609).

Paternalism has been demonstrated in other ways. Josselin was on a number of occasions employed as a matchmaker (see, for example, Josselin 74, 585). James Woodforde cared for others' money, paying interest and requiring six months notice for repayment; a mutually advantageous arrangement (Woodforde, 1.55).

In the exercise of pastoral authority, a shrewd understanding of human nature has been indispensable. George Herbert's country parson kept 'God's watch' over his people, but prevented wicked speech or quarrelling less by direct rebuke than by the use of humour: 'A pleasantness of disposition is of great use, men being willing to sell the interest and engagement of their discourses for no price sooner than that of mirth' (Herbert, XVIII). J. C. Atkinson** wanted a difficult piece of land drained; the local poacher was eminently qualified for the work but his profession was an obstacle; so Atkinson made a treaty with him that he should have the work if he did not poach while engaged on it (Addison, 200).

Atkinson's concern was an example of another clerical characteristic – tenderness towards the outcast. Thomas Traherne* wrote: 'The worse they [bad men] are the more they were to be pitied and tended and desired, because they had more need, and were more miserable' (Traherne, 4.26). 'A special kindness,' W.C.E. Newbolt declared, 'will lead him [the priest] towards those whom the world regards as the unfortunate, the disagreeable, the unprepossessing' (Newbolt, 117–8). When Arthur Stanton* was dying he gave £10 to be distributed among 'the *undeserving* poor' (Russell, *Stanton* 309).

The clergy are often in a position to observe social extremes. William Bennett* wrote of his experiences in London: 'Many an evening walk ... has brought me, by some pastoral duty ... from one extreme right into the midst of the other. I have gone forth from the lowest degradation of squalid misery and filth, into the glittering display of festivity and magnificence. I have come forth from the sound of wailing children wanting food, and sat down in the brilliant assemblies of joyous, thoughtless, self-indulging creatures, without a desire ungratified or a want unsupplied' (Bennett, 48).

Impressed by such contrasts and driven by the imperatives of their calling some clergy have discriminated in favour of the disadvantaged. 'I am a clergyman, sir,' declared Mrs Oliphant's Frank Wentworth. 'If a man in my position is good for anything, it is his business to help the helpless' (Oliphant,

PC 402). Faced with the agricultural riots of the 1830s, the magistrates' bench at North Walsham, Norfolk, which consisted of five clergymen and three laymen, published a document condemning threshing machines and the low pay of labourers. They also discharged thirty machine breakers (Virgin, 10–11). It was said of Julius Hare* that the only persons with whom he was never harsh were his sister-in-law Maria and the poor. Walter Hook* received the poor daily; the times set aside for other parishioners were less frequent (Stephens, *Hook* 284). In 1851 T.T. Carter, rector of Clewer, Berkshire, assisted with the creation of the Community of St John Baptist, an order of nuns dedicated to helping the poor; the order spread widely (Pickering, 131). Robert Hawker* said: 'The poor man ought to be called Master and Lord for so he is' (Brendon, *Hawker* 114). Dick Sheppard*, though he treated everyone with distinction, recognized a special vocation to the poor and dispossessed; from his first months in the East End he discerned Christ in them (Roberts, *Sheppard* 39).

A special instance of this ministry has been a concern for prisoners. Charles Simeon* visited both the local Cambridge gaol and the notorious Newgate. He prompted conversions in a number of criminals condemned to death and remarked of one that he had 'good hopes he will go from gallows to glory' (Hopkins, *Simeon* 53).

A preoccupation with the disadvantaged has sometimes proved costly. Trollope's Mr Crawley got into trouble with the local farmers because he crowded out Hogglestock church with the brickmakers whom his assiduous ministry had attracted (Trollope, *LC* 131). More commonly, however, the costliness has been of an opposite character: the great mass of working-class people have always been indifferent to the Church of England. No one tried harder, or with more success, than Walter Hook; but even he wrote, in the heyday of Victorian religion: 'Christianity scarcely exists among the mass. They are no longer sectarians, but are utterly indifferent to religion, looking upon it generally as a luxury for the rich' (Stephens, *Hook* 419). The greatest of the Victorian slum priests were doing well if they attracted one in ten of the population to church.

Perhaps the most characteristic pastoral experience for priests in working-class areas is that of failure. Cosmo Lang** concluded that, as a curate in Leeds, he failed both in bringing the poorest to Christ and in helping any one of the street boys in whom he took a special interest to make good (Lockhart, *Lang* 98). Lang, of course, was not in Leeds for long; but even slum heroes such as Arthur Stanton and Robert Dolling* loved their people more for what they were than for what they were able to help them to become.

It has been important therefore to remember that the function of the priest, as R.W. Evans taught in *The Bishopric of Souls*, is to minister to Christ in the other; so the reaction of the person concerned is not of great importance (Evans, ch. 14). Nor of course is his or her character. 'The true call to the priesthood is tested and shown in the power to love people who are unattractive or downright horrible.' Thus Joseph Williamson**, a slum priest of our own time. He was himself a graceless lad; but he was saved for Christ and the priesthood by Fr Dawson, of St Saviour's, Poplar, who spent time and trouble on him and provided a role model: 'We East End lads looked up to our priests ... What they said we believed; what they did was right' (Williamson, 50, 52).

Driven by Christian ideals of love and neighbourliness, clergy have sought to live on close terms with their parishioners. George Herbert's country parson thought Sunday evenings 'a very fit time ... to entertain some of his neighbours, or to be entertained of them, where he takes occasion to discourse of such things as are both profitable and pleasant' (Herbert, VIII). Walter Hook relied on simple friendliness, to such effect that one of his parishioners asked him to have his photograph printed and sold cheaply, so that his people could hang it up in their houses (Stranks, *Hook* 90). Harold Hosking** was one of those modern parsons who have set dignity aside in order to identify themselves with parish activities. In his case the activity was dramatics, provoking the comment: 'Tis coming to a pretty pass ... the Vicar chasing a lot of naked maids round the stage' (Hosking, 63). Setting dignity aside in another way, Father Joe Williamson of Stepney went 'straight from an early Holy Communion service to carry coal, light the fire, sweep up, and make tea for some old lady who is too old or ill to go down four flights of stairs to fetch coal for herself' (Williamson, 137–8).

Nicolas Stacey** has put this point in general terms. 'It is difficult for priests to be dispassionate about the congregations committed to their care ... It is difficult not to love those whose secrets one knows, whose sorrows one has shared and whose battles one helps to fight ... we coaxed them and cuddled them. We scolded them and sometimes swore at them, and laughed with them too. We prayed with them in private and did knees-up-Mother-Brown with them at parish socials in public. We visited them when they were sick and held their hands as they died' (Stacey, 123–4).

Unfortunately the nature of the flock has sometimes militated against close relations. John Newton's* bell ringers at Olney were, he related, 'often drunk and when drunk no better than Mad' (Martin, *Newton* 237). Sidney Smith* described the people of Combe Florey as 'drunken, wretched and degraded' (Bell, *Smith* 149). Francis Kilvert loved the people of Clyro, but we learn from his diary that they were obstinate and backward, and capable of gratuitous cruelty to the weak. In the course of his ministry there he came across drunkenness, prostitution, illegitimacy, violence and theft. Later, he wrote of a conversation with a parishioner at Langley Burrell: 'He and his wife told me things about the parish which drew aside the veil from my eyes and showed me in what an atmosphere and abyss of wickedness we are living and how little many people are to be trusted whom we thought respectable and good' (Kilvert, 2.444). Robert Hawker was surrounded with viciousness and brutality, by cruelty to animals and drunkenness. For fear of violence he kept a revolver and searched his house every night before bedtime. Cosmo Lang, remembering the district of Leeds which he served as a curate, wrote of his people: 'Some of them, especially the women … were worse than beasts, for beasts are not degraded. I seem to see now their unkempt hair, their tattered clothes, their bleared eyes looking out at me with sullen suspicion' (Lockhart, *Lang* 96). Gethyn Owen, parish priest of the Suffolk village of Akenfield in the years after the Second World War said of his people 'at the imaginative or creative level … all … had been blunted and crushed by toil' (Blythe, 77).

The root cause of most barbarism has been poverty, a fact which some of the clergy have had to learn by experience. Margaret Oliphant's Cicely St John explained to the ingenuous young clergyman who has come to take over her father's ministry: 'You don't know the village people. If you speak to them of high ideals, they would only open their mouths and stare. If it was something to make a little money by, poor souls! or to get new boots for their children, or even to fatten the pigs. Now you are disgusted, Mr Mildmay; but you don't know how poor the people are, and how little time they have for anything but just what is indispensable for living' (Oliphant, *CC* 106–7).

More generally, a parish priest has not been able to assume that he would be regarded with warmth and good will. Ralph Josselin was hurt when no single person welcomed him to Earls Colne, 'which seemed to mee an unkind part'. In 1652 he complained: 'I find … in people a coldnes towards mee, and little of love and affection, which,' he resolved, 'shall not dampe but quicken mee, knowing my worke shall not bee in vaine in the lord whatsoever entertainment it meete withall from men.' He could also count his blessings. After a visit to a clerical relation he wrote: 'My uncle hath a great living, but a bad people, I preferre my condicion to his' (Josselin, 10, 275, 177). John Skinner* was literally driven to distraction by his people's hostility. In a typical incident he worked hard to secure the release from prison of one of his servants, only to hear that local gossip was naming him the father of of the family's baby (Skinner, 51–5). R.W. Evans warned his readers that in the early days of parochial ministry 'the warmth of approbation is succeeded by the coolness of criticism'. He also made a point which every active parish priest has validated in his own experience: 'The more you do, the more they [your flock] will think lies in your power, and the more they will expect from you' (Evans, 25, 10).

Parsons have reacted to ill-usage on the part of their parishioners both with charity and with indignation. Josselin reported in 1647: 'The lord tried mee with scornes and reproaches … I was taxed for lording, and domineering … in some measure god gave mee patience and wisedome to silence the mouth of such persons' (Josselin, 100). In 1755 George Woodward's** garden was damaged by parishioners. In response Woodward nailed on his church door a manifesto 'showing my concern at such ill usage from a parish, wherein I had always behaved as a friend to them all … assuring them, that I heartily forgave them this time; but if ever I should find any one guilty of the same another time, they were not to expect such indulgence, for it was transportation if not felony [which carried the death penalty] by the Black Act' (Woodward, 70–2). Henry Alford** turned the other cheek in his reply to a parishioner who had responded to a rebuke by charging Alford with negligence. 'Regarding my own pastoral deficiencies, I heartily thank you [for his remarks]. I am deeply aware that I am not "sufficient for these things", and only wish my place were better filled. At the same time the deficiencies of one man do not excuse another. Let us both strive and pray that we may be found diligent in our business, fervent in spirit, serving the Lord our God, and so our best to live in charity and peace with one another and with all men' (Alford, 170–1).

In the face of indifference or hostility among their parishioners clergy have sought solace in personal friendships. Josselin was devoted to the unmarried Mary Church, who was good to him both emotionally and financially. She cared for him in sickness, assisted with the delivery of a child, and supported him when the baby died. The months of May and June 1650 when he lost both her and two of his children was one of the bleakest periods of his life. He was not helped by his personal theology, since the message he received from the Lord was 'sin no more lest a worse thing happen unto thee' (Josselin, 80, 111, 114, 90, 210, 205).

Josselin made friends with someone of his own class. Trollope's Frank Fenwick was less wise. He was rebuked by the local squire for his association with Sam Brattle, scapegrace son of the local miller and Fenwick's companion on ferreting and fishing expeditions. Fenwick's rueful response was: 'I ... know very well I have got to choose between two things. I must be called a hypocrite or else I must be one. I have no doubt that as years go on with me I shall see the advantage of choosing the latter' (Trollope, *VB* 114).

Fenwick was an exception. Parish priests' personal friends have, at least until recent times, usually been drawn from the higher orders of society, thus increasing their dependence upon their affluent neighbours' good will and distancing them from their poorer parishioners. Conscious of this difficulty, some clergy have deliberately avoided forming personal friendships with parishioners, in order to be seen to be equally accessible to all. William Andrew's* refusal to dine out was for this reason.

A sort of distancing has been a necessity if a parson is to be free to do his work properly. Josselin declared: 'I love no quarrells, I seeke peace, but I will not offend god to gayne the same.' He sought out a woman 'to admonish her in respect of her peevishnes the worke was solemne, and the lord I blesse him was with mee in the same ... the lord in mercy perswade her heart thoroughly' (Josselin, 25, 242). Bishop Jeremy Taylor advised: 'Let no minister be governed by the opinion of his people, and destroy his duty by unreasonable compliance with their humours ... Strive to get the love of the congregation, but let it not degenerate into popularity' (*CI* 70, 72). Charles Simeon is said to have directed his trustees never to appoint any clergyman whom the parishioners wished for, because they were the worst judges of what they stood in need (Garratt, 213). I incurred local odium when I offered ministry to a group of travellers who ensconced themselves within this parish. Fortunately, although sensitive to the dislike of others, I am, as an ex-headmaster, used to surviving it.

Since the seventeenth century most parish priests have numbered Dissenters among their parishioners. Their attitudes to Dissent have some-times been of unmitigated and reciprocated hostility. In a pamphlet published in 1740, William Bowman, vicar of Dewsbury, Yorkshire, described Methodists as 'furious disciples of Antichrist, reverend scavengers, filthy pests and plagues of mankind' (Balleine, 33). A tract written by John Kirby, rector of Blackmanstone, Kent, was entitled *A full discovery of the horrid Blasphemies taught by those Diabolical Seducers called Methodists* (Balleine, 32). Returning to his parish of Muston in 1805 after thirteen years of absenteeism, George Crabbe** found a diminished congregation and a thriving Wesleyan community. He underwent the humiliation of seeing two of his own servants join the more extreme Huntingdonians, in the case of one of them as a preacher (Crabbe, 1.181–2). He took his revenge in verse:

See yonder Preacher! to his people pass,
Borne up and swell'd by tabernacle gas; ...
He rails, persuades, explains and moves the will
By fierce bold words and strong mechanic skill.

(Crabbe 3.87; from 'The Borough: Sects and Professions in Religion'. It should be added that in his final parish of Trowbridge Crabbe both preached and practised toleration and co-operation – see Crabbe 1.221–2.)

Robert Hargreaves, who succeeded William Grimshaw* at Todmarden was accused by the local Methodists of using 'grievous and ireful' language about them. He retorted that they had described him as 'not being an orthodox shepherd caring for his sheep and protecting them, but more like a wolf-dog always barking at them, and scaring them away from the fold, and minded neither their bleatings nor their rendings asunder so he got the fleece' (Baker, *Grimshaw* 107). Patrick Bronte's** curates at Haworth were so virulent against Dissent that they provoked a refusal to pay the Church rate (Gaskell, *Bronte* 173–5). As late as 1898 the young Cyril Garbett** caused embarrassment by attacking the credentials of Dissent in a lecture in his late father's parish (Smyth, *Garbett* 491).

Nor have parish priests confined themselves to verbal violence. In 1748 George White, curate of Colne, Lancashire, incited a mob against Methodists led by his fellow Anglican priests John Wesley and William Grimshaw (Barrow, 99). In 1800 a Baptist minister who held a cottage meeting was brought before a parson magistrate who fined him, his host and the members of his congregation (Addison, 137). 'Starve you we will,' said a nineteenth-century clerical Poor Law Guardian to a widow, 'unless you forsake these meetings' (Brendon, *Hawker* 171). In the 1830s a parson arranged for a Primitive Methodist preacher and those listening to him at Newark market to be hosed by the local fire engine (Chadwick, *VC* 1.388). In the 1870s the vicar of Owston Ferry, Lincolnshire, refused to allow the gravestone of a Wesleyan minister to bear the inscription 'Reverend' (Chadwick, *VC* 2.204; the case was taken to the Privy Council and the vicar lost).

Hostility stood in the way of ministry. In the 1830s the curate of Milford, Yorkshire, refused to read the burial service over the unbaptized child of Baptist parents, and John Henry Newman** refused to conduct the marriage of the unbaptized daughter of a Baptist pastrycook (Chadwick, *VC* 1.63). Both were technically within their rights. The young John Keble* recognized only a limited pastoral responsibility to Dissenters and took a grim view of their condition: 'They may be ... in a certain sense exempted from one's care, but I think one would do better not to consider them as being so in theory – one would have one's eye on them ... just as one would watch over people guilty of other sins, humanly speaking incurable' (Battiscombe, *Keble* 55).

There were grounds for Anglican hostility and suspicion. Memories of the Commonwealth and Protectorate were not easily exorcised. Oliver Heywood, the seventeenth-century dissenting minister and diarist, made a practice of preaching in local churches, sometimes when no clergyman had turned up to take service, but on occasion excluding the clergyman from his own pulpit (Heywood, passim; see especially 1.263). Josselin, noticing some Anabaptists in church, wondered if they were planning a takeover. He also feared, with some justice, that a service he took at Gaines Colne might be disrupted by the local 'quakers nest'. The Quakers of his own parish 'set up a paper on the church door' accosted him with argument or caused minor disturbances in his church (Josselin, 308, 348, 350).

George Crabbe wrote passionately about the local Huntingdonians: 'There is yet their imagined contention with the powers of darkness, that is at once so lamentable and so ludicrous. There is the same offensive familiarity with the Deity, with a full trust and confidence both in the immediate efficacy of their miserably delivered supplications, and in the reality of numberless small miracles wrought at their request and for their convenience ... it is painful to the mind of a soberly devout person, when he hears every rise and fall of the animal spirits, every whim and motion of enthusiastic ignorance, expressed in the venerable language of the apostles and evangelists' (Crabbe, 3.66–7). In Robert Hawker's part of Cornwall a Methodist sect, called the Bryanites after their leader, was strong. Their worship was exuberant, ecstatic and occasionally corybantic and added substance to Hawker's contentions that Methodism originated in sexual feeling and gave rise to sexual immorality. He referred to

John Wesley as 'that father of English fornication', and was convinced that the central Evangelical experience of instantaneous conversion was akin to an orgasm (Brendon, *Hawker* 70, 168).

It was a further cause of offence that the Bryanites were of low social standing. Hawker was on better terms with the wealthy local farmer and Dissenting preacher who was his churchwarden. But he declared: 'I never spare heresy or schism ministerially.' He attacked Dissent and Dissenters savagely, referring to a visit from a Nonconformist minister as an 'audacious intrusion' and preaching about a Nonconformist minister to the text: 'Abide ye here with the ass, while I and the lad go yonder and worship' (Brendon, *Hawker* 170–4).

Hawker rightly saw Dissent as an attack on social as well as ecclesiastical order; it was thus doubly offensive to Churchmen who saw themselves as the defenders of both. In times when it was almost unthinkable not to be a professing Christian, the chapel offered (as in Trollope's Bullhampton) an opportunity of repudiating the established order without repudiating the faith (Trollope, *VB* 385).

Inevitably there have been local power struggles between Church and Dissent. In John Conybeare's** parish dissenting employers deliberately kept men at work on festival days to prevent them going to church (Colloms, 255). Francis Kilvert noted in 1872 that an election for a Poor Law Guardian was creating high party feeling between Church and Chapel. 'The dissenters are behaving badly.' He recorded an anecdote about the Methyr Dissenters being preached into voting for a candidate in a General Election, and commented: 'Talk about being priest-ridden, 'tis nothing to being ridden by political dissenting preachers'. Attending a meeting for the Liberation Society (which sought disestablishment) in Chippenham in 1876, he rejoiced that the church-warden he had invited left the meeting with 'a profound contempt for the lecturer, the Liberation Society and Dissent generally' (Kilvert, 2.166, 189; 3.296–7).

John Skinner's journal describes in some detail relationships between one parish priest and his Methodist parishioners. The story is not a happy one, though Skinner's faults of temperament excuse us from concluding that it was typical. It was a constant source of exasperation to Skinner, who was a faithful visitor, to find Methodists ministering at the bedside of the Methodist sick. Though he grudgingly admitted on one occasion that their constant attendance had been of service, he felt that they were poaching on his preserves, and disapproved of their emphasis on instantaneous conversion and their tendency to regard a death-bed repentance as 'a sufficient satisfaction for an ill-spent life'. He came across cases of individuals panicked by brimstone teaching, and took a severe line with a woman who claimed to have had visions of Jesus. He engaged in theological argument with Methodist leaders, rather weakening the intellectual force of his case by threatening them with the law if they continued to meet for worship in private houses. Perhaps ignoring the difference between their means and his, he accused them in his journal of lack of practical generosity to each other. He scornfully described parishioners moving from Church to Chapel and back again as economic advantage prescribed.

None the less, Skinner called on the teacher of the local Methodist school to enquire whether any of his pupils might wish to be confirmed. Many of his Methodist parishioners attended church, especially to communicate, and he was vigilant to observe any falling-off. Using their own weapons against them, he pointed out that John Wesley had advocated frequent communion in the parish church; but he was not prepared to adapt his preaching to make them feel welcome. He preached with intent on the text: 'In the latter time shall come those who have itching ears, and will not endure sound doctrine' (Skinner, passim; see especially 26–7, 40, 66, 81, 91–4, 185, 205, 213, 232, 340, 443).

There have been more kindly attitudes to Dissent. George Herbert's country parson thought it his duty to bring holders of 'strange doctrines' back to the 'common faith', but his methods were gentle. He prayed for Dissenters, and engaged in 'a very loving and sweet usage of them, both in going to and sending for them often, and in finding out courtesies to place upon them; as in their tithes, or otherwise' (Herbert, XXIV). Ralph Josselin argued with the anabaptist Samuel Oates, father of the notorious Titus, but 'without passion'. He secured the release of a pacifist anabaptist from military service (Josselin, 63, 38).

William Jones** wrote approvingly in 1806: 'Mr Millar, the vicar of Harlow, Essex, who is a very mild, benevolent man is, I am told, often seen "arm in arm" with the dissenting Minister, who is settled in his parish' (Hart, *ECCP* 70). John Henry Newman, visiting as a young curate in St Clement's, Oxford, took 'care always to speak kindly of Mr Hinton, the dissenting minister' (Faber, 152). William Bennett who, as we shall see below, had strong views, was on good personal terms with local Dissenters because he abolished the church rate (Bennett, 213). Even Robert Hawker was careful not to discriminate between church people and Dissenters when it was a question of supplementing labourers' wages (Brendon, *Hawker* 106).

Clerical reactions to Dissent have even included admiration. William Grimshaw wrote: 'I love all denominations ... so far ... as I find them endued with the Holy Spirit' (Baker, *Grimshaw* 241). Sydney Smith told Quakers 'you obtain something which we do not' (Bell, *Smith* 105). J.C. Atkinson was quite prepared to let his 'good old friends' the Quakers wear their hats in church for funerals. Robert Dolling attributed national loyalty to the English Bible and the English Sunday largely to non-conformist influence, and declared: 'It makes me ... sick at heart to hear the way in which the newly-ordained, strong in the orthodoxy of his High Church collar ... speaks of these class leaders, at whose feet he is unworthy to sit' (Osborne, *Dolling* 211). Samuel Garratt** wrote to the Mayor of Ipswich in 1881 to say that the work of the Salvation Army 'however little in some of its details it is in accordance with our own taste, is as a whole God's work, and therefore to be cordially welcomed'. He asked the Mayor to give the Army fair play and to use the police to protect them from the mob (Garratt, 85).

Although many Anglicans were repelled as Garratt was by the vulgarities of the Salvation Army, many more were moved by its enthusiasm and its success with the poor. Salvationists were invited to Anglican services, and came. In 1882 large numbers of them communicated at Eucharists held in York and Northallerton. They were afforded the sincerest form of flattery when the Kensington curate Wilson Carlile (1847–1942) founded the Church Army (Chadwick, *VC* 2.295–9).

Tolerance made good sense when, as we have seen in the case of John Skinner's parish, Dissenters continued their connection with the parish church as well as worshipping elsewhere. Even after the Methodists became to all intents a separate denomination in 1795, most of them continued to be married and buried by local incumbents and many went to both church and chapel. Henry Fardell* was very gratified when in 1851 the local Methodist minister came to hear him preach and congratulated him on a sermon. The same minister came with several of his congregation to take the sacrament on Christmas Day. Fardell also noted instances of other Dissenters attending church, and of one applying for a pew (Fardell, 120). As late as 1870 there were chapels where the Eucharist was not celebrated and where there was no worship at the times of church services (Chadwick, *VC* 1.370–1). Not all clergy thought this eirenicism appropriate, however. William Bennett told the Frome Dissenters that to go to both church and chapel imperilled their salvation. 'It is either of great consequence to be a Dissenter, or it is not. If it is not, then why do they not come forth out of their schism, and rejoin the Church … But if it be of consequence to be a Dissenter, then why do they come and play with the church and amuse themselves with hearing sermons, and partake in worship which in their own opinion and by their own showing is sinful and injurious?' (Bennett, 244).

Tolerance can both disarm and weaken. William Jones argued for friendliness on those grounds: 'If they are obdurate, such conduct will melt them down: if they have any gall, this will extract it' (Hart, *ECCP* 70). Trollope's Mr Puddleham, dissenting minister at Bullhampton, was 'painfully conscious of the guile of this young man [the vicar Frank Fenwick], who had, as it were, cheated him out of that appropriate acerbity of religion, without which a proselytizing sect can hardly maintain its ground beneath the shadow of an endowed and domineering Church' (Trollope, *VB* 239). Henry Alford, who advocated generosity and moderation as principles, added 'above all, should we be anxious to maintain our hold upon them by being constant comforters in their hours of distress, and attendants by their beds of sickness and death' (Alford, 124). R.W. Evans advised his readers to minister assiduously to separatists, taking advantage of the fact that Anglican clergy had more time available than Dissenting ministers, who were for the most part part-timers, and playing upon superior 'education and status in society' (Evans, 18–19).

Even before modern times, when it is taken for granted, active co-operation was not unknown. The Puritans set a precedent; Josselin wrote with approval: 'My neighbours at Halsted, entered into fellowship with the neighbour Independent church lord direct their hearts therein unto thee only, and let them beautify the gospel, and bring honour to thy name thereby' (Josselin, 322). George Bull**, who fell out with Bradford dissenters over a number of issues, continued to work with them in the temperance cause (Gill, *Bull* 108–9). Walter Hook, who had suffered at dissenting hands, co-operated with them over the creation of a local Penitentiary [refuge for prostitutes]. He referred to the local Dissenters as 'that respectable body of men ... I would never refuse to co-operate with dissenters, when I could do so without compromising the principles of the Church.' He went on to say: 'There is a line between us, but over that line we shake hands' (Stephens, *Hook* 88, 104). Robert Dolling worked closely with the local Baptist minister at Landport to try and lessen the excessive hours worked by shop assistants. He was a leading light in the interdenominational Portsmouth Social Purity Organization, founded in 1893 (Osborne, *Dolling* 122, 139).

The natural allies of Dissent within the Church of England were the Evangelicals; both because of a shared history and theology and because of a common hostility to Roman Catholicism. John Newton got on well with all who preached the gospel of salvation through Jesus Christ; he was friendly with the Baptists of Olney and with Dissenters generally. He told his wife that he could see nothing wrong in her communicating when she attended a Congregational chapel, though he thought himself precluded from doing so as a minister of the Establishment (Martin, *Newton* 254, 301 and passim). Edward Bickersteth** was one of the founding figures of the Evangelical Alliance, set up in 1846 and uniting Protestants of all denominations against Popery and Puseyism. In a letter he put a view which has become common since but which most of his brother clergy at the time would have vehemently repudiated: 'The Church of England is not the whole church of Christ in England. It probably was once; but for our sins ... it might to a great extent have been so now ... though we should aim at this [unity] in the way truth, forbearance and love, we must also humble ourselves before God for our exceeding church sinfulness, which has prevented our dissenting brethren from recovering the light of truth which we really enjoy, and has ... engaged their Zeal even directly against what we believe to be the truth of God' (Hennell, 48–9).

For Dissenters Anglican clergy have often felt dislike and contempt; for Roman Catholics Evangelicals in particular have often felt active hatred. The gentle John Fletcher* greeted the news of a Roman Catholic church in Madeley with the words: 'I have declared war ... and propose to strip the Whore of

Babylon, and expose her nakedness tomorrow' (Benson, *Fletcher* 117). Hugh Stowell, a much loved parish priest in a difficult area of Manchester in the early nineteenth century served his own people admirably but was also a tribal leader against the Irish Roman Catholic population (Clark, 71–2). Even the generally charitable Samuel Garratt attacked the stirrings of ecumenism in the 1860s by arguing that to unite with Rome, or indeed with the Orthodox churches, would be 'to commit fornication with the mystical Babylon, and to involve ourselves in her plagues' (Garratt, 78).

Inevitably, we turn to John Skinner for an example of hostility between a parish priest and a Roman Catholic parishioner. For years Skinner was on uneasy terms with Samuel Day, a Roman Catholic farmer of his parish. He supected Day of cheating him of his ecclesiastical revenue, and sniped at him for not observing Good Friday. Day annoyed Skinner by trying to get vestries changed from a Sunday to a Monday, and at a vestry so bandied words with him that he vowed to stay away in future.

All this was small beer, however, compared with an event in 1824. Day had insisted on being tithed in kind, instead of making a composition and paying a sum in cash. This made for inconvenience all round, and Skinner took exception to the way the tithing of a field of barley was carried out. An altercation with Day took a religious turn, with Skinner saying that *his* religion was not one of tricks. Day, not unnaturally infuriated, offered such provocation to Skinner that the latter struck him. In his defence at the ensuing court action Skinner alleged that Day's behaviour had been 'supported and encouraged' by the staff of Downside and that his refusal to compound was through dislike to the Defendant as a Protestant Ecclesiastic'. None the less Skinner had to pay £50 damages (Skinner, 187, 198, 239, 261–3, 272–4, 282–3).

Even before the nineteenth century and Tractarianism there were, however, parish priests who felt a kinship with Roman Catholics on both religious and social grounds. Richard Hooker** maintained that 'the church of Rome, though not pure or perfect, yet is a true church; so that such who live and die therein ... may be saved' (Fuller, *CH* 3.142). William Cole, who socialized with a Benedictine monk, quoted from Roman Catholic literature and used dates from the Roman calendar in his diary. He wrote of the Catholic Church 'supposing it much debased and corrupted, yet minds its Externals, and takes [more] Care of the Morals of its People ... than ours can pretend to'. When he was asked by his bishop for a list of local Papists, he reflected: 'Why don't the Bps enquire after the growth of Dissenters of multifarious denominations? After Atheists, Deists and Libertines, surely these are more dangerous to our Constitution and Christianity in general than Papists, whose tenets are submission to Government and Order' (Cole, 5, 23, 255–6). Cole's attitude was shared by many eighteenth-century clergy, especially in the North, who had considerable numbers of Roman Catholics in their parishes and thought it essential to live on good terms with them (Addison, *ECCP* 67–8). In addition, gentry were gentry, no matter their denomination. In the early eighteenth century Nicholas Blundell, a Roman Catholic country gentleman of Lancashire, was friendly with several Anglican clergy; though parson Ellison, rector of Formby, once laid an information against him and cost him £2 7s 9d in fees and payments (Blundell, 75–6, 81). After a conversation in 1824 with the highly civilized Lord Arundel even John Skinner was inclined to look more kindly on Catholic claims: 'Are not these likely to become as good citizens and subjects as the puritanical levelling Methodists and Presbyterians?' (Skinner, 259).

The growth of ecumenism has been one of the most important spiritual changes of the twentieth century. It has of course been in large part the product of a sense of weakness, but more positive and generous attitudes have not been lacking either. In the little Kentish village of Shepherdswell in the 1990s, parents of all denominations, as of none, allowed their children to receive 'Church teaching' from the parish priest; there were regular shared services and frequent shared activities; house groups were interdenominational; and I was as sure of a warm welcome in Free Church and Roman Catholic homes as in Anglican ones. So far as local Christians were concerned it was unthinkable that things should be otherwise; and in this the village was typical rather than exceptional.

The editor of Henry Fardell's* diary contends: 'The portrait of the Church [in Wisbech at the time of his ministry] ... is not that of a gathered congregation with a mission to the wider community of the Parish. Rather, the Church is the Town at prayer; and the work of the Town is the church at work' (Fardell, 211). Despite the presence of Dissenters and Roman Catholics, that has often been the case, in the country even more than in the town; but today the situation is different. Perhaps the greatest tension in modern Anglican pastoral ministry has been created by the obligation to care both for those who are active members of the Christian community and for those who are not.

The tension is not entirely new. At no time has it been the case that a priest could expect his ministry to be universally accepted. Ralph Josselin's vast and detailed diary contains references to only 250 local inhabitants out of a total at any one time of about 1100. He lamented in 1661 'persons wonderfull profane and neglective of gods worship'. On the departure of a parishioner from Earls Colne he lamented: 'the lord thins our towne of christian people much, the lord in mercy make up our losses herein' (Josselin, 484, 140). But Josselin set exacting standards of commitment. Then and until the nineteenth century people who would claim they were not Christians were rare indeed. Even in the nineteenth and early twentieth centuries professed non-Christians were a tiny minority, and about half the population were churchgoers. But in the later twentieth century the decline in churchgoing and in even nominal Christian allegiance has been catastrophic, and has challenged the clergy to decide what should be their pastoral obligations to the unchurched majority.

The most usual strategy has been to know and be known to as many people as possible, and to be available to churchgoer and non-churchgoer alike. When Nicolas Stacey was a curate in Portsea in the 1950s he was one of a team of seven priests serving 6000 households. About 10% of the population went to church but the clergy reckoned that they were in touch with 80% of their people (Stacey, 45–6). In the 1990s about 240 of the population of 1800 of Shepherdswell, Kent, were in some kind of meaningful contact with the parish church (a figure not including those who made use of the rites of passage but were not seen in church again). I knew all of them well, but was also on personal terms with nearly a thousand other people in the village, who between them absorbed a substantial proportion of pastoral time.

The spiritual effect of ministering to the secularized can be considerable. As I have visited scores of people, shared their joys and sorrows, and reflected on any help I have been able to give them, I have found it less and less possible to believe that effective ministry invariably requires the use of Christian references and terminology. I have seemed to be doing something useful simply by being there and by listening, by being what I am and by talking about any topic my interlocutors have chosen. I have concluded that the parish priest is still in the old sense a parson – a person who is seen to embody the values of the local community, and whose ministry structures personal experience by setting it in a wider context. His value to the bulk of his parishioners depends upon a commitment which they do not share but none the less value. They are unlikely to make much in the way of a positive response; but in the contact of the priest with the parishioner the Church has served the world.

Visiting

George Herbert's* country priest went visiting on weekday afternoons. He blessed each house as he entered it and then spoke as he found. He fortified those engaged in religious activity and commended those attending to their work, warning them, however, not to give too great a priority to worldly affairs or to the acquisition of wealth. With the poor he opened 'not only his mouth but his purse to their relief'. The idle or ill employed he rebuked: those of the lower class bluntly and those of the higher tactfully, not refraining simply because other people were about. In all cases he questioned the household about their religious practice, and whenever possible heard the children read (Herbert, XIV).

Although his methods were more intrusive than has been usual, Herbert's parson stood in a long tradition. Jeremy Taylor wrote that 'every minister ought frequently to converse with his parishioners; to go to their houses, but always publicly with witness, and with prudence, lest what is charitably intended be scandalously reported' (*CI* 180). Bishop Burnet (1643–1715) gave similar advice, though his demands on time were modest: in town parishes an hour of brief visits twice or thrice a week (*CI* 177–8). John Newton* was an assiduous visitor at Olney; his visits were a refreshment to women spending ten hours a day lace-making. As soon as he became curate of St Clement's, Oxford, John Henry Newman** undertook a house to house visitation (Faber, 152). At about the same time W.M. Praed was writing in his poem 'The Vicar':

And he was kind and loved to sit
In the low hut or garnished cottage,
And praise the farmer's homely wit,
And share the widow's homelier pottage;
At his approach complaint grew mild;
And when his hand unbarred the shutter,
The clammy lips of fever smiled
The welcome which they could not utter.

The Victorians took visiting very seriously. George Wagner (1818–57), curate to a non-resident Vicar at Dallington, Sussex, from 1842 to 1848, visited each of his 600 parishioners every six weeks (Wagner, 93). After Sunday service John Keble* walked to the homes of parishioners who lived at a distance (Battiscombe, *Keble* 349). R.W. Evans, writing in the middle of the century, suggested that in a parish spread over 12 square miles and containing 1500 people, the priest should over six days visit the whole area of the parish on foot, making about fifty calls (Evans, 30). Brenda Colloms has calculated that Francis Kilvert* visited regularly at least 90 out of the 130 families in Clyro and 24 out of the 34 at Bettws (Colloms, 187). At Bredwardine he tried to see every parishioner at least once a fortnight (Grice, *Kilvert* 82). Edward King** advised his clergy to visit every home in the parish five times a year (Elton, *King* 120). Writing at the turn of the century W.C.E. Newbolt stressed that missions were no substitute for systematic visiting (Newbolt, 49).

Nor has the tradition of regular visiting been lost in our own century. A curate under J.W. Willink, rector of St Helens, Lancashire, from 1891 to 1904, was told that apart from the statutory services and staff meetings the vicar did not wish to see him for three months. But at the end of that time he would expect a case history of every family in his assigned district (Gummer, *Chavasse* 40). Cyril Garbett** visited four hours a day five days a week as a curate in Portsea; and when he became vicar expected his curates to do the same (Smyth, *Garbett* 62). Mervyn Stockwood** made it a rule to make at least three visits a day (Stockwood, 92).

Afternoon visiting has been the norm; additional evening visiting has often been advocated. Cyril Garbett pointed out the obvious facts that most men are at home only in the evenings, and that the best way to win the whole family is to win the man (Smyth, *Garbett* 121).

The burden of visiting in town parishes has been so great that the clergy have often shared it with the laity. At Holy Trinity, Cambridge, Charles Simeon* organized a Visiting Society. The parish was divided into areas and a man and woman visitor cared for each. In Simeon's words the Society's purpose was 'to find out the modest and industrious poor in a time of sickness, and to administer to them relief for their bodies, and at the same time instruction for their souls' (Hopkins, *Simeon* 47–8). The district visitor was a common feature in Victorian parishes, and provided a distinguished and effective precedent for similar arrangements in our own time.

Despite the strenuous support of those who believe in it, the principle of general visiting has not always found favour either with the parson or with his people. It is an old saying that some clergy have foot and mouth disease – they won't visit and can't preach. Mrs Gaskell reported that many Yorkshiremen's 'surly independence would revolt from the idea of any one having a right from his office to enquire into their condition'. She asked a Yorkshireman what sort of clergyman his parish priest was. 'A rare good one,' came the reply. 'He minds his own business, and ne'er troubles us with ours.' Patrick Bronte** was of that ilk; cherishing his own privacy, he was 'perhaps over-delicate' in intruding upon that of others (Gaskell, *Bronte* 37).

For that reason or for others, there have been parish priests who have taken visiting lightly. James Woodforde* was of his time in eschewing it except in emergencies. Henry Alford** was not a regular visitor at Wymeswold during his time there from 1838 to 1853; a friend charitably suggested that this was because regular visiting was not yet general practice, and that his parishioners did not expect it. Cosmo Lang** at Portsea left routine visiting to his curates, though he ministered attentively to individuals in need (Lockhart, *Lang* 124). Ernest Raymond wrote of his Canon Welcome that: 'Visiting ... was not an activity in which he delighted at all ... while full of hearty affection for people who would come to him, he had not that urgent love of souls which would drive him into dismal and depressing byways to look for them ... Posters, handbills and Baynes [his curate] were his substitute for visiting' (Raymond, 33).

Because visiting is time-consuming, and often apparently fruitless, there is a temptation for busy clergy to avoid it. The outcome is unforgettably described by W.C.E. Newbolt: 'Your great organizer ... has a meeting of the Diocesan Fund in the morning in the cathedral town; he has to attend a committee meeting of local charities in the afternoon ... and at night ... there is a meeting of Church Defence ... at which he must make a speech. And the poor woman with a sick child hesitates to approach so great a man for so trivial an object. And he does not know that, could he have gone with her, he would have found that the child was not baptized; he does not know that, if he had gone that night, he would have found the father nursing it; he does not know that the elder brother would have come in from work, rough and tired and suspicious; and that he would have found out from him as the roughness wore off that he wished to be confirmed, only he had been afraid to apply. He does not know that there would have been a man sitting by the door of the church on the following Sunday, very shabbily dressed, and unused to his surroundings, who had come there simply because he thought there must be some good in a person who would turn out at night to see a sick child' (Newbolt, 36–7).

The value Newbolt ascribes to visiting depends of course upon the use made of it. When William Grimshaw* was a young clergyman at Todmorden, he is said to have visited his parishioners only 'in order to drink and be merry with them' (Baker, *Grimshaw* 30). Mr Ellison of Lark Rise called at every home in his parish each year. His arrival provoked a scurry of preparation and he was greeted with 'respectful tolerance'. Conversation was difficult and stilted. 'The Rector never mentioned religion. This was looked upon in the parish as one of his chief virtues, but it limited the possible topics ... the gulf ... was too wide; neither he nor his hostess could bridge it' (Thompson, 221–2). When the visitor was gentry and the visited were not, visiting could be an embarrassment or an intrusion. Sabine Baring-Gould**, who visited in a trap driven by his coachman, gave warning in advance (Colloms, 244–5). W.C.E. Newbolt thought it necessary to remind his priestly readers that it was essential to knock at the door of a cottage, and to wait to be invited in (Newbolt, 119).

I knew a parish priest who used visiting to share his woes with his parishioners, rather than to listen to theirs. Listening is, of course, of the essence. Richard Watson Dixon (1833–1900), the scholarly vicar of Hayton, Cumberland, was forgiven his erudite sermons by his parishioners because 'he was the best listener in the village, and always had time to stop and hear some-one's troubles' (Colloms, 215).

It was long the custom that the visiting priest should pray with those visited. Ralph Josselin's* practice was to spend days of prayer in his people's homes, often with their neighbours gathered too (see for example Josselin, 255). Practice has not usually been so intense, and has died away with increasing secularism. John Collins** recounts how, serving his first curacy in Whitstable in the late 1920s, he found it impossible to propose prayer even to regular members of the congregation, and how grateful he was when an old lady asked for it (Collins, 40). Visiting in the 1990s, I have suggested prayer only when I have thought it might be welcome, and even so have occasionally been rebuffed.

The standard picture of the visiting parson is of tea and polite conversation in the parlour. In fact, visiting has often needed a strong stomach. One of Walter Hook's* curates wrote of visiting a dying girl: 'I could at first discern nothing but what seemed a dark bundle of rags. By degrees, however, I became conscious of a dirty cotton gown, with two legs sticking out, partly covered with some remnant of stockings, and in the extreme corner, propped up against the wall, a ghastly head; the face pallid and emaciated to the last degree, the eyes sunk, the nose sharp as before death, the lips vivid, the teeth set in convulsions. Under the dying woman was a handful of filthy straw, and this was all there was between her and the boards on which she was laid' (Stranks, *Hook* 93). In an equally vivid fashion Francis Kilvert described taking communion to a sick man: 'What a scene it was, the one small room up in the roof of the hovel, almost dark, in which I could not stand upright, the shattered window, almost empty of glass, the squalid bed, the close horrid smell, the continual crying and wailing of the children below, the pattering of the rain on the tiles close overhead, the ceaseless moaning of the sick man with his face bound about by a napkin' (Kilvert, 1.238). Dick Sheppard* used to say that the most Christian thing he ever did was to use the pin an old lady removed from her hair to prise out the winkles she served him for tea (Scott, *Sheppard* 41). A priest of our own time, Tom Walker** visited a blind old lady who was unable to observe that the best china cups in which she proudly served tea were thick with filthy grease (Walker, 68). I have had the same experience.

Visiting has also called for composure in unusual circumstances. John Newton 'visited a poor thoughtless man much addicted to drink (tho' sober at the time) who was suddenly struck with a Phrenzy' (Martin, *Newton* 237). Harold Hosking** at Newlyn was asked to visit an old man at 1.00 a.m. and to conduct his ministrations by his bed, with his wife 'snoring away quite contentedly beside him' (Hosking, 42). Roy Catchpole** approached a sick man in an upper room through a hole in the floor because the stairs had been burned as part of a desperate attempt to keep warm (Catchpole, *GMDC* 28–9). Visiting an elderly parishioner, I found him crawling naked round the floor in the first stages of acute mental illness; my first task was to clothe him, my second to summon his doctor.

Edward Boys, a nineteenth-century country parson, wrote that he had always believed that a house-going parson produced a church-going people (Goodenough, 119). There is some evidence to support this view. Newman's visiting at St Clement's immediately filled his church to overflowing. The vast congregations at St Helens under J.W. Willink were attributed in large part to his system of district visitors backed by the clergy. It was customary in some Kentish villages as late as the twentieth century for people who had been visited in their homes to return the courtesy in church the following Sunday; on the other hand, the parson's failure to visit gave a cast-iron reason for staying away.

But Boys' aphorism no longer holds generally good, if indeed it ever did. David Watson* began his ministry at St Cuthbert's, York, with visiting, and found it unproductive (Saunders, *Watson* 101). I found that, while my initial general visitation of my parish flushed out a number of people who needed only the mildest stimulus to renew their church allegiance, the positive effects on churchgoing thereafter were not great. I cannot tell, of course, what would have happened had I ceased to visit; it is reasonable to assume that the numbers in church would actually have fallen.

There is an element of drudgery about visiting, especially general visiting, which calls for rule and discipline if the priest is to persevere. But the spiritual rewards can be very great. 'Often does he find in some obscure individual,' wrote R.W. Evans, 'natural graces which delight him, mental gifts which surprise him, moral worth which he respects; spiritual attainments which he reverences' (Evans, 229). One of the most delightful aspects of Kilvert's diary is the sense it leaves of the loving intimacy which constant visiting created, an intimacy which met the emotional and spiritual needs both of the one visited and of the visitor. So, as a fitting conclusion to this section, here is Kilvert's account of a visit to the elderly Mr Whitcombe: 'The old man, ninety years old, leaned on me and fondled my hand, talking earnestly but incoherently and repeating himself every moment. He said the Lord's Prayer and Creed like a child to let me see that he knew them and he kept on muttering fragments of church prayers, anxiously complaining that his memory was gone and that he had no one to read or talk to him and bring things to his remembrance. I repeated some of the Church prayers for him and he joined in eagerly at the end or wherever the old familiar words struck a chord in his memory. Then putting his hands together reverently like a child he repeated, speaking in a low voice as if to himself, "Thank God for hearing my prayers". It was very touching. It was like teaching and soothing and reassuring a very little child' (Kilvert, 2.119–20).

Healing

Even when general visiting has not been customary, sick visiting has always been regarded as a fundamental duty of the clergy. *The Clergyman's Instructor* (sixth edition 1865) contains advice from Bishops Jeremy Taylor and Gilbert Burnet on the subject. Taylor advocates stressing the love of God, Burnet the dangers of judgment. The clergy have conveyed both messages, with varying degrees of emphasis.

Richard Hooker** visited the sick even when not sent for, 'supposing that the fittest time to discover to them those errors to which health and prosperity had blinded them'. He invited confession and offered communion (Walton, 156). George Herbert's* country parson readily undertook the same office, having 'thoroughly digested all the points of consolation'. These included 'the benefit of affliction, which softens and works the stubborn heart of man ... the certainty both of deliverance and reward if we faint not ... the miserable comparison of the moment of griefs here with the weight of joys hereafter.' As well as delivering these exhilarating messages, he enjoined the sick person to confession and communion (Herbert, XV).

Herbert took the same line in his personal life, writing to his sick mother: 'Madam, as the earth is but a point in respect of the heavens, so are earthly troubles compared with heavenly joys; therefore, if either age or sickness lead you to these joys, consider what advantage you have over youth and health, who [meaning his mother] are now so near these true comforts' (Walton, 195–6). Two hundred years later R.W. Evans advocated pointing out the sick person's sinfulness at the first opportunity, conceding, however, that 'the great difficulty ... is that of giving an effectual shake, so as to rouse the sinner's conscience, but yet one not so rude and violent as to tempt him to shut the door on your future visits' (Evans, 78).

Ralph Josselin* frequently visited the seriously ill. Attending at the death-bed of a young married man with two children he mused, with typical spiritual egocentricity: 'Its good to bee sometimes in the house of mourning, the lord I hope will make me more closely to endeavour a spiritual communion with him, in the sight of the creatures emptynes.' It is only fair to add that his diary entries often include a prayer for the person visited, and that he could take the trouble to call in order to give 'a day of praise to god' for recovery (Josselin, 67, 278, 375). William Cole** visited housebound old Dame Mollard twelve times in four months, taking her the sacrament and twice sending her dinner (Cole, passim). James Woodforde* read prayers with the sick, took them communion, and sent them little comforts. He was, however, selective, in at least one case praying in church for a seriously ill parishioner without calling on her (Wood-forde, 3.231). An elderly Wiltshire incumbent in the 1830s was still more economical of his time. He sent sick parishioners a shilling saying it would do more good than his presence or his prayers (Hammond, 143).

There is a kind of urgency about sick visiting which is brought home only by experience. During his time at Whitstable John Collins** missed a weekly visit to an elderly blind man, because of the superior attractions of a tennis match. Calling as usual a week later, he was confronted by the old man in his coffin (Collins, 48–9). I received a request to visit an old lady, mortally afraid of dying, in hospital, but decided I was too busy to call until the next day. I walked up the ward to find the old lady sitting dead in her chair with a cup of tea still in her hand; she had died a few seconds before my arrival. It is easy to see why Cyril Garbett** insisted that his curates at Portsea should respond to news of sickness or bereavement that very day (Smyth, *Garbett* 131).

Faced with human agony, the clergy have sometimes felt helpless. Ralph Josselin was baffled by a sick man who refused to consider the prospect of recovery: 'Lord hath he puld his heart absolutely out of thy hands. lord I will cleave to thee in thy worship though others will not and I will eye thy providence to that man' (Josselin, 613). When Margaret Oliphant's Roger Mildmay 'saw a man of his own age growing into a great gaunt skeleton with consumption ... what could the young rector say? ... he would read the prayers with a faltering voice, and, going away wretched, would lavish wine and soup ... upon the invalid; but what could he *say* to him, he whose very health and wealth and strength and well-being seemed an insult to the dying?' (Oliphant, *CC* 199). John Skinner* attended a woman whose only child, born after eleven years of marriage, was dying. He noted: 'She does not seem to bear up at all; but who can reason against the feelings of a parent over a dying infant? You may tell her whatever is right, but that is but poor consolation. I repeated to her the excellent moral inculcated in Parnell's *Hermit*. The poor woman listened and cried; well might she have replied with our immortal bard "Oh, who can hold a fire in his hand by thinking of the frosty Caucasus?" or in the words of Job to his friends, "All this I know as well as ye"' (Skinner, 245–6).

A flood of light is cast upon Skinner's spirituality by a reading of the poem he quoted to his parishioner. It is a story about a hermit who undertakes a journey back into the world. On the journey he is joined by a youth, who engages in a series of inexplicable actions, including killing a child, the apple of his father's eye. Eventually the youth reveals himself as an angel, fulfilling God's purposes. The child had been killed because his father loved him too much:

> Long had our pious friend in virtue trod
> But now the child half-wean'd his heart from God ...
> To what excesses had this dotage run!
> But God, to save the father, took the son ...
> The poor fond parent, humbled in the dust,
> Now owns in tears the punishment was just.

There is of course a healing property in spiritual ministration. Francis Kilvert* wrote of his visit to a madwoman shut up by her family in a room where she had smashed both the window and her crockery. 'It was a mad skeleton with such a wild scared animal's face as I never saw before.' Kilvert's conversation with her, and his successful attempt to remind her of the Lord's Prayer, left her more settled, and anxious that he should come again (Kilvert, 2.24–5).

But the clergy have not relied on spiritual methods alone. In days when doctors were not numerous and cost money the clergyman often took their place. George Herbert's country priest might commission his wife to be the village doctor, or have a doctor as a member of his household, or enter into an agreement with a physician living nearby. But Herbert thought it best if the priest himself undertook the work, familiarizing himself with herbal remedies, and drawing in particular on local ones, which his wife could grow in the garden. 'Surely hyssop, valerian, mercury, adder's tongue, yarrow, melilot, and Saint-John's-wort, made into a salve, and elder, camomile, mallows, comfrey, and smallage, made into a poultice, have done great and rare cures' (Herbert, XXIII).

George Crabbe** was in a good position to render medical assistance since he trained as a surgeon-apothecary before ordination. At Stathern he dispensed medicines and assisted at childbirth (Crabbe, 1.130). James Woodforde gave his servants emetics, and when one of them had a touch of ague, Woodforde gave him a dram of gin, pushed him headlong into a pond and ordered him to bed (Woodforde, 2.86; 1.252). John Skinner prescribed quite frequently for his people, providing rhubarb dissolved in brandy for a bowel complaint (Skinner, 359). Sydney Smith* rather fancied himself as a medical practitioner. He had attended lectures and clinical classes to prepare himself for medical ministry at Foston-le-Cray, and was the village doctor. He wrote:

> I know all drugs, all simples and all pills;
> I cure diseases and I send no bills.
> The poor old women now no lameness know;
> Rheumatics leave their hand, the gout their toe.
> Full atrophy has fled from Foston's vale,
> And health, and peace, and joy and love prevail.

At Combe Florey he pumped out the stomach of a manservant who had eaten rat poison by accident. Called to baptize a baby thought to be dying, he reported on his return: 'Why, I first gave it a dose of castor oil, and then I christened it; so now the poor child is ready for either world' (Bell, *Smith* 105, 107, 200).

William Andrew* applied brandy and salt both internally and externally for what he described as a liver complaint, with pleasing results. He noted: 'She is very grateful. May it be an open door for me to her soul. Lord, leave not her soul unhealed!' On another occasion he offered to extract a parishioner's tooth. He succeeded only in breaking it off 'which,' he reflected, 'perhaps was better than extracting the fangs' (Chadwick, *Andrew* 53, 55). In Arthur Stanton's* day, the students at Cuddesdon Theological College were given 'a lecture to give us some clue how to treat some of the more ordinary casualties which come under the scope of clerical assistance' (Stanton, 31). J. Edmund Long, rector of White Roothing, Essex, from 1893 to 1925 did practically all the doctoring in his parish (Addison, 220).

More prosaically, James Woodforde paid a medical bill of £0 10s 3d for his neighbour, Anne Gooch. He had been introduced while in Somerset to the virtues of inoculation against smallpox by his bother-in-law Dr Clarke, and when the disease was plaguing Weston in 1791, he did what he could to encourage the preventive (Woodforde, 3.252, 255, 264–5). John Skinner paid for a doctor to attend a collier who had broken his back, as well as attending to his spiritual needs; he supplied a sick woman with port wine as well as the eucharist, and a broken-down old man with a loan of sheets and blankets and a gift of half a crown as well as having 'a long and serious conversation' with him (Skinner, 229–30, 323, 458). In 1848 W.J. Butler, a great vicar of Wantage, Berkshire, encouraged the creation of the order of Nursing Sisters of St John the Divine; the order became the Community of St Mary the Virgin, working throughout the Anglican communion (Pickering, 130).

The clergy have played a major part during epidemics. The London clergy were ordered on pain of dismissal to stay at their posts during the Great Plague of 1665. Eleven of them died (Barrow, 68). When cholera came to Bilston, Staffordshire, in 1832 the incumbent William Leigh created and headed a Board of Health, equipped a barracks as a hospital, hired a nurse and an ambulance, distributed free lime for the whitewashing of houses, organized cleaners and the provision of coffins, and set up an orphan school (Hammond, 146). Walter Hook's* curate William Stanley Monck ventured into cellars full of fever-stricken people to do what little he could for them. In consequence he caught typhus, and died (Stranks, *Hook* 95). In the cholera epidemic of 1849 William Bennett* arranged days of fasting and humiliation and read the commination service, but this was the least part of his activity. 'The clergy of St Barnabas' might be found at all hours by the bedside of the sick and dying, not only administering the consolations of religion but also assisting in kindly offices for the sick; giving them their medicines and incurring personal danger by rubbing their cold and cramped limbs, watching for hours by their pillows, and exhibiting those fruits of holiness which can only emanate from a pure love' (Bennett, 15). The strain involved, and the motivation behind the clergy's activity, was summarized by Hook in a letter during an epidemic in Leeds: 'We are to have a parochial fast ... I pray that I may be able to speak home to the hearts of some who may be at church then, but who seldom come at other times. I have the care of two cholera hospitals ... I have taken the chief place of danger, because I am the chief clergyman in the parish, and also to punish myself for my cowardice, for I confess that as regards the natural man I am a little frightened; but I have full trust in God. I feel the post of danger to be the post of honour' (Stephens, *Hook* 435).

We are able to observe in detail John Skinner's reactions when Camerton was affected by the cholera epidemic of 1832. On news of the first outbreak he distributed camphor and aromatic vinegar, and had affected houses fumigated with tobacco which he provided. He gave money to stricken families, and insisted that the local drains should be improved and dung-heaps buried, brooking no resistance from the official who said 'It was the Lord's will they should die; that he could not prevent it'. He arranged for a deep grave to be dug in the consecrated part of the churchyard but away from the other graves, and was prepared to provide glebe land for burials should it be needed. Unlike some of his colleagues he conducted a funeral service, partly at least for the practical reason that if he was seen to be unwilling to go near dead bodies others would be unprepared to bring them to the place of burial. It appears, however, that as the epidemic continued he allowed bodies to be buried without formality. He provided a glass of spirits for the men who carried coffins, and, having closed the school, wine for the schoolmistress and her daughter because they were terrified, and thus liable to infection. In a sermon he urged practical usefulness rather than 'wordy professions and unavailing lamentations', and implicit obedience to the medical men.

A friend invited Skinner to stay with her while the pestilence continued. He wrote her 'as lively a note as I could ... saying I should be a poltroon to desert my post when the enemy was about to attack it.' Indeed, Skinner appears at his most attractive in this crisis in his parish's affairs. Although his actions were sometimes misguided and his spiritual ministry overshadowed by his determination to be of practical use, he behaved admirably (Skinner, 452–7).

This kind of ministry required great courage, and courage has sometimes been lacking. Woodforde does not appear to have visited the sick during the 1791 smallpox epidemic, and one of his parishioners died without his priest even knowing he was ill (Woodforde, 3.252–7). When there was fever at Foston-le-Clay in 1816, Sydney Smith visited his flock daily, but prudently stood at the door (Bell, *Smith* 106). Thackeray's Dr Tusher showed a nice discrimination when confronted with an outbreak of smallpox: 'We are not in a Popish country; and a sick man does not absolutely need absolution and confession ... in a case where the life of a parish priest in the midst of his flock is highly valuable to them, he is not called upon to risk it (and therewith the lives, future prospects, and temporal, even spiritual, welfare of his own family) for the sake of a single person, who is not very likely in a condition to understand the religious message whereof the priest is the bringer – being uneducated, and likewise stupefied or delirious by disease. If your ladyship or his lordship, my excellent good friend and patron were to take it ... for your sake I would lay my life down' (W.M. Thackeray, *The History of Henry Esmond*, 1940, 79–80).

That Thackeray was drawing from life is confirmed by the reactions of John Skinner, called to the death-bed of a young man who had caught typhus. He reflected: 'What ignorance in the parents to think the merely having a clergyman at that time could be of the smallest benefit!' (Skinner, 74).

In general, attendance at death-beds has been a prime example of the healing ministry, as the dying person has been delivered from fear and restlessness. The methods traditionally used have been stringent: an insistence that the sufferer recognize the weight of sin as a preliminary to accepting the saving work of Christ. Confronted with a dying boy of fifteen, John Fletcher* 'spent an hour in setting before him the greatness of his guilt ... that he had been so long under the rod of God, and had not been whipped out of his careless unbelief to the bosom of Jesus Christ'. To his joy the boy responded 'and spent his last hours testifying ... that the kingdom was come, and he was going to the King' (Benson, *Fletcher* 101). John Skinner, ministering to a dying collier, was concerned that he was more preoccupied with his pain than with the state of his soul. Coming back the next day he found the collier dead, and was indignant to hear that a Methodist 'had been to him in his last moments and extorted from him a declaration that he had faith in Christ, which is considered as a sufficient satisfaction for an ill-spent life and as a sure passport to Heaven. What delusive, what diabolical doctrines …!' (Skinner, 40). It is not clear what Skinner himself would have attempted had the matter been left to him; so perhaps he was suffering from professional pique. The young John Henry Newman** at the bed of a dying coachman 'spoke *very* strongly on our being sinful and corrupt till death … this he seemed to admit, and thanked me very fervently' (Faber, 157). As a curate in the 1960s Tom Walker** was impressed by the way his rector Geoffrey Shaw 'pleaded, gently cajoled, and firmly warned' a dying man 'of the consequences of dying without Christ' (Walker, 77). Despite the element of coercion involved in ministry of this nature, however, R.W. Evans ruefully reflected that only rarely could 'true repentance' be expected of those at death's door (Evans, 94).

It was a common belief among the clergy in the eighteenth and early nineteenth centuries that the age of miracles was over. This view inhibited resort to spiritual healing; but views changed as the nineteenth century went on. Samuel Garratt**, impressed by a spectacular cure, believed that a restoration of gifts of healing might well be a presage of the Second Coming for which he was eagerly looking (Garratt, 192–3). Even those who did not share his millenarianism gradually emancipated themselves from an undue reverence for physical regularities.

In our own century spiritual healing has again become respectable and has been set in a wider context of co-operation with the healing professions. Percy Dearmer (1867–1936), vicar of St Mary's, Primrose Hill, Hampstead, and Conrad Noel** were among the founders in 1904 of the Guild of Health which had these functions. When the Guild became interdenominational in 1915 the Anglican Guild of St Raphael was set up. Arthur Hopkinson**, a member of the Guild, was one of many parish priests who introduced the healing ministry into their parishes. Howard Cobb (*c.* 1885–*c.*1950) was healed from sleeping sickness by the laying on of hands and prayer. When he became rector of Crowhurst, Sussex, in 1928 he founded the Crowhurst home of healing, which endures today (Morris Maddocks, *The Christian Healing Ministry*, SPCK 1981, 100–3).

Tom Walker instituted a healing ministry in his parish despite the grave doubts of senior members of his congregation, and was convinced that it bore fruit in the lives of individuals (Walker, 117–18). After intensive prayer a member of Nicholas Rivett-Carnac's** congregation recovered completely from lung cancer; his doctor said: 'We can't give any rational explanation' (Cooke, 170–3). The processes involved are indeed mysterious. I have myself conducted healing services instituted by my rector, Lawrence Smith of the Eythorne benefice, Kent, but without a consciousness of any gift for the work.

I felt indeed at the outset that the whole cast of my temperament and spirituality made it unlikely that I possessed one. I was the more taken aback to be told by several people that they had positively benefited from my laying on of hands.

Benefit is of course a matter of definition. Only the smallest part of the healing ministry has been concerned with dramatic and inexplicable 'cures'. Usually, the gain is emotional and spiritual. Harold Hosking** tells the story of a nurse with a terminal illness whose aggressive refusal to accept her condition was changed into a gentle and grateful acceptance after prayer and holy unction. She continued to decline physically but 'Who would question for one moment that this [the change of character] was the form of healing that is far better and far more lasting than any other?' (Hosking, 64).

The subtlety of the spiritual factors at work in the healing ministry is evinced by the experience of a contemporary clergyman who felt drawn to offer the laying on of hands to a young woman dying of multiple sclerosis. At her wish he called in an experienced colleague; after the latter's ministry the young woman walked, but three days later collapsed and died. Her father, who had been strongly anti-religious, came in tears to the priest to thank him for giving his daughter back to him, however briefly, as she used to be; and became a committed Christian (personal information).

The most dramatic form of healing to which priests are called is that associated with exorcism and its related rites. The Protestant and gentlemanly strains in the history of the Anglican ministry have sometimes militated against claims that their powers in this respect should be taken seriously. An old lady asked J.C. Atkinson** to lay the spirits which possessed her house. Atkinson said he did not profess to be able to do so, and was told, 'Ay, but if I had sent for a priest o' t'oud church, he would a'deean it, they were a vast mair powerful conjurers than you Church-priests' (Atkinson, 59n).

Common sense has been a useful weapon. Ralph Josselin, confronted with a claim that a parishioner was a witch and had made a child ill 'tooke the fellow alone into the feild, and dealt with him solemnely, and I conceive the poore wretch is innocent as to that evill' (379). Faced with a woman raving after childbirth and terrified that the Evil One was destroying her soul, John Skinner concluded that she was suffering from the effects of living in a damp house, and prescribed Scott's pills (Skinner, 317–18).

None the less, the clergy have engaged in the deliverance ministry where circumstances have appeared to warrant it. Tom Walker tells of delivering a student from a life committed to Satan, and of praying with tongues over a possessed woman to give her peace (Walker, 117–21). I have purified a house tainted by a succession of unhappy events, to the relief of the occupants (see for a large number of other examples *Deliverance*, ed. Michael Perry, SPCK 1987). Since a notorious disaster in the 1970s every diocese has a priest or team of priests equipped to practise and to advise on the deliverance ministry, and, despite theological controversy about the forces involved, the ministry itself is firmly established as a proper part of the duties of a priest.

Almsgiving and Social Concern

On Maundy Thursday 1872 Francis Kilvert* was on his way home from Clyro school when he was stopped by a man who told him he was a hatter walking from Shropshire to Cardiff in search of work. The man was penniless, fasting and soaked through by the rain. 'He was a fine manly-looking fellow with a black moustache and his address was manly and pleasant, respectful and self-respectful. But there was a mute appeal in his dark fine eyes, which I could not resist ... My heart melted within me ... and I took a shilling from my purse. "For the sake of the old county," I said. "My family are from Shropshire too. Cheer up. Better luck tomorrow." "God bless you, Sir, for your kindness," he said. And as he spoke I thought there was a tear in his eye' (Kilvert, 2.162).

And, no doubt, in that of the sentimental Kilvert too. Constrained by the Dominical commands, by human sympathy, and by the view that their income should be regarded as in trust for the public good, the clergy have always been expected to exercise spontaneous charity. In greater or lesser measure they have done so. We have seen numerous examples already, so will confine ourselves here to episodes which illustrate the spirit in which help has been given, and the principles which have been seen to be involved.

George Herbert* makes one principle clear in 'The Church Porch':

Man is God's image; but a poor man is
Christ's stamp to boot: both images regard.

Herbert supplemented the principle with advice on practice in *A Priest to the Temple*. His country parson welcomes the poor to his table, and treats them with distinction 'for his own humility and their comfort'; but prefers to give them money which they can employ to their best advantage. He uses the Poor Law to assist the indigent, but is always prepared to employ his own cash if needs be. He assists the beggar at his door, giving him the benefit of the doubt about being deserving. 'At hard times and dearths, he even parts his living and life among them [the poor], giving some corn outright, and selling other at under rates; and when his own stock serves not, working those that are able to the same charity.' His giving, however, is with strings. He gives preference to the deserving, 'so is his charity in effect a sermon', and asks casual mendicants to say prayers or recite the Creed and the Commandments (Herbert, XI, XII).

As a curate in a Bristol slum in the 1930s Mervyn Stockwood** concluded that scroungers who were prepared to make a show did better from almsgiving than the truly deserving. He tells the tale of an old woman who, seeing him approaching, hurriedly spread out a Bible on her knees. "'There's nothing better than reading the Good Book, Mister", she said. "Yes, there is," I replied, "and that's reading it the right way up." She was impenitent and added with a wicked grin, "Right side up or wrong side down, how about a coal ticket for Christmas?"' (Stockwood, 29).

William Andrew*, sallying out in snowy weather to relieve the inhabitants of a nearby parish, essayed to do so in the spirit of the Sermon on the Mount. He 'tried to go as a stranger but there was scarcely a cottage in which I was not recognized … O what a privilege to be the Lord's Almoner! Remember me, O God, for good! Enlarge my heart! Let not my left hand know what my right has done!' (Chadwick, *Andrew* 54).

Robert Hawker, vicar of Charles church, Plymouth, from 1784 to 1827, and grandfather of the vicar of Morwenstow, put another New Testament principle into practice. He was a sacrificial giver. He subvented the poor with such generosity that his own family was sometimes in want. The bedroom doors 'had to be locked, so often had he stripped the beds in order to supply the needs of the poor' (Balleine, 64).

Thoughtful giving has often evinced itself as practical helpfulness. Confronted with a man who had lost an eye and the use of a leg from the bursting of a cannon, John Skinner* agreed with the cripple that he should learn netting in order to make a living, and paid for his lessons. Coming across an unemployed parishioner he promised to find him occasional work (Skinner, 300, 438). Octavius Pickard-Cambridge** offered the vats in his malt-house so that on Saturday nights the boys and girls of his Sunday School could be bathed (Collums, 78). At Flora Thompson's Lark Rise THE BOX arrived with every new baby. THE BOX was supplied by the Rector's daughter. 'It contained half a dozen of everything – tiny shirts, swathes, long flannel barrows, nighties, and napkins, made, kept in repair and lent for every confinement by the clergyman's daughter. In addition to the loaned clothes it would contain, as a gift, packets of tea and sugar and a tin of patent groats for making gruel.' The clergyman's daughter provided a substantial meal for the new mother and christening robes, which, as with THE BOX's contents, she had made and repaired herself. THE BOX saw mothers through the first weeks of their confinement. It was so popular that a second one had eventually to be provided (Thompson, 133–5).

As well as giving in person the clergy have organized giving. The *Book of Common Prayer* directs that at the service of Holy Communion there should be an offertory to be put 'to such pious and charitable uses, as the Minister and Church-wardens shall think fit'. The custom had died out at Weston Longueville when Woodforde became rector; he re-introduced it. His own contribution was usually half a crown (Woodforde, 1.152; 2.211). He gave more generously than Mr Ormerod, rector of Presteigne, near Clyro, in Kilvert's time. He would declare he had no change, and put his pocket knife in the collection plate. After the service, however, he 'returns the knife to his pocket, but (it is stated) invariably forgets to *redeem* it' (Kilvert, 3.116).

John Skinner spent part of Christmas Day 1820 walking round his parish distributing the sacrament money; forty communicants had provided just under £4 between them (Skinner, 156). William Andrew discovered that at Witchingham the custom was to distribute the sacrament money as soon as the service was over. He was shocked when the clerk demanded a shilling for himself (Chadwick, *Andrew* 30).

The practice of making collections for special purposes at services other than the Communion has a long history. One Sabbath in 1644 Ralph Josselin* 'gatherd liberally for a poore Ministers widdow who was plunderd and housband slain.' In 1651 'I moved for poore Mighill whose house was burnt downe, wee gathered beare £3 for him, the lord bee blessed for this mercy in my people who gave them an heart to give.' During the plague of 1665 he appealed, though without much effect, for those affected in nearby Colchester, and in the following year for those rendered destitute by the fire of London. Nor did he neglect the claims from overseas. In 1655 he and his people collected £8 12s 2d for Milton's 'slaughtered saints', the Protestant people of Savoy; in 1658 £6 9s 10d for persecuted Poles and Bohemians (Josselin, 30, 253, 523, 531, 347, 423).

John Skinner raised £20 in 1822 towards relief for an Irish famine, partly by direct application and partly by a collection in church (Skinner, 207). In 1831 Henry Fardell* raised £55 to the same end. Fardell also preached to raise money to assist the inhabitants of Quebec and of St John's, Newfoundland, after disastrous fires; and regularly for the Society for the Propagation of the Gospel (Fardell, 129). Robert Hawker* was one of the first clergy to introduce a weekly offertory for charity (Brendon, *Hawker* 104–5). Kilvert began a monthly afternoon offertory for the sick and needy at Bredwardine in 1878 and was pleased that 'the people responded kindly. Most of them gave something.' On that occasion he raised 6s 1d. Four years previously his father's parish of Langley Burrell had raised £5 12s 10d for the Bengal Famine Mansion House Fund (Kilvert, 3.413, 20).

The clergy have organized general giving among their people, and have been trusted to disburse funds on behalf of Christian laity. Ralph Josselin and his friends took up a collection for a 'French Baron' who had made a sacrificial conversion from Popery; after one house meeting 'we releived divers poore persons with what wee gathered', and at another he raised 8 shillings which sufficed to buy a widow a load of logs (Josselin, 21, 183, 374). In 1822 Francis Witts** distributed clothing, coal and money to the elderly on behalf of Lady Elcho (Witts, 25). One of George Bull's** wardens, after visiting the parish schools, authorized Bull to spend up to £1 a week on his behalf on necessitous children (Gill, *Bull* 138).

As a matter of course the clergy have taken a leading role in the raising and disbursing of money for local emergency relief. During the bread famine of 1788–9 Charles Simeon* used the subscriptions of the affluent to enable bread to be sold at half-price to the poor of the villages near Cambridge (Hopkins, *Simeon* 51). After the disastrous harvest of 1817 Robert Hawker the elder sold a thousand sixpenny loaves to the poor every Sunday at half price, raising the difference by church collections (Brendon, *Hawker* 34). In the cold winter of 1830 John Skinner kept a boiler of soup made from 'coarse beef' always available for those who wanted it (Skinner, 394). During his time at St Matthew's, Duddesdon, George Bull was secretary of a committee which disbursed £2,383 during the famine winter of 1840–1 (Gill, *Bull* 138). Over the same period William Andrew gave soup to people who walked up to eight miles to get it. 'I purpose (DV) to boil forty pounds of beef into soup weekly … which together with about a peck of peas, a bundle of leeks and three papers of groats, boiled for ten hours [sic], will afford nourishing food for upwards of forty families' (Chadwick, *Andrew* 54).

During the cholera epidemic of 1849 William Bennett* set up a board of gentry who provided a soup kitchen, a dispensary and medical help, together with a lay visitor who ensured that the charity was administered properly and investigated the complaints of the poor (Bennett, 205–6).

Another form of organized help has been by way of local charities, to which parish priests have given both money and time. Robert Hawker senior opened a 'Female Penitentiary' for Plymouth prostitutes, and, after the fashion of Gladstone, recruited for it in person (Brendon, *Hawker* 34). Vaughan Thomas, an incumbent in the Oxford and Gloucester dioceses between 1836 and 1856, reformed the Radcliffe Infirmary and the Radcliffe lunatic asylum; he became chairman of the Oxford Board of Health (Clark, 201). Henry Wagner** of Brighton was a donor to, and governor of, the Sussex County Hospital, the Brighton Dispensary, the local Eye Infirmary, the local asylums for the deaf and dumb and the blind, and the local branch of the RSPCA (Wagner, 81–2).

Charitable endeavour has not necessarily evoked gratitude on the part of the beneficiaries. George Herbert advised his readers to contrive it (of course for the highest spiritual purposes) by never appearing to give on a regular basis, so that each gift was a cause for fresh thanksgiving (Herbert, XII). By comparison R.W. Evans wrote: 'The clergyman … will never complain of ingratitude, for his heart looks not to gratitude as its object' (Evans, 265). The good sense of both pieces of advice is evinced by the way the women at Lark Rise regarded the regular supply of THE BOX as a 'provision of Nature' and gave the Rector's daughter no credit for it (Thompson, 134).

Gratitude has been inhibited by the distance between the affluence of the giver and the poverty of the recipient; by the often justified belief that the giving had strings attached; and by a gross disproportion between the need and the means available to meet it. With grudging minimalism, George Woodward**, confronted with the bad winter of 1756–7, contributed a guinea to the local relief fund (admittedly 'to begin with'), but, at the age of 48, thought the snow too heavy to allow him to accompany the Poor Law officers on their rounds (Woodward, 94). When Samuel Garratt** went to Trinity Church, Waltham Cross, he found a custom by which those who sought aid from Church funds sat in what was called 'Hypocrites' Aisle'. Later, slaving away in St-Giles-in-the-Fields, he wrote 'There is much to discourage. Poor dissatisfied with relief given. Cannot obtain work for them and have no way of relieving them. So much could be done if I had but the means' (Garratt, 38, 41). Woodforde had a similar experience during the harsh winter of 1799: 'The Poor complain of the small Quantity of Bread given to them on Sunday at church almost as much as if they had none given' (Woodforde, 5.227).

The ungrateful have had one strong argument at their disposal. Almsgiving, however commendable in itself, can actually stand in the way of human dignity and social justice. As Simone Weil remarks: 'Almsgiving when it is not supernatural is like a sort of purchase. It buys the sufferer' (Simone Weil, *Waiting on God*, Collins 1973, 104). It can be a sort of voluntary tax on the affluent, paid to quieten guilty consciences and maintain the unjustly treated poor in subservience. Samuel Barnett* wrote scathingly about the Lord Mayor of London's Mansion House fund, set up to alleviate misery in the bad year 1885: 'Suddenly the advertisement appeared that £60,000 were to be given away. People whose imaginations hardly grasp the meaning of £100 felt this sum to be sufficient to meet all needs. They came forward in crowds to make their applications, and found themselves face to face with administrators without organization, without principles [of giving], without even time to listen patiently ... The poor are rightly angry ... The struggling workers who know that the wages weekly earned are insufficient, protest that the fund is being wasted. The idle threaten to break more windows if their wants be not more easily satisfied. The servants of the poor break their hearts. They see the work of years undone, as some of their friends give up trying, and waste their days begging for relief ... They see people of goodwill hurried and anxious to give money, forgetful of the real needs of other men, and they lose hope' (Barnett, 2.236).

Some almsgiving has been highly insensitive. Mervyn Stockwood describes how his predecessor in St Matthew's, Moorfields, in the nineteenth century, 'living in his iron fortress, had a carriage and horses. He and his four curates wore top hats and frock coats. On Sundays ... at evening service a bread ticket was placed in every tenth Prayer Book. A celestial bingo session!' Stockwood himself was disgusted by the relationships created by the need for alms, and welcomed the social changes which made the poor no longer dependent upon 'Lady Bountifuls in clerical collars ... I prefer to meet parishioners as equals, without enforced patronage on my side or false subservience on theirs' (Stockwood, 57, 28).

A few clergy have protested, as Barnett did, against the principle of almsgiving. Thomas Hancock** preaching to a middle-class congregation in 1869 said: 'The spirit of the Son of Man speaking to the Church through the artisans and the labourers of our time asks for justice, for rights. We ask Him to be content with alms and charities' (Clark, 287–8). John Collins** reluctantly concluded that his ordination committed him to 'a ministry of ambulance work to individuals within society, the essential nature of which is divinely ordained and needs to be preserved' (Collins, 39).

The least radical way of meeting such criticism has been by helping the poor to help themselves. In rural society the provision of land for private cultivation has been particularly important. Sydney Smith* provided allotments for local people both at Foston-le-Clay and at Combe Florey (Goodenough, 129). The clergy of Northamptonshire were the moving force behind the practice, by 1834 almost universal, of letting out small plots of land to labourers. Sydney Godolphin Osborne, the reforming rector of Durweston, Dorset, from 1841 to 1875, divided the whole of his glebe into allotments (Colloms, 200). In the most developed scheme Stephen Demainbray, rector of Broad Somerford, Wiltshire, ensured that when the parish was enclosed in 1806 half an acre of land was attached to every cottage. The land was vested in the rector and wardens so that it could not be used for building, and the use of it granted yearly to prevent neglect. In addition, the rector's glebe was let out to smallholders (Clark, 169).

There have been other ways of encouraging self-help. The clergy have helped the poor of their parishes by such devices as savings banks and clothing clubs. Francis Kilvert took his turn at staffing both institutions at Clyro. In one of his few attempts to put his social teaching into practice, Charles Kingsley* set up a tailors' co-operative. It collapsed when the man in charge ran away with the funds (Chitty, *Kingsley* 133n). While at Holy Trinity, Coventry, Walter Hook* opened a savings bank and a dispensary (Stephens, *Hook* 125–6). A measure of the poverty of those assisted is provided by the existence of blanket clubs. A poor woman would borrow a blanket from November to June at 6d a year for two years, and 4d a year for four years; then the blanket was hers (Clark, 183).

Another constructive approach to the problems of poverty and disadvantage has been by way of attacking social abuses. John Skinner fought a lonely war against drunkenness and misbehaviour at Camerton. He opposed the opening of an additional public house and was very critical of the local magistrates because of their failure to control licensed premises or to deal properly with disorders caused by drunkenness (Skinner, passim; see expecially 77). It may be that in this matter, as in others, Skinner's zeal outran his discretion; but there is no doubt that drunkenness was then, as it has always been, a major social evil, and that the efforts of the parochial clergy were legitimately directed against it. The Evangelical Spencer Thornton, vicar of Wendover, created his own parish temperance society in 1839 (Hennell, 19). In many nineteenth-century parishes a reading-room was established as an alternative to the local inn (Russell, 163).

George Bull campaigned against drunkenness to such effect that he lost the affection of some of the working-class people he strove so hard to help (Gill, *Bull* 115). In 1876 Osbert Mordaunt opened a public house in his parish of Hampton Lucy, Warwickshire. One of his servants was its manager. The opening hours were shorter than usual, and spirits were on sale only for medicinal purposes (Barrow, 164). This oblique approach may have been more effective than a frontal assault. J.C. Atkinson** pointed out how a violent advocacy of temperance could discomfit moderate drinkers, and alienate them (Atkinson, 29–30).

Sometimes a zeal for temperance has meant campaigning against Conservative candidates at an election. Cosmo Lang**, Bernard Wilson and Cyril Garbett**, all three vicars of Portsea and all three Conservatives themselves, took this course. Garbett was at daggers drawn with the wealthy, churchgoing chairman of the Brewers' Company, and secured his resignation from the treasurership of the ruridecanal conference by pointing to the character of a public house for which he was responsible. He also attacked local owners of slum property, brothel-keepers and vendors of pornographic literature (Lockhart, *Lang* 78n; Smyth, *Garbett* 102–4).

Robert Dolling*, who said that 'every social question was a question of the Lord Jesus Christ' constantly campaigned against the twin abuses of drunkenness and unchastity. To set an example he was a total abstainer for much of his life. He shamed landlords into closing brothels, in one instance by naming the offender during a service (Osborne, *Dolling* 128, 135, 141). One aspect of Dolling's work became the pastoral thrust of Joe Williamson's** ministry in Stepney after the Second World War. Horrified by the growth of prostitution in his parish, and the failure of the authorities to act effectively against it, he opened Church House, part of his freehold, as a hostel for prostitutes seeking to escape their profession. He also agitated about local conditions in terms which secured him national attention and made him unpopular with some of his superiors (Williamson, 138–98).

In a differing but equally useful vein, in the days before effective local utilities clergymen sometimes did their job. In 1754 Stephen Hales, Vicar of Twickenham, installed a decent water supply in his parish (Barrow, 102). W.J. Butler, who became vicar of Wantage, Berkshire, in 1847 was responsible for the renewal of the town's drainage (Clark, 209). At Haworth Patrick Bronte** secured improvements to the local prison and to local roads, and the provision of clean water and gas (Colloms, 90, 92). George Denison** built a water-works for the people of Brent Knoll (Denison, *FY* xi). Henry Fearon, rector of Loughborough from 1848, attempted, with the help of other local clergy, to secure a local sewerage and water supply. Because a rate was necessary, it took him ten years to get the first and twenty the second (Clark, 211).

In scores of parishes the incumbent has anticipated the provisions of the Welfare State. William Champneys, rector of Whitechapel from 1837 to 1860, set up a Provident Society, a refuge and industrial home for vagrant boys, and a local association for the health and comfort of the working-classes (Clark, 72). When in 1850 the new church of St Stephen's, Rochester Row, was consecrated, the provision included a soup kitchen, temperance rooms and a self-help club (Barrow, 150). Dick Sheppard* used the funds of St Martin's to put unemployed tradesmen to repair and decorate hospitals and orphanages (Roberts, *Sheppard* 113–4). In 1924 Basil Jellicoe (1899–1935), Anglo-Catholic curate of the parish of Somers Town, founded the St Pancras House Improvement Society. His driving personality and his social connections brought in £160,000 in four years, and inspired similar initiatives all over the country (Hastings, 180–1).

A few parish priests created welfare instutions which have far outgrown their origins. During the cholera epidemic of 1849 James Gillman, vicar of Holy Trinity, Lambeth, started a very cheap life insurance scheme which became in due course the mighty Prudential (Hammond, 146). In 1953 Chad Varah, rector of St Stephen's, Walbrook, founded the first branch of what is now the worldwide organization of the Samaritans.

It has often been a part of the parson's function to seek to protect the poor from the insufficiencies of public arrangements for relief. John Skinner visited a couple in their eighties who had been denied proper assistance from the parish poor rate because of the miserliness of their ex-master, a local magistrate. He wrote in his diary: 'If there is any crime which calls upon the Almighty for His vengeance it is surely this of oppressing the poor,' and in strong terms to the magistrate in question; alas unavailingly. He intervened energetically when he discovered a pauper in Camerton workhouse who, crippled through rheumatism, 'had actually been left for ten days in his filth, so that maggots had bred in his flesh and left great holes in his body' Skinner was also prepared to supplement Poor Law provision. Visiting old Mrs Moon he gave her daughter, a dwarf, some money because she received only 6d a week from the parish, and offered her the chance to earn more by weeding (Skinner, 426–7, 450, 250, 437). Nearly a century later Arthur Hopkinson** used his position as chaplain to a workhouse to make friends with Guardians, staff and inmates and to work discreetly for very necessary improvements (Hopkinson, 110–11).

From 1932 Gilbert Shaw, loosely attached to All Saints, Poplar, and in 1938 to become incumbent of St Nicholas, Blackwall Stairs, worked among the unemployed, using as his base, after various temporary expedients, a disused beer-hall, The Sydney. He provided clothes and footwear, cheap meals and recreation. He helped the unemployed in their dealings with Public Assistance Committees, set up a law surgery, and with his friend and ally Fr St John Groser created a Tenants' Defence Association. He led a successful rent strike in 1939. In his newsletter *Poplar News* he wrote: 'The Christian religion is concerned with the whole life of man, the material things of life, food and clothing; the material social order in which the reign of righteousness must be established as well as the mental outlook and those things more specifically termed as religious, and until the Christian Church as a whole realizes the importance of the material field of spiritual operation there can be no hope for revival' (Hacking, *Shaw* 42–51).

The dramatic change in the extent of Christian responsibility for deprivation is illustrated by W.H. Vanstone's** experiences. As a boy in a vicarage between the two world wars he 'could not ... assess the volume of the traffic of kindness which passed through, and was stimulated by, my father's church in those hard times.' As a parish priest in the 50s and 60s he experienced a world in which the Welfare State had in large measure taken the place of the Church. In the first parish in which he served, the Church continued, through its schools and the sports facilities it provided, to enrich the life of the community which its worship expressed and sustained. He then moved to a parish where local life appeared totally self-sufficient and where he had to learn that, in that place at least, 'the importance of the Church lies in something other than its service to, or satisfaction of, the needs of man' (Vanstone, 5–16).

Vanstone's experiences were not, however, identical with those of other parish priests in recent years. We have already seen how Nicolas Stacey found a social role for his parish in the 1960s. Similarly, in Moss Side, Manchester, Gerald Wheale and his congregation tackled the problems of multiple deprivation and wholesale clearance and redevelopment by creating the Moss Side Pastoral Centre, which is home to groups both sacred and secular, including a church Housing Association and a Community Project designed to lessen the harm Council policy was doing (Melinsky, 212–13). With the increasing expectations and declining State provision of the 1980s the Church was again challenged to make a major contribution to social provision. Roy Catchpole** experienced actual starvation among his parishioners in Broxtowe, Nottingham, in the 1980s (Catchpole, *GMDC* 123). By the 1990s scores of parish priests were engaged in such enterprises as housing associations or the welfare provisions associated with the use of the Church Urban Fund. As the corporatist ideals which had flourished since the Second World War were replaced by a philosophy of aggressive self-seeking, it became increasingly apparent that the clergy, though from a far weaker position than previously, would have to resume their traditional role as the protectors of the poor.

There is a point, easier to discern in principle than in practice, at which almsgiving and good works evolve into an attempt to re-order society. The tension between social conservatism and a lively understanding of the plight of the poor has turned some clergy into 'reactionary interventionists' (Louis Cazamian's expression, quoted Brendon, *Hawker* 104–5). Robert Hawker, in many respects profoundly conservative, was unwilling to see his parishioners starve. He used Sunday offertories to subsidize the wages of twenty-three labourers, each with a wife and four children to support, by adding a shilling a week to the seven they were paid by their employers. He was criticized for distorting economic processes which, it was argued, would ensure that the labourers received a higher wage before they and their families actually dropped dead. Knowing local employers, he remained unconvinced. He was also one of the tiny number of clergy who faced the wrath of the landowning classes by seeking the repeal of the Corn Laws (Brendon, *Hawker* 104–110).

Another priest exemplifies the tradition of caring Toryism which in the early nineteenth century opposed the aggressive individualism espoused by the Manchester School, and which regarded Peelite 'Conservatism ... [as] the dilution of a pure principle'. George Bull of Byerley espoused a Toryism which, according to his biographer, 'was recognizably Christian, springing from a sense of social justice and the Christian view of the nature of Man'. Bull defended the Tolpuddle Martyrs and attacked the Poor Law Amendment Act of 1834. He contended that 'the poor had a right to a share of God's bounty; that this was scriptural and bound up in the law of the land'; and that a true Tory preserves all that is good, destroying 'all oppression, cruelty, tyranny and Malthusianism'. His approach was thoroughly paternalistic. He did not believe in universal suffrage and opposed Chartism, but said memorably about the election of MPs that he hoped 'the representatives of the people would take care of the poor; the rich would take care of themselves' (Gill, *Bull* 73–4, 106, 108, 119).

Bull was a leading supporter of the Ten Hours movement, which sought to limit the hours worked in factories. When the original leader of the movement lost his seat in Parliament, it was Bull who persuaded Lord Ashley (later Lord Shaftesbury) to take up the cause. He wrote pamphlets, helped arrange demonstrations and gave evidence to Select Committees. His philosophy was summed up in one of his sermons: 'Until legislators will obey the Word of God and begin at the right end by protecting the wages of the labourer and guarding them from the grasp of the speculator or the avaricious capitalist, nothing can go well – no class can prosper – and no nation can continue great, wealthy or happy' (Gill, 140).

A touchstone of the clergy's social concern has been their attitude to trade unions. For the most part they have been true to their class, and have been hostile to them, as Francis Kilvert was; or have tried to stand neutral between employer and employee. The second stance has enabled the priest to act as a mediator. A country parson writing to *The Spectator* in 1873 declared: 'Farmers, although they will bear to be told about the low wages, hovel cottages and poor fare of their men ... will not tolerate the wholesale, whole-hog advocacy of the labourer's side by a clergyman who should be the friend of all' (Clark, 258). Walter Hook was arbitrator between masters and men during a colliery strike in the late 1850s, at the men's request. Samuel Barnett intervened in fourteen trade disputes in a single year.

There have been examples of identification with the union cause. The vicar of Leintwardine, Herefordshire, chaired a local Agricultural Labourers Union with twenty clergymen as vice-presidents. The union, which claimed 30,000 members, encouraged emigration and migration but did not strike (Chadwick, *VC* 2.155; Clark, 180). Jack Putterill** started a branch of the National Union of Agricultural Workers after the Second World War while he was vicar of Thaxted, and was its chairman (Putterill, 116).

Sometimes parish priests have aided strikers and their families, thus making a statement about what is, and what is not, acceptable in economic warfare. Patrick Bronte, who had put his life in danger by criticizing the Luddite machine-breakers, later took the mill-workers' side in a local dispute, and, though severely criticized by the mill-owners, did what he could to save the men from starving or from falling irretrievably into debt (Gaskell, *Bronte* 41). During the 1889 dock strike Samuel Barnett did all he could to support the strikers, 'aiding by relief', his wife wrote, 'those who without it would have been starved into unrighteous submission' (Barnett, 2.66). Charles Marson** supported a cab-drivers' strike in 1895 while he was at St Mary's, Somers Town (Reckitt, 112). While he was Conrad Noel's** curate at Thaxted, Jack Putterill took the men's side during a bus strike (Putterill, 35). In the small village of Shepherdswell, Kent, the vicar Cuthred Compton and his helpers provided lunch for up to 60 women and children throughout the miners' strike of 1921 (*SPM*, Aug. 1921). By contrast, an attempt on my own part to raise money for a similar purpose during the Dover seamen's strike of 1988 was almost entirely unsuccessful. Local circumstances and public attitudes had changed, and the influence of the parish priest was less.

An extreme example of social commitment has occurred when a priest has become a local councillor (he cannot by law become an MP) in order to help the weak. We may in charity assume that some of the priests who have become Conservative councillors have had this end in view; but less obviously than those who have supported Labour. Jack Putterill, while Conrad Noel's curate at Thaxted, put himself up for election to the Rural District Council in opposition to the owner of Beverley Mansions, a group of damp army huts let at high rents. He was elected, and got the Mansions demolished as part of a programme of slum clearance. Later he was elected to the county council, and when Labour gained a majority in 1946 he was deeply involved in governance (Putterill, 49, 103–6). Mervyn Stockwood joined the Labour party because of a passion for social justice. As a member of Bristol City Council he pioneered the then new idea of a health centre (Stockwood, 68).

Stockwood remained first and foremost a parish priest. One remarkable parish priest lived out much of his vocation as a politician. Charles Jenkinson**, a Labour councillor on Leeds City council, was chairman of the Housing Committee from 1933 to 1936 and embarked upon a massive programme of slum clearance which, among other achievements, wiped his own parish of St John and St Barnabas, Holbeck, off the residential map. The work involved was so overwhelming that he offered his resignation to the Bishop; it was refused because of the opposition of his own parishioners, who were content that during his chairmanship he did no more in the parish than take services. His work, highly contentious at the time, gave him a national reputation. He served on a variety of national bodies and became chairman of the Stevenage Development Corporation (Hammerton, *Jenkinson* passim).

Parochial Morals

George Herbert's* country parson kept close watch over the morals of his people, seeking to curb both the more and the less evident vices. It is the parson's duty to ensure that a careful provision for family does not become covetousness, nor a proper care of the body gluttony. Feeding servants badly is covetousness; so is using a neighbour's spade when you can afford to buy one of your own. To the 'heavy and carnal' the parson supplies practical rules about wise eating; but some one 'with a refined and heavenly disposition' he encourages to abstinence, knowing that, just as Jesus supplied the needs of those who sought him in the wilderness, so God will ensure that self-discipline in His service will not pass to extremes (Herbert, XXVI).

Such refined and meticulous supervision has been unusual. For the most part the clergy have cared for local morals in a more rough and ready fashion. Their concern has been for social discipline as much as for the spiritual nurture of individuals. They have played a part in the enforcement of secular law; to enforce certain aspects of morality they have been able to call upon church courts as well. In earlier centuries the archdeacon's or bishop's visitation included a requirement that churchwardens should present those guilty of such derelictions as sexual offences, absence from church, sabbath-breaking, drunkenness and swearing (Hart, *CC* 77). Herbert's country priest preferred spiritual suasion but was not afraid to invoke ecclesiastical power: 'The parson's punishing of sin and vice is rather by withdrawing his bounty and courtesies from the parties offending, or by private or public reproof ... than by causing them to be presented, or otherwise complained of. And yet as the malice of the person, or heinousness of the crime may be, he is careful to see condign punishment inflicted, and with truly godly zeal, without hatred to the person, hungereth and thirsteth after righteous punishment of unrighteousness' (Herbert, XX).

Church courts could operate vigorously against the recalcitrant, as they notoriously did in the time of Archbishop Laud. Many of the clergy lived in the spirit of Tillotson's remark to a legalistic prebendary: 'Doctor, doctor, charity is above all rubrics' (Addison, 67); but they worked against the background of a system which could, as in the seventeenth century, excommunicate a man with the consequence that he lost his job (Matthews, *Walker* 336); or, as happened in 1839, gaol a cobbler who refused to pay his local church rate (Chadwick, *VC* 1.149–50). Until 1855 an ecclesiastical court could impose on a person found guilty of defamation or of a sexual offence the penalty of standing in a white sheet in church and reading a confession of guilt. James Woodforde* noted that 'one Sarah Gore came to me ... and brought me an instrument from the court of Wells, to perform publick Penance next Sunday at C. Cary Church for having a child, which I am to administer to her publickly after Divine Service' (Woodforde, 1.69–70).

William Grimshaw* employed ecclesiastical discipline freely, and to more effect than some of his later colleagues. 'At Fen Ditton near Cambridge on Sunday 6 May 1849, the village fiddler, convicted of calling the rector's wife a whore, did penance amid catcalls and riot and hassock-throwing and pew-breaking, and was carried shoulder-high for drinks at the Plough after the service' (Chadwick, *VC* 1.489).

Legal sanctions apart, it was for long expected that the parish priest would enforce law and order. John Fletcher* 'burst in' upon the 'licentious assemblies' of young people spending the night in 'dancing, revelling, drunkenness and obscenity ... with a holy indignation making war upon Satan in places peculiarly appropriated to his service,' and with some success. 'After standing the first shock of their rudeness and brutality, his exhortations ... [were] generally received with silent submission, and ... sometimes produced a partial if not entire reformation' (Benson, *Fletcher* 54). James Woodforde policed Castle Cary. In December 1769 'Brother Heighes, Jack and myself, all armed, took a walk at twelve this evening round the parish to see if we could meet any idle folk' (Woodforde, 1.95). John Skinner* walked about Camerton on Sundays between morning and evening service 'to see that things are tolerably quiet'; and personally investigated a case of alleged sexual assault before referring it to the bench (Skinner, 41, 21–3). The historian J.A. Froude, himself a clergyman's son, wrote that a typical parson in the 1830s 'was spoken of in the parish as "the master" – the person who was responsible for keeping order there, and who knew how to keep it' (Quoted in Brendon, *Hawker* 81–2). When William Andrew* was at Cromer he used to walk the streets in the evenings to ensure that the children were not about; to such effect that some refused to do errands for their mothers for fear of meeting him (Chadwick, *Andrew* 25). Edward Elton, who was vicar of Wheatley, near Oxford, from 1851 told his grandson: 'I had not only to be an active clergyman but perform duty also as a quasi-policeman and keep order among a turbulent population' (Elton, *King* 32–3). In 1882 John Conybeare** of Barrington saved the proprietor of a local cement works from an angry crowd of his workpeople (Colloms, 260).

In the interests of good order the clergy have used both physical and moral suasion. William Grimshaw would leave church in the psalm before the sermon to urge, and if necessary, flog idlers in inn or churchyard within the sacred walls. George Bull** who measured 5 feet 2 inches, used to visit the ginshops and alehouses of the notorious Sticker Lane in Brierley at the request of wives, and drag out offending husbands by the ear (Gill, *Bull* 56). On Easter Monday 1835 William Andrew brought the customary festivities at Witchingham to an early and unusually peaceful close by standing in the front room of the public house till the people dispersed (Chadwick, *Andrew* 31–2). John Keble*, called by one of his parishioners 'a very stern gentleman', never hesitated to lay his stick over the shoulders of any village boy who failed to touch his cap to him (Battiscombe, *Keble* 178). John Conybeare excommunicated a parishioner because of an assault on a woman, and secured repentance (Colloms, 260). Christopher Chavasse**, while a curate at St Helens, joined the rest of the ministry team for their Saturday night routine. At 11.00 p.m. the team visited the parish's public houses and invited their occupants to the mission where they were given a hot drink and a gospel message, and then sent home more sober than would otherwise have been the case. Often the clergy could not leave the mission until 2.00 or 3.00 a.m.; and the duties of Sunday lay ahead (Gummer, 44).

Informal social discipline has had its dangers. In 1842 Henry Michell Wagner**, who had given a boy who had cheeked him several strokes with his riding-crop, was summoned for assault by the boy's father and was fined £2. The case was unusual, however, in that Wagner was widely unpopular in Brighton at the time; his political enemies took advantage of the opportunity to embarrass him (Wagner, 65–7). Another priest was luckier. In 1882 Mr Lee-Warner, vicar and schoolmaster of Tarrant Gunville, Dorset, was sued by the father of one of his pupils after he had dragged a boy from his home and beaten him for committing an indecent offence against a girl and boasting of it. The judge dismissed the assault charge and levied a nominal fine of one shilling for the offence of pulling the boy out of his home (Barrow, 166).

On the whole the clergy have been cautious about policing the morals of the rich. There was a tradition of outspoken criticism directed against them in the earlier centuries of our period. Thomas Becon, the sixteenth-century Puritan incumbent of St Stephen's, Walbrook, was not untypical when he criticized 'gorgeous houses and sumptuous mansions' and 'vain and foolish light apparel'; nor when he ferociously attacked enclosers – 'the greedy gentlemen which are sheepmongers and graziers' (Bailey, *Becon* 62). Later that tradition died away. John Skinner regretted the sabbath-breaking of the gentry and the coal proprietors, but was not prepared to challenge them directly (Skinner, 99–100). The reliance was now on example. In a chapter entitled 'The Clergyman in Society' R.W. Evans advocated being in it but not of it: 'Even the stranger will discover his office, not by his black clothes, nor yet by unreasonable intrusion of subjects too solemn for the occasion; but by the indescribable propriety, that modest dignity, that gentleness and serenity which is derived from the habitual exercize of his profession' (Evans, 216). The distinction between these indirect methods and the more stringent approach to the poor did not pass unnoticed. Sydney Smith*, criticizing the activities of the Society for the Suppression of Vice in the early nineteenth century observed: 'They should denominate themselves a society for suppressing the vices of persons whose income does not exceed £500 per annum' (Bell, *Smith* 72). However, Tom Keble, John's brother and incumbent of Bisley, refused communion to a local gentleman who was causing open scandal (Battiscombe, *Keble* 179).

For reasons both sacred and secular, the supervision of sexual morals has been a special concern. Ralph Josselin brought his characteristic theology to the subject. He reported that a woman 'gott with child by a weaver, afterwards was married to him, was deliverd before her time, and died. god make such things to bee warnings to us.' He rejoiced when he was able to prevent 'an eminent wickednes' between 'an old fellow and a youth lord helpe mee to improve it for thy glory and their good in rescuing them out of the bonds of iniquity' (Josselin, 430, 465–6).

Two novelists describe contrasting clerical approaches to sexual morals. Jane Austen's Mr Collins took a strong line with Mr and Mrs Bennett about the elopment of their daughter Lydia with Mr Wickham, even though she subsequently married him: 'I must not ... neglect the duties of my station, or refrain from declaring my amazement, at hearing that you received the young couple into your house as soon as they were married. It was an encouragement to vice ... You ought certainly to forgive them as a Christian, but never to admit them in your sight, or allow their names to be mentioned in your hearing' (Austen, *PP* 382). In contrast, Trollope's Frank Fenwick spoke to the mother of Carry Brattle, disgraced and forbidden her home because of a love affair, 'never calling her [daughter] a castaway, talking of her as Carry, who might yet be worthy of happiness here and of all joy hereafter; [so] that when she [Mrs Brattle] thought of him as a minister of God, whose duty it was to pronounce God's threats to erring human beings, she was almost alarmed' (Trollope, *VB* 45).

In real life, when Will, James Woodforde's servant, contracted venereal disease in 1781 Woodforde arranged for him to receive medical treatment and made no moral comment (Woodforde, 1.331). In a stricter age, Kilvert approved of the action of Mrs Venables, the wife of his vicar at Clyro, in reprimanding publicly a woman who had allowed her daughter to sit up at night with her young man while she and her husband went to bed (Kilvert, 1.233). Indeed, in country parishes of the time the clergy could often expect to be supported by public opinion in any stand they took against loose morals. At Clyro Kilvert was approached by parishioners indignant that an unmarried couple were living together. He regretfully informed them that there was no law against people living in concubinage (Kilvert, 1.84).

The tension between the parish priest's pastoral and disciplinary roles is illustrated in Henrietta Barnett's* description of her husband's responses to cases of homosexuality. 'One sinner he drew to repentance, another to justice, a third he comforted in his crippling sorrow, the wife of a fourth he induced to remain with him' (Barnett, 1.268). Certainly, a sensitive priest, confronted with the complexity of human nature and motives, is likely to be cautious about dealing in rigid moral categories. Harold Hosking**, encountering a young homosexual in unpermissive Newlyn in the 1960s, found his previous certainties eroded by the experience; pastoral care became more important than condemnation (Hosking, 95–8).

A concern for sexual morals has had positive results other than the obvious ones. One of the driving forces behind attempts to provide better housing in the nineteenth century was distaste for the consequences of throwing the sexes together higgledy-piggledy (see, for example, Atkinson, 20–2).

I came across a variety of departures from Christian sexual norms in a Kentish village in the 1980s and 1990s. The difference from the past was that morals had changed; there was little tendency for villagers to show active disapproval. Finding that I was more valued and valuable as a listening ear than as an arbiter of morals, I usually kept my opinions to myself. When asked for ethical comment I supplied it; but that was very rarely the part required of me.

The clergy have a special stake in ensuring the proper use of Sundays. For obvious reasons they have felt bound to practice the sabbatarianism they have enjoined upon others. Ralph Josselin asked God's pardon for journeying on a Sunday: 'It was a worke of mercy' (Josselin, 442). Alarmed by a razor breaking as he stropped it, James Woodforde resolved 'not to shave on the Lord's Day or do any other work to profane it pro futuro'. It has to be said, however, that when Woodforde was away from his Norfolk parish in Somerset he was not a regular churchgoer. Once he read the family a sermon instead; on another occasion they 'read ... Books at home'; on another 'Dinner Time interfered with the time of Service' (Woodforde, 1.85; 2.269, 272, 266). It seems that he had enough conscience to make excuses for staying at home, but not enough invariably to attend.

Few clergy have gone as far as Parson Froude of Knowstone, Devonshire, in the eighteenth century, who is said to have fired the hay-ricks of backsliders (Goodenough, 111), but they have, as one would expect, unanimously advocated church-going, and for much of our period had the law to support them. John Fletcher used to rise at 5.00 a.m. and traverse Madeley bell in hand to rouse sluggard parishioners (Benson, *Fletcher* 55).

The divisive question has been how the rest of Sunday should be employed. In Elizabethan times relaxed mediaeval attitudes still prevailed, and the clergy could suffer for advocating strict observance. Two men who were bowling in the churchyard of Deighton, Yorkshire, set upon the curate when he reprimanded them and 'bett him grevowslie' (Hart, *CC* 45–6).

The curate was ahead of his time. It was not until Nicholas Bound (or Bownde), rector of Norton, Suffolk, 1585–1611 published in 1595 *The true doctrine of the Sabbath* that any serious attempt was made to equate Sunday with the Jewish Sabbath, and to prevent recreation and unessential work altogether. He taught, among other things, that only one church bell should be rung, and that conversation on worldly matters was to be avoided (Fuller, *CH* 3.159).

Bound appealed to the economic as well as the spiritual sensibilities of Puritans by arguing that with strict Sabbath observance should go a reduction in the number of holy days in case 'men should be hindered from the necessary works of their callings' (Hill, 85). Royal and episcopal sentiments were, however, against him. Sabbatarianism was criticized as 'galling men's necks with a Jewish yoke, against the liberty of Christians' (Fuller, *CH* 3.160). Gerard Prior, vicar of Elsfield, Worcestshire, was suspended for preaching against Sabbath dancing in defiance of James I's *Declaration of Sports*, and for praying that 'the King's heart might be turned from profaneness, vanity and popery' (Hart, *CC* 73). Contrariwise, many of the evicted clergy of the period 1642–60 were accused of the profanation of the Sabbath. Thomas Darnell, vicar of Thorpe le Soken, Essex, was accused not only of playing games, but of cleaning out his cowhouse; Nicholas Lowes, vicar of Great Bentley in the same county, of leading his parish by example to spend the greater part of Sundays in games and drinking (Matthews, *Walker* 149, 158).

Sabbatarians were battling against strong traditions of wakes – festivities after Sunday service on the parish's annual Feast Day – and ales – Church-ales to raise money for church repairs, clerk-ales to raise money to pay the parish clerk, bid-ales to raise money for the poor. Charles I's bishops supported these occasions, both because they judged them innocent and because they prevented the people gathering 'into tippling-houses and there on their ale benches talking matters of Church and State, or else into conventicles' (Hart, *CC* 96). James Woodforde taught that while the Christian should abstain from 'bodily labour and worldly cares' and dedicate the greater part of the day to devotion, 'innocent amusements may justly be allowed' (quoted by N. Sykes in *Theology*, vol. 38, 342–3). John Keble was in the same tradition; he encouraged cricket after Sunday evensong until compelled by strong local opposition to abandon it (Battiscombe, *Keble* 180).

Some eighteenth-century clergy organized concerts on Sundays, provoking the Evangelical poet Cowper to write:

If apostolic gravity be free
To play the fool on Sundays, why not we?
If he the tinkling harpsichord regards
As inoffensive, what offence in cards?

Strike up the fiddles, let us all be gay!
Laymen have leave to dance, if parsons play. (Martin, *Newton* 299)

Cowper was speaking for the sabbatarian tradition which took root during the seventeenth century and which gradually prevailed thereafter both in law and custom. Ralph Josselin 'routed' young people playing cat on the green on the Sabbath (Josselin, 476). William Grimshaw did not hesitate to bring Sunday games-players before the archdeacon's court. John Skinner visited a local inn to check that the law confining the serving of drink to travellers was being observed. He rebuked his clerk when he observed him picking plums on a Sunday (Skinner, 97–8, 170). Samuel Ashe, rector of Langley Burrell before the Kilverts' time (and squire as well as parson) stopped games of Sunday football on Langley Common by puncturing any football he could get hold of (Kilvert, 2.232). Henry Michell Wagner became vice-president of the Brighton branch of the Early Closing Association, a body which sought to limit shop hours not so much to preserve the health of employees as to lessen the likelihood that they would be tempted to spend their one day off in 'pleasure and recreation' (Wagner, 83). Francis Close** prevailed on Cheltenham shop-keepers not to open on Sunday. He prevented trains from stopping in the town on the sacred day, and advised worshippers not to use public transport to come to church, thus giving weary animals a chance to rest. A walk in the afternoon was permissible, but the part of the day not spent in worship should for the most part be spent with interesting scriptural material (Hennell, 106).

An insistence on Sabbath observance was a hallmark of Evangelicals, but not all were guilty of the rigorism of some. Charles Simeon* showed his usual sanctified common sense when he wrote: 'I think that many Judaize too much, and that they would have joined the Pharisees in condemning our Lord on many occasions. I do not think that they err in acting up to their own principles ... but that they err in making their own standard a standard for all others ... They will in effect argue thus: "*I* do not walk out on a Sabbath day; therefore an artisan may not walk out into the fields for an hour on that day." They forget that the poor man is confined all the rest of the week, which they are not; and that they themselves will walk in their garden, when the poor have no garden to walk in' (Hopkins, *Simeon* 172).

Simeon was echoing views expressed by Dr Paul Micklethwaite at the height of seventeenth-century Sabbatarian controversy: 'Gentlefolk were obliged to a stricter observation of the Lord's day, than labouring people ... Such as are not annihilated with labour, have no title to be recreated with liberty. Let servants, whose hands are ever working while their eyes are waking; let such, who all the foregoing week had their cheeks moistened with sweat and hands hardened with labour; let such on the Lord's day have some recreation ... indulged to them; while persons of quality ... are concerned in conscience to observe the Lord's day with greater abstinence from recreations' (Fuller, *CH* 3.419–221).

Viewed thus, Sabbatarianism has a strongly positive aspect. It protected the labourer from his employer, as George Crabbe** noted in 'The Village':

> Their careful masters brood the painful thought;
> Much in their mind they murmur and lament,
> That one fair day should be so idly spent;
> And think that Heaven deals hard, to tithe their store
> And tax their time for preachers and the poor.

John Skinner, ruminating that Sabbath-breaking was undoubtedly a 'forerunner' of the French Revolution and observance 'an express command of God', believed the law on the matter 'replete in benevolence to the race of man, especially to the lower part of the community' (Skinner, 98–9). Taking the argument further, Samuel Barnett advocated that the day should be used for 'enlargement'. His view that educational and cultural activities were to be encouraged brought him into collision with those, such as Francis Close, who taught that picture galleries and museums should be closed (Barnett, 2.101; Hennell, 106).

Both Close and Barnett would have been horrified by the way in which Sundays are used and regarded in the late twentieth century. There are those who wish the day to be like any other; those who wish otherwise argue almost exclusively in secular terms. Perhaps this is as it should be. Those clergy, such as myself, who wish to keep Sunday special are only to a limited degree seeking to protect religious observance; the thrust of our argument is more general, resting on the belief that society is better served by a rhythmic rather than a monotonous weekly calendar.

With pastoral care, as with priestly work in general, it is hard to measure effects. But there can be no doubt that the efforts of the parochial clergy over the centuries have had a softening and civilizing effect, and that against their occasional narrowness of vision must be set both the magnitude of the evils against which they have fought and the amount of good they have done. To conclude with a striking example: Bishop Blomfield of London built ten churches in Bethnal Green. When the first was being built in 1839 a canvasser for sixpences was told that people would give him a shilling in order to hang a bishop but not sixpence in order to build a church; a cow was used to disrupt the ceremony of laying the foundation-stone. Eleven years later the tenth church was opened to general approval; the work the Church had done for children was particularly appreciated. The women of clerical households, originally insulted in the street, were now greeted kindly everywhere. A police inspector told an incumbent that before his church was built a policeman on his own would not dare make an arrest in the streets behind it; now women visited freely in the same area (Chadwick, *VC* 1.331–2).

10

Private Practice

Your enjoyment of the world is never right, till
every morning you wake in Heaven (Traherne 1.28).

The Use of Time

To an extent unparalleled in other professions the clergy of the Church of
England have been free to determine the length of their working hours and
what they do within them. The outcome has been indolence and also dedication
which beggar belief. Bishop Hensley Henson (1863–1947) remarked that the
Church of England contained the half-dozen idlest and the half-dozen most
hard-working men in the country (Melinsky, 163). Hours of work apart, the
spiritual question in some cases has been that of the division of time between
responsibilities; in others that of the quality of response to circumstance.

It is possible to describe with great exactness the public clerical duties
performed by William Cole** in the year 1766. He presided at Matins in his
own parish on 82 occasions, and at Vespers (his word for Evening Prayer) on
50, preaching twice on a Sunday only once. He celebrated Holy Communion 4
times. He conducted 15 baptisms, 13 churchings, 9 marriages and 9 funerals.
He paid 25 visits to sick persons. He catechized the children of the parish at
Vespers throughout Lent. He examined three groups of persons for confirmation and took them to the Bishop. He thrice took services for other clergy. He
attended an Archdeacon's Visitation. He performed a few minor clerical duties,
and spent some time in business connected with his prospective resignation of
the parish. On the most generous construction it is impossible to believe that he
averaged as much as two hours a day on these public duties (Cole, 3–172).

A similar exercise undertaken in respect of James Woodforde* yields a like
result. In the year 1791 Woodforde's recorded clerical duties consisted of duty
at a single service each Sunday, 14 christenings, 6 churchings, 2 marriages, 11
funerals, a single sick visit, a service on Good Friday, and attending the
Bishop's and Archdeacon's visitations (Woodforde, vol. 3). The year was
untypical only in the respects that Woodforde took no time off to go to
Somerset and that he undertook no duties for colleagues. The amount of time
Woodforde devoted to public duties must have been even less than that spent
by Cole.

A clergyman has, of course, duties other than public ones; notably those of
private devotion, study and sermon preparation. So far as the evidence Woodforde provides allows us to judge, he did not spend great tracts of time on any
of the three; nor was Cole much more conscientious.

Examples of restricted commitment are not confined to the eighteenth century. The diaries of two of Robert Hawker's neighbours – John Davis (1779–1857), rector of Kilkhampton, Cornwall, from 1804 to 1857, and Oliver Rouse (1781–1846), rector of Tetcott, Devon, for the last thirty years of his life – suggest lives of extraordinary intellectual and spiritual poverty, devoted for the most part to eating and drinking, shooting and socializing (Brendon, *Hawker* 156–8).

It has been argued that idleness is a besetting – perhaps even an unavoidable – clerical sin. William Paley** wrote: 'If there be any principal objection to the life of a clergyman ... it is this – that it does not supply sufficient engagements to the time and thoughts of an active mind' (Charge (1785), p.15, quoted Russell, 114). In a sermon preached in 1809 Sydney Smith* asserted: 'The most inveterate disease to which a clerical life is exposed is that of indolence' (Bell, *Smith* 102). Walter Hook* declared: 'The temptations of a young clergyman are to idleness, hypocrisy and malignity' (Stephens, *Hook* 503). A country doctor in the 1870s said that the great disease which afflicted the mass of the clergy was a lack of work; in the 1880s a country parson was described as a 'spiritually minded vegetable' (Chadwick, *VC* 2.166).

Nor has the lack of occupation been regarded as a shameful secret. When the advowson of John Skinner's* parish of Camerton was for sale *c.*1800 the patron wrote: 'The duty is very easy, viz. only once a Sunday, and occasional burials, etc., etc.' (Skinner, vii; 'etc, etc.' presumably referred to the other rites of passage). John Skinner did a great deal more than the essential minimum; but he was still left with abundant time for scholarship, for business and for family matters.

The state of affairs so far described has been seen, however, as a dereliction of duty. 'Sir,' said Dr Johnson, 'the life of a parson, of a conscientious clergyman, is not easy ... No, Sir, I do not envy a clergyman's life as an easy life, nor do I envy the clergyman who makes it an easy life' (Boswell's *Life* quoted Smyth, *Garbett* 98). 'It is better,' said Edward Bickersteth**, in the 1830s, 'to wear out than to rust out' (Chadwick, *VC* 1.443). 'The great lesson which ought to be stamped irrevocably upon the clerical mind,' wrote Henry Liddon, 'is the preciousness of time – its brevity and irrevocableness, the strict account which must be given of it, the overwhelming interests which hang upon its due employment ... Labour is the portion of the servants of God, leisure is a misery' (Liddon, 42–3).

'I suppose,' said Bishop Lang** in 1904, 'there is no body of clergy in the world so energetic as the clergy of our English church' (Smyth, *Garbett* 75). Lang knew what he was talking about. In every age the work load accepted by many clergy has been phenomenal. They have followed the example of William Grimshaw* who, when urged by friends to spare himself, used to reply: 'Let me labour now, I shall have enough rest by and by. I cannot do enough for Christ Who has done so much for me' (Cragg, *Grimshaw* 64). Grimshaw's conscience in the matter is illustrated by an entry in his diary: 'To Day I have trifled. I have loitered it away doing little, or I fear but little to God's Glory. Let it not come into the number of my Months. Be ashamed, O my soul, before ye Lord, for so embezzling thy golden Moments!' (Barker, *Grimshaw* 112).

Here is a description of the use of golden moments in Walter Hook's parish of Leeds in the mid-1840s, given by one of his curates: 'We rose at six, and within a few minutes were assembled for a short service ... At half-past seven two of us were at church, beginning the early morning service ... Before breakfast we had our own family worship. At nine the day schools had to be opened with prayer, and afterwards religious instruction given to the older scholars. From school the transition was naturally to the districts, where the anxiously expected visits were made until half-past ten, at which hour those of us who had not already been to Morning Prayer had to hasten to church to take the ordinary forenoon service, preceded by marriages and followed by baptisms and churchings, while the others continued to visit in their districts. In the afternoon, at three, came baptisms again, with churchings and burials, and a full choral service; the latter to be repeated at half-past seven, but now only read ... At the last service ... only one curate was usually present, the rest being otherwise fully occupied, some with classes of candidates for Confirmation, or of communicants, others at evening schools, but all in one way or another. It was usually ten o'clock before we had wearily reached home, to eat our simple supper, have our night's devotion, and go gladly to rest. Sunday, however sacred, was no Sabbath, being the day least of all the seven a day of rest' (Stranks, *Hook* 58–9).

The clergy's day at Portsea under Cyril Garbett** began with a voluntary Eucharist at 7.30 a.m. followed by a compulsory Matins at 8.10 a.m. Breakfast was followed by study, which occupied the time till Sext at 1.00 p.m. and lunch, the only formal corporate meal of the day. An hour afterwards was given over to recreation, but by 2.30 the team were out visiting until high tea at 6.00 p.m. Clubs and more visiting followed, with evening prayer for the most part said privately. Cocoa and biscuits at 10.00 were followed by Compline; after which, one curate recorded, 'the rest of the day was our own' (Smyth, *Garbett* 107–8). When Nicolas Stacey went to Portsea in the 1950s the discipline was more genial but the working day just as long (Stacey, 44).

We have already had occasion to comment on the way in which Dick Sheppard* lived his life, periods of frenetic activity alternating inevitably with periods of collapse. In a letter he describes a Sunday in 1934:

Up writing at 6 a.m.
Celebrated Charing Cross Hospital 7.30.
Assisted at [St] Martin's 8.15.
Ward services; three different short sermons 9.0–10.0.

Assisted Martin's 10.15.

Took service Martin's 11.30.

Beardoe Grundy ... to sandwich lunch, and pipe 1–2.15.

Saw two people 2.30.

3.30 Christened Frank Williams' second baby.

4.0–6.0 Charing Cross Hospital ... four different short sermons in wards.

6.15 Preached at Martin's.

7.30 Dined with pal ...

9.0–10.0 In crypt [a refuge for the homeless].

10.15 BBC Epilogue.

11.30 to now 4.0 a.m. Writing!!! (Roberts, *Sheppard* 240–1)

Two final examples from recent times: Arthur Hopkinson**, ruminating in the 1940s on the delights of retirement, described the chief of them as ceasing to be the slave of time. 'For forty years life has been stretched on the rack of a time-table. Over and over again a job has had to be left unfinished because some other job has got to be begun. Duties have waged a perpetual war for precedence. And rest has been marred by the remembrance of the things left undone and waiting to be done' (Hopkinson, 25). Roy Catchpole**, writing of the 1970s and 1980s claims: 'The work was never-ending. Junior doctors may complain at eighty-hour stretches, but at least they have a rest after it. We don't. It's eighty hours and then another eighty hours, and maybe after twenty years you'll get a sabbatical because you're on the verge of cracking up. It's a good life for a work-a-holic though' (Catchpole, *GMDC* 54).

These examples are, however, as extreme in one direction as those of Woodforde and Cole in the other. In every case cited, the priest relied on others for domestic support; in most there were no other than ministerial claims upon his time. When the circumstances have been different, so has been the response.

Ralph Josselin* reproached himself: 'I found my selfe backward to my studies, oh the time that I loose, wheras I should redeeme the same' (Josselin, 181). He was reporting the mutterings of an over-sensitive conscience; by most standards he was a paragon of industry. Yet a great deal of his time was not devoted to ministry. It was devoted to business, to family affairs, above all to agriculture. He was as much a farmer as a minister, to the extent that he once considered abandoning the latter occupation for the former. Nor did these non-ecclesiastical calls upon his time ever cause him conscientious scruples; he accepted them as an integral part of his life.

Josselin actually put his hand to the plough (see for example Josselin, 500). For the most part, later clergy did not; but vast tracts of their time were spent on the work of a gentleman householder and farmer. Woodforde fell into this category. That he had a conscience about the use of time is shown by the agreement he made with Nancy that each of them would rise before 7.00 a.m.

except on Sundays, on pain of forfeiting 6d (Woodforde, 1.317); but his conscience remained unwrung by the amount of time he devoted to non-ministerial activities. So did that of John Skinner; who wrote in typical vein that: 'The great secret of life, if we look for comfort (Happiness I will put out of the question), is to be constantly occupied' (Skinner, 383).

In similar vein James Newton** wrote: 'The Distance from the Cradle to the Grave is Short ... & the Days of our Pilgrimage soon come to an End, & since this is the Case let me be the more careful & frugal in the Management of my Time, for it is that only that will intitle me to a happy Death.' True to his principles, he berated himself for late rising: 'Not up till about 9 O'Clock M. & shameful thing' (James Newton, 22,138). Yet Newton was often away from his parish on visits to Oxford and London; and when he was at home his specifically clerical duties took only a fragment of his time. He felt he must not waste time; he did not feel that he was bound to devote most or even much of it to his work as a clergyman.

Financial considerations have persuaded many clergy to spend much of their time on other than ministerial work. The problem has been to maintain a proper balance. Daniel Falconer, rector of Aldham, Essex, was accused to the Parliamentary Commissioners in 1644 of giving 'much of his tyme about worldly imployments as dressing corne, pitching cart, and that sometymes on Satterday Nine a clock at night when it were better he were in his study' (Matthews, *Walker* 151). James Layton, curate and only clergyman in three Norfolk parishes at the beginning of the nineteenth century, did no more than the bare minimum of duty. When financial exigency compelled him to take pupils he had to work long hours with them. Whatever time was left was devoted to his wife. He was honest about his laziness: 'My activity,' he wrote, 'is only that of [a] bottled small bee which flies about and plentifully if shaken, but otherwise is still enough' (Virgin, 243–4).

It has always been acknowledged that a married clergyman should find time for his wife and family. Stern souls have seen this as an argument for celibacy; but family time need no more be a distraction from ministry than time given to private devotion. Charles Kingsley's* plan for his days at Eversley was both systematic and uxorious. He rose at 6.00 a.m.; family prayers took place at 7.30, and breakfast at 8.00; 8.30–10.00 was given over to household matters; 10.00 to 1.00 p.m. to the study of divinity with Fanny 'having our door open for *poor* parish visitants' (he was not interested in purely social callers). In the afternoon he taught in the school and visited. After dinner at 5.00 he and Fanny would 'draw and feed our intellect and fancy all evening with your head on my bosom and our lips meeting every now and again to tell each other something that is too deep for words'. The day ended with family prayers and bed at 11.00 (Chitty, *Kingsley* 97).

Many clergy have followed the extraordinary English tradition by which children are handed over to the care of nursemaids, governesses and schoolteachers. William Grimshaw sent his children to the Methodist school at Kingswood, John Skinner his sons to Winchester, Dick Sheppard his girls to board at St Paul's school. In other cases children have been educated at home by their parents; sometimes with good effects, as in the case of the Wesleys, sometimes with bad, as in the case of Samuel Butler's Theobald Pontifex: 'He hears the children their lessons, and the daily oft-repeated screams that issue from the study during the lesson hours tell their own horrible story over the house' (Butler, 97).

Scholarship and recreation have sometimes taken up unconscionable proportions of a clergyman's time. Mere ecclesiastical busy-ness is equally to be deprecated. Ernest Raymond's Canon Welcome 'delegated to his curates all weekday services ... all urgent visiting, and all the unimportant weddings and funerals. As the GOC, he would say, he was almost entirely confined to Headquarters; most unfortunately he had little time to accompany his subalterns into the Front Line. A vicar and rural dean had an immense amount of correspondence to attend to, and ... there was always a multitude of small activities to be discharged ... This committee and that committee claimed him, this board and that council' (Raymond, 38).

The case of Welcome serves as a reminder that the hours spent on clerical duties do not tell the whole story. More important are the quality of the work and the spirit in which it is done. George Carey** tells the story of how, having ranted at God for giving him too much to do, he said to himself: 'Whose work is it anyway? If it is God's work – why should I do God's worrying for him?' He handed his problems back to God; 'the weight was lifted from my shoulders and each and every job got done!' (Carey, 52).

Nor is a well-organized day the only characteristically Christian use of time. Monica Furlong's remark that the main thing she asked of a priest was that he should always have plenty of time was a plea not for laziness but for a readiness to respond to the call of the moment. Those who knew Alexander Mackonochie** remarked on 'his ready response to each separate demand upon his time and attention. When each five minutes was of value, and when ... the stress of work must last from early morning to late at night, he would bear with repeated and often unnecessary interruptions without the slightest manifestation of impatience ... For the time being only three persons existed for him, God, himself, and the soul with which he had to deal' (Towle, *Mackonochie* 90–1). Catherine Treasure has suggested that one thing women might contribute to the ministry would be the lack of a need to justify their existence by having a full diary (Treasure, 15).

An unhurried priest invites confidences. Nicolas Stacey**, not a paragon in this regard, writes of a time when he gave space to a man whose errand was declared to be the disposal of his mother-in-law's clothes. He discovered that the man wanted to talk about an incestuous relation with a daughter (Stacey, 95). I regard it as one of the failures of my ministry at Shepherdswell that people constantly comment on how 'busy' I am; the more so because, by comparison with the great souls of the past, the observation is misplaced.

It is even a question how far being fully occupied is an essential characteristic of priestly spirituality. John Keble* is one of only four parish priests included in the Anglican calendar (the others are Charles Simeon, George Herbert, and Richard Hooker). Keble's family responsibilities took up much of his time; but, by the standard of many of his contemporaries, he was indolent. Perhaps this characteristic was one of the limitations which Georgina Battiscombe refers to in the sub-title of her biography; perhaps it gave him the space to be the quality of man he was.

A more extreme example still is that of Thomas Traherne*. Of the outward circumstances of his life we know very little, but his *Centuries* contains a few tantalizing clues. His remark 'When I came into the country, and saw that I had all time in my own hands' seems to refer to the period when he was parish priest at Credenhill; and to suggest that his parochial duties weighed far less heavily upon him than his dedication to 'the study of Felicity' (Traherne, 3.52). The eventual outcome of this study was literature of which the most significant part survived only by chance, and remained unknown until the beginning of this century. Traherne's use of his time bore most of its fruit only hundreds of years after his death; an interesting example of the divine economy at work.

Prayer

All spirituality displays what might be called the iceberg effect: the visible phenomena give only a restricted idea of the vast unseen below.

In nothing is this effect more apparent than in prayer. Not only is prayer hidden by its very nature; it is also an intensely private activity, concealed behind silence or self-deprecating humour. Henry Liddon wrote: 'Partly from our habitual national reserve, and partly from our dread of all unreality and cant in religious matters, it is usual even for religious Englishmen to avoid any reference whatever to their private spiritual life. The feeling is, that you would just as soon refer to a man's income, or to the character of his near relations, as to his daily prayers' (Liddon, 62). Cyril Tomkinson, Harry Williams's** vicar at All Saints, Margaret Street, prayed for long hours, but in public was only heard to say: 'People speak about prayer. But the only prayer I ever say is to thank God that my father was a stockbroker' (Williams, 115).

James Woodforde* may be a further case in point. His diary contains only very occasional references to personal prayer: 'I did not go to Church today, but hope what I did in my Closet was acceptable to the Divine Goodness;' 'We did not go to Church today, but I hope we did what was acceptable to God at home.' (Woodforde, 2.38; 4.261). Yet, if he followed the practice he enjoined upon his people in sermons (and there is no reason to think him a hypocrite), he prayed regularly and with perseverance. We are entitled to hope that his normal practice is reflected in an entry made when Mrs Custance, the squire's wife, was ill: 'It is my daily, Morning and Evening Prayer, that she might get over it, and soon' (N.Sykes in *Theology*, vol. 38, 345–6; Woodforde, 3.326).

Similarly, John Skinner's* references to prayer are rare and fleeting, except on the single occasion when he summarizes a sermon he intended to give on the subject. He enjoins on the laity the morning and evening use of the Lord's Prayer; memorizing collects and psalms; communing 'with their own hearts in their chambers, and be[ing] still'; and engaging in 'secret communications of devotion' throughout the working day. Skinner's character suggests that what he recommended for others he practised himself (Skinner, 277–8).

In the case of Ralph Josselin* reticence is not a problem. It may be surmised, and is to be hoped, that his practice was typical of many others who have not left a like record.

In his fretful old age Josselin noted: 'My bed was uncomfortable, its best to bee up early and with god'; but it did not take a bad night to put him to prayer. He reminds himself in passing 'not to forgett the condicon of my son Thomas in my daily prayers', and frequently records the setting aside of all or part of a day for extended devotion. In 1651 he spent 'part of this day in prayer at my house in seeking god in behalfe of my wife and the kingdome'. Later the same year he gave the whole day to fasting and to prayer 'in regard of the illnesse of my sonne John ... to seeke god to make me more profitable in the ministry of the word, and that the word might prosper to begett and strengthen soules, and to blesse our fellowship ... [and] ... that god would discover to me ... his operations that he is acting in the world, that so I may serve him therein, and not stumble at [sic] fall against any of them.' In 1658 he set apart the first available day of the school holidays 'to humble my soule before god for all my sins in my relations ... to beg his presence in my studdies, ministry, his blessing on my little ones in their education and course of life, and that the lord would provide for me, and mine.' To give him the privacy his prayer life required he erected a 'litle house in the orchard ... for a retiring, meditating place to contemplate and view my god with delight in his word and works and doings in the world.'

One diary entry takes us especially deeply into Josselin's prayer life. On his fortieth birthday on 26 January 1655 he 'set this day apart to seeke gods presence with me in all my wayes'. He records the reflections which occurred to him as the day went on. He appears to have sat with a Bible before him, finding texts which followed or guided the progress of his thought. He gives his whole self over to be God's slave ('I desire thee this day to boare my eare'); he prays to be accepted as a servant and a son, and to be given strength to bear trials and to grow in faith and joy; he prays for 'the soule of those I call mine, wife, children, sister freinds, kindred, people: my worke of ministry, and educacon of youth, that I might be fruitfull unto thy glorie'; he resigns his need of 'outward things' to God's disposal, at the same time stressing his gratitude for needed bounties and his hope that they might continue. His egotism is as apparent in Josselin's prayers as in the rest of his life; but there can be no doubt about his sincerity or his perseverance (Josselin, 606, 426, 254, 262, 428, 449, 360–1).

A trawl through the centuries produces other examples of prayerful devotion. Robert Bolton, the Puritan incumbent of Broughton, Northampton-shire, in the early seventeenth century prayed six times a day: twice by himself, twice with his family, and twice with his wife (Hart, *CC* 143). Charles Simeon* rose at 4.00 a.m. to give four hours to prayer and Bible study (Jones, *Spirituality*, 461). Walter Hook* wrote to a friend: 'I have found it necessary ... to dedicate an hour or two at midnight ... to serious meditation, self-examina-tion and prayer. Between 10 and 1 are usually my happy hours' (Stephens, *Hook* 296). When the First World War broke out, Cyril Garbett** made it a daily practice to go into an unheated church at 6.30 a.m. to pray for an hour before the 7.30 a.m. Eucharist (Garbett, 130).

Two great Evangelicals – William Grimshaw* and John Fletcher* – were pre-eminently men of prayer. Grimshaw rose very early, having already meditated in bed. 'As soon as you awake in the Morning, employ an Hour in five things: – Bless God for the Mercies of Night past – Praise Him for a New Day, and pray for the Blessing of it – Examine well your own Hearts – Meditate upon some Spiritual Subject – and lastly, plan out the Business of the Day.' He dressed singing a hymn or praying, spent a further half hour in private worship in his study, and then led family worship. Prayer punctuated the rest of the day; when he had no preaching duties he would spend up to six further hours praying, in addition to time spent in reading. The day ended with yet more family and private prayer. 'At going to Bed, revise the Thoughts, Words and Actions of the Day. W[ha]t is amiss, Beg Pardon of; what is well, bless God alone for. Conclude with Prayer. Undress and lye down with Prayer. And never fall asleep with an unforgiven sin upon your Conscience' (Baker, *Grimshaw* 170, 172).

Much of his prayer time was given to self-examination, to an unending search for sin. At least as much was given to meditation on the Bible; as he put it, the soul needs food as well as medicine. 'Meditation,' he said 'may be called the soul's chewing.' A typical entry in his diary for 1756 reads: 'A day of Net-Mending; No preaching – Reading, Meditation and prayer have been my chief Exercise and Imployment' (Baker, *Grimshaw* 69, 112).

Constantly praying, he saw into the depths of prayer in a manner worthy of the great spiritual masters. He looked for fervency, but understood dryness: 'Though the indifference I am ... speaking of be never so great, insomuch that you can hardly utter a word with your lips, nor perceive the least motion of your heart thereto; yet the soul, if you observe attentively, is all the while uneasy, grieves that it cannot pray, yea, grieves that it cannot grieve to pray, and languishes for want of enlargement therein. This uneasiness, you may assure yourselves, is the spirit's conatus, if I may so speak, to pray; and this conatus, or anxious desire after liberty to prayer, is indeed the best of prayer' (Baker, *Grimshaw* 68). St Teresa might have written so – indeed, did.

In a book of personal devotions written about 1756 John Fletcher resolved: 'Pray upon my knees as often as possible' (Macdonald, *Fletcher* 38). Faced with a problem, he prayed so often and so long that his breath deeply stained the wall against which he knelt. An extract from one of his letters serves to show his mastery of the art: 'Get recollection. Recollection is a dwelling within ourselves; being abstracted from the creature, and turned towards God ... Outward recollection consists in *silence* ... and a wise disentanglement from the world ... Inward recollection ... consists in a deep attention to the presence of God ... For want of continuing in a recollected frame all the day, our times of prayer are frequently dry and useless ... whereas we pass easily from recollection to delightful prayer' (Benson, *Fletcher* 109, 81).

In his stress on recollection Fletcher went deeper than other spiritual guides. A characteristic, and perhaps a weakness, of Anglican teaching on prayer has been to regard it chiefly as speaking with God. C. J. Stranks believes that the approach derives from the *Book of Common Prayer*. 'Its prayers are the expressions of a filial relationship between a child and his father ... Anglican writers ... are content to accept prayer as a natural activity of the soul, as ordinary ... as converse between human beings' (Stranks, 276). *The Whole Duty of Man* teaches that the parts of prayer are confession, petition, deprecation, intercession and thanksgiving; there is no mention of meditation, contemplation or silence (*WDM* 90–3). Woodforde was aware of wider dimensions, but the thrust of his definition is petitionary: 'A solemn act of worshipping the Supreme Being, wherein we on the one hand acknowledge our weakness and indigence, on the other His power and ability to afford us relief' (N. Sykes in *Theology*, vol. 38, 344–6).

Trollope, not a notably spiritual author, uses the person of archdeacon Grantly to illuminate the experience of prayer as constraint. The archdeacon finds himself wishing for the speedy death of his father, to open the way for his own preferment. 'The effect was a salutary one ... the proud, wishful, worldly man sank on his knees by the bedside, and taking the bishop's hand within his own, prayed eagerly that his sins might be forgiven him.' On another occasion the archdeacon, infuriated by his son's intended marriage 'went about his parish, intending to continue to think of his son's iniquity, so that he might keep his anger hot, – red hot. Then he remembered that the evening would come, and that he would say his prayers; and he shook his head in regret ... as he reflected that his rage would hardly be able to survive that ordeal' (Trollope, *BT* 4; *LC* 333).

In one crisis the Archdeacon was driven to prayer; in the other his regular practice of prayer steadied him. In both situations habit was decisive. Habits must be formed. Liddon's *Clerical Life and Work* begins by regretting that many of the clergy have no rule of prayer: 'Many ... [priests] do not lead a devotional life, because they do not comprehend the truth that such a life is a work in itself, and, being so, must be treated methodically. They imagine religion to be a sentiment to which they occasionally surrender themselves, rather than a service which lays all the energies of the soul under perpetual obligation' (Liddon, 4). If the clergy fail to pray systematically, who will do so? A clergyman who allows business to stand in the way of devotion is like a sailor who cares more about painting his ship's superstructure than about maintaining her engines.

As Ralph Josselin realized, a serious prayer life calls not only for method but also for periods of extended devotion. Thomas Jones, the Evangelical curate of Creaton, Northamptonshire, at the end of the eighteenth century, organized a retreat for the Evangelical clergy of the surrounding counties in the week after Easter, until the bishop of Peterborough forbade the use of the church for the purpose (Balleine, 83). Richard Benson** of Cowley is said to have instituted modern practice with a retreat for clergy at Cuddesdon in 1858 (Woodgate, *Benson* 44).

Not every clergyman who believes in retreats has wanted conducted ones. Arthur Stanton*, like Charles Lowder**, preferred 'a few days' quiet in a house where the 'Hours' were said and a rule of silence observed, wholly or in part' (Russell, *Stanton* 118). Indeed, not every clergyman has taken retreats with due seriousness. John Robinson** was sent on retreat with a fellow curate by his vicar Mervyn Stockwood**. After a few hours' experience of what the Cowley Fathers had to offer, the two curates repaired to a nearby inn, 'where they remained until – much refreshed by reading, walking and what the hostelry had to offer – it was time for them to return to Bristol' (James, *Robinson* 39).

Other Disciplines

Anglicanism is nothing if not biblical. The clergy read the scriptures daily as they say the office, but few have rested content with that. Ralph Josselin* passed naturally from his assiduous Bible reading to prayer. He constantly refers to his 'course' – shorthand for 'my ordinary course of [Bible] reading'. A passage in Isaiah 'smott my heart' and led him to pray 'ever Lord give me a tender spirit'. Another passage in the same book 'tasted ... as speaking of the deliverances god in the end of dayes will aford his people and we shall see much of it in my day.' Reading Acts 14 'of the impotent man in his feete' his mind turned to the persistent sore on his leg 'with faith god would keepe my distemper from hurt, would heale it and doe mee good'. When his much loved daughter Mary was dying 'divers texts in the psalms I read this day cheered my heart'. Josselin's Bible was an indispensable handbook on his spiritual journey (Josselin, 225, 62, 623, 606, 201).

Young Henry Martyn, when Charles Simeon's* curate, read his Bible three times a day, having risen at half-past five after the example of William Law (Jones, *Spirituality*, 462). Walter Hook* described his practice in a letter to a friend: 'I know nothing more conducive to bring me to a devotional disposition than to read some portion of the Bible, till I gradually sink off into a holy reverie' (Stephens, *Hook* 154).

Literature other than the Bible has provided food for the spirit. Hook was deeply affected by William Law's *A Serious Call*: 'You will think the first day that he commands impossibilities, but you will on the second day think those impossibilities less impossible' (Stephens, *Hook* 70). John Keble's* regard for the same book was evinced when he said to Hurrell Froude: 'You said ... that ... [it] was a clever book; it seemed to me as if you had said that the Day of Judgment would be a pretty sight' (Battiscombe, *Keble* 73). John Skinner* gave his erring son Owen his own copy of the *Works of Thomas a Kempis*, 'in a small pocket volume which has been my companion in all my travels many years; ... [it] has frequently administered consolation when nothing else has had the power of doing it' (Skinner, 386).

The practices of fasting and abstinence are commanded on Fridays, during Lent, and on thirty-one other vigils, Ember and Rogation days, in the *Book of Common Prayer*. *The Whole Duty of Man* teaches that fasting goes with repentance (*WDM* 109–10). W.C.E. Newbolt enjoined it on the clergy, remarking 'the priest has laid low his appetites, lest they should lay low him' (Newbolt, 63). Even the less stringent *Alternative Service Book* nominates Fridays and the week-days of Lent for discipline and self-denial. Anglican practice has reflected this teaching. George Herbert** writes in 'The Size':

> To be in both worlds full
> Is more than God was, who was hungry here.
> Wouldst thou his laws of fasting disannul?
> Exact good cheer?

Richard Hooker** locked himself in church to fast on Fridays and during Ember Weeks (Walton, 155). At a ludicrously lower level James Woodforde*, well aware of his gluttony, made occasional attempts at self-discipline: 'I have made a promise today concerning a certain thing [in eating]; which every time I break that promise I pay 1s' (Woodforde, 1.40). Woodforde's contemporary James Newton** observed the fasts proclaimed by secular authority with some strictness: 'This being a National Fast, Self fasted till Candle Light, & suffer none of my Family to Eat, till after NP [night prayer] were over' (James Newton, 11. Newton was a bachelor; his 'family' were his servants). Robert Hawker* fasted habitually, to the benefit, he believed, of both body and soul

(Brendon, *Hawker* 158–9). William Andrew* noted: 'I have felt the benefit of great abstinence today;' but his suggestion at a clerical meeting that spirituality might be improved by fasting was laughed at (Chadwick, *Andrew* 56).

The principle of fasting has been extended to other acts of self-denial. George Herbert's poem 'The Size', quoted above, enjoins moderation in pleasure:

> The Saviour sentenced joy,
> And in the flesh condemned it as unfit,
> At least in lump: for such doth oft destroy;
> Whereas a bit
> Doth 'tice us on to hopes of more,
> And for the present health restore.

Abstinence has been advocated as a general principle. John Fletcher* said: 'In the beginning of my spiritual course, I heard the voice of God, in an articulate, but inexpressibly awful, sound, go through my soul in these words: "If any man will be my disciple, let him deny himself"' (Macdonald, *Fletcher* 126). John Skinner wrote: 'I am perfectly indifferent to what I eat, and what I drink, and wherewithal I am clothed, so that what I use be only neat and clean ... the more we depend upon the things of this world, the more we become enslaved' (Skinner, 383). We have already seen how often the clergy have denied themselves common pleasures.

A stoic acceptance of discomfort has frequently been expected or taken for granted. The meals at Charles Lowder's** clergy house ruined his digestion. A curate recalled: 'Anyone was good enough to be our cook, and I shudder to think of what we suffered. On one occasion I sent down my cup of cocoa to the cook with ... the remark that *cockroaches* were not the necessary ingredient ... The good woman thought I was very dainty' (Ellsworth, *Lowder* 70). A friend who slept in Cosmo Lang's** bed while Lang was a curate in Leeds discovered that the bed had only a blanket and a sheet over a chain mattress. The bed accompanied Lang for the rest of his career, but he left behind in Leeds the tiny condemned house he had occupied, with two rooms and no bathroom. Lang recalled: 'This was my home for nearly three years, and I found it quite sufficient' (Lockhart, *Lang* 90). Cyril Garbett** describes the accommodation of Bernard Wilson, his vicar in Portsea: 'His bedroom was the smallest and most uncomfortable in the Vicarage, a small attic, in which it was impossible for a tall man to stand upright – he had given up his own room for one of his clergy who was ill, and had never resumed possession of it' (Smyth, *Garbett* 72).

Naturally, Lent has been the time when clergy have imposed the strictest disciplines upon themselves. Francis Kilvert* noted in 1876 that the new curate at Chippenham did not dine out during the season (Kilvert, 3.247). Charles Marson** abstained from meat, tobacco, snuff and alcohol; curiously, his health is said to have suffered (Reckitt, 113). In a pathological instance, the young Charles Kingsley, consumed with desire for his Fanny, fasted severely, slept on the floor and rose at 3.00 a.m. to pray. 'I went into the woods at night and lay naked upon thorns and when I came home my body was torn from head to foot. I never suffered so much. I began to understand Popish raptures and visions that night, and their connection with self-torture. I saw such glorious things' (Chitty, *Kingsley* 75).

Asceticism has been relatively rare. More common among Anglo-Catholics, it has not been unknown among Evangelicals. Charles Lowder's rule as a member of the Society of the Holy Cross included celibacy, daily communion, extensive prayer and frequent self-examination, daily study and meditation, control of the senses, restraint in speech and recreation, abstinence and fasting (Ellsworth, *Lowder* 21). Richard Benson** 'had become independent of comfort, and impervious to hunger, or cold, or lack of sleep. He denied himself all food from the evening of Maundy Thursday until after mid-day on the following Sunday.' A fellow Cowley Father described him as living 'apparently untouched by self-consideration, self-pity, self-indulgence ... There must have been continual questions arising for him to decide how much of his time, money, rest, convenience should be given up to Christ; but ... there was never any question as to the principle ... that was always absolute – his self-sacrifice must be complete' (Woodgate, *Benson* 86–7).

John Fletcher 'lived on vegetables, watched throughout two nights a week and on other nights went to sleep only when he could no longer stay awake' (Benson, *Fletcher* 22). John Wesley said of him: 'He did not allow himself such food as was necessary to sustain nature.' His biographer comments: 'His rigid self-denial, his almost unearthly indifference to the common comforts and recreations of human life, his carefully ordered devotions, were not the travail of a soul going about to establish its own righteousness, nor the half-expiatory sacrifices of one who seeks to pacify his conscience ... Beneath his ascetic practice was evangelical doctrine, and a living faith. He did not fast, nor give whole days to study nor whole nights to prayer, because he was in doubt and distress concerning his soul, but from his very joy in God ... His was the asceticism of love, and not of bondage or of fear' (Macdonald, *Fletcher* 35, 36).

Asceticism of this kind, filling weaker souls with awe, is most attractive when, as in the case of Fletcher, it is combined with loving-kindness; there was about Benson an austerity which even those closest to him often found uncongenial. John Keble was more typically Anglican when he taught that austerities which harmed health were actively undesirable because they hindered the performance of duty. In addition there was the danger of pride: 'There is more charity lost than sobriety gained in any unnecessary austerity.' A desire for discomfort should be satisfied by the performance of uncongenial duties; there was no need to deny oneself incidental pleasures. He advised a friend 'not to be afraid to take, as they come, the little refreshments and amusements which God in His Mercy provides for you' (Battiscombe, *Keble* 270–1).

A century later Harry Williams** came to a more radical view. He reacted against what he saw as the idolatrous view that God demanded abnegation. He derided the view that 'God wanted me to be an emotional dwarf so that I might give my stunted heart wholly to him ... God wanted you to enjoy him, and how could you enjoy him if you had too great a relish for gin or smoked salmon or Noel Coward or a long lie-in? ... If they became over-enjoyable, they might ... become God's competitors ...' (Williams, 131–2). There is a pleasing irony about the fact that Williams found his way to fullness of spiritual life first by abandoning the ideal of abnegation, and then by becoming a monk.

Most clergy who have taken their devotional life seriously have come to think with John Fletcher 'that the impulses, even of the regenerate life, may not be left to themselves with entire confidence in their sufficient working.' Fletcher formulated a rule of life. As well as the injunction recorded above, to pray on his knees as often as possible, his resolutions of *c.* 1756 read: 'Sing frequently penitential hymns. Eat slowly, and upon my knees, three times a day and never more. Always speak gently. Neglect no outward duty. Beware of a fire thou kindlest thyself; the fire that God kindles is bright, mild, constant, and burns night and day. Think always of death, and of the Cross, the hardness of thy heart, and the blood of Christ. Beware of relaxing, and of impatience; God is faithful, but He owes thee nothing. Speak only when necessary. Do not surrender thyself to any joy. Rise in the morning without yielding to sloth. Follow always thy first motion. Be a true son of affliction. Write down every evening whether thou hast kept these rules' (Macdonald, *Fletcher* 41, 38–9).

Whether they have followed a rule of life or not, many clergy have engaged in periodic self-assessment. In the first earnestness of his conversion William Grimshaw kept spiritual accounts. 'In a large folio he daily set down his sins on one page, and his good works on the other, and kept his accounts ... as regularly as any merchant; in whatever he imagined he had sinned, he did as many good works as he supposed would atone for his offences; and then crossing his book, thought he kept an even account with God ... In this matter he proceeded for seven years' (Baker, *Grimshaw* 37), presumably giving up when he accepted the full significance of justification. He was in the tradition of *The Whole Duty of Man*, which advocated a weekly accounting (WDM 105).

A less significant figure, Joseph Price**, engaged in an annual personal stock-taking in which financial and secular considerations bulked largest, but in which spiritual matters were not entirely overlooked. He noted his reading, from which devotional and theological and biblical works were not lacking. One year he meditated: 'I lie too long in bed, but cannot charge myself with being extravagant.' His scale of values is revealed in the further comment: 'French rather neglected, along with whist and sermonizing' (Ditchfield, *Price* 167–70).

No doubt the vast majority of parish priests have, in the severity of their self-discipline and self-assessment, lain somewhere between Grimshaw and Price, and have been of the school of John Keble.

II

Persecution and Affliction

The Cross is the abyss of wonders, the centre of
desires, the school of virtues, the house of wisdom,
the throne of love, the theatre of joys, and the place
of sorrows; it is the root of happiness, and the gate of
Heaven. (Traherne, 1.58)

Persecution

Being a priest of the Church of England has not been as a rule a physically
dangerous occupation. Few clergy have been called upon to exhibit heroism in
the face of violent death. Many, however, have had to make hard decisions
about conformity under threat of sanctions; and, as we shall see in the second
section of this chapter, very many have had to suffer because of the conscientious performance of their ministry.

Of the three hundred or so Marian martyrs, only a few were parish priests
(for what follows, see Foxe, passim). The proto-martyr, John Rogers, was
incumbent of St Sepulchre's and of St Margaret Moyses, London. He was
followed to the stake by Laurence Saunders, incumbent of Church Langton,
Leicestershire, and of Allhallows, Bread Street, London, and by Saunders's
one-time curate George Marsh; by Rowland Taylor, vicar of Hadley, Suffolk,
and his curate Richard Yeoman; by John Bland and John Frankesh, incumbents
respectively of Adisham and Rolvenden, Kent; by three Essex clergy, Robert
Drakes of Thundersley, William Tyms of Hockley and Thomas Whittle; by
Robert Samuel of Barholt or Barfold, Suffolk; by John Hullier, one time curate
of Babraham, Cambridgeshire, and later of King's Lynn; and by John Rouch
who had held a benefice in Hull.

The martyrs resisted strenuous attempts to make them recant. Thomas
Whittle recanted, only to withdraw his recantation. Robert Samuel withstood
being starved while chained to a post in such a way that he had to support his
weight on his toes. Impugned by the challenge: 'Thou wilt not burn ... when it
cometh to the purpose, I know that', John Rogers replied: 'Sir, I cannot tell,
but I trust in my Lord God'. In the spirit of Thomas More, he greeted the
news, given to him as he lay in bed, that his execution day had come, with: 'If it
be so, I need not tie my points'. Laurence Saunders embraced the stake before
his execution, saying 'Welcome, thou cross of Christ! welcome, everlasting life!'
George Marsh went to his death Bible in hand; his suffering was prolonged by
an unskilfully built fire, and born with such fortitude that the Bishop of
Chester thought it necessary to preach against him afterwards declaring that he
was now 'a firebrand in hell' (Foxe, 7.722–4, 373; 6.596, 609 [points were the

strings which, in the interests of neatness, attached one garment to another]; 6.628; 7.53).

Additional pathos was added to the martyrdoms by the fact that the martyrs were in most cases married. Many of the letters which Foxe preserved were to wives and children. One of Laurence Saunders to his wife reads, in small part: 'Dear wife, riches I have none to leave behind me, wherewith to endow you after the worldly manner: but that treasure of tasting how sweet Christ is unto hungry consciences ... that I bequeath unto you ... to retain the same in sense of heart always. Pray, pray. I am merry, and I trust I shall be merry, maugre the teeth of all the devils in hell ... Pray, pray, pray!' In another letter he asked her to send him a shirt to be burnt in, adding the heart-breaking detail: 'Let it be sewed down on both the sides, not open' (Foxe, 6.622–3, 635).

On his journey to the place of execution Rowland Taylor prayed with his family, embraced his wife, and declared: 'Be of good comfort, for I am quiet in my conscience. God shall stir up a father for my children.' He was 'joyful and merry, as one that accounted himself going to a most pleasant banquet or bridal', and made a joke of the fact that his burning would deprive the worms of his parochial churchyard of the 'jolly feeding on this carrion' which they had anticipated (Foxe, 6.694–6).

He died on Aldham Common, near Hadleigh, in the presence of a large crowd. 'When he had prayed he went to the stake and kissed it, and set himself into a pitch barrel ... with his hands folded together, and his eyes towards heaven, and continually prayed. At last they kindled the fire; and Dr Taylor holding up both his hands, calling upon God, and said, "Merciful Father of heaven! for Jesus Christ, my Saviour's sake, receive my soul into Thy hands!" So he stood still without either crying or moving, with his hands folded together, until Soyce, with a halberd struck him on the head until his brains fell out, and the corpse fell down into the fire' (Foxe, 6.699–700).

These parish priests died for such offences as disbelieving in transubstantiation, rejecting communion in one kind, denying the necessity of auricular confession, asserting that there were only two sacraments, and refusing to part from their wives. By their deaths they sanctified Protestantism far more successfully than by their lives. The blood of the martyrs was the seed of the reformed Church of England.

It is one thing to be prepared for suffering, another to invite it. Bernard Gilpin* adopted a moderate Protestantism, but he was extremely careful both in formulating and in promulgating his opinions. He said: 'Be assured, I should never have thrown myself voluntarily into the hands of my enemies; but I am fully resolved to persevere in doing my duty, and shall take no measures to avoid them' (Collingwood, *Gilpin* 111). He returned home from the Continent while the Marian persecution was raging, and took up his post at Houghton. His clerical enemies, numerous because of his attacks on clerical abuses, delated him successively to his own bishop and to Bishop Bonner of London, who had a general commission to discover heresy. Gilpin could have fled, but decided not to do so. Instead, he prepared a long garment to be his burning sheet, and wore it daily. Summoned to London, he escaped trial and survived to undertake a notable ministry only because Queen Mary died while he was on his journey.

Since the time of Mary, no parish priest of the Church of England has died specifically for his faith, though, as we shall see, some have died because of it. Many, however, have suffered deprivation or the threat of it. About 200 clergy unwilling to accept the Prayer Book of 1559 were evicted early in Elizabeth's reign. The next to suffer were the Puritans. About 40 London clergy were deprived for refusing to accept the 1566 *Advertisements* of Archbishop Parker, with their insistence on ritual conformity. Archbishop Whitgift, although in doctrine a strict Calvinist, harried unmercifully clergy who would not toe the line; 45 Suffolk clergy were suspended in a single day. An uncertain number of Puritan ministers – possibly 90, possibly rather more – were ejected from their livings after the failure of the Hampton Court Conference of 1604 (Roger Lockyer, *Tudor and Stuart Britain* Longmans 1964, 177, 197, 231).

When the Civil War of 1642–6 broke out, many of the parochial clergy took an active part on the royalist side and thus exposed themselves to the vicissitudes of war. Many, such as John Squire, vicar of St Leonard's, Shoreditch, were imprisoned, and their families left to starve. Nicholas Andrews, rector of St Nicholas, Guildford, Surrey, was one of those incarcerated on prison ships; he died under the ill treatment he received. Parson Prolfe of Tarrington, Herefordshire, was murdered by a Parliamentary soldier for saying he was for God and the King. Michael Hudson, rector of Uffington, Lincolnshire and King's Cliffe, Northamptonshire, bore arms and was killed at the siege of Woodcroft House, Northamptonshire, in 1646. Thomas Cooper, rector of Little Barningham, Norfolk, was hanged in 1650 'for being concern'd in a Rising in favour of his Majesty' (Matthews, *Walker* 58, 349, 194, 252, 266; Hart, *CC* 122).

There were not wanting those who suffered from their attachment to the Church rather than to the Crown. Despite the danger of heavy sanctions clergy continued to lead Prayer Book services. Matthew Gifford, sometime rector of two London parishes, read Common Prayer 'by stealth ... for poor Cavaliers'; for doing this he was, it was said, assaulted seven times and imprisoned five. Charles Forbench, already sequestered from his parish of Great Henny, Essex, and living in great poverty, was imprisoned for using the Prayer Book. On his release he said: 'If I must not read it, I am resolved I will say it by Heart, in spight of all the Rogues in England' (Matthews, *Walker* 49, 152).

Throughout the period 1642–60 parochial clergy were evicted in numbers, for a variety of causes. Evictions were sometimes savagely conducted. The elderly John Prince, rector of Little Shefford, Berkshire, was carried from a sick-bed to a nearby barn, where he died. William Prestell, rector of Cole

Orton, Leicestershire, received 'above 100 blows of a skeane [dagger, presumably scabbarded] on his back armes and shoulders till all was black as a shooe' (Matthews, *Walker* 71, 242).

Provision was sometimes made from parochial income for the wife and children of the evicted parson; from 1657 even for the minister himself. They benefited from private charity too; Thomas Fuller and the poet Robert Herrick** were both subvented by Viscount Scudamore. Others scratched a living by teaching, or medical practice, or even manual work. Many families and individuals however suffered grievously. Robert Clarke of Andover, Hampshire, who was imprisoned twelve times, plundered eleven, and fined continually was 'always threadbare, often barefoot'. (Matthews, *Walker* xxvi, 181). Thomas Campbell, rector of Swafield, Norfolk, established himself in a cottage in a village near his parish with his wife and four children. One freezing day a visitor found him without firing, with only water to drink, and with no food save some barley dumplings. He told his horror-stricken guest that God gave such as he the strength to bear suffering with courage and contentment (Hart, *CC* 131–2). The staunchness of the evicted clergy was in fact remarkable. Only ten or so sought a new career in the arms of Rome, and only one turned informer in return for a living (Matthews, *Walker* xxvi–xxvii).

The extent of this persecution has sometimes been overlooked. Between 1642 and 1660 about 2425 benefices were sequestered (Matthews, *Walker* xv). By comparison, between 1660 and 1662 ejections and resignations numbered only about 1760. On the other hand, the later departures were all occasioned by the return of the previous incumbent or were on grounds of principle; the sequestrations were on grounds of pluralism, scandal and inefficiency as well as of 'malignancy'. If they were justly accused, it is hard to regard as a martyr Jeremiah Ravens, rector of Great Blakenham, Suffolk, who was a drunkard, kept a whore and had 'hunge his wife upp by the heels ... and whipped her'; or William Lange, vicar of Bradworthy, Devon, whose offences included forgery, employing a poisoner, conspiring to kill his predecessor, failing to take services, and keeping a tavern at the vicarage (Matthews, *Walker* 342, 117–18). In addition, while the sequestrations were usually with compensation, the ejections were not (Hill, 242).

The Restoration of 1660 brought a fresh crop of departures. Those ministers who were ejected by returning Royalists or who vacated their livings on St Bartholomew's day 1662 cannot, however, be regarded as Anglican martyrs; they belong to the hagiography of the free churches. Had the Restoration been marked with generous comprehensiveness, as Charles II wished, the history of English Christianity would have been very different; but, alas, religious generosity was not the seventeenth-century way.

The political vicissitudes of the sixteenth and seventeenth centuries claimed one other group of victims. About four hundred parish priests, holding firm to the principles of the Divine Right of Kings and of passive obedience, gave up their offices after the Glorious Revolution of 1688 rather than swear allegiance to William III. One of their number was John Kettlewell, vicar of Coleshill, Warwickshire since 1682 and a distinguished devotional author. An exemplary parish priest, who supplied all the poor families of his parish with Bibles and with copies of *The Whole Duty of Man*, he was described by bishop Ken as 'as saint-like a man as ever I knew'. None the less, he was deprived in 1690 because of his uncompromising teaching of passive obedience (*DNB*).

Most of the non-jurors lived in obscurity or poverty, the latter mitigated occasionally by the kindness of lay sympathizers. Others engaged in controversy and suffered for it, such as Hilkiah Bedford (1663–1724), incumbent of Whittering, Northamptonshire, who was fined and imprisoned for his part in the publication of a book querying the Hanoverian succession. He was later to be one of the first non-juring bishops. The attempt to perpetuate the movement failed, however, and by the end of the eighteenth century it had virtually disappeared (Overton, 198–203).

We must set against the persecuted clergy of the sixteenth and seventeenth centuries the less heroic majority who quietly conformed. The brave souls who died or who were prepared to die were exceptions. More typical of the clergy as a whole was 'one Fairebanke, who sometimes had been a married priest, and served the cure of Warbleton [Sussex], where he had often persuaded the people not to credit any other doctrine but that which he preached, taught and set forth, in King Edward's days: and afterward, in the beginning of Queen Mary's reign, the said Fairebanke, turning head to tail, preached clean contrary to that which he had before taught' (Foxe, 8.333). Clergy of this ilk were not necessarily cowards. They were often humble souls who did what most human beings do in times of turmoil – conform to what at the time constitutes authority.

Less than 300 of 8000 parish priests were deprived after the accession of Elizabeth (though it has also to be said that the Act of Uniformity was not rigorously enforced). John Stalworth, who died as rector of Greatworth, Northamptonshire, in 1590, had been pensioned off from a monastery in 1539, and had subsequently held livings under Henry VIII, Edward, Mary and Elizabeth (Owen Chadwick, *The Reformation*, Penguin 1982, 134). Thomas Fuller immortalized another character, best known for a song which transferred his pliancy into the seventeenth-century setting: 'The vivacious vicar hereof [of Bray, Berkshire] living under King Henry VIII, King Edward VI, Queen Mary, and Queen Elizabeth, was first a Papist, then a Protestant, then a Papist, then a Protestant again. He had seen some martyrs burnt ... at Windsor, and found this fire too hot for his tender temper. This vicar being taxed by one for being a turncoat and an inconstant changeling, "Not so", said he, "for I always keep my principle, which is this, to live and die the vicar of Bray"' (Fuller, *WE* 113).

It is a corollary of the sequestrations during the Interregnum that about two-thirds of the clergy retained their livings; and by no means all of these men were Puritans. Richard Baxter, the great Puritan divine, wrote that there were left undisturbed of the Worcestershire clergy: 'near one half ... that were not good enough to do much service, nor bad enough to be cast out as utterly intollerable' (quoted Matthews, *Walker* xvii). Among the surprising survivors was Thomas Fuller, who persuaded the parliamentary commissioners to leave him in place at Waltham Abbey (Addison, *WDF* 170).

Retaining one's living was not of itself evidence of turpitude. Charles Butler (d. 1647), vicar of Wotton St Lawrence, Hampshire, for forty-eight years and a staunch follower of Laud, obtained the reward of his scholarship, piety and good works, and was left unmolested throughout the Interregnum (Hart, *CC* 160–1, *DNB*).

The last formal persecution of parochial clergy occurred in the nineteenth century, and was directed against Anglo-Catholics. By previous standards it was small beer. In consequence of the Public Worship Regulation Act of 1874 five priests were imprisoned – Arthur Tooth of Hatcham, Deptford; Thomas Pelham Dale of St Vedast's, Foster Lane, London; R.W. Enraght of Bordesley, Birmingham; S.F. Green of St John's, Miles Platting, Manchester; and Bell Cox of St Margaret's, Liverpool. The numbers were tiny and the longest incarceration – that of Green – less than two years. But because central government was involved, and because official persecution was associated with the huge and often highly organized unofficial attempts to make the position of Anglo-Catholic clergy intolerable, the episode is dealt with here.

An account of the experiences of Arthur Tooth and Henry Aston Walker at St James, Hatcham, serves to illustrate in detail how the persecution of Anglo-Catholic priests operated both at the formal and at the informal level (for what follows see Coombs, passim). Tooth was 'an ascetic, devoted, earnest, honest man incapable of seeing two sides of a question, ... endowed less with a great power of will than with an enormous power of won't' (Coombs, 24; the remark about his 'power of won't' was also made about Alexander Mackonochie: see Towle, *Mackonochie* 188). He was inducted at Hatcham in 1868, after his brother had purchased the presentation, and set about his rundown church and parish with a will. The church was redecorated and restored. The main altar was moved to the east end, and another placed in a side chapel. A rood screen was installed. A newly built north transept contained a baptistry and a confessional. A convent and an orphanage were founded nearby, the latter providing the choir.

For eucharistic worship Tooth introduced all six of the practices then causing most controversy: the eastward position, unleavened bread, the mixed chalice, lighted candles on the altar, vestments and incense. He attracted a large congregation, mainly of poor people, and by the mid-1870s the parish was teeming with life.

After the passage of the Public Worship Regulation Act in 1874 St James's was one of the first targets of the militantly Protestant Church Association. Tooth was prosecuted in the Court of Arches. He was accused of the alterations and practices already mentioned, and of others running, the full gamut of Catholic ceremonial – genuflecting, elevating the sacrament, using the sign of the cross, singing the Agnus Dei, tolling the church bell at the consecration, employing acolytes, and celebrating when there were less than three communicants. Tooth refused to acknowledge the competence of a secular court; notionally he was prepared to submit to his bishop, but, like many other Anglo-Catholics then and since, he combined a high theology of the episcopal office with considerable unreadiness to do as he was told. Others fought his court battles for him, but the outcome was against him. He was instructed to abandon his Catholic practices and to re-order his church. He refused and was inhibited. He and his congregation turned away the clergyman sent to take over from him, but found it less easy to deal with the vast crowds (in part, it was alleged, paid hooligans) who disrupted worship towards the end of 1876. After several strenuous Sundays Tooth went away to recover; meanwhile the legal steps were taken which would punish his continued contumacy with imprisonment.

Early in 1877 the police closed St James's on the bishop's instructions. When Tooth returned to London he was consigned to the Horsemonger jail. He did not suffer acute discomfort. He was placed among the debtors; extra furniture was brought in and his meals cooked and brought in by nuns; he paid another prisoner to do his cleaning and he was allowed regular visitors. He attended worship daily and was afforded the devoted support of his own congregation and of many other sympathizers. A protest meeting of the Church of England Working Mens Society (an Anglo-Catholic body) attracted an attendance of 2000, and the authorities feared trouble unless Tooth were released. Less than a month after his arrest an appeal on his behalf succeeded and he went away for a long rest. Later in the year an appeal against the original condemnation succeeded on a technical point. Tooth was free to return to his parish, which in the meantime had been the scene of constant and debilitating conflict. Vindicated, but badly affected by the long struggle, Tooth announced his intention of resigning. His worst punishment was to come. At the age of thirty-eight 'he would never be offered so much as an unpaid curacy, let alone a living or an honorary canonry, by any diocesan bishop in the next 53 years of his life' (Coombs, 133).

The battles at St James's went on; it had now become a point of honour on both sides to try and secure the parish for a party. Tooth nominated as his successor Henry Aston Walker, who had been one of Alexander Mackonochie's curates. The historian of these events reflects: 'If there are candidates for palms as a reward for martyrdom in the ritualist controversy, Henry Aston Walker's name should stand high on the list ... [he was] broken in the grinding daily round of petty persecutions' (Coombs, 167).

It was Walker's misfortune that his principal antagonist was a fanatical Protestant, William Sanders, 'rich, clever and single-minded in an almost megalomaniacal way' (Coombs, 177). Sanders had been elected as a church-warden at the 1878 vestry, and he used this point of vantage to make Walker's life impossible. The points at issue were far fewer and less substantial than those in the time of Tooth. Sanders protested against the presence of a cross and candlesticks on the altar and eventually after a long battle secured a faculty for their removal. He destroyed one Sunday School crucifix and raided the School supported by thirty or forty roughs in search of another. Disapproving of the antiphonal singing of the psalms by the vicar and the congregation, he and some of his supporters insisted on singing with the vicar. He challenged visiting preachers to produce their letters of order, and once prevented a sermon on a technicality. He came to week-day communions to ensure that wafers were not used, and on one occasion sought to stop a celebration on the grounds that there were fewer than three communicants.

Sanders' party in the congregation were at constant loggerheads with Walker's supporters. Worship was frequently disrupted, on one occasion by a struggle over the offertory bag. He was prosecuted on several occasions and was once fined £2 for brawling. Eventually he vacated his place as warden and, remarkable as it may seem, successfully sought ordination. His cause was taken up by others, who accused Walker of further illegalities, such as employing a server. The bishop took his side but by now it was too late. In 1884, after a vestry meeting which, like the previous five he had experienced, was conten-tious and acrimonious to a degree, Walker had a complete breakdown. He resigned the following year, to become in due course the honoured and loved vicar of Chettisham, Cambridgeshire, until his death in 1906 (Coombs, 167–232).

Walker was defeated by a species of low-level persecution; Tooth by the full majesty of statute. The first kind of Protestant activity persisted: as late as 1932 militants of the Protestant Truth Society wrecked the interior of an Anglo-Catholic Cornish church and in 1936 forced the resignation of the incumbent, Bernard Walke, by continued zealotry (*Church Times*, 12 July 1991). But the Public Worship Regulation Act failed in its purpose. Prosecutions were few because bishops, including low church bishops, decided that the scandal created by imprisoning upright if misguided clergymen would be greater than that occasioned by their ritualistic practices. They vetoed the great majority of prosecutions, and thus left the way open for changes in ceremonial which in due course spread far beyond Anglo-Catholic circles. The normal eucharistic practice of a central Anglican church today would have been thought blatantly Roman by William Sanders and his ilk. It remains a question whether the advance of Catholic practices owes more to cautious moderates than to un-accommodating zealots; but in any event the martyrs did not suffer in vain.

Affliction

'Ministers of good things,' wrote Richard Hooker**, 'are like torches, a light to others, waste and destruction to themselves' (quoted D. Edwards, *Leaders of the Church of England*, Oxford 1978, 328). There are countless examples of parochial clergy suffering because of the exercise of their vocation; suffering not in any extreme fashion, but in the ways to be expected when men stand in judgment, directly or by implication, on the world. As Henry Liddon put it (Liddon, 236), clergy are commending 'a cause which can never be popular, in face of an opposition which can never sleep'; they must expect painful consequences.

The commonest of all causes of affliction has been the clash of personalities, aggravated as often as not by a tendency on both sides towards the self-righteous acrimony characteristic of squabbles over religion, and by the minister's vulnerability.

> When things go wrong it's rather tame
> To find we are ourselves to blame,
> It gets the trouble over quicker
> To go and blame things on the Vicar.
> (John Betjeman, *Church Poems* 1981, 63)

Differences of temperament and character generate friction, hard feelings and worse. Samuel Wesley**, who viewed his flock at Epworth, 'in the temper of an exasperated missionary among savage tribes', suffered at their hands the molestation of his property, the maiming of his cattle, and (it appears possible) the burning of half his house in 1702 (Ayling, *Wesley* 17). John Skinner* was constantly exposed to surliness, abuse or defiance, and occasionally to interference with his property, in part because of his dogged attempts to do his duty, in part because of his irascibility. He wrote with some truth after an altercation with a parishioner: 'I was ready enough to acknowledge I was frequently angry, but the fault was with those with whom I had to deal as much as with myself; that when they did everything to insult and provoke me, flying in my face on every trivial occasion, and, what was worse, when they even offered insults to the Deity, whose Minister I was, by the grossest misbehaviour in the sacred house of God, I then could not but take warning; that I knew my own disposition sufficiently to assure him that if my parishioners had taken half the pains to please me and to discharge their several duties they would never have had reason to complain of the warmth of my temper' (Skinner, 57–8).

Milder characters have suffered too. With perceptive tenderness, Henry Alford's** wife wrote of his time at Wymeswold: 'It was not the most congenial work to one of his disposition, endowed with a refined, intellectual, and sensitive temperament, and with a peculiarly generous, open nature. He was brought into intercourse constantly with some who did not understand him, and into collision occasionally with some who could not sympathize with him' (Alford, 107–8). In such situations it is only rarely that the laity are put on the defensive in the way they were in a Southwark parish when Cyril Garbett** was bishop. A pious faction had driven the vicar into a breakdown. Garbett descended on the parish to proclaim from the pulpit: 'Your Vicar is very ill, and may die; if he dies, you will be as much his murderers as the Scribes and Pharisees were murderers of our Lord' (Smyth, *Garbett* 166).

It cannot be assumed that a priest's people will welcome his teaching and practice. Elizabethan fanatics dragged their parish priests from their pulpits, tore off their gowns, and beat them, because of lack of sympathy with their doctrine (Hart, *CC* 35). The congregation of Samuel Butler's Theobald Pontifex would have been 'equally horrified at hearing the Christian religion doubted, and at seeing it practised' (Butler, 94). For this reason or for others life can be lonely and miserable. Bishop Edward King** said that parochial clergy 'often are not understood, not wanted, not cared for, isolated, unnoticed' (Elton, *King* 120).

Moralists are rarely popular, and clerical moralists no exception. George Herbert*, imagining his country parson proceeding against a parishioner at law, describes him treating him 'as a brother still' and doing all he can to maintain good personal relations; but this aspiration, admirable in principle, is hard to achieve in practice (Herbert, XXV). Thomas Fuller** anticipated that the faithful minister would be disliked: 'I should suspect his preaching had no salt in it, if no galled horse did wince ... though he ever whips the vice and spares the person' (Fuller, *HS* 73). It was, however, also Fuller who wrote: 'Sure I am those are the best Christians who least censure others, and most reform themselves' (Fuller, *CH* 3.426).

John Fletcher* wrote in 1761: 'You cannot well imagine how much the animosity of my parishioners is heightened, and with what boldness it discovers itself against me, because I preached against drunkenness, shows and bull-baiting' (Macdonald, *Fletcher* 63). Henry Moule, vicar of Fordington, Dorset, told Kilvert that when he first went to the parish in the 1820s he put a stop to a local race meeting. For five years afterwards he was insulted whenever he went into Dorchester; young men jeered at him and his congregation as they went into church each Sunday; and all the shrubs and flowers in his garden were annually uprooted (Kilvert, 2.438). But such affliction can often only be avoided at the cost of a dereliction of duty. 'Woe unto you, if your time pass on without vexation! It will be the plainest of proofs that you have never stirred the waters' (Evans, 11).

A priest worth his salt is almost certainly an instrument of change; and for that there is a price to be paid. Henry Alford explained in 1848 why he wanted to leave Wymeswold: 'It is well known that when a clergyman has made extensive alterations in his parish he works at a disadvantage, he has stirred up ill-will, or provoked coldness among many of his people; he has passed through bricks and mortar, and bears the stain upon him; he has been mixed in tangled worldly business, and is distrusted; and therefore a successor has greatly the advantage over him' (Alford, 108).

One of the saddest of pastoral situations occurs when a priest's duty to some of his people alienates him from others. Charles Marson** scandalized many of his rural parishioners in Hambridge, Somerset, when he took a gipsy family into his vicarage to save the father from dying of pneumonia (Reckitt, 134). I had an analogous experience when a group of travellers settled for some months in the parish of Shepherdswell. I thought myself bound to minister to them, and to give them what assistance I could. My actions earned me some odium, and in particular made it impossible, despite my efforts, for me to minister to the family who had suffered most from the incursion.

Attempts to assist deprived parishioners have not always been welcome to affluent ones. John Newton's* attempts to help the poor in and around Olney were opposed by the local farmers and landowners, who wanted a cowed and beggarly workforce. To raise money he was forced to turn to friends in London (Martin, *Newton* 232–4). John Keble*, trying to provide allotments, was forced by the local farmers to specify that none might be larger than a quarter of an acre and that none should grow corn (Colloms, 27). When J.S. Henslow, Darwin's mentor, divided his glebe land into 150 allotments the local farmers resolved at the 1852 vestry meeting that they would 'refuse all employment and show no favour to any day-labourer who should hold an allotment' (Goodenough, 129). A Hampshire parson was locked out of his church for three Sundays because he had criticized his wardens for spending more on themselves on market day than they paid a ploughman for a week's work (Colloms, 33). A parson writing in the *Spectator* in 1872 claimed that many farmers had left his congregation because he had spoken about the dangers of pregnant women working in the fields (Clark, 258). When Edward Girdlestone of Halberton, Devonshire, encouraged labourers to emigrate overseas or elsewhere in Britain, thus forcing local farmers to put up their wages, he was obscenely abused at a vestry, there were disturbances in church, and an attempt on the part of some farmers to defect to the Methodists (Clark, 173–5, 179; the Methodist minister refused to accept the defectors).

Problems with rich parishioners did not disappear with the nineteenth century. When Arthur Hopkinson** was appointed to rural Winchfield, Hampshire, in 1909 he was appalled by local housing conditions, but fought his nine year battle against them alone; everyone else in the parish was either a landlord or under the thumb of a landlord. 'A blight of evil hung over the place; fear and suspicion made life a tragedy.' Hopkinson felt his experience marked him with a 'brand of bitterness which has left a permanent wound on my soul' (Hopkinson, 107–9).

It is possible that the Christianity which Evangelicals have commended has been more out of tune with ordinary life than the Christian vocation actually demands. Be that as it may, there has been no doubt that they have suffered for their devotion. Charles Simeon* ended his ministry as an icon; but in its early days he was a laughing-stock. He was frequently hooted and abused by town and gown alike. He was ostracized in the street, and when on one occasion a poor man took off his hat to him, he was so moved that he broke down in tears on regaining his rooms. He was pelted with dirt and eggs, and his services were constantly disrupted. He accepted attacks on his person without retaliation, but responded vigorously to interruptions in church. Several trouble-makers were jailed, and not released until they had made a contribution to the poor of the parish (Hopkins, *Simeon* 79–81).

A more general cause of affliction has been a sense of failure. In every age priests are confronted by the sheer intractability of those to whom they minister. Thomas Fuller tells a sad tale about Richard Greenham, in Elizabethan times parish priest of Dry-Drayton, near Cambridge. 'Dry-Drayton indeed; which – though often watered with Mr Greenham's tears, and oftener with his prayers and preaching, who moistened the rich with his counsel, the poor with his charity – neither produced proportionable fruitfulness. The generality of the parish remained ignorant and obstinate, to their pastor's great grief, and their own greater damage and disgrace.' Their broken-hearted pastor resigned, to undertake a more profitable ministry as a spiritual director (Fuller, *CH* 3.147).

John Skinner wrote in 1821: 'Alas! my labours in the Vineyard, I feel more and more convinced are of no avail: when I look for good fruit the grapes still continue to tart [sic]; they set my teeth on edge' (Skinner, 167). Sabine Baring-Gould** referred to 'the prospect of a life and best efforts being, as far as man can see, wholly thrown away. Many an earnest and devout clergyman is planted in some most unsuitable living, among untractable people, without token of his labours producing any effect. A thousand such hearts have been broken, a thousand such lives wasted, long cherished and fervent hopes killed.' He evinced as an example his fellow-curate at Horbury, Mr Davies, who was destroyed by the rural parish of One House, Suffolk, and who became 'a broken-hearted, silly old man' (Purcell, *Baring-Gould* 64–5).

The price exacted by integrity can be failure. Edward Girdlestone's campaign to raise labourers' wages created an unhappy parish in which he could no longer minister effectively (Chadwick, *VC* 2.156–7). William Tuckwell, incumbent of Stockton, Warwickshire from 1878 to 1893 wrote ruefully of the penalties of Radicalism. They included the social ostracism of himself and his family, the emptying of his church and the drying up of subscriptions (Clark, 181). Samuel Barnett* prophesied in 1886: 'For some time to come it may be the glory of a preacher to empty rather than fill his church as he reasons about the Judgment to come, when twopence a gross to the match-makers will be laid alongside of the 22% to the shareholders, and penny dinners for the poor compared with 16 courses for the rich' (Article 'Distress in East London' in *The Nineteenth Century*, November 1886, 689). His own experience was along those very lines.

A sense of failure can be evoked simply by a failure to make progress. Charles Curzon, a bishop of Stepney used to say: 'Parish work in North or East London is like walking up a moving-staircase which is coming down all the time: if at the end of a year you find yourself where you were at the beginning of it, you have made progress!' (Smyth, *Garbett* 180). He need not have confined his remarks to the districts he mentioned. In recent years the trend to secularization is so strong that the staircase moves down faster than most clergy can walk up it. George Carey** was told by a colleague: 'I'm here to officiate at a funeral – that of my church. I have not had a new member for eight years. In five years' time they will close us down' (Carey, 85).

W.C.E. Newbolt puts his finger on a fundamental point when he writes: 'We [clergy] are all of us a little apt to feel ... that we only need to put the truth before people in its strong beauty, and they must needs give in ... a very slight experience corrects this estimate' (Newbolt, 98). Arthur Stanton* – of all people – recalled his own experience thus: 'I had come up from Cuddesdon in December full of enthusiasms and anticipations ... Would not London yield to the Gospel if it were preached in the streets? would it not bring light into the dark lives of myriads? would not the sweet story bring out the love that must lie somewhere in the hearts of men, and could not I do this? So I dreamed when I saw the lights as I came into the great city ... Then ... the reality – dirt, squalor, indifference, hatred, misery; and ere the year died out the disillusionment had set in, and now ... I dream no more' (Russell, *Stanton* 40–1).

Nicolas Stacey** echoes Stanton: 'It took twelve years of hard work and much anguish to work out of my system the conviction that the Gospel vividly presented would lead to changed lives and full churches' (Stacey, 41. The printed sentence reads 'would not' but the context makes the intended meaning clear). More specifically he lamented: 'The agony of so much of our pastoral work at Woolwich was that the things people did want from us – the name of a safe, cheap abortionist; the loan of £20; a roof over their heads, or a new husband – we were unwilling or unable to provide. But the things that we were able to give they did not appear to greatly want' (Stacey, 158).

The price affliction exacts can be a high one. Had John Skinner done the bare minimum of duty and spent his days with his books and his archaeological digs he might have survived the pressures of his temperament, without being driven to suicide. The hatred of local farmers contributed to Robert Hawker's paranoia and persecution mania; he referred to himself as 'the Victim of Morwenstow' (Brendon, *Hawker* 112). Robert Dolling*, who conducted a ministry to clerical drunkards, included among the afflictions which were his colleagues' undoing 'an inward rebellion against their own work; they feel more or less that their preaching and teaching is humbug' (Dolling, *TY* 85–6).

A conclusive response to affliction has been the abandonment of ministry. Richard Syms, a team vicar in Hitchin, Hertfordshire, decided to go in 1978 because of what he called 'a bunch of last straws'. They included reactions to an article in the parish magazine which had been less than enthusiastic about the Royal Jubilee celebrations of 1977; the insistence of the PCC on an expensive refurbishing of the church organ; criticism of an experimental harvest festival service in a local community centre; and a failure among his people to support a week-end of festivity on a council estate within the parish. Behind these immediate causes lay concern over wider issues, such as the failure of the attempt to reunite Anglicans and Methodists, reluctance to marry divorced persons in church, and, chiefly, the institutional nature of the Church. Syms looked for a radicalism like his own among his parishioners and among the church authorities; failing to find it, he decided to pursue a ministry in the more open situation of the professional theatre (Syms, passim).

In a farewell sermon Nicholas Stacey, another who left parochial ministry, tried to cope with his sense of failure by invoking the analogy with Good Friday and Easter, and by pointing to the unexpected triumphs of his ministry (Stacey, 292–3). The theological point is valid, though Stacey was perhaps not in the best position to make it convincingly. R.W. Evans, who stuck to his post, suggests another constructive line of thought: 'You will not count anything for failure. You will only put it to the account of delay knowing that the Lord ... may not think fit to crown our labours with visible success, lest we should be vainglorious ... The Lord is sometime pleased to try the faith and patience of his servants, and hides from them the increase of their labours, and lets them sow in tears, that their successors may reap in joy' (Evans, 22, 118).

Stacey and Evans were not whistling in the dark. Affliction need not be a wholly negative experience. Ralph Josselin* wrote: 'I have some experience of sorrowes, and trials in the world, and they make mee the more to prize my god knowing nothing is sweete or good without him' (Josselin, 210). Many of the priests with whom we have been dealing were equipped to deal with affliction because they did not share the extraordinary modern delusion that happiness is a right rather than a gift. Alexander Mackonochie** wrote in one of his letters: 'I do not think there is one promise in the Gospel that we shall be *happy* in this world' (Towle, *Mackonochie* 236). Walter Hook* wrote: 'It is absolutely necessary ... for my soul's health that I should undergo a good deal of obloquy and hatred, for I am over-desirous of being loved, and of returning love for love' (Stephens, *Hook* 354). John Keble believed the Christians must expect to be despised and rejected, and that if they achieved success they should be suspicious of it. He wrote: 'It would be a charity if people would sometimes in their litanies pray for the *very* healthy, *very* prosperous, *very* light-hearted, *very* much be-praised.' (Battiscombe, *Keble* 336–7).

In typical Evangelical fashion Charles Simeon sought help at a time when he was subjected to much contempt and derision by opening the Bible at random.

His eye lighted on the story of Simon of Cyrene. 'Simon is the same name as Simeon. What a word of instruction was here – what a blessed hint for my encouragement! to have the Cross laid upon me, that I might bear it after Jesus – what a privilege! ... Now I could leap and sing for joy as one whom Jesus was honouring with a participation in his sufferings ... I henceforth bound persecution as a wreath of glory round my brow!' (Hopkins, *Simeon* 81).

W.C.E. Newbolt suggests indeed that a priest wear his affliction as a badge of office. He: 'must not hesitate to let it be seen that there is of necessity about him that undertone of sorrow ... He has been at Gethsemane himself; the lines of anguish are still there' (Newbolt, 293). His undeserved suffering is more likely than that of other people to assist the Christian cause, because more likely to be associated with it. In her brilliant short novel *Amos Barton* George Eliot tells of a throughly commonplace curate who has no gifts to attract his parishioners and who alienates them by an indiscretion; but who wins them by his suffering on the death of his wife. 'Amos failed to touch the spring of goodness by his sermons, but he touched it effectually by his sorrows' (Eliot, *SCL* 113).

At the end of the day, the only certain way a priest can deal with affliction is to remain convinced of the significance of his work. That significance was superbly expressed by one of the greatest of Victorian churchmen, Henry Liddon: 'It may seem to the servants of Christ, amid the steady monotony of their daily work and their incessant conflict with evil, that they are but as children writing on the sands of time their little alphabet, which must presently be effaced by the waters of the rising tide. Brethren, it is not so ... the message which we write upon the minds of a generation would be indelible, even if it were not destined to be re-written by our successors ... As each soul passes from a pastor's care, enlightened, repentant, sanctified, ... to enter upon its rest in that better world beyond the stars, it bears with it the spiritual results of sanctified toil, which are as immortal as itself' (Liddon, 231). Interestingly, Liddon spent only two years in parochial work. Perhaps the onlooker sees most of the game.

Intimate Experience

> As it becometh you to retain a glorious sense of the
> world, because the Earth and the Heaven and the Heaven
> of Heavens are the magnificent and glorious territories
> of God's Kingdom, so are you to remember always the
> unsearchable extent and illimited greatness of your own
> soul; the length and breadth and depth, and height of your
> own understanding. (Traherne, 2.92)

Vocation

'A man under authority; a man with supernatural powers; a man who was chosen a life of duties without end: at once delegate and representative: man's servant and God's: God's servant for man's sake: man's servant for God's sake … every priest is what his Master is – at once priest and victim. All things to all men, and yet permanently one's self, … God's pledged man' (Roberts, *Sheppard* 46–7).

It was with such a sense of his calling that Dick Sheppard* approached ordination. For a man to undertake so exalted a responsibility a compelling summons is required; and for Sheppard: 'The man is chosen rather than the maker of a choice' (Roberts, *Sheppard* 46). Chosen, of course, by God. No one can serve effectively as a minister unless he believes himself so chosen. But since God usually works through circumstances, it is possible to write in human terms about vocation; and necessary to point out that the motivation of individuals has sometimes been all too human.

The most frequent cause of vocation has been the experience of being brought up in a clerical family. James Woodforde*, son of a parish priest, accepted ordination as unreflectively as he did everything else in the even tenor of his days. Henry Alford**, the only child of a widowed clerical father, was what William James would have called a once-born. Devout from infancy, he followed almost automatically in his father's footsteps (Alford, 1–91), as did John Keble*, Francis Kilvert* and Walter Hook*. Christopher Chavasse** said: 'My father was a parson and I wanted nothing else but to follow him. I would frequently as a tiny boy don my white nightshirt as though it were a surplice and preach sermons to my brothers and sisters' (Gummer, *Chavasse* 29).

A more dramatic path has been that followed by a man who, after conversion, decides to express his commitment through ordination. Charles Simeon* is a paradigm of this process. The religious training of his youth had affected him little, but his conscience was pricked when the Provost of King's College required him to make his communion a few weeks after he came up to Cambridge. He embarked on a course of religious reading which in due course led him to the characteristic Evangelical experience in which he laid his guilt on Jesus and was himself liberated from it. Thereafter he never looked back. He survived three years of spiritual loneliness, and was ordained deacon at the first opportunity (Hopkins, *Simeon* 26–34).

Others have walked Simeon's way. Confined to bed after a riding accident William Andrew* experienced conversion and dedicated himself to ministry (Chadwick, *Andrew* 16). Roy Catchpole** was converted in prison, and, fortunate in the support and guidance he received, went forward to ordination after his release (Catchpole, *KTF* passim). David Watson* was converted at Cambridge University, was placed under the tutelage of the future bishop David Sheppard, and, much influenced by his experiences on the staff of camps for public schoolboys, moved naturally to thoughts of ministry.

Some come to ministry chiefly because of their love of God, others because of their love of humankind. Dick Sheppard found his vocation through his work in the East End of London. W.H. Vanstone**, already impressed by the love and care his parents brought to parochial and family life, discovered his personal vocation when in his teens he caught a boy stealing apples from the family tree, and was overwhelmed by his poverty and hunger (Vanstone, 5). Nicolas Stacey** resigned from the Royal Navy to seek ordination because of his experience of human suffering in the Far East at the end of the Second World War (Stacey, 13–20). Nicholas Rivett-Carnac**, who came from a titled and affluent background, found his way to ministry through work in Bede House, a Christian settlement in Bermondsey, and in the probation service (Cooke, *Rivett-Carnac* 24–35).

Sometimes in the past and often in modern times a call to ministry has emerged from a shorter or longer period of service as a Christian layman. George Herbert* held a number of university posts as a layman, and was for a short time an MP before in his thirties seeking orders. The faith inculcated in George Bull** by his clerical family survived five years in the Royal Navy. He was then trained as a schoolmaster by the Church Missionary Society, and worked in Sierra Leone until ill health drove him home in 1820, and opened the way for two years' further study as a prelude to ministry (Gill, *Bull* 15–44).

Some have been called to Anglican orders by way of ministry in other denominations. An extreme case was that of the Victorian William Edward Addis, who was a Roman Catholic priest, a Presbyterian minister, and a Unitarian professor before becoming an Anglican incumbent (Chadwick, *VC* 2.127). In recent years a steady trickle of Roman Catholic priests have been licensed as Anglican clergy, often because they have decided to get married.

Of the few women who have been ordained, many felt their vocation long before they were able to exercise it. One interviewed by Catherine Treasure had wanted to be ordained since her 'teens but had to wait till her thirties for the diaconate to be open to her (Treasure, 22). Margaret Cundiff was converted early in life. She was successively a parish worker, licensed to officiate, and a deaconess. Before ordination she gave the ministry all she was allowed to, and ordination itself was inevitable once the opportunity was there (Margaret Cundiff, *Called to be Me*, Triangle 1988, passim).

Some have been born ministers; others have had ministry thrust upon them. With regard to the former: 'I confess my childhood was taken with ministers and I heard with delight and admiracion and desire to imitate them from my youth, and would be acting in corners.' Thus Ralph Josselin* (Josselin, 1). Arthur Stanton*, devoted both to God and to his fellow-men, never thought of any other profession (Russell, *Stanton* 26). From earliest youth Samuel Barnett too was determined to take orders; an intriguing decision since, by his own account, he lacked a strong religious sense (Barnett, 1.7). Although George Dolling* worked as a land agent for a time, his biographer is undoubtedly right in referring to him as 'a little priest from the cradle' (Osborne, *Dolling* 7).

John Fletcher* too was always drawn to ministry. In his teens he abandoned the idea for a time, because of a mistrust of Calvinist doctrine and a concern lest he should be prompted by secular motives. However, attempts to become a soldier were thwarted by circumstances. He came to England to act as a tutor, and underwent a conversion experience which impelled him to revert to his original intentions (Macdonald, *Fletcher* 14–20).

With regard to those who have had ministry thrust upon them, Thomas Fuller** complained that there were 'many nowadays, who begrutch their pregnant [that is, promising] children to God's service, reserving straight timber to be beams in other buildings, and only condemning crooked pieces for the temple; so that what is found unfit for city, camp and court (not to add ship and shop) is valued of worth enough for the Church' (quoted in Addison, *WDF* 10). He was referring to the practice by which the income from a living was retained within a patron's family through the ordination of a son. Jane Austen's Edmund Bertram was recruited in this fashion; fortunately he was no crooked piece (Austen, *MP* passim). Sydney Smith*, who would have preferred the law, was railroaded into ordination by his overbearing father on grounds of expense (Bell, *Smith* 7–8). It was said of John Conybeare**: 'It was no secret that economic need and family tradition had dictated the course [of ordination]' (Colloms, 251). None the less, Smith and Conybeare proved ornaments to their profession. Smith spoke for others as for himself when he wrote: 'I hope I am too much a man of honour to take an office without fashioning my manners and conversation so as not to bring it into disrepute' (Bell, *Smith* 165).

In past centuries ordination was often in a narrow sense a career choice. Educated young men were brought up in an environment in which ministry was one of a very restricted range of options. Choice among them might be almost fortuitous. Lord Chesterfield advised a friend to guide his sons in terms of their temperaments: 'to a good dull and decent boy the Church' (Russell, 32). There was no tradition of ordination in William Bennett's* family. He seems to have sought orders because it was a natural thing for an Oxford man to do (Bennett, 11). John Skinner* and Robert Hawker* flirted with the law before deciding upon ministry. Augustus Hare* was a brilliant but light-hearted and lazy young man. Because of the latter characteristic his family thought he might be better suited to the church than to the law, but he resisted the suggestion and became a college tutor. Then he fell in love and had to secure an adequate source of income. At about the same time one of his best friends died, leaving him thinking to himself: 'If I were to die now without ever having been of use ...' (Hare, 1.215). The same evening he decided to take orders. His wifely biographer felt it necessary to point to his zealous work as a parish priest as evidence that he had not been exclusively influenced by worldly motives.

Ministry used to offer the best opportunity for a poor but bookish boy to lead a professional life. George Crabbe**, seeking a career as a writer, was taken under the patronage of Edmund Burke. Burke supported him in his wish for ordination, and by the use of influence overcame the difficulties created by his protege's lack of formal education (Crabbe, 1.97–103). Patrick Bronte** was the son of a poor farmer; he made his way by teaching until he could afford to go to university at the age of twenty-five and from there be ordained (Gaskell, *Bronte* 27–8).

William Grimshaw* wrote that a frequent motive for seeking ordination was simply 'getting a good living ... I confess it was mine' (Baker, *Grimshaw* 24). Thomas Scott who succeeded Newton at Olney in 1781 started life as a farm worker. Study made ordination possible, but his own description of his motives was 'a desire of a more comfortable way of procuring a livelihood, the expecta-tion of more leisure to employ in reading, and a vain-glorious imagination that I should sometime distinguish myself in the literary world' (Balleine, 77). It is pleasant to record that Scott was converted after ordination, and later wrote a notable Bible Commentary.

Scott was not alone in finding his true vocation after ordination. Thomas Adam, parish priest of Winteringham, Lincolnshire, from 1726 to 1784 took orders for worldly reasons. In 1745 or thereabouts, however, he read William Law's *A Serious Call*, and was thrown into a spiritual crisis which lasted three years. A reading of Romans completed the process of conversion, and he became a leading Evangelical teacher. Samuel Walker came to Truro as a curate in 1746 because of his love of the cards and dancing which the local Assembly Rooms afforded. He was converted by another local clergyman, and thereafter ministered to extraordinary effect until he died in 1761 (Balleine, 55–6, 65).

The class structure of English society has operated effectively to stifle all save the most energetically pursued vocations among the working-class.

Certain exceptions have already been described. Others have included Charles Jenkinson**, who came to ministry by way of St Stephen's, Poplar, socialism, work with Conrad Noel**, and a government grant after army service in the First World War (Hammerton, *Jenkinson* 15–31). He was academically able; more remarkable is the story of Joe Williamson**. He came from a poverty-stricken Poplar home, but was fortunate in his Anglo-Catholic parish church of St Saviour's and in the saintly priests who saw through his graceless exterior to the potential within. While he was still a choir boy Williamson had a religious experience which convinced him he was called to ordination. The experience improved neither his manners nor his prospects, and he was condemned to a number of unrewarding jobs on leaving school. War service matured him, and after demobilization he went to an Ordination Test School, situated in an old prison, at government expense. He made little progress because of lack of grounding. He was about to go into Church work as a layman when a quiet conspiracy of clergy secured him at place at St Augustine's College, Canterbury. Further generous conspiracy spirited him through his deacon's examination and provided the money to set him up for ordination. The fact that the first years of his ministry were disastrous and the later fruitful, testifies to the long-sightedness of the wise men who defied the system to save him for his vocation (Williamson, passim).

Williamson was no exception in his reliance upon the guidance of clergy. Jack Putterill** had embarked on a career in banking when he met Conrad Noel and Harold Mason, his curate. It was their influence which determined him to seek orders (Putterill, 19–25). Indeed, a factor in almost every ordination has been the influence of parish priests. Imitation has been the sincerest form of flattery.

It is most unlikely that anyone would become a priest nowadays from a desire for affluence, distinction or a professional life. But that is not to say that motives are never mixed. I am convinced that my own vocation was in large measure genuinely spiritual; but I am also well aware that it owed something to a lifelong belief that I can commend myself to other people only when I possess the standing afforded by a professional role, and something to a lifelong desire to be the central figure in a creative enterprise. I trust that God has sanctified these traits of character, but I recognize that they are largely self-directed and that they constitute the shadow-side of what might appear an altruistic decision. No doubt most contemporary clergy could point to a similar shadow-side in their own vocation.

Spiritual Experience

It is not always easy to discover what has gone on within the hearts even of those whose interiority is their stock in trade. Inarticulacy is part of the English tradition, reticence of the Anglican. Samuel Barnett* was representative in believing that it is neither healthy nor modest either to examine other people's souls or to expose one's own (Barnett, 1.12). Even some Evangelicals have thought in those terms; one of his curates said of Charles Simeon* that he 'was not ordinarily communicative, never obtrusive, on subjects of personal feeling in religion. These he regarded as matters between God and the soul, not lightly to be divulged' (Hopkins, *Simeon* 33).

Perhaps inarticulacy is inevitable and reticence desirable. The profoundest religious experiences are indescribable. Whereof one cannot speak, thereof one must, or at least should, be silent. John Fletcher* 'was favoured, like Moses, with a supernatural discovery of the glory of God, in an ineffable converse with Him, face to face; so that, whether I was in the body or out of the body, I cannot tell' (Macdonald, *Fletcher* 126). On waking one morning Nicholas Rivett-Carnac** 'suddenly felt weightless and a marvellous peace and joy rolled all over him ... while one part of him knew that God, the almighty and ineffable, was in this mystery, the other part relaxed totally into the hundred per cent feeling of physical, mental, emotional and spiritual wholeness. He sparkled with joy ... he was responding ... to someone' (Cooke, *Rivett-Carnac* 23–4). The word 'ineffable' is of the essence. To ask for more detail would be impertinent, and, if details were given, they would in all probability convey little.

Fortunately there have been exceptional priests with literary as well as spiritual gifts who have been able to communicate some part of their interiority. Francis Kilvert* described in masterly fashion one of those extraordinary experiences which come and go without warning and often without any apparent reason, but which assume an immense significance if they are regarded as a momentary rending of the veil. He was walking in the country-side: 'As I came down from the hill into the valley across the golden meadows and along the flower-scented hedges a great wave of emotion and happiness stirred and rose up within me. I know not why I was so happy, nor what I was expecting, but I was in a delirium of joy, it was one of the supreme few moments of existence, a deep delicious draught from the strong sweet cup of life. It came unsought, unbidden, at the meadow stile, it was one of the flowers of happiness scattered for us and found unexpectedly by the wayside of life. It came silently, suddenly, and it went as it came, but it left a long lingering glow and glory behind as it faded slowly like a gorgeous sunset, and I shall ever remember the place and the time which such great happiness fell upon me' (Kilvert, 3.190–1).

Thomas Traherne* looked to the common things of life for enlightenment: 'When I came into the country, and saw that I had all time in my own hands, having devoted it wholly to the study of Felicity ... I was guided by an implicit faith in God's goodness; and therefore led to the study of the most obvious and common things. For thus I thought within myself: God being ... infinite in goodness, it is most consonant and agreeable with His nature, that the best things should be the most common ... Air, Light, Heaven and Earth, Water, the Sun, Trees, Men and Women, Cities, Temples etc. ... Rubies, Pearls, Diamonds, Gold and Silver; these I found scarce and to the most denied. Then began I to consider and compare the value of them which I measured by their serviceableness ... And I saw clearly, that there was a real valuableness in all the common things; in the scarce, a feigned' (Traherne, 3.52, 53).

Traherne was incapable of thinking negatively; but he could experience and learn from negative feelings. 'In a sad and lowering evening, being alone in the field, when all things were dead and quiet, a certain want and horror fell upon me, beyond imagination. The unprofitableness and silence of the place dissatis-fied me; its wideness terrified me: from the utmost ends of the earth fears surrounded me ... Yet something also of hope and expectation comforted me from every border. This taught me that ... I was made to hold a communion with the secrets of Divine Providence in all the world: that a remembrance of all the joys I had from my birth ought always to be with me ... and that these things being absent to my eyes, were my joys and consolations, as present to my understanding (Traherne, 3.23).

John Fletcher's experience of alienation was, typically, on behalf of others: 'About the time of my entering into the ministry, I one evening wandered into a wood, musing on the importance of the office I was going to undertake. I then began to pour out my soul in prayer; when such a sense of the justice of God fell upon me, and such a sense of his displeasure at sin, as absorbed all my powers, and filled my soul with an agony of prayer for poor, lost sinners. I continued therein until the break of day; and I considered this as designed of God to impress upon me more deeply the meaning of those solemn words, "Knowing therefore the terror of the Lord, we persuade men"' (Macdonald, *Fletcher* 126–7).

Tom Walker** was so overcome with doubt and fear while in hospital waiting for an exploratory operation that he concluded he was under attack by Satan. He engaged him in conflict with prayer and scriptural quotations; and as he did so 'the whole of my surroundings seemed to change. I was no longer conscious of the dimly lit ward and the hospital smells. It was as though I was high up on a mountain, worshipping God in a quiet sanctuary. The shaded light above my bed seemed to be transformed so that there was a translucent quality about the scene. There, for hours, I was carried with praise into the presence of God. The fight with Satan was over. He had left – a defeated foe' (Walker, 133).

Other Christians might have described Walker's experience in different terms; but the battle with the self, and the need for self-knowledge if the battle is to be won, is a recurring theme. John Newton* remembered an occasion when a lion was brought to Olney Cherry Fair: 'The lion was wonderfully tame: as familar with his keeper, as docile and obedient as a spaniel; yet the man told me he had his surly fits, when he durst not touch him. No looking-glass could express my face more justly than the lion did my heart. I could trace every feature. As wild and fierce by nature, yea, much more so; but grace has in some measure tamed me. I know and love my Keeper, and sometimes watch His looks that I may learn His will. But oh! I have my surly fits too – seasons when I relapse into the savage again – as though I had forgotten all. I got a hymn out of this lion ...' (Pollock, *Newton* 171).

All Christians seek for guidance in particular situations. Some receive it in dramatic circumstances. Conrad Noel**, visiting Thaxted church after the patron had offered the parish to him, and unimpressed by what he saw, knelt in a side-chapel and asked for guidance from St Thomas of Canterbury. 'I felt his hand on my shoulder and his voice telling me that this was the work God was giving me to do.' He rose, his mind made up; to discover that the chapel was dedicated to St Thomas (Dark, *Noel* 87).

God may be known as joy and love, as wrath and judgment, in weakness and perplexity. He may also be known as absence. The contemporary priest and poet R.S. Thomas writes:

> Why no! I never thought other than
> That God is that great absence
> In our lives, the empty silence
> Within, the place where we go
> Seeking, not in hope to
> Arrive or find. (R.S. Thomas, 'Via Negativa', in *Later Poems* 1984)

We turn to the pentecostal experience. As a curate in Rotherhithe Nicholas Rivett-Carnac failed to offer deliverance to a young man involved in black magic. After several days of intense prayer he asked a group of friends to lay hands on him: 'It was all over in the few moments, but Nicholas felt as if something had burst within him, a torrent of feelings and longings all poured out in that one, single-syllabled cry in another tongue. For over an hour he cried out in this way. All his stiff-upper-lip reserve melted in the joy and peace that flooded through him. It was like coming home, like the end of a long journey.' Thereafter Rivett-Carnac was released into fluent praying in tongues and conducted a continuing healing ministry (Cooke, *Rivett-Carnac* 41–2).

Rivett-Carnac was lucky in finding himself among the like-minded. David Watson* too had the experiences of being filled with the Spirit and of speaking with tongues. Sharing the one with a fellow clergyman he was accorded the embarrassed rejoinder 'I think it may rain today.' After experimenting with the other he was asked to leave the Biblical Research Centre where he was living (Watson, *YAMG* 54–5, 64–5).

In recent times charismatic experience has become more respectable, not least because it has not been the preserve of any one group within the Church. In 1964 the Evangelical Michael Harper resigned his curacy at All Souls', Langham Place, to found the Fountain Trust as an ecumenical instrument for renewal. Another Evangelical George Carey** received the Spirit in 1972. A few months later the Anglo-Catholic John Gunstone, laid hands upon him and prayed in tongues. Carey wrote: 'That time ... made me take seriously the ecumenical movement; that God is working through his Spirit in all the traditions' (Carey, 8–10).

At an opposite pole of spiritual experience lies the demand of the moral imperative; in large measure a product of personal upbringing, yet ultimately depending for its validity on a perception of the divine sanction behind it. There has been a grim tradition within Anglicanism, represented and in part created by the widely-read seventeenth-century religious primer *The Whole Duty of Man*, by which morality has been regarded as accountancy and as the enemy of pleasure. This approach is seen at its best in the injunction: 'One plain coat thou puttest upon a poor man's back, will better become thee, than twenty rich ones thou shalt put upon thine own'; at its worst in the remark: 'As men use not to take physic for pleasure, but remedy, so neither should they eat', and in the description of marrying without parental consent as stealing. 'Children are so much the goods, the possessions of their Parent, that they cannot, without a kind of theft, give away themselves without the allowance of those that have the right in them' (*WDM* 169–70, 144, 242).

As one would expect, Thomas Traherne takes a more genial line: 'I do not speak much of vice ... because I am entirely taken up with the abundance of worth and beauty in virtue, and have so much to say of the positive and intrinsic goodness of its nature ... since a strait line is the measure both of itself, and of a crooked one, ... the very glory of virtue ... will make all vice appear like dirt before a jewel when they are compared together' (Traherne, *Christian Ethics*, quoted in Stranks, *AD* 108).

In matters of morality John Keble* appealed to the Spirit rather than to the letter. He said of Jesus's moral teaching: 'Consider these commandments as so many instances of *friendly advice* rather than so many tasks set us ... as practices and tempers of the mind flowing naturally from what we know to be the truth of our condition and God's dealing with us. For instance ... we are not to be nicely enquiring as to how much money is to be given in alms, but we are to consider whether it is not natural and reasonable for one who seriously believes the Gospel to lay out every farthing in some way which deserves to be called alms ie in providing for the reasonable wants of others rather than his own superfluities, however innocent in themselves these latter may be' (Battiscombe, *Keble* 56).

Traherne and Keble were proclaiming the supremacy of grace over law in moral issues. More generally, every priest needs to learn and to be reminded that the ground of Christianity is the experience of being unconditionally loved. This is of course a truth which he constantly holds in his head, but for the refreshment of his spiritual life and ministry he needs also to feel it in his heart. Charles Simeon made the point in a typically orotund fashion: 'O how desirable is it for all, but especially for ministers, to have their souls deeply and devoutly impressed! What is religion without this? What are duties without this? Alas! a dry, insipid, unsatisfying, unproductive form. Surely this is happiness, to taste the love of God' (Hopkins, *Simeon* 139).

As an ordinand John Robinson** wrote: 'Tonight God has spoken to me forcibly ... the experience had about it that double quality of absolute sweetness, fruition, repose and of absolute demand, searching, condemning and exhausting – which I have so often written about and never completely experienced' (Robinson, 19). With a question mark against the word 'condemning', the experience Robinson describes is a necessary validation of the routine of the Christian life, referring it back to the experiential truths on which it rests. My own need in this respect has been met most fully in recent years by the Cursillo movement, the spread of which within the Church of England is one of the hopeful signs of modern times; not least because the movement combines Catholic devotion with Evangelical exuberance.

We examine in detail the spiritual experience of William Grimshaw*. Grimshaw was one of those whose spiritual lives are a perpetual drama, whose souls are a perpetual battleground. He learned in childhood to fear eternal punishment, but it was not until after he was ordained that spiritual awakening came. 'For long years he believed himself to be engaged in a losing battle against the powers of darkness, for long years the moments of radiant joy were followed by hours of bitter self-reproach.' The pleasures of his first marriage distracted him from spiritual matters, but in 1738 came a fresh reformation, to be followed, after his wife died in the following year, by a depression so deep as almost to deprive him of his reason. His grief and his enforced chastity reinforced a sense of sin which was already unusually strong, and he battled with temptations to curse God and to believe that He was 'a cruel implacable Being'. He was plagued with physical symptoms, which he was not yet wise enough to deal with by way of diet and medicine. He felt himself in the grip of Satan, and study of a seventeenth-century best-seller *Precious Remedies against Satan's Devices* did no more than confirm him in that conviction. He once exclaimed in the middle of a service: 'My friends, we are all in a damnable state, and I scarcely know how we are to get out of it!' He even considered suicide (Baker, *Grimshaw* 31, 42, 44).

Another book worked a total transformation. As his friend Joseph Williams described the scene: 'At the house of one of his friends he lays his hand on a book and opens it with his face towards the pewter-shelf; and instantly an uncommon heat flashes in his face. He is surprised, and turning about cannot imagine how the pewter could reflect fire at such a distance. He turns to the title-page and finds it to be Dr Owen on Justification, and immediately his face is saluted with such another flash.' From Owen Grimshaw learned total dependence upon God and to look to Christ alone for salvation; a doctrine in which he was confirmed by his reading of the epistles of St Paul. The outcome was a 'great joy ... a Bridal Bliss in Christ' (quoted in Baker, *Grimshaw* 44, 47), which brought with it physical fitness and energy. This endured only for a time; then the old depression returned, though in a less virulent form.

A later experience confirmed the earlier one. One Sunday in 1744 Grimshaw fell so ill after the morning church service that he was thought to be dying. As he lay in a nearby inn he had a vision in which God the Father conferred with the Son about him. The Father would have condemned him because he had not fully set aside his claims to righteousness, but Jesus pleaded for him; and in his vision Grimshaw saw his wounds. By the time of afternoon service he was sufficiently recovered to preach for four hours.

Grimshaw said of this experience: 'I have had a glorious vision from the Third Heaven'. However, he did not claim, as some other Evangelicals have done, to have achieved sinless perfection. His spiritual struggles continued; indeed he saw temptation as a sign of spiritual vitality. 'So long as I resist the temptations of Satan, I am a Gainer, and for many Reasons I would rather be assaulted by them than not ... Never ... is faith stronger, nor grace fuller, than when you feel most your filthiness, weakness and unworthiness' (Baker, *Grimshaw* 72, 75). But, side by side with temptation, he experienced rapture; the strife was not over, but victory was now certain.

Spirituality and Character

The Minutes of the 1786 Methodist conference include the question and answer: 'Who has died this Year? John Fletcher*, a pattern of all holiness, scarce to be paralleled in a century.' A contemporary said of him: 'Fletcher is a seraph who burns with the ardour of Divine love. Spurning the fetters of mortality, he almost habitually seems to have anticipated the rapture of the beatific vision.' His biographer writes: 'He possessed in an exceptional degree the qualities that constitute saintliness: deep humility and transparent purity, absolute unworldliness, with love unfailing, and patience that had its perfect work' (Macdonald, *Fletcher* 4, 7, 5).

Fletcher was a phenomenon, unusual even among saints in that he had no apparent weaknesses. It might seem perplexing that it is not he who represents the Evangelical tradition in the Anglican calendar but the deeply flawed Charles Simeon*. But the choice of Simeon can be defended; not on the ground that he is more 'important', whatever that means, but on the ground that he illustrates more graphically the truth that grace uses and refines nature, but does not abolish it. In Fletcher grace and personality fused so perfectly that the one could not be distinguished from the other; in most of us awkward excrescences of character jut out so far that, even if they are washed by the silver sea of grace, they are never wholly covered.

John Skinner* provides a case in point. His diary is given a painful and salutary interest by the way in which he wrestles with his depression and paranoia, calling Christian faith to his aid, but rarely convincing his readers that head-religion has effectually touched his heart. He battled, ultimately in vain, against traits of character which he knew in principle how to sanctify, but which in practice remained obstinately destructive. He lacked the self-knowledge which would have enabled him to distinguish between the real difficulties of his life and his morbid reactions to them; and he did not receive the medical and spiritual help which might have saved him.

Self-knowledge is a protection against the spiritually dangerous practice, which Skinner did not avoid, of harnessing questionable aspects of character to a religious cause and thereby justifying them. A perceptive critic wrote of Charles Kingsley* after his frenetic patriotism at the time of the Crimean War had impelled him to write the bloodthirsty *Westward Ho!*: 'What an unspeakable relief and joy for a Christian, like Mr Kingsley, whom God has made boiling over with animal eagerness and fierce aggressive instincts, to feel that he is not called upon to control these instincts, but only to direct them; and that once having, or fancying he has, in view a man or institution that is God's enemy as well as his, may hate it with a perfect hatred' (Chitty, *Kingsley* 171).

In another sense too Kingsley's character warred against his spirituality. His periodic depressions hampered his work and undermined his faith. In 1855 He wrote to F.D. Maurice: 'A period of collapse has come upon me. I live in dark nameless dissatisfaction and dread.' He doubted his commitment to reform, his trust in the Bible was weakened, and he was unable to complete work on which he embarked (Chitty, *Kingsley* 186).

Depression, like other weaknesses of character, can, however, be turned to good use. Sydney Smith*, who 'suffered from the constitutional melancholy of the jovial', was well placed to support an aristocratic lady with a 'tendency to despair'. In a letter he supplied twenty nostrums against low spirits which seem as wise now as they must have done then. They vary from 'Short views of human life not farther than dinner or tea' and 'Keep good blazing fires' to 'Don't expect too much of human life, a sorry business at the best' and 'Make no secret of low spirits to your friends but talk of them fully; they are always the worse for dignified concealment'; and culminate in 'Be firm and constant in the exercise of rational religion' (Bell, *Smith* 137–8).

Despite his world-wide reputation David Watson* was plagued by an insecurity of which his asthma was an outward and visible sign. He was subject to depression and dogged by a sense of failure. He was temperamentally unsuited to two of the enterprises to which Bible study and conscience drew him – living in community and sharing leadership with others. His devotion to his work led him to neglect the needs of those closest to him: Anne and the children, and the team who accompanied him on tour. He had a limited gift for personal friendship and was often thought aloof.

But this is to say no more than that, as Watson was himself the first to admit, he had personal spiritual battles to fight. On the positive side his quality as a man of God was manifested in his teaching, leadership and writing; his faith and courage were beyond question, and never clearer than in his behaviour in the months before his death. He wrote that during a bad asthma attack at that time: 'between one and three a.m. God spoke to me so powerfully and painfully that I have never felt so broken before him ... He showed me that all my preaching, writing and other ministry was absolutely *nothing* compared to my love-relationship with him ... God also showed me that any "love" for him meant *nothing* unless I was truly able to love from my heart my brother and sister in Christ' (Watson, *FNE* 171). Watson had come to value his capacity for love above all his achievements; and that is one definition of holiness.

The impressive thing about Watson was what he did with limited gifts; the impressive thing about Dick Sheppard* was the way he harnessed great gifts which might otherwise have led him magnificently astray. His personality was almost irresistible, and he had perpetually to struggle against abusing it. He could sway great masses of men to do and believe whatever he wished, and at the same time he evinced the mastery of detail and the grasp of complicated arrangements which are the hallmarks of a great organizer. 'It was only by continual prayer and humility that this great and elemental force was so completely turned to the service of God.' The extent of his success was epitomized by a cockney coster woman who was one of the 100,000 who filed past his coffin: 'He's all right now. He's happy. But what's going to happen to the rest of us?' (Scott, *Sheppard* 58, 18).

We look in detail at the characters of two of the men who have bulked large throughout this book – Charles Simeon and John Keble*.

An acute observer described Charles Simeon as 'a truant from the green-room, studying in clerical costume for the part of Mercutio, and doing it scandalously ill ... beset ... by inveterate affectations, by the want of learning, by the want of social talents, by the want of general ability of any kind, by the want of interest in the pursuits of his neighbours' (Hopkins, *Simeon* 154, 45). His manners were affected to the point of absurdity, his care for his appearance excessive, his self-importance offensive. The admirer might have added that Simeon was intolerant, quick-tempered, unsociable except with the like-minded, and insensitive in personal relations. He was deeply dependent upon friendship, yet all too apt to forfeit it through arrogance and prickliness.

Weaknesses of character dogged Simeon throughout his life. He remained impetuous and high-handed, deploying Evangelical colleagues with scant regard to their own opinions of those of others. He said himself that a 'besetting sin in a state of nature will most generally remain so ... in a state of grace; with this difference only, that in the former case it has the entire ascendant ... – in the latter it meets with continual checks and is not suffered to have dominion' (Hopkins, *Simeon* 100).

It is, however, a measure of Simeon's spirituality that he both partially remedied his faults, and learned to rise above them. He was chastened by the experience of unpopularity, and realized that patience and humility could grow in him only if he were given the opportunity to exercise them. He learned to know himself and to come to terms with himself. He learned to overcome weaknesses of temperament by leaning to the side opposite to his natural bias; learned to remain within the god-given limits of his strength and to practise, in his phrase, 'self-denying moderation' (Hopkins, *Simeon* 132); accepted rebuke from his friends when he lost his temper; learned to offer and to seek for forgiveness with equal alacrity.

Simeon was affluent, and took advantage of the fact. His establishment was luxurious, his horses expensive, his wine cellar extensive, his hospitality lavish. On the other hand, he was generous with his means. As a young man he allocated a third of his income to good causes. Later he devoted the whole interest on a legacy of £15,000 to charitable ends and gave away the £5,000 profit from his *Horae Homileticae*. He was conscious of the needs of the poor, and in the village parish of Stapleford, which he took on to provide the house and income for a curate, he established a small factory for the plaiting of straw, to provide employment.

One vice which did not trouble Simeon was that of sloth. He was of course exempted from the claims on his time which poverty, domestic duties or a family would have imposed, but none the less his industry was deeply impressive. It was said that behind most of his sermons there lay not less than twelve hours of study. He conducted a huge ministry by correspondence. He followed the characteristic Evangelical practice of accounting for his time. He trained himself to early rising (normally 4.00 a.m.), fining himself if he overlay.

Simeon was gifted with other good qualities. Only a man of steely determination could have sustained the weight of hostility which he experienced. He was devoid of jealousy, and rejoiced in the achievements of his friends and followers, saying of one curate 'he must increase, and I must decrease'.

It could be argued that these qualities were not innate, but arose from his conversion. Certainly his intense earnestness came from that source; so did his joyous vitality. He once told a congregation: 'There are but two lessons for the Christian to learn: the one is, to enjoy God in everything; the other is, to enjoy everything in God' (Hopkins, *Simeon* 203). He was not naturally humorous or light-hearted, but he made great efforts to be cheerful, and succeeded. In this, as in other respects, he was aided by his constant practice of prayer, sometimes all night long, and with considerable emphasis on a habit uncommon among Evangelicals, of silence.

Had Simeon given himself entirely to a ministry to large numbers he would in all probability have been confirmed in the egotism which came naturally to him. Fortunately, he realized from the outset that he had a first duty to individuals. He was a spiritual director of extraordinary insight and empathy, in large part because, knowing his own inner self, he was able to see into the selves of others.

The acid test of a sanctified character is its depth of humility. In this respect, as in others, Simeon's nature warred with his Christian intentions. His intentions triumphed only incompletely and after struggle. He spent his birthdays as days of humiliation, on which he recalled and lamented his sins, but he did not engage in extensive self-denigration; instead he humbled himself by contemplating the greatness of God. He once wrote: 'That God calls and does work by the meanest instruments, I am a living witness,' continuing: 'Yet I have lived to see the triumph of my own principles throughout the land' (Hopkins, *Simeon* 118–19). He was unworried about his reputation, but he kept careful copies of his correspondence to avoid false accusations. He was reluctant to provide material for a biography, and during his last illness requested that nothing laudatory said of him should be repeated to him.

The observer (Sir James Stephen) who described Simeon in the terms quoted at the beginning of this passage went on to marvel at the use he made of his life, and wrote: 'He was ... one of those on whom the impress of the Divine image was distinct and vivid' (Hopkins, *Simeon* 166). He is indeed a remarkable example of an unprepossessing character sanctified by grace. The Church of England has done well to follow Stephen's own suggestion and number him among those she delights to remember with reverence.

A reviewer of *The Christian Year* wrote 'We are conscious of the presence of one more humble indeed, more subdued and self-forgetting than ourselves, oppressed with a sense of infirmities and errors, of unsatisfied responsibilities, and unrequited mercies, yet still a recluse more holy and pure than ourselves, in whose presence we are ashamed to indulge in any worldly, impure, or ungoverned imaginations' (quoted in Stranks, 266n).

That picture of John Keble does justice to his character only in part. Certainly he was humble; certainly he shared with all devout Christians of his age a profound sense of sin. But his vast attractiveness depended upon other qualities. John Henry Newman described him as gentle, courteous and unaffected, and remarked on his hatred of humbug, his playfulness and his tender love for others. Geoffrey Faber writes of the 'unabashed emotionalism of his temperament, which might perhaps have seemed sloppy had it not been boxed in by scholarship and blessed by religion' (quoted by Battiscombe, *Keble* 67). He was sunny and even-tempered, and in youth especially he gave an impression of innocence and gaiety. These qualities fell into the background as he grew older, but until the end of his life he possessed the gift of setting anxiety aside and entering whole-heartedly into the smallest of everyday pleasures. There was a radiance about him, compounded of wisdom, kindliness and humour. He attracted the devotion and the reverence of those who knew him best.

To a degree Keble's qualities, like Simeon's, represented the triumph of grace over nature. There was a depressive element in his character – or perhaps it would be truer to say that he recognized and felt deeply the tragic aspect of life. Nor was he indiscriminate in the affection he offered others. His natural sociability was tempered by a severity which characterized many of his dealings with his humbler parishioners and which made him a stern judge of social equals of whom he disapproved. He broke decisively not only with friends who went over to Rome, but also with fellow-Anglicans such as Thomas Arnold whose religious opinions differed from his own.

Keble approached life sacramentally, and saw in the rites of the church a distillation of the wider sacrament of nature. He was not an ascetic in the sense of rejecting God's gifts in the process of rejecting the abuse of them. He taught a thankful enjoyment. He dressed neatly and ate well, and counselled others against excesses of self-punishment. The calmness and sweetness which emanated from him arose in part from his refusal to hurry (he called hurry 'want of faith and dutifulness'); perhaps too from his lack of competitiveness and business sense, and from the streak of indolence in his character which denied him the pinnacles of scholarly achievement which his friends Newman and Pusey attained.

Indolence was not his only shortcoming. Georgina Battiscombe sub-titles her book *John Keble* (to which I owe nearly all the material in these paragraphs) 'A Study in Limitations'. 'His mind ran in a deep but narrow channel, and, to vary the metaphor slightly, he could not, or would not, look out over the channel's bank' (Battiscombe, *Keble* xviii). Keble's background and upbringing closed his eyes to social and intellectual change and to the need for social reform. It bred into him an impregnable Toryism, political and religious, which a lifetime of thought and experience confirmed and which allowed no merit whatever to opposing views. While it was said of him that he never said a sharp word about those who differed from him without immediately correcting himself, it was also remarked that he was unhappy in the common room at Oriel because he soon lost his temper in discussion; no one could get on with him unless they entirely agreed with him. Nor did he allow any virtue to doubt. Rocklike in his own orthodoxy, he not only had no sympathy with those who were less certain than himself, but ascribed their doubts to weakness or sinfulness.

Yet he remained the exemplar of thousands who knew him or who read his works. Keble revivified the supernatural element in Anglicanism. He taught the centrality of holiness by being holy himself; and the fact that he was a country parson rather than a bishop or a don made his influence all the greater. His holiness had a distinctive character, which Georgina Battiscombe summarizes as 'reticence', and which Keble himself called sobriety; and that too was, for good and ill, a legacy to his Church.

Old Age and Dying

'Give me Grace evermore, O my God, to be in readiness for my latter End, and no ways to be terrified at the Thoughts of my approaching Dissolution. A Conscience void of Offence towards God and Man is the best Preparation, and its my Study to acquire such a Conscience' (James Newton, 2). Thus James Newton** at the age of 44. He was not anticipating unduly. Death among the clergy with whom we have been concerned, as among our ancestors generally, was not always preceded by old age. Francis Kilvert* died at 39 of peritonitis, George Dolling* of disease and exhaustion at 51, George Herbert* at 40 from tuberculosis.

Augustus Hare* died in middle life in Italy, where he had gone in the hope of recovering his health. The course of his illness gave him ample time for preparation. He received the sacrament 'with a joy and brightness I cannot describe', wrote his sister-in-law; and said good-bye individually to his friends and family. His wife described their farewell: 'He said "There is only one thing left now, that is, to take leave of *you* – when shall it be?" Fearful every hour might be the last, I said it had better be now ... he raised himself up with astonishing strength, and, embracing me, said "I must press you once more to my heart; you have been the dearest, tenderest, the most affectionate of wives"; and then he prayed that I might be strengthened and comforted. When I spoke of meeting again he said, "No, not for many years. You have too many on earth to love you." Some time after, "I did not say what I ought – the *truest* of wives; it has been that truth I so delighted in." Then he gave me messages for all, and then he said, "Everything in the world is now done; now let me be alone, I must go to sleep." He begged me to put the locket on the chain around his neck, "The first thing you ever gave me." ... When a bad coughing fit came on, he thought it was the last, and, taking my hand in both his, he raised it up saying, "Dearest Mia", and lifted up his eyes to heaven, as if in prayer' (Hare, 2.19–20).

In letters written after he died six days later his wife recounted how she had read the Bible to him, and how he had given her the text 'In patience possess ye your souls'. He had been much 'pressed down' by a sense of his unworthiness but had repeatedly said that he hoped he was 'in the fold'. 'He had been for two months looking the moral eye of God's justice in the face, and he felt that if it were not for his faith in Christ all his hopes for heaven would sink under him.' He had had a strong persuasion of Satan's agency and had feared that if he suffered greatly he might dishonour his Christian character. 'Never was a fear less realized, nor was faith ever less tried.' In death as in life Hare's earthly and heavenly loves were intertwined. In death as in life God's judgment was as real to him as God's mercy; no doubt he was preserved from the one by his faith in the other (Hare, 2.25, 23).

Hare was only 41. For the most part, however, the clergy have been long-lived by the standards of their day; possibly because of the health conferred by active spirituality, possibly because they have enjoyed more ease and comfort than most. They have been fortunate in being able to pursue their vocation to the end unless seriously incapacitated. George Denison** of East Brent was carried to his church in extreme old age and preached from a chair in the chancel (Denison, xi). Less satisfactorily, until well into this century many incumbents retained their posts without discharging their duties, regarding their stipends as pensions and using a fraction of them to pay curates.

James Woodforde* began to decline at the age of 55, in the cold winter months which began 1795. He contracted gout, cancelled services, and then obtained substitutes to take them. In due course he recovered sufficiently to resume his duties and to make one of his regular excursions to Somerset. On his return to Weston Longueville in November he appointed a curate to assist him and thereafter almost ceased to attend church; when he did so it was as a member of the congregation. He performed occasional services in his own home and was well enough to maintain his social life.

By early 1797 Woodforde was finding the fact that it was 'rather dirty etc.' or 'very damp' a sufficient reason for staying at home. At the year's end he wrote: 'It grieves me much that I am rendered unable to do it [lead worship] myself or to attend at Church being so very infirm.'

Thereafter Weston Church remained unserved when Woodforde's curate had business elsewhere. The severe winter of 1798–9 aggravated his ills; he was 'very low' and complained that 'Fear seems to have got great Power over me of late days.' He retained charge of his household and agricultural affairs, received guests and continued his charitable routines. His diary ends appropriately, ten weeks before his death in 1803, with notes that the curate had taken church service, that his friends from the gentry had attended, and that 'Dinner to day [was] Rost Beef etc.'.

Woodforde grew old and died as he had lived, unreflectively. He was less concerned with his spiritual responsibilities and his eternal destiny than with his comfortable and no doubt consoling secular routines. It may not be too uncharitable to suggest that the last pages of his diary give a fair picture of the balance of values in his life (Woodforde, vols 4 and 5 passim).

Another diarist who died in post philosophized about old age in a way Woodforde did not. In 1830, at the age of 58, John Skinner* wrote: 'I ask no pre-eminence, I seek no honours: ambition and pride, if ever I entertained such guests, they have long since deserted me. I am more and more inclined to anchor my frail and more than half-decayed bark in this its anchoring place, and lay its timbers where it is in port. I get more and more weary of common topics, yet I am only high-minded in one particular, which is to court the converse of purer spirits, and to endeavour to avoid everything which will estrange my mind from such communion when I hold converse with my own heart as I do now in my chamber and am still' (Skinner, 416).

As so often, poor Skinner was expressing aspiration rather than achievement. The air of weary tranquillity which this passage breathes soon gives place in his journal to the usual catalogue of family, parochial and wider affairs, accompanied by the usual plenitude of unregulated emotion. In due course came derangement and the *Liber Niger* in which he exulted over the varying fates of his old enemies. Not long afterwards he shot himself. Unhappy in his death, often almost intolerable during life, he remains an ultimately sympathetic figure, a good man overwhelmed by psychological forces beyond his control.

Others of the clergy with whom we have been principally concerned died in harness or without formally relinquishing their cures. At the age of 81 William Bennett* suffered a stroke while he was preparing to celebrate, and died two days later (Bennett, 289). Dick Sheppard* died at his desk (Roberts, *Sheppard* 311). Sydney Smith* slowed down gently, taking an interest in parish and Chapter affairs almost to the last (Bell, *Smith* 216–17). John Keble's* ministry too tapered away gradually. He and his wife suffered both bodily weakness and acute anxiety about each other. They died less than six weeks apart; the money to build Keble college, his memorial, was subscribed in the shortest of times (Battiscombe, *Keble* 337–53).

Henry Fardell*, always plagued with influenza and bronchitis, left his parish for his home in Ely after a serious illness, and died six months later (Fardell, 142–3). Julius Hare* was frequently ill from 1851 onwards. He died peacefully; his last words were 'Upwards, upwards' (Hare, 2.361–2). Charles Kingsley*, waiting at Eversley in terror for his wife's expected death, was carried off by pneumonia; the last words he uttered were a recitation of the burial service (Chitty, *Kingsley* 294–6). Arthur Stanton* fell ill at the end of 1912, and, as soon as his health permitted, moved to the family home in Gloucestershire. In his correspondence he gave priority to his 'rough lads'. As he lay dying in March 1913, he spoke twice: once to thank his nurse, and once to reply to the quotation: 'The beloved of the Lord shall dwell in safety'. He responded: 'If He wills it, I am willing.' His funeral was attended by thousands, and brought London to a standstill (Russell, *Stanton* 298–314).

Even before the days of pensions from the Church Commissioners some clergy vacated their posts instead of using them as sinecures. A stroke incapacitated William Andrew*; he resigned his parish and moved away, dying two years later. Samuel Garratt** thought himself too old at 77 to run a parish, and resigned. He told his congregation: 'I do not think it is for the honour of God that I should retain such a post as this till compelled by the infirmities of age to cease to do its duties. In that case the work of the parish would … dwindle and grow feeble' (Garratt, 103–4).

Garratt did not abandon ministry with his parish. He continued to preach and did not resign as rural dean of Ipswich until 1906 when he was 88 (Garratt, 163). He was an early example of what has become a widespread phenomenon – the retired priest still in reasonable health, and much in demand as a guest, a substitute, a locum tenens or an unpaid curate. At the time of writing more than half the living clergy of the Church of England are retired, and a high proportion of them are active.

An alternative to retirement has been a move to a less demanding parish. George Bull** retired from an inner city Birmingham parish to Almeley in Herefordshire for the last year of his life. Not inappropriately, he called the bishop who had offered him the post his relieving officer (Gill, *Bull* 150).

The great Evangelicals spent their last days as men who had nothing to fear and no occupation other than serving their Lord. Dying of typhus contracted while visiting, William Grimshaw* received streams of visitors 'who rekindled the flame of their devotion at the dying man's faith'. Didactic in death as in life, Grimshaw was buried according to his instructions in 'a plain poor man's coffin' inscribed 'for me to live is Christ, and to die is gain' (Baker, *Grimshaw* 261, 263).

John Newton* was ready for death well before it came. In old age he wrote: 'I am like a labourer in a harvest, who does not wish to leave the field until he has finished his day's work, yet who looks now and then at the sun, and is glad to see the approach of evening, that he may go to rest.' He could not bear to abandon ministry and preached almost to the last (Martin, *Newton* 36, 357, 365).

Charles Simeon* retained his parish and his faculties to the end. He refused treatment which might artificially prolong life. He had his bed moved into a large room so that he could conveniently receive callers, but in one respect was an exception for his time, telling a party which had gathered in his room: 'You want to see what is called a *dying scene*. That I abhor from my inmost soul. I wish to be *alone*, with my God, and to lie before him as a poor, wretched, hell-deserving sinner ... but I would also look to him as my all-forgiving God.' He died in the spirit of the doctrines he had preached for so many years; it was fitting that text for his very last sermon was: 'Come with me and see my zeal for the Lord' (Hopkins, *Simeon* 210–12).

As one would expect, John Fletcher* awaited death with serenity and was well aware of the blessings of old age. He wrote: 'I keep in my sentry-box till Providence remove me; my situation is quite suited to my little strength. I do as much or as little as I please, according to my weakness. And I have an advantage which I can have nowhere else in such a degree; my little field of action is just at my door; so that if I happen to overdo myself, I have but a step from my pulpit to my bed, and from my bed to my grave' (Macdonald, *Fletcher* 183). In his last illness he constantly repeated 'God is love' (Benson, *Fletcher* 350). On the day before his death his wife said to him: 'My dear, I ask not for myself, but for the sake of others; if Jesus is very present with thee, lift thy right hand.' He did so. 'If the prospect of glory opens before thee, repeat the sign.' He did (Macdonald, *Fletcher* 191).

Our ancestors loved improving death bed scenes such as Fletcher's. They have in fact often occurred. Bernard Gilpin* spoke in turn to the poor, his schoolboys, his servants, and a group of those who had not previously responded to him; he spent his last hours in prayer interspersed with conversation (Collingwood, *Gilpin* 269–70). It was noted by a nun present at the death of the sometime parish priest Gilbert Shaw in 1967 that his appearance was so transformed that 'it was the nearest thing to a death bed transfiguration I've ever seen' and that 'the remembrance of the sight continues to be a source of joy to all those who witnessed it' (Hacking, *Shaw* 137).

David Watson* died in exemplary fashion, despite the fact that the circumstances provided a severe test of faith. Cancer was diagnosed early in 1983, and set a speedy term to the evangelistic work he was just beginning with the Belfrey Trust. He was surrounded by prayer and attended by leading practitioners of the healing ministry. Yet what remissions there were were very brief. The disease took its course, and killed him in just over a year. Where was the hand of God in all this?

Watson answered the question in two ways. First, the ministry he undertook during that final year was charged with a consciousness, both on his part and on that of his hearers, of the fact that he was dying and was correspondingly effective. When he preached at St Michael-le-Belfry for the last time, he stood at the door for an hour and a half after the service ended, greeting individually the huge congregation who had come to say good-bye.

Secondly, he wrote *Fear No Evil*, which tells the story of his last months almost to the end. It is a book which comforts because it is in such large measure a confession of weakness and dereliction. Watson died in faith, but not without a struggle; his last journey gave the lie to the facile attitudes not uncommon among his followers and to which he had perhaps sometimes succumbed himself. Before the end he had learned to surrender himself. The last paragraph of his book reads: '"Father, not my will but yours be done." In that position of security I have experienced once again his perfect love, a love that casts out all fear' (Watson, *FNE* 171).

Watson had to battle his way to tranquillity. He was not alone in his doubts and fears. At the age of 40 Ralph Josselin* had 'frequent thoughts and feares of death: With if I should miscarry, and be eternally miserable how sad would bee my condition the mercy of god in christ Jesus is alone that which upholds my heart' (Josselin, 386). Walter Hook* had 'a constitutional dread of dying' (Stephens, *Hook* 570). Robert Hawker* too dreaded what lay ahead: 'The earth has many trials, sorrows, anxieties, pains, but what are all these ... compared with the severance and gulph of death?' 'At all times and in every rank ... the last journey of a separated soul is a very awful path.' In fact he died calmly, possibly because he had been received into the Roman Catholic church a few hours beforehand. (Brendon, *Hawker* 188, 227–232).

It might be expected that the clergy, more than most, would wish to know that they were dying, so that they might prepare themselves. Yet such has not always been the case. Henrietta Barnett* was told three years before her husband's death that his time was limited. 'The Canon,' she recalled, 'was never told, and as one bears great sorrows best in silence no one ever knew, but each day was treasured more, each pregnant suggestion remembered, every gay glad incident enfolded deep.' The sentence throws a flood of light on Henrietta's character, and on her relationship with her husband. When the time actually came, Barnett died firm in the faith which his adversaries had so often accused him of lacking, constantly reiterating: 'The Everlasting Arms will sustain me'. By his wish, his funeral was at St Jude's; Henrietta received 1100 letters of sympathy (Barnett, 2.371).

'If it be now, 'tis not to come; if it be not to come, it will be now; if it be not now, yet it will come: the readiness is all' (*Hamlet*, 5.2). Not all perhaps; but much. William Jones** kept a coffin in his study and looked out from his bedroom window on the yew tree under which he expected to be buried (Addison, *ECCP* 59). That, though prescient, may be thought macabre, so let the last word lie with a parson-poet who loved the sweetness of this world but who was well prepared, in thought at least, for the next. Contemplating his grave Robert Herrick** wrote:

Here down my wearyed limbs I'le lay;
My Pilgrim's staffe; my weed of gray;
My Palmer's hat; my Scallops shell
My Crosse; my Cord; and all farewell.
For having now my journey done,
(Just at the setting of the Sun)
Here have I found a Chamber fit,
(God and good friends be thanked for it)
Where if I can a lodger be
A little while from Tramplers free;
At my up-rising next, I shall,
If not requite, yet thank ye all.

Afterword

It becometh His Goodness to make all things treasures:
and his Power is able to bring Light out of Darkness,
and Good out of Evil. (Traherne, 3.31)

A case could be made for saying that the Church of England in her present form has outlived her usefulness to God and nation. The number of regular churchgoers has been in relative decline since the middle of the nineteenth century, in absolute decline throughout the twentieth century, and in catastrophic decline in recent years. The Church has never won the working class, and she now has little influence among the well educated. Never fully the Church *of* the nation, she is losing the claim to be the Church which *serves* the nation. She baptizes fewer children, confirms fewer people, marries fewer adults, conducts a smaller proportion of funerals. Lack of resources makes the pastoral ideals which have been her greatest strength less attainable. Her contributions to education and to social service, though not insignificant, are increasingly marginal. Her political influence is waning. There are those who seek her disestablishment; should it take place, her place in national life would become even more peripheral than it is now. Above all, the parochial system, which is of the essence of historic Anglicanism, is collapsing under the strains imposed upon it by declining human and financial resources. In 1993 there were 5293 parishes with a place of worship but no resident minister. The question of how the system can be preserved is rapidly giving way to the question of what should take its place.

It may be that the Church of England, which has been closely associated with characteristics of English society which have lost their potency – the Crown, the countryside, a socially cohesive class structure, a culture deeply rooted in the past – is now simply out of date. The fact that active church members form a smaller percentage of the population in England than in any other Western European country suggests that the Church principally responsible for serving them must have something badly wrong with her. The fact that there are now more Roman Catholic churchgoers than Anglicans, despite the Church of England having twice as many clergy, points to the same conclusion. So, it might persuasively be argued, the Church as she is has no useful future.

Nor would it be surrender if the Church of England were to seek a new structure and a different mission. Anglicanism is like cricket or football; it is an English invention which has been imitated worldwide and is now stronger overseas than in the land of its birth. Worldwide Anglicanism survives without establishment or the parochial system; it may be that the daughter Churches have valuable lessons to teach their mother. Perhaps the Church of England is called to retain only that part of her heritage which she shares with the rest of the Anglican communion. Perhaps she is even called to abandon her identity within some wider ecumenical grouping. In either event she would have a part to play in the continuing work of the whole Church of God. Drastic alterations of role and character might well lie within the providence of God, and it would be no grounds for despair should they occur. Anglicans should be prepared to face such eventualities. It is less certain, however, that they should invite them.

For this declining Church retains old virtues and has developed new ones. She preserves a tradition of worship valued even by unbelievers and has grafted on to it a modern liturgy which serves the needs of those left unmoved by the *Book of Common Prayer*. She stands for much which society is losing, and which society may become anxious to regain. She articulates the inchoate spirituality of the ordinarily irreligious at turning-points in their lives. She 'remains a venerable social institution which continues to be acknowledged by the State as in some sense guardian of the nation's morals and a vehicle for the ritual expression of national aspirations and achievements' (Tiller, 15). She is a bulwark against the individualism and the withdrawal from collective activity which is wearing away the foundations of our society. She is heard, if not attended to. She is still, on the whole, conservative, but far from being Conservative. She harbours, if sometimes reluctantly, exceptional individuals: 'It is a strength of the Church of England ... that it is ... unable to control its prophetic mavericks' (Hastings, 432). Establishment, no longer an expression of triumphalism, has become a mark of a servant Church; of a Church which exists not to serve the interests of her own committed membership but to minister to a wider and often ungrateful society. The historic revenues of the Church enable her to perform beyond her present strength; her management of contemporary giving has a healthily redistributive effect, as the affluent suburbs support struggling inner city and rural parishes. Her clergy are now the only professional group serving everyone on a roughly equal basis and not only ministering to the deprived but living among them. The parish priest and his congregation symbolize the universal availability of Christian service. The very moral weaknesses which are eroding the Church's strength make her role more vital.

The parochial system has a further merit which even church people are in danger of undervaluing. Because of the constraints of history and the complexities of the relationship between each parish priest and his people, the system remains healthily untidy. This characteristic is one aspect of a wider witness which the Church is still qualified to undertake – a witness against centralized authority, against management by objectives, against quantified results, against market forces, against cost benefit analysis, against the profit motive. In a society where the ideal of public service has been subverted and where almost everything has been reduced to a business, we need an institution which remains obstinately wedded to the human and particular, to relationship and idiosyncrasy, to intuitional leadership and unrewarded service, to bringing about unquantifiable changes in the hearts of men and women, to a local loyalty which does not deny but puts into perspective wider responsibilities.

God's ways are not man's. There is a well-known story about a French priest who worked for years in a slum without any measurable results. Asked what he thought was the value of his work, he replied that his task was to ensure that the rumour of God did not entirely disappear. That has been and will continue to be the vocation of some parochial clergy, and it should be the privilege and responsibility of 'successful' priests and their congregations to ensure that the 'failures' are sustained in their costly witness. This idea makes no sense in human terms but it accords with the divine economy.

What are the implications of these reflections for the ordained ministry? There are clergy who would welcome a more clear-cut role. They chafe under the ambiguities of the present situation, and, without denying the need for service, long for a starker distinction between the Church and the world – for congregationalism and believer's baptism; for the warmth of a community of the wholly committed; for permission to talk about 'them' and 'us'.

The bulk of the clergy, however, wish both to sustain the committed and to minister to the casual. They bear with resigned cheerfulness the abrasions constantly inflicted upon them by work with the unchurched. They extend a generous tolerance to those who turn to the Church only to make use of her. They think that the boundaries of the Kingdom neither coincide with those of the Church nor are subsumed within them.

But can the parochial ministry be retained in anything like its present form in the face of continuing decline? It can, with adjustments. 'The shape of the ordained ministry is, and always has been, one of "variable geometry", a model derived from advanced aircraft design where an aeroplane can change the shape of its wings according to the demands of the flight' (Melinsky, xiii). Change there must be; but, to continue Melinsky's metaphor, it should be in order to enable the plane to fly on in the same direction in differing weather conditions. In the terms used by Anthony Russell, the Church should opt for an 'adaptionist future' (Russell, 300).

Change is nothing new. Russell has identified four changes in the nature of ministry which have taken place over the past century. The clergy have increasingly concentrated upon specifically priestly tasks; much which they used to do is now done by others; they have been affected by the privatization of personal and family life; and they spend more time than formerly on routine paper work and on meetings (Russell, 274).

Adaptations of this nature are inevitable. Others, to deal with dysfunctions which Russell identifies as causing conflict and tension in the contemporary role of the clergyman, such as the tendency to consign the laity to passivity, may be called for. As has already been pointed out, however, the clergy cannot adopt a role thoroughly congenial to modern attitudes and continue to do their job properly. To be seen as anomalous is part of the price of ministry today.

Some adaptations threaten the essential character of the ministry. The attack on the parson's freehold, however justifiable in terms of good discipline and necessary change, weakens the traditional independence of the parish priest, and concedes too much to the twentieth-century mania for managerial structures and bureaucratic efficiency. The tendency to claim that the parsonage should be in the ordinary sense a private house and preferably a modern one is fostered by dioceses for dubious economic reasons and supported by some clergy for reasons of familial privacy. The tradition, however, requires both a policy of the open door and large parsonages which can serve parochial uses within a context of personal hospitality (William Hurdman, 'The Privatization of the Parsonage' 1985, unpublished). The fact that the average stay of an incumbent in a parish is now about six years suggests that too little attention is being given to the benefits of stability and pastoral knowledge which only the years can accumulate.

The grouping of parishes so that they may be served by teams of clergy constitutes a fourth threat. As an expedient to meet staffing shortages the arrangement is defensible; but a benefice is not as well served by the corporate ministry of several clergy as its constituent parishes would be by the exclusive ministry of one. The clergy spend too much time with each other; the laity are marginalized because they are confronted with the corporate decisions of the team; administration becomes more cumbrous and time-consuming; pastoral and liturgical arrangements work well only if team members behave as if they were in fact independent parish priests; the advantages which accrue could for the most part be garnered through informal co-operation; and the usual rule operates, that the actual benefit of the smaller units is frequently sacrificed to the notional benefit of the large one.

Fifthly, there is an increasing tendency to enhance the power of the bishop at the expense of his clergy. It is true that in the early Church the bishop was the leader and priests his surrogates; but that was in days when dioceses were small. The present diocesan structure removes the bishops far from the scene of action, and is a relic of prelacy rather than a pastoral arrangement. A Church which took traditional episcopacy with true seriousness would ordain a bishop to every deanery. While this remains undone, the parochial clergy must continue to exercise an *episcope* unknown in the early Church. There must of course be constant interplay between the bishop, representing the wider Church, and the parish priest, representing the basic unit of worship and service; but for the interplay to be fruitful it must be reciprocal.

There is indeed much to be said for a ramshackle system of authority. Organizations are usually run by those within them furthest from the actual work they exist to do. When the work is the care of souls that kind of distancing is especially damaging. By a paradox of history the Church of England, despite apparently being fettered by law and bureaucracy to an uncommon degree, gives her clergy and people considerable freedom to be themselves in the context of their parochial life. It is a heritage to be cherished.

Turning from threats to promise, five recent initiatives, all in part engendered by weakness, could become major sources of strength to the parochial system. First, the Church has in her hands a potentially invaluable instrument in the body of non-stipendiary ministers. At present they are used for the most part as auxiliaries and stop-gaps; a decision to employ them widely and to trust them with real responsibility would go far towards ensuring the maintenance of the parochial system, and would have the additional advantage of reinforcing the Church's stated objective of asking the laity to shoulder heavier obligations. The same is true, secondly, of the use of local ministers, raised up by their own congregations and relying heavily upon them.

Thirdly, ecumenical projects – desirable in themselves – can sustain the Church where the efforts of separate denominations would be insufficient. This is at least as important in the countryside as in towns. The suggestion in the Tiller Report (Tiller, 34) that the laity rather than the clergy should sustain rural ministry is unrealistic; but an active laity working across denominational boundaries can compensate for the fact the clergy often have several communities or congregations to serve.

Fourthly, the increasing authority and responsibility accorded the laity should enable the clergy to concentrate on the tasks for which they have been ordained, and thus to spread themselves more widely. 'It is a limitation of the image of pastor that – as an image of oversight – it leaves no room for a growth to maturity and participation by the sheep' (ACCM report *Ordained Ministry Today*, 1969, p. 37, quoted Tiller, 84). When the clergy have the opportunity and the good sense to hand over administration to others, they may be less able to run things but they are more able to serve people. It may well be that the one essential and major departure from the tradition should be a readiness on the part of the clergy to work with their people rather than to direct them. This attitude would facilitate a fifth initiative – the use of retired clergy to serve parishes in a purely priestly capacity, on a house for duty basis.

Precedents for these initiatives can be found in the ministry's history. Very many clergy in the past have relied only in part, and occasionally not at all, on the Church's finances for their living. A high proportion of the parochial clergy have in practice been part-timers. Sixteenth-century parish priests were for the most parts local products. Many a parish priest has been constrained to share his authority with the laity. Many clergy have continued to give useful service in old age. It may be argued that these are not altogether happy precedents; but if the choice were to be between a bewildering patchwork of ministries support-ing the traditional system, and tidy centralizing which would make parishes retail outlets of policies manufactured wholesale by dioceses or deaneries, there is not much doubt which alternative would be truer to the genius of the Church of England.

It is probable that the decision to ordain women as priests will reinforce the parochial clergy numerically. Certainly the ordination of women will give parochial ministry dimensions which now it lacks. It has already increased the readiness of laywomen to take leadership roles in the Church (*Deacons Now*, 27–8). In due course it will do more. It is unfashionable to argue that the sexes differ in anything save biological function; but, leaving questions of nature or nurture on one side and allowing for any number of exceptions, it is likely that women will enrich ministry with the distinctive virtues which the deacons interviewed by Catherine Treasure singled out: a readiness to listen, a reliance on intuition, a freer expression of feelings and hence an ability to help others (especially women) to release theirs, a reliance on first-hand rather than on bookish experience (Treasure, 11–12). Consequences of the priesting of women may include a stronger tendency towards consensual leadership and a rediscovery of the servant nature of the ministry. It would be a tragedy if the rich spirituality with which women's ministry will increasingly endow the Church were to be stifled by the creation of male-made systems which subjugate individual genius to central planning and policies.

Of course the parochial principle should be adapted to local circumstances; it always has been. It makes sense to regard the rector of a City church as pastor to the people who work nearby on week-days rather than of the exiguous congregation who gather in his church on Sundays. Guild churches can concentrate on specialized ministries, and close at week-ends. 'In a city or heavily urbanized area the parish church should serve to hold together different working units' (Melinsky, 144). The team idea has real value in city centres. Sector ministries criss-cross with parochial ones to the benefit of both. Ministers in secular employment are often better able to minister to their colleagues at work than priests who know them, if at all, only at home. These arrangements are, however, acceptable only as exceptions. As Martin Thornton wrote three decades ago: 'Whatever the answer to our practical problems, we should realize that huge parishes, group ministries, industrial chaplaincies, eclectic congregations, and so on, are basically ascetical matters which are opposed to the Prayer Book system of spirituality' (Thornton, 259).

More generally, the way any parish lives its Christian life should reflect the perceptions of its priest and congregation and the nature of the locality. Whatever is done will fall far short of what needs to be done; it is for local Christians to determine their priorities and the pattern of their witness. So it is to be expected that one parish priest will concentrate on keeping the flame of worship burning, and another on serving the wider community; that one will give priority to visiting and another to lay training; that the life of one congregation will be distinguished by its intensity, and that of another by its generosity. Such decisions must evolve in the light of personalities and local circumstances. The recommendation in the Tiller Report that each vacancy should have a precise job specification attached to it (Tiller, 101) denies the parish priest the freedom he has always possessed to write his own job specification from within, and places him at the mercy of those who wish to define his ministry in their own terms.

Administrative manipulation misses the point. At the end of the day, in the Anglican tradition, it is the relationship between priest and people which counts. W.C.E. Newbolt wrote: 'In some parts of England there is a custom, when the parish priest dies, of burying him with his feet towards the west, that at the Resurrection Day he may be able ... to stand up and face his people' (Newbolt, 52). The assumption of life-long service to a single parish no longer obtains, and the implication of a continuing distinction between leader and led is theologically faulty. But the image of a bond forged to eternity illustrates the pastoral emphasis which has been at the heart of the tradition. Earthen vessels the parochial clergy admittedly have been; they might reply, with St Paul, 'Who is sufficient for these things?' (II Cor. 2.16). Within their human limitations they have served, and to a greater or lesser degree embodied, a pastoral ideal. Bishop Ken described that ideal in terms appropriate to his time; with surprisingly few adjustments it speaks to our own day too:

> Give me the Priest these Graces shall possess;
> Of an Ambassador the just Address,
> A Father's Tenderness, a Shepherd's Care,
> A leader's Courage, which the Cross can bear,
> A Ruler's Awe, a Watchman's wakeful Eye,
> A Pilot's Skill, the Helm in Storms to ply,
> A Fisher's Patience, and a Lab'rer's Toil,
> A Guide's Dexterity to disembroil,
> A Prophet's Inspiration from Above,
> A Teacher's Knowledge, and a *Saviour's* Love.
> ('Edmund: an Epic Poem', Book VIII)

Bibliography

Dates refer to the editions used. The words in brackets are those used in the references in the text. Books not listed here are given a full reference in the text.

Individual biographical material, arranged under the names of the clergy concerned

Henry Alford   *Life, Journals and Letters*, edited by his widow, Rivingtons 1873 (Alford)

William Andrew   Owen Chadwick, *Victorian Miniature*, Hodder and Stoughton 1960 (Chadwick, *Andrew*)

J.C. Atkinson   J.C. Atkinson, *Forty Years in a Moorland Parish*, Macmillan 1891 (Atkinson)

Thomas Becon   D.S. Bailey, *Thomas Becon and the Reformation in England*, Oliver and Boyd 1952 (Bailey, *Becon*)

Sabine Baring-Gould   W. Purcell, *Onward Christian Soldier*, Longmans Green 1957 (Purcell, *Baring-Gould*)

Samuel Barnett   H. Barnett, *Canon Barnett, His Life, Work and Friends*, 2 vols, 1919 (Barnett)

William Bennett   F. Bennett, *The Story of W.J.E. Bennett*, 1909 (Bennett)

Richard Benson   M.V. Woodgate, *Father Benson of Cowley*, Bles 1953 (Woodgate, *Benson*)

Patrick Bronte   Mrs Gaskell, *Life of Charlotte Bronte*, John Grant 1924 (Gaskell, *Bronte*)

George Bull   J.C. Gill, *Parson Bull of Byerley*, SPCK 1963 (Gill, *Bull*)

George Carey   George Carey, *The Church in the Market Place*, Kingsway 1990 (Carey)

Roy Catchpole   Roy Catchpole, *Grown Men Do Cry*, Triangle 1990 (Catchpole, *GMDC*)
     Roy Catchpole, *Key to Freedom*, Lutterworth 1974 (Catchpole, *KTF*)

Christopher Chavasse	Selwyn Gummer, *The Chavasse Twins*, Hodder and Stoughton 1963 (Gummer, *Chavasse*)
William Cole	*Blecheley Diary of William Cole*, ed. F.G. Stokes, 1931 (Cole)
John Collins	L.J. Collins, *Faith under Fire*, Leslie Frewin 1966 (Collins)
George Crabbe	*Life and Poems of the Rev. George Crabbe*, edited by his son, 1847 (Crabbe)
	Howard Mills (ed.), *George Crabbe; Tales*, 1812 and other selected poems, (Mills, *Crabbe*)
George Denison	L.E. Denison, *Fifty Years at East Brent*, 1902 (Denison)
Robert Dolling	R.R. Dolling, *Ten Years in a Portsmouth Slum*, 1896 (Dolling, *TY*)
	C.E. Osborne, *Life of Father Dolling*, 1903 (Osborne, *Dolling*)
Henry Fardell	*View from the Vicarage: The Diary of Henry Fardell*, ed. Arnold Nicholas – unpublished (Fardell)
John Fletcher	J. Benson, *Life of the Rev. John W. de la Flechere*, 1825 (Brown, *Fletcher*)
	F.W. Macdonald, *Fletcher of Madeley*, 1885 (Macdonald, *Fletcher*)
Thomas Fuller	William Addison, *Worthy Dr Fuller*, Dent 1951 (Addison, *Fuller*)
Cyril Garbett	Charles Smyth, *Cyril Foster Garbett*, Hodder and Stoughton 1959 (Smyth, *Garbett*)
Samuel Garratt	Samuel Garratt, *Life and Personal Recollections*, J. Nisbet 1908 (Garratt)
Bernard Gilpin	C.S. Collingwood, *Memoirs of Bernard Gilpin*, 1884 (Collingwood, *Gilpin*)
William Grimshaw	Frank Baker, *William Grimshaw*, Epworth 1963 (Baker, *Grimshaw*)
	G.G. Cragg, *Grimshaw of Haworth*, 1947 (Cragg, *Grimshaw*)
Julius and Augustus Hare	Augustus Hare, *Memorials of a Quiet Life*, 2 vols, 1872 (Hare)
Robert Hawker	Piers Brendon, *Hawker of Morwenstow*, Anthony Mott 1975 (Brendon, *Hawker*)
George Herbert	G. Herbert, *A Priest to the Temple* (Herbert)
	Amy Charles, *A Life of George Herbert*, Cornell University Press 1977 (Charles, *Herbert*)

Robert Herrick	Robert Herrick, *Poems*, ed. L.C. Martin, Clarendon 1965 (Herrick)
	F.W. Moorman, *Robert Herrick*, 1910 (Moorman, *Herrick*)
John Hester	John Hester, *Soho is my Parish*, Lutterworth 1970 (Hester)
Walter Hook	C.J. Stranks, *Dean Hook*, Mowbrays 1954 (Stranks, *Hook*)
	W.R.W. Stephens, *Life of Walter Farquhar Hook*, 1880 (Stephens, *Hook*)
Arthur Hopkinson	A. Hopkinson, *Pastor's Progress*, Michael Joseph 1942 (Hopkinson)
Harold Hosking	Harold Hosking, *It's only the Vicar*, Gooday 1987 (Hosking)
Charles Jenkinson	H.J. Hammerton, *This Turbulent Priest*, Lutterworth 1952 (Hammerton, *Jenkinson*)
Rowland Jones	W. Rowland Jones, *Diary of a Misfit Priest*, Allen and Unwin 1960 (Jones)
Ralph Josselin	Ralph Josselin, *Diary*, ed. Alan Macfarlane, The British Academy 1976 (Josselin)
	A. Macfarlane, *Family Life of Ralph Josselin*, Cambridge University Press 1970 (Macfarlane, *Josselin*)
John Keble	G. Battiscombe, *John Keble*, Constable 1963 (Battiscombe, *Keble*)
Francis Kilvert	Francis Kilvert, *Diary*, ed. William Plomer, 3 vols, Cape 1980 (Kilvert)
	F. Grice, *Francis Kilvert and His World*, Caliban nd (Grice, *Kilvert*)
Edward King	Lord Elton, *Edward King and Our Times*, Bles 1958 (Elton, King)
	Edward King, *Spiritual Letters*, ed. B.W. Randolph, 1910 (King, *Letters*)
	G.W.E. Russell, *Edward King*, Bishop of Lincoln, 1912 (Russell, *King*)
Charles Kingsley	S. Chitty, *The Beast and the Monk*, Hodder and Stoughton 1974 (Chitty, *Kingsley*)
J.G. Lockhart,	*Cosmo Gordon Lang*, Hodder and Stoughton 1949 (Lockhart, *Lang*)
Charles Lowder	L.E. Ellsworth, *Charles Lowder*, Darton, Longman and Todd 1982 (Ellsworth, *Lowder*)
Alexander Mackonochie	E.A. Towle, *Alexander Heriot Mackonochie* ed. E.F. Russell, 1890 (Towle, *Mackonochie*)

James Newton	*The Deserted Village*, ed. Gavin Hannah, Alan Sutton 1992 (James Newton)
John Newton	Bernard Martin, *John Newton*, Heinemann 1950 (Martin, *Newton*)
John Pollock,	*Amazing Grace*, Hodder and Stoughton 1981 (Pollock, *Newton*)
Conrad Noel	*Autobiography of Conrad Noel*, ed. S. Dark, 1945 (Dark, *Noel*)
Thomas Phelps	Gerald Van Loo, *A Victorian Parson*, Self Publishing Association 1989 (Loo, *Phelps*)
Joseph Price	*A Kentish Parson, Selections from the Private Papers of Joseph Price*, ed. G.M. Ditchfield and B. Keith-Lucas, Kent Arts and Libraries 1991 (Price)
Jack Putterell	J. Putterell, *Thaxted Quest for Social Justice*, Precision Press 1977 (Putterell)
Richard Randall	J.F. Briscoe and H.F.B. Mackay, *A Tractarian at Work*, 1932 (Briscoe, *Randall*)
Nicholas Rivett-Carnac	Jenny Cooke, *Upon this Rock*, Hodder and Stoughton 1989 (Cooke, *Rivett-Carnac*)
John Robinson	Eric James, *A Life of Bishop John A.T. Robinson*, Collins 1987 (James, *Robinson*)
John Rous	J. Rous, *Diary 1625–42*, ed. M.A.E. Green, 1856 (Rous)
Gilbert Shaw	R.D. Hacking, *Such a Long Journey*, Mowbray 1988 (Hacking, *Shaw*)
Dick Sheppard	R. Ellis Roberts, *H.R.L. Sheppard*, John Murray 1942 (Roberts, *Sheppard*)
	Carolyn Scott, *Dick Sheppard*, Hodder and Stoughton 1977 (Scott, *Sheppard*)
Charles Simeon	H.E. Hopkins, *Charles Simeon of Cambridge*, Hodder and Stoughton 1977 (Hopkins, *Simeon*)
John Skinner	John Skinner, *Journal of a Somerset Rector*, ed. H. and P. Coombs, Oxford Univeristy Press 1985 (Skinner)
Sydney Smith	Alan Bell, *Sydney Smith*, Oxford University Press 1980 (Bell, *Smith*)
Nicolas Stacey	Nicolas Stacey, *Who Cares*, Hodder and Stoughton 1971 (Stacey, *WC*)
Arthur Stanton	G.W.E. Russell, *Life of Arthur Stanton*, Longmans 1917 (Russell, *Stanton*)
Mervyn Stockwood	Mervyn Stockwood, *Chanctonbury Ring*, Hodder and Stoughton 1982 (Stockwood)

Richard Syms | Richard Syms, *Working Like the Rest of Us*, SCM Press 1979 (Syms)

Thomas Traherne | Thomas Traherne, *Centuries*, Mowbrays 1975 (Traherne)

William Vanstone | W.H. Vanstone, *Love's Endeavour, Love's Expense*, Darton, Longman and Todd 1977 (Vanstone)

Arthur and Henry Wagner | Anthony Wagner and Anthony Dale, *The Wagners of Brighton*, Phillimore 1983 (Wagner)

Tom Walker | Tom Walker, *From Here to Heaven*, Hodder and Stoughton 1987 (Walker)

David Watson | Teddy Saunders and Hugh Sansom, *David Watson*, Hodder and Stoughton 1992 (Saunders, *Watson*)
David Watson, *Fear No Evil*, Hodder and Stoughton 1983 (Watson, *FNE*)
David Watson, *You are My God*, Hodder and Stoughton 1983 (Watson, *YAMG*)

Gilbert White | Gilbert White, *The Natural History of Selborne*, ed. R. Mabey, Century 1988 (White)

Harry Williams | H.A. Williams, *Some Day I'll Find You*, Collins 1984 (Williams)

Joseph Williamson | Joseph Williamson, *Father Joe*, Abingdon 1963 (Williamson)

Francis Witts | *The Diary of a Cotswold Parson, Reverend F.E.Witts* ed. David Verey, Alan Sutton 1986 (Witts)

James Woodforde | James Woodforde, *Diary of a Country Parson 1758–1802*, ed. J. Beresford 5 vols, 1924–31 (Woodforde)

George Woodward | *George Woodward's Letters from East Hendred 1753–61 – a Parson in the Vale of the White Horse*, ed. Donald Gibson, Alan Sutton 1982 (Woodward)

Other Works

Addison, William, *The English Country Parson*, Religious Book Club 1947 (Addison)

Aubrey, John, *Brief Lives*, ed. Andrew Clark, 1898 (Aubrey)

Austen, Jane, *Mansfield Park*, Folio Society 1959 (Austen, *MP*)

Austen, Jane, *Pride and Prejudice*, Daily Express Publications 1933 (Austen *PP*)

Ayling, Stanley, *John Wesley*, Collins 1979 (Ayling, *Wesley*)

G.R. Balleine, *History of the Evangelical Party in the Church of England*, 1911 (Balleine)

Andrew Barrow, *The Flesh is Weak*, Hamish Hamilton 1980 (Barrow)

Lewis Bayly, *The Practice of Piety*, 1612 (Bayly)

Blundell, Margaret (ed.), *Blundell's Diary and Letter Book*, Liverpool University Press 1952 (Blundell)

Ronald Blythe, *Akenfield*, Penguin 1969 (Blythe, *Akenfield*)

Shelagh Brown (ed.), *Married to the Church*, Triangle 1983 (Brown)

S. Butler, *The Way of All Flesh*, Penguin 1986 (Butler)

S.C. Carpenter, *Winnington-Ingram*, Hodder and Stoughton 1949 (Carpenter, *Winnington-Ingram*)

Owen Chadwick, *The Victorian Church*, SCM Press, 2 vols 1966, 1970 (Chadwick, *VC*)

F.E. Christmas, *The Parson in English Literature*, Hodder and Stoughton 1950 (Christmas)

G. Kitson Clark, *Churchmen and the Condition of England*, Methuen 1973 (Kitson Clark)

Brenda Colloms, *Victorian Country Parsons*, Constable 1977 (Colloms)

Joyce Coombs, *Judgement on Hatcham*, Faith Press 1969 (Coombs)

G.R. Cragg, *The Church and the Age of Reason*, Penguin 1960 (Cragg)

Adrian Desmond and James R. Moore, *Darwin*, Michael Joseph 1991 (Desmond & Moore)

John Earle: *Microcosmographie* (Earle)

George Eliot, *Scenes from Clerical Life*, Penguin 1985 (Eliot, *SCL*)

George Eliot, *Silas Marner*, Penguin 1985 (Eliot, *SM*)

R.W. Evans, *The Bishopric of Souls*, 4th ed., 1856 (Evans)

Geoffrey Faber, *Oxford Apostles*, Penguin 1954 (Faber)

Henry Fielding, *Joseph Andrews*, Dent, Everyman 1987 (Fielding)

R.P. Flindall (ed.), *The Church of England 1815–1948*, SPCK 1972 (Flindall)

John Foxe, *Acts and Monuments*, ed. Pratt and Stoughton, 1843–9 (Foxe)

Thomas Fuller, *The Church History of Britain*, ed. James Nichols, 1868 (Fuller, *CH*)

Thomas Fuller, *The History of the Worthies of England*, ed. P.A. Nuttall, 1840 (Fuller, *WE*)

Thomas Fuller, *The Holy State and the Profane State*, 1840 (Fuller, *HS*)

Oliver Goldsmith, *The Vicar of Wakefield*, Daily Express Publications 1933 (Goldsmith)

Simon Goodenough, *Country Parsons*, David and Charles 1983 (Goodenough)

Peter C. Hammond, *The Parson and the Victorian Parish*, Hodder and Stoughton 1977 (Hammond)

Thomas Hardy, *Tess of the D'Urbervilles*, Penguin 1986 (Hardy)

A. Tindal Hart, *The Country Clergy 1558–1660*, Phoenix House 1958 (Hart CC)

A. Tindal Hart, *The Curate's Lot*, J. Baker 1970 (Hart TCL)

A. Tindal Hart, *The Eighteenth Century Country Parson*, Wilding 1955 (Hart, *ECCP*)

Adrian Hastings, *A History of English Christianity 1920–90*, SCM Press 1991 (Hastings)

Brian Heeney, *Mission to the Middle Classes*, SPCK 1969 (Heeney)

M. Hennell, *Sons of the Prophets*, SPCK 1979 (Hennell)

Christopher Hill, *The Century of Revolution*, Nelson 1961 (Hill)

Rev. Oliver Heywood's Diary, 1603–1702, ed. J. Horsfall Turner 4 vols, 1882 (Heywood)

Susan Howatch, *Glamorous Powers*, Fontana 1988 (Howatch, *GP*)

Susan Howatch, *Glittering Images*, Fontana 1987 (Howatch, *GI*)

Susan Howatch, *Scandalous Risks*, Fontana 1991 (Howatch, *SR*)

Cheslyn Jones, Geoffrey Wainwright, Edward Yarnold (eds), *The Study of Spirituality*, SPCK 1986 (Jones, *Spirituality*)

William Law, *A Serious Call*, Griffith, Farran, Browne nd (Law)

H.P. Liddon, *Clerical Life and Work*, 1897 (Liddon)

A.G. Matthews, *Walker Revised*, 1948 (Matthews, *Walker*)

M.A.H. Melinsky, *The Shape of the Ministry*, The Canterbury Press 1992 (Melinsky)

P.E. More and F.L. Cross (eds), *Anglicanism*, 1935 (More)

W.C.E. Newbolt, *Speculum Sacerdotum*, 1894 (Newbolt)

E. Norman, *The Victorian Christian Socialists*, Cambridge 1987 (Norman)

Margaret Oliphant, *The Perpetual Curate*, Virago 1987 (Oliphant, *PC*)

Margaret Oliphant, *The Curate in Charge*, Alan Sutton 1987 (Oliphant, *CC*)

J.H. Overton, *The Nonjurors*, 1902 (Overton)

Paul, Leslie, 'The Role of the Village Parson', article in *The Countryman*, Winter 1978 (Paul)

W.S.F. Pickering, *Anglo-Catholicism*, SPCK 1991 (Pickering)

Ernest Raymond, *The Witness of Canon Welcome*, Cassell 1950 (Raymond)

M.B. Reckitt (ed.), *For Christ and the People*, SPCK 1968 (Reckitt)

Anthony Russell, *The Clerical Profession*, SPCK 1984 (Russell)

Laurence Sterne, *Tristram Shandy*, Penguin 1967 (Sterne)

C.J. Stranks, *Anglican Devotion*, SCM Press 1961 (Stranks)

Flora Thompson, *Lark Rise to Candleford*, Penguin 1976 (Thompson)

Martin Thornton, *English Spirituality*, SPCK 1963 (Thornton)

John Tiller, *A Strategy for the Church's Ministry*, Church Information Office 1983 (Tiller)

Catherine Treasure, *Walking on Glass*, SPCK 1991 (Treasure)

A. Trollope, *Barchester Towers*, Oxford 1989 (Trollope, *BT*)

A. Trollope, *Framley Parsonage*, Penguin 1986 (Trollope, *FP*)

A. Trollope, *Dr Thorne*, Pan 1968 (Trollope, *DT*)

A. Trollope, *The Last Chronicle of Barset*, Pan 1967 (Trollope, *LC*)

A. Trollope, *The Vicar of Bullhampton*, Alan Sutton 1991 (Trollope, *VB*)

P. Virgin, *The Church in an Age of Negligence: Ecclesiastical Structure and Problems of Church Reform, 1700–1840*, J. Clarke 1989 (Virgin)

Gordon S. Wakefield (ed.), *A Dictionary of Christian Spirituality*, SCM Press 1983 (*DCS*)

Izaak Walton, *Lives*, ed. W.E. Henley, 1895 (Walton)

John Whale, *One Faith, One Lord*, SCM Press 1979 (Whale)

The Clergyman's Instructor, 6th ed. 1865 (*CI*)

The Dictionary of National Biography (*DNB*)

The Homilies, Focus Christian Ministries Trust 1986 (Homilies)

The Oxford Dictionary of the Christian Church, ed. F.L. Cross, Oxford 1958 (*ODCC*)

Shepherdswell Parish Magazine (*SPM*)

The Whole Duty of Man, 1842 (*WDM*)

Index of Parochial Clergy